# HTML

## in an *instant*

**Visual**

*From*
**maranGraphics**

&

Wiley Publishing, Inc.

D1361635

## HTML In an Instant

Published by
**Wiley Publishing, Inc.**
909 Third Avenue
New York, NY 10022

Published simultaneously in Canada

Copyright© 2001 by maranGraphics Inc.
    5755 Coopers Avenue
    Mississauga, Ontario, Canada
    L4Z 1R9

Library of Congress Control Number: 2001091979

ISBN: 0-7645-3627-3

Manufactured in the United States of America

10  9  8  7  6  5  4  3  2

1B/RU/QY/QS/MG

## Trademark Acknowledgments

## Important Numbers

For U.S. corporate orders, please call maranGraphics at 800-469-6616 or fax 905-890-9434.

For general information on our other products and services or to obtain technical support, please contact our Customer Care Department within the U.S. at 800-762-2974, outside the U.S. at 317-572-3993 or fax 317-572-4002.

## Permissions

Wiley Publishing, Inc.     is a trademark of Wiley Publishing, Inc.

| U.S. Corporate Sales | U.S. Trade Sales |
|---|---|
| Contact maranGraphics at (800) 469-6616 or fax (905) 890-9434. | Contact Wiley at (800) 762-2974 or fax (317) 572-4002. |

# Some comments from our readers...

"I have to praise you and your company on the fine products you turn out. I have twelve of the *Teach Yourself VISUALLY* and *Simplified* books in my house. They were instrumental in helping me pass a difficult computer course. Thank you for creating books that are easy to follow."

—*Gordon Justin (Brielle, NJ)*

"I commend your efforts and your success. I teach in an outreach program for the Dr. Eugene Clark Library in Lockhart, TX. Your *Teach Yourself VISUALLY* books are incredible and I use them in my computer classes. All my students love them!"

—*Michele Schalin (Lockhart, TX)*

"Thank you so much for helping people like me learn about computers. The Maran family is just what the doctor ordered. Thank you, thank you, thank you."

—*Carol Moten (New Kensington, PA)*

"I would like to take this time to compliment maranGraphics on creating such great books. Thank you for making it clear. Keep up the good work."

—*Kirk Santoro (Burbank, CA)*

"I write to extend my thanks and appreciation for your books. They are clear, easy to follow, and straight to the point. Keep up the good work!"

—*Seward Kollie (Dakar, Senegal)*

"What fantastic teaching books you have produced! Congratulations to you and your staff. You deserve the Nobel prize in Education in the Software category. Thanks for helping me to understand computers."

—*Bruno Tonon (Melbourne, Australia)*

"Over time, I have bought a number of your 'Read Less, Learn More' books. For me, they are THE way to learn anything easily."

—*José A. Mazón (Cuba, NY)*

"I was introduced to maranGraphics about four years ago and YOU ARE THE GREATEST THING THAT EVER HAPPENED TO INTRODUCTORY COMPUTER BOOKS!"

—*Glenn Nettleton (Huntsville, AL)*

"Compliments To The Chef!! Your books are extraordinary! Or, simply put, Extra-Ordinary, meaning way above the rest! THANK YOU THANK YOU THANK YOU! for creating these."

—*Christine J. Manfrin (Castle Rock, CO)*

"I'm a grandma who was pushed by an 11-year-old grandson to join the computer age. I found myself hopelessly confused and frustrated until I discovered the Visual series. I'm no expert by any means now, but I'm a lot further along than I would have been otherwise. Thank you!"

—*Carol Louthain (Logansport, IN)*

"Thank you, thank you, thank you...for making it so easy for me to break into this high-tech world. I now own four of your books. I recommend them to anyone who is a beginner like myself. Now... if you could just do one for programming VCRs, it would make my day!"

—*Gay O'Donnell (Calgary, Alberta, Canada)*

"You're marvelous! I am greatly in your debt."

—*Patrick Baird (Lacey, WA)*

**maranGraphics is a family-run business located near Toronto, Canada.**

**At *maranGraphics*,** we believe in producing great computer books–one book at a time.

Each maranGraphics book uses the award-winning communication process that we have been developing over the last 25 years. Using this process, we organize screen shots and text in a way that makes it easy for you to learn new concepts and tasks.

We spend hours deciding the best way to perform each task, so you don't have to!

Our clear, easy-to-follow screen shots and instructions walk you through each task from beginning to end.

We want to thank you for purchasing what we feel are the best computer books money can buy. We hope you enjoy using this book as much as we enjoyed creating it!

Sincerely,

***The Maran Family***

Please visit us on the Web at:

# www.maran.com

## CREDITS

**Author:**
Ruth Maran

**Copy Development Director:**
Kelleigh Johnson

**Copy Editor:**
Raquel Scott

**Technical Consultants:**
Paul Whitehead
Joel Desamero

**Project Manager:**
Judy Maran

**Editors:**
Teri Lynn Pinsent
Luis Lee
Norm Schumacher
Faiza Jagot

**Screen Captures & Editing:**
Stacey Morrison

**Layout & Screen Artist:**
Paul Baker

**Indexer:**
Teri Lynn Pinsent

**Permissions Coordinator:**
Jennifer Amaral

**Wiley Vice President and
Executive Group Publisher:**
Richard Swadley

**Wiley Vice President
and Publisher:**
Barry Pruett

**Wiley Editorial Support:**
Jennifer Dorsey
Sandy Rodrigues
Lindsay Sandman

**Post Production:**
Robert Maran

## ACKNOWLEDGMENTS

Thanks to the dedicated staff of maranGraphics, including
Jennifer Amaral, Roderick Anatalio, Paul Baker, Joel Desamero,
Darryl Grossi, Faiza Jagot, Kelleigh Johnson, Wanda Lawrie, Luis Lee,
Treena Lees, Cathy Lo, Jill Maran, Judy Maran, Robert Maran,
Ruth Maran, Russ Marini, Suzana G. Miokovic, Stacey Morrison,
Teri Lynn Pinsent, Steven Schaerer, Norm Schumacher, Raquel Scott,
Roxanne Van Damme and Paul Whitehead.

Finally, to Richard Maran who originated the easy-to-use
graphic format of this guide. Thank you for your
inspiration and guidance.

# TABLE OF CONTENTS

# 6 Work With Images

# 7 Create Links

# 8 Create Tables

# TABLE OF CONTENTS

# THE INTERNET AND THE WORLD WIDE WEB

The Internet is the largest computer network in the world. More than 275 million people worldwide use the Internet to access information, exchange electronic mail, participate in discussion groups, shop online and more.

## THE INTERNET

### HISTORY OF THE INTERNET

The Internet began as a military research project in the late 1960s. The U.S. Defense Department created a network, called ARPANET, that covered a large geographic area and that would continue to function even if part of the network failed. The improved, high-speed network that developed from this technology became the Internet. In the 1980s, most of the people accessing the Internet were scientists and researchers. In the early 1990s, companies began to offer Internet access to home users and the Internet eventually grew to include organizations and individuals around the world.

### STRUCTURE OF THE INTERNET

The Internet consists of thousands of connected networks around the world. Each government agency, company, college, university and organization on the Internet is responsible for maintaining its own network. When you transfer information over the Internet, these organizations allow the information to pass through their networks.

Computers on the Internet use a collection of protocols called Transmission Control Protocol/Internet Protocol (TCP/IP) to transfer information over the Internet. A protocol is a set of rules controlling the transfer of information between computers. TCP/IP allows computers on the Internet to communicate as if they were directly connected.

## WHAT THE INTERNET OFFERS

### ELECTRONIC MAIL

Electronic mail (e-mail) is the most popular feature on the Internet. You can exchange e-mail with people around the world.

### ONLINE SHOPPING

You can order products on the Internet without leaving your home. You can purchase items such as books, computer programs, flowers, music CDs, stocks and cars.

### INFORMATION AND ENTERTAINMENT

The Internet gives you access to information on every subject imaginable. You can review newspapers, government documents, television show transcripts, famous speeches, recipes, job listings and airline schedules. You can also play games, watch videos, listen to music and chat with people around the world.

### DISCUSSION GROUPS

You can join discussion groups to meet people with similar interests around the world. You can ask questions and discuss topics such as food, music, politics and sports. Usenet newsgroups are the most popular discussion groups on the Internet. You can also find discussion groups on many Web sites.

# in an instant

## THE WORLD WIDE WEB

The World Wide Web is a part of the Internet and consists of a huge collection of documents stored on computers around the world. The World Wide Web is commonly known as the Web.

A Web page is a document on the Web. Web pages can include information such as text, images, pictures, sounds and videos.

Web pages are stored on computers called Web servers. Once a Web page is stored on a Web server, it is available for other people to view. Many colleges, universities, government agencies, companies, organizations and individuals create and maintain collections of Web pages called Web sites.

### URLS

Each page on the Web has a unique address, called a Uniform Resource Locator (URL). People can instantly display a Web page if they know its URL.

A Web page URL consists of a scheme, a Web server name and a path. The scheme identifies the language, or protocol, used to access the Web page. Web page URLs usually use the http (HyperText Transfer Protocol) scheme. The Web server name, also known as a domain name, indicates the name of the server that stores the Web page. The path specifies the location of the Web page on the Web server. For example, the URL http://www.maran.com/ws–documents/new.html has the scheme http, the Web server name www.maran.com and the path /ws–documents/new.html.

### WEB BROWSERS

A Web browser is a program that allows people to view and explore information on the Web. A Web browser retrieves Web pages and other files from a Web server and displays them on a user's computer. Two popular Web browsers are Microsoft Internet Explorer and Netscape Navigator. The latest versions of these two programs are available at the www.microsoft.com/ie and www.netscape.com Web sites.

### LINKS

Web pages contain highlighted text or images, called links, that connect to other pages on the Web. Links are also known as hyperlinks. Links help save time since people do not have to enter the URL of each Web page they want to view. This allows people to move through a vast amount of information by jumping from one Web page to another.

Links are easy to identify on a Web page. Text links appear underlined and in color, while image links usually display a colored border.

# WHO USES THE INTERNET

People of all ages and backgrounds use the Internet. The Internet makes available a vast amount of information and services that can help everyone from children and students, to researchers and people at work.

## WHO USES THE INTERNET

### CHILDREN

The Internet can help children improve their reading and communication skills. Children can send e-mail messages to their friends and explore information on the Internet. There are many security products available that allow children to access the Internet without being exposed to inappropriate material.

### PEOPLE AT HOME

There are many services and resources available for people who use the Internet at home. People can use the Internet to access information about their community, such as local newspaper reports, television listings and movie theater showtimes. People can also use the Internet to find restaurant reviews and purchase tickets for sporting events.

### STUDENTS

Many students can access the Internet directly from school. The Internet contains a vast amount of information that can assist students with school projects. Students can also use the Internet to communicate with students in other parts of the world to learn new languages and learn about different cultures. High school students can use the Internet to find information on colleges or universities they are interested in attending. Schools and universities also offer courses that people can complete using the Internet.

### RESEARCHERS

One of the original uses for the Internet was to help researchers and scientists at institutions around the world exchange information and work on joint projects. Information displayed on the Internet allows researchers from different parts of the world to work together.

### PEOPLE AT WORK

Many people use the Internet at work. People can communicate with colleagues and clients using e-mail or videoconferencing over the Internet. People can also use the Internet to perform many business tasks, such as ordering products from other companies, shipping packages around the world and performing banking transactions. The Internet also offers Web sites that can help people with career planning and advancement, or help people search for a new job.

# GETTING CONNECTED

There are several ways you can get connected to the Internet. You require a connection device, such as a modem or ISDN line, and a company that provides access to the Internet, such as an Internet service provider or commercial online service, in order to connect.

## TYPES OF CONNECTIONS

### MODEM

Most people use a modem to connect to the Internet through a regular telephone line. A modem with a speed of 56 Kbps is recommended for browsing the Web. Slower modems will take longer to display information on a screen.

### ISDN

An Integrated Services Digital Network (ISDN) line is a digital phone line offered by telephone companies in most cities. An ISDN line can transfer information at speeds from 64 Kbps to 128 Kbps.

### CABLE MODEM

A cable modem allows you to connect to the Internet with the same cable that attaches to a television set. A cable modem can transfer information at a speed of up to 3,000 Kbps. You can contact your local cable company to determine if they offer cable Internet services.

### DSL

Digital Subscriber Line (DSL) is a service offered by telephone companies in many cities. DSL can transfer information at speeds from 1,000 Kbps to 9,000 Kbps.

## HOW TO CONNECT

### INTERNET SERVICE PROVIDER

An Internet Service Provider (ISP) is a company that offers access to the Internet. Most ISPs offer a certain number of hours on the Internet each month for a set fee. If you exceed the total number of hours, you are usually charged for every extra hour that you use the Internet. Some ISPs offer unlimited access to the Internet for a set fee.

### SCHOOL OR COMPANY

Universities and colleges often provide students and teachers with free access to the Internet. Many companies also provide free Internet access for their employees.

### COMMERCIAL ONLINE SERVICE

A commercial online service is a company that offers access to the Internet and provides well-organized information and services such as daily news, weather reports, encyclopedias and chat rooms. Popular commercial online services include America Online and The Microsoft Network.

Most commercial online services offer a certain number of hours each month for a set fee. If you exceed the total number of hours, you are usually charged for every extra hour that you use the service.

# REASONS FOR CREATING WEB PAGES

Before you begin creating Web pages, you should consider your reasons for creating the pages. You may want to create personal Web pages to share information about your family, interests or an area of expertise. Alternatively, you may want to create commercial Web pages to share information about your business, such as press releases, online catalogs or job postings.

## PERSONAL

### SHARE PERSONAL INFORMATION

Many people create Web pages to share information about their families, pets, vacations or favorite hobbies. Some people create Web pages to present a résumé to potential employers.

### SHARE KNOWLEDGE

Many scientists and business professionals make their work available on the Web. If you are experienced in an area that many people are unfamiliar with, you can create Web pages to share your knowledge.

### ENTERTAIN USERS

Many people create Web pages to display collections of jokes or humorous stories. You can also create Web pages to display information, pictures, sound clips and videos about a favorite celebrity, sports team or TV show.

### PROMOTE INTERESTS

You can create Web pages to display information about an organization or club to which you belong. You can include a schedule of upcoming events and detailed information about the goals of the organization.

## COMMERCIAL

### PROVIDE INFORMATION

Companies often place pages on the Web to provide information about their company and the products and services they offer. Companies can use Web pages to keep the public informed about new products and interesting news. Many companies display their press releases on the Web.

### SHOPPING

Many companies create Web pages that allow users to order products and services over the Internet. Companies can display descriptions and pictures of products to help users determine which products they want to purchase.

### JOB LISTINGS

Many companies use Web pages to advertise jobs that are available within the company. Some companies also allow users to submit résumés through their Web site.

### CONTACT INFORMATION

Companies can display their office addresses and phone numbers on their Web pages. This helps users contact the company to ask questions and express opinions.

# STEPS FOR CREATING WEB PAGES

Before you begin creating Web pages, decide what you want to accomplish with your Web pages. Decide on a main topic or theme for the Web pages and then determine the type of information you want to include. You may want to use the following steps as a guideline to help you create attractive and useful Web pages.

## STEPS FOR CREATING WEB PAGES

### 1) GATHER INFORMATION

Collect the information you want to include on your Web pages, such as text, images, diagrams and contact numbers. Make sure the information you gather directly relates to the main topic or theme of your Web pages and will appeal to your intended audience. When gathering information, keep in mind that you must have permission to use any information that you did not create yourself.

### 2) ORGANIZE INFORMATION

Divide the information you gathered into sections. Each section will be a separate Web page that discusses a different concept or idea. Each Web page should contain enough information to fill a single screen. When organizing your information, consider that adding many elements to a single Web page will increase the file size of the Web page. A larger file size can increase the time the page takes to transfer to a user's computer.

### 3) ENTER INFORMATION

Enter the text you want to appear on your Web pages in a word processor or text editor. Each Web page should be a separate document. You can then add HyperText Markup Language (HTML) tags to the text to convert the documents into Web pages. HTML tags also allow you to add elements such as images, sounds, videos and tables to the Web pages.

### 4) ADD LINKS

Adding links is an important step in creating Web pages. Links are text or images that users can select to display other pages on the Web. The links you add to your Web pages should allow users to easily move through information of interest.

### 5) PUBLISH WEB PAGES

When you finish creating your Web pages, you can transfer the pages to a computer that makes pages available on the Web. You should then test the Web pages to ensure your links work properly and your information appears the way you want.

# WEB PAGE CONTENT CONSIDERATIONS

When creating your Web pages, you should carefully consider the content you want the pages to include. The following suggestions can help you design well-organized Web pages that contain useful information.

## WEB PAGE CONTENT CONSIDERATIONS

### EMPHASIZE IMPORTANT INFORMATION

Always display the most important information at the top of each Web page. Some users will not scroll through a Web page to read all the information. These users will miss important information if you do not display the information at the top of each page.

Including a table of contents that contains links to important areas of a Web page can help users access any important information that appears later in the page.

Headings can also help emphasize important information, allowing users to glance through a Web page and quickly find information of interest.

### AVOID "UNDER CONSTRUCTION" LABELS

You should avoid using "under construction" labels for Web pages that are not complete. You will frustrate users when they visit a Web page that does not contain useful information. Do not make your Web pages available on the Web until the pages are complete.

### PAGE LENGTH

Web pages should not be too short or too long. If a Web page is shorter than half a screen of information, try to combine the information with another page. If a Web page is longer than five screens, try to break up the page into several shorter pages. Users may become frustrated if they have to scroll through a large amount of information on a page.

### CONSIDER FILE SIZES

When determining the content for a Web page, keep in mind that including many elements with large file sizes, such as embedded sounds and videos, will increase the time it takes for the page to transfer to a user's computer. Whenever possible, you should limit the number of large files you include on a Web page.

### AVOID SPECIFIC WEB BROWSER INSTRUCTIONS

Avoid giving detailed instructions on how to perform tasks using a specific Web browser. People who use a different Web browser may not be able to perform the task using the instructions you provide. For example, adding a Web page to a list of favorite Web pages is a different process in Internet Explorer than in Netscape Navigator.

# in an *instant*

## COPYRIGHT CONSIDERATIONS

If you plan to use text, images or other information you did not create, make sure the information is not copyrighted. Many pages on the Web offer information and images that do not have copyright restrictions. If you want to use copyrighted information, you must obtain permission from the author.

## WEB PAGES WITHOUT IMAGES

Some people turn off the display of images to browse the Web more quickly, while others use Web browsers that cannot display images. Always design your Web pages so that users who do not see images will still get valuable information from your pages.

## INCLUDE CONTACT INFORMATION

Always include your name and e-mail address on Web pages you create. This allows users to contact you if they have questions or comments.

When providing contact information, you may want to set up a separate e-mail address for messages about your Web site. This will help prevent your personal e-mail inbox from becoming overloaded with messages if your Web site becomes popular.

## UPDATE INFORMATION

You should update your Web pages on a regular basis. If the information on your Web pages never changes, people will read the pages only once and will not revisit them in the future. You should include the date on your Web pages to let users know when you last updated the pages.

## USE WARNINGS

If your Web pages display information that some users may consider offensive, place a warning on your main page. When users visit your Web site, they will see the warning and can then decide whether they want to view your pages.

## PROVIDE A FAQ

A FAQ is a list of Frequently Asked Questions about a topic. A FAQ can help answer questions that users have about your Web pages and can help prevent users from sending you e-mail messages asking the same questions over and over.

If you are not sure what information to include in your FAQ, you may want to wait until you have received some questions and comments about the Web pages before creating the FAQ.

Carefully planning your Web site before you begin creating your Web pages can help you avoid having to re-organize the Web pages later. You should decide how many Web pages you want the Web site to contain and consider how the pages will link to each other. Once you have determined a layout for the Web site, you should plan the home page for the site.

## WEB SITE LAYOUT

### LINEAR

A linear layout organizes Web pages in a straight line. This layout is ideal for Web pages that people should read in a specific order, such as pages containing a story or step-by-step instructions. Each Web page in a linear layout usually links to the next and previous pages in the Web site, allowing users to move both forward and backward through the Web pages.

### HIERARCHICAL

In a hierarchical layout, all Web pages branch off a home page. The home page provides a general summary of the information in the Web site, while the other pages provide more specific information. Users select links on the home page to access Web pages that contain detailed information.

### WEB

A Web layout has no overall structure. Each Web page in a Web layout contains multiple links to other Web pages in the site. This type of layout is ideal for Web pages that people do not need to read in a specific order.

### COMBINATION

Combining layouts provides you with the most flexibility when creating your Web site. For example, combining a hierarchical layout with a Web layout lets you create a Web site that has an overall structure, while allowing users to randomly browse through information.

## PLAN YOUR HOME PAGE

The home page is usually the first page users will see when they visit your Web site. The home page is usually named index.html or index.htm. You should check with the company that makes your Web pages available on the Web to determine what name to use.

Your home page should contain a brief summary of your Web site, a table of contents and links that users can select to quickly access information of interest.

When planning your home page, make sure the page will work well with the layout of your Web site. For example, the home page for a Web site with a linear layout should contain a link to the next page in the Web site.

HyperText Markup Language (HTML) is a computer language used to create Web pages. Web pages are HTML documents that consist of text and HTML tags. A Web browser interprets the tags in an HTML document and displays the document as a Web page.

## HTML ESSENTIALS

### HTML DOCUMENTS

HTML documents have the .html or .htm extension (example: index.html). You do not have to create different HTML documents for different types of computers. Any computer that has a Web browser installed can display Web pages, including computers running a Unix, Windows or Macintosh operating system.

### HTML TAGS

HTML tags tell a Web browser about the structure and formatting of a Web page. Each tag gives a specific instruction and is surrounded by angle brackets < >. Most tags have an opening tag and a closing tag that affect the text between the tags. The closing tag has a forward slash (/). Some tags have only an opening tag. Tags can be displayed in uppercase or lowercase letters, but using uppercase letters can help make the tags stand out from the main text.

Many tags have attributes that offer options for the tags. For example, the <FONT> tag has a COLOR attribute that lets you change the color of text.

### WEB BROWSERS

A Web page may not look the same when displayed in different Web browsers. Each Web browser may interpret HTML tags differently and many Web browsers do not support all of the features of HTML.

Some companies that make Web browsers, such as Netscape and Microsoft, have developed additional tags and attributes that Web browsers made by other companies may not understand. When a Web browser does not understand a tag or attribute, the information is usually ignored.

### HTML VERSIONS

There are several versions of HTML. The HTML specification, also known as the HTML standard, is constantly evolving and a new version of HTML is released every few years. Each version offers new features to give people more control when creating Web pages. An organization called the World Wide Web Consortium (W3C) regulates the versions of HTML. HTML version 4.01 is the latest version of HTML. Information about HTML and its versions is available at the www.w3.org Web site.

# PROGRAMS FOR CREATING WEB PAGES

You can choose from several types of programs to create Web pages. Text editors, word processors, HTML editors and visual editors are all popular tools for creating Web pages.

## TEXT EDITOR OR WORD PROCESSOR

### TEXT EDITOR

A text editor is a simple program you can use to create and edit documents that contain only text. Popular text editors include

Notepad for Windows and SimpleText for Macintosh.

### WORD PROCESSOR

A word processor is a program that provides advanced editing and formatting features to help you create documents. Any formatting you apply to text will not appear when you view documents you create on the Web. Popular word processors include Microsoft Word and Corel WordPerfect.

To create a Web page using a text editor or word processor, you must type the text for the Web page and then add HTML tags to specify how you want the text to appear on the Web page. You need a Web browser to see how the Web page will appear on the Web.

## HTML EDITOR

An HTML editor is a program you can use to create Web pages. HTML editors offer menus and toolbars that you can use to add HTML tags to your Web pages. You need to know HTML to create a Web page using an HTML editor.

Some HTML editors allow you to see how Web pages you create will appear on the Web, while others require you to use a Web browser to view your Web pages. BBEdit (www.barebones.com) and HomeSite (www.allaire.com) are popular HTML editors.

## VISUAL EDITOR

A visual editor is a program you can use to graphically create Web pages. Visual editors enter HTML tags for you as you create a Web page. You do not need to know HTML to create a Web page using a visual editor.

Visual editors hide HTML tags from view, so you can see how your Web pages will look as you create the Web pages. HoTMetaL PRO (www.hotmetalpro.com) and Microsoft FrontPage (www.microsoft.com/frontpage) are popular visual editors.

You can get ideas for creating your Web pages by viewing the HTML code used to create other pages on the Web. Viewing HTML code can help improve your understanding of HTML since it allows you to see how other people use HTML tags. Examining the code for other Web pages can also help you troubleshoot problems with your own Web pages.

## VIEW HTML CODE FOR A WEB PAGE

**1** Start the Web browser you want to use. In this example, we started Microsoft Internet Explorer.

**2** Display the Web page for which you want to view the HTML code.

**3** Click **View**.

**4** Click **Source**.

*Note: If you are using Netscape Navigator, click **Page Source**.*

**●** A window appears, displaying the HTML code used to create the Web page.

**5** When you finish viewing the HTML code, click ☒ to close the window.

*Note: Although you can use the HTML code you find on the Web, you should never copy any content on a Web page without first obtaining permission from the author.*

# SET UP A WEB PAGE

You can enter the text you want to appear on your Web page in a word processor or text editor. You must add HTML tags to the text to convert the document into a Web page. HTML tags provide instructions for formatting and structuring a Web page.

## SET UP A WEB PAGE

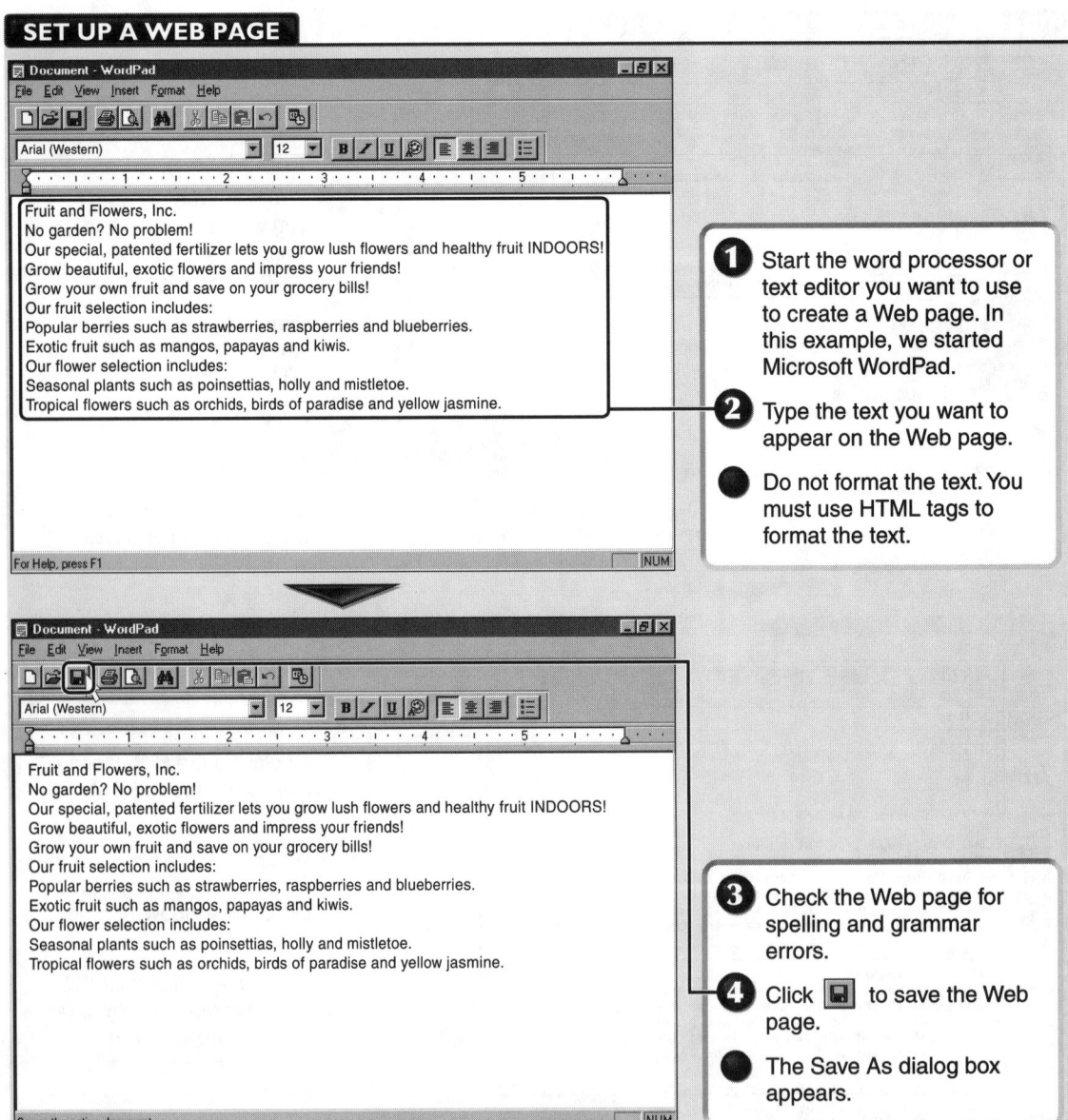

1 Start the word processor or text editor you want to use to create a Web page. In this example, we started Microsoft WordPad.

2 Type the text you want to appear on the Web page.

● Do not format the text. You must use HTML tags to format the text.

3 Check the Web page for spelling and grammar errors.

4 Click 💾 to save the Web page.

● The Save As dialog box appears.

# in an *instant*

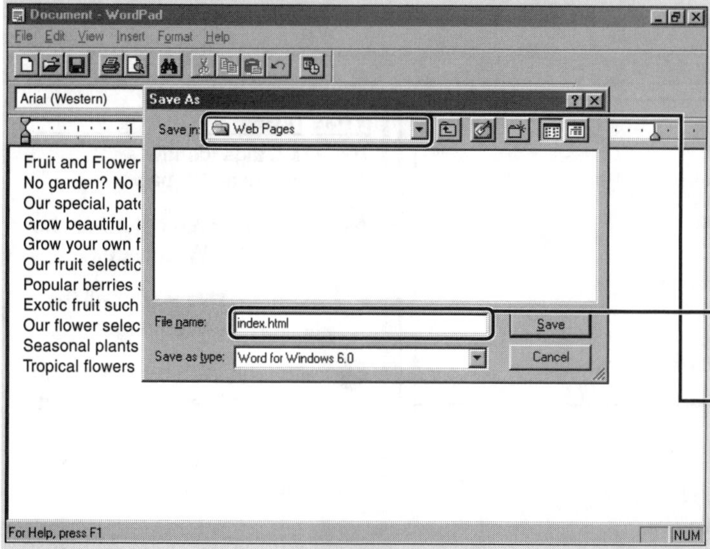

**5** Type a name for the Web page. Make sure you add the **.html** or **.htm** extension to the Web page name.

*Note: A Web page name can contain letters and numbers, but no spaces. The main Web page is usually named **index.html**.*

● This area shows the location where the program will store the Web page. You can click this area to change the location.

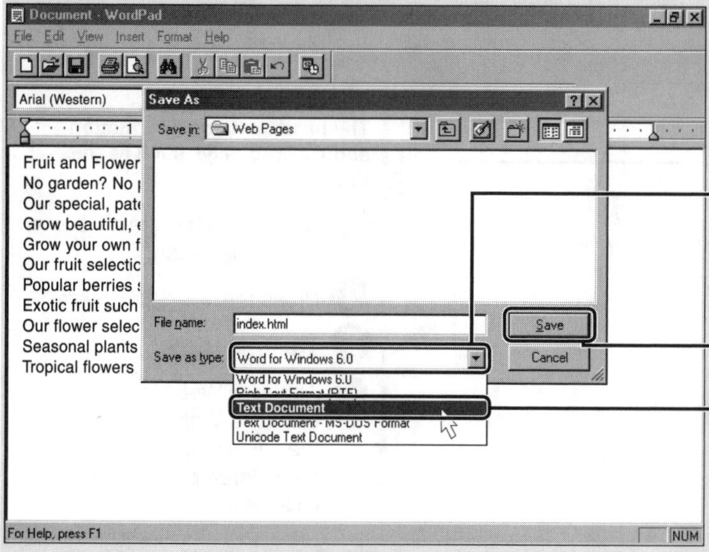

**6** Click this area to list the ways you can save the Web page.

**7** Click **Text Document**.

**8** Click **Save**.

● A dialog box will appear, stating that all formatting will be removed from the Web page. Click **Yes** to save the Web page.

CONTINUED

# SET UP A WEB PAGE

There are some basic HTML tags that you should add to every Web page you create. These tags include the HTML, HEAD, TITLE and BODY tags. Each tag gives a specific instruction and is surrounded by angle brackets <>. You can use uppercase or lowercase letters when typing tags.

## SET UP A WEB PAGE (CONTINUED)

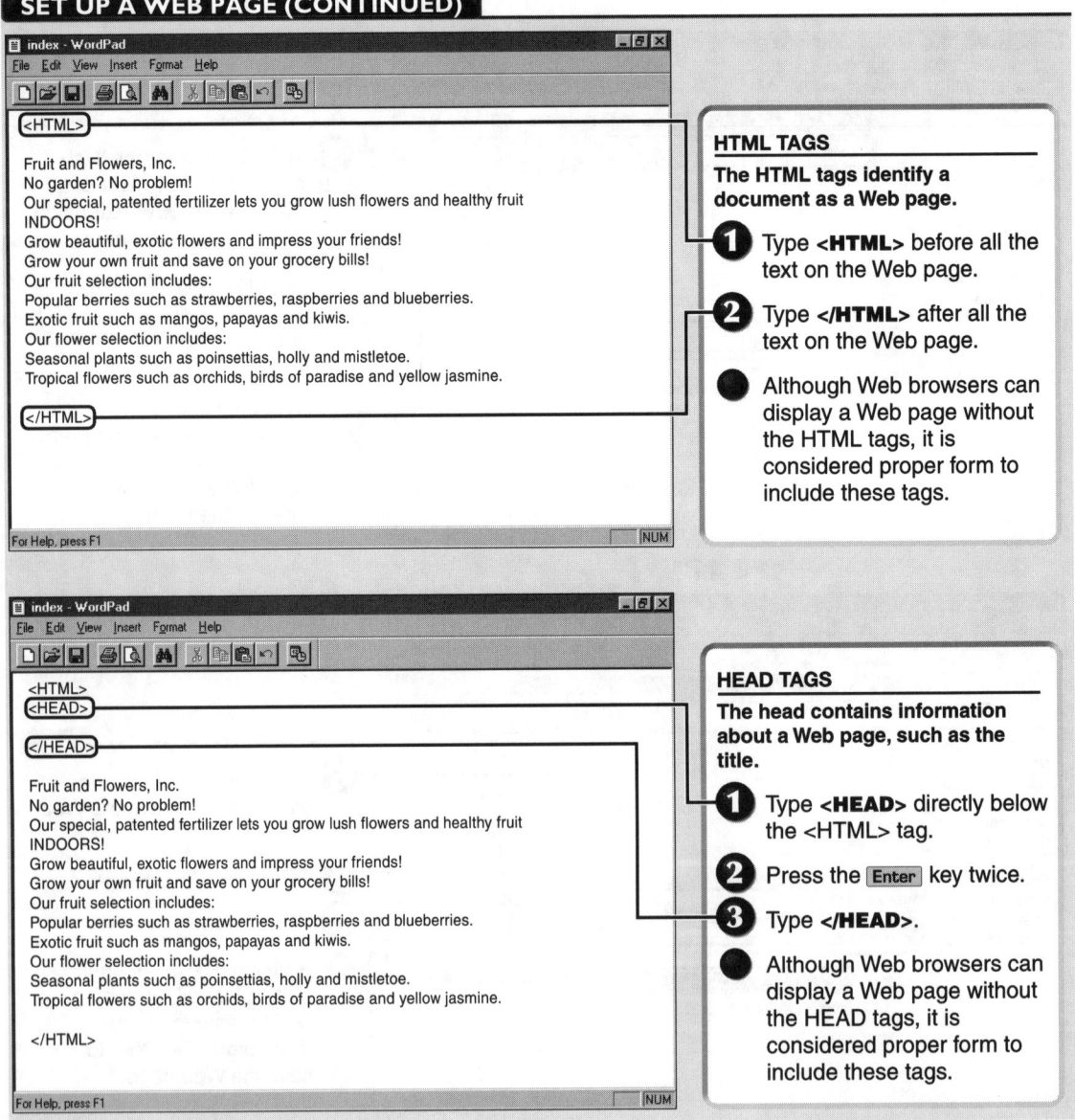

### HTML TAGS

**The HTML tags identify a document as a Web page.**

**1** Type **<HTML>** before all the text on the Web page.

**2** Type **</HTML>** after all the text on the Web page.

● Although Web browsers can display a Web page without the HTML tags, it is considered proper form to include these tags.

### HEAD TAGS

**The head contains information about a Web page, such as the title.**

**1** Type **<HEAD>** directly below the <HTML> tag.

**2** Press the Enter key twice.

**3** Type **</HEAD>**.

● Although Web browsers can display a Web page without the HEAD tags, it is considered proper form to include these tags.

## in an instant

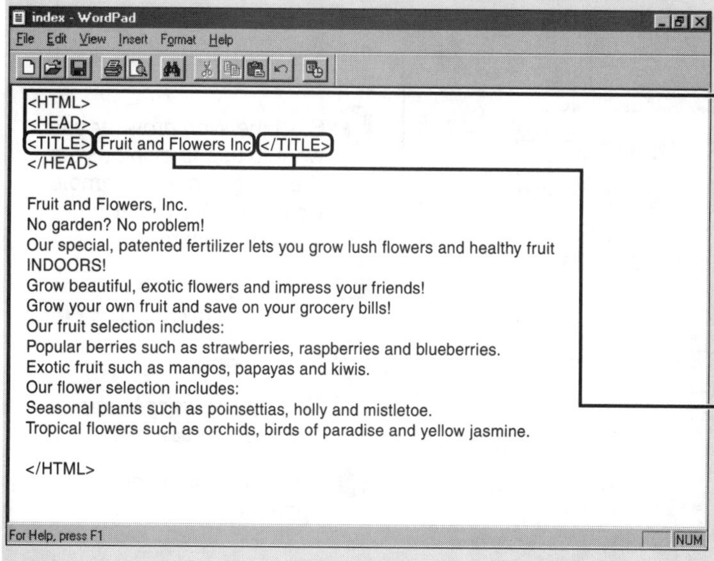

---

index - WordPad

File Edit View Insert Format Help

```
<HTML>
<HEAD>
<TITLE> Fruit and Flowers Inc </TITLE>
</HEAD>

Fruit and Flowers, Inc.
No garden? No problem!
Our special, patented fertilizer lets you grow lush flowers and healthy fruit
INDOORS!
Grow beautiful, exotic flowers and impress your friends!
Grow your own fruit and save on your grocery bills!
Our fruit selection includes:
Popular berries such as strawberries, raspberries and blueberries.
Exotic fruit such as mangos, papayas and kiwis.
Our flower selection includes:
Seasonal plants such as poinsettias, holly and mistletoe.
Tropical flowers such as orchids, birds of paradise and yellow jasmine.

</HTML>
```

For Help, press F1                                                          NUM

### TITLE TAGS

**You must give a Web page a title that describes its contents. The title usually appears in the title bar of a Web browser window.**

**1** Type **<TITLE>** directly below the <HEAD> tag.

**2** Type the title of the Web page, using only letters and numbers (A to Z and 0 to 9).

**3** Type **</TITLE>**.

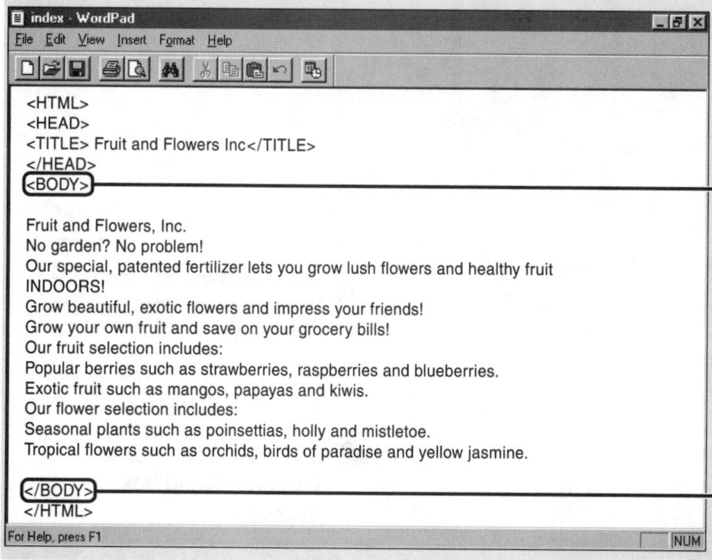

---

index - WordPad

File Edit View Insert Format Help

```
<HTML>
<HEAD>
<TITLE> Fruit and Flowers Inc</TITLE>
</HEAD>
<BODY>

Fruit and Flowers, Inc.
No garden? No problem!
Our special, patented fertilizer lets you grow lush flowers and healthy fruit
INDOORS!
Grow beautiful, exotic flowers and impress your friends!
Grow your own fruit and save on your grocery bills!
Our fruit selection includes:
Popular berries such as strawberries, raspberries and blueberries.
Exotic fruit such as mangos, papayas and kiwis.
Our flower selection includes:
Seasonal plants such as poinsettias, holly and mistletoe.
Tropical flowers such as orchids, birds of paradise and yellow jasmine.

</BODY>
</HTML>
```

For Help, press F1                                                          NUM

### BODY TAGS

**You must place the BODY tags around the contents of a Web page.**

**1** Type **<BODY>** directly below the </HEAD> tag.

**2** Type **</BODY>** directly above the </HTML> tag.

You can display your Web page in a Web browser, such as Microsoft Internet Explorer or Netscape Navigator, to preview how the page will appear on the Web. Keep in mind that other people on the Web cannot view the Web page until the page is transferred to a Web server on the Internet.

## DISPLAY WEB PAGE IN WEB BROWSER

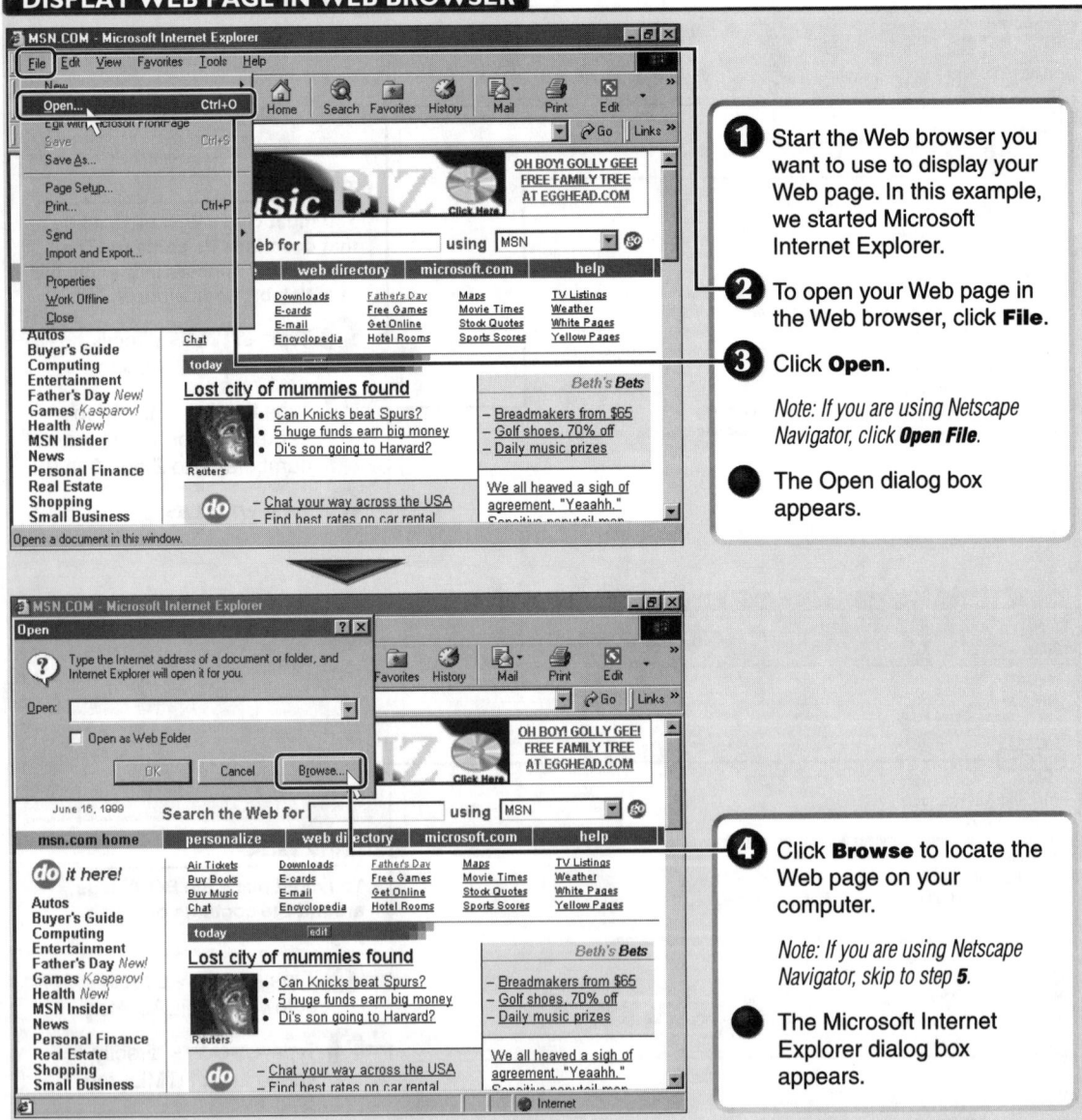

**1** Start the Web browser you want to use to display your Web page. In this example, we started Microsoft Internet Explorer.

**2** To open your Web page in the Web browser, click **File**.

**3** Click **Open**.

*Note: If you are using Netscape Navigator, click **Open File**.*

● The Open dialog box appears.

**4** Click **Browse** to locate the Web page on your computer.

*Note: If you are using Netscape Navigator, skip to step 5.*

● The Microsoft Internet Explorer dialog box appears.

# in an *instant*

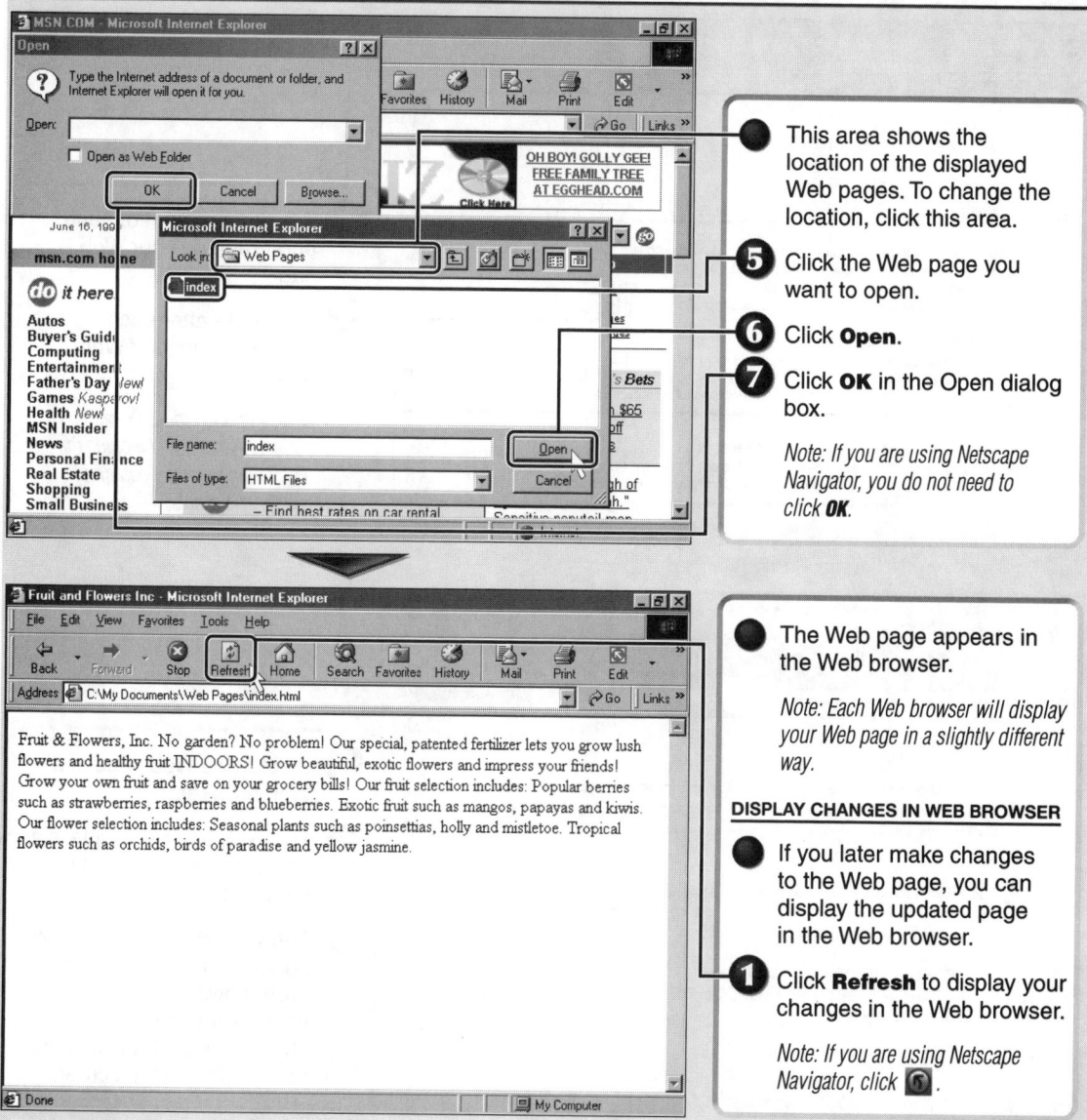

This area shows the location of the displayed Web pages. To change the location, click this area.

**5** Click the Web page you want to open.

**6** Click **Open**.

**7** Click **OK** in the Open dialog box.

*Note: If you are using Netscape Navigator, you do not need to click OK.*

The Web page appears in the Web browser.

*Note: Each Web browser will display your Web page in a slightly different way.*

### DISPLAY CHANGES IN WEB BROWSER

If you later make changes to the Web page, you can display the updated page in the Web browser.

**1** Click **Refresh** to display your changes in the Web browser.

*Note: If you are using Netscape Navigator, click* 🔄 *.*

# START A NEW PARAGRAPH

When creating a Web page, you must specify where you want each paragraph to begin. Web browsers usually ignore line breaks you type in your text editor. Starting a new paragraph can help improve the layout of your Web page by breaking up large sections of text.

## START A NEW PARAGRAPH

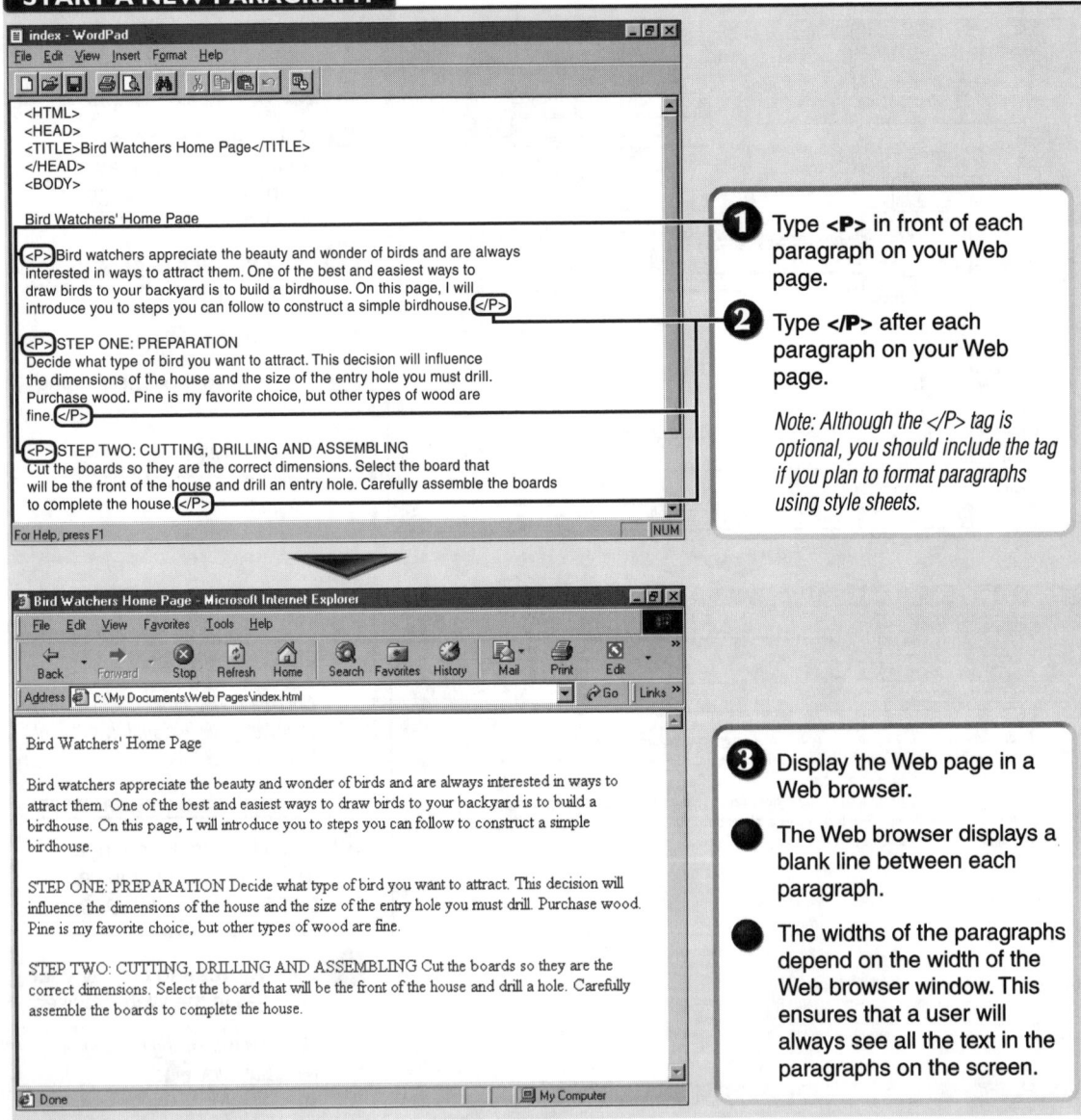

**1** Type **<P>** in front of each paragraph on your Web page.

**2** Type **</P>** after each paragraph on your Web page.

*Note: Although the </P> tag is optional, you should include the tag if you plan to format paragraphs using style sheets.*

**3** Display the Web page in a Web browser.

■ The Web browser displays a blank line between each paragraph.

■ The widths of the paragraphs depend on the width of the Web browser window. This ensures that a user will always see all the text in the paragraphs on the screen.

# CHANGE PARAGRAPH ALIGNMENT

You can change the alignment of the paragraphs on your Web page. Paragraphs can be left aligned, centered, right aligned or justified. By default, all paragraphs are left aligned, but changing the alignment of an important paragraph can make the paragraph stand out from the rest of the Web page.

## CHANGE PARAGRAPH ALIGNMENT

```
align - WordPad
File  Edit  View  Insert  Format  Help

<HTML>
<HEAD>
<TITLE>Change Paragraph Alignment</TITLE>
</HEAD>
<BODY>

<P ALIGN=left>This paragraph is left aligned. This paragraph is left aligned. This paragraph is left
aligned. This paragraph is left aligned. </P>

<P ALIGN=center>This paragraph is centered. This paragraph is centered. This paragraph is
centered. This paragraph is centered. This paragraph is centered. This paragraph is centered. </P>

<P ALIGN=right>This paragraph is right aligned. This paragraph is right aligned. This paragraph is
right aligned. This paragraph is right aligned. </P>

<P ALIGN=justify>This paragraph is justified. This paragraph is justified. This paragraph is justified.
This paragraph is justified. This paragraph is justified. This paragraph is justified. This paragraph is
justified. This paragraph is justified. This paragraph is justified. This paragraph is justified. This
paragraph is justified. This paragraph is justified. This paragraph is justified. This
paragraph is justified. This paragraph is justified. </P>

</BODY>

For Help, press F1                                                                    NUM
```

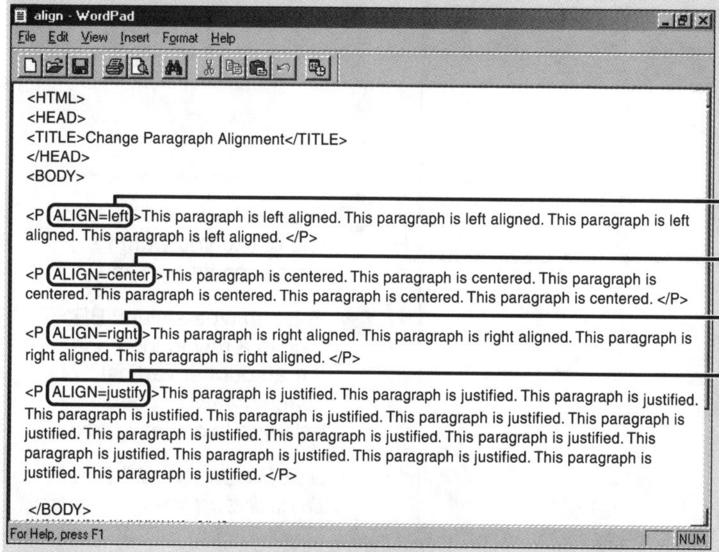

**1** In the **<P>** tag for the paragraph you want to change, type **ALIGN=?** replacing **?** with the way you want to align the paragraph (**left**, **center**, **right** or **justify**).

Repeat step **1** for each paragraph you want to change.

```
Change Paragraph Alignment - Microsoft Internet Explorer
File  Edit  View  Favorites  Tools  Help

← Back ▾ → ▾ 🗙 🗋 🖄 | 🔍 Search 🔚 Favorites 🕓 History | 🔹 ▾ 🖨 🗗 ▾ 📄 🚇
Address 🗋 C:\My Documents\Web Pages\align.html                         ▾ 🔗 Go  Links »

This paragraph is left aligned. This paragraph is left aligned. This paragraph is left aligned. This
paragraph is left aligned.

     This paragraph is centered. This paragraph is centered. This paragraph is centered. This paragraph
                is centered. This paragraph is centered. This paragraph is centered.

          This paragraph is right aligned. This paragraph is right aligned. This paragraph is right aligned. This
                                              paragraph is right aligned.

This paragraph is justified. This paragraph is justified. This paragraph is justified. This paragraph is
justified. This paragraph is justified. This paragraph is justified. This paragraph is justified. This
paragraph is justified. This paragraph is justified. This paragraph is justified. This paragraph is
justified. This paragraph is justified. This paragraph is justified. This paragraph is justified. This
paragraph is justified.

Done                                                             My Computer
```

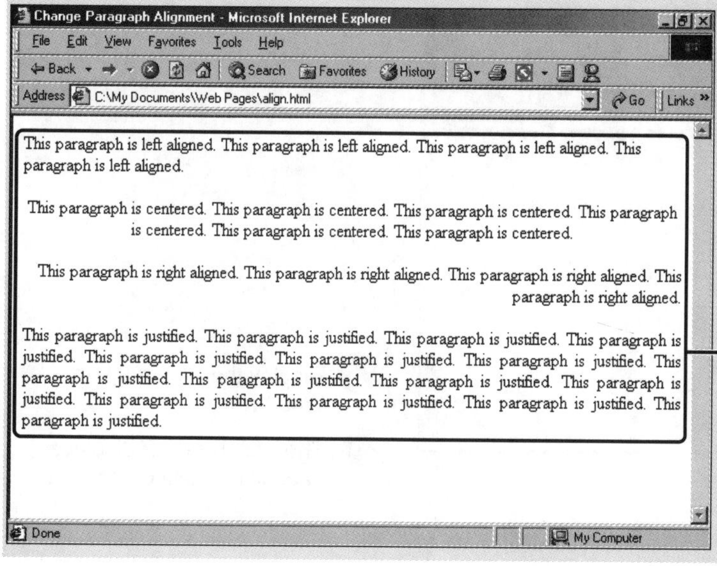

**2** Display the Web page in a Web browser.

The Web browser displays the paragraphs with the alignments you specified.

*Note: The ALIGN attribute is still supported by Web browsers, but the use of style sheets is now preferred.*

**21**

# START A NEW LINE

You must specify where you want each new line of text to begin on a Web page. Starting a new line is useful for separating short lines of text, such as the text in a mailing address or poem, or for increasing the amount of space between elements on a Web page.

## START A NEW LINE

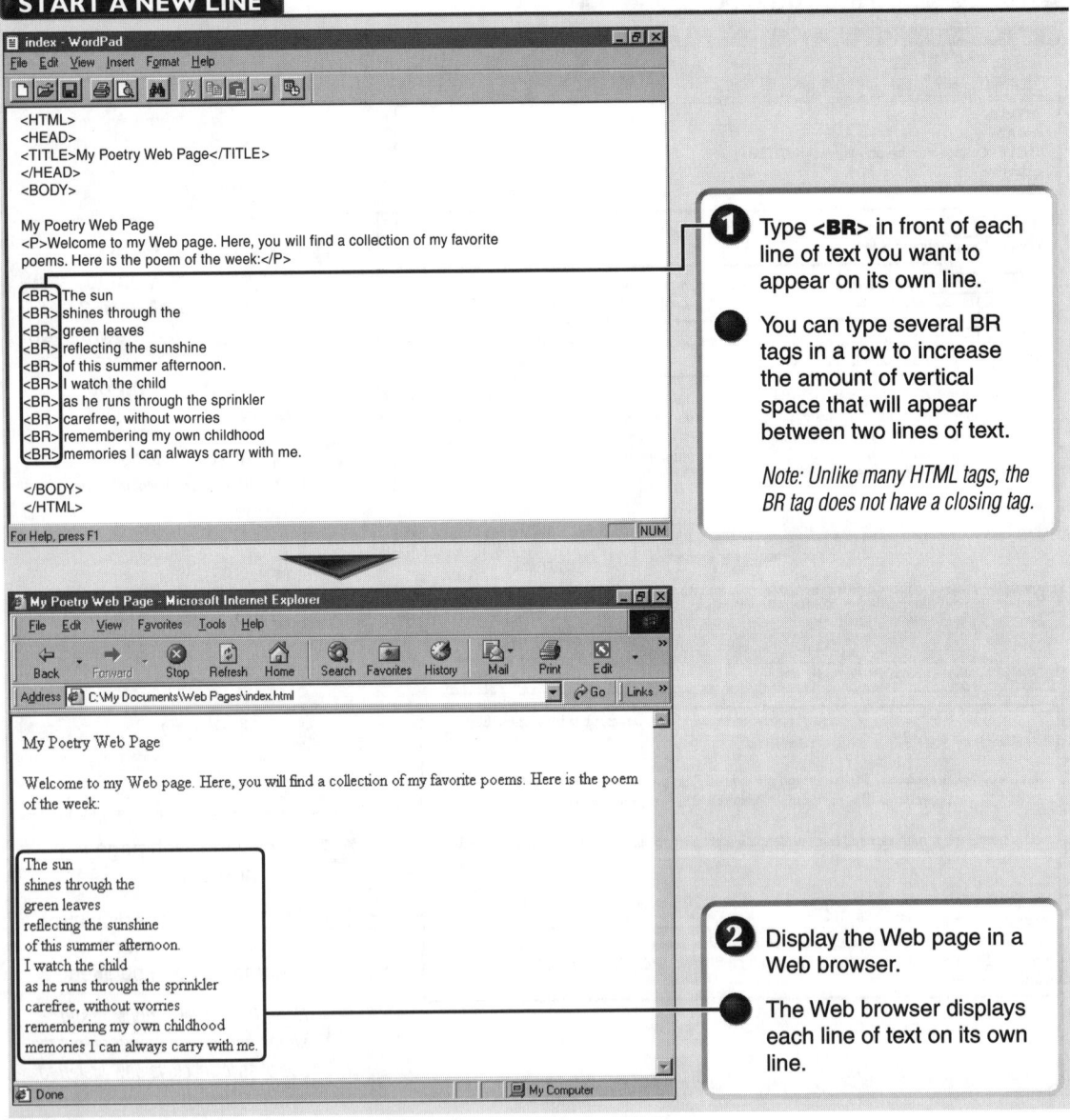

**1** Type **<BR>** in front of each line of text you want to appear on its own line.

● You can type several BR tags in a row to increase the amount of vertical space that will appear between two lines of text.

*Note: Unlike many HTML tags, the BR tag does not have a closing tag.*

**2** Display the Web page in a Web browser.

● The Web browser displays each line of text on its own line.

A Web browser usually ignores extra spaces you include when typing the text for a Web page. To add extra blank spaces to your Web page, you must use a special code. Inserting blank spaces is useful for indenting the first line of a paragraph or separating elements, such as images, on a Web page.

## INSERT BLANK SPACES

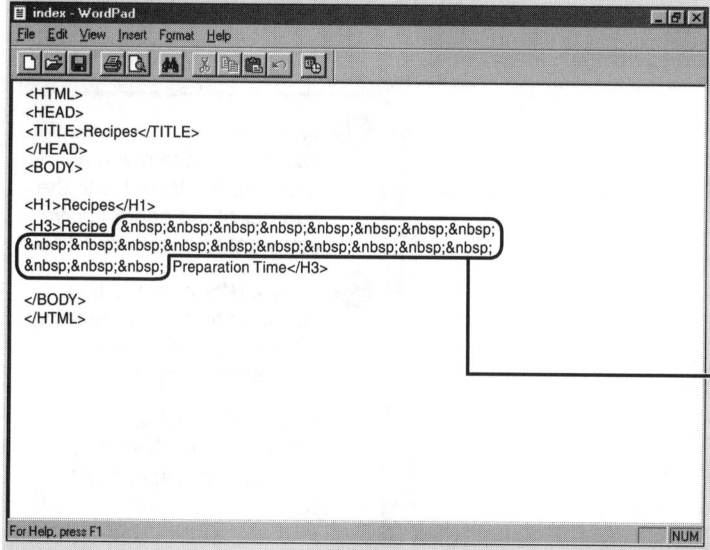

```
index - WordPad
File  Edit  View  Insert  Format  Help

<HTML>
<HEAD>
<TITLE>Recipes</TITLE>
</HEAD>
<BODY>

<H1>Recipes</H1>
<H3>Recipe         
          
    Preparation Time</H3>

</BODY>
</HTML>

For Help, press F1                                    NUM
```

**1** Position the cursor where you want blank spaces to appear on your Web page.

**2** Type ** ** for each blank space you want to add.

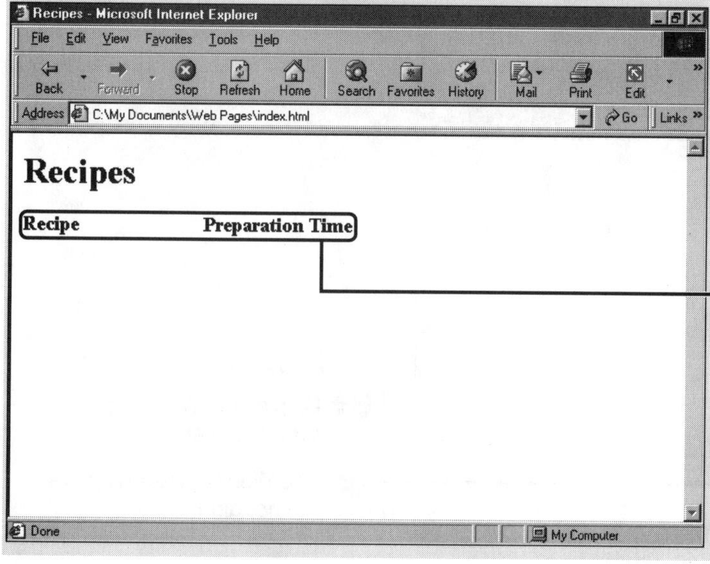

```
Recipes - Microsoft Internet Explorer
File  Edit  View  Favorites  Tools  Help

Back  Forward  Stop  Refresh  Home  Search  Favorites  History  Mail  Print  Edit

Address  C:\My Documents\Web Pages\index.html          Go  Links

Recipes

Recipe            Preparation Time

Done                                     My Computer
```

**3** Display the Web page in a Web browser.

● The Web browser displays the blank spaces on your Web page.

*Note: You can also use   between two words on a Web page to prevent the words from being separated when a Web browser wraps text to fit in the window.*

**23**

You can use headings to help organize the information on your Web page. There are six heading levels you can use. Heading level 1 is the largest and level 6 is the smallest. Heading level 4 is usually the same size as the main text on a Web page.

## ADD A HEADING

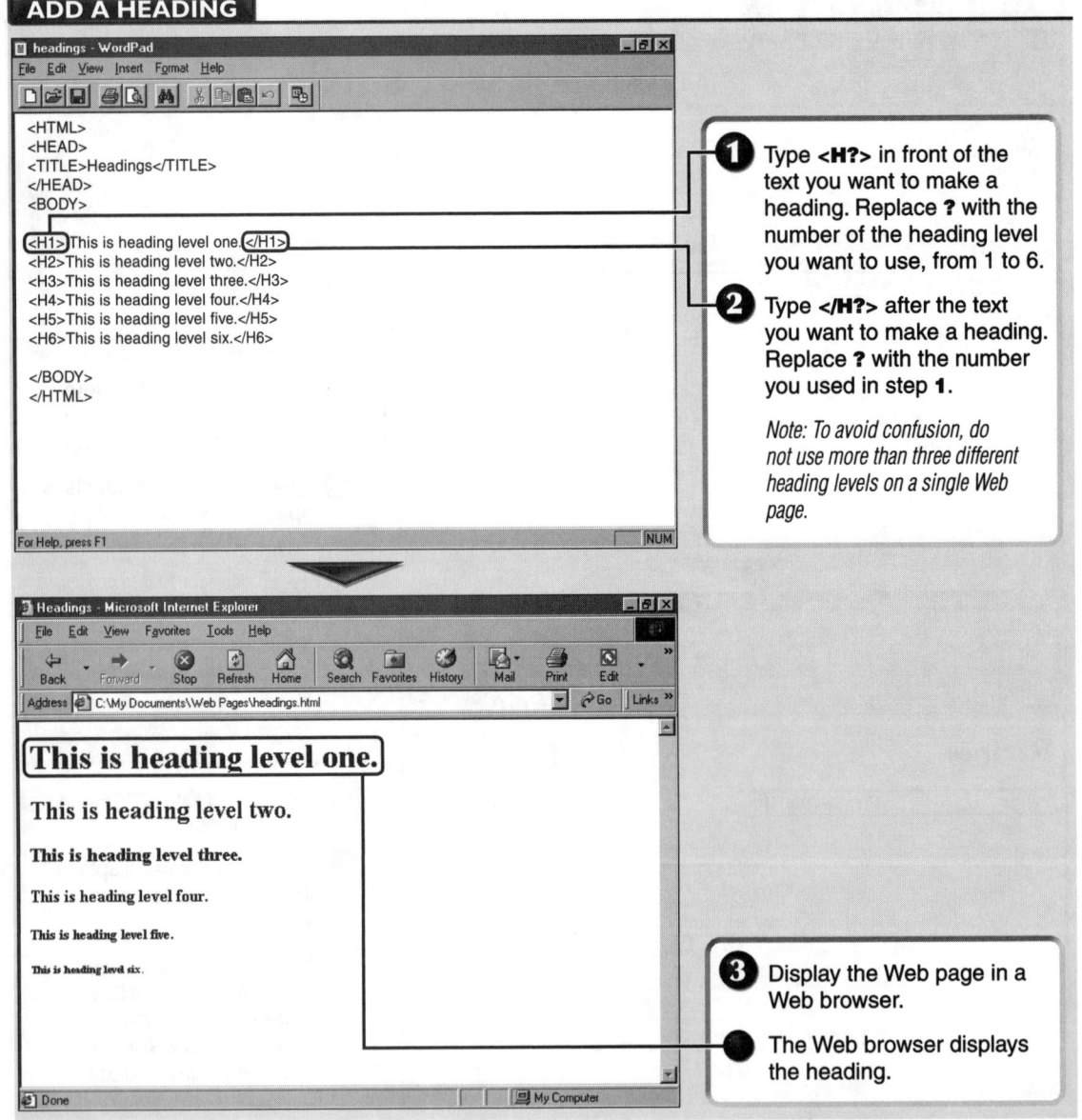

**1** Type **<H?>** in front of the text you want to make a heading. Replace **?** with the number of the heading level you want to use, from 1 to 6.

**2** Type **</H?>** after the text you want to make a heading. Replace **?** with the number you used in step **1**.

*Note: To avoid confusion, do not use more than three different heading levels on a single Web page.*

**3** Display the Web page in a Web browser.

■ The Web browser displays the heading.

You can change the alignment of headings on your Web page. In most Web browsers, headings are displayed left aligned, but you can center or right align headings to give the headings a distinctive look. Using heading styles and alignments consistently will help users understand the structure of your Web page.

## CHANGE HEADING ALIGNMENT

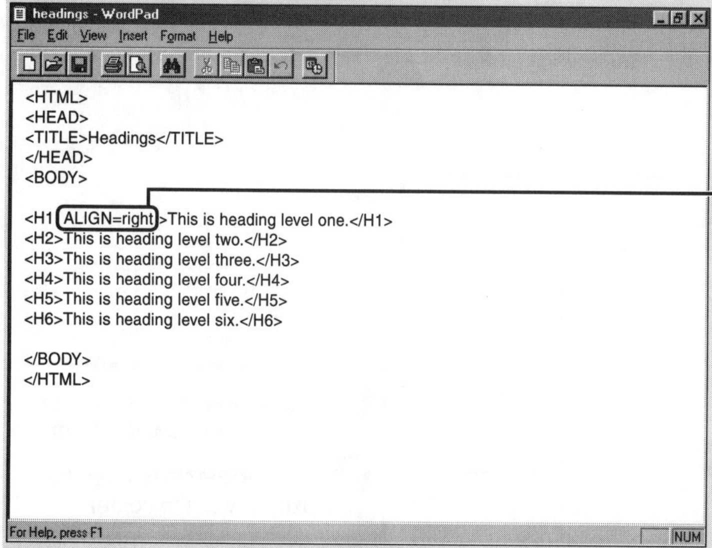

```
headings - WordPad
File  Edit  View  Insert  Format  Help

<HTML>
<HEAD>
<TITLE>Headings</TITLE>
</HEAD>
<BODY>

<H1 ALIGN=right>This is heading level one.</H1>
<H2>This is heading level two.</H2>
<H3>This is heading level three.</H3>
<H4>This is heading level four.</H4>
<H5>This is heading level five.</H5>
<H6>This is heading level six.</H6>

</BODY>
</HTML>

For Help, press F1                                    NUM
```

**1** In the <H> tag for the heading you want to change, type **ALIGN=?** replacing **?** with the way you want to align the heading (**left**, **center** or **right**).

*Note: By default, headings are displayed left aligned.*

```
Headings - Microsoft Internet Explorer
File  Edit  View  Favorites  Tools  Help

Back  Forward  Stop  Refresh  Home  Search  Favorites  History  Mail  Print  Edit
Address  C:\My Documents\Web Pages\headings.html              Go  Links

                                    This is heading level one.

This is heading level two.

This is heading level three.

This is heading level four.

This is heading level five.

This is heading level six.

Done                                          My Computer
```

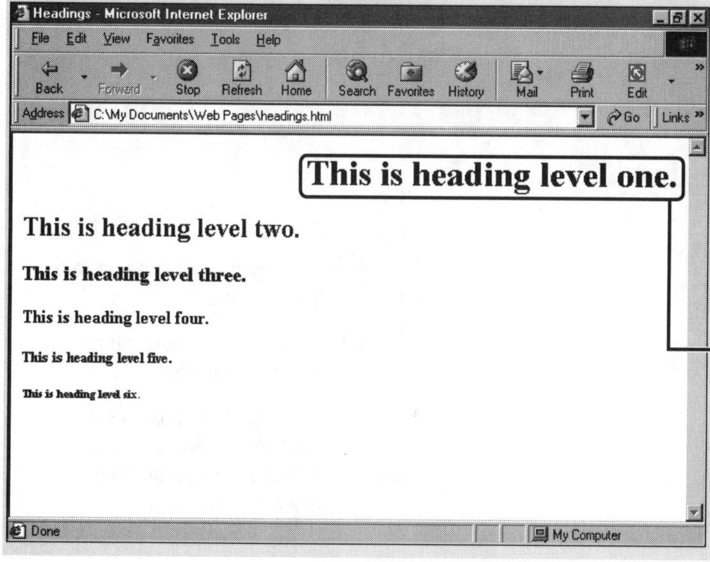

**2** Display the Web page in a Web browser.

The Web browser displays the heading with the alignment you specified.

*Note: The ALIGN attribute is still supported by Web browsers, but the use of style sheets is now preferred.*

**25**

# CENTER TEXT

You can center text on your Web page. Centering text can help you emphasize important information. You should center only short lines of text, such as a title or heading, since long paragraphs can be difficult to read when centered.

## CENTER TEXT

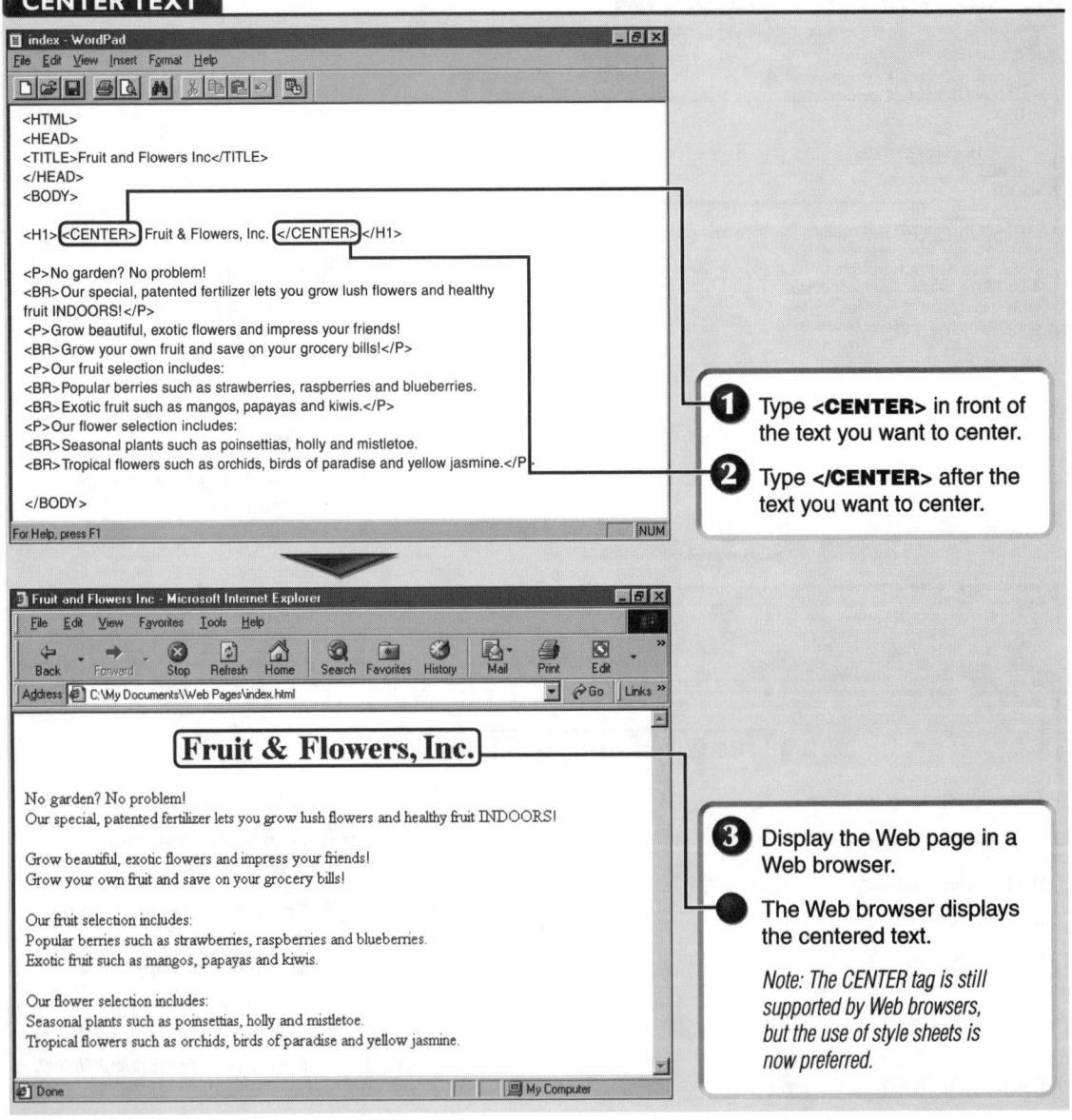

**1** Type **<CENTER>** in front of the text you want to center.

**2** Type **</CENTER>** after the text you want to center.

**3** Display the Web page in a Web browser.

■ The Web browser displays the centered text.

*Note: The CENTER tag is still supported by Web browsers, but the use of style sheets is now preferred.*

Web browsers automatically wrap the text in your paragraphs to fit on a user's screen. You can make sure certain words or phrases on your Web page will appear on the same line. For example, you may want to keep a name and phone number on the same line.

## CONTROL LINE BREAKS

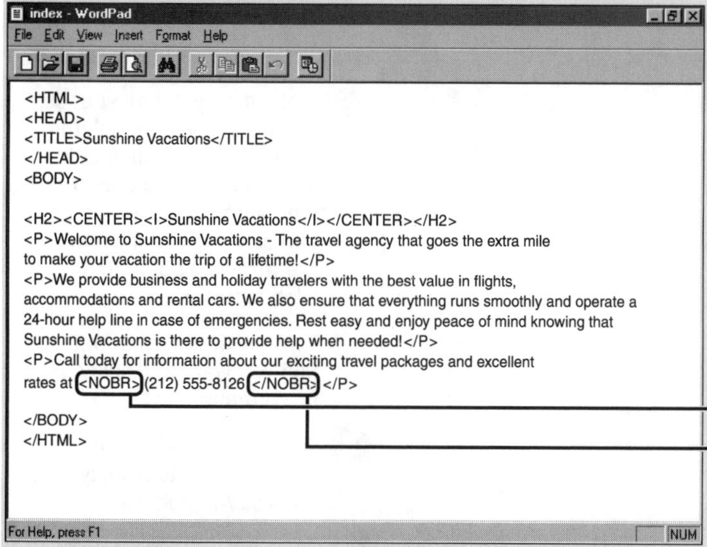

---

**index - WordPad**

File  Edit  View  Insert  Format  Help

```
<HTML>
<HEAD>
<TITLE>Sunshine Vacations</TITLE>
</HEAD>
<BODY>

<H2><CENTER><I>Sunshine Vacations</I></CENTER></H2>
<P>Welcome to Sunshine Vacations - The travel agency that goes the extra mile
to make your vacation the trip of a lifetime!</P>
<P>We provide business and holiday travelers with the best value in flights,
accommodations and rental cars. We also ensure that everything runs smoothly and operate a
24-hour help line in case of emergencies. Rest easy and enjoy peace of mind knowing that
Sunshine Vacations is there to provide help when needed!</P>
<P>Call today for information about our exciting travel packages and excellent
rates at <NOBR>(212) 555-8126 </NOBR> </P>

</BODY>
</HTML>
```

For Help, press F1                                                      NUM

**1** Type **<NOBR>** in front of the text you want to appear on the same line.

**2** Type **</NOBR>** after the text you want to appear on the same line.

---

**Sunshine Vacations - Microsoft Internet Explorer**

File  Edit  View  Favorites  Tools  Help

Back  Forward  Stop  Refresh  Home  Search  Favorites  History  Mail  Print  Edit

Address  C:\My Documents\Web Pages\index.html     Go  Links »

### *Sunshine Vacations*

Welcome to Sunshine Vacations - The travel agency that goes the extra mile to make your vacation the trip of a lifetime!

We provide business and holiday travelers with the best value in flights, accommodations and rental cars. We also ensure that everything runs smoothly and operate a 24-hour help line in case of emergencies. Rest easy and enjoy peace of mind knowing that Sunshine Vacations is there to provide help when needed!

Call today for information about our exciting travel packages and excellent rates at (212) 555-8126

Done                                            My Computer

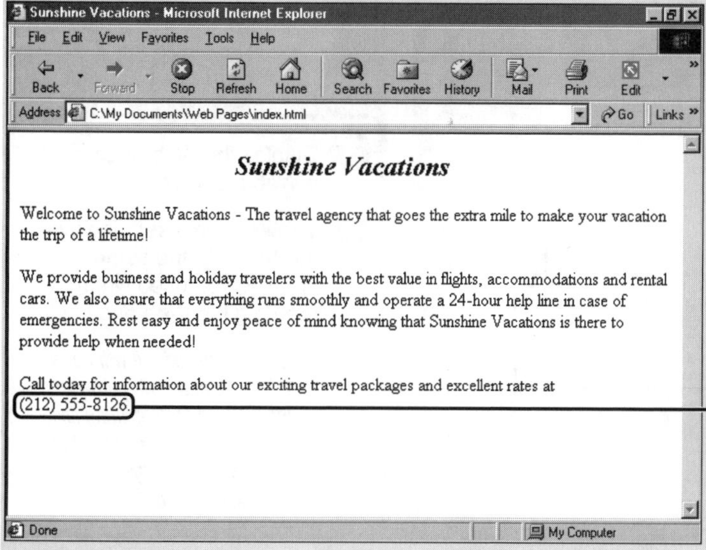

**3** Display the Web page in a Web browser.

● The Web browser displays the text on the same line.

*Note: A Web browser will keep the text on the same line even if the text extends beyond the edge of the window.*

# PREFORMAT TEXT

A Web browser usually ignores blank lines and extra spaces you add when typing the text for your Web page. You can preformat text to retain the spacing of text you type in a text editor. Preformatting text is useful when creating simple tables.

## PREFORMAT TEXT

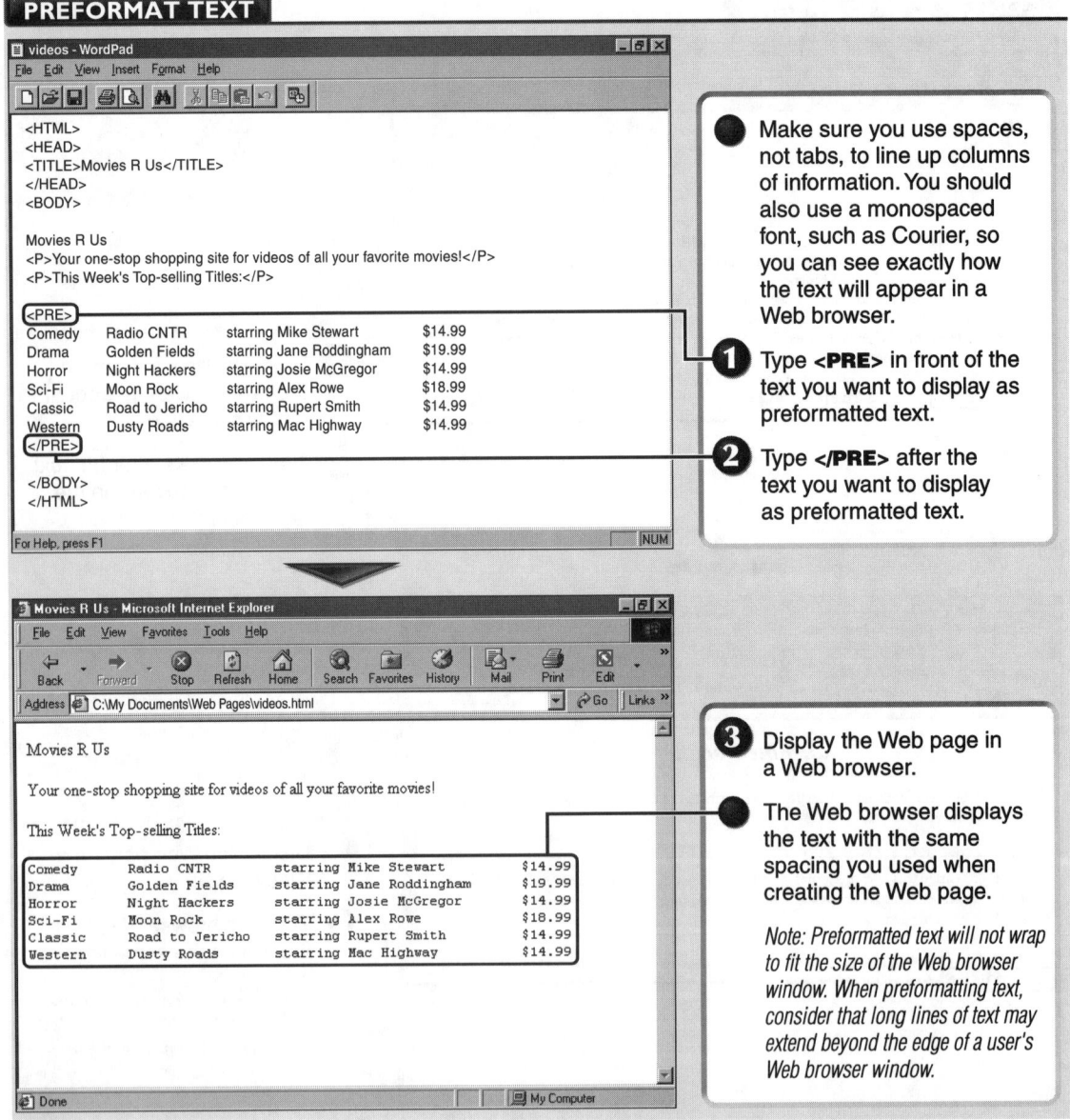

● Make sure you use spaces, not tabs, to line up columns of information. You should also use a monospaced font, such as Courier, so you can see exactly how the text will appear in a Web browser.

**1** Type **<PRE>** in front of the text you want to display as preformatted text.

**2** Type **</PRE>** after the text you want to display as preformatted text.

**3** Display the Web page in a Web browser.

● The Web browser displays the text with the same spacing you used when creating the Web page.

*Note: Preformatted text will not wrap to fit the size of the Web browser window. When preformatting text, consider that long lines of text may extend beyond the edge of a user's Web browser window.*

# ADD A COMMENT

You can add a comment to your Web page. Comments will not appear when users view your Web page. Comments are useful for reminding yourself to update a section of text, indicating why you used a specific tag or hiding Web page elements that some Web browsers may not recognize.

## ADD A COMMENT

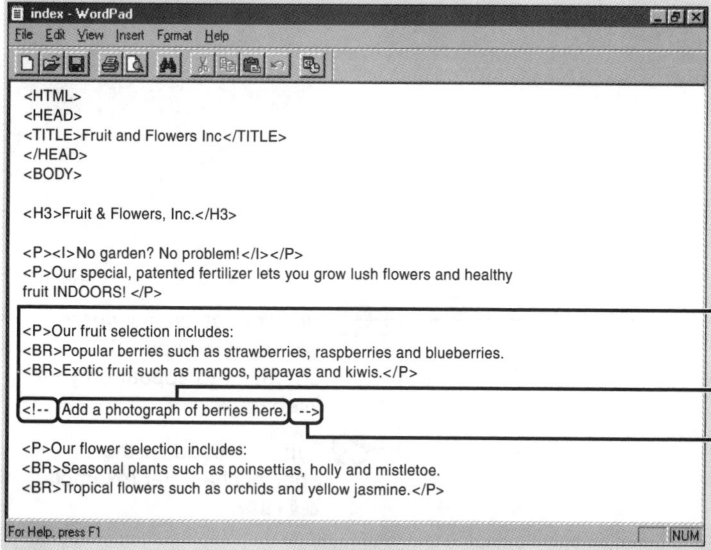

```
index - WordPad
File  Edit  View  Insert  Format  Help

<HTML>
<HEAD>
<TITLE>Fruit and Flowers Inc</TITLE>
</HEAD>
<BODY>

<H3>Fruit & Flowers, Inc.</H3>

<P><I>No garden? No problem!</I></P>
<P>Our special, patented fertilizer lets you grow lush flowers and healthy
fruit INDOORS! </P>

<P>Our fruit selection includes:
<BR>Popular berries such as strawberries, raspberries and blueberries.
<BR>Exotic fruit such as mangos, papayas and kiwis.</P>

<!-- Add a photograph of berries here. -->

<P>Our flower selection includes:
<BR>Seasonal plants such as poinsettias, holly and mistletoe.
<BR>Tropical flowers such as orchids and yellow jasmine.</P>

For Help, press F1                                        NUM
```

**1** Type **<!--** where you want to add a comment. Then press the **Spacebar**.

**2** Type the comment. Then press the **Spacebar**.

**3** Type **-->** to complete the comment.

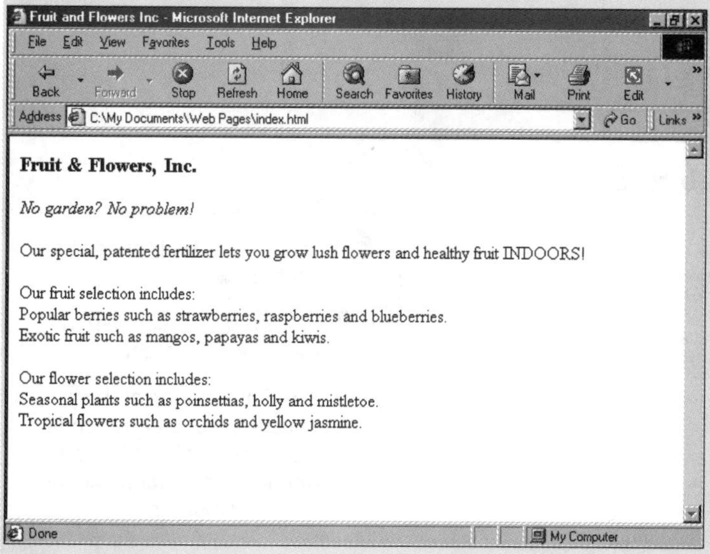

```
Fruit and Flowers Inc - Microsoft Internet Explorer
File  Edit  View  Favorites  Tools  Help

Back  Forward  Stop  Refresh  Home  Search  Favorites  History  Mail  Print  Edit

Address  C:\My Documents\Web Pages\index.html                    Go  Links

Fruit & Flowers, Inc.

No garden? No problem!

Our special, patented fertilizer lets you grow lush flowers and healthy fruit INDOORS!

Our fruit selection includes:
Popular berries such as strawberries, raspberries and blueberries.
Exotic fruit such as mangos, papayas and kiwis.

Our flower selection includes:
Seasonal plants such as poinsettias, holly and mistletoe.
Tropical flowers such as orchids and yellow jasmine.

Done                                          My Computer
```

**4** Display the Web page in a Web browser.

● The Web browser does not display the comment on your Web page.

● Keep in mind that users who view the HTML tags for your Web page will be able to read any comments you added.

# INSERT SPECIAL CHARACTERS

You can use character codes to add special characters that do not appear on your keyboard to your Web pages. Using character codes is also useful for adding characters that are used for creating Web pages, such as <, >, " and &, since Web browsers may misinterpret these characters. For example, Web browsers usually interpret the < character as the beginning of a tag.

## INSERT SPECIAL CHARACTERS

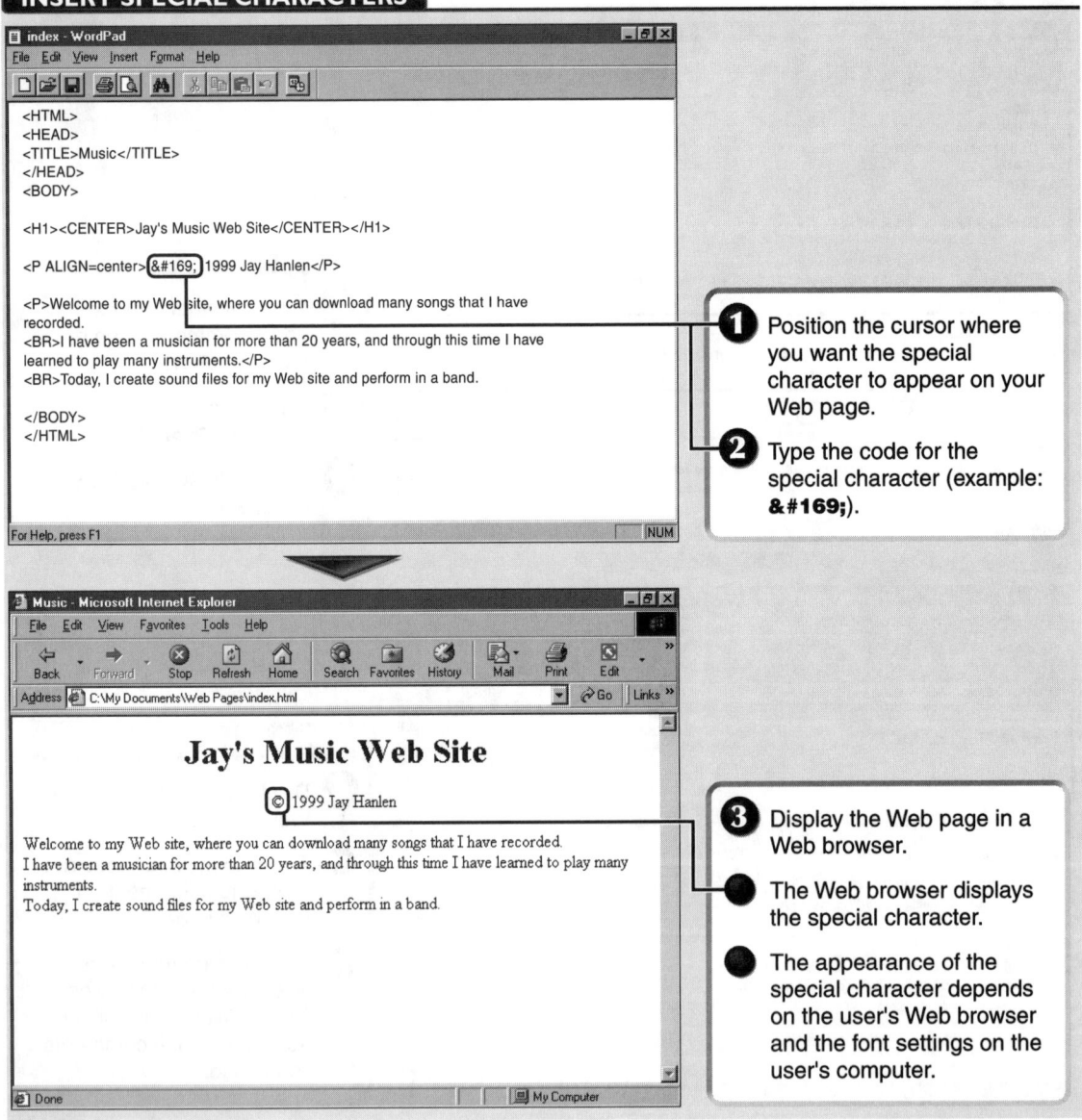

**1** Position the cursor where you want the special character to appear on your Web page.

**2** Type the code for the special character (example: **&#169;**).

**3** Display the Web page in a Web browser.

● The Web browser displays the special character.

● The appearance of the special character depends on the user's Web browser and the font settings on the user's computer.

# in an *instant*

## SPECIAL CHARACTERS

| CHARACTER | CODE | CHARACTER | CODE | CHARACTER | CODE | CHARACTER | CODE |
|-----------|------|-----------|------|-----------|------|-----------|------|
| " | &#34; | · | &#183; | Ð | &#208; | é | &#233; |
| & | &#38; | ¸ | &#184; | Ñ | &#209; | ê | &#234; |
| < | &#60; | ¹ | &#185; | Ò | &#210; | ë | &#235; |
| > | &#62; | ° | &#186; | Ó | &#211; | ì | &#236; |
| ¡ | &#161; | » | &#187; | Ô | &#212; | í | &#237; |
| ¢ | &#162; | ¼ | &#188; | Õ | &#213; | î | &#238; |
| £ | &#163; | ½ | &#189; | Ö | &#214; | ï | &#239; |
| ¤ | &#164; | ¾ | &#190; | × | &#215; | ð | &#240; |
| ¥ | &#165; | ¿ | &#191; | Ø | &#216; | ñ | &#241; |
| ¦ | &#166; | À | &#192; | Ù | &#217; | ò | &#242; |
| § | &#167; | Á | &#193; | Ú | &#218; | ó | &#243; |
| ¨ | &#168; | Â | &#194; | Û | &#219; | ô | &#244; |
| © | &#169; | Ã | &#195; | Ü | &#220; | õ | &#245; |
| ª | &#170; | Ä | &#196; | Ý | &#221; | ö | &#246; |
| « | &#171; | Å | &#197; | Þ | &#222; | ÷ | &#247; |
| ¬ | &#172; | Æ | &#198; | ß | &#223; | ø | &#248; |
| ® | &#174; | Ç | &#199; | à | &#224; | ù | &#249; |
| ¯ | &#175; | È | &#200; | á | &#225; | ú | &#250; |
| ° | &#176; | É | &#201; | â | &#226; | û | &#251; |
| ± | &#177; | Ê | &#202; | ã | &#227; | ü | &#252; |
| ² | &#178; | Ë | &#203; | ä | &#228; | ý | &#253; |
| ³ | &#179; | Ì | &#204; | å | &#229; | þ | &#254; |
| ´ | &#180; | Í | &#205; | æ | &#230; | ÿ | &#255; |
| µ | &#181; | Î | &#206; | ç | &#231; | | |
| ¶ | &#182; | Ï | &#207; | è | &#232; | | |

# BOLD OR ITALICIZE TEXT

You can bold or italicize text to emphasize information on your Web page. Bold text and italicized text are useful for introducing new terms and highlighting important phrases on a Web page.

## BOLD OR ITALICIZE TEXT

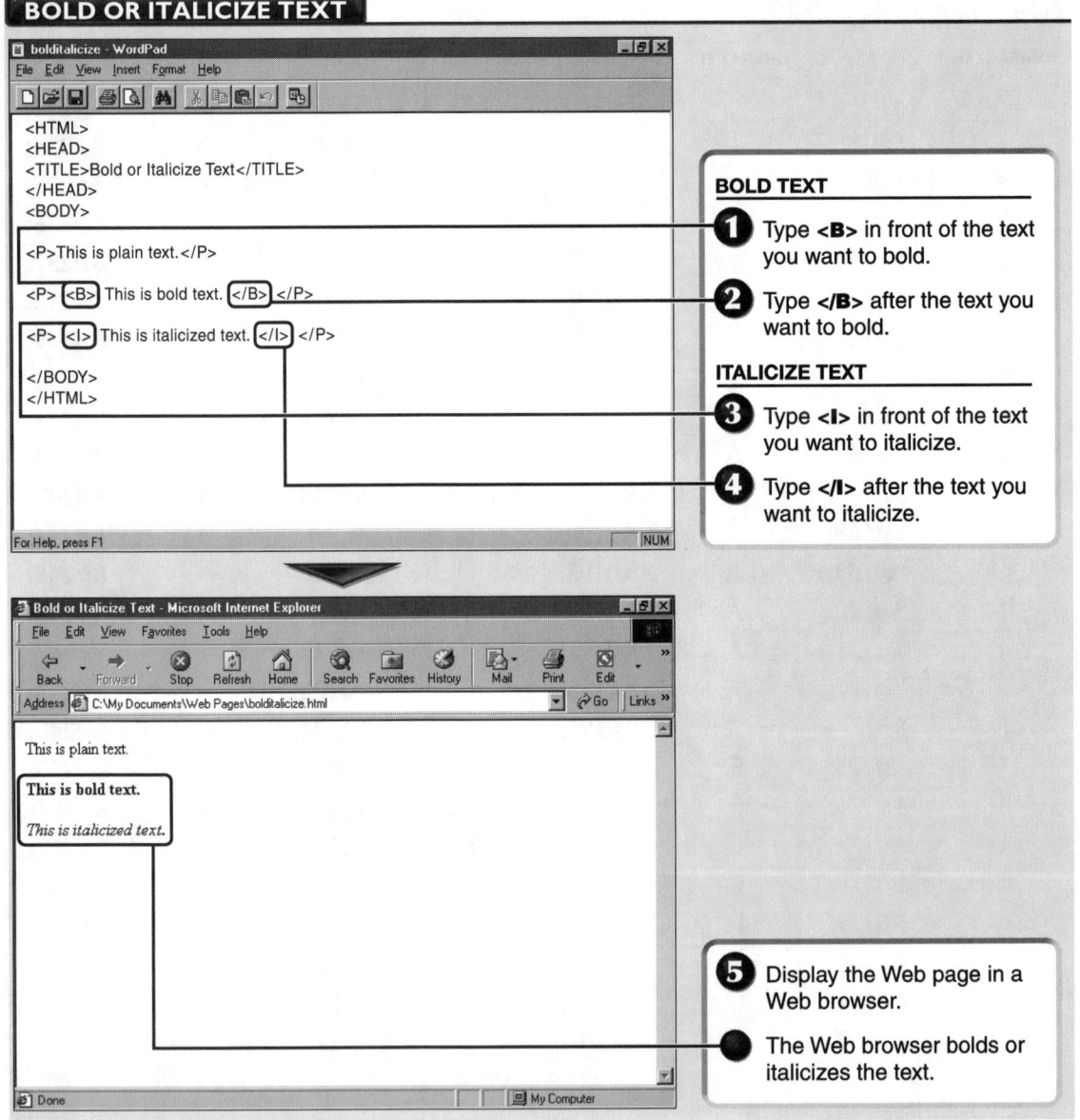

**BOLD TEXT**

**1** Type **&lt;B&gt;** in front of the text you want to bold.

**2** Type **&lt;/B&gt;** after the text you want to bold.

**ITALICIZE TEXT**

**3** Type **&lt;I&gt;** in front of the text you want to italicize.

**4** Type **&lt;/I&gt;** after the text you want to italicize.

**5** Display the Web page in a Web browser.

● The Web browser bolds or italicizes the text.

# STRIKE OUT OR UNDERLINE TEXT

You can place a line through text to show changes to information. Companies often strike out old prices to show that new prices are lower. You can also underline text to emphasize information. You should be careful when underlining text on a Web page, however, since users may think the text is a link.

## STRIKE OUT OR UNDERLINE TEXT

```
strikeout - WordPad
File  Edit  View  Insert  Format  Help

<HTML>
<HEAD>
<TITLE>Strike Out or Underline Text</TITLE>
</HEAD>
<BODY>

<P>This is plain text.</P>

<P><STRIKE> You can strike out this text. </STRIKE></P>

<P><U> This text is underlined. </U></P>

</BODY>
</HTML>

For Help, press F1                                    NUM
```

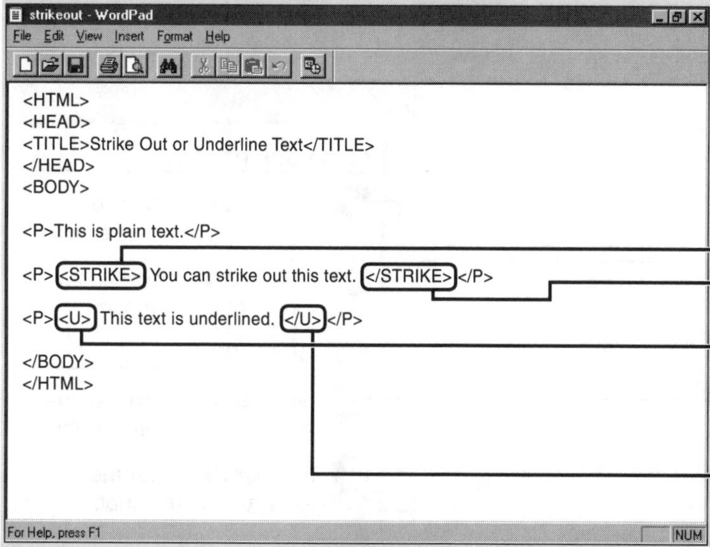

### STRIKE OUT TEXT

**1** Type **<STRIKE>** in front of the text you want to strike out.

**2** Type **</STRIKE>** after the text you want to strike out.

### UNDERLINE TEXT

**3** Type **<U>** in front of the text you want to underline.

**4** Type **</U>** after the text you want to underline.

```
Strike Out or Underline Text - Microsoft Internet Explorer
File  Edit  View  Favorites  Tools  Help

Back  Forward  Stop  Refresh  Home   Search  Favorites  History   Mail  Print  Edit

Address  C:\My Documents\Web Pages\strikeout.html              Go   Links

This is plain text.

You can strike out this text.

This text is underlined.



Done                                          My Computer
```

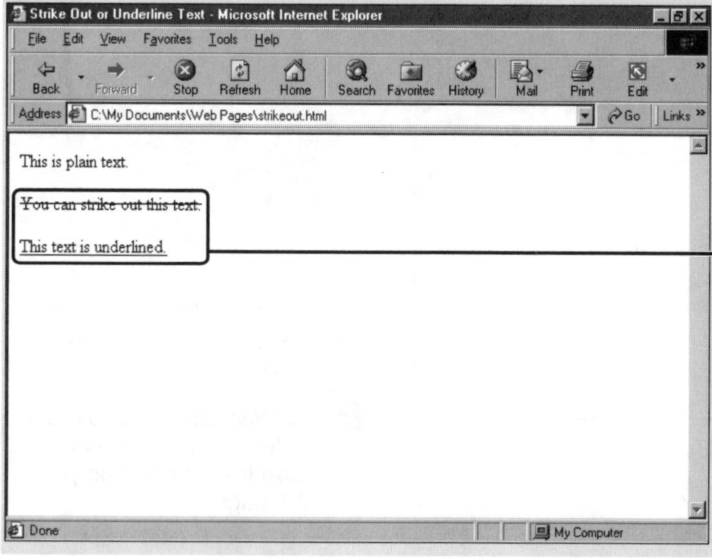

**5** Display the Web page in a Web browser.

● The Web browser displays a line through or under the text.

*Note: The STRIKE and U tags are still supported by Web browsers, but the use of style sheets is now preferred.*

# SUPERSCRIPT OR SUBSCRIPT TEXT

You can place text or numbers slightly above or below the main text on your Web page. Superscripts and subscripts are ideal for displaying mathematical equations. When superscripting or subscripting text, keep in mind that some Web browsers may display superscript or subscript text in a smaller font size than the main text on the Web page.

## SUPERSCRIPT OR SUBSCRIPT TEXT

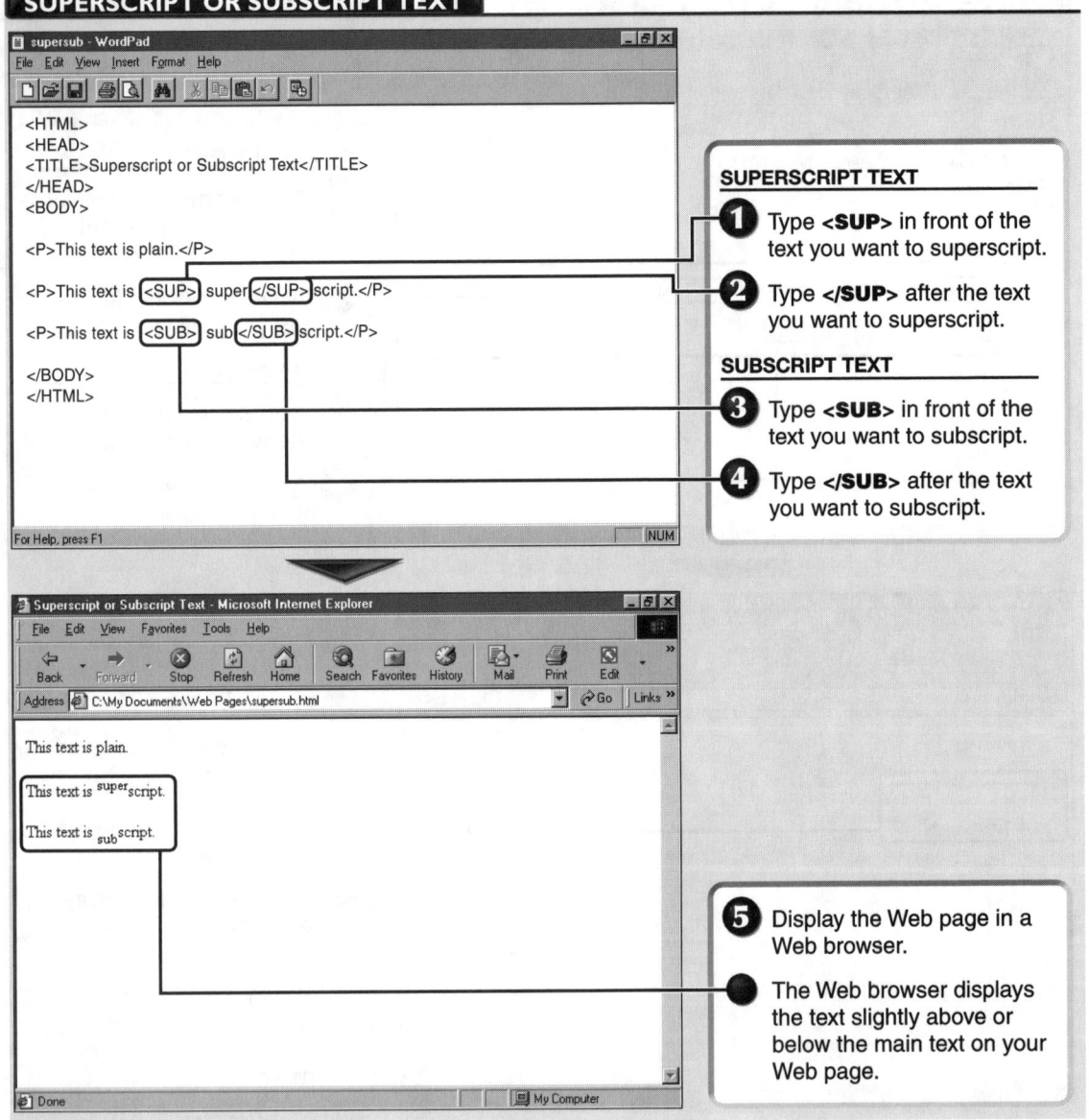

**SUPERSCRIPT TEXT**

**1** Type **<SUP>** in front of the text you want to superscript.

**2** Type **</SUP>** after the text you want to superscript.

**SUBSCRIPT TEXT**

**3** Type **<SUB>** in front of the text you want to subscript.

**4** Type **</SUB>** after the text you want to subscript.

**5** Display the Web page in a Web browser.

● The Web browser displays the text slightly above or below the main text on your Web page.

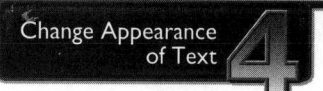

You can make text on your Web page larger or smaller than the surrounding text. The size of the surrounding text determines the size of the text you enlarge or reduce. When you change the size of the surrounding text, the size of the enlarged or reduced text also changes proportionally.

## ENLARGE OR REDUCE TEXT

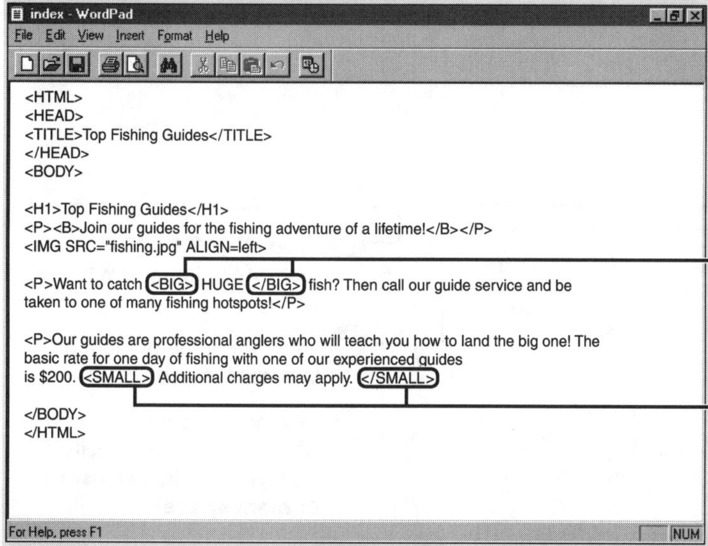

```
index - WordPad
File  Edit  View  Insert  Format  Help

<HTML>
<HEAD>
<TITLE>Top Fishing Guides</TITLE>
</HEAD>
<BODY>

<H1>Top Fishing Guides</H1>
<P><B>Join our guides for the fishing adventure of a lifetime!</B></P>
<IMG SRC="fishing.jpg" ALIGN=left>

<P>Want to catch <BIG> HUGE </BIG> fish? Then call our guide service and be
taken to one of many fishing hotspots!</P>

<P>Our guides are professional anglers who will teach you how to land the big one! The
basic rate for one day of fishing with one of our experienced guides
is $200. <SMALL> Additional charges may apply. </SMALL>

</BODY>
</HTML>

For Help, press F1                                                     NUM
```

### ENLARGE TEXT

**1** Type **<BIG>** in front of the text you want to enlarge.

**2** Type **</BIG>** after the text you want to enlarge.

### REDUCE TEXT

**3** Type **<SMALL>** in front of the text you want to reduce.

**4** Type **</SMALL>** after the text you want to reduce.

```
Top Fishing Guides - Microsoft Internet Explorer
File  Edit  View  Favorites  Tools  Help

Back  Forward  Stop  Refresh  Home  Search  Favorites  History  Mail  Print  Edit
Address  C:\My Documents\Web Pages\index.html                    Go   Links
```

# Top Fishing Guides

**Join our guides for the fishing adventure of a lifetime!**

Want to catch HUGE fish? Then call our guide service and be taken to one of many fishing hotspots!

Our guides are professional anglers who will teach you how to land the big one! The basic rate for one day of fishing with one of our experienced guides is $200. Additional charges may apply.

```
Done                                      My Computer
```

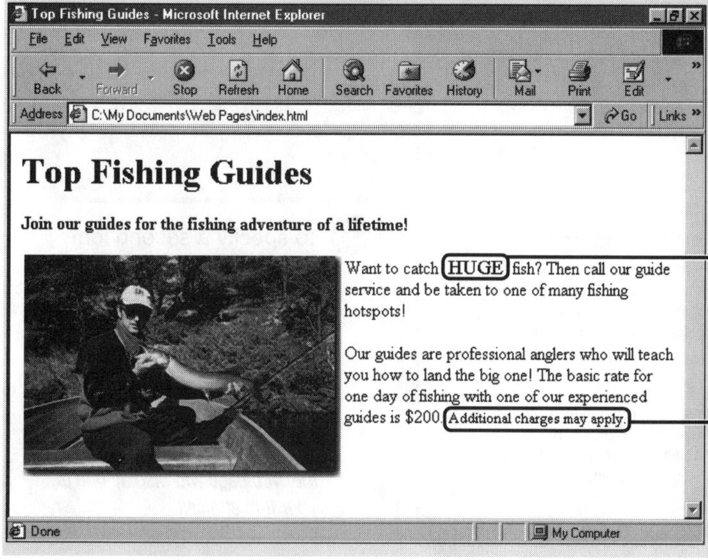

**5** Display the Web page in a Web browser.

● The Web browser enlarges or reduces the size of the text relative to the surrounding text.

You can change the font of a section of text to customize the appearance of your Web page. You should specify more than one font in case your first font choice is not available on a user's computer. You can specify a font by name or by font type.

## CHANGE THE FONT

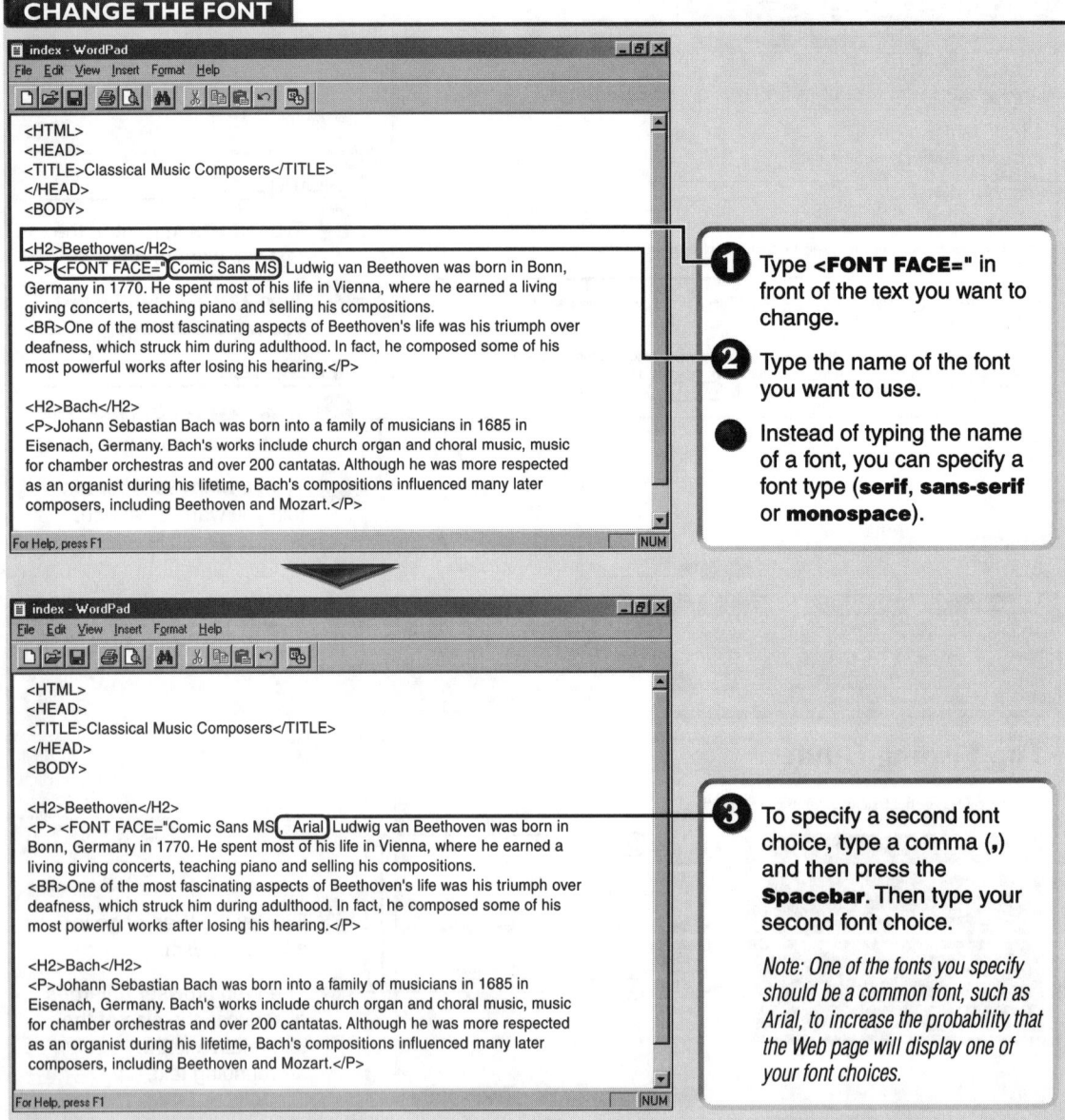

**1** Type **<FONT FACE="** in front of the text you want to change.

**2** Type the name of the font you want to use.

● Instead of typing the name of a font, you can specify a font type (**serif**, **sans-serif** or **monospace**).

**3** To specify a second font choice, type a comma (**,**) and then press the **Spacebar**. Then type your second font choice.

*Note: One of the fonts you specify should be a common font, such as Arial, to increase the probability that the Web page will display one of your font choices.*

# in an Instant

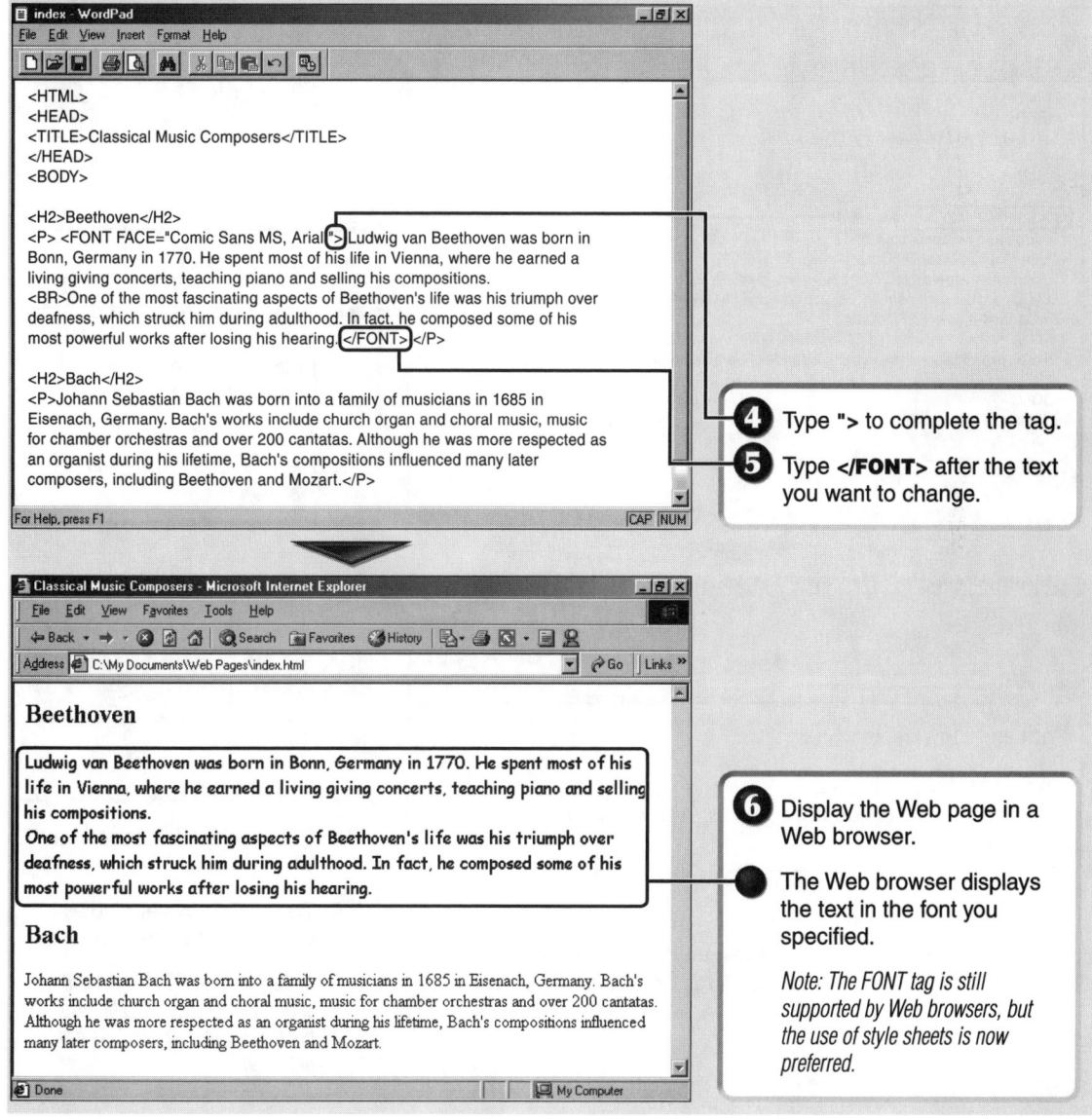

**4** Type "**>**" to complete the tag.

**5** Type **</FONT>** after the text you want to change.

**6** Display the Web page in a Web browser.

● The Web browser displays the text in the font you specified.

*Note: The FONT tag is still supported by Web browsers, but the use of style sheets is now preferred.*

# CHANGE FONT SIZE

You can change the size of all the text on your Web page, a section of text or even individual characters. Larger text is easier to read, but smaller text allows you to fit more information on a screen. There are seven font sizes you can use. The smallest font size is 1 and the largest font size is 7.

## CHANGE FONT SIZE

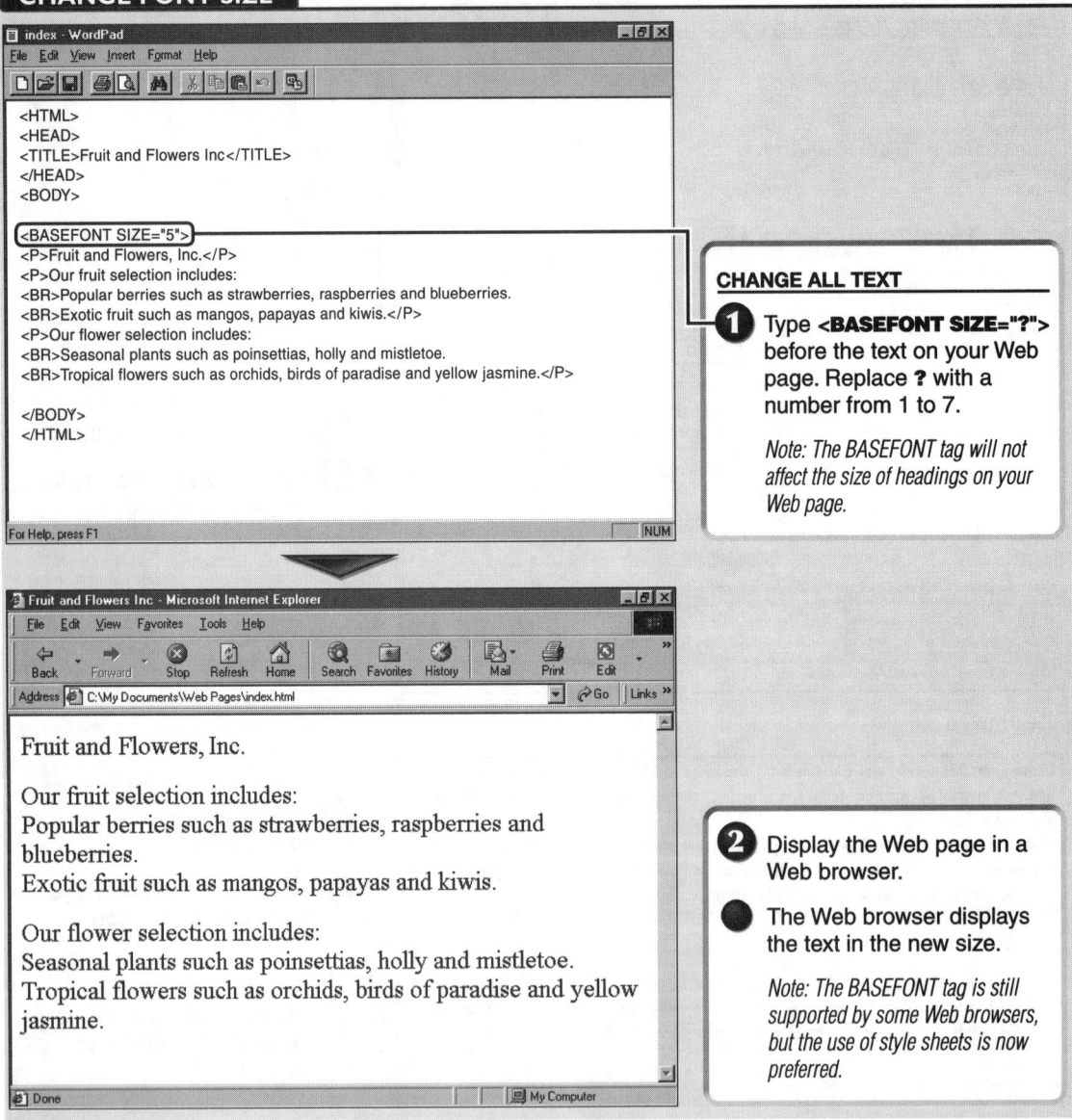

**CHANGE ALL TEXT**

**1** Type **<BASEFONT SIZE="?">** before the text on your Web page. Replace **?** with a number from 1 to 7.

*Note: The BASEFONT tag will not affect the size of headings on your Web page.*

**2** Display the Web page in a Web browser.

● The Web browser displays the text in the new size.

*Note: The BASEFONT tag is still supported by some Web browsers, but the use of style sheets is now preferred.*

in an *instant*

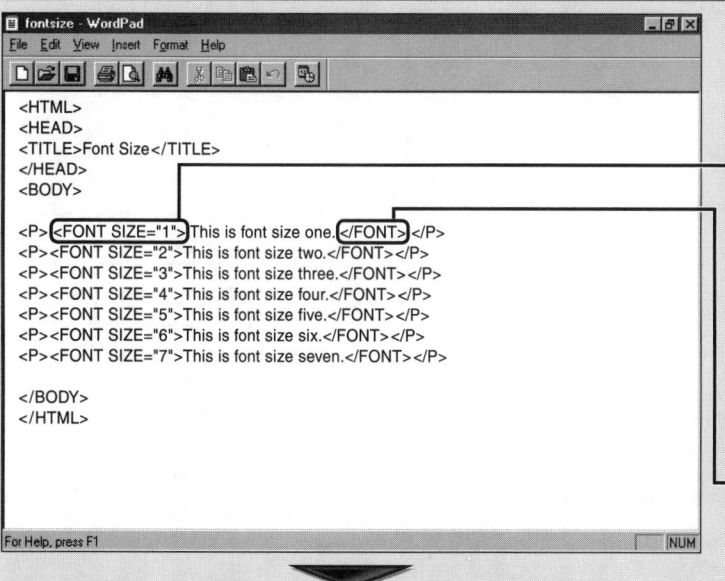

**CHANGE A SECTION OF TEXT**

**1** Type **<FONT SIZE="?">** in front of the text you want to change. Replace **?** with a number from 1 to 7.

*Note: You can type a plus (+) or minus (-) sign before the number to specify a size relative to the surrounding text. For example, type **+2** to make the text two sizes larger than the surrounding text.*

**2** Type **</FONT>** after the text you want to change.

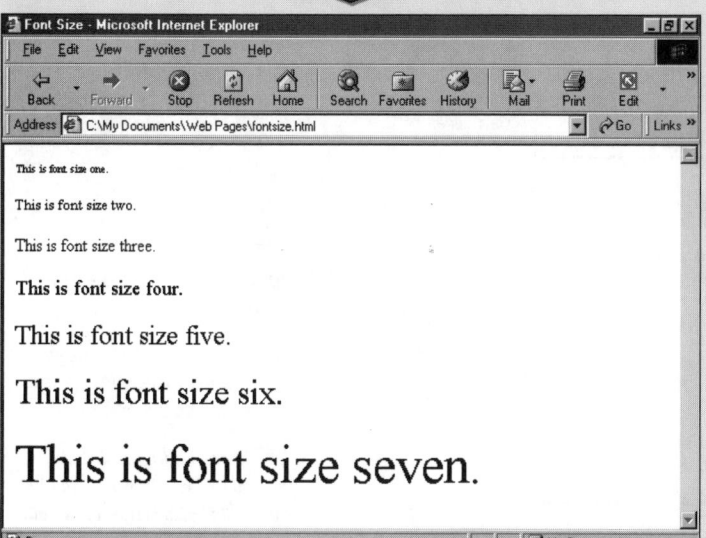

**3** Display the Web page in a Web browser.

● The Web browser displays the text in the new size.

*Note: The FONT tag is still supported by Web browsers, but the use of style sheets is now preferred.*

You can change the color of text on all or part of your Web page. The colors you choose for the text on your Web page may not appear the way you expect on some computers since some users can set their Web browsers to display the colors they prefer.

## CHANGE TEXT COLOR

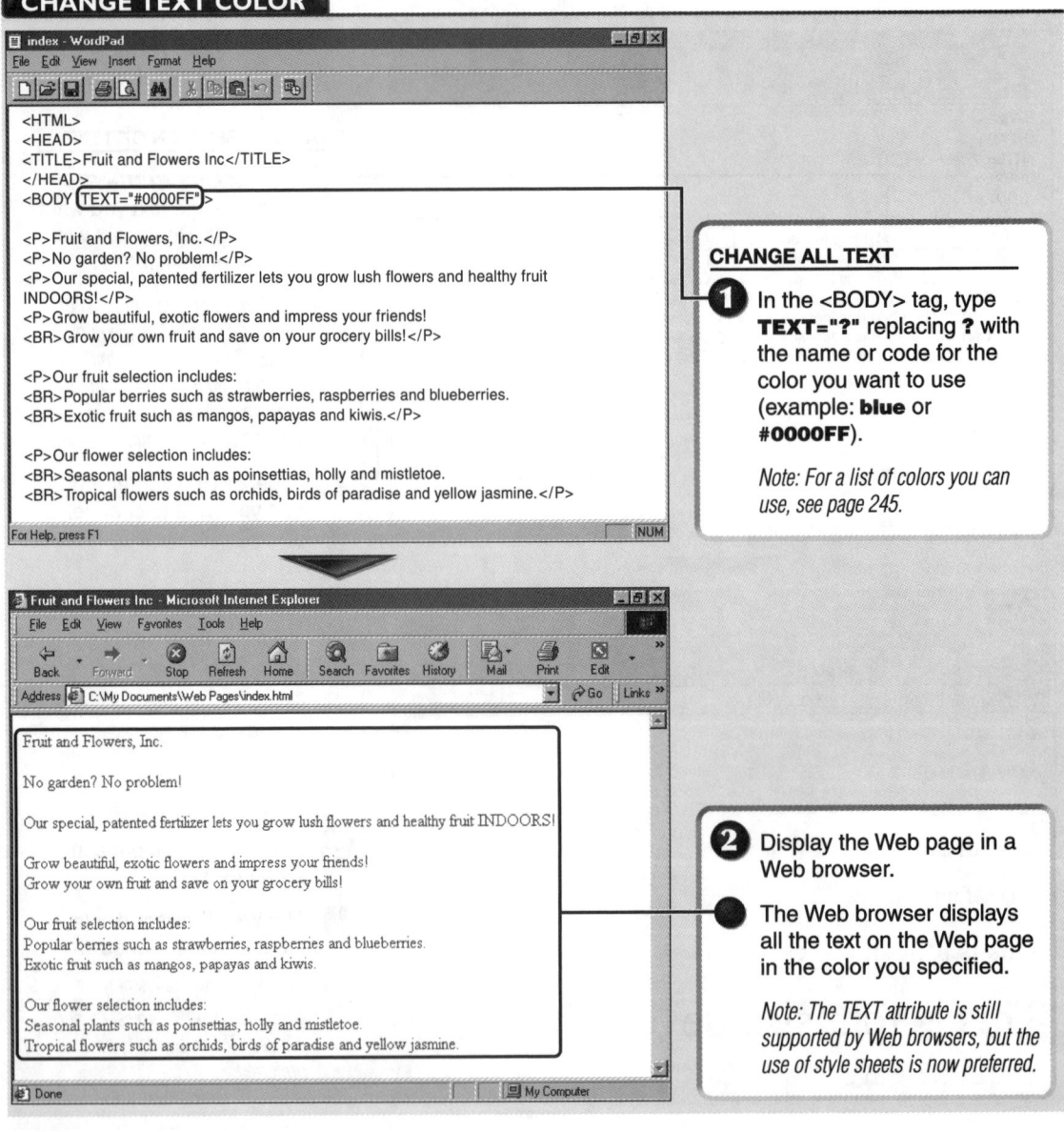

**CHANGE ALL TEXT**

**1** In the <BODY> tag, type **TEXT="?"** replacing **?** with the name or code for the color you want to use (example: **blue** or **#0000FF**).

*Note: For a list of colors you can use, see page 245.*

**2** Display the Web page in a Web browser.

The Web browser displays all the text on the Web page in the color you specified.

*Note: The TEXT attribute is still supported by Web browsers, but the use of style sheets is now preferred.*

in an *instant*

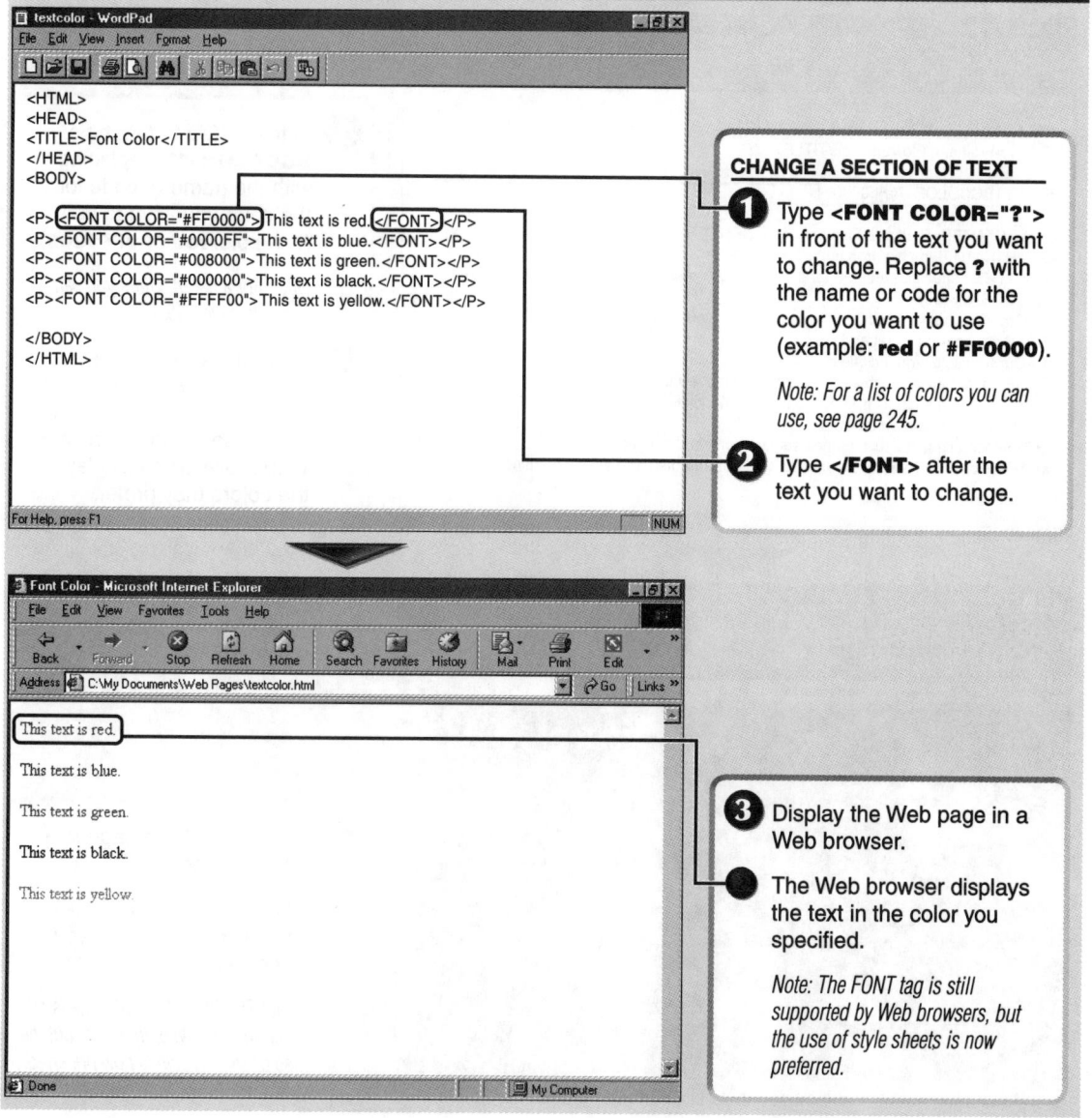

**CHANGE A SECTION OF TEXT**

**1** Type **<FONT COLOR="?">** in front of the text you want to change. Replace **?** with the name or code for the color you want to use (example: **red** or **#FF0000**).

*Note: For a list of colors you can use, see page 245.*

**2** Type **</FONT>** after the text you want to change.

**3** Display the Web page in a Web browser.

The Web browser displays the text in the color you specified.

*Note: The FONT tag is still supported by Web browsers, but the use of style sheets is now preferred.*

**41**

You can change the background color of your Web page. Make sure you choose a background color that works well with the color of your text. For example, red text on a blue background can be difficult to read.

## CHANGE BACKGROUND COLOR

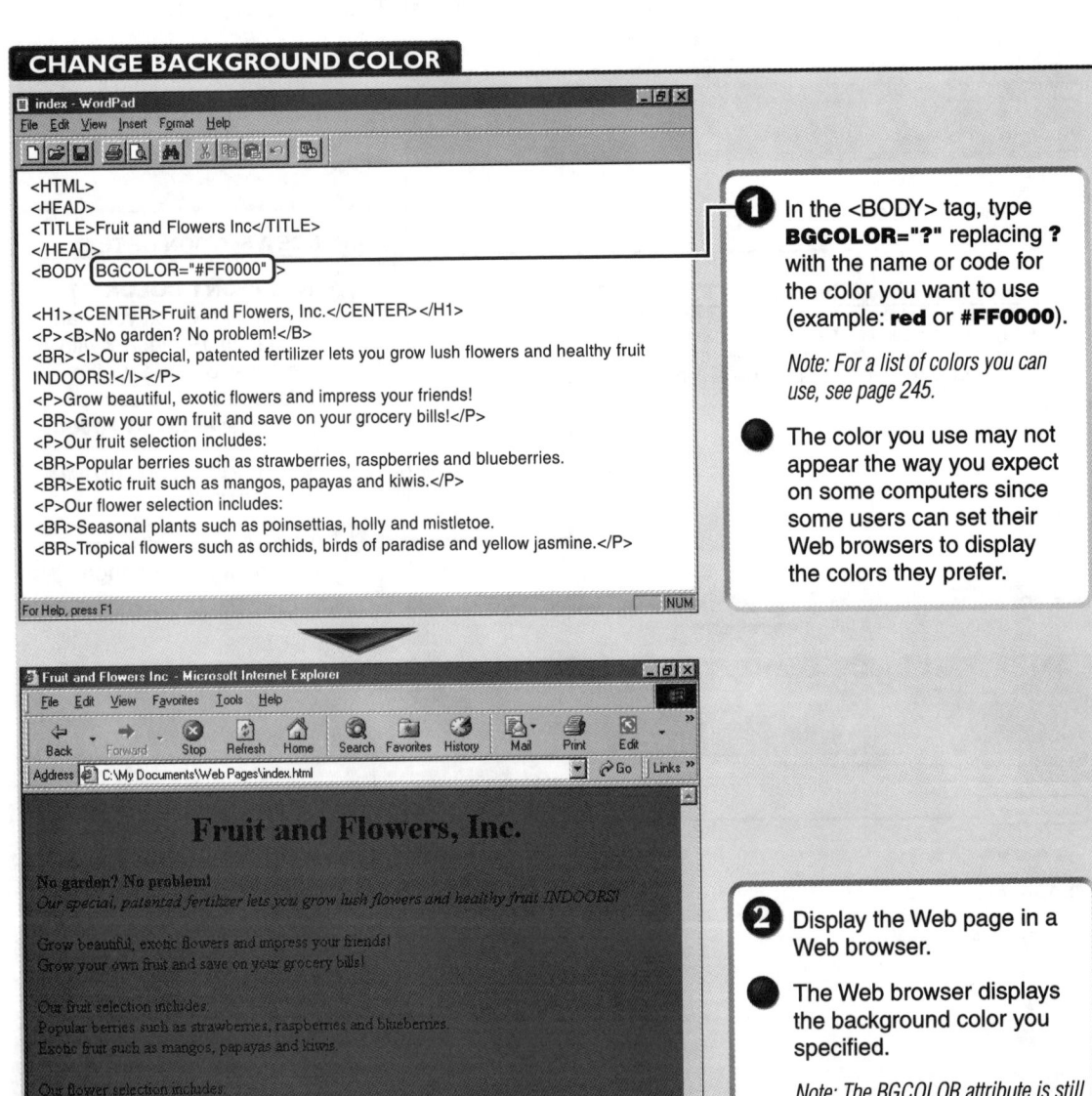

**1** In the <BODY> tag, type **BGCOLOR="?"** replacing **?** with the name or code for the color you want to use (example: **red** or **#FF0000**).

Note: For a list of colors you can use, see page 245.

● The color you use may not appear the way you expect on some computers since some users can set their Web browsers to display the colors they prefer.

**2** Display the Web page in a Web browser.

● The Web browser displays the background color you specified.

Note: The BGCOLOR attribute is still supported by Web browsers, but the use of style sheets is now preferred.

# USING TYPEWRITER TEXT

You can make text on your Web page look like it was
produced by a typewriter. Typewriter text is often used
to display instructions or information a user can enter
into a computer. Typewriter text uses a monospaced
font, which means that each character takes up the
same amount of space.

## USING TYPEWRITER TEXT

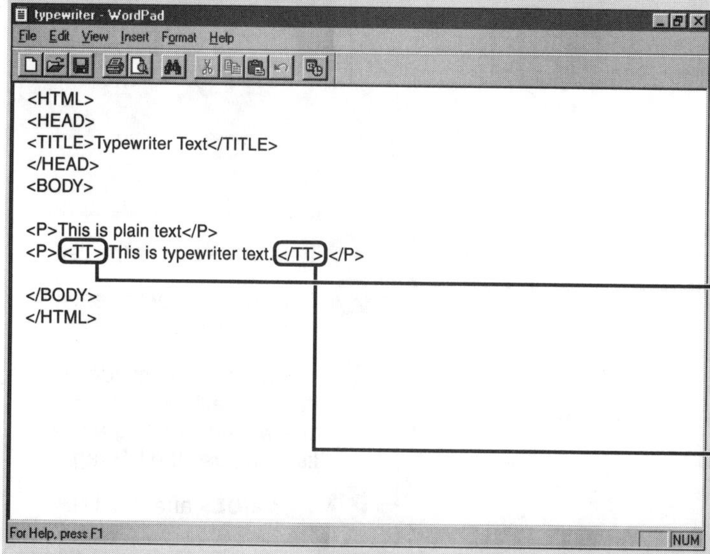

```
<HTML>
<HEAD>
<TITLE>Typewriter Text</TITLE>
</HEAD>
<BODY>

<P>This is plain text</P>
<P><TT>This is typewriter text.</TT></P>

</BODY>
</HTML>
```

*typewriter - WordPad*
File Edit View Insert Format Help

For Help, press F1 — NUM

**1** Type **<TT>** in front of the
text you want to display as
typewriter text.

**2** Type **</TT>** after the text
you want to display as
typewriter text.

*Typewriter Text - Microsoft Internet Explorer*
File Edit View Favorites Tools Help

Back  Forward  Stop  Refresh  Home  Search  Favorites  History  Mail  Print  Edit

Address C:\My Documents\Web Pages\typewriter.html

This is plain text.

```
This is typewriter text.
```

Done — My Computer

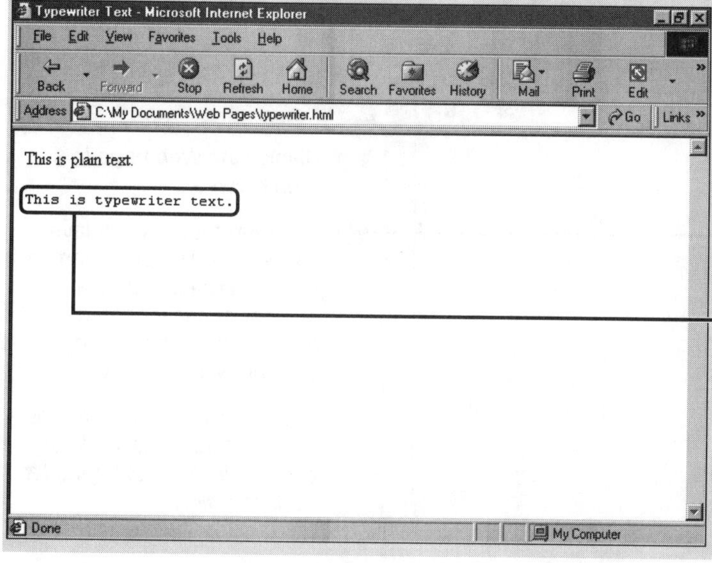

**3** Display the Web page in a
Web browser.

■ The Web browser displays
the text as typewriter text.

*Note: The typewriter text is
displayed using the monospaced
font set in the user's Web browser.
The default monospaced font is
usually Courier New.*

43

# CREATE AN ORDERED LIST

You can create an ordered list to display items in a specific order, such as a set of instructions or a table of contents. You should try to limit each item in the list to one or two lines to help improve the readability of the list. After creating an ordered list, you can change the number style for the list or change the starting value.

## CREATE AN ORDERED LIST

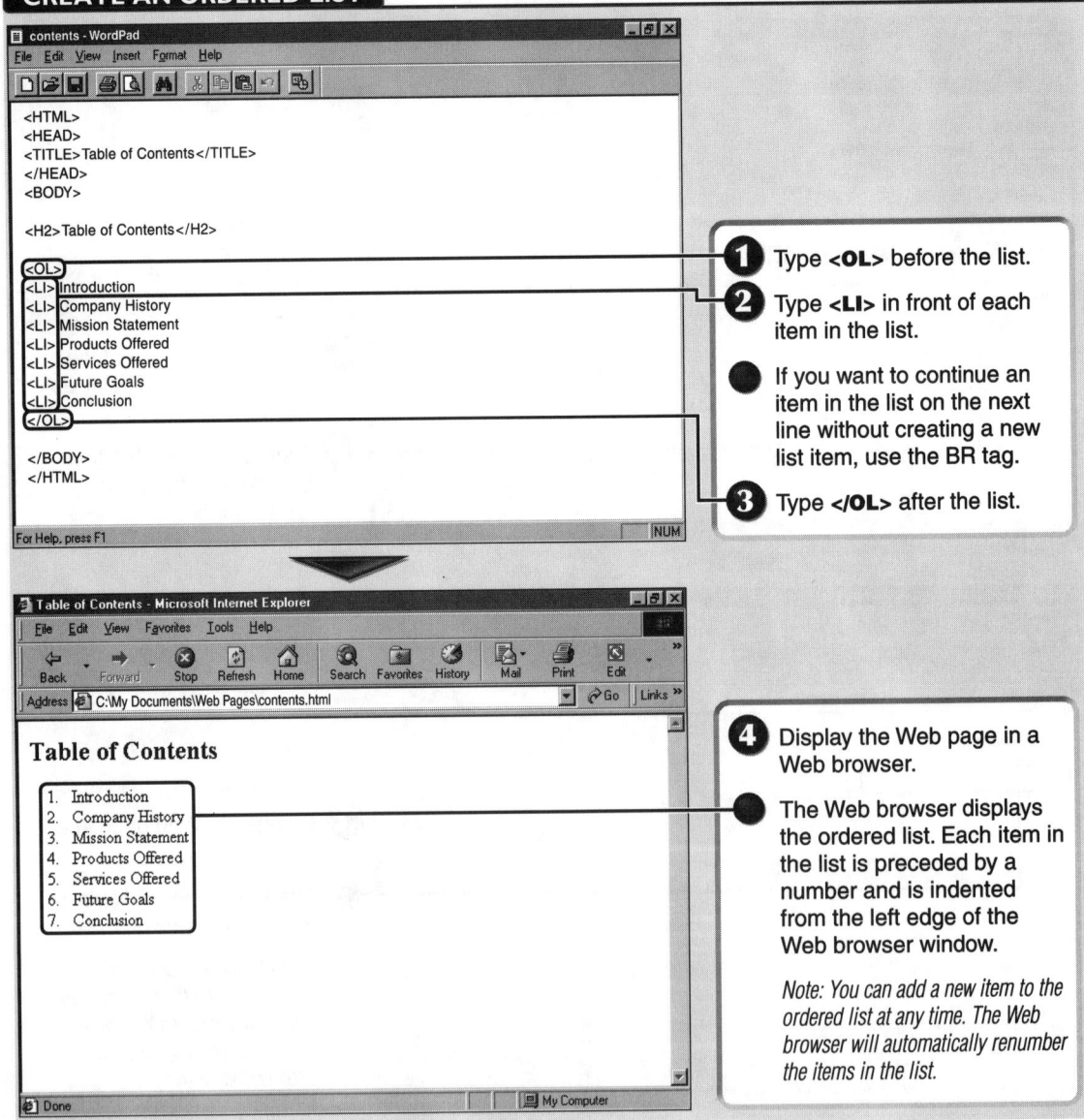

**1** Type **<OL>** before the list.

**2** Type **<LI>** in front of each item in the list.

■ If you want to continue an item in the list on the next line without creating a new list item, use the BR tag.

**3** Type **</OL>** after the list.

**4** Display the Web page in a Web browser.

■ The Web browser displays the ordered list. Each item in the list is preceded by a number and is indented from the left edge of the Web browser window.

*Note: You can add a new item to the ordered list at any time. The Web browser will automatically renumber the items in the list.*

in an *Instant*

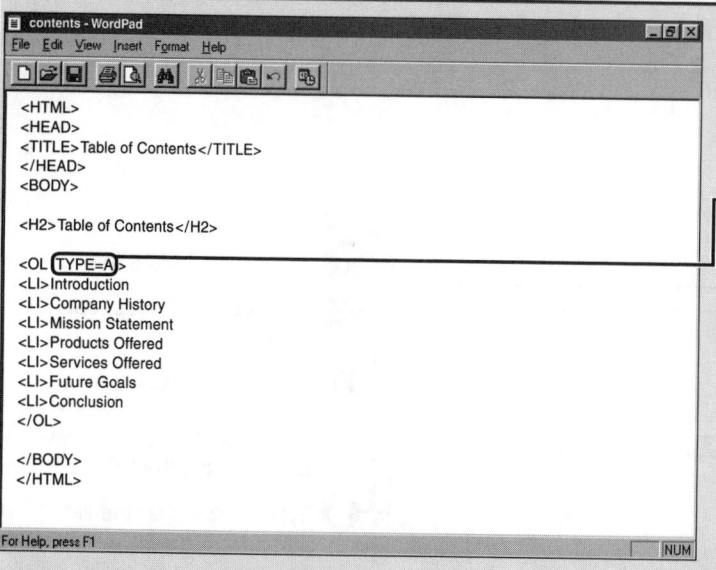

**CHANGE NUMBER STYLE**

**1** In the <OL> tag, type **TYPE=?** replacing **?** with the number style you want to use.

**A** - A, B, C

**a** - a, b, c

**I** - I, II, III

**i** - i, ii, iii

**1** - 1, 2, 3

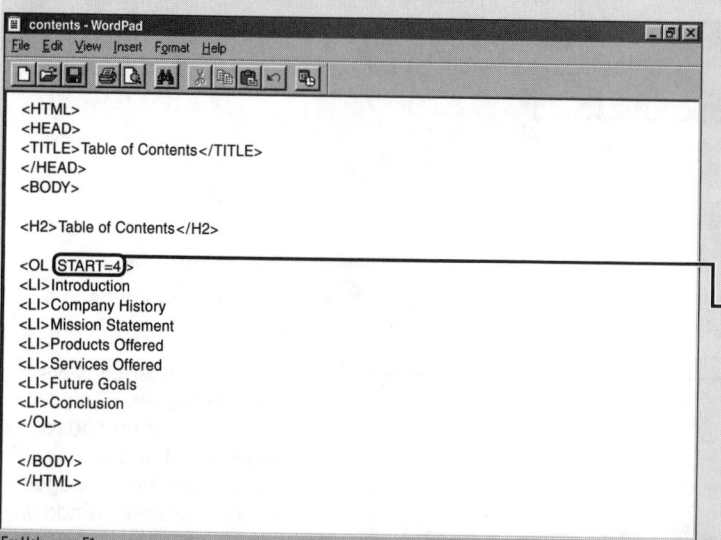

**CHANGE STARTING VALUE**

**1** In the <OL> tag, type **START=?** replacing **?** with the value you want to start the list.

*Note: The TYPE and START attributes are still supported by Web browsers, but the use of style sheets is now preferred.*

# CREATE AN UNORDERED LIST

You can create an unordered list to display items that are in no particular order, such as a list of products or Web sites. After creating an unordered list, you can specify a different bullet style for the items in the list.

## CREATE AN UNORDERED LIST

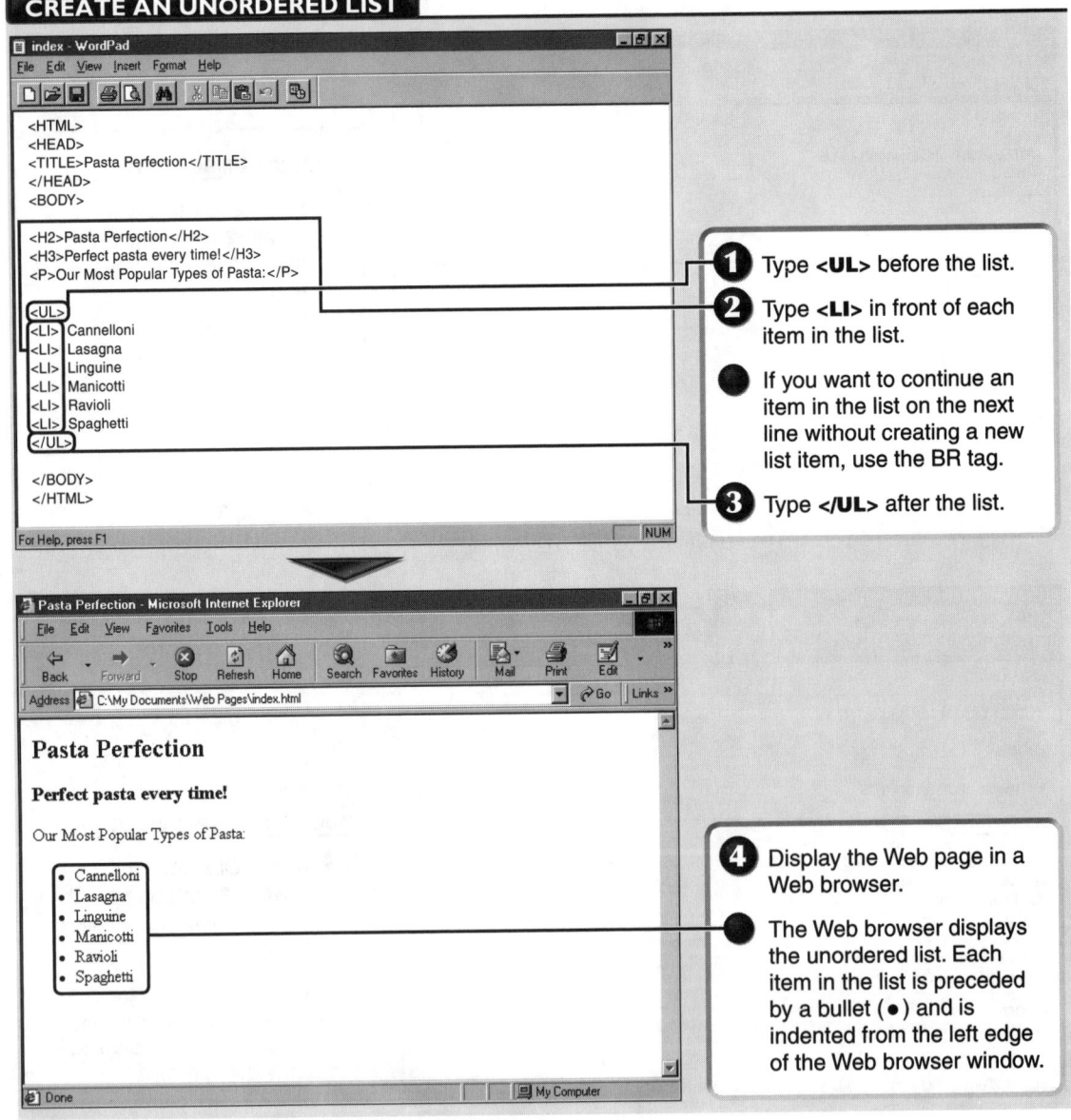

**1** Type **<UL>** before the list.

**2** Type **<LI>** in front of each item in the list.

■ If you want to continue an item in the list on the next line without creating a new list item, use the BR tag.

**3** Type **</UL>** after the list.

**4** Display the Web page in a Web browser.

■ The Web browser displays the unordered list. Each item in the list is preceded by a bullet (●) and is indented from the left edge of the Web browser window.

in an *instant*

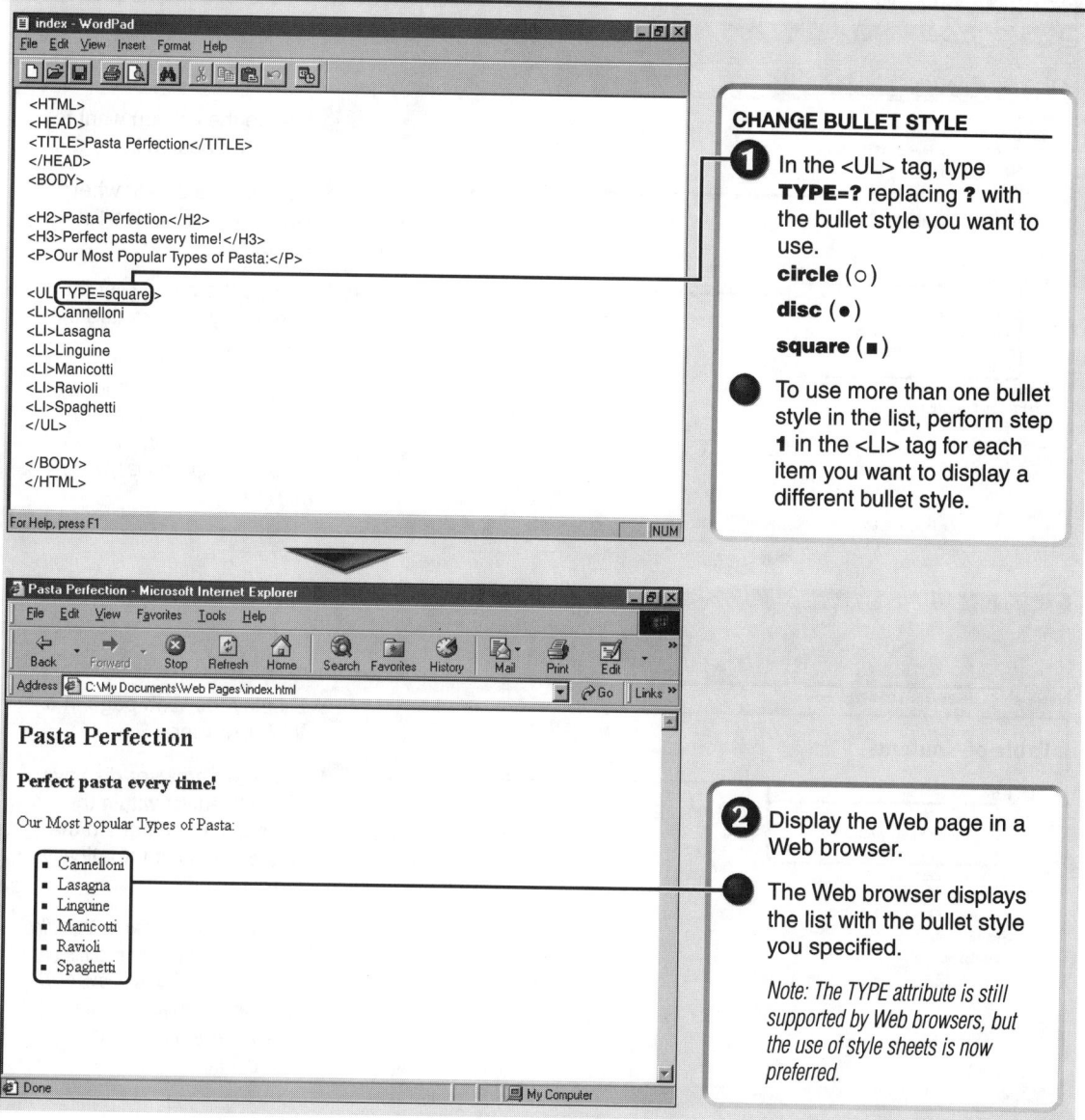

```
index - WordPad
File  Edit  View  Insert  Format  Help

<HTML>
<HEAD>
<TITLE>Pasta Perfection</TITLE>
</HEAD>
<BODY>

<H2>Pasta Perfection</H2>
<H3>Perfect pasta every time!</H3>
<P>Our Most Popular Types of Pasta:</P>

<UL TYPE=square>
<LI>Cannelloni
<LI>Lasagna
<LI>Linguine
<LI>Manicotti
<LI>Ravioli
<LI>Spaghetti
</UL>

</BODY>
</HTML>

For Help, press F1                                          NUM
```

**CHANGE BULLET STYLE**

**1** In the <UL> tag, type
**TYPE=?** replacing **?** with
the bullet style you want to
use.

circle ( o )

disc ( • )

square ( ■ )

● To use more than one bullet
style in the list, perform step
**1** in the <LI> tag for each
item you want to display a
different bullet style.

```
Pasta Perfection - Microsoft Internet Explorer
File  Edit  View  Favorites  Tools  Help

Back  Forward  Stop  Refresh  Home  Search  Favorites  History  Mail  Print  Edit
Address  C:\My Documents\Web Pages\index.html                    Go  Links

Pasta Perfection

Perfect pasta every time!

Our Most Popular Types of Pasta:

    ■ Cannelloni
    ■ Lasagna
    ■ Linguine
    ■ Manicotti
    ■ Ravioli
    ■ Spaghetti

Done                                          My Computer
```

**2** Display the Web page in a
Web browser.

● The Web browser displays
the list with the bullet style
you specified.

*Note: The TYPE attribute is still
supported by Web browsers, but
the use of style sheets is now
preferred.*

**47**

# CREATE A NESTED LIST

A nested list is a list within a list. You can create a nested list to provide additional information about an item in a list. This allows you to create a list with several levels of items, such as a project outline. A nested list can be an ordered or unordered list, regardless of the type of the main list.

## CREATE A NESTED LIST

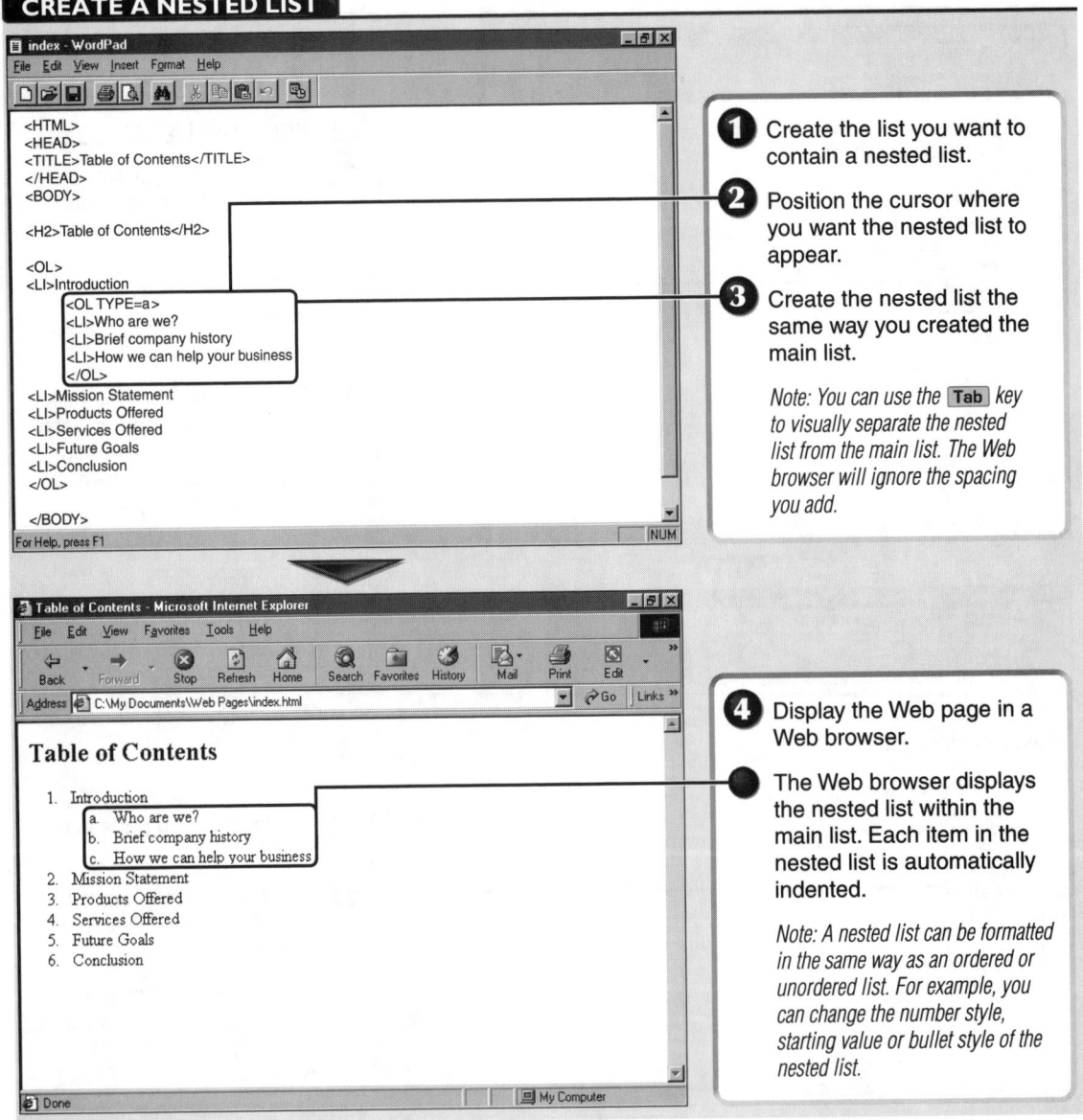

**1** Create the list you want to contain a nested list.

**2** Position the cursor where you want the nested list to appear.

**3** Create the nested list the same way you created the main list.

*Note: You can use the* **Tab** *key to visually separate the nested list from the main list. The Web browser will ignore the spacing you add.*

**4** Display the Web page in a Web browser.

■ The Web browser displays the nested list within the main list. Each item in the nested list is automatically indented.

*Note: A nested list can be formatted in the same way as an ordered or unordered list. For example, you can change the number style, starting value or bullet style of the nested list.*

# CREATE A DEFINITION LIST

You can create a definition list to display terms and their definitions. This type of list is ideal for a glossary. Web browsers automatically left align the terms in a definition list. The definitions appear below the terms and are indented from the left side of the Web page.

## CREATE A DEFINITION LIST

```
glossary - WordPad
File  Edit  View  Insert  Format  Help

<HTML>
<HEAD>
<TITLE>Internet Glossary</TITLE>
</HEAD>
<BODY>

<H2>Internet Glossary</H2>

<DL>
<DT>Anonymous FTP
<DD>A way to transfer files between computers on the Internet without needing a password.
<DT>Anti-virus software
<DD>Software viruses are annoying bits of code that can corrupt your program files. To protect your
computer, you should use anti-virus software.
</DL>

</BODY>
</HTML>

For Help, press F1                                                          NUM
```

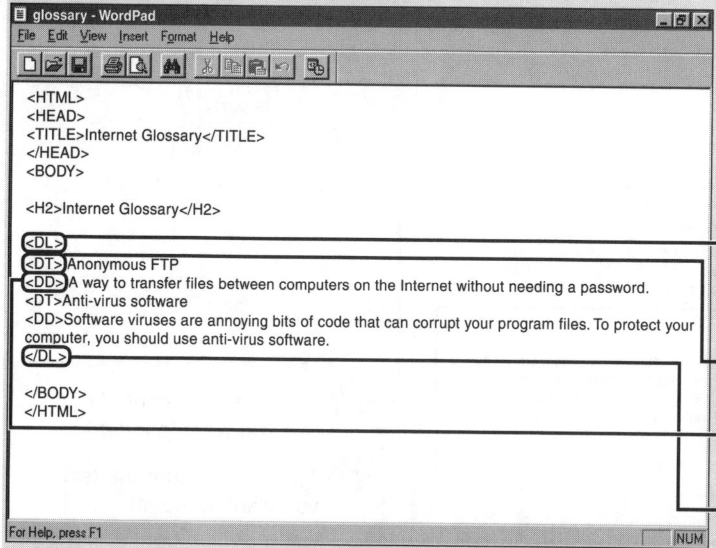

**1** Type **<DL>** before the list.

**2** Type **<DT>** in front of each term in the list.

**3** Type **<DD>** in front of each definition in the list.

**4** Type **</DL>** after the list.

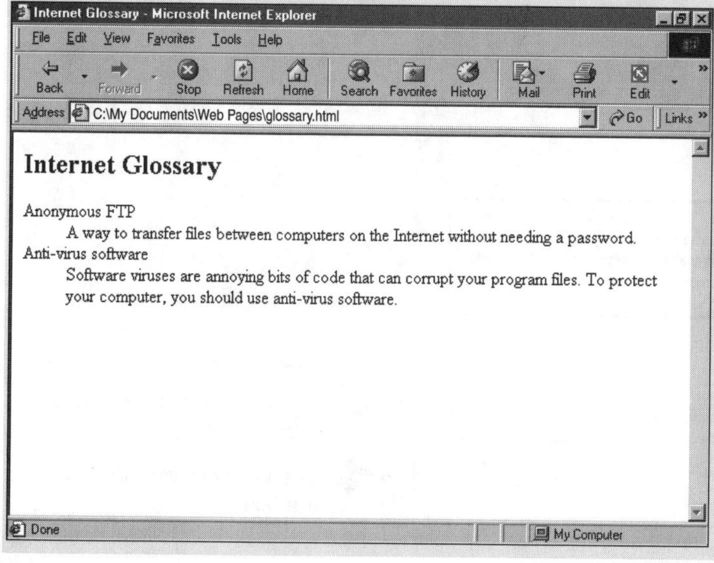

```
Internet Glossary - Microsoft Internet Explorer
File  Edit  View  Favorites  Tools  Help

Back  Forward  Stop  Refresh  Home  Search  Favorites  History  Mail  Print  Edit

Address  C:\My Documents\Web Pages\glossary.html              Go   Links
```

### Internet Glossary

Anonymous FTP
    A way to transfer files between computers on the Internet without needing a password.
Anti-virus software
    Software viruses are annoying bits of code that can corrupt your program files. To protect your computer, you should use anti-virus software.

```
Done                                          My Computer
```

**5** Display the Web page in a Web browser.

● The Web browser displays the definition list. Each definition is indented from the left side of the Web page.

# INDENT TEXT USING LISTS

You can indent text to set off paragraphs on your Web page. When you indent text, you use the same tag you would use to create an unordered list. Web browsers will indent every line in the section of text you specify.

## INDENT TEXT USING LISTS

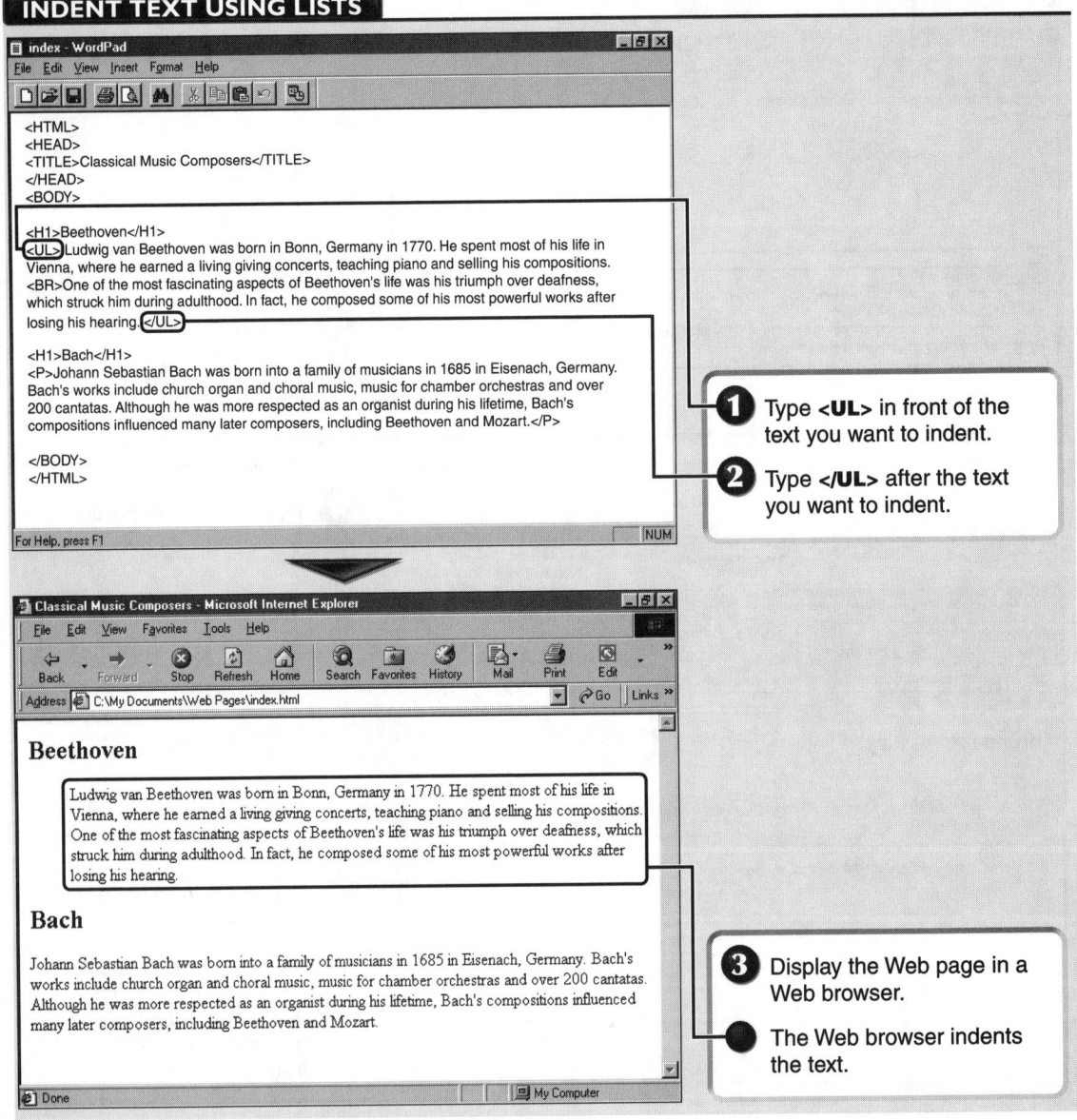

**1** Type **<UL>** in front of the text you want to indent.

**2** Type **</UL>** after the text you want to indent.

**3** Display the Web page in a Web browser.

● The Web browser indents the text.

You can create a block quote to separate a section of text from the rest of the text on your Web page. Block quotes usually appear indented from both sides of a Web page and are often used for displaying long quotations. You can include any amount of text in a block quote.

## CREATE A BLOCK QUOTE

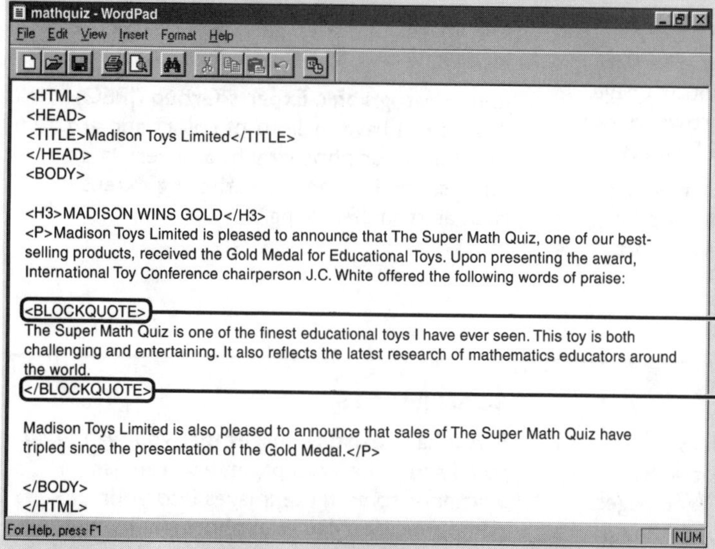

```
mathquiz - WordPad
File  Edit  View  Insert  Format  Help

<HTML>
<HEAD>
<TITLE>Madison Toys Limited</TITLE>
</HEAD>
<BODY>

<H3>MADISON WINS GOLD</H3>
<P>Madison Toys Limited is pleased to announce that The Super Math Quiz, one of our best-
selling products, received the Gold Medal for Educational Toys. Upon presenting the award,
International Toy Conference chairperson J.C. White offered the following words of praise:

<BLOCKQUOTE>
The Super Math Quiz is one of the finest educational toys I have ever seen. This toy is both
challenging and entertaining. It also reflects the latest research of mathematics educators around
the world.
</BLOCKQUOTE>

Madison Toys Limited is also pleased to announce that sales of The Super Math Quiz have
tripled since the presentation of the Gold Medal.</P>

</BODY>
</HTML>

For Help, press F1                                                    NUM
```

**1** Type **<BLOCKQUOTE>** in front of the text you want to display as a block quote.

**2** Type **</BLOCKQUOTE>** after the text you want to display as a block quote.

```
Madison Toys Limited - Microsoft Internet Explorer
File  Edit  View  Favorites  Tools  Help

Back  Forward  Stop  Refresh  Home   Search  Favorites  History   Mail  Print  Edit
Address  C:\My Documents\Web Pages\mathquiz.html                          Go  Links
```

**MADISON WINS GOLD**

Madison Toys Limited is pleased to announce that The Super Math Quiz, one of our best-selling products, received the Gold Medal for Educational Toys. Upon presenting the award, International Toy Conference chairperson J.C. White offered the following words of praise:

> The Super Math Quiz is one of the finest educational toys I have ever seen. This toy is both challenging and entertaining. It also reflects the latest research of mathematics educators around the world.

Madison Toys Limited is also pleased to announce that sales of The Super Math Quiz have tripled since the presentation of the Gold Medal.

Done                                                      My Computer

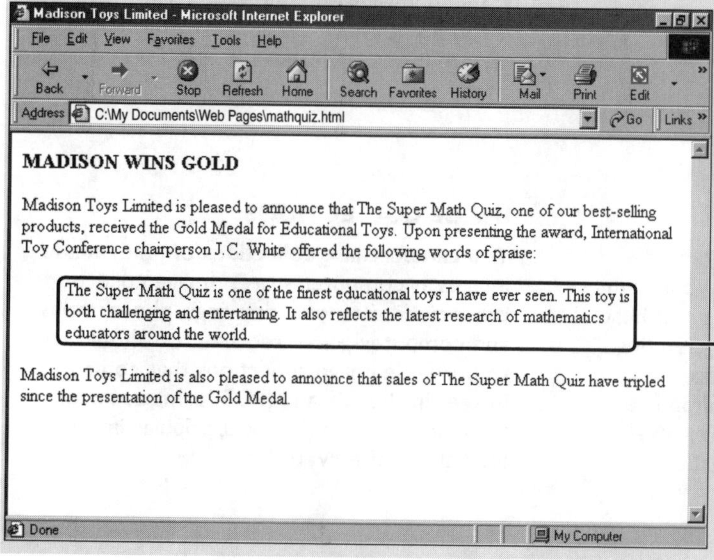

**3** Display the Web page in a Web browser.

■ The Web browser displays the text as a block quote. Block quotes are usually indented from both sides of the Web page and display a blank line before and after the text.

# INTRODUCTION TO IMAGES

You can add images, such as photographs, drawings, picture bullets and navigation buttons, to your Web pages. Images can help illustrate ideas, add visual interest and help break up long sections of text on a Web page.

## TYPES OF IMAGES

When adding images to your Web pages, you should use GIF or JPEG images. The GIF and JPEG formats are the most popular image formats on the Web. Most Web browsers can display images in the GIF and JPEG formats.

Graphics Interchange Format (GIF) images are limited to 256 colors and are often used for logos, banners and computer-generated art.

GIF images have the .gif extension, such as logo.gif.

Joint Photographic Experts Group (JPEG) images can have millions of colors and are often used for photographs and very large images. JPEG images have the .jpg extension, such as stonehenge.jpg.

## OBTAIN IMAGES

### INTERNET

Many Web sites offer images, such as computer-generated art and photographs, that you can use for free on your Web pages. Make sure you have permission to use any images you obtain on the Web. You can find images at the following Web sites.

www.allfree-clipart.com

www.clipartconnection.com

www.noeticart.com

### SCAN IMAGES

If you have existing images that you want to add to your Web pages, you can use a scanner to scan the images into your computer. You can scan photographs, logos or drawings and then place the scanned images on your Web pages. If you do not have a scanner, many service bureaus will scan images for a fee.

### CREATE IMAGES

You can use an image editing program to create your own images. Creating your own images allows you to design images that best suit your Web pages. Popular image editing programs include Adobe Photoshop (www.adobe.com) and Jasc Paint Shop Pro (www.jasc.com). If you are creating a Web site for your company, you may want to hire a graphic artist to create images for you.

### IMAGE COLLECTIONS

You can purchase collections of ready-made images at computer stores. Image collections can include cartoons, drawings, photographs and computer-generated art. You should try to purchase image collections that contain images in the GIF and JPEG formats, since these formats are the most popular image formats on the Web.

# in an *instant*

## IMAGE CONSIDERATIONS

### IMAGE SIZE

Images increase the time Web pages take to transfer and appear on a user's screen. If a Web page takes too long to appear, users may lose interest and move to another page. Whenever possible, you should use images with small file sizes since these images will transfer faster.

If you want to include a large image on a Web page, consider adding a thumbnail image. A thumbnail image is a small version of an image that users can select to display the larger image. Displaying a thumbnail image on a Web page allows users to decide if they want to wait to view the larger image.

### IMAGE RESOLUTION

The resolution of an image refers to the clarity of the image. Higher resolution images are sharper and more detailed, but take longer to transfer and appear on a user's screen. Since most computer monitors display images at a resolution of 72 dots per inch (dpi), images you add to your Web pages do not need to have a resolution higher than 72 dpi.

### VIEW WEB PAGES WITHOUT IMAGES

Make sure your Web pages will look attractive and make sense if the images do not appear. Some users turn off the display of images to browse the Web more quickly, while others use Web browsers that cannot display images. You can provide alternative text that will appear on a Web page if the images do not appear on a user's screen.

### REUSE IMAGES

When the same image appears on several Web pages in a Web site, the image transfers only once to a computer. The computer temporarily stores a copy of the image and displays the copy each time the image appears. Using the same image on several Web pages in your Web site can help reduce the time the pages take to transfer and appear on a user's screen.

### COPYRIGHT

You may find images in books, newspapers, magazines and on the Internet that you want to add to your Web pages. If the images you want to use are copyrighted, make sure you have permission to use any of these images on your Web pages.

# ADD AN IMAGE

You can add an image to a Web page. When adding images to your Web pages, you should use GIF or JPEG images, which are the most popular types of images on the Web. Whenever possible, you should use images with small file sizes since these images will transfer faster to a user's computer.

## ADD AN IMAGE

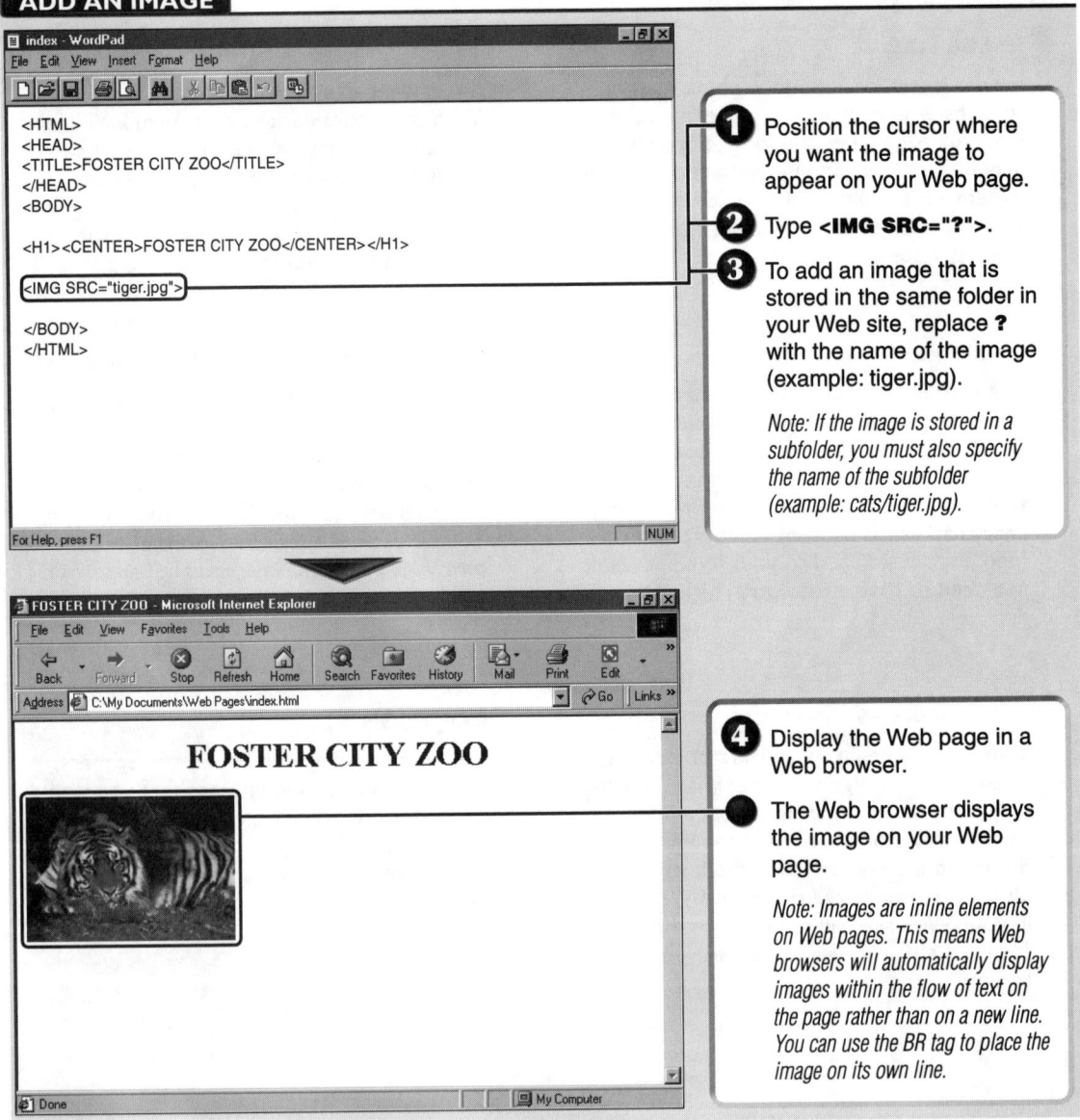

**1** Position the cursor where you want the image to appear on your Web page.

**2** Type **<IMG SRC="?">**.

**3** To add an image that is stored in the same folder in your Web site, replace **?** with the name of the image (example: tiger.jpg).

*Note: If the image is stored in a subfolder, you must also specify the name of the subfolder (example: cats/tiger.jpg).*

**4** Display the Web page in a Web browser.

■ The Web browser displays the image on your Web page.

*Note: Images are inline elements on Web pages. This means Web browsers will automatically display images within the flow of text on the page rather than on a new line. You can use the BR tag to place the image on its own line.*

You can center an image on your Web page to enhance the appearance of the page. If the image is on the same line as another element, such as a line of text or another image, centering the image will automatically display the image on its own line.

**CENTER AN IMAGE**

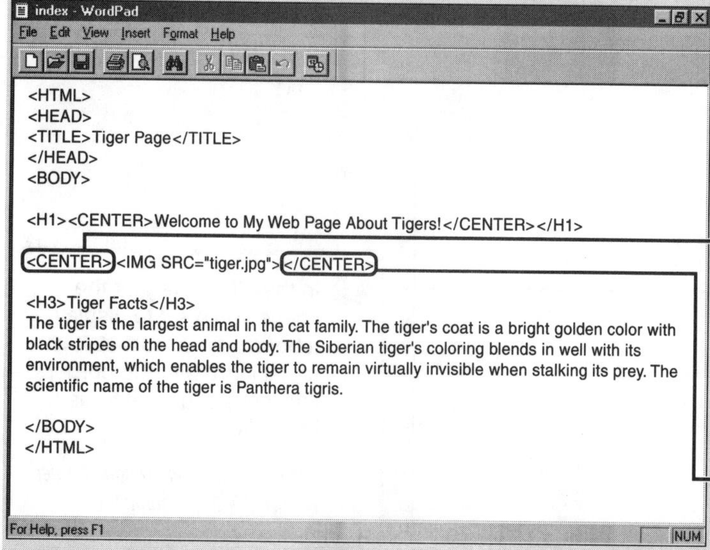

```
index - WordPad
File  Edit  View  Insert  Format  Help

<HTML>
<HEAD>
<TITLE>Tiger Page</TITLE>
</HEAD>
<BODY>

<H1><CENTER>Welcome to My Web Page About Tigers!</CENTER></H1>

<CENTER><IMG SRC="tiger.jpg"></CENTER>

<H3>Tiger Facts</H3>
The tiger is the largest animal in the cat family. The tiger's coat is a bright golden color with
black stripes on the head and body. The Siberian tiger's coloring blends in well with its
environment, which enables the tiger to remain virtually invisible when stalking its prey. The
scientific name of the tiger is Panthera tigris.

</BODY>
</HTML>

For Help, press F1                                                    NUM
```

**1** Type **<CENTER>** in front of the image you want to center.

**2** Type **</CENTER>** after the image you want to center.

```
Tiger Page - Microsoft Internet Explorer
File  Edit  View  Favorites  Tools  Help

Back  Forward  Stop  Refresh  Home  Search  Favorites  History  Mail  Print  Edit
Address  C:\My Documents\Web Pages\index.html                    Go  Links
```

## Welcome to My Web Page About Tigers!

**Tiger Facts**

The tiger is the largest animal in the cat family. The tiger's coat is a bright golden color with black

Done                                          My Computer

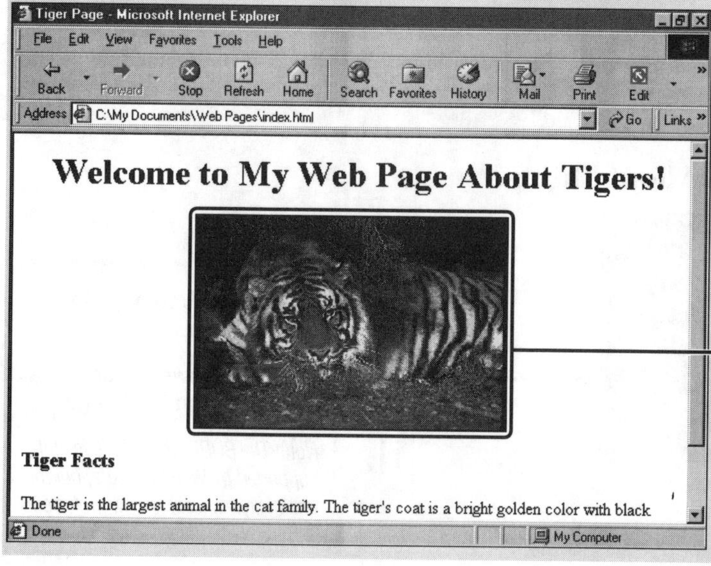

**3** Display the Web page in a Web browser.

● The Web browser centers the image.

*Note: The CENTER tag is still supported by Web browsers, but the use of style sheets is now preferred.*

# ADD A BORDER

You can improve the appearance of a Web page by adding a border to an image on the page. When adding a border, you must specify a thickness for the border. The border should be large enough to be visible, but small enough that it will not draw attention away from your image.

## ADD A BORDER

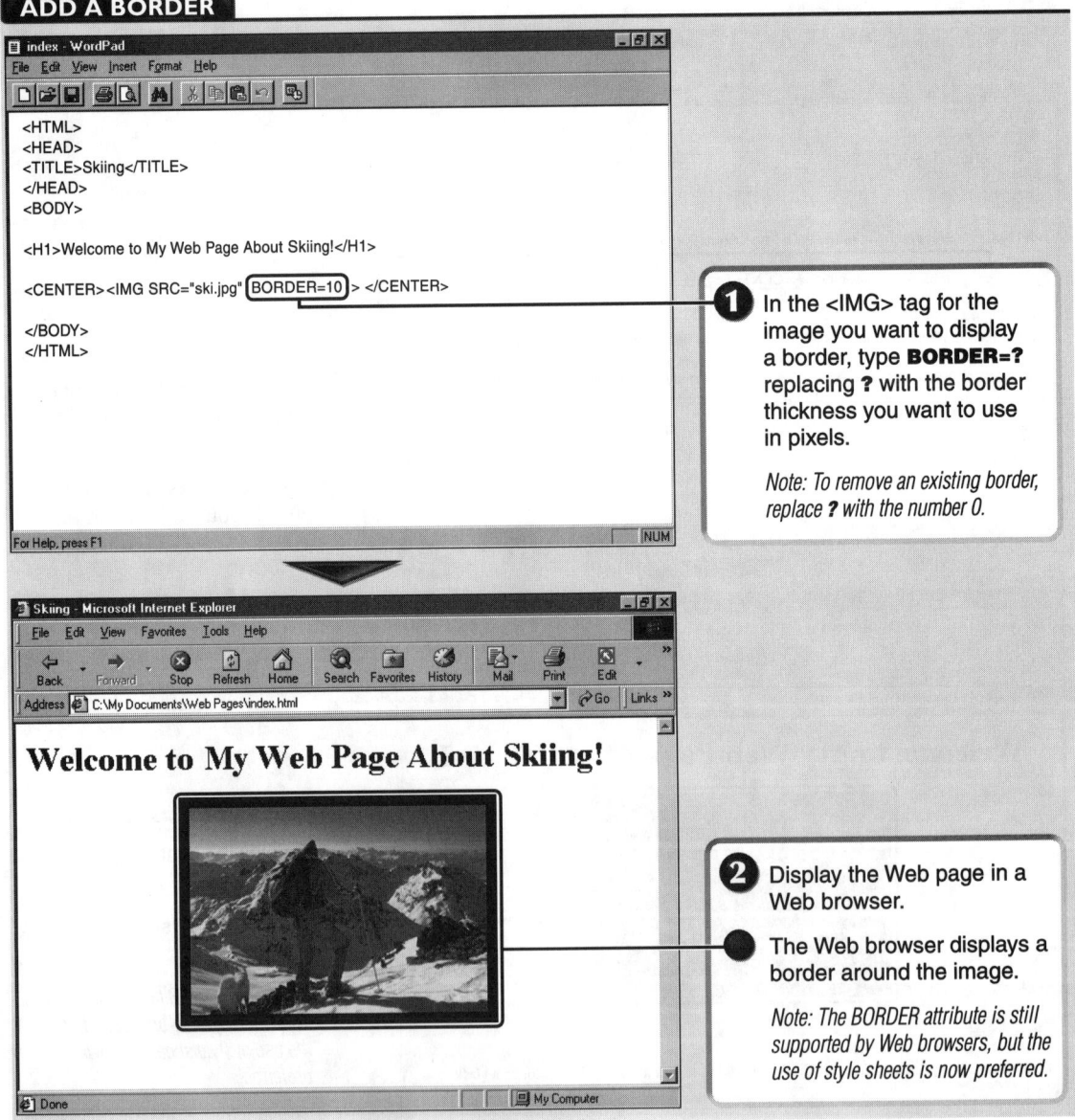

**1** In the <IMG> tag for the image you want to display a border, type **BORDER=?** replacing **?** with the border thickness you want to use in pixels.

*Note: To remove an existing border, replace **?** with the number 0.*

**2** Display the Web page in a Web browser.

■ The Web browser displays a border around the image.

*Note: The BORDER attribute is still supported by Web browsers, but the use of style sheets is now preferred.*

You can provide text that you want a Web browser to display if an image on your Web page does not appear. This will provide information about the image for users whose Web browsers cannot display images or who may have turned off the display of images to browse the Web more quickly.

## PROVIDE ALTERNATIVE TEXT

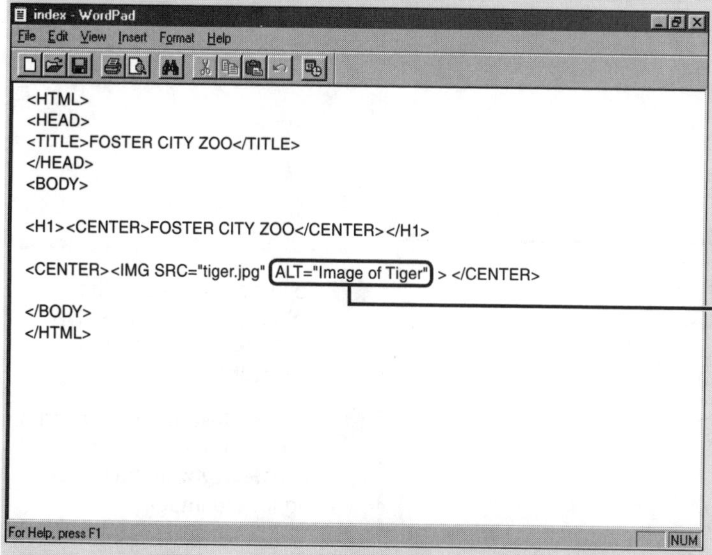

**index - WordPad**

File   Edit   View   Insert   Format   Help

```
<HTML>
<HEAD>
<TITLE>FOSTER CITY ZOO</TITLE>
</HEAD>
<BODY>

<H1><CENTER>FOSTER CITY ZOO</CENTER></H1>

<CENTER><IMG SRC="tiger.jpg" ALT="Image of Tiger" > </CENTER>

</BODY>
</HTML>
```

For Help, press F1                                                    NUM

**①** In the <IMG> tag for the image you want to offer alternative text, type **ALT="?"** replacing **?** with the text you want to display if the image does not appear.

● The text should provide a clear and concise description of the image.

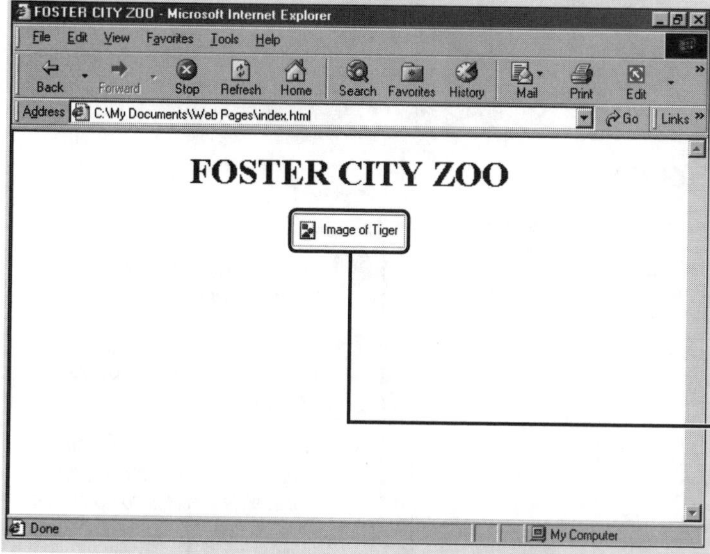

**FOSTER CITY ZOO - Microsoft Internet Explorer**

File   Edit   View   Favorites   Tools   Help

Back   Forward   Stop   Refresh   Home   Search   Favorites   History   Mail   Print   Edit

Address   C:\My Documents\Web Pages\index.html                    Go   Links »

# FOSTER CITY ZOO

Image of Tiger

Done                                                            My Computer

**②** Display the Web page in a Web browser.

● If the image does not appear, the Web browser will display the text you specified.

# WRAP TEXT AROUND AN IMAGE

You can wrap text around the right or left side of an image on your Web page. Wrapping text around an image can give the Web page a professional look. If you have aligned an image with text, you cannot wrap text around the image.

## WRAP TEXT AROUND AN IMAGE

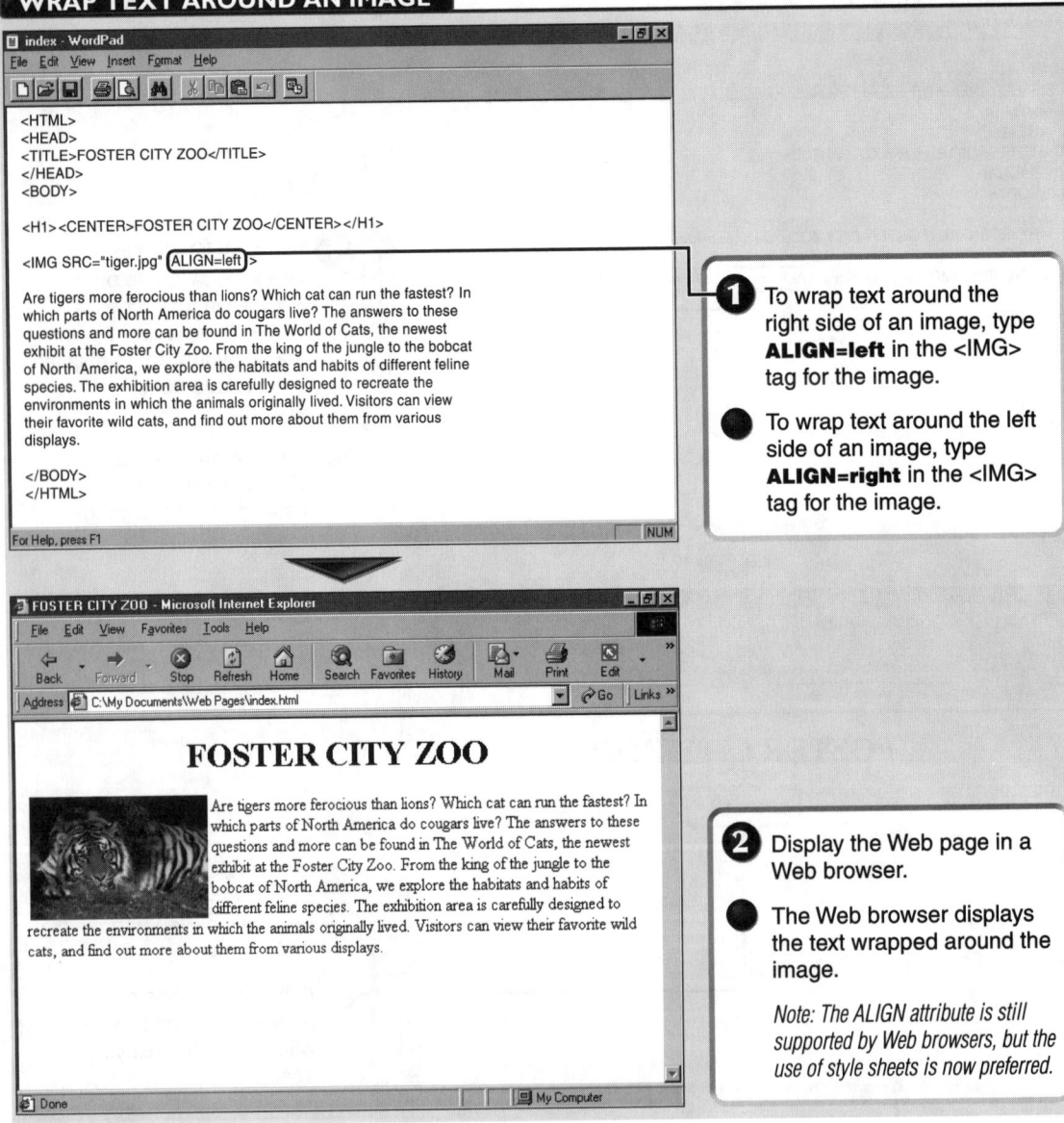

**1** To wrap text around the right side of an image, type **ALIGN=left** in the <IMG> tag for the image.

● To wrap text around the left side of an image, type **ALIGN=right** in the <IMG> tag for the image.

**2** Display the Web page in a Web browser.

● The Web browser displays the text wrapped around the image.

*Note: The ALIGN attribute is still supported by Web browsers, but the use of style sheets is now preferred.*

You can stop text from wrapping around an image and have the text continue only when the left, right or both margins are clear of images. Stopping text from wrapping is useful when you want only some of a section of text to wrap around an image.

## STOP TEXT WRAP

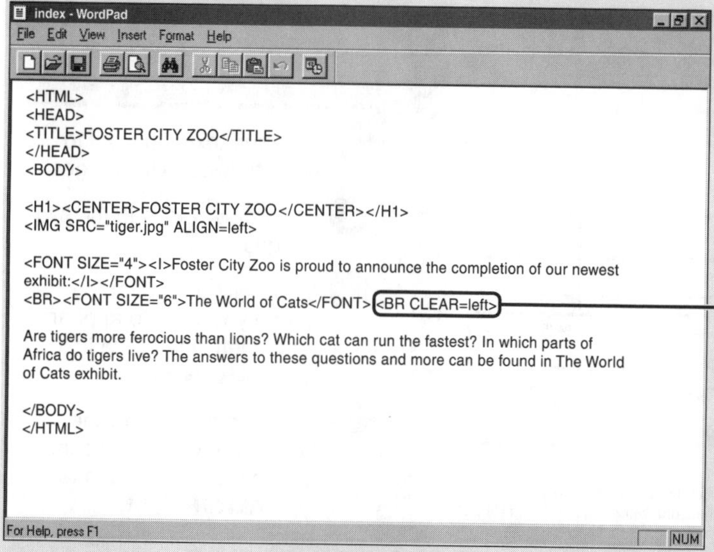

```
index - WordPad
File  Edit  View  Insert  Format  Help

<HTML>
<HEAD>
<TITLE>FOSTER CITY ZOO</TITLE>
</HEAD>
<BODY>

<H1><CENTER>FOSTER CITY ZOO</CENTER></H1>
<IMG SRC="tiger.jpg" ALIGN=left>

<FONT SIZE="4"><I>Foster City Zoo is proud to announce the completion of our newest
exhibit:</I></FONT>
<BR><FONT SIZE="6">The World of Cats</FONT><BR CLEAR=left>

Are tigers more ferocious than lions? Which cat can run the fastest? In which parts of
Africa do tigers live? The answers to these questions and more can be found in The World
of Cats exhibit.

</BODY>
</HTML>

For Help, press F1                                                              NUM
```

**1** Position the cursor where you want to stop text from wrapping around an image.

**2** Type **<BR CLEAR=?>** replacing **?** with the margin(s) you want to be clear of images before the text continues (**left**, **right** or **all**).

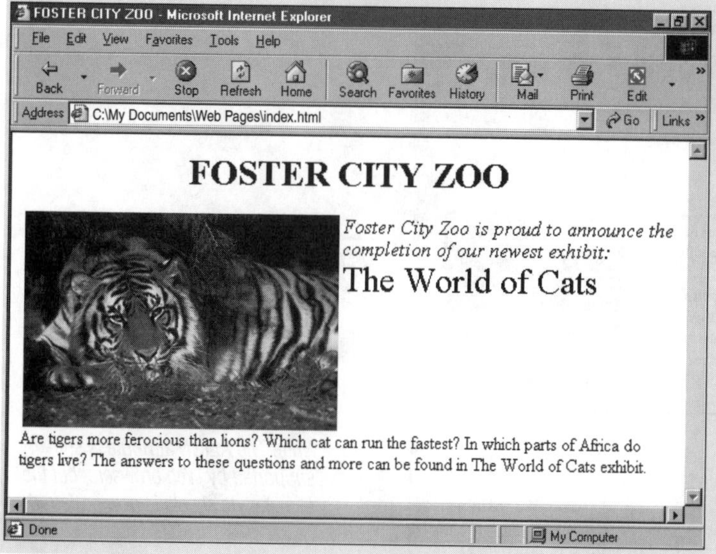

```
FOSTER CITY ZOO - Microsoft Internet Explorer

File   Edit   View   Favorites   Tools   Help

Back   Forward   Stop   Refresh   Home   Search   Favorites   History   Mail   Print   Edit

Address  C:\My Documents\Web Pages\index.html                          Go   Links
```

# FOSTER CITY ZOO

*Foster City Zoo is proud to announce the completion of our newest exhibit:*

The World of Cats

Are tigers more ferocious than lions? Which cat can run the fastest? In which parts of Africa do tigers live? The answers to these questions and more can be found in The World of Cats exhibit.

```
Done                                                          My Computer
```

**3** Display the Web page in a Web browser.

● The Web browser stops the text wrap where you specified.

*Note: The CLEAR attribute is still supported by Web browsers, but the use of style sheets is now preferred.*

You can wrap text between two images to improve the layout of your Web page. The images must appear directly above the text you want to wrap between them. If you have previously aligned the images with text, you cannot wrap text between the images.

## WRAP TEXT BETWEEN TWO IMAGES

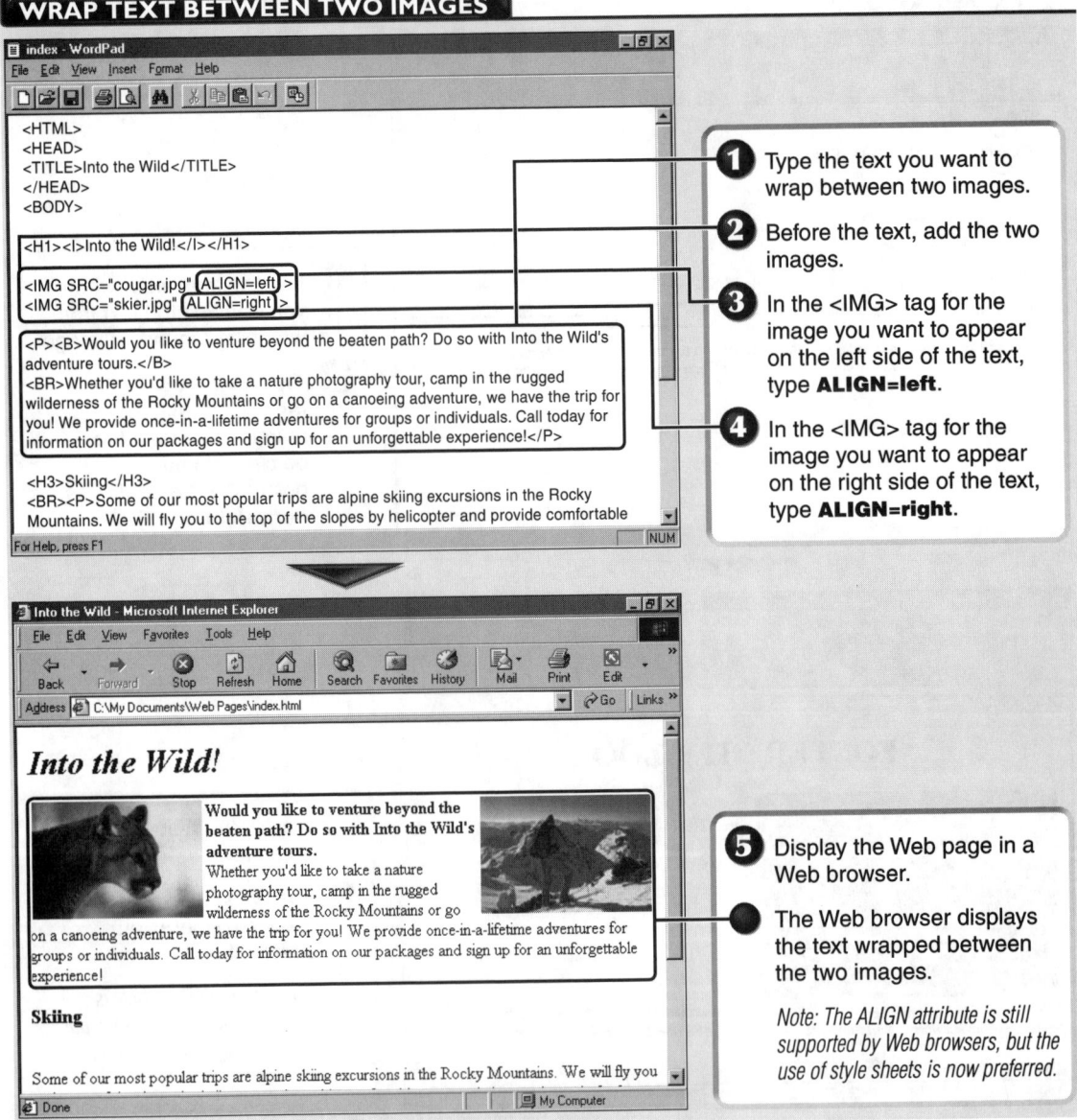

**1** Type the text you want to wrap between two images.

**2** Before the text, add the two images.

**3** In the <IMG> tag for the image you want to appear on the left side of the text, type **ALIGN=left**.

**4** In the <IMG> tag for the image you want to appear on the right side of the text, type **ALIGN=right**.

**5** Display the Web page in a Web browser.

■ The Web browser displays the text wrapped between the two images.

*Note: The ALIGN attribute is still supported by Web browsers, but the use of style sheets is now preferred.*

You can vertically align an image with text on your Web page. You can choose to align the top, middle or bottom of the image with text. If you have wrapped text around an image, you cannot align the image with text.

## ALIGN AN IMAGE WITH TEXT

```
alignimage - WordPad
File  Edit  View  Insert  Format  Help

<HTML>
<HEAD>
<TITLE>Images</TITLE>
</HEAD>
<BODY>

<P><IMG SRC="scuba.jpg" ALIGN=top>This text appears at the top
of an image.</P>
<P><IMG SRC="scuba.jpg" ALIGN=middle>This text appears at the
middle of an image.</P>
<P><IMG SRC="scuba.jpg" ALIGN=bottom>This text appears at the
bottom of an image.</P>

</BODY>
</HTML>

For Help, press F1                                          NUM
```

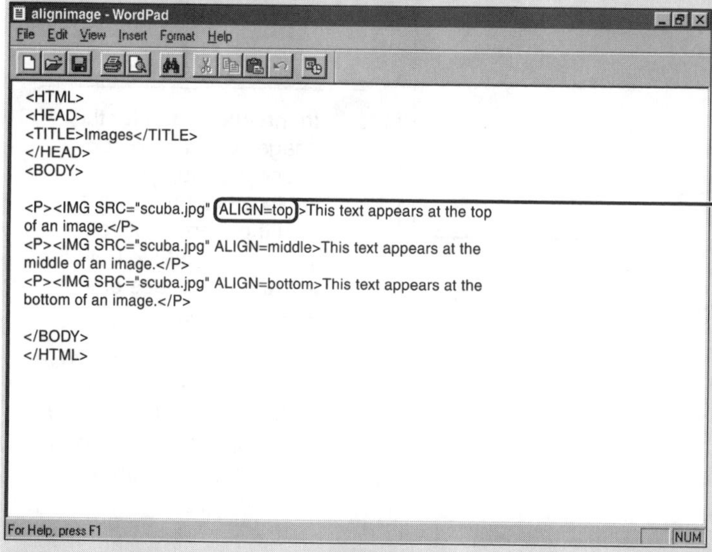

**1** In the <IMG> tag for the image you want to align with text, type **ALIGN=?** replacing **?** with the way you want to align the image with the text (**top**, **bottom** or **middle**).

● By default, Web browsers align the bottom of an image with the bottom of a line of text.

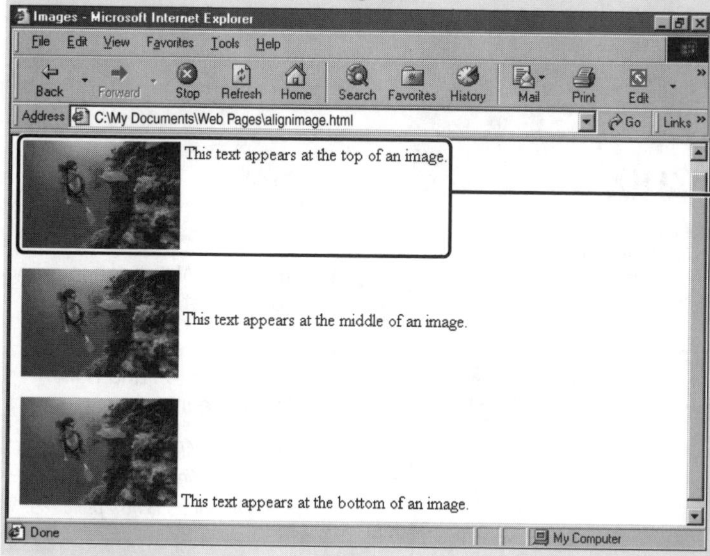

```
Images - Microsoft Internet Explorer
File  Edit  View  Favorites  Tools  Help

Back  Forward  Stop  Refresh  Home  Search  Favorites  History  Mail  Print  Edit
Address  C:\My Documents\Web Pages\alignimage.html            Go   Links »

        This text appears at the top of an image.

        This text appears at the middle of an image.

        This text appears at the bottom of an image.

Done                                              My Computer
```

**2** Display the Web page in a Web browser.

● The Web browser aligns the image with the text.

● The alignment you specify may not turn out the way you expect if you have more than one image on the same line.

*Note: The ALIGN attribute is still supported by Web browsers, but the use of style sheets is now preferred.*

# ADD SPACE AROUND AN IMAGE

You can increase the amount of space around an image to enhance the appearance of your Web page. Increasing the amount of space between an image and the surrounding text will make the text easier to read. Increasing the amount of space between two adjacent images will prevent the images from appearing as one large image.

## ADD SPACE AROUND AN IMAGE

```
index - WordPad
File  Edit  View  Insert  Format  Help

<HTML>
<HEAD>
<TITLE>FOSTER CITY ZOO</TITLE>
</HEAD>
<BODY>

<H1><CENTER>FOSTER CITY ZOO</CENTER></H1>

<IMG SRC="tiger.jpg" ALIGN=left HSPACE=30>Are tigers more ferocious
than lions? Which cat can run the fastest? In which parts of North America
do cougars live? The answers to these questions and more can be found in
The World of Cats, the newest exhibit at the Foster City Zoo. From the king of
the jungle to the bobcat of North America, we explore the habitats and habits
of different feline species. The exhibition area is carefully designed to
recreate the environments in which the animals originally lived. Visitors can
view their favorite wild cats, and find out more about them from various
displays. Learn how the wild cats hunt and how mothers rear their cubs. The
highlight of the exhibit is a Siberian tiger and her six-month-old cub. The
World of Cats is open six days a week during regular zoo hours.

</BODY>
</HTML>

For Help, press F1                                           NUM
```

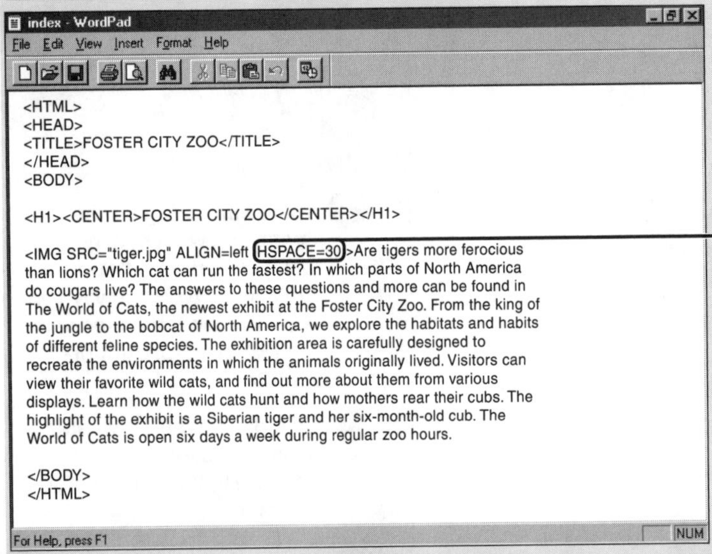

### LEFT AND RIGHT SIDES

**1** In the <IMG> tag for the image you want to add space around, type **HSPACE=?** replacing **?** with the amount of space you want to add to both the left and right sides of the image in pixels.

*Note: You cannot add space to just one side of an image using the HSPACE attribute. To add space to just one side of an image, modify the image using an image editing program.*

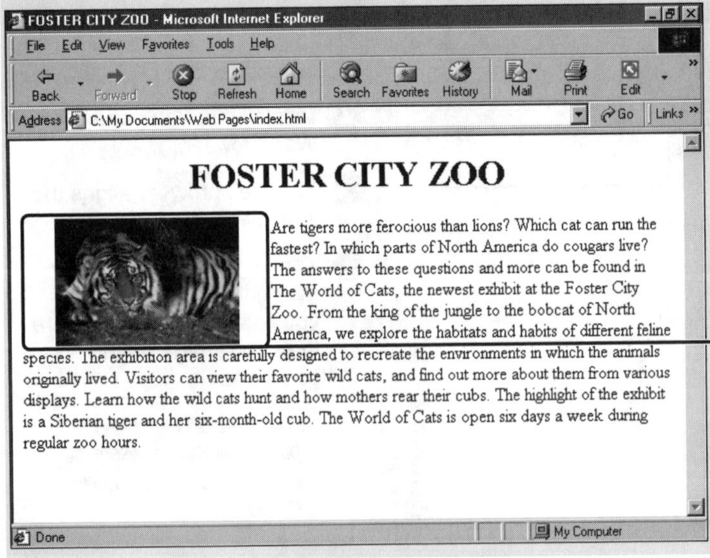

---

```
FOSTER CITY ZOO - Microsoft Internet Explorer
File  Edit  View  Favorites  Tools  Help

Back  Forward  Stop  Refresh  Home  Search  Favorites  History  Mail  Print  Edit

Address  C:\My Documents\Web Pages\index.html                    Go   Links
```

# FOSTER CITY ZOO

Are tigers more ferocious than lions? Which cat can run the fastest? In which parts of North America do cougars live? The answers to these questions and more can be found in The World of Cats, the newest exhibit at the Foster City Zoo. From the king of the jungle to the bobcat of North America, we explore the habitats and habits of different feline species. The exhibition area is carefully designed to recreate the environments in which the animals originally lived. Visitors can view their favorite wild cats, and find out more about them from various displays. Learn how the wild cats hunt and how mothers rear their cubs. The highlight of the exhibit is a Siberian tiger and her six-month-old cub. The World of Cats is open six days a week during regular zoo hours.

```
Done                                                   My Computer
```

**2** Display the Web page in a Web browser.

● The Web browser adds space to the left and right sides of the image.

*Note: The HSPACE attribute is still supported by Web browsers, but the use of style sheets is now preferred.*

# in an *instant*

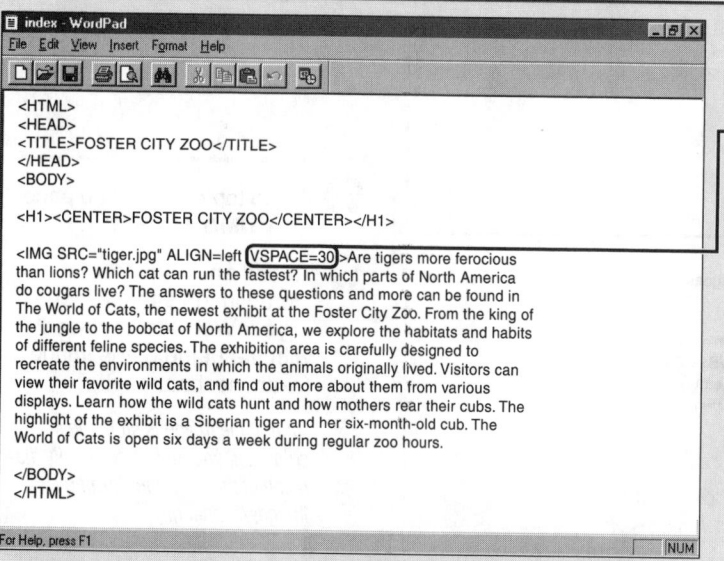

```
index - WordPad

File  Edit  View  Insert  Format  Help

<HTML>
<HEAD>
<TITLE>FOSTER CITY ZOO</TITLE>
</HEAD>
<BODY>

<H1><CENTER>FOSTER CITY ZOO</CENTER></H1>

<IMG SRC="tiger.jpg" ALIGN=left VSPACE=30>Are tigers more ferocious
than lions? Which cat can run the fastest? In which parts of North America
do cougars live? The answers to these questions and more can be found in
The World of Cats, the newest exhibit at the Foster City Zoo. From the king of
the jungle to the bobcat of North America, we explore the habitats and habits
of different feline species. The exhibition area is carefully designed to
recreate the environments in which the animals originally lived. Visitors can
view their favorite wild cats, and find out more about them from various
displays. Learn how the wild cats hunt and how mothers rear their cubs. The
highlight of the exhibit is a Siberian tiger and her six-month-old cub. The
World of Cats is open six days a week during regular zoo hours.

</BODY>
</HTML>

For Help, press F1                                          NUM
```

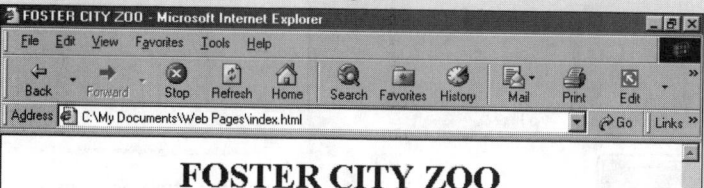

**FOSTER CITY ZOO**

Are tigers more ferocious than lions? Which cat can run the fastest? In which parts of North America do cougars live? The answers to these questions and more can be found in The World of Cats, the newest exhibit at the Foster City Zoo. From the king of the jungle to the bobcat of North America, we explore the habitats and habits of different feline species. The exhibition area is carefully designed to recreate the environments in which the animals originally lived. Visitors can view their favorite wild cats, and find out more about them from various displays. Learn how the wild cats hunt and how mothers rear their cubs. The highlight of the exhibit is a Siberian tiger and her six-month-old cub. The World of Cats is open six days a week during regular zoo hours.

## TOP AND BOTTOM

**1** In the <IMG> tag for the image you want to add space around, type **VSPACE=?** with the amount of space you want to add to both the top and bottom of the image in pixels.

*Note: You cannot add space to just the top or the bottom of an image using the VSPACE attribute. To add space to just the top or the bottom of an image, modify the image using an image editing program.*

**2** Display the Web page in a Web browser.

The Web browser adds space to the top and bottom of the image.

*Note: The VSPACE attribute is still supported by Web browsers, but the use of style sheets is now preferred.*

**63**

# ADD A BANNER

You can add a banner to the top of a Web page to display information such as a company logo or advertisement. Adding the same banner to all your Web pages can help give the pages a consistent design. Banner images are usually in the GIF format and are approximately 100 pixels high and 450 pixels wide.

## ADD A BANNER

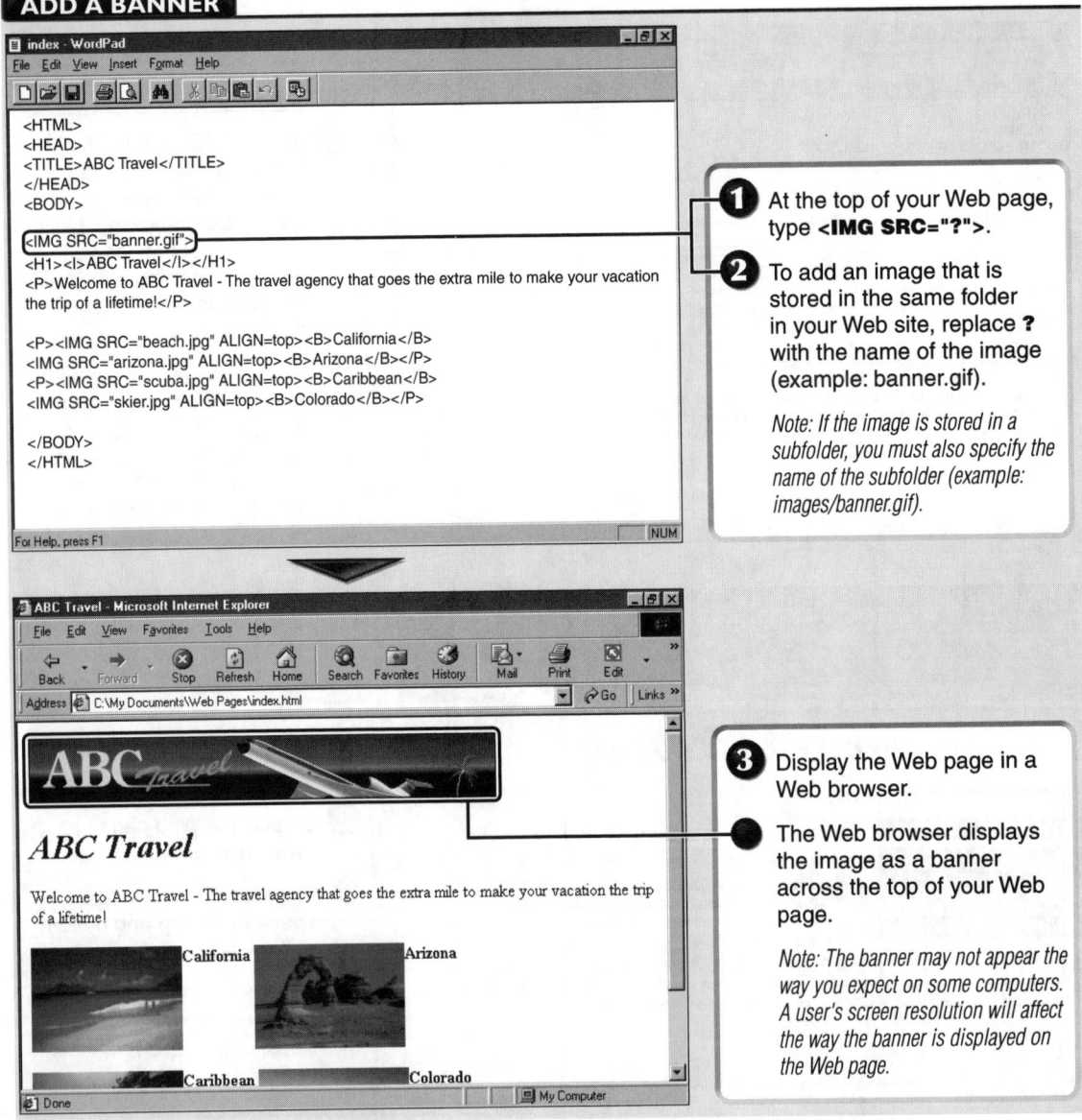

1 At the top of your Web page, type **<IMG SRC="?">**.

2 To add an image that is stored in the same folder in your Web site, replace **?** with the name of the image (example: banner.gif).

*Note: If the image is stored in a subfolder, you must also specify the name of the subfolder (example: images/banner.gif).*

3 Display the Web page in a Web browser.

■ The Web browser displays the image as a banner across the top of your Web page.

*Note: The banner may not appear the way you expect on some computers. A user's screen resolution will affect the way the banner is displayed on the Web page.*

You can add an interesting background design to your Web page by having a small image repeat to fill the entire page. The background image should not be overwhelming or make your Web page difficult to read. Some interesting background images are available at the imagine.metanet.com and www.nepthys.com/textures Web sites.

## ADD A BACKGROUND IMAGE

```
<HTML>
<HEAD>
<TITLE>Chocolate</TITLE>
</HEAD>
<BODY BACKGROUND="chocolate.jpg" >

<FONT COLOR="#FFFFFF">
<H1><CENTER>Chocolate Lovers' Web Page!</CENTER></H1>
<P ALIGN=center> <B>This page is dedicated to the millions of people who love
chocolate!
<BR>It is designed for those who cannot get enough of the most wonderful food
on earth!
<BR><I>CHOCOLATE!</I></B></P>
</FONT>

</BODY>
</HTML>
```

**index - WordPad** — File Edit View Insert Format Help — For Help, press F1 — NUM

**1** In the <BODY> tag, type **BACKGROUND="?"**.

**2** To add a background image that is stored in the same folder in your Web site, replace **?** with the name of the image (example: chocolate.jpg).

*Note: If the image is stored in a subfolder, you must also specify the name of the subfolder (example: images/chocolate.jpg).*

**Chocolate - Microsoft Internet Explorer**
File Edit View Favorites Tools Help
Back Forward Stop Refresh Home Search Favorites History Mail Print Edit
Address C:\My Documents\Web Pages\index.html

### Chocolate Lovers' Web Page!

This page is dedicated to the millions of people who love chocolate!
It is designed for those who cannot get enough of the most wonderful food on earth!
*CHOCOLATE!*

Done — My Computer

**3** Display the Web page in a Web browser.

● The Web browser repeats the image to fill the entire Web page.

*Note: The BACKGROUND attribute is still supported by Web browsers, but the use of style sheets is now preferred.*

# ADD A HORIZONTAL RULE

You can add a horizontal rule to visually separate sections of your Web page. For example, you may want to use a horizontal rule to separate sections of text or set off headings. You should try not to place more than one horizontal rule on each screen, since overusing horizontal rules can distract users and make your Web page difficult to read.

## ADD A HORIZONTAL RULE

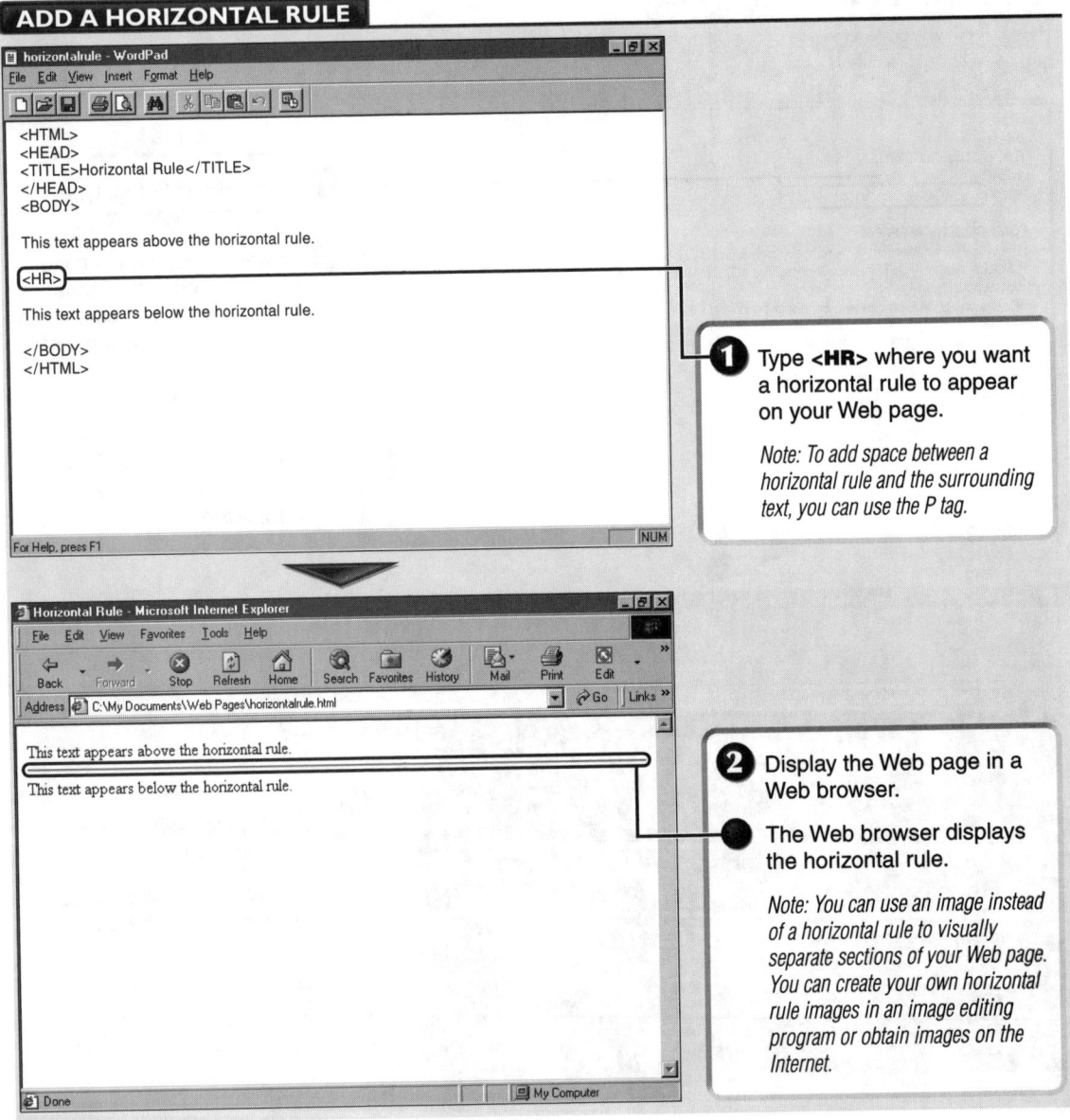

**1** Type **<HR>** where you want a horizontal rule to appear on your Web page.

*Note: To add space between a horizontal rule and the surrounding text, you can use the P tag.*

**2** Display the Web page in a Web browser.

■ The Web browser displays the horizontal rule.

*Note: You can use an image instead of a horizontal rule to visually separate sections of your Web page. You can create your own horizontal rule images in an image editing program or obtain images on the Internet.*

in an *instant*

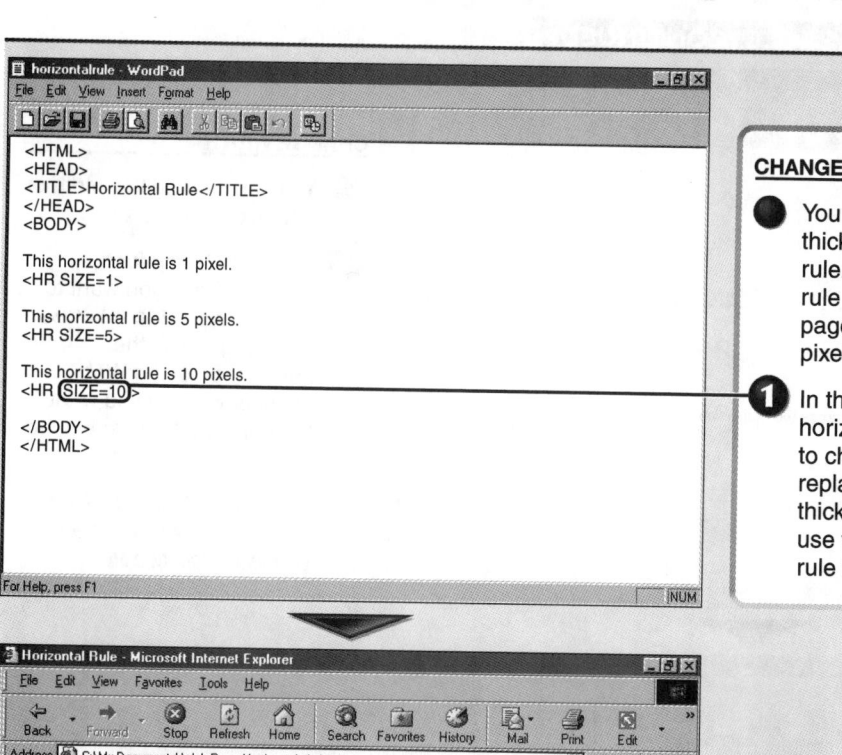

```
<HTML>
<HEAD>
<TITLE>Horizontal Rule</TITLE>
</HEAD>
<BODY>

This horizontal rule is 1 pixel.
<HR SIZE=1>

This horizontal rule is 5 pixels.
<HR SIZE=5>

This horizontal rule is 10 pixels.
<HR SIZE=10>

</BODY>
</HTML>
```

**CHANGE THICKNESS**

● You can change the thickness of a horizontal rule. By default, a horizontal rule you add to your Web page has a thickness of 2 pixels.

**1** In the <HR> tag for the horizontal rule you want to change, type **SIZE=?** replacing **?** with the thickness you want to use for the horizontal rule in pixels.

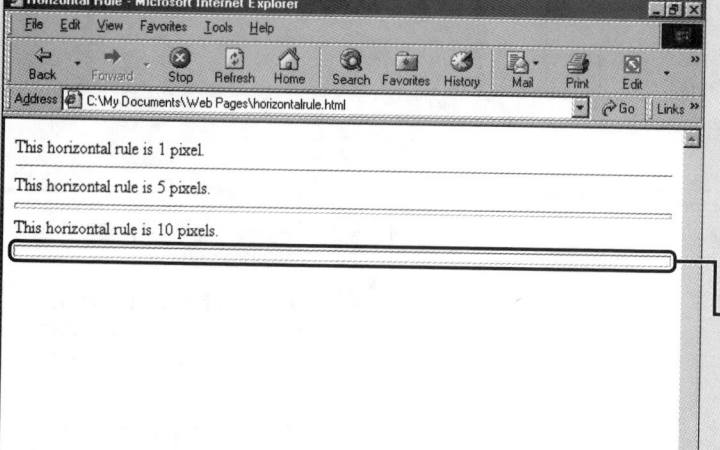

This horizontal rule is 1 pixel.

This horizontal rule is 5 pixels.

This horizontal rule is 10 pixels.

**2** Display the Web page in a Web browser.

● The Web browser displays the horizontal rule with the thickness you specified.

*Note: The SIZE attribute is still supported by Web browsers, but the use of style sheets is now preferred.*

CONTINUED ▶

# ADD A HORIZONTAL RULE

If you do not want a horizontal rule to extend across the entire Web browser window, you can change the width of the rule. You can specify a new width as a percentage of the Web browser window. After changing the width, you can also change the alignment of the horizontal rule.

## ADD A HORIZONTAL RULE (CONTINUED)

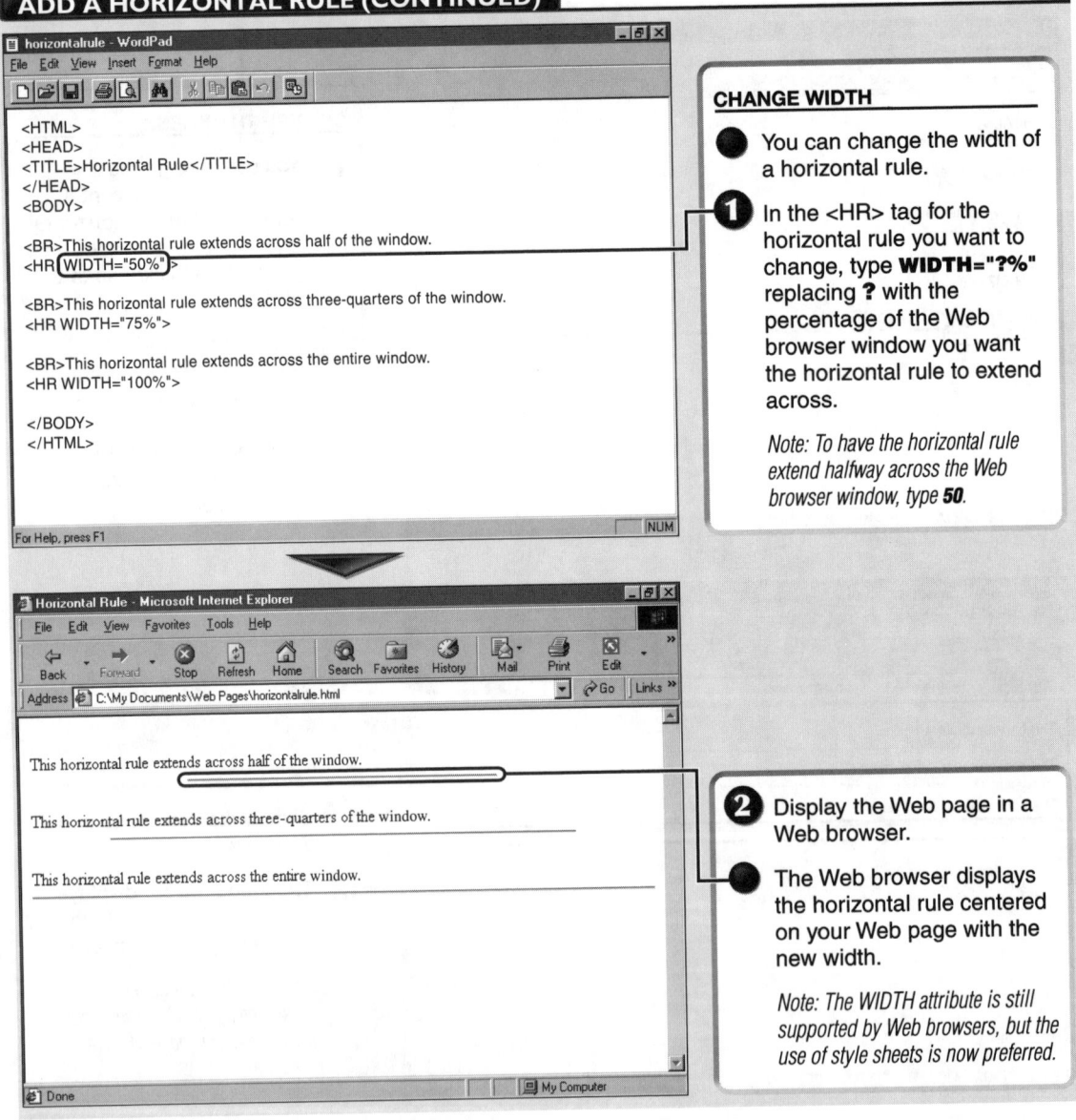

**CHANGE WIDTH**

● You can change the width of a horizontal rule.

❶ In the <HR> tag for the horizontal rule you want to change, type **WIDTH="?%"** replacing **?** with the percentage of the Web browser window you want the horizontal rule to extend across.

*Note: To have the horizontal rule extend halfway across the Web browser window, type **50**.*

❷ Display the Web page in a Web browser.

● The Web browser displays the horizontal rule centered on your Web page with the new width.

*Note: The WIDTH attribute is still supported by Web browsers, but the use of style sheets is now preferred.*

in an *instant*

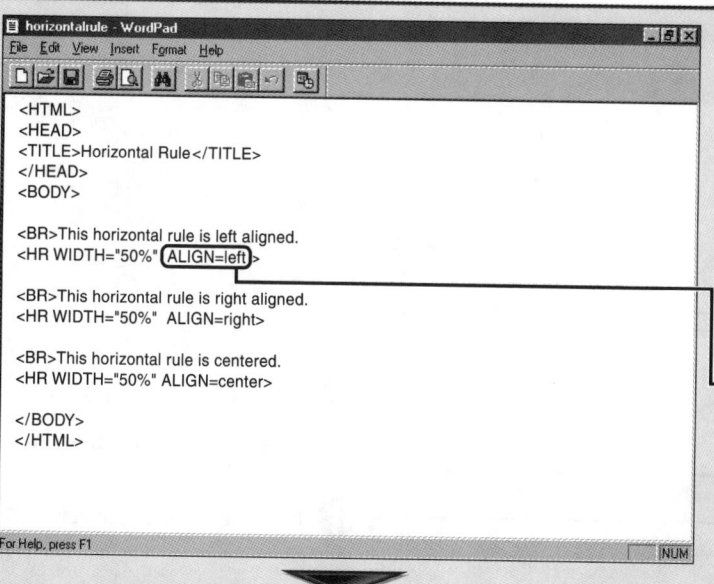

**CHANGE ALIGNMENT**

● After changing the width of a horizontal rule, you can change the alignment of the rule.

**1** In the <HR> tag for the horizontal rule you want to change, type **ALIGN=?** replacing **?** with the way you want to align the horizontal rule (**left**, **center** or **right**).

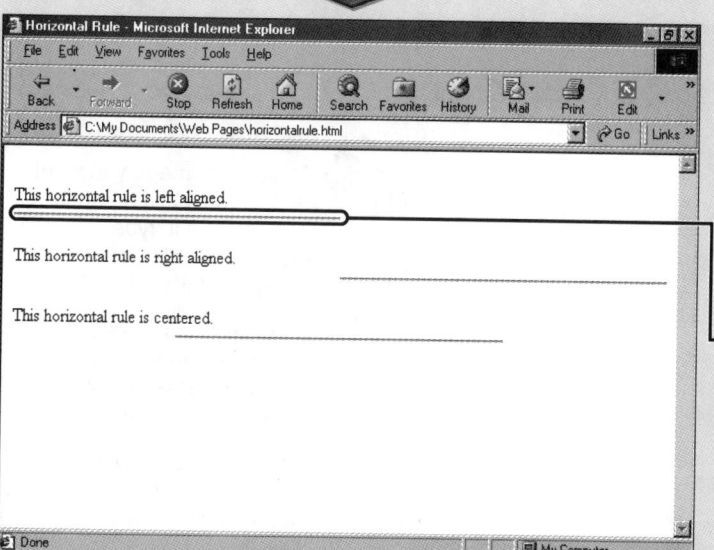

**2** Display the Web page in a Web browser.

● The Web browser displays the horizontal rule with the alignment you specified.

*Note: The ALIGN attribute is still supported by Web browsers, but the use of style sheets is now preferred.*

# USING IMAGES IN A LIST

You can create an eye-catching list that uses images instead of bullets. For example, you may want to display a small version of your company logo beside each item in a list of products. The image should be small enough to fit neatly beside each item in the list. Interesting bullet images are available at the www.grapholina.com/Graphics and www.theshockzone.com Web sites.

USING IMAGES IN A LIST

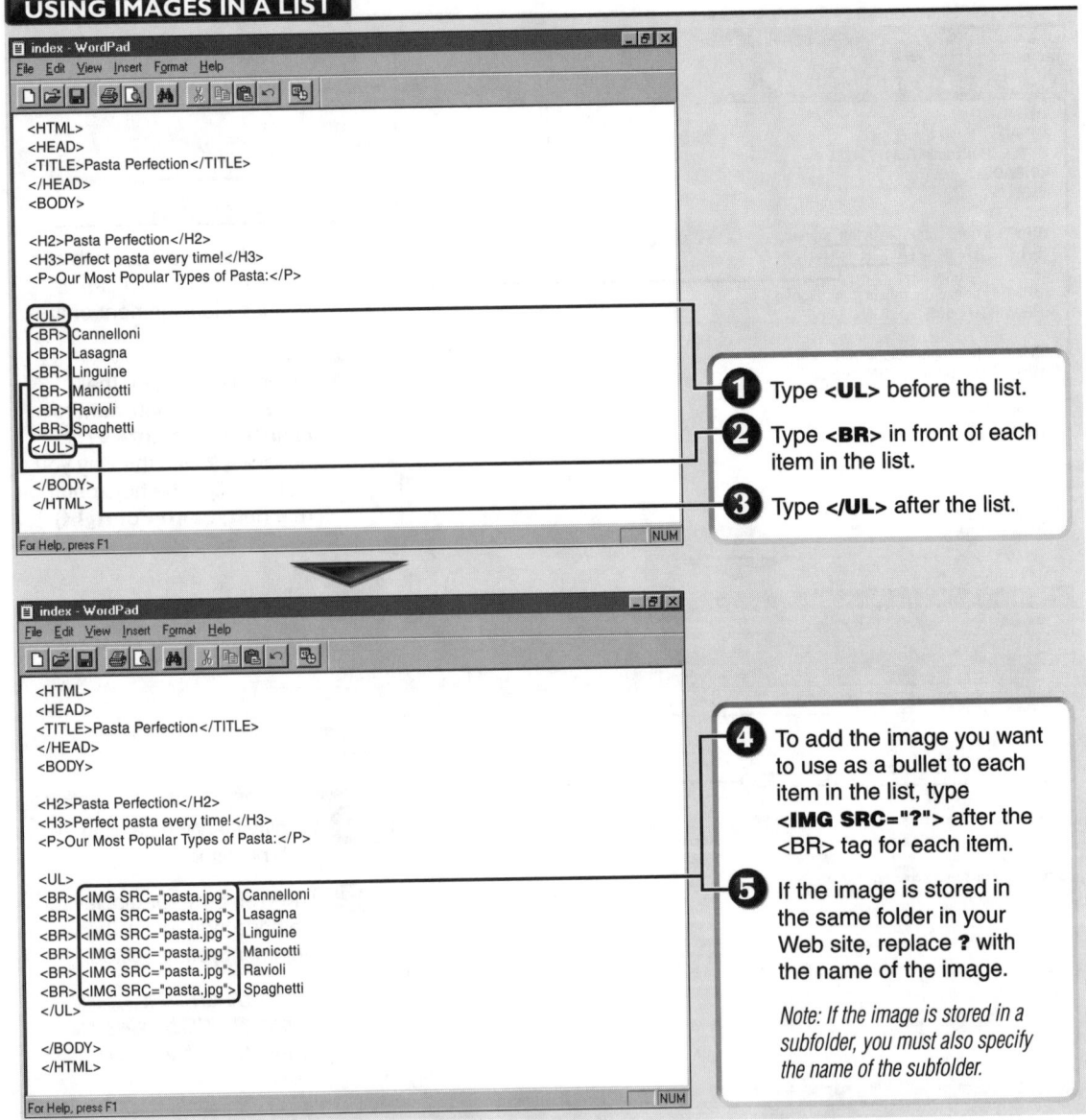

**1** Type **<UL>** before the list.

**2** Type **<BR>** in front of each item in the list.

**3** Type **</UL>** after the list.

**4** To add the image you want to use as a bullet to each item in the list, type **<IMG SRC="?">** after the <BR> tag for each item.

**5** If the image is stored in the same folder in your Web site, replace **?** with the name of the image.

*Note: If the image is stored in a subfolder, you must also specify the name of the subfolder.*

# in an instant

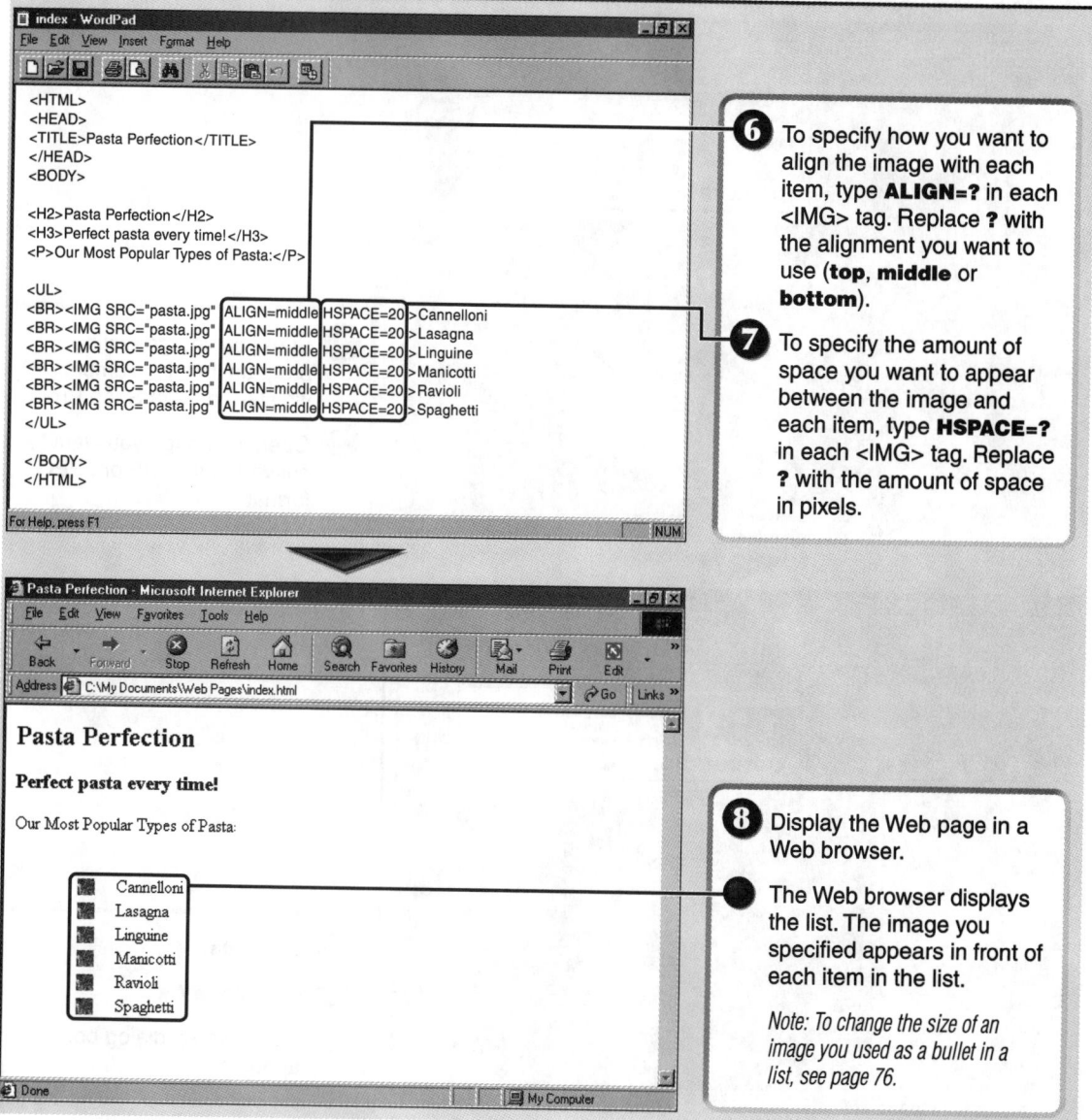

**6** To specify how you want to align the image with each item, type **ALIGN=?** in each <IMG> tag. Replace **?** with the alignment you want to use (**top**, **middle** or **bottom**).

**7** To specify the amount of space you want to appear between the image and each item, type **HSPACE=?** in each <IMG> tag. Replace **?** with the amount of space in pixels.

**8** Display the Web page in a Web browser.

The Web browser displays the list. The image you specified appears in front of each item in the list.

*Note: To change the size of an image you used as a bullet in a list, see page 76.*

You can convert an image you want to add to your Web page to the GIF or JPEG format. The GIF and JPEG formats are the most popular image formats on the Web. To convert an image, you need an image editing program such as Paint Shop Pro. Paint Shop Pro is available at computer stores or at the www.jasc.com Web site.

## CONVERT AN IMAGE TO GIF OR JPEG

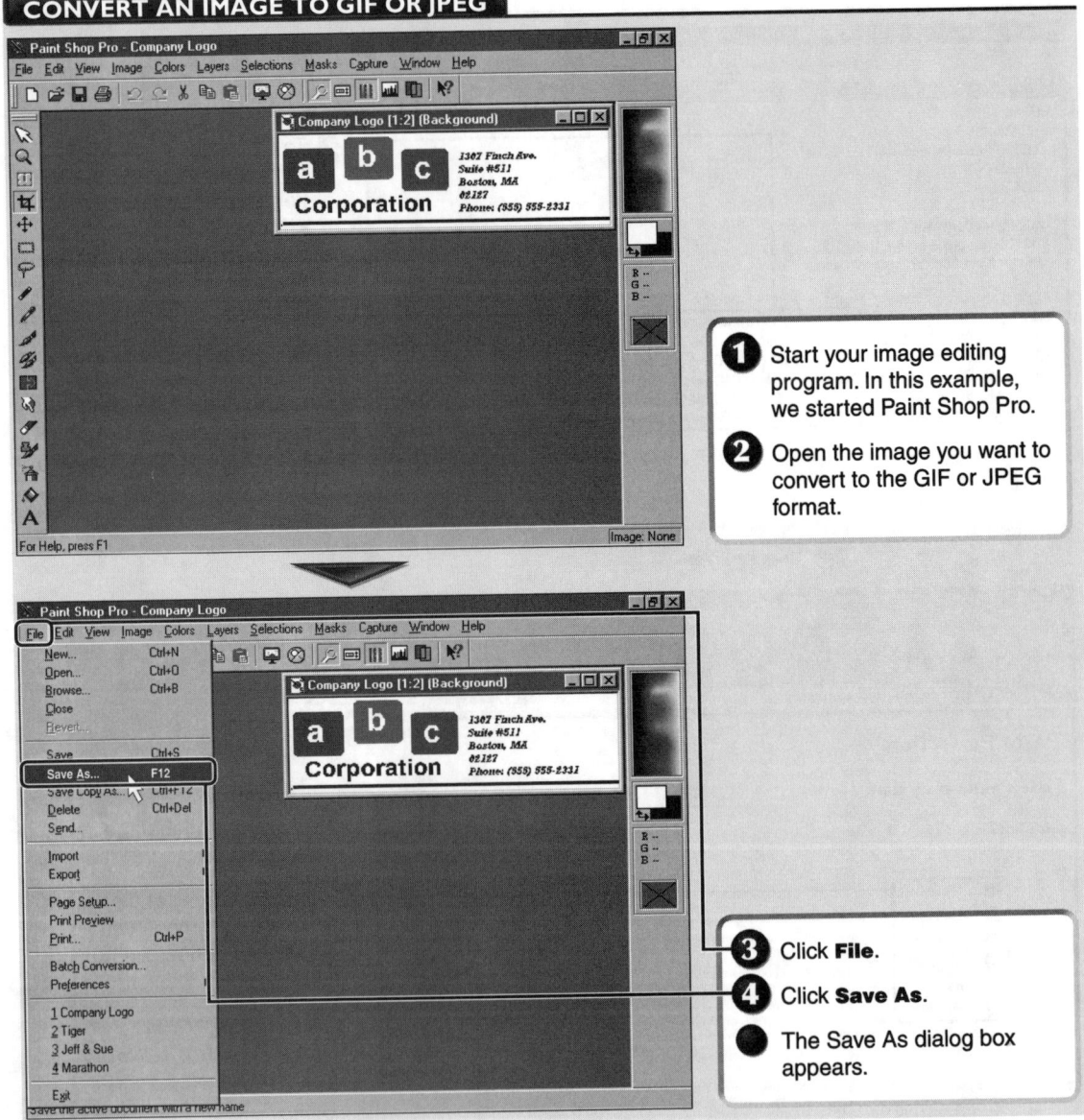

**1** Start your image editing program. In this example, we started Paint Shop Pro.

**2** Open the image you want to convert to the GIF or JPEG format.

**3** Click **File**.

**4** Click **Save As**.

● The Save As dialog box appears.

# in an instant

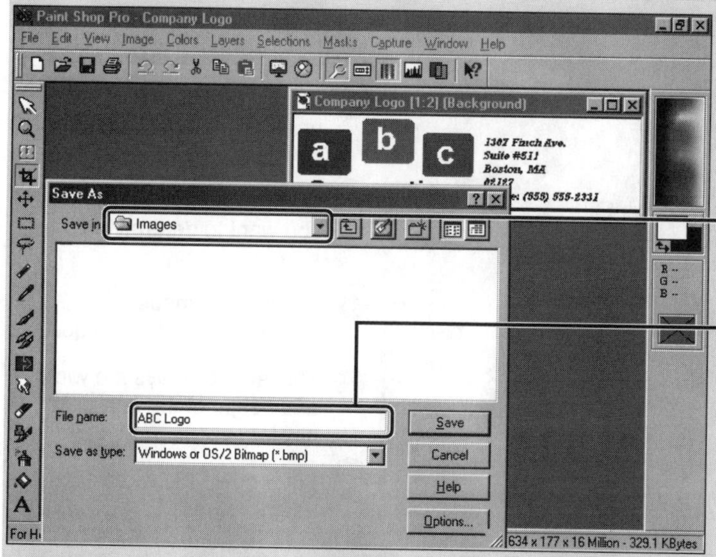

**5** If you want to rename the image, type a new name.

● This area shows the location where the program will store the image. You can click this area to change the location.

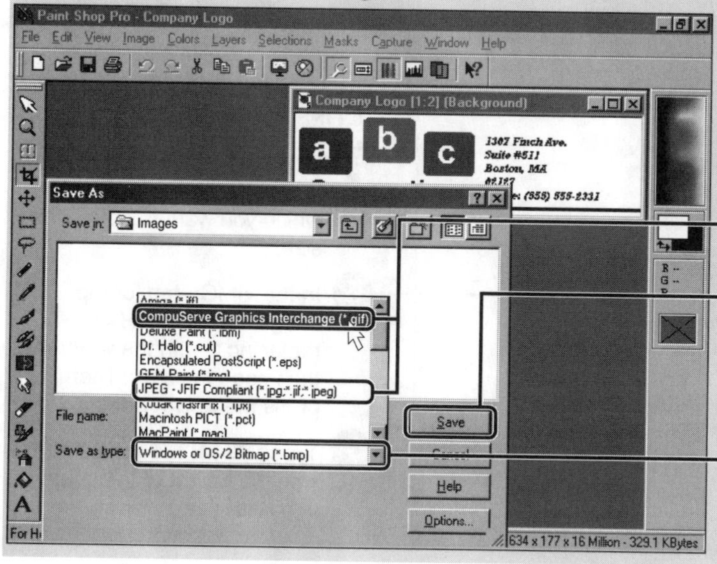

**6** Click ▣ in this area to list the available image formats.

**7** Click the image format you want to use.

**8** Click **Save**.

● If you selected the GIF format in step **7**, a dialog box appears, stating that the image will be limited to a maximum of 256 colors. Click **Yes** to convert the image.

# DEFINE IMAGE SIZE

You can define the width and height of an image on your Web page. Defining the size of an image will help your Web page appear on a screen more quickly since Web browsers do not have to calculate the image size. Before defining the size of an image, you must first determine the size of the image using an image editing program.

## DEFINE IMAGE SIZE

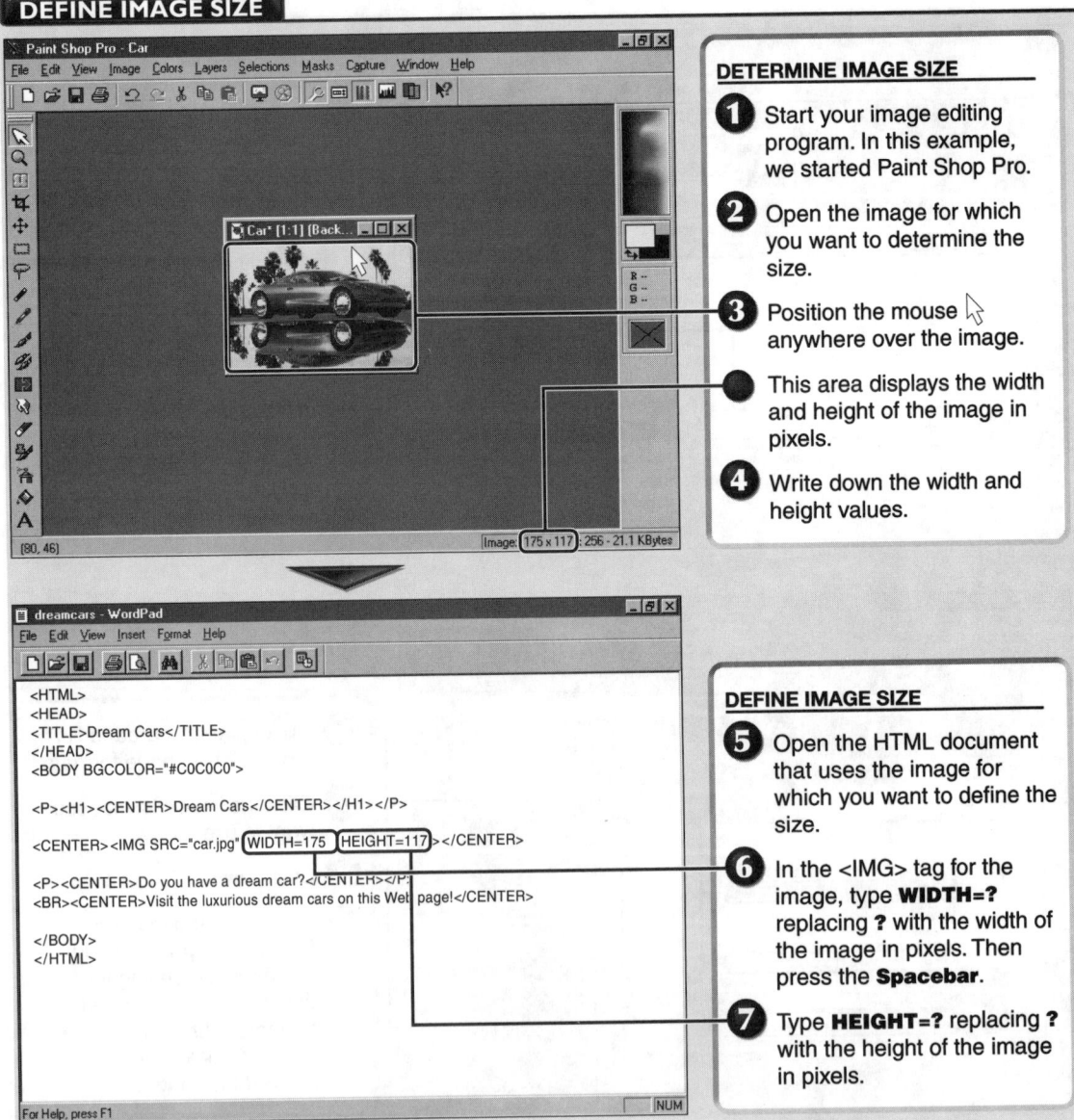

### DETERMINE IMAGE SIZE

**1** Start your image editing program. In this example, we started Paint Shop Pro.

**2** Open the image for which you want to determine the size.

**3** Position the mouse anywhere over the image.

● This area displays the width and height of the image in pixels.

**4** Write down the width and height values.

### DEFINE IMAGE SIZE

**5** Open the HTML document that uses the image for which you want to define the size.

**6** In the <IMG> tag for the image, type **WIDTH=?** replacing **?** with the width of the image in pixels. Then press the **Spacebar**.

**7** Type **HEIGHT=?** replacing **?** with the height of the image in pixels.

You can increase the size of an image on a Web page by specifying a new width and height for the image. You should avoid making images too large since the images may appear grainy. You should also ensure that the width and height values are proportional to avoid distorting the image.

## INCREASE IMAGE SIZE

**dreamcars - WordPad**

File  Edit  View  Insert  Format  Help

```
<HTML>
<HEAD>
<TITLE>Dream Cars</TITLE>
</HEAD>
<BODY BGCOLOR="#C0C0C0">

<P><H1><CENTER>Dream Cars</CENTER></H1></P>

<CENTER><IMG SRC="car.jpg" WIDTH=325 HEIGHT=218 ></CENTER>

<P><CENTER>Do you have a dream car?</CENTER>
<BR><CENTER>Visit the luxurious dream cars on this Web page!</CENTER></P>

</BODY>
</HTML>
```

For Help, press F1                                                          NUM

**1** In the <IMG> tag for the image you want to change, type **WIDTH=?** replacing **?** with the width you want to use in pixels. Then press the **Spacebar**.

**2** Type **HEIGHT=?** replacing **?** with the height you want to use in pixels.

*Note: You may want to first determine the original size of the image using an image editing program. For more information, see page 74.*

**Dream Cars - Microsoft Internet Explorer**

File  Edit  View  Favorites  Tools  Help

Back  Forward  Stop  Refresh  Home  Search  Favorites  History  Mail  Print  Edit

Address  C:\My Documents\Web Pages\dreamcars.html                Go   Links

## Dream Cars

Do you have a dream car?
Visit the luxurious dream cars on this Web page!

Done                                                    My Computer

**3** Display the Web page in a Web browser.

● The Web browser displays the image with the new size.

# REDUCE IMAGE SIZE

You can reduce the size of an image so the image will take up less space on your Web page. Reducing the size of an image decreases the file size of the image. This allows the image to transfer faster and appear on a screen more quickly. You should use an image editing program to reduce the size of an image.

## REDUCE IMAGE SIZE

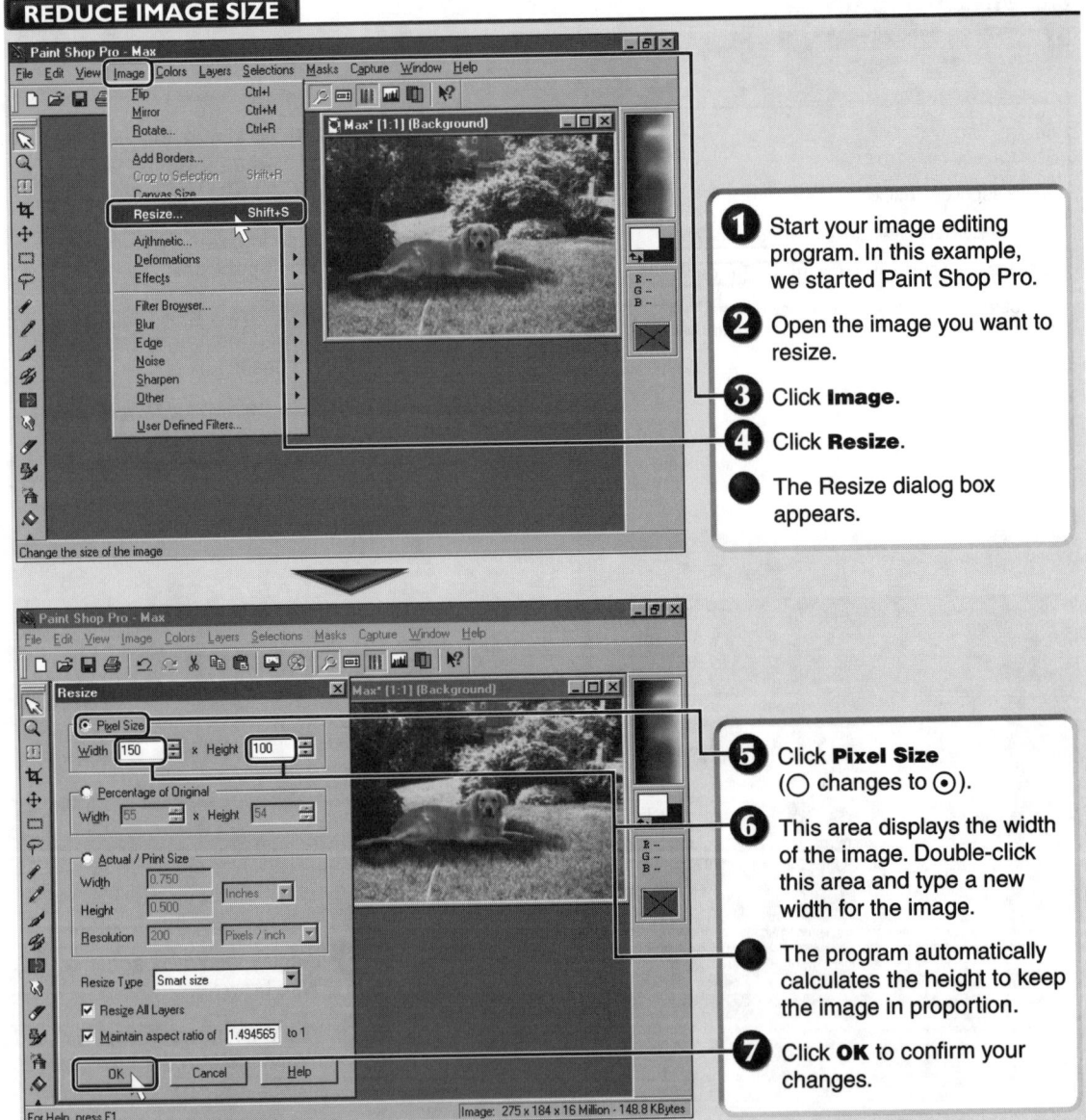

1 Start your image editing program. In this example, we started Paint Shop Pro.

2 Open the image you want to resize.

3 Click **Image**.

4 Click **Resize**.

● The Resize dialog box appears.

5 Click **Pixel Size** (○ changes to ⊙).

6 This area displays the width of the image. Double-click this area and type a new width for the image.

● The program automatically calculates the height to keep the image in proportion.

7 Click **OK** to confirm your changes.

# in an *Instant*

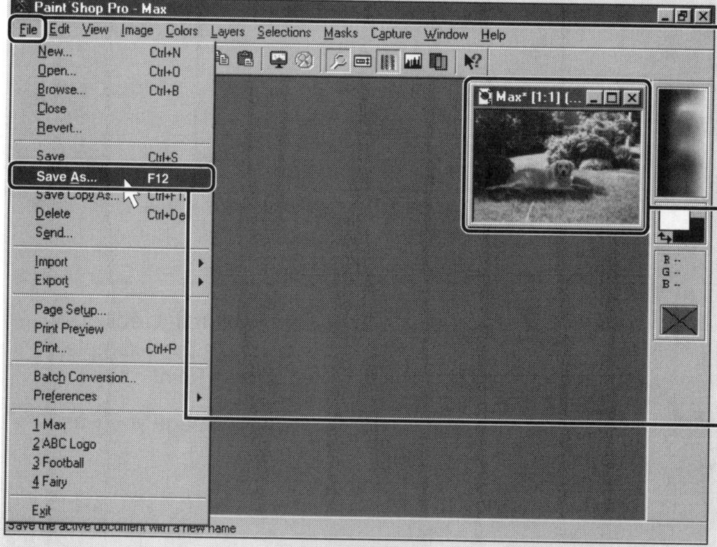

**Paint Shop Pro - Max**

File Edit View Image Colors Layers Selections Masks Capture Window Help

| | |
|---|---|
| New... | Ctrl+N |
| Open... | Ctrl+O |
| Browse... | Ctrl+B |
| Close | |
| Revert... | |
| Save | Ctrl+S |
| Save As... | F12 |
| Save Copy As... | Ctrl+T |
| Delete | Ctrl+De |
| Send... | |
| Import | ▶ |
| Export | ▶ |
| Page Setup... | |
| Print Preview | |
| Print... | Ctrl+P |
| Batch Conversion... | |
| Preferences | ▶ |
| 1 Max | |
| 2 ABC Logo | |
| 3 Football | |
| 4 Fairy | |
| Exit | |

Save the active document with a new name

Max* [1:1] (...

● The image appears in the new size.

**SAVE CHANGES**

**1** To create a new file that will store the image with your changes, click **File**.

**2** Click **Save As**.

● The Save As dialog box appears.

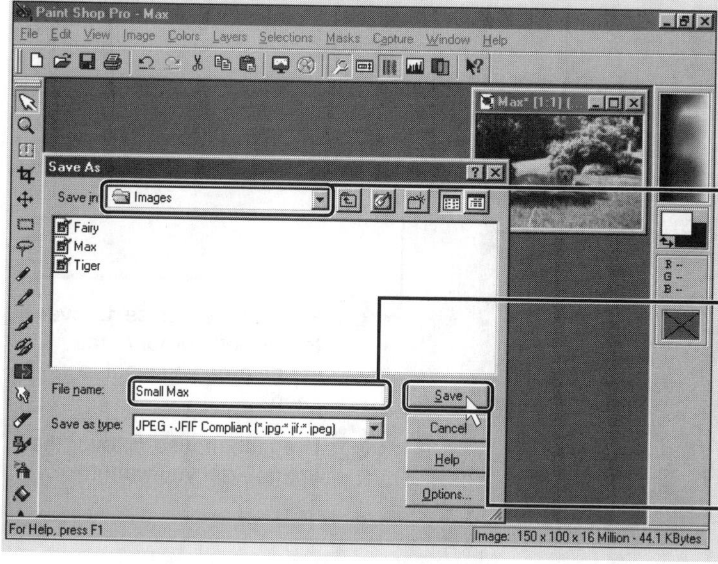

---

**Paint Shop Pro - Max**

File Edit View Image Colors Layers Selections Masks Capture Window Help

**Save As**

Save in: Images

Fairy
Max
Tiger

File name: Small Max

Save as type: JPEG - JFIF Compliant (*.jpg;*.jif;*.jpeg)

Save
Cancel
Help
Options...

For Help, press F1

Image: 150 x 100 x 16 Million - 44.1 KBytes

**3** Type a name for the new image.

● This area shows the location where the program will store the image. You can click this area to change the location.

**4** Click **Save**.

# CROP AN IMAGE

You can use an image editing program to remove parts of an image you do not need. Cropping an image is useful when you want to focus a user's attention on an important part of the image. Cropping an image also reduces the file size of the image, allowing the image to transfer faster to the user's computer.

## CROP AN IMAGE

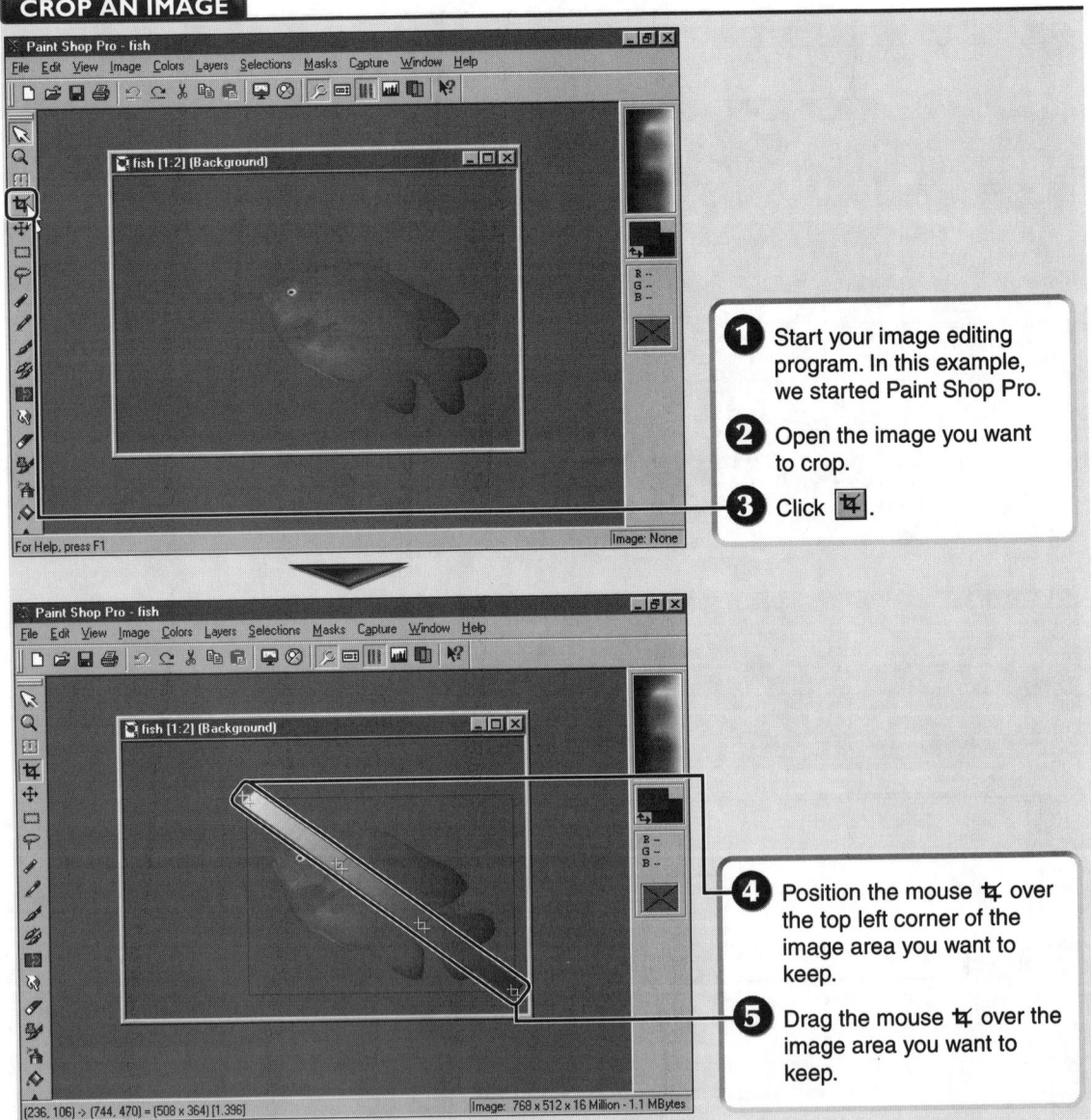

1 Start your image editing program. In this example, we started Paint Shop Pro.

2 Open the image you want to crop.

3 Click ⊬.

4 Position the mouse ⊬ over the top left corner of the image area you want to keep.

5 Drag the mouse ⊬ over the image area you want to keep.

in an *instant*

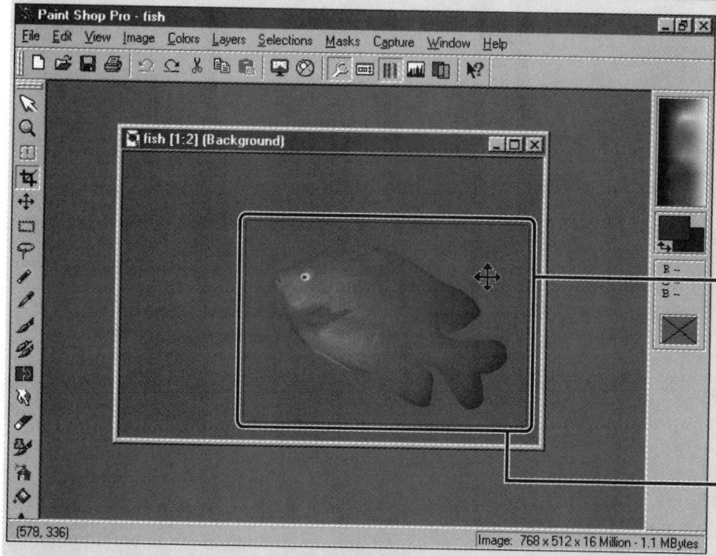

A box appears around the area you selected.

*Note: If you make a mistake when selecting the area, right-click the image and then repeat steps **4** and **5**.*

**6** Double-click within the area you selected.

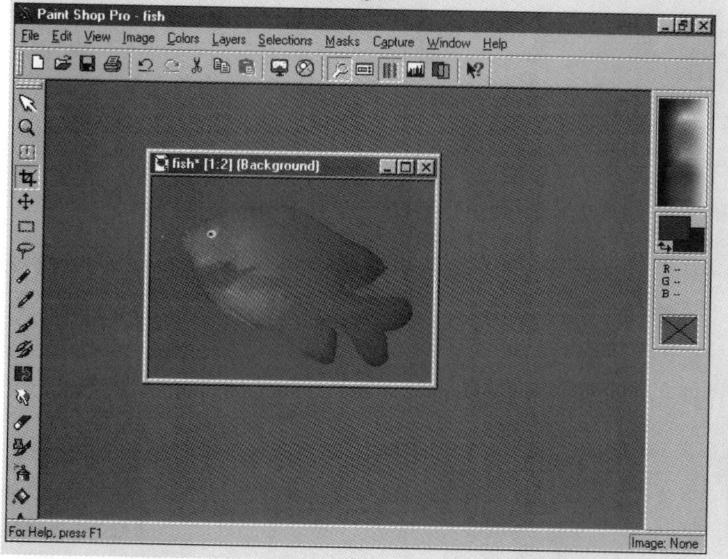

The areas of the image you did not select disappear.

**7** To create a new file that will store the cropped image, perform steps **1** to **4** on page 77.

*Note: Saving the cropped image in a new file allows you to crop the original image again later if you are not satisfied with the results.*

**79**

# REDUCE COLORS IN AN IMAGE

You can reduce the number of colors in an image using an image editing program. Reducing colors will decrease the file size of an image so the image can transfer more quickly over the Internet. You should not reduce the number of colors in a JPEG image, since in many cases, this will increase the file size of the image.

## REDUCE COLORS IN AN IMAGE

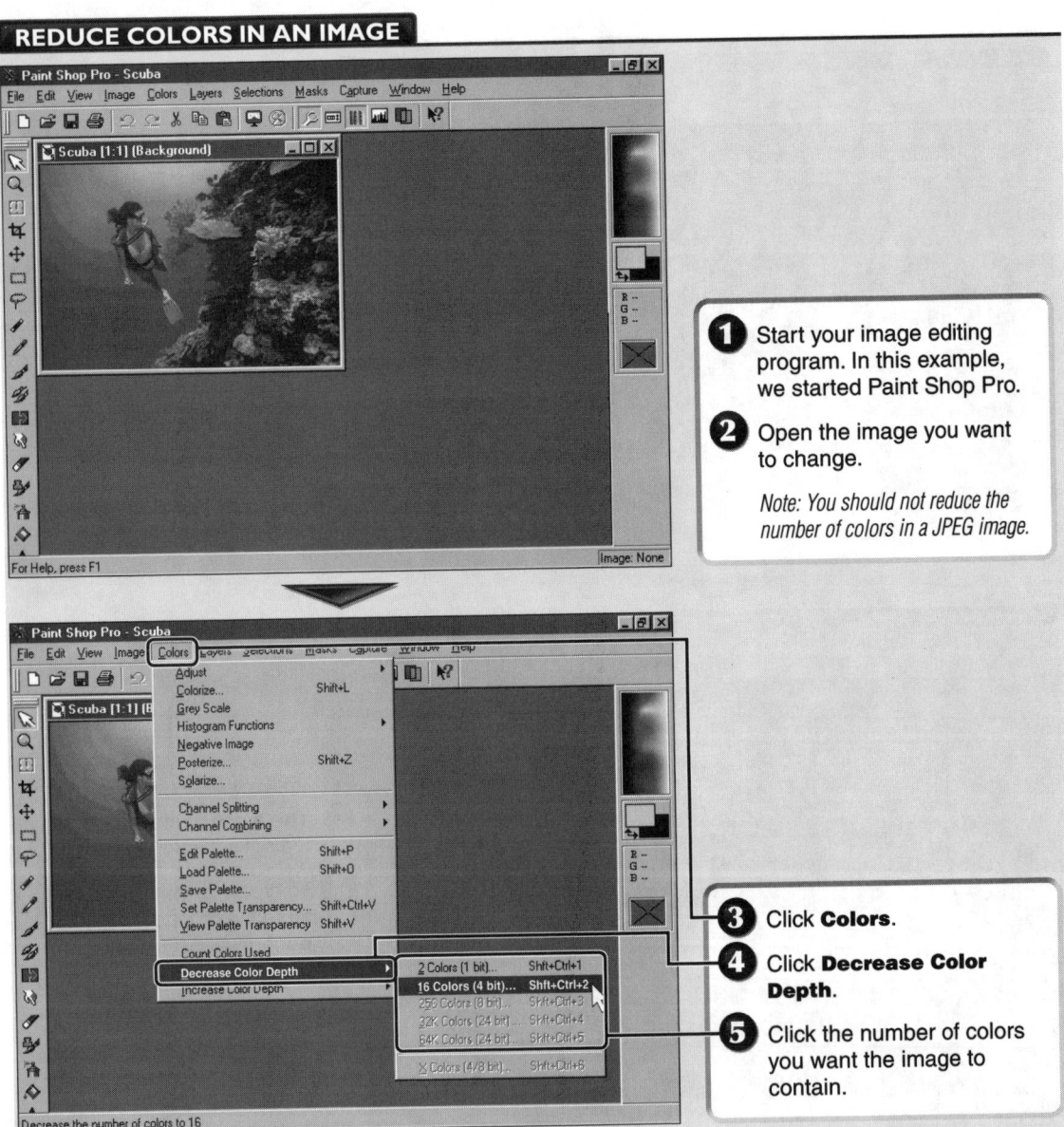

**1** Start your image editing program. In this example, we started Paint Shop Pro.

**2** Open the image you want to change.

*Note: You should not reduce the number of colors in a JPEG image.*

**3** Click **Colors**.

**4** Click **Decrease Color Depth**.

**5** Click the number of colors you want the image to contain.

# in an *instant*

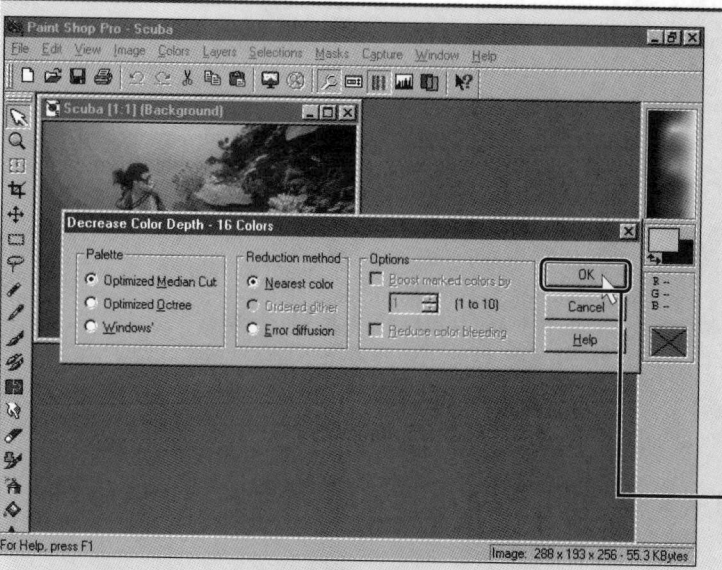

The Decrease Color Depth dialog box appears.

*Note: The dialog box that appears on your screen may offer different options.*

**6** Click **OK** to confirm your change.

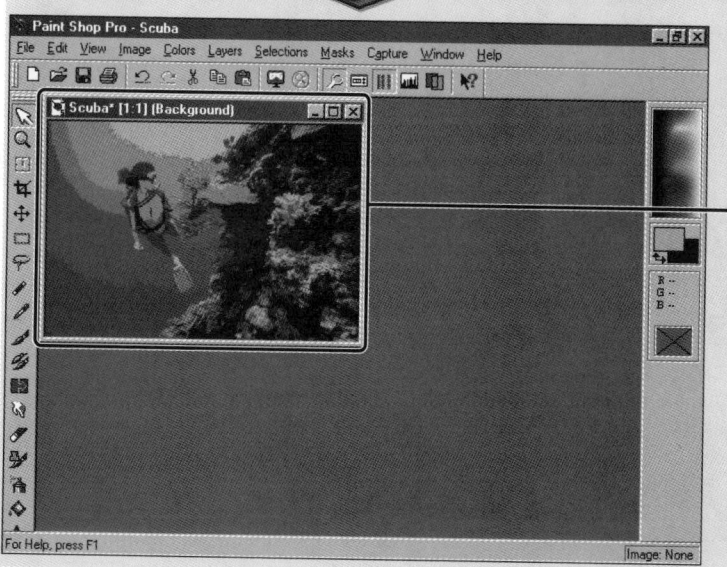

The image displays the new number of colors.

**7** To create a new file that will store the image with the new number of colors, perform steps **1** to **4** on page 77.

*Note: Saving the image in a new file allows you to reduce the colors in the original image again later if you are not satisfied with the results.*

# MAKE IMAGE BACKGROUND TRANSPARENT

You can use an image editing program to make the solid background of a GIF image transparent so the background will blend into a Web page. You should make sure the background color does not appear in the image itself. When you make an image background transparent, parts of the image that display the same color as the background will also become transparent.

## MAKE SOLID BACKGROUND TRANSPARENT

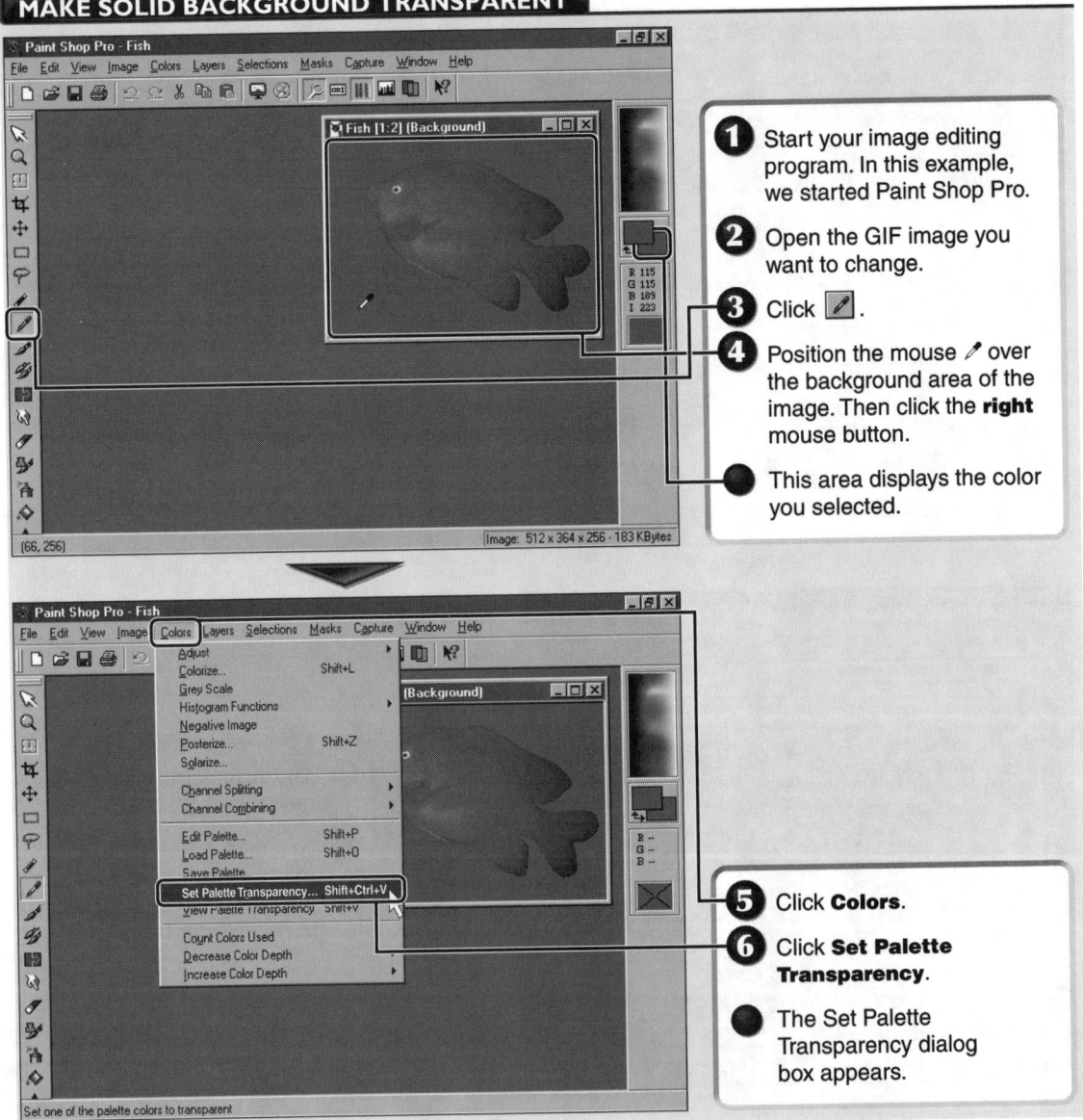

1 Start your image editing program. In this example, we started Paint Shop Pro.

2 Open the GIF image you want to change.

3 Click ✏.

4 Position the mouse ✏ over the background area of the image. Then click the **right** mouse button.

● This area displays the color you selected.

5 Click **Colors**.

6 Click **Set Palette Transparency**.

● The Set Palette Transparency dialog box appears.

# in an *instant*

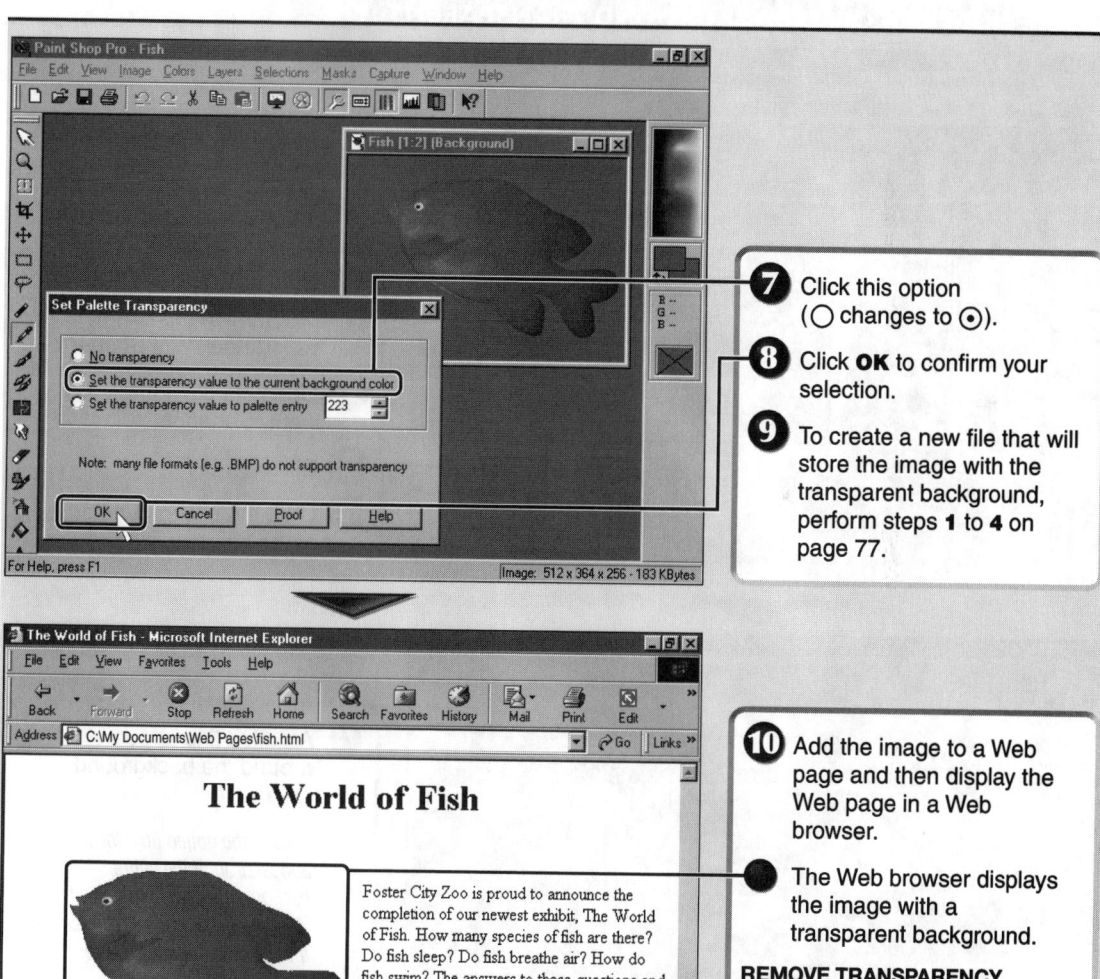

**7** Click this option
(○ changes to ⊙).

**8** Click **OK** to confirm your
selection.

**9** To create a new file that will
store the image with the
transparent background,
perform steps **1** to **4** on
page 77.

**10** Add the image to a Web
page and then display the
Web page in a Web
browser.

● The Web browser displays
the image with a
transparent background.

**REMOVE TRANSPARENCY**

**1** To no longer display the
image with a transparent
background, repeat steps
**1** to **8**, selecting **No
transparency** in step **7**.

CONTINUED

# MAKE IMAGE BACKGROUND TRANSPARENT

You can use an image editing program to make the multicolored background of a GIF image transparent so the background will blend into a Web page. To make a multicolored background transparent, you must first change the background to one color.

## MAKE MULTICOLORED BACKGROUND TRANSPARENT

**1** Start your image editing program. In this example, we started Paint Shop Pro.

**2** Open the GIF image you want to change.

**3** Click 🖉.

**4** Click the background area of the image.

● A dotted line appears around the background area.

*Note: If the dotted line does not appear around the entire background area, hold down the* **Shift** *key and click other areas of the background until you select the entire background.*

**5** Press the **Delete** key.

● The background area you selected changes to one color.

# in an instant

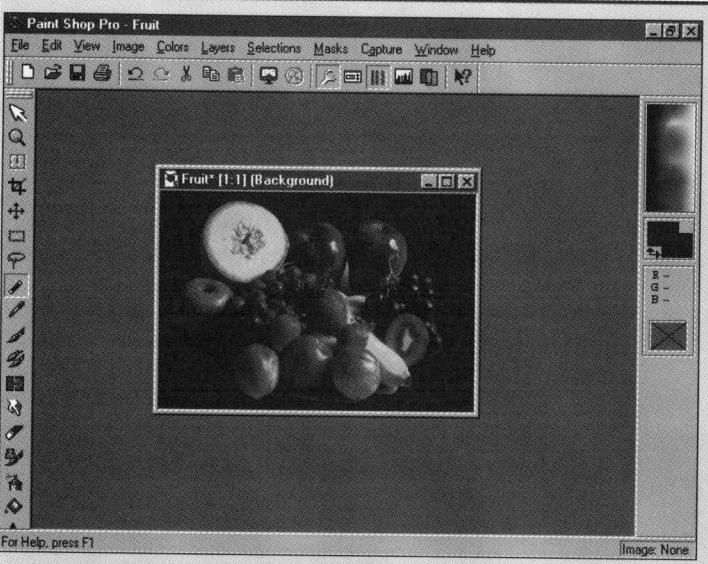

**6** To make the background transparent, perform steps **5** to **8** starting on page 82.

**7** To create a new file that will store the image with the transparent background, perform steps **1** to **4** on page 77.

*Note: Saving the image in a new file allows you to make the original image transparent again later if you are not satisfied with the results.*

**8** Add the image to a Web page and then display the Web page in a Web browser.

● The Web browser displays the image with a transparent background.

# INTERLACE A GIF IMAGE

You can use an image editing program to interlace a GIF image. An interlaced GIF image first appears blurry in a Web browser window and then gradually sharpens as it transfers. This gives users some idea of what the final Web page will look like. Noninterlaced images must fully transfer to a computer before appearing on the screen.

## INTERLACE A GIF IMAGE

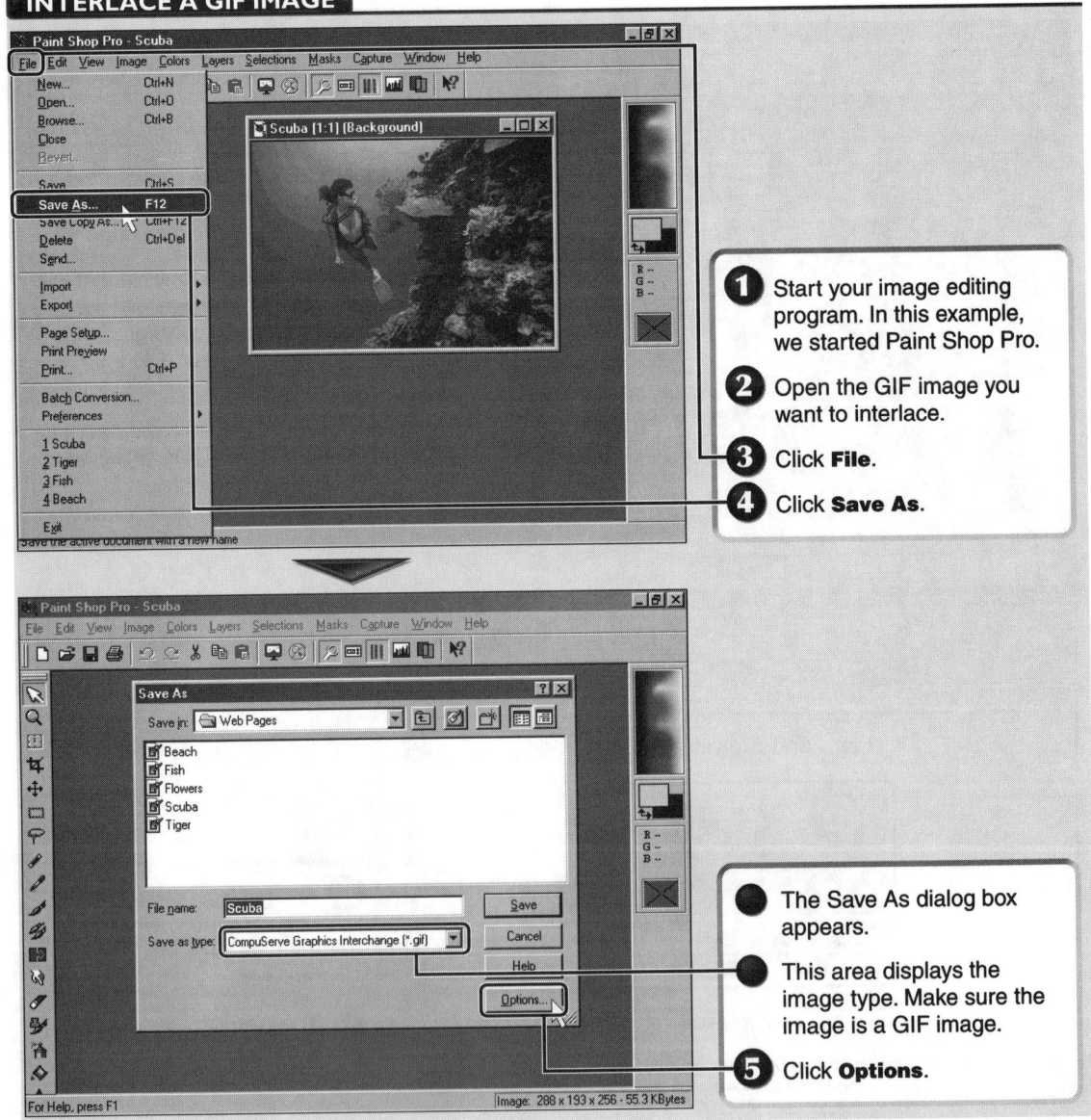

**1** Start your image editing program. In this example, we started Paint Shop Pro.

**2** Open the GIF image you want to interlace.

**3** Click **File**.

**4** Click **Save As**.

■ The Save As dialog box appears.

■ This area displays the image type. Make sure the image is a GIF image.

**5** Click **Options**.

# in an instant

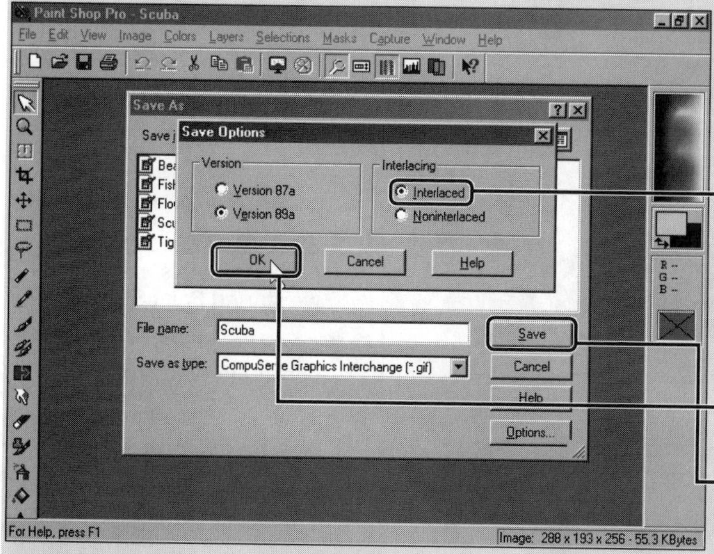

- The Save Options dialog box appears.

**6** Click **Interlaced** (○ changes to ⊙).

**7** Click **OK** to confirm your change.

**8** Click **Save** to save your change.

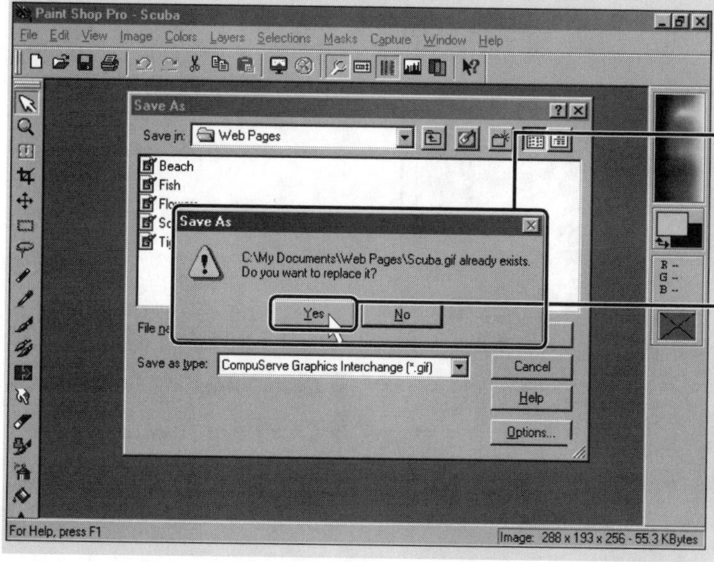

- A dialog box appears, stating that you will replace the original image.

**9** Click **Yes** to replace the original image.

- The image is now interlaced.

**REMOVE INTERLACING**

**1** To remove interlacing from an image, repeat steps **1** to **9**, selecting **Noninterlaced** in step **6**.

# CONVERT TO WEB BROWSER SAFE COLORS

You can use an image editing program to convert an image to Web browser safe colors. This can help ensure the image will appear the way you expect when displayed in a Web browser. Web browser safe colors are a set of 216 colors that can be accurately displayed on computers that display only 256 colors.

## CONVERT TO WEB BROWSER SAFE COLORS

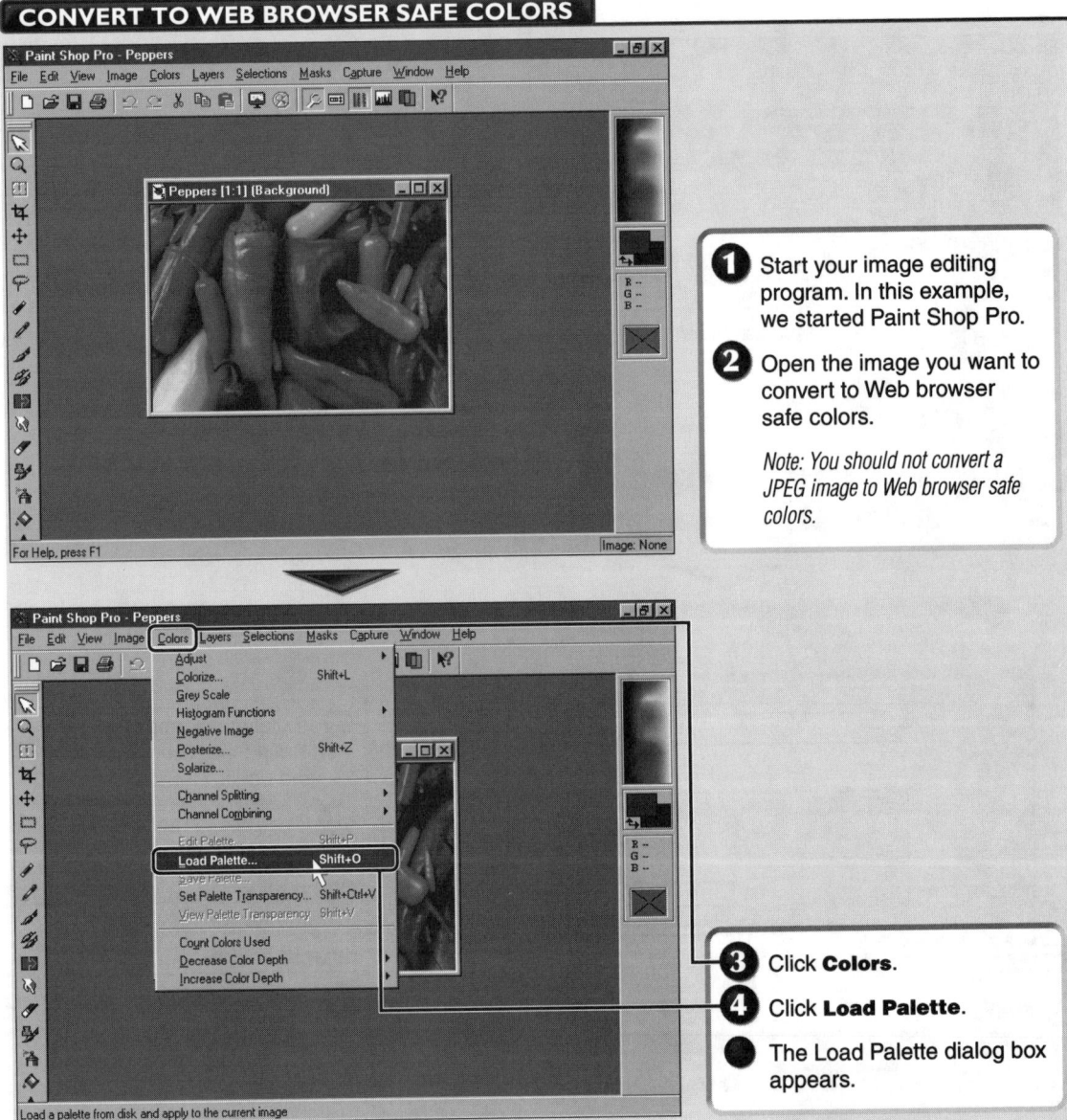

**1** Start your image editing program. In this example, we started Paint Shop Pro.

**2** Open the image you want to convert to Web browser safe colors.

*Note: You should not convert a JPEG image to Web browser safe colors.*

**3** Click **Colors**.

**4** Click **Load Palette**.

● The Load Palette dialog box appears.

# in an *instant*

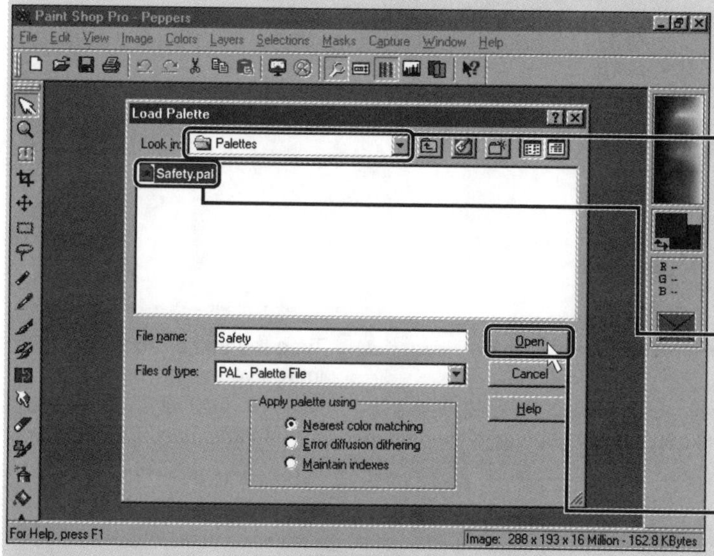

This area shows the
location of the displayed
files.

**5** Click the **Safety.pal** file.
This file contains the Web
browser safe colors.

*Note: The Safety.pal file is located
in the Palettes folder.*

**6** Click **Open** to open the file.

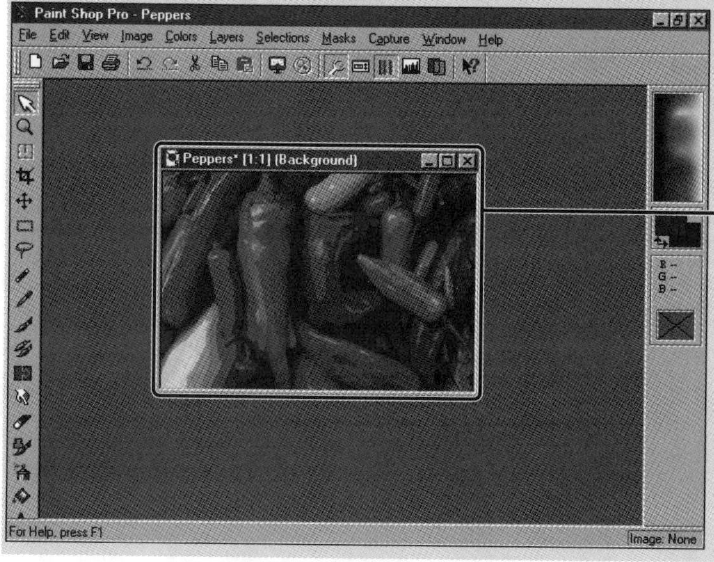

**7** The program converts the
image to Web browser safe
colors.

**8** To create a new file that
will store the image with
the Web browser safe
colors, perform steps
**1** to **4** on page 77.

*Note: Saving the image in a new
file allows you to use the original
image again later if you are not
satisfied with the results.*

You can link a word, phrase or image on your Web page to another page on the Web or in your own Web site. When a user selects the link, the other Web page will appear. You should ensure the text or image you use for a link clearly indicates where the link will take users.

## CREATE A LINK TO ANOTHER WEB PAGE

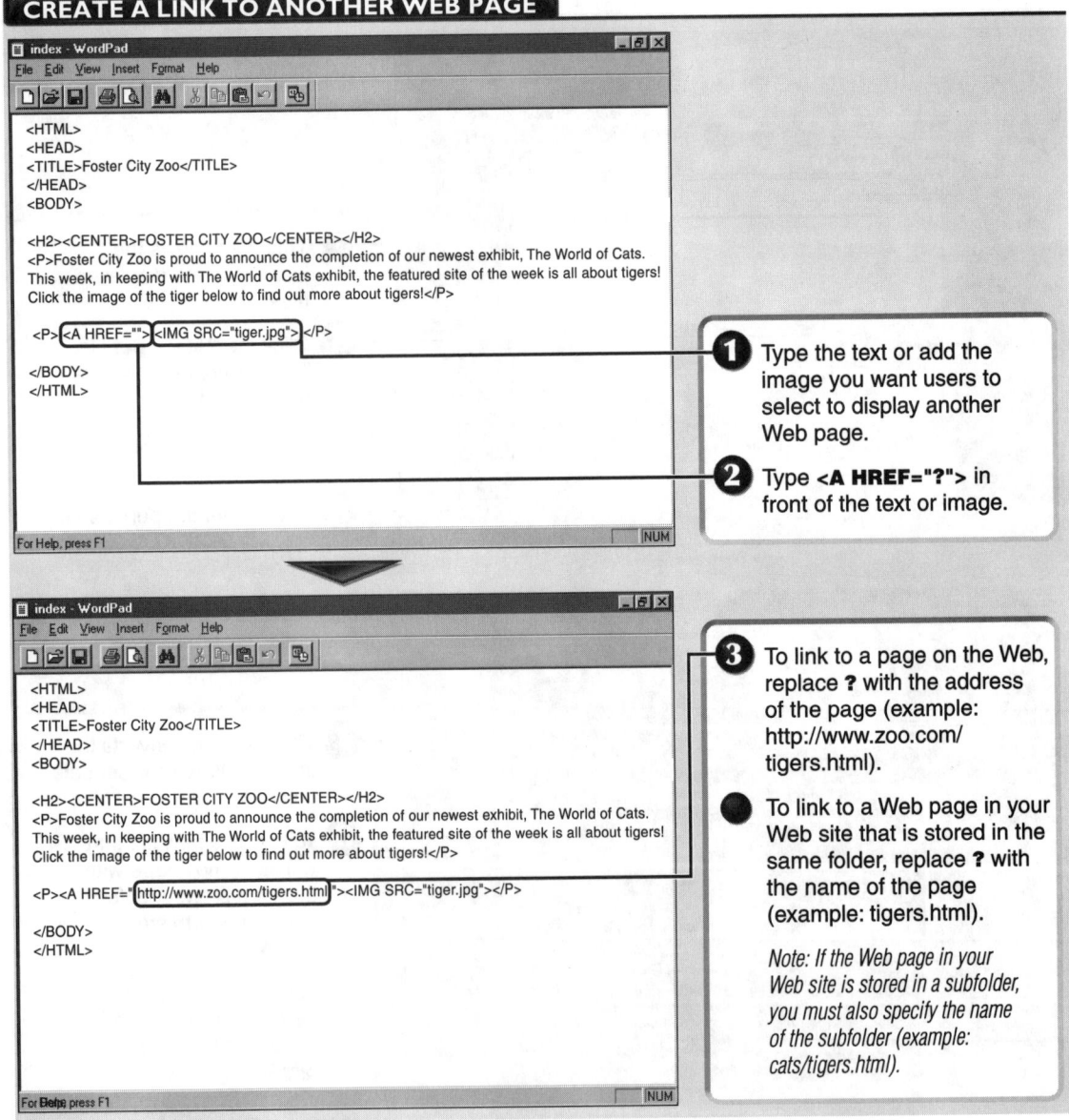

**1** Type the text or add the image you want users to select to display another Web page.

**2** Type **<A HREF="?">** in front of the text or image.

**3** To link to a page on the Web, replace **?** with the address of the page (example: http://www.zoo.com/tigers.html).

● To link to a Web page in your Web site that is stored in the same folder, replace **?** with the name of the page (example: tigers.html).

*Note: If the Web page in your Web site is stored in a subfolder, you must also specify the name of the subfolder (example: cats/tigers.html).*

# in an instant

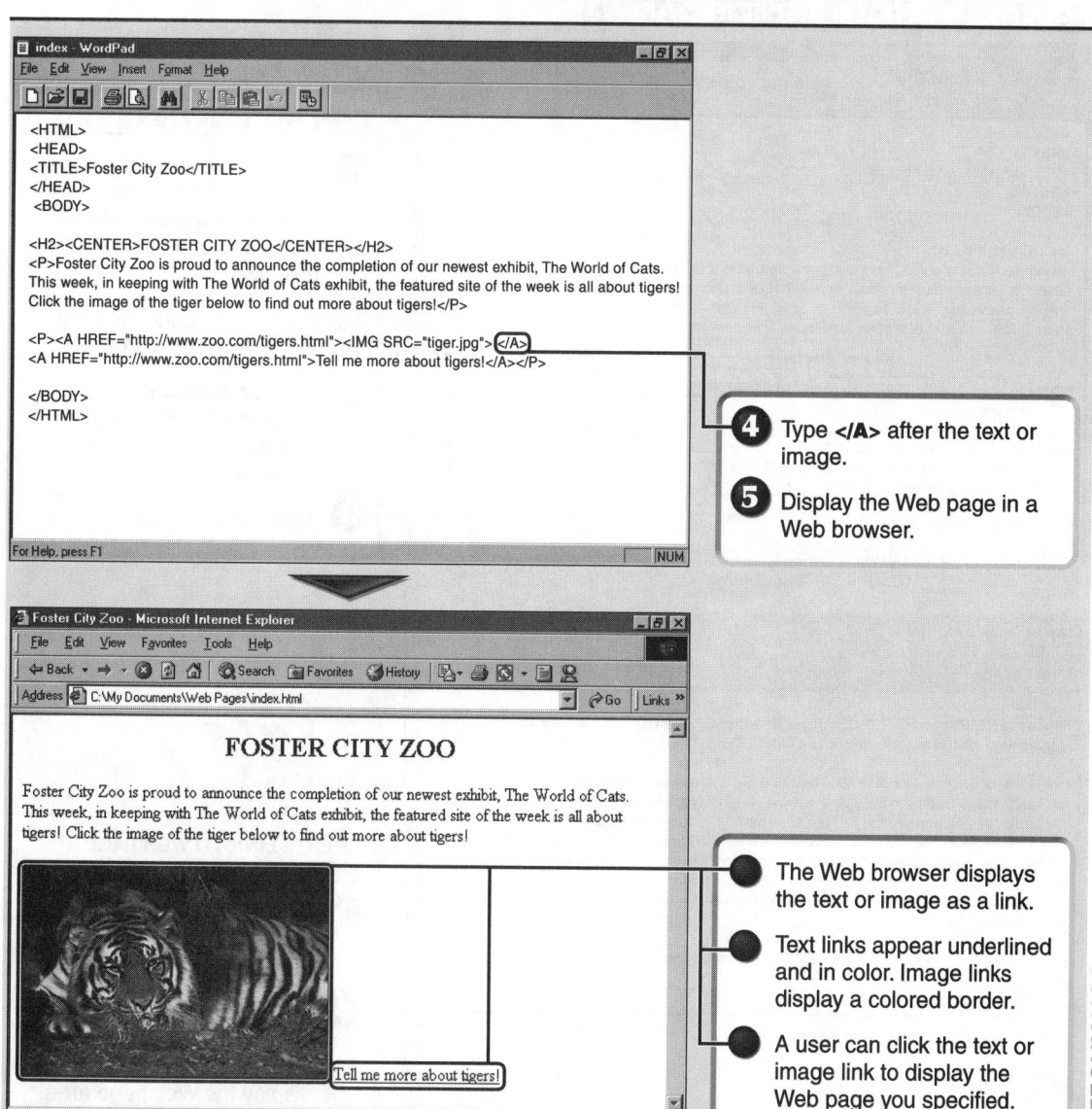

**4** Type **</A>** after the text or image.

**5** Display the Web page in a Web browser.

● The Web browser displays the text or image as a link.

● Text links appear underlined and in color. Image links display a colored border.

● A user can click the text or image link to display the Web page you specified.

CONTINUED

# CREATE A LINK TO ANOTHER WEB PAGE

You can create a link that will take users to a specific area on another Web page in your Web site. This lets users quickly display information of interest. For example, you can create a link that will take users directly to a specific area on an address list, price list or glossary.

## CREATE A LINK TO A SPECIFIC AREA

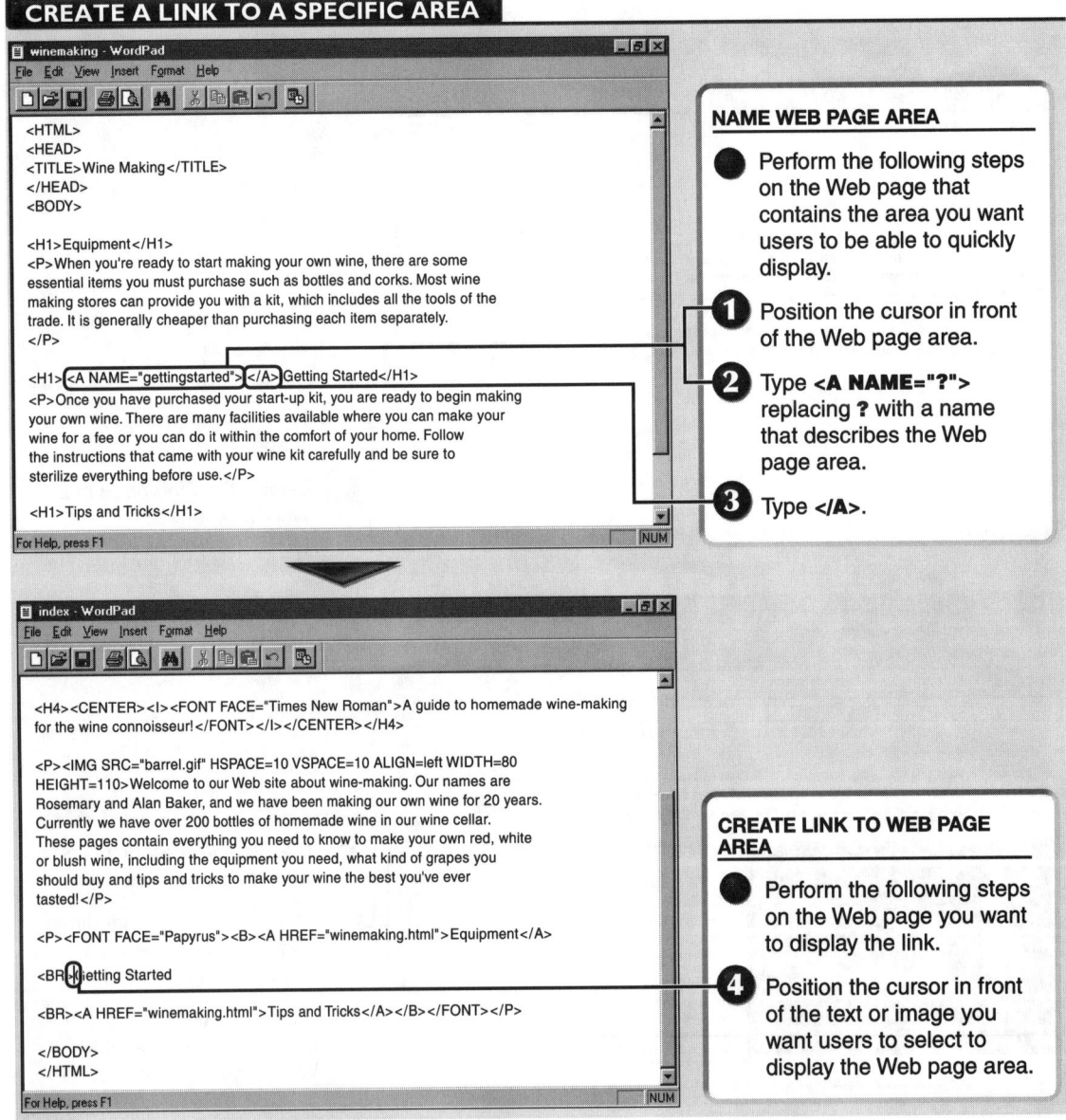

### NAME WEB PAGE AREA

● Perform the following steps on the Web page that contains the area you want users to be able to quickly display.

**1** Position the cursor in front of the Web page area.

**2** Type **<A NAME="?">** replacing **?** with a name that describes the Web page area.

**3** Type **</A>**.

### CREATE LINK TO WEB PAGE AREA

● Perform the following steps on the Web page you want to display the link.

**4** Position the cursor in front of the text or image you want users to select to display the Web page area.

# in an instant

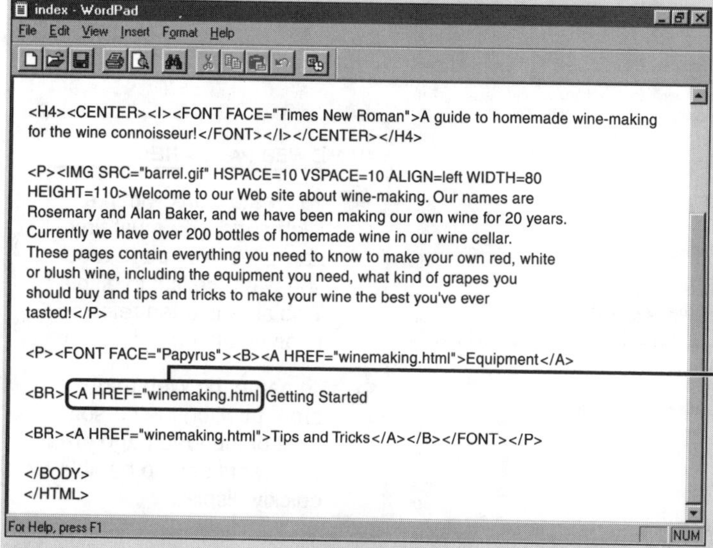

---

**index - WordPad**

File  Edit  View  Insert  Format  Help

<H4><CENTER><I><FONT FACE="Times New Roman">A guide to homemade wine-making for the wine connoisseur!</FONT></I></CENTER></H4>

<P><IMG SRC="barrel.gif" HSPACE=10 VSPACE=10 ALIGN=left WIDTH=80 HEIGHT=110>Welcome to our Web site about wine-making. Our names are Rosemary and Alan Baker, and we have been making our own wine for 20 years. Currently we have over 200 bottles of homemade wine in our wine cellar. These pages contain everything you need to know to make your own red, white or blush wine, including the equipment you need, what kind of grapes you should buy and tips and tricks to make your wine the best you've ever tasted!</P>

<P><FONT FACE="Papyrus"><B><A HREF="winemaking.html">Equipment</A>

<BR><A HREF="winemaking.html" Getting Started

<BR><A HREF="winemaking.html">Tips and Tricks</A></B></FONT></P>

</BODY>
</HTML>

For Help, press F1                                                          NUM

**5** Type **<A HREF="?**.

**6** If the Web page you want to link to is stored in the same folder in your Web site, replace **?** with the name of the page (example: winemaking.html).

*Note: If the page is stored in a subfolder, you must also specify the name of the subfolder (example: pages/winemaking.html).*

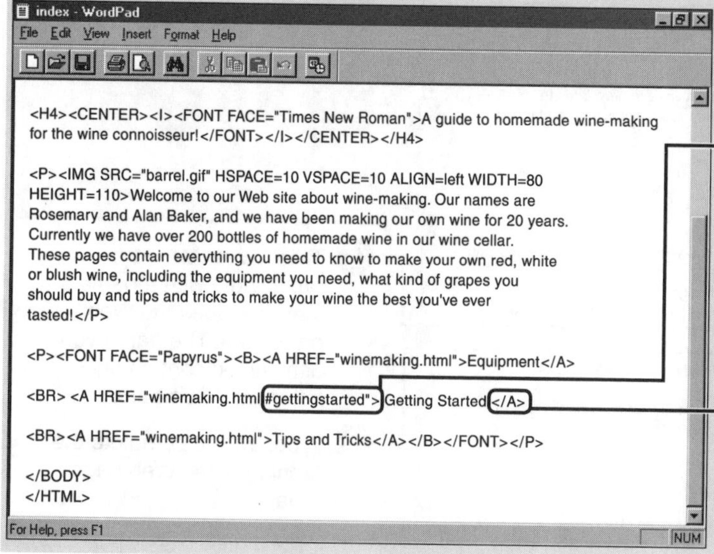

---

**index - WordPad**

File  Edit  View  Insert  Format  Help

<H4><CENTER><I><FONT FACE="Times New Roman">A guide to homemade wine-making for the wine connoisseur!</FONT></I></CENTER></H4>

<P><IMG SRC="barrel.gif" HSPACE=10 VSPACE=10 ALIGN=left WIDTH=80 HEIGHT=110>Welcome to our Web site about wine-making. Our names are Rosemary and Alan Baker, and we have been making our own wine for 20 years. Currently we have over 200 bottles of homemade wine in our wine cellar. These pages contain everything you need to know to make your own red, white or blush wine, including the equipment you need, what kind of grapes you should buy and tips and tricks to make your wine the best you've ever tasted!</P>

<P><FONT FACE="Papyrus"><B><A HREF="winemaking.html">Equipment</A>

<BR> <A HREF="winemaking.html#gettingstarted">Getting Started</A>

<BR><A HREF="winemaking.html">Tips and Tricks</A></B></FONT></P>

</BODY>
</HTML>

For Help, press F1                                                          NUM

**7** Type **#?">** replacing **?** with the name you specified for the Web page area in step **2**.

**8** Type **</A>** after the text or image.

● When the Web page is displayed in a Web browser, the Web browser will display the link.

● A user can click the link to display the Web page area you specified.

You can create a link that will take users to another area of the same Web page. This lets users quickly display information of interest in a Web page. For example, you can create a table of contents that contains links to different sections of a long Web page.

## CREATE A LINK WITHIN A WEB PAGE

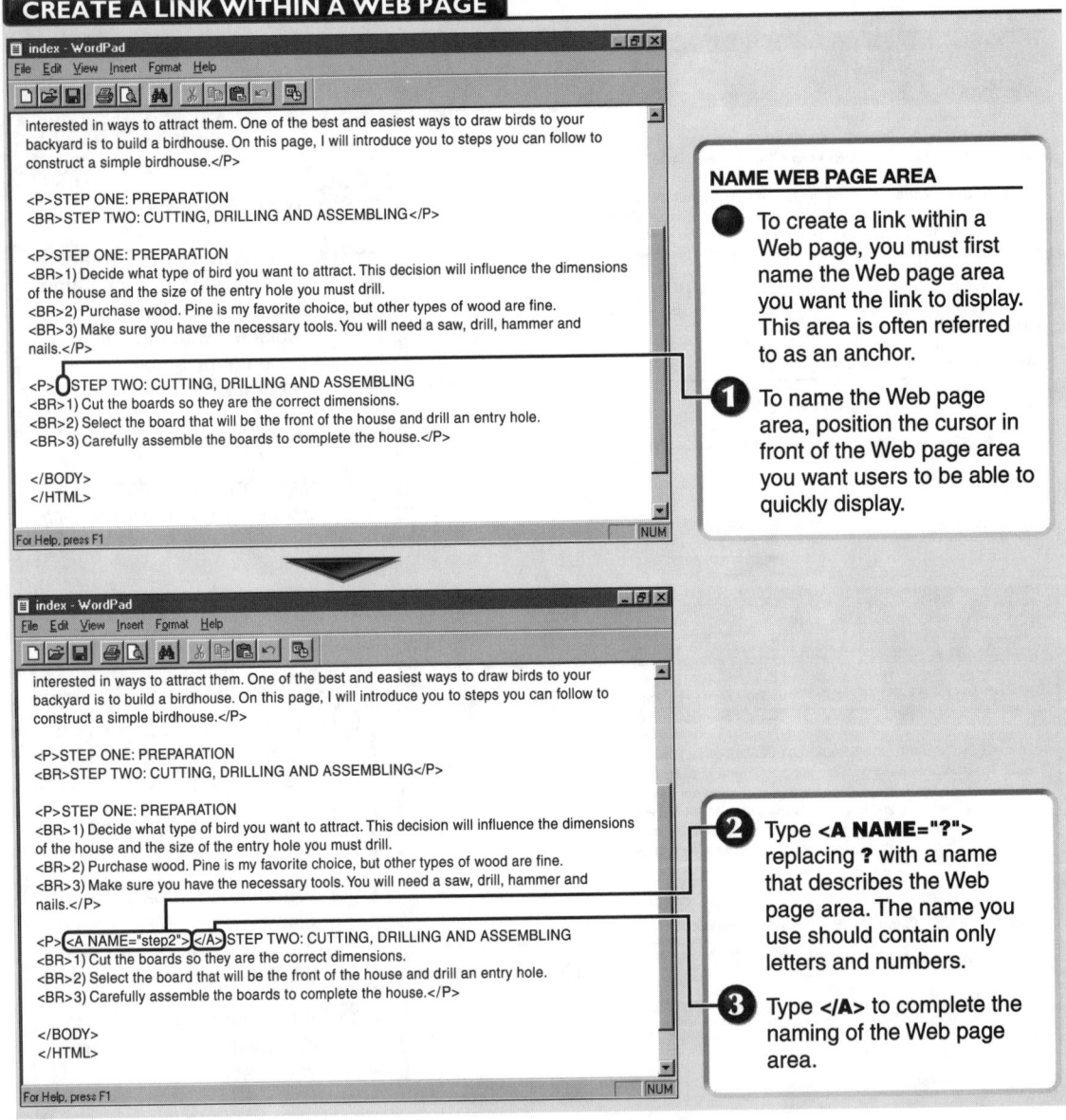

**NAME WEB PAGE AREA**

● To create a link within a Web page, you must first name the Web page area you want the link to display. This area is often referred to as an anchor.

① To name the Web page area, position the cursor in front of the Web page area you want users to be able to quickly display.

② Type **<A NAME="?">** replacing **?** with a name that describes the Web page area. The name you use should contain only letters and numbers.

③ Type **</A>** to complete the naming of the Web page area.

# in an instant

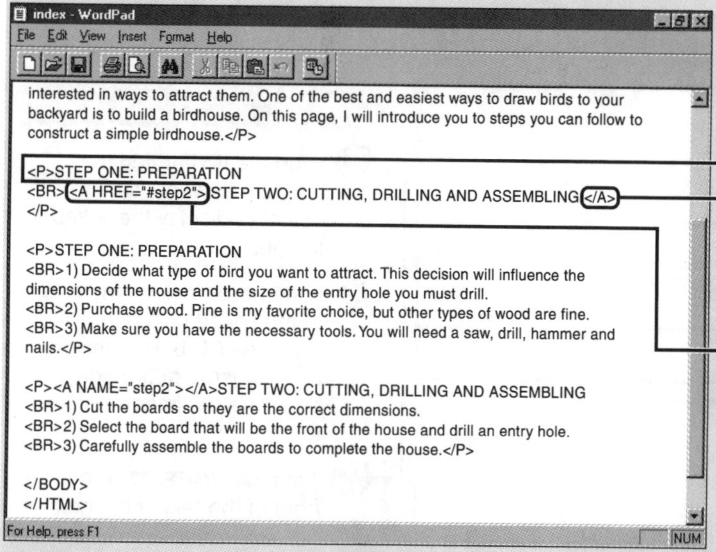

---

**index - WordPad**

File   Edit   View   Insert   Format   Help

interested in ways to attract them. One of the best and easiest ways to draw birds to your
backyard is to build a birdhouse. On this page, I will introduce you to steps you can follow to
construct a simple birdhouse.</P>

<P>STEP ONE: PREPARATION
<BR> <A HREF="#step2"> STEP TWO: CUTTING, DRILLING AND ASSEMBLING </A>
</P>

<P>STEP ONE: PREPARATION
<BR>1) Decide what type of bird you want to attract. This decision will influence the
dimensions of the house and the size of the entry hole you must drill.
<BR>2) Purchase wood. Pine is my favorite choice, but other types of wood are fine.
<BR>3) Make sure you have the necessary tools. You will need a saw, drill, hammer and
nails.</P>

<P><A NAME="step2"></A>STEP TWO: CUTTING, DRILLING AND ASSEMBLING
<BR>1) Cut the boards so they are the correct dimensions.
<BR>2) Select the board that will be the front of the house and drill an entry hole.
<BR>3) Carefully assemble the boards to complete the house.</P>

</BODY>
</HTML>

For Help, press F1                                                              NUM

## CREATE LINK TO WEB PAGE AREA

**4** To create the link, position the cursor in front of the text or image you want users to select to display the Web page area you named on page 94.

**5** Type **<A HREF="#?">** replacing **?** with the name you specified for the Web page area in step **2**.

**6** Type **</A>** after the text or image.

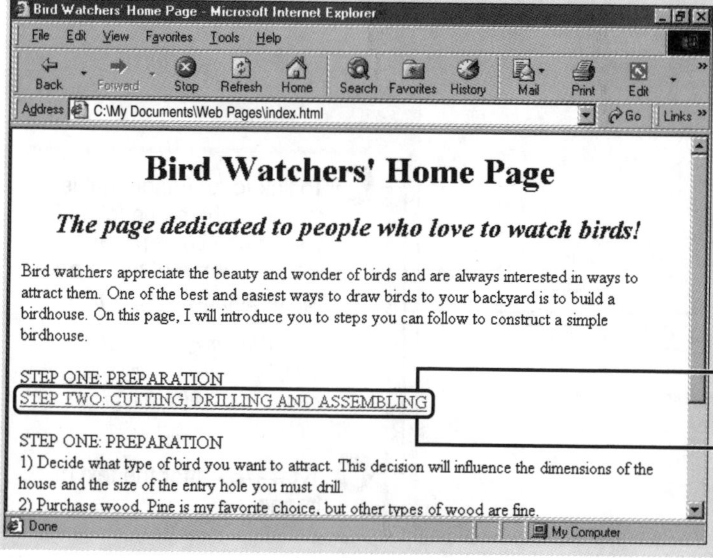

---

**Bird Watchers' Home Page - Microsoft Internet Explorer**

File   Edit   View   Favorites   Tools   Help

Back   Forward   Stop   Refresh   Home   Search   Favorites   History   Mail   Print   Edit

Address  C:\My Documents\Web Pages\index.html                          Go   Links »

## Bird Watchers' Home Page

### *The page dedicated to people who love to watch birds!*

Bird watchers appreciate the beauty and wonder of birds and are always interested in ways to
attract them. One of the best and easiest ways to draw birds to your backyard is to build a
birdhouse. On this page, I will introduce you to steps you can follow to construct a simple
birdhouse.

STEP ONE: PREPARATION
STEP TWO: CUTTING, DRILLING AND ASSEMBLING

STEP ONE: PREPARATION
1) Decide what type of bird you want to attract. This decision will influence the dimensions of the
house and the size of the entry hole you must drill.
2) Purchase wood. Pine is my favorite choice, but other types of wood are fine.

Done                                                              My Computer

**7** Display the Web page in a Web browser.

● The Web browser displays the link.

● A user can click the link to display the Web page area you specified.

# CREATE A LINK TO AN IMAGE

You can create a link that will take users to an image. Linking to an image is useful for linking a small image to a larger version of the image. This gives users access to the image without increasing the transfer time of your Web page and lets users decide if they want to wait to view the larger image.

## CREATE A LINK TO AN IMAGE

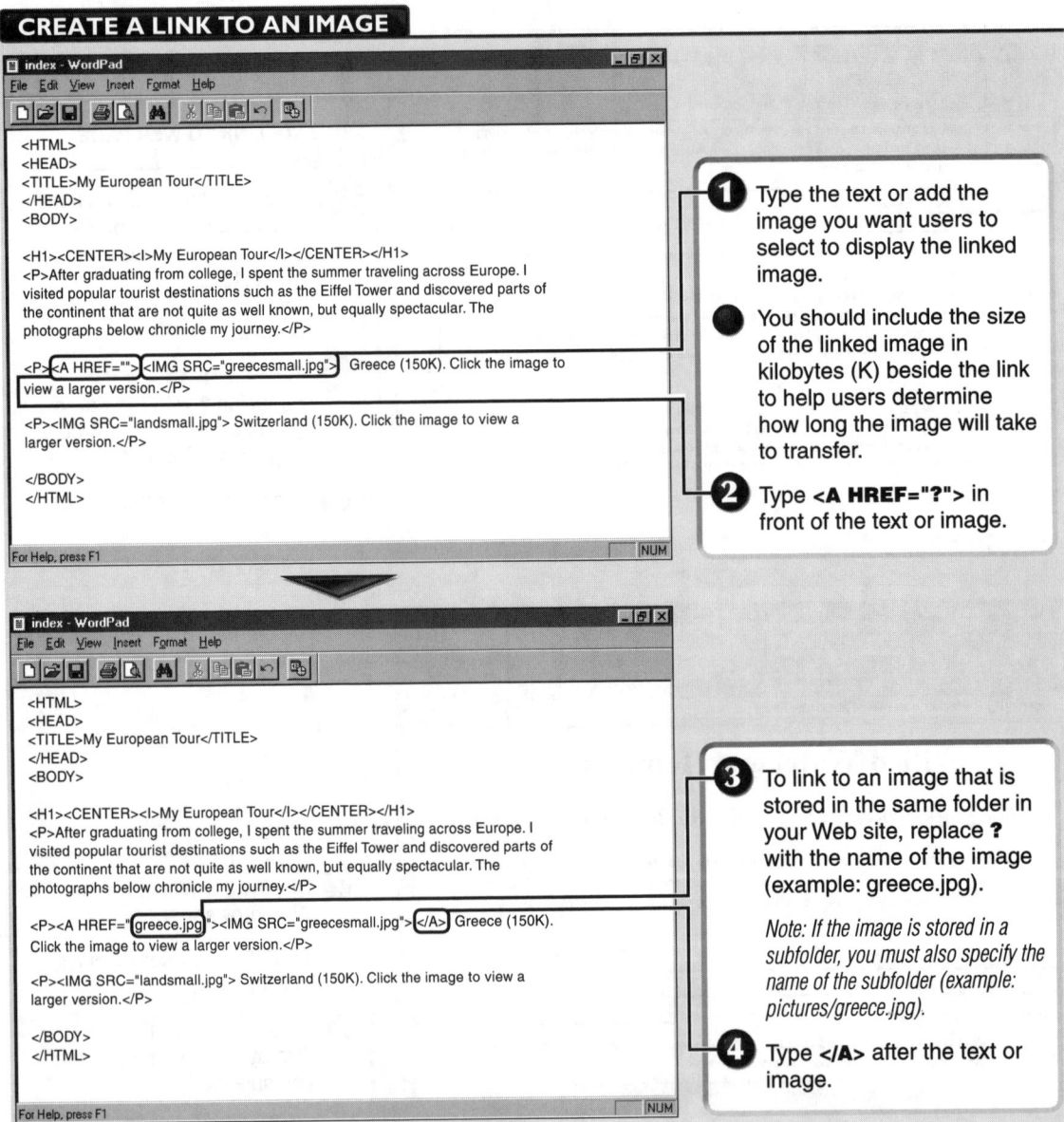

1 Type the text or add the image you want users to select to display the linked image.

● You should include the size of the linked image in kilobytes (K) beside the link to help users determine how long the image will take to transfer.

2 Type **<A HREF="?">** in front of the text or image.

3 To link to an image that is stored in the same folder in your Web site, replace **?** with the name of the image (example: greece.jpg).

*Note: If the image is stored in a subfolder, you must also specify the name of the subfolder (example: pictures/greece.jpg).*

4 Type **</A>** after the text or image.

# in an instant

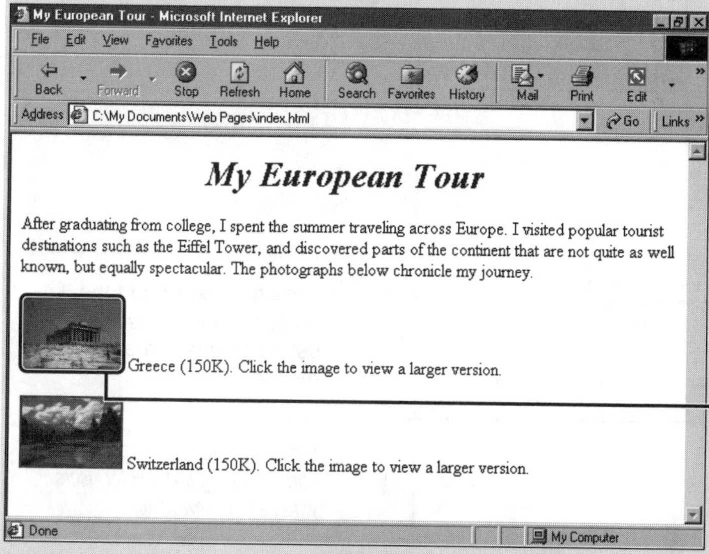

---

**My European Tour - Microsoft Internet Explorer**

File  Edit  View  Favorites  Tools  Help

Back  Forward  Stop  Refresh  Home  Search  Favorites  History  Mail  Print  Edit

Address  C:\My Documents\Web Pages\index.html

## *My European Tour*

After graduating from college, I spent the summer traveling across Europe. I visited popular tourist destinations such as the Eiffel Tower, and discovered parts of the continent that are not quite as well known, but equally spectacular. The photographs below chronicle my journey.

Greece (150K). Click the image to view a larger version.

Switzerland (150K). Click the image to view a larger version.

Done                    My Computer

**5** Display the Web page in a Web browser.

● The Web browser displays the link.

● A user can click the link to display the linked image.

---

**C:\My Documents\Web Pages\greece.jpg - Microsoft Internet Explorer**

File  Edit  View  Favorites  Tools  Help

Back  Forward  Stop  Refresh  Home  Search  Favorites  History  Mail  Print  Edit

Address  C:\My Documents\Web Pages\greece.jpg

Done                    My Computer

● When a user selects the link, the image you specified appears.

*Note: Some Web browsers cannot display certain types of images, such as Windows bitmap images. If the image cannot be displayed, the Web browser may allow the user to view the image in a different program.*

# CREATE AN E-MAIL LINK

Your Web page can include a link that allows users to quickly send an e-mail message. An e-mail link allows users to send questions and provide feedback that can help improve your Web pages. Many companies include e-mail links that allow users to contact company employees.

## CREATE AN E-MAIL LINK

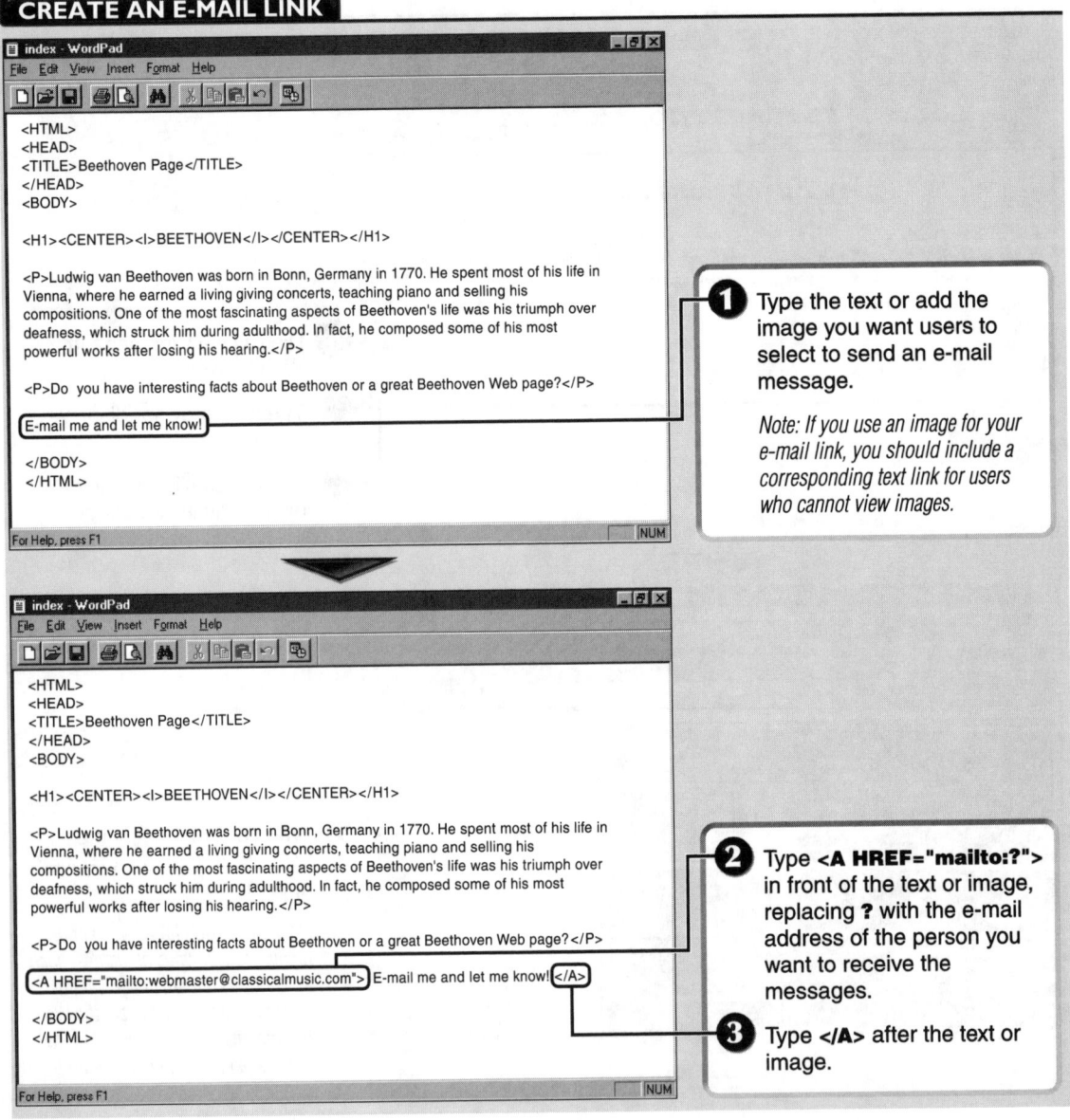

**1** Type the text or add the image you want users to select to send an e-mail message.

*Note: If you use an image for your e-mail link, you should include a corresponding text link for users who cannot view images.*

**2** Type **<A HREF="mailto:?">** in front of the text or image, replacing **?** with the e-mail address of the person you want to receive the messages.

**3** Type **</A>** after the text or image.

# in an *instant*

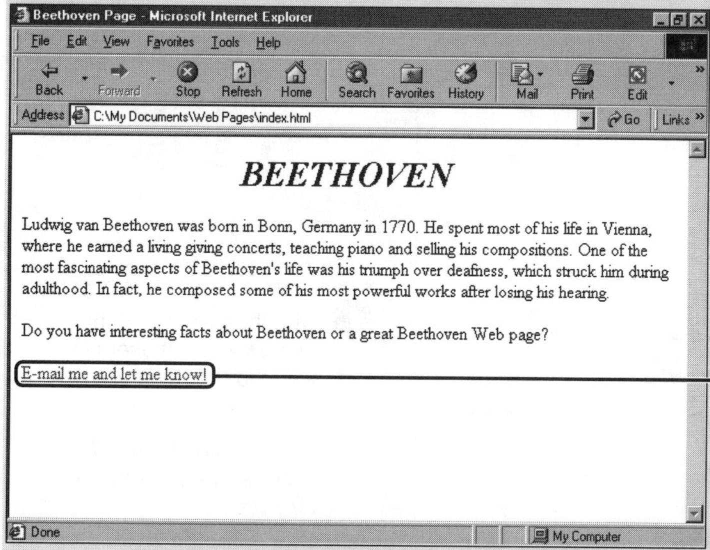

---

**Beethoven Page - Microsoft Internet Explorer**

File  Edit  View  Favorites  Tools  Help

Back  Forward  Stop  Refresh  Home  Search  Favorites  History  Mail  Print  Edit

Address  C:\My Documents\Web Pages\index.html     Go  Links

### *BEETHOVEN*

Ludwig van Beethoven was born in Bonn, Germany in 1770. He spent most of his life in Vienna, where he earned a living giving concerts, teaching piano and selling his compositions. One of the most fascinating aspects of Beethoven's life was his triumph over deafness, which struck him during adulthood. In fact, he composed some of his most powerful works after losing his hearing.

Do you have interesting facts about Beethoven or a great Beethoven Web page?

E-mail me and let me know!

Done     My Computer

---

**4** Display the Web page in a Web browser.

● The Web browser displays the e-mail link.

● A user can click the link to send a message to the e-mail address you specified.

---

**Untitled - Message (Plain Text)**

File  Edit  View  Insert  Format  Tools  Actions  Help

Send    Options...

To...  webmaster@classicalmusic.com

Cc...

Subject:

---

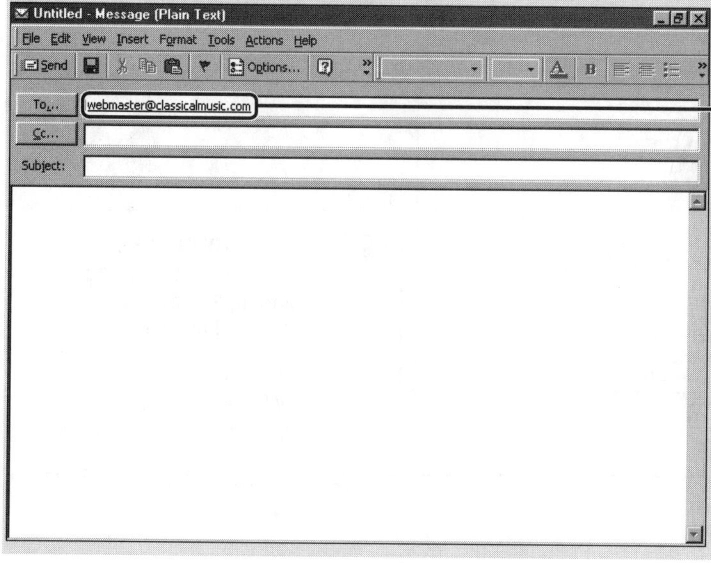

● When a user selects an e-mail link, the user's e-mail program will start.

● The e-mail program will automatically display the e-mail address you specified to ensure the message will reach the correct person.

---

# CREATE A LINK TO AN FTP SITE

You can create a link on your Web page that will take users to an FTP site. File Transfer Protocol (FTP) sites store files that users can transfer to their computers. Many colleges, universities, government agencies and companies maintain FTP sites on the Internet. Some popular FTP sites include ftp.cdrom.com and ftp.digital.com.

## CREATE A LINK TO AN FTP SITE

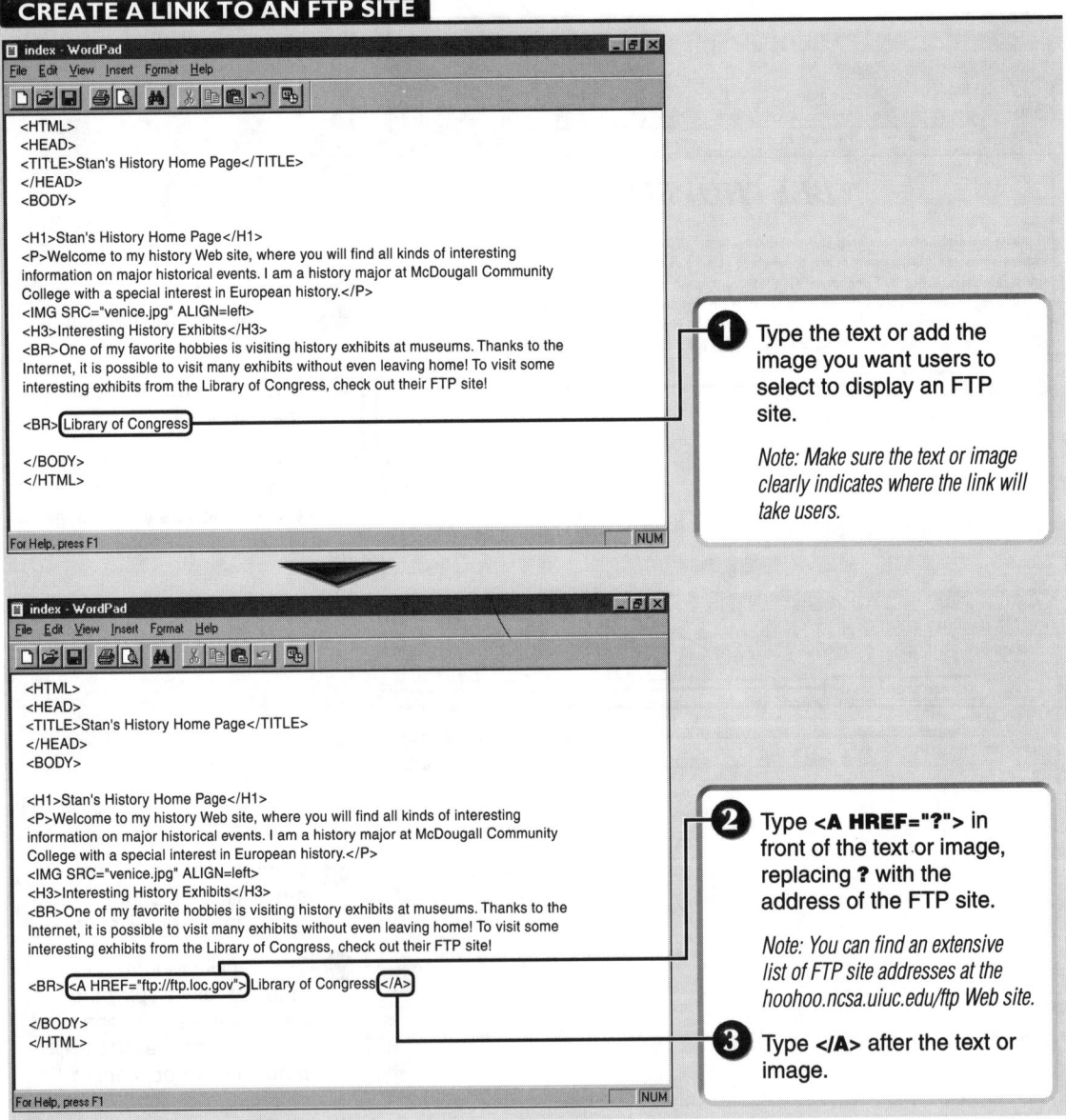

**1** Type the text or add the image you want users to select to display an FTP site.

*Note: Make sure the text or image clearly indicates where the link will take users.*

**2** Type **<A HREF="?">** in front of the text or image, replacing **?** with the address of the FTP site.

*Note: You can find an extensive list of FTP site addresses at the hoohoo.ncsa.uiuc.edu/ftp Web site.*

**3** Type **</A>** after the text or image.

# in an *instant*

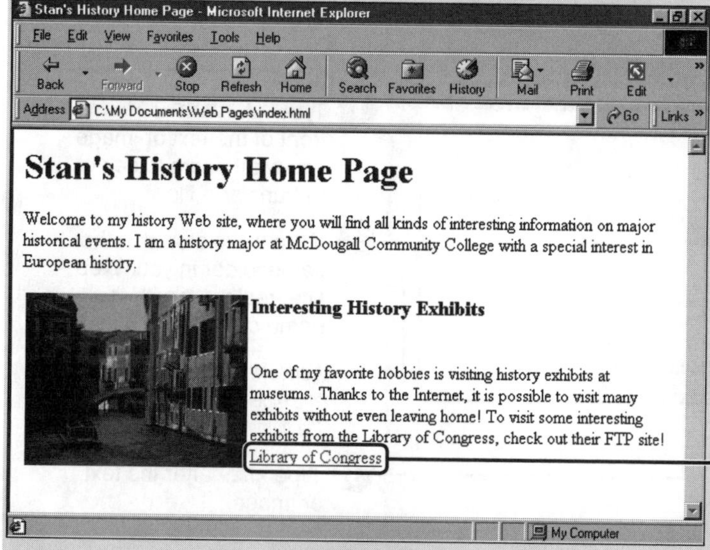

---

**Stan's History Home Page** — Microsoft Internet Explorer

File Edit View Favorites Tools Help

Back Forward Stop Refresh Home Search Favorites History Mail Print Edit

Address C:\My Documents\Web Pages\index.html

## Stan's History Home Page

Welcome to my history Web site, where you will find all kinds of interesting information on major historical events. I am a history major at McDougall Community College with a special interest in European history.

### Interesting History Exhibits

One of my favorite hobbies is visiting history exhibits at museums. Thanks to the Internet, it is possible to visit many exhibits without even leaving home! To visit some interesting exhibits from the Library of Congress, check out their FTP site!
Library of Congress

My Computer

---

ftp://ftp.loc.gov/ — Microsoft Internet Explorer

File Edit View Go Favorites Help

Back Forward Up Cut Copy Paste Undo Delete Properties Views

Address ftp://ftp.loc.gov/

bin   etc   lib   pub   usr   .profile

User: Anonymous   Internet

---

**4** Display the Web page in a Web browser.

● The Web browser displays the link to the FTP site.

● When a user selects the link, the FTP site you specified appears.

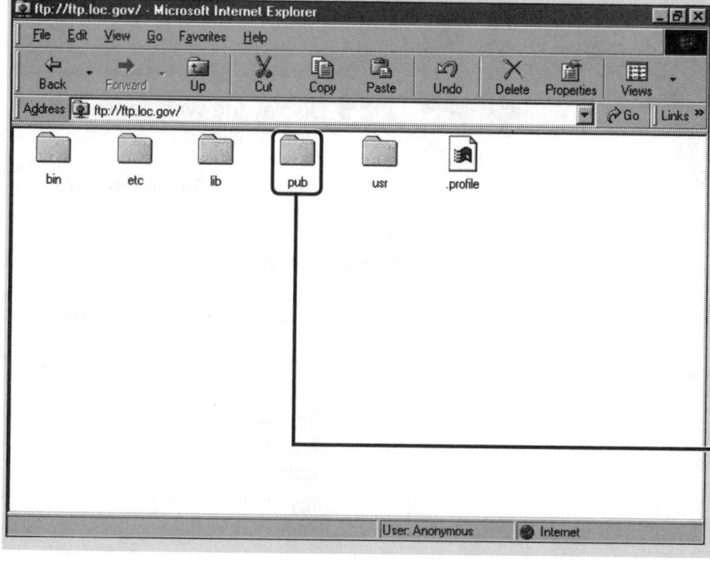

● Files at FTP sites are stored in different directories.

● Users can usually find files of interest in the **pub** or **public** directory.

**101**

# CREATE A LINK TO A FILE

You can create a link that allows users to transfer files such as sounds, videos and programs to their computers. You should provide a short description of the linked file, including the file type and size. This information can help users decide if they want to transfer the file to their computers.

## CREATE A LINK TO A FILE

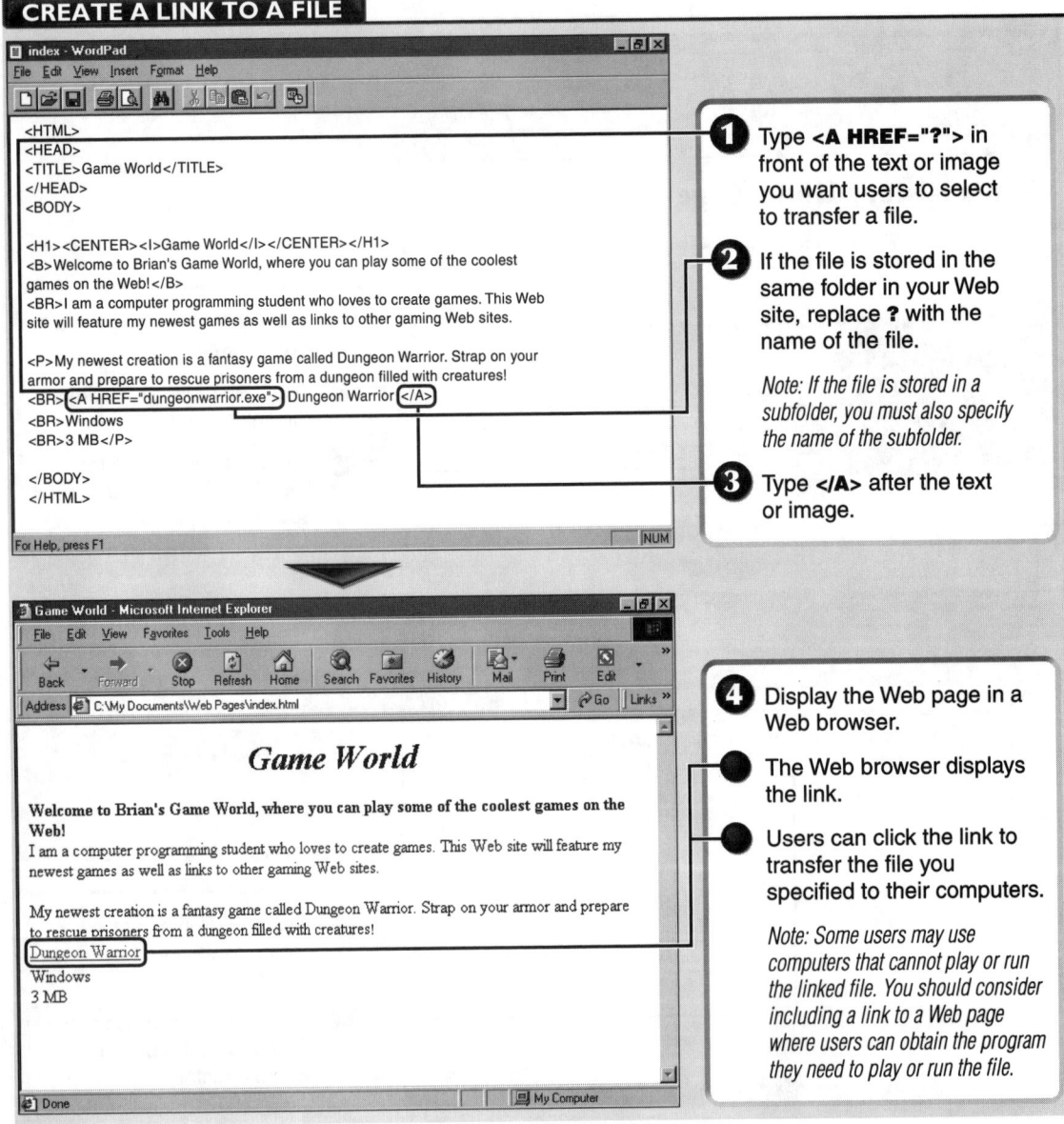

**1** Type **<A HREF="?">** in front of the text or image you want users to select to transfer a file.

**2** If the file is stored in the same folder in your Web site, replace **?** with the name of the file.

*Note: If the file is stored in a subfolder, you must also specify the name of the subfolder.*

**3** Type **</A>** after the text or image.

**4** Display the Web page in a Web browser.

● The Web browser displays the link.

● Users can click the link to transfer the file you specified to their computers.

*Note: Some users may use computers that cannot play or run the linked file. You should consider including a link to a Web page where users can obtain the program they need to play or run the file.*

You can have linked information open in a new window.
The Web page containing the link will remain open. This
allows users to quickly return to the Web page when
they have finished viewing the linked information.

## OPEN A LINK IN A NEW WINDOW

```
index - WordPad
File  Edit  View  Insert  Format  Help

<HTML>
<HEAD>
<TITLE>Into the Wild</TITLE>
</HEAD>
<BODY>

<H1><I>Into the Wild!</I></H1>

<IMG SRC="cougar.jpg" ALIGN=left>

<P><B>Would you like to venture beyond the beaten path? Do so with Into the Wild's adventure
tours.</B></P>
<P>Whether you'd like to take a nature photography tour, camp in the rugged wilderness of the
Rocky Mountains or go on a canoeing adventure, we have the trip for you!</P>

<IMG SRC="skier.jpg" ALIGN=right>

<BR><H3><A HREF="skiing.html" TARGET="_blank" >Skiing</A></H3>
<P>Some of our most popular trips are alpine skiing excursions in the Rocky Mountains. We will fly
you to the top of the slopes by helicopter and provide comfortable accommodations at the end of a
fun-filled day! Cross-country ski packages are also available!</P>

For Help, press F1                                                        NUM
```

**1** Create the link you want
users to select to view the
linked information in a new
window.

**2** In the <A> tag for the link,
type **TARGET="_blank"**.

```
Into the Wild - Microsoft Internet Explorer
File  Edit  View  Favorites  Tools  Help

Back  Forward  Stop  Refresh  Home  Search  Favorites  History  Mail  Print  Edit

Address  C:\My Documents\Web Pages\index.html                      Go  Links
```

## *Into the Wild!*

**Would you like to venture beyond the beaten path? Do so
with Into the Wild's adventure tours.**

Whether you'd like to take a nature photography tour, camp in
the rugged wilderness of the Rocky Mountains or go on a
canoeing adventure, we have the trip for you!

Skiing

Some of our most popular trips are alpine skiing excursions in the Rocky
Mountains. We will fly you to the top of the slopes by helicopter and
provide comfortable accommodations at the end of a fun-filled day! Cross-
country ski packages are also available!

My Computer

**3** Display the Web page in a
Web browser.

The Web browser displays
the link.

A user can click the link to
open the linked information
in a new window.

You can change the color of unvisited and visited links on your Web page. An unvisited link is a link a user has not previously selected. A visited link is a link a user has previously selected. Make sure you choose different colors for unvisited and visited links.

## CHANGE UNVISITED LINKS

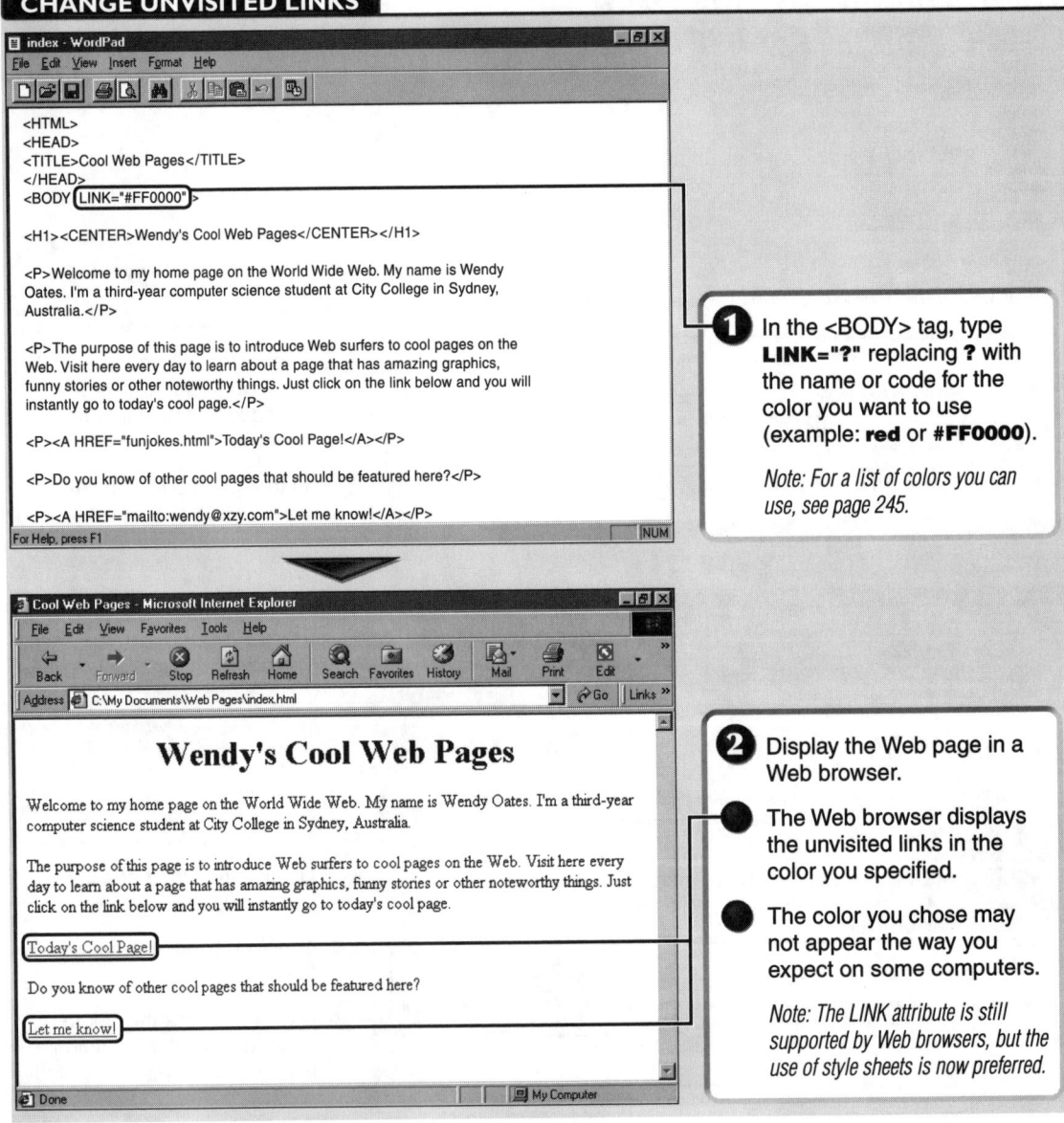

**1** In the <BODY> tag, type **LINK="?"** replacing **?** with the name or code for the color you want to use (example: **red** or **#FF0000**).

*Note: For a list of colors you can use, see page 245.*

**2** Display the Web page in a Web browser.

● The Web browser displays the unvisited links in the color you specified.

● The color you chose may not appear the way you expect on some computers.

*Note: The LINK attribute is still supported by Web browsers, but the use of style sheets is now preferred.*

# in an *instant*

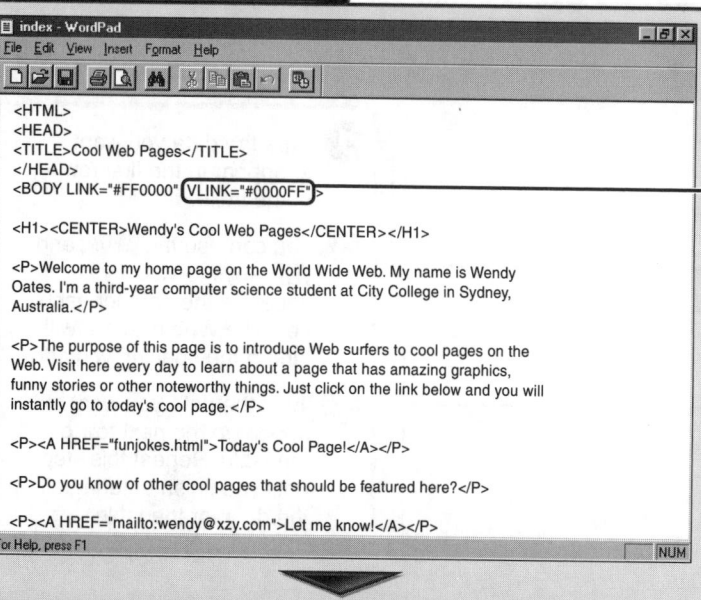

```
<HTML>
<HEAD>
<TITLE>Cool Web Pages</TITLE>
</HEAD>
<BODY LINK="#FF0000" VLINK="#0000FF">

<H1><CENTER>Wendy's Cool Web Pages</CENTER></H1>

<P>Welcome to my home page on the World Wide Web. My name is Wendy
Oates. I'm a third-year computer science student at City College in Sydney,
Australia.</P>

<P>The purpose of this page is to introduce Web surfers to cool pages on the
Web. Visit here every day to learn about a page that has amazing graphics,
funny stories or other noteworthy things. Just click on the link below and you will
instantly go to today's cool page.</P>

<P><A HREF="funjokes.html">Today's Cool Page!</A></P>

<P>Do you know of other cool pages that should be featured here?</P>

<P><A HREF="mailto:wendy@xzy.com">Let me know!</A></P>
```

**1** In the <BODY> tag, type **VLINK="?"** replacing **?** with the name or code for the color you want to use (example: **blue** or **#0000FF**).

*Note: For a list of colors you can use, see page 245.*

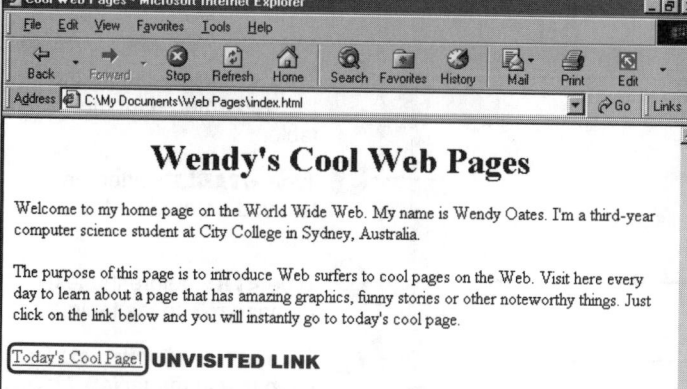

# Wendy's Cool Web Pages

Welcome to my home page on the World Wide Web. My name is Wendy Oates. I'm a third-year computer science student at City College in Sydney, Australia.

The purpose of this page is to introduce Web surfers to cool pages on the Web. Visit here every day to learn about a page that has amazing graphics, funny stories or other noteworthy things. Just click on the link below and you will instantly go to today's cool page.

Today's Cool Page! **UNVISITED LINK**

Do you know of other cool pages that should be featured here?

Let me know! **VISITED LINK**

**2** Display the Web page in a Web browser.

The Web browser displays the visited links in the color you specified.

The color you chose may not appear the way you expect on some computers.

*Note: The VLINK attribute is still supported by Web browsers, but the use of style sheets is now preferred.*

# CREATE A TABLE

You can create a table to neatly display information on a Web page. You use tags to create rows, header cells and data cells in a table. A row is a horizontal line of data. Header cells usually describe the data in a row or column, while data cells contain the information in the table.

## CREATE A TABLE

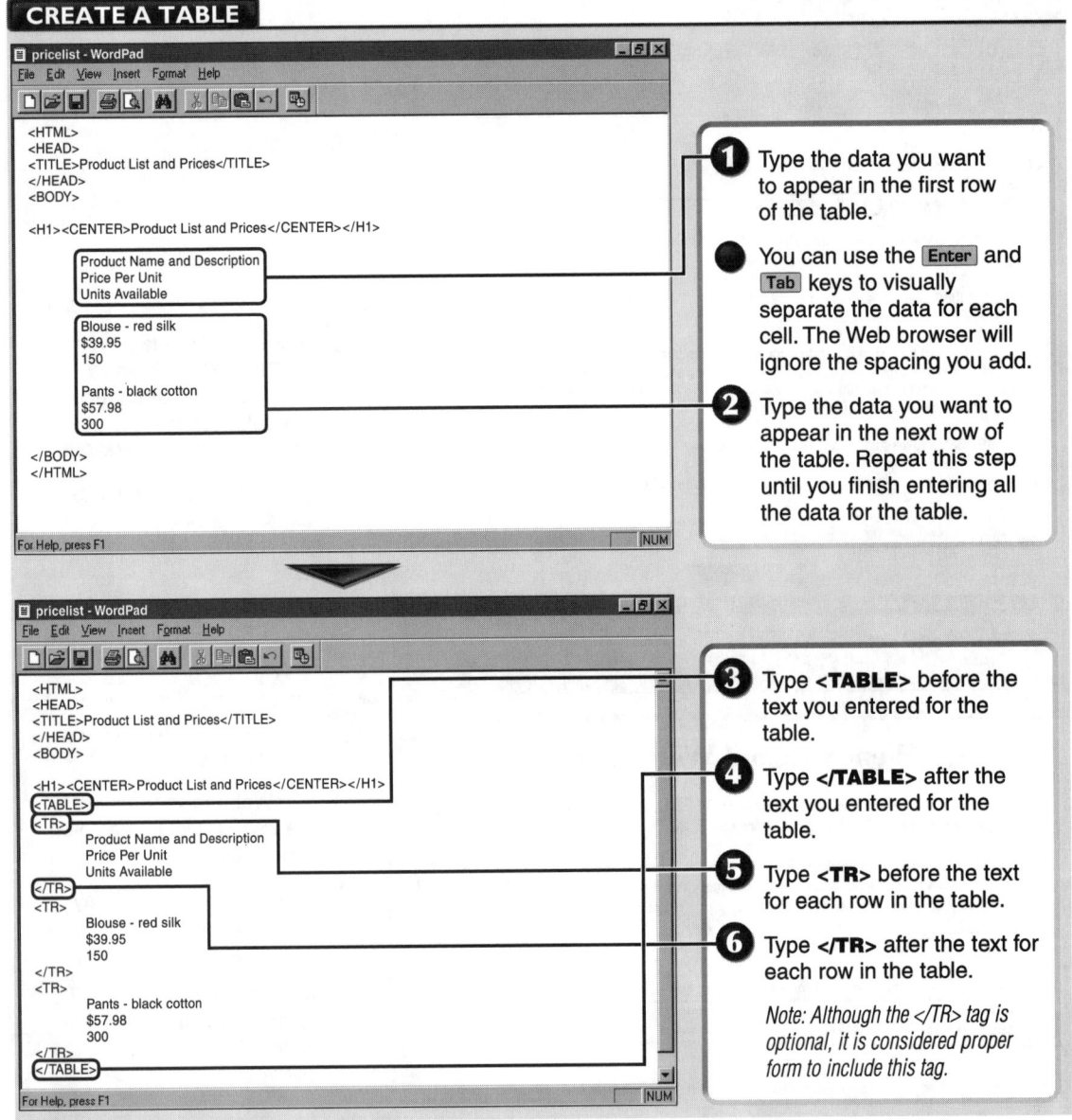

**1** Type the data you want to appear in the first row of the table.

● You can use the `Enter` and `Tab` keys to visually separate the data for each cell. The Web browser will ignore the spacing you add.

**2** Type the data you want to appear in the next row of the table. Repeat this step until you finish entering all the data for the table.

**3** Type **<TABLE>** before the text you entered for the table.

**4** Type **</TABLE>** after the text you entered for the table.

**5** Type **<TR>** before the text for each row in the table.

**6** Type **</TR>** after the text for each row in the table.

*Note: Although the </TR> tag is optional, it is considered proper form to include this tag.*

# in an *Instant*

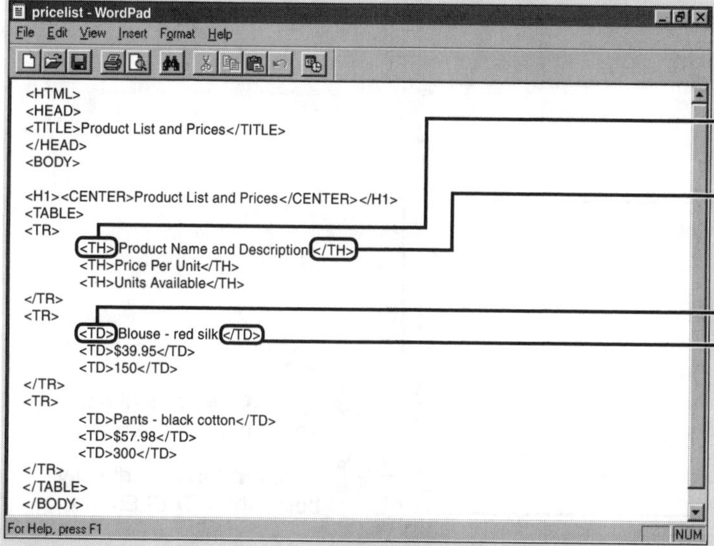

---

**pricelist - WordPad**

File  Edit  View  Insert  Format  Help

```
<HTML>
<HEAD>
<TITLE>Product List and Prices</TITLE>
</HEAD>
<BODY>

<H1><CENTER>Product List and Prices</CENTER></H1>
<TABLE>
<TR>
        <TH>Product Name and Description</TH>
        <TH>Price Per Unit</TH>
        <TH>Units Available</TH>
</TR>
<TR>
        <TD>Blouse - red silk</TD>
        <TD>$39.95</TD>
        <TD>150</TD>
</TR>
<TR>
        <TD>Pants - black cotton</TD>
        <TD>$57.98</TD>
        <TD>300</TD>
</TR>
</TABLE>
</BODY>
```

For Help, press F1                                           NUM

---

**7** Type **<TH>** in front of the text for each header cell.

**8** Type **</TH>** after the text for each header cell.

**9** Type **<TD>** in front of the text for each data cell.

**10** Type **</TD>** after the text for each data cell.

*Note: Although the </TH> and </TD> tags are optional, it is considered proper form to include these tags.*

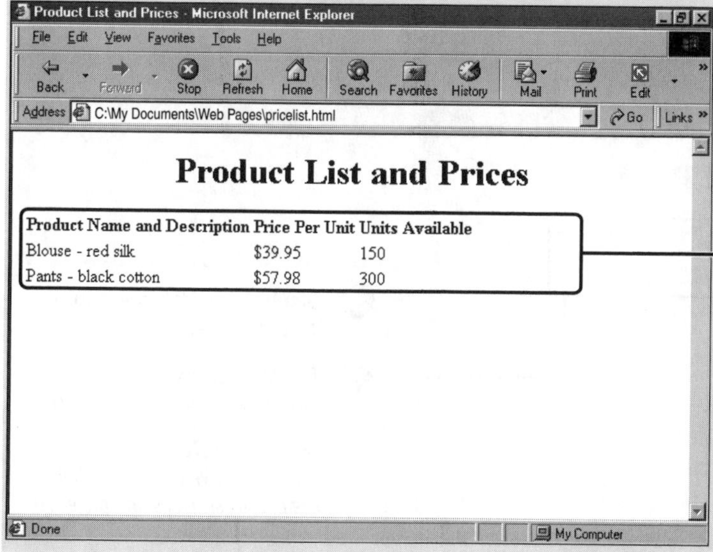

---

**Product List and Prices - Microsoft Internet Explorer**

File  Edit  View  Favorites  Tools  Help

Back  Forward  Stop  Refresh  Home  Search  Favorites  History  Mail  Print  Edit

Address  C:\My Documents\Web Pages\pricelist.html    Go   Links »

## Product List and Prices

| Product Name and Description | Price Per Unit | Units Available |
|---|---|---|
| Blouse - red silk | $39.95 | 150 |
| Pants - black cotton | $57.98 | 300 |

Done                                              My Computer

---

**11** Display the Web page in a Web browser.

● The Web browser displays the table.

● You can use tables to present information in newspaper-style columns. Create a table with one row that contains three cells.

● You can also use tables to place a three-dimensional border around text or an image. Place the text or image in a table with one row that contains one cell.

# CENTER A TABLE

You can center a table horizontally on your Web page to improve the overall appearance of the Web page. Centering a small table can also make the table stand out from the other elements on a Web page. By default, tables appear left aligned in a Web browser.

## CENTER A TABLE

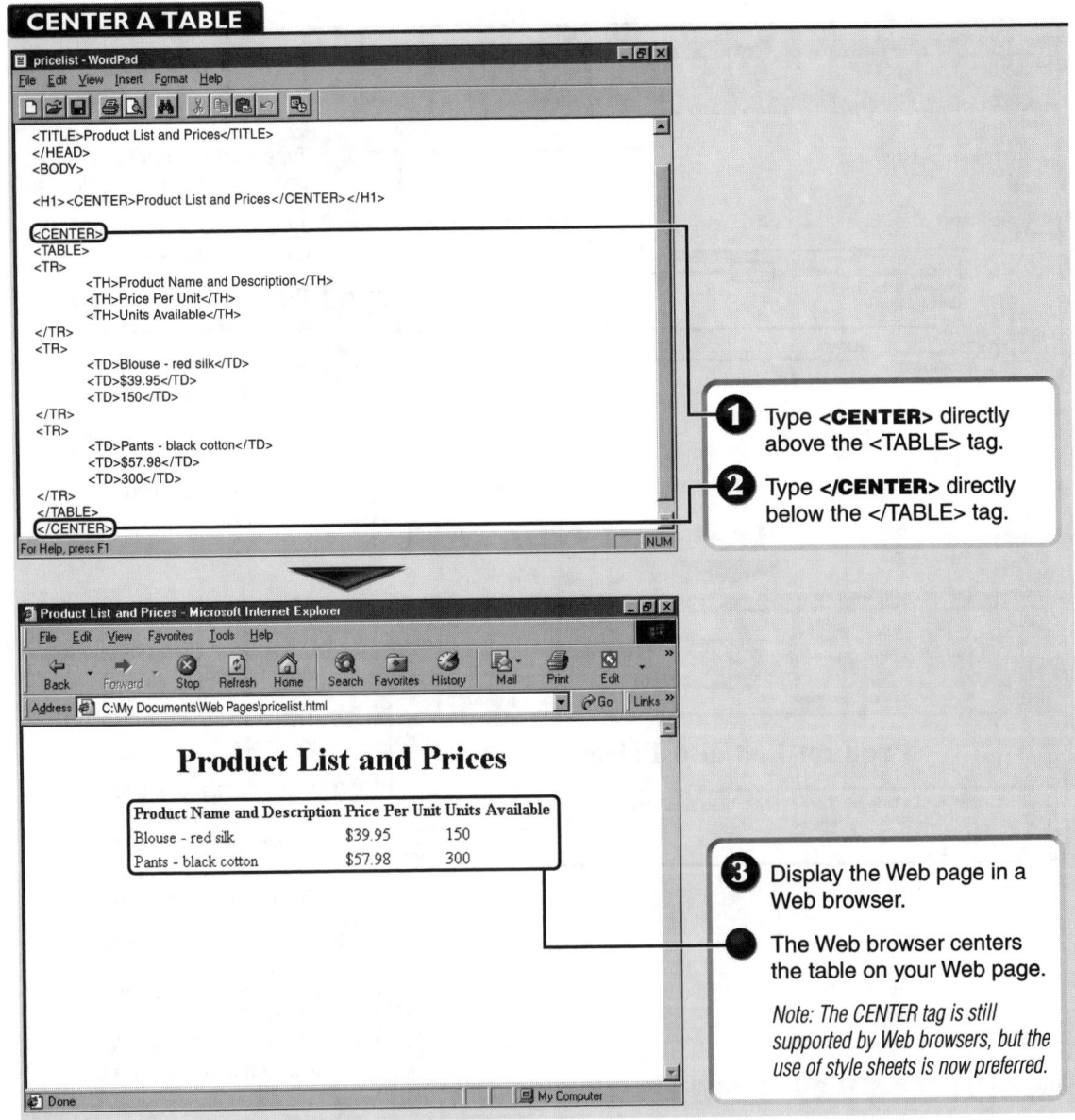

① Type **<CENTER>** directly above the <TABLE> tag.

② Type **</CENTER>** directly below the </TABLE> tag.

③ Display the Web page in a Web browser.

● The Web browser centers the table on your Web page.

*Note: The CENTER tag is still supported by Web browsers, but the use of style sheets is now preferred.*

You can add a border to a table to separate each cell in the table and make the data easier to read. If you are using a table to organize the layout of your Web page, you may want to temporarily add a border to help you see where to place text, images and other elements.

## ADD A BORDER

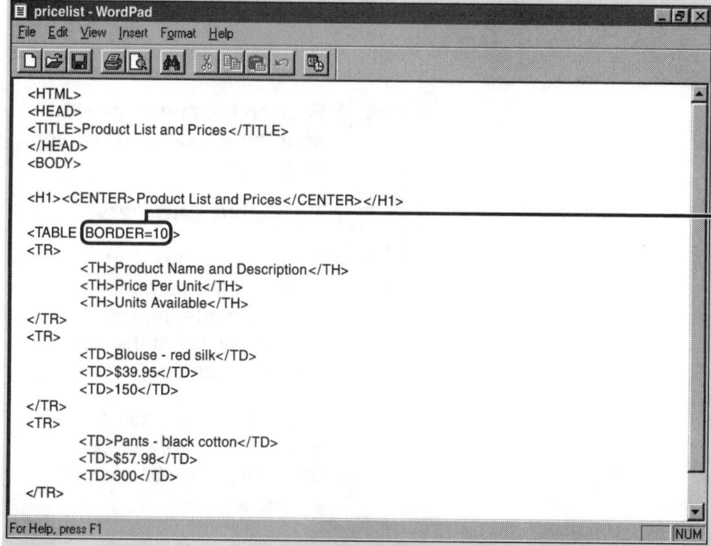

```
pricelist - WordPad

File  Edit  View  Insert  Format  Help

<HTML>
<HEAD>
<TITLE>Product List and Prices</TITLE>
</HEAD>
<BODY>

<H1><CENTER>Product List and Prices</CENTER></H1>

<TABLE BORDER=10>
<TR>
        <TH>Product Name and Description</TH>
        <TH>Price Per Unit</TH>
        <TH>Units Available</TH>
</TR>
<TR>
        <TD>Blouse - red silk</TD>
        <TD>$39.95</TD>
        <TD>150</TD>
</TR>
<TR>
        <TD>Pants - black cotton</TD>
        <TD>$57.98</TD>
        <TD>300</TD>
</TR>

For Help, press F1                                          NUM
```

**1** In the <TABLE> tag for the table you want to display a border, type **BORDER=?** replacing **?** with the thickness you want to use for the border in pixels.

*Note: The thickness you specify will affect only the border around the outside of the table. To change the thickness of the border between cells in the table, see page 121.*

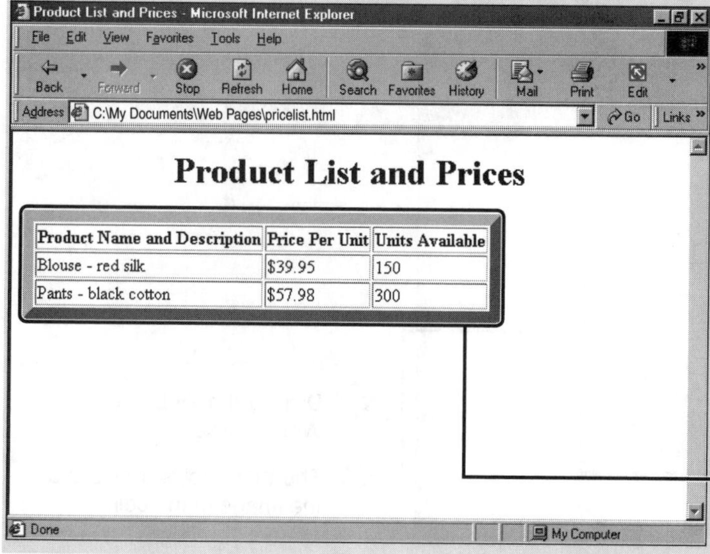

```
Product List and Prices - Microsoft Internet Explorer

File  Edit  View  Favorites  Tools  Help

Back  Forward  Stop  Refresh  Home  Search  Favorites  History  Mail  Print  Edit

Address  C:\My Documents\Web Pages\pricelist.html                    Go   Links
```

# Product List and Prices

| Product Name and Description | Price Per Unit | Units Available |
|---|---|---|
| Blouse - red silk | $39.95 | 150 |
| Pants - black cotton | $57.98 | 300 |

Done                                                My Computer

**2** Display the Web page in a Web browser.

■ The Web browser displays the table with a border.

109

# ADD AN IMAGE

Adding an image to a cell in a table can help you control the placement of the image on your Web page. This is useful when you want to use a table to organize and display a collection of images.

## ADD AN IMAGE

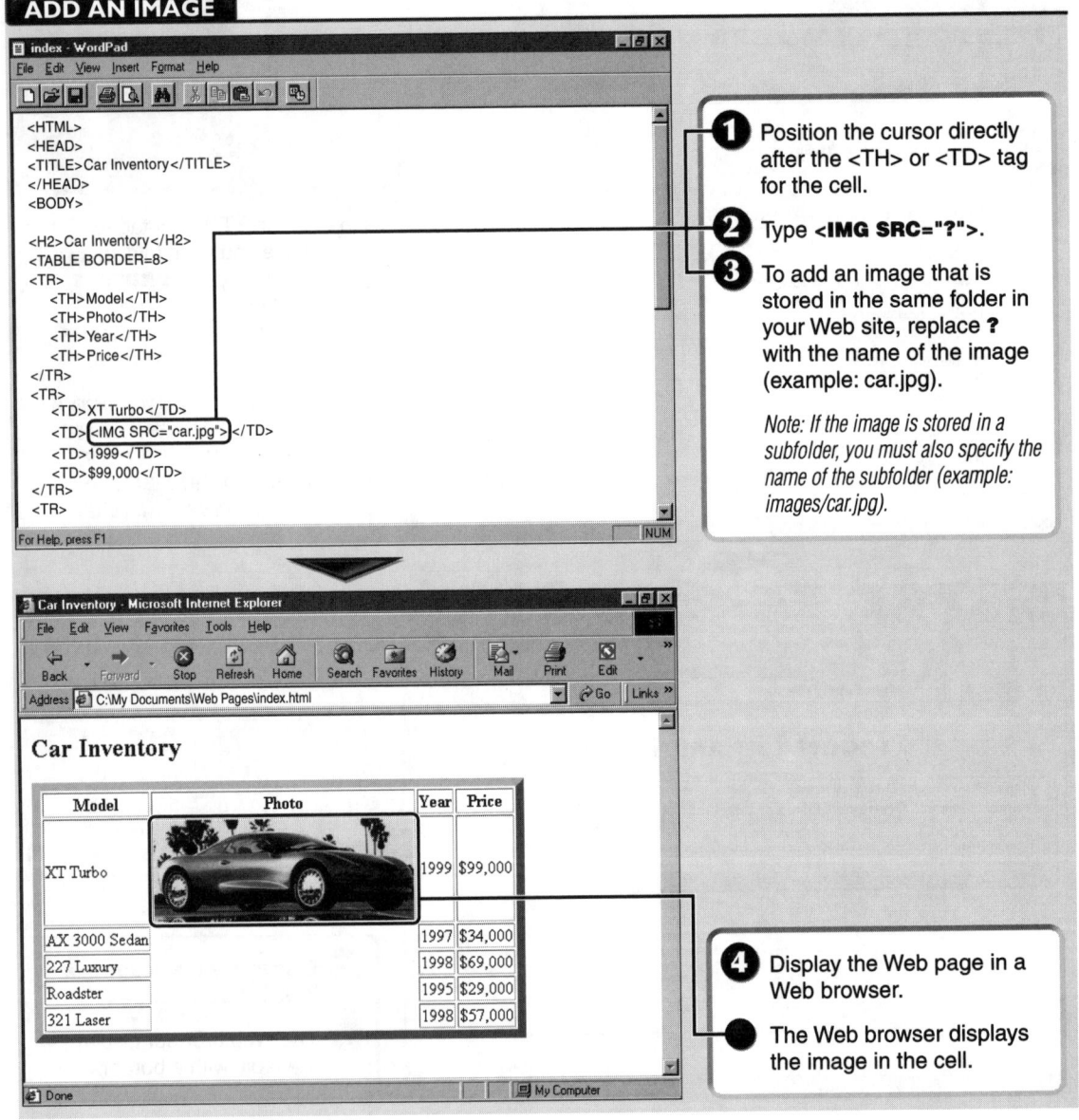

1. Position the cursor directly after the <TH> or <TD> tag for the cell.

2. Type **<IMG SRC="?">**.

3. To add an image that is stored in the same folder in your Web site, replace **?** with the name of the image (example: car.jpg).

   *Note: If the image is stored in a subfolder, you must also specify the name of the subfolder (example: images/car.jpg).*

4. Display the Web page in a Web browser.

● The Web browser displays the image in the cell.

You can add a caption to summarize the information in a table on your Web page. This is useful for displaying a title for a table. Although some Web browsers support the use of multiple captions, adding more than one caption to a table is not recommended.

## ADD A CAPTION

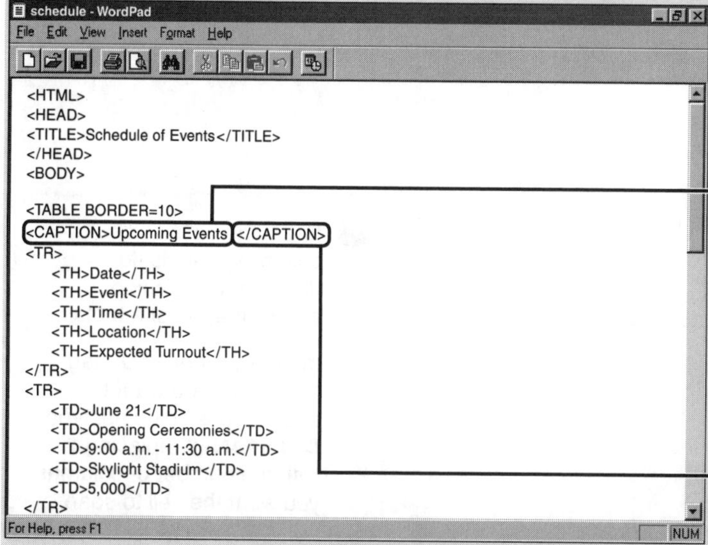

```
<HTML>
<HEAD>
<TITLE>Schedule of Events</TITLE>
</HEAD>
<BODY>

<TABLE BORDER=10>
<CAPTION>Upcoming Events </CAPTION>
<TR>
    <TH>Date</TH>
    <TH>Event</TH>
    <TH>Time</TH>
    <TH>Location</TH>
    <TH>Expected Turnout</TH>
</TR>
<TR>
    <TD>June 21</TD>
    <TD>Opening Ceremonies</TD>
    <TD>9:00 a.m. - 11:30 a.m.</TD>
    <TD>Skylight Stadium</TD>
    <TD>5,000</TD>
</TR>
```

*schedule - WordPad*
File Edit View Insert Format Help

**1** Type **<CAPTION>** directly below the <TABLE> tag for the table you want to display a caption.

**2** Type the caption you want the table to display.

**3** Type **</CAPTION>** after the caption.

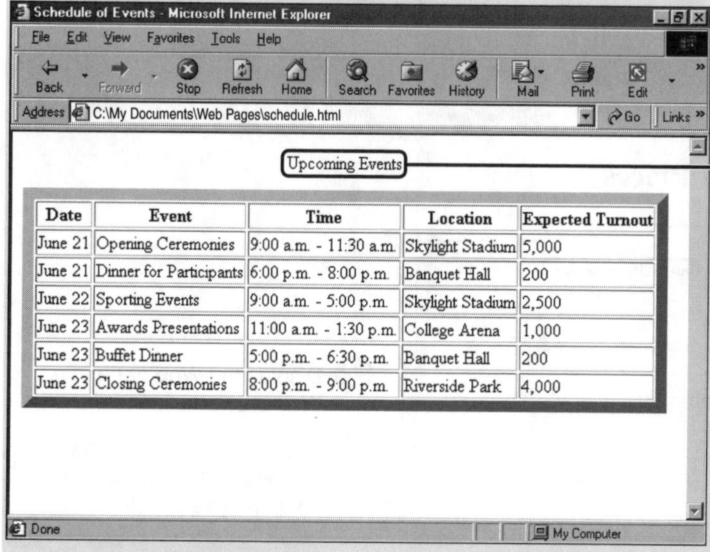

---

*Schedule of Events - Microsoft Internet Explorer*
File Edit View Favorites Tools Help

Address C:\My Documents\Web Pages\schedule.html

Upcoming Events

| Date | Event | Time | Location | Expected Turnout |
|------|-------|------|----------|------------------|
| June 21 | Opening Ceremonies | 9:00 a.m. - 11:30 a.m. | Skylight Stadium | 5,000 |
| June 21 | Dinner for Participants | 6:00 p.m. - 8:00 p.m. | Banquet Hall | 200 |
| June 22 | Sporting Events | 9:00 a.m. - 5:00 p.m. | Skylight Stadium | 2,500 |
| June 23 | Awards Presentations | 11:00 a.m. - 1:30 p.m. | College Arena | 1,000 |
| June 23 | Buffet Dinner | 5:00 p.m. - 6:30 p.m. | Banquet Hall | 200 |
| June 23 | Closing Ceremonies | 8:00 p.m. - 9:00 p.m. | Riverside Park | 4,000 |

**4** Display the Web page in a Web browser.

● The Web browser displays the caption centered above the table.

**111**

# SPAN CELLS

You can combine two or more cells in a row or column into one large cell. To prevent problems when spanning cells, you should sketch your table on a piece of paper before you begin so you can clearly see the layout of your table.

## SPAN CELLS ACROSS COLUMNS

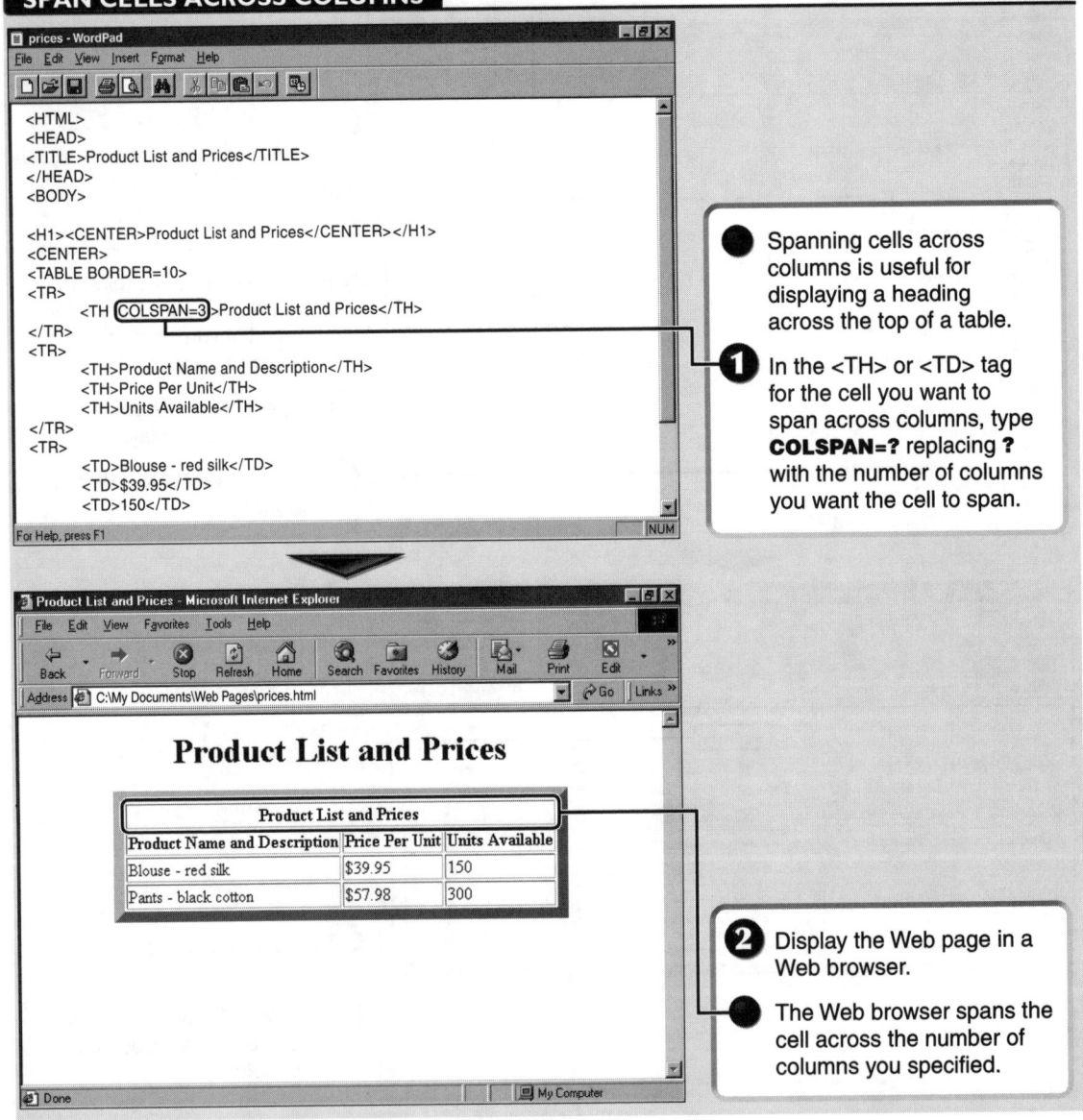

● Spanning cells across columns is useful for displaying a heading across the top of a table.

**1** In the <TH> or <TD> tag for the cell you want to span across columns, type **COLSPAN=?** replacing **?** with the number of columns you want the cell to span.

**2** Display the Web page in a Web browser.

● The Web browser spans the cell across the number of columns you specified.

# in an instant

## SPAN CELLS DOWN ROWS

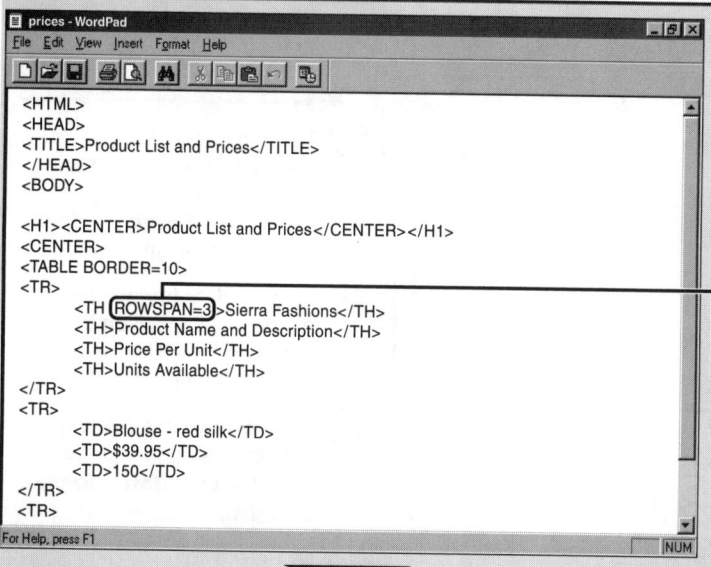

```
prices - WordPad
File  Edit  View  Insert  Format  Help

<HTML>
<HEAD>
<TITLE>Product List and Prices</TITLE>
</HEAD>
<BODY>

<H1><CENTER>Product List and Prices</CENTER></H1>
<CENTER>
<TABLE BORDER=10>
<TR>
        <TH ROWSPAN=3>Sierra Fashions</TH>
        <TH>Product Name and Description</TH>
        <TH>Price Per Unit</TH>
        <TH>Units Available</TH>
</TR>
<TR>
        <TD>Blouse - red silk</TD>
        <TD>$39.95</TD>
        <TD>150</TD>
</TR>
<TR>

For Help, press F1                                              NUM
```

- Spanning cells down rows is useful for displaying a title down the side of table.

**1** In the <TH> or <TD> tag for the cell you want to span down rows, type **ROWSPAN=?** replacing **?** with the number of rows you want the cell to span.

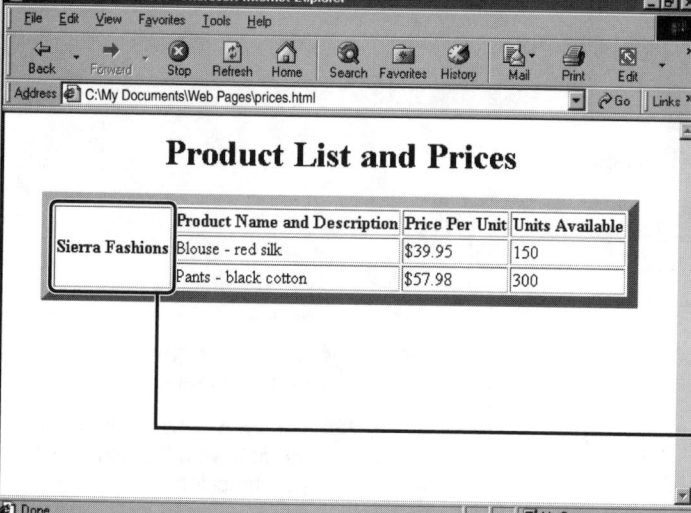

```
Product List and Prices - Microsoft Internet Explorer
File  Edit  View  Favorites  Tools  Help
Back  Forward  Stop  Refresh  Home  Search  Favorites  History  Mail  Print  Edit
Address  C:\My Documents\Web Pages\prices.html                    Go   Links »
```

## Product List and Prices

| | Product Name and Description | Price Per Unit | Units Available |
|---|---|---|---|
| Sierra Fashions | Blouse - red silk | $39.95 | 150 |
| | Pants - black cotton | $57.98 | 300 |

`Done`                                          `My Computer`

**2** Display the Web page in a Web browser.

- The Web browser spans the cell down the number of rows you specified.

# ALIGN DATA HORIZONTALLY

You can change the horizontal alignment of a row of data or of a single cell in a table on your Web page. By default, data in header cells is centered and data in data cells is left aligned.

ALIGN DATA HORIZONTALLY

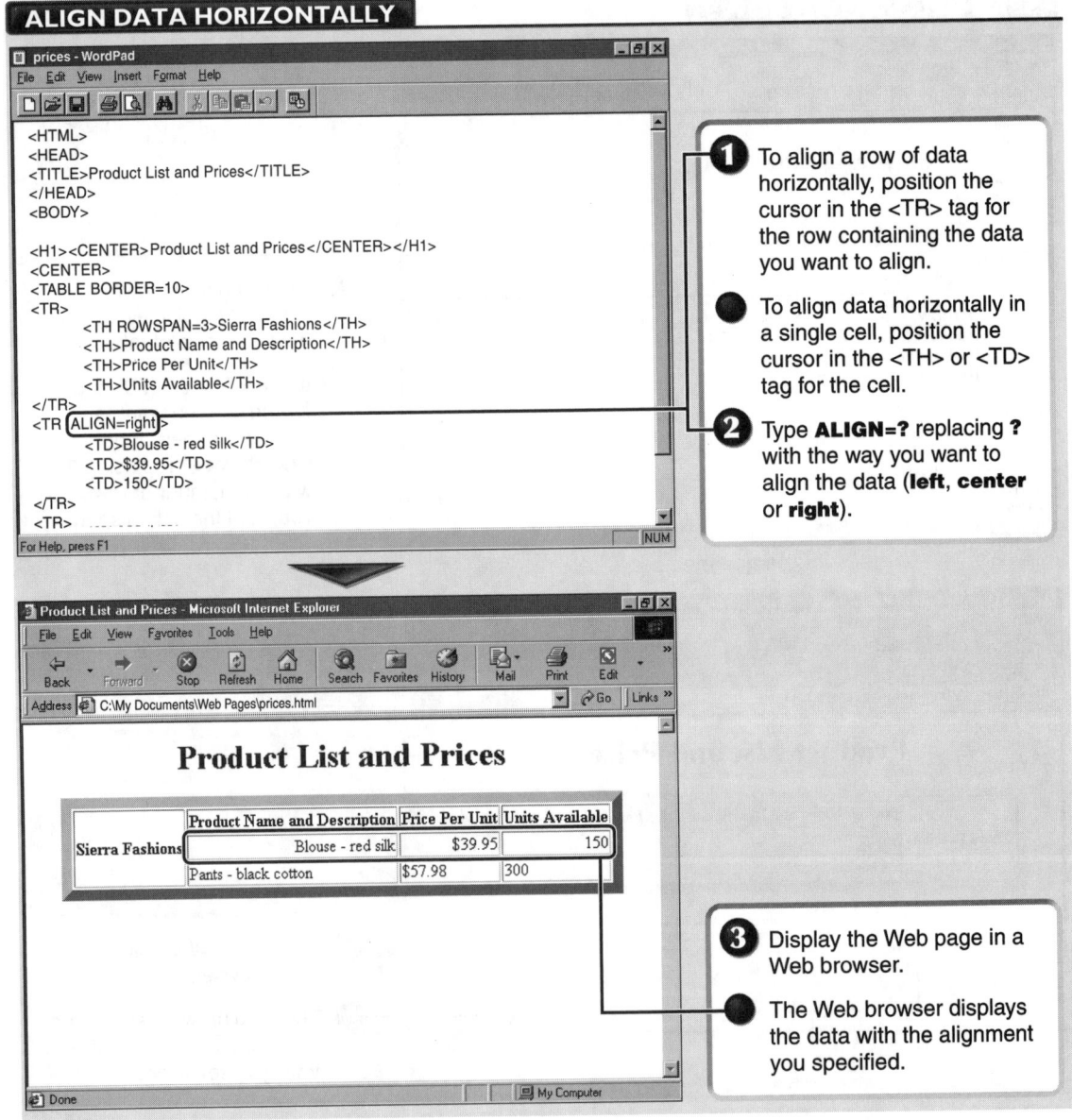

**1** To align a row of data horizontally, position the cursor in the <TR> tag for the row containing the data you want to align.

● To align data horizontally in a single cell, position the cursor in the <TH> or <TD> tag for the cell.

**2** Type **ALIGN=?** replacing **?** with the way you want to align the data (**left**, **center** or **right**).

**3** Display the Web page in a Web browser.

● The Web browser displays the data with the alignment you specified.

# ALIGN DATA VERTICALLY

You can change the vertical alignment of an entire row of data or of a single cell in a table on your Web page. You can choose to align the data with the top, middle or bottom of the cell. By default, data is vertically aligned in the middle of each cell in a table.

## ALIGN DATA VERTICALLY

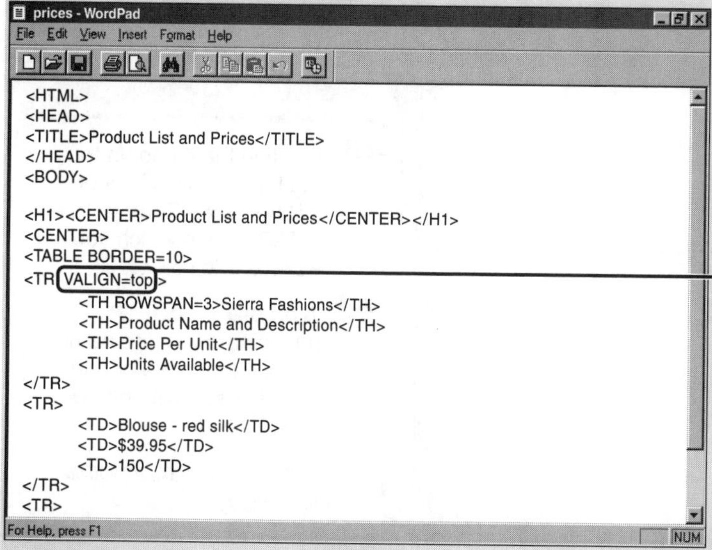

```
prices - WordPad
File  Edit  View  Insert  Format  Help

<HTML>
<HEAD>
<TITLE>Product List and Prices</TITLE>
</HEAD>
<BODY>

<H1><CENTER>Product List and Prices</CENTER></H1>
<CENTER>
<TABLE BORDER=10>
<TR VALIGN=top>
        <TH ROWSPAN=3>Sierra Fashions</TH>
        <TH>Product Name and Description</TH>
        <TH>Price Per Unit</TH>
        <TH>Units Available</TH>
</TR>
<TR>
        <TD>Blouse - red silk</TD>
        <TD>$39.95</TD>
        <TD>150</TD>
</TR>
<TR>

For Help, press F1                                          NUM
```

**1** To align a row of data vertically, position the cursor in the <TR> tag for the row containing the data you want to align.

● To align data vertically in a single cell, position the cursor in the <TH> or <TD> tag for the cell.

**2** Type **VALIGN=?** replacing **?** with the way you want to align the data (**top**, **middle** or **bottom**).

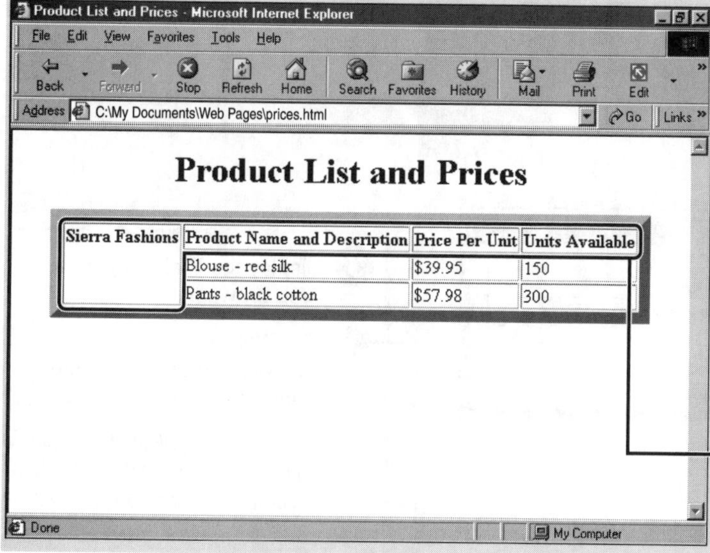

```
Product List and Prices - Microsoft Internet Explorer
File  Edit  View  Favorites  Tools  Help

Back   Forward   Stop   Refresh   Home   Search  Favorites  History   Mail   Print   Edit

Address  C:\My Documents\Web Pages\prices.html                    Go   Links
```

## Product List and Prices

| Sierra Fashions | Product Name and Description | Price Per Unit | Units Available |
|---|---|---|---|
| | Blouse - red silk | $39.95 | 150 |
| | Pants - black cotton | $57.98 | 300 |

```
Done                                        My Computer
```

**3** Display the Web page in a Web browser.

● The Web browser displays the data with the alignment you specified.

Adding color to a table helps emphasize important information. You can add color to a cell, a row or an entire table. If the color you choose affects the readability of your table, you may need to change the color of text to make the table easier to read.

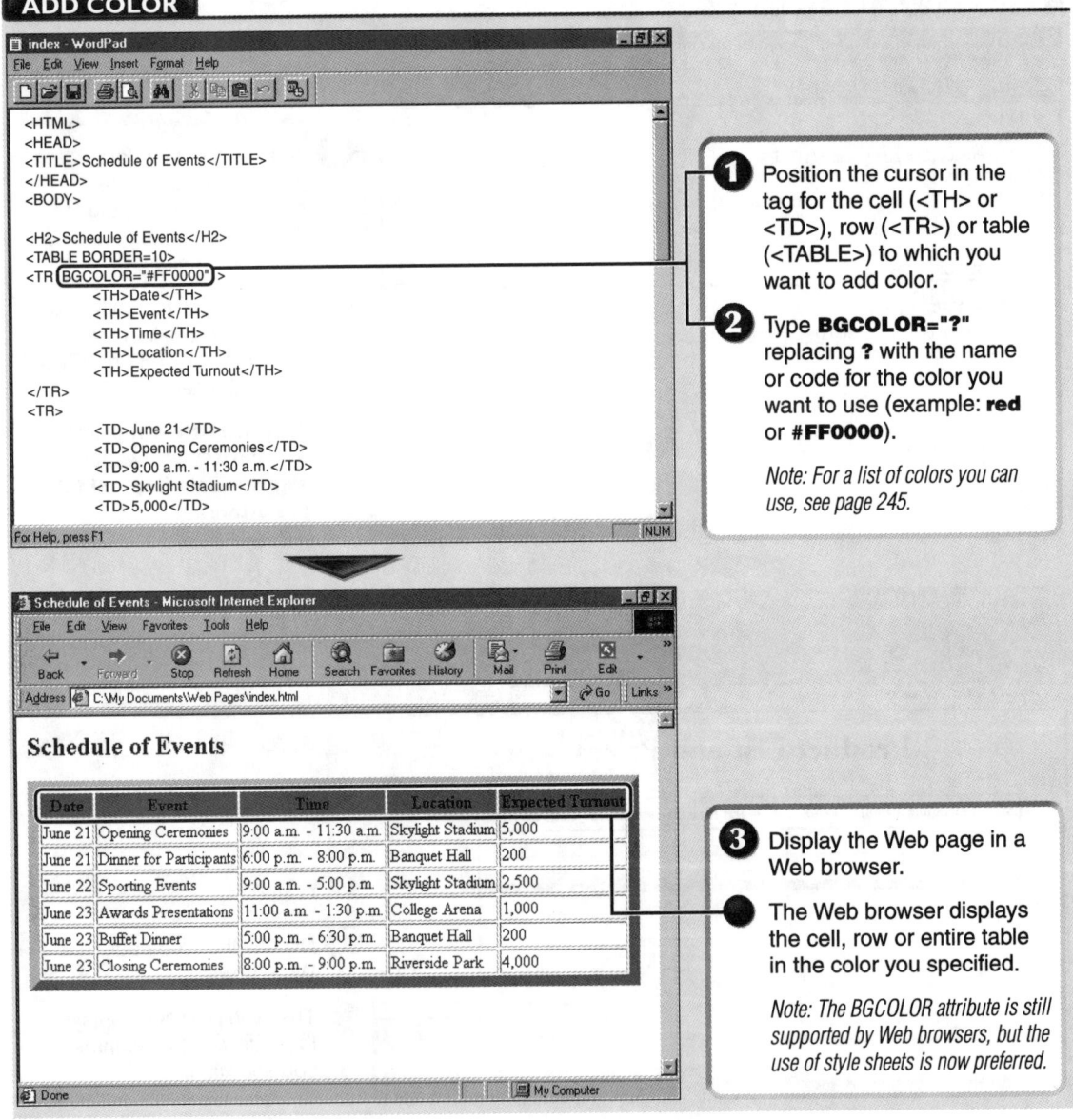

**1** Position the cursor in the tag for the cell (<TH> or <TD>), row (<TR>) or table (<TABLE>) to which you want to add color.

**2** Type **BGCOLOR="?"** replacing **?** with the name or code for the color you want to use (example: **red** or **#FF0000**).

*Note: For a list of colors you can use, see page 245.*

**3** Display the Web page in a Web browser.

■ The Web browser displays the cell, row or entire table in the color you specified.

*Note: The BGCOLOR attribute is still supported by Web browsers, but the use of style sheets is now preferred.*

You can add a background image to a table to enhance the appearance of the entire table. You can also add a background image to a single cell to emphasize the information in the cell. Some interesting background images are available at the www.pixelfoundry.com/bgs.html and www.grsites.com/textures Web sites.

## ADD A BACKGROUND IMAGE

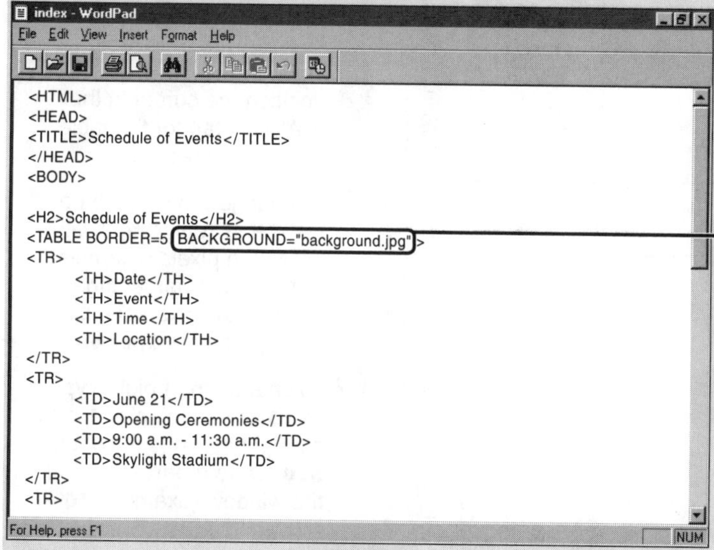

```
index - WordPad
File Edit View Insert Format Help

<HTML>
<HEAD>
<TITLE>Schedule of Events</TITLE>
</HEAD>
<BODY>

<H2>Schedule of Events</H2>
<TABLE BORDER=5 BACKGROUND="background.jpg">
<TR>
      <TH>Date</TH>
      <TH>Event</TH>
      <TH>Time</TH>
      <TH>Location</TH>
</TR>
<TR>
      <TD>June 21</TD>
      <TD>Opening Ceremonies</TD>
      <TD>9:00 a.m. - 11:30 a.m.</TD>
      <TD>Skylight Stadium</TD>
</TR>
<TR>
```
For Help, press F1                                    NUM

**1** Position the cursor in the tag for the cell (<TH> or <TD>) or table (<TABLE>) you want to display a background image.

**2** Type **BACKGROUND="?"**.

**3** If the background image is stored in the same folder in the Web site, replace **?** with the name of the image.

*Note: If the image is stored in a subfolder, you must also specify the name of the subfolder.*

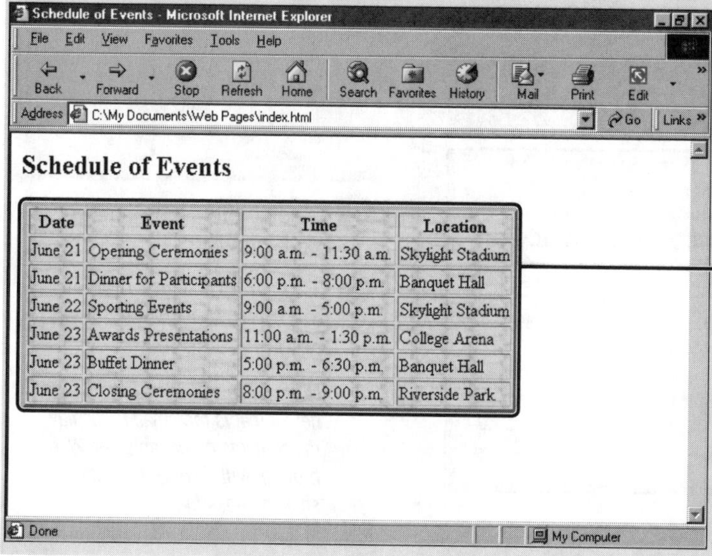

---

Schedule of Events - Microsoft Internet Explorer
File Edit View Favorites Tools Help

Back  Forward  Stop  Refresh  Home  Search  Favorites  History  Mail  Print  Edit

Address  C:\My Documents\Web Pages\index.html          Go  Links »

### Schedule of Events

| Date | Event | Time | Location |
|------|-------|------|----------|
| June 21 | Opening Ceremonies | 9:00 a.m. - 11:30 a.m. | Skylight Stadium |
| June 21 | Dinner for Participants | 6:00 p.m. - 8:00 p.m. | Banquet Hall |
| June 22 | Sporting Events | 9:00 a.m. - 5:00 p.m. | Skylight Stadium |
| June 23 | Awards Presentations | 11:00 a.m. - 1:30 p.m. | College Arena |
| June 23 | Buffet Dinner | 5:00 p.m. - 6:30 p.m. | Banquet Hall |
| June 23 | Closing Ceremonies | 8:00 p.m. - 9:00 p.m. | Riverside Park |

Done                                    My Computer

**4** Display the Web page in a Web browser.

■ The Web browser displays the table with the background image you specified.

■ Internet Explorer repeats the image to fill the entire table. Netscape Navigator repeats the image in each cell.

# CHANGE THE SIZE OF A TABLE

You can change the size of a table on your Web page. You can specify a width or height for the table in pixels or as a percentage of the Web browser window. When specifying a width in pixels, use a width of 600 pixels or less to ensure the entire table will fit on a user's screen.

CHANGE THE SIZE OF A TABLE

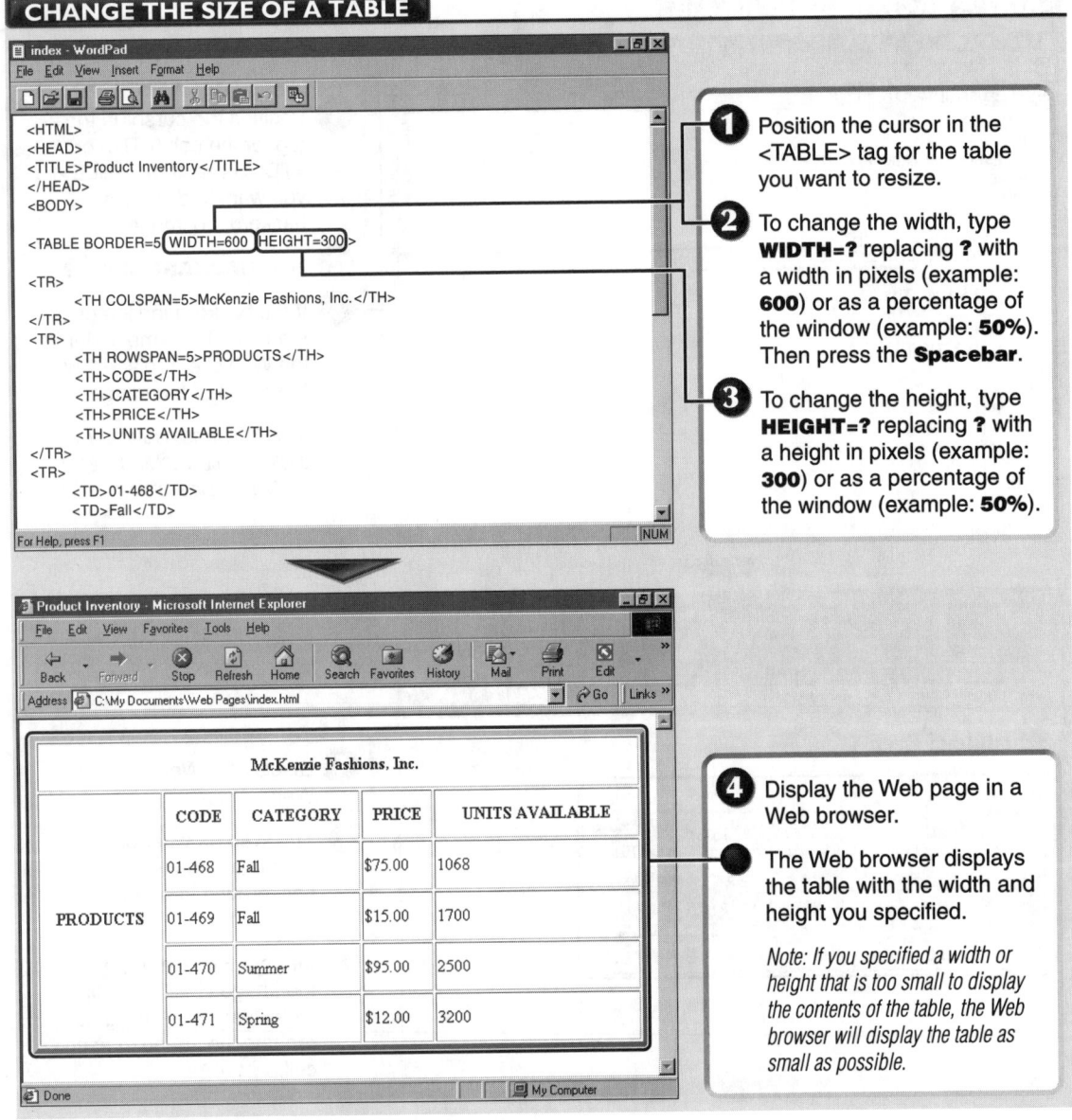

**1** Position the cursor in the <TABLE> tag for the table you want to resize.

**2** To change the width, type **WIDTH=?** replacing **?** with a width in pixels (example: **600**) or as a percentage of the window (example: **50%**). Then press the **Spacebar**.

**3** To change the height, type **HEIGHT=?** replacing **?** with a height in pixels (example: **300**) or as a percentage of the window (example: **50%**).

**4** Display the Web page in a Web browser.

■ The Web browser displays the table with the width and height you specified.

*Note: If you specified a width or height that is too small to display the contents of the table, the Web browser will display the table as small as possible.*

You can change the size of a cell to improve the layout of a table. When you change the width of a cell, all the cells in the same column will display the new width. Changing the height of a cell also changes the height of all the cells in the same row.

## CHANGE THE SIZE OF A CELL

```
index - WordPad                                              _ 8 X
File   Edit   View   Insert   Format   Help

<HTML>
<HEAD>
<TITLE>Recipes</TITLE>
</HEAD>
<BODY>

<H2>Recipes</H2>
<TABLE BORDER=5>
<TR>
          <TH WIDTH=200 HEIGHT=100>Recipe</TH>
          <TH>Food Group</TH>
          <TH>Preparation Time</TH>
          <TH>Notes</TH>
</TR>
<TR>
          <TD>Vegetarian Lasagna</TD>
          <TD>Pasta</TD>
          <TD>45 Min.</TD>
          <TD>Good vegetarian dish</TD>
</TR>
<TR>
For Help, press F1                                           NUM
```

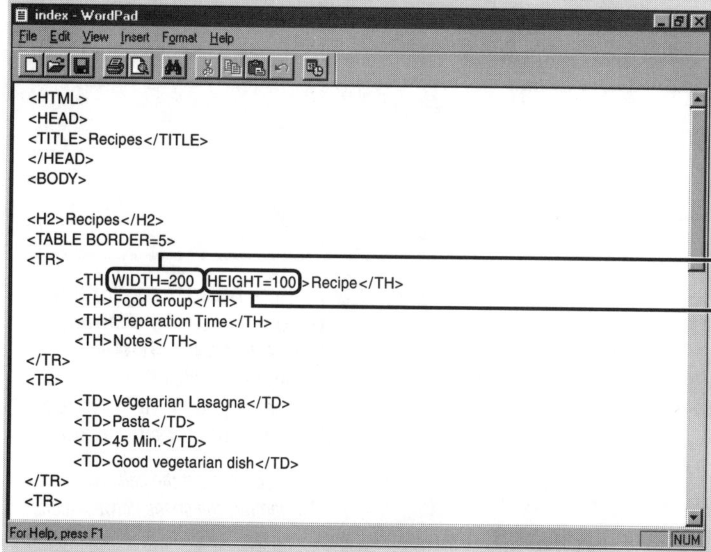

① Position the cursor in the <TH> or <TD> tag for the cell you want to resize.

② To change the width, type **WIDTH=?** replacing **?** with a width in pixels (example: **200**) or as a percentage of the table (example: **50%**). Then press the **Spacebar**.

③ To change the height, type **HEIGHT=?** replacing **?** with a height in pixels (example: **100**).

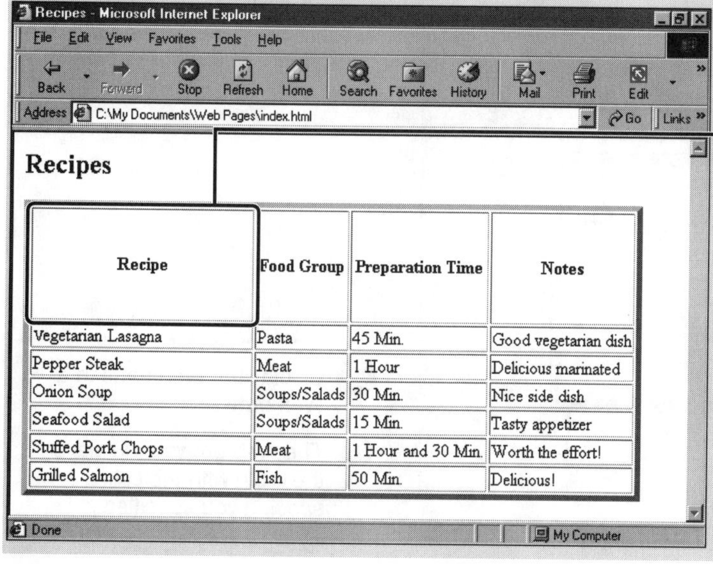

```
Recipes - Microsoft Internet Explorer                        _ 8 X
File   Edit   View   Favorites   Tools   Help

 ⇦        ⇨        ⊗       ↻      ⌂       ◉       ▣      ◈      ▣▾     ▤     ▣      ▾
Back    Forward    Stop   Refresh  Home   Search  Favorites History  Mail   Print    Edit
Address  C:\My Documents\Web Pages\index.html                    ⮕ Go   Links »
```

## Recipes

| Recipe | Food Group | Preparation Time | Notes |
|---|---|---|---|
|  |  |  |  |
| Vegetarian Lasagna | Pasta | 45 Min. | Good vegetarian dish |
| Pepper Steak | Meat | 1 Hour | Delicious marinated |
| Onion Soup | Soups/Salads | 30 Min. | Nice side dish |
| Seafood Salad | Soups/Salads | 15 Min. | Tasty appetizer |
| Stuffed Pork Chops | Meat | 1 Hour and 30 Min. | Worth the effort! |
| Grilled Salmon | Fish | 50 Min. | Delicious! |

④ Display the Web page in a Web browser.

● The Web browser displays the cell with the size you specified.

● If you specified a width or height that is too small to display the contents of the cell, the Web browser will display the cell as small as possible.

*Note: The WIDTH and HEIGHT attributes are still supported by Web browsers, but the use of style sheets is now preferred.*

# CHANGE CELL SPACING

You can change the amount of space between each cell in a table. Changing the cell spacing will change the size of the border between cells. This can improve the layout and readability of your table. The default cell spacing is 2 pixels.

## CHANGE CELL SPACING

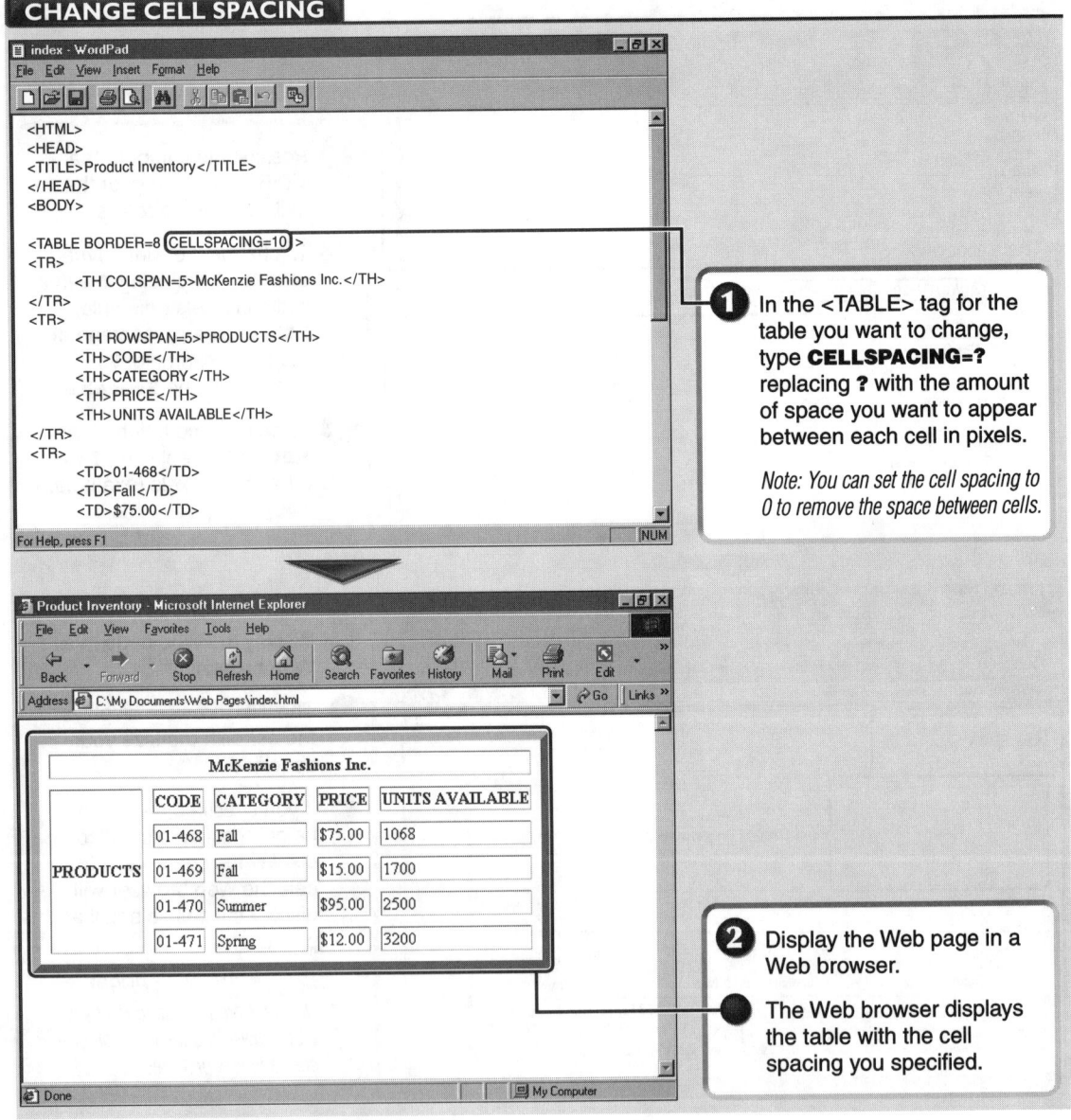

**1** In the <TABLE> tag for the table you want to change, type **CELLSPACING=?** replacing **?** with the amount of space you want to appear between each cell in pixels.

*Note: You can set the cell spacing to 0 to remove the space between cells.*

**2** Display the Web page in a Web browser.

■ The Web browser displays the table with the cell spacing you specified.

You can change the cell padding to increase or decrease the amount of space around the contents of each cell in a table. Increasing the cell padding can make a table appear less cluttered. The default cell padding is 1 pixel.

## CHANGE CELL PADDING

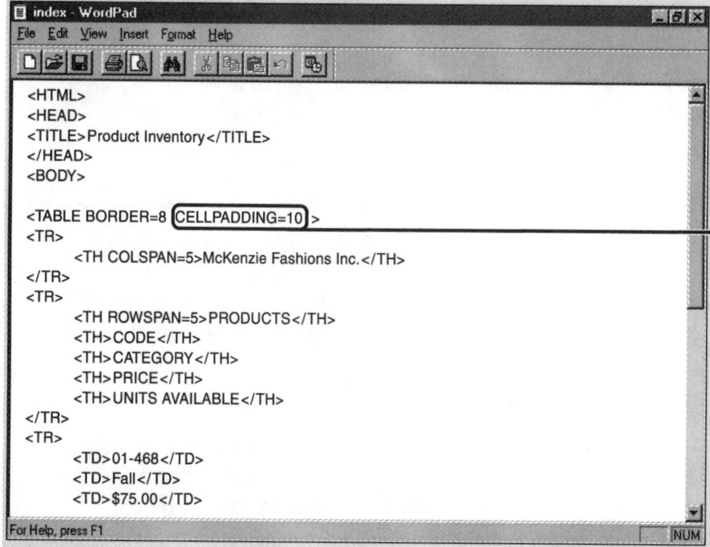

```
index - WordPad
File  Edit  View  Insert  Format  Help

<HTML>
<HEAD>
<TITLE>Product Inventory</TITLE>
</HEAD>
<BODY>

<TABLE BORDER=8 CELLPADDING=10 >
<TR>
        <TH COLSPAN=5>McKenzie Fashions Inc.</TH>
</TR>
<TR>
        <TH ROWSPAN=5>PRODUCTS</TH>
        <TH>CODE</TH>
        <TH>CATEGORY</TH>
        <TH>PRICE</TH>
        <TH>UNITS AVAILABLE</TH>
</TR>
<TR>
        <TD>01-468</TD>
        <TD>Fall</TD>
        <TD>$75.00</TD>
```
For Help, press F1                                          NUM

**1** In the <TABLE> tag for the table you want to change, type **CELLPADDING=?** replacing **?** with the amount of space you want to appear around the contents of each cell in pixels.

*Note: You can set the cell padding to 0 to remove the space around the contents of each cell.*

```
Product Inventory - Microsoft Internet Explorer
File  Edit  View  Favorites  Tools  Help

Back  Forward  Stop  Refresh  Home  Search  Favorites  History  Mail  Print  Edit

Address  C:\My Documents\Web Pages\index.html                    Go  Links
```

| McKenzie Fashions Inc. | | | | |
|---|---|---|---|---|
| | CODE | CATEGORY | PRICE | UNITS AVAILABLE |
| | 01-468 | Fall | $75.00 | 1068 |
| PRODUCTS | 01-469 | Fall | $15.00 | 1700 |
| | 01-470 | Summer | $95.00 | 2500 |
| | 01-471 | Spring | $12.00 | 3200 |

Done                                          My Computer

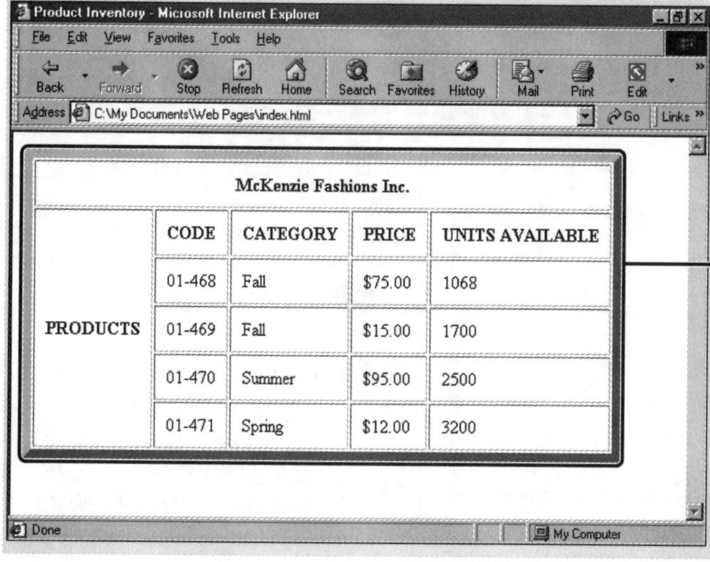

**2** Display the Web page in a Web browser.

The Web browser displays the table with the cell padding you specified.

*Note: Changing the cell padding may affect the alignment of data in a table. The data may not appear the way you expect. To change the alignment of data in a table, see pages 114 and 115.*

# CONTROL LINE BREAKS IN A CELL

You can keep all the text in a cell on one line. This is useful when you want a small amount of text, such as a product name or date, to appear on one line. Controlling line breaks in a cell that contains a large amount of text may cause your table to extend past the edge of a Web browser window.

## CONTROL LINE BREAKS IN A CELL

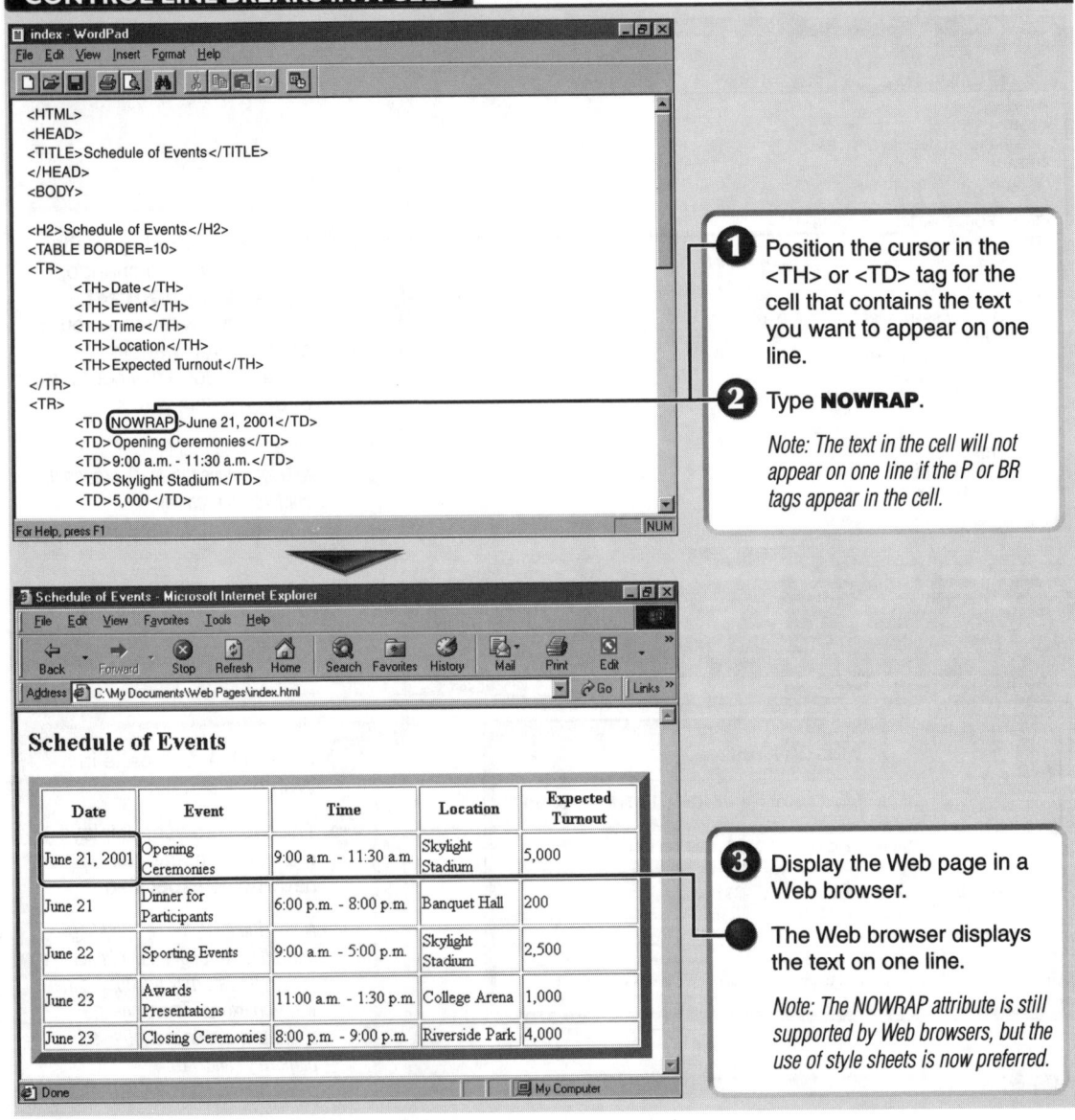

① Position the cursor in the &lt;TH&gt; or &lt;TD&gt; tag for the cell that contains the text you want to appear on one line.

② Type **NOWRAP**.

*Note: The text in the cell will not appear on one line if the P or BR tags appear in the cell.*

③ Display the Web page in a Web browser.

● The Web browser displays the text on one line.

*Note: The NOWRAP attribute is still supported by Web browsers, but the use of style sheets is now preferred.*

# CREATE NESTED TABLES

You can nest a table within another table to create a more complex table layout. To nest a table, you create a new table in an empty cell of the main table. When creating a nested table, make sure you include all the end tags (</TH>, </TD>, </TR> and </TABLE>) for both the main table and the nested table.

## CREATE NESTED TABLES

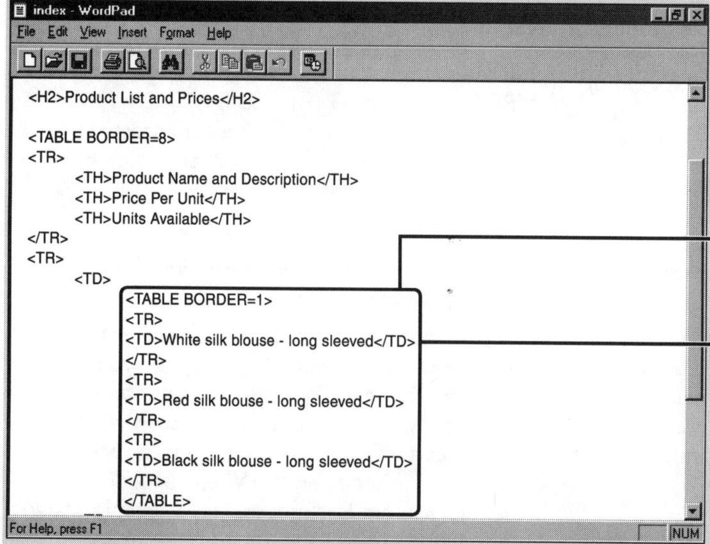

```
index - WordPad
File  Edit  View  Insert  Format  Help

<H2>Product List and Prices</H2>

<TABLE BORDER=8>
<TR>
        <TH>Product Name and Description</TH>
        <TH>Price Per Unit</TH>
        <TH>Units Available</TH>
</TR>
<TR>
        <TD>
                <TABLE BORDER=1>
                <TR>
                <TD>White silk blouse - long sleeved</TD>
                </TR>
                <TR>
                <TD>Red silk blouse - long sleeved</TD>
                </TR>
                <TR>
                <TD>Black silk blouse - long sleeved</TD>
                </TR>
                </TABLE>

For Help, press F1                                    NUM
```

**1** Create the table you want to contain a nested table, leaving an empty cell for the nested table.

**2** Position the cursor in the cell you want to contain the nested table.

**3** Create the nested table as you created the main table.

*Note: You can use indents to visually separate the nested table from the main table. A Web browser will ignore the indents you add.*

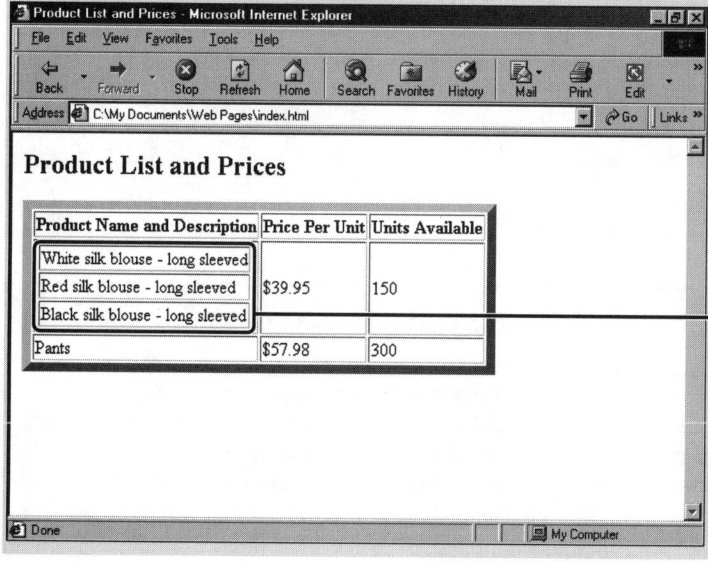

```
Product List and Prices - Microsoft Internet Explorer
File  Edit  View  Favorites  Tools  Help

Back  Forward  Stop  Refresh  Home  Search  Favorites  History  Mail  Print  Edit

Address  C:\My Documents\Web Pages\index.html          Go  Links

Product List and Prices
```

| Product Name and Description | Price Per Unit | Units Available |
| --- | --- | --- |
| White silk blouse - long sleeved<br>Red silk blouse - long sleeved<br>Black silk blouse - long sleeved | $39.95 | 150 |
| Pants | $57.98 | 300 |

```
Done                                          My Computer
```

**4** Display the Web page in a Web browser.

**●** The Web browser displays the nested table within the main table.

*Note: You can format a nested table as you would format any other table. For example, you can add color or a background image to a nested table.*

**123**

# INTRODUCTION TO SOUNDS

One of the most popular reasons for including sounds on Web pages is for entertainment. You can include sound clips from television shows, famous speeches and theme songs. Adding sounds to Web pages is also useful for selling products such as music CDs or audio tapes. People may be more likely to buy a product if they can listen to a sample of the product first.

## TYPES OF SOUNDS

There are several types of sounds commonly used on Web pages. The most popular type of sound is WAV. You can determine the type of a sound by the file extension that appears at the end of the sound filename (example: birdchirp.wav).

| TYPE OF SOUND | EXTENSION | USED FOR |
|---|---|---|
| MIDI | .mid | Instrumental music |
| MPEG | .mp3 | Songs |
| RealAudio | .ra | Live broadcasts |
| WAV | .wav | Short sound clips |

## WHERE TO GET SOUNDS

### THE INTERNET

There are many places on the Internet that offer sounds you can use on your Web pages for free. Make sure you have permission to use any sounds you obtain on the Internet. You can find sounds at the wavcentral.com and soundamerica.com Web sites.

### COMPUTER STORES

Most computer stores offer collections of sounds that you can purchase. Sound collections can include theme songs, nature sounds and special effects. Make sure sounds you purchase are in a format commonly used on the Web, such as WAV.

### RECORD SOUNDS

If your computer has sound capabilities, you can use a sound recording program to record sounds. You can connect a microphone to your computer to record your own voice or connect a CD or cassette player to record music or other sounds. When recording a sound you did not create, make sure you have permission to use the sound on your Web page.

## SOUND CONSIDERATIONS

### PROVIDE DESCRIPTIONS

You should provide a short description of a sound you add to a Web page. Include the sound type, size and length of time the sound will play. Visitors to your Web page can use this information to decide if they want to play the sound.

### PROVIDE ALTERNATIVES

Some users may be hearing impaired or use computers that cannot play sounds. Other users may not be able to play certain types of sounds. You should consider including a text version of important sounds on your Web page.

You can create a link on your Web page that users can
select to play a sound. When creating a link to a sound,
you should make sure the sound is in a format commonly
used on the Web, such as WAV or MPEG. You should
also use small sound files whenever possible, since large
files can take a long time to transfer to a computer.

## CREATE A LINK TO A SOUND

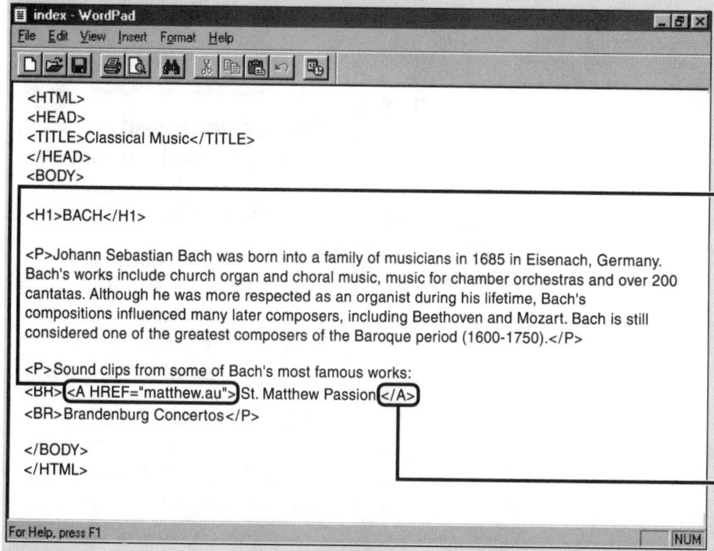

```
index - WordPad
File  Edit  View  Insert  Format  Help

<HTML>
<HEAD>
<TITLE>Classical Music</TITLE>
</HEAD>
<BODY>

<H1>BACH</H1>

<P>Johann Sebastian Bach was born into a family of musicians in 1685 in Eisenach, Germany.
Bach's works include church organ and choral music, music for chamber orchestras and over 200
cantatas. Although he was more respected as an organist during his lifetime, Bach's
compositions influenced many later composers, including Beethoven and Mozart. Bach is still
considered one of the greatest composers of the Baroque period (1600-1750).</P>

<P>Sound clips from some of Bach's most famous works:
<BR><A HREF="matthew.au">St. Matthew Passion</A>
<BR>Brandenburg Concertos</P>

</BODY>
</HTML>

For Help, press F1                                                       NUM
```

**1** In front of the text or image
you want users to select to
play a sound, type
**<A HREF="?">**.

**2** If the sound is stored in
the same folder in your
Web site, replace **?** with
the name of the sound
(example: matthew.au).

*Note: If the sound is stored in a
subfolder, you must also specify
the name of the subfolder
(example: clips/matthew.au).*

**3** Type **</A>** after the text or
image.

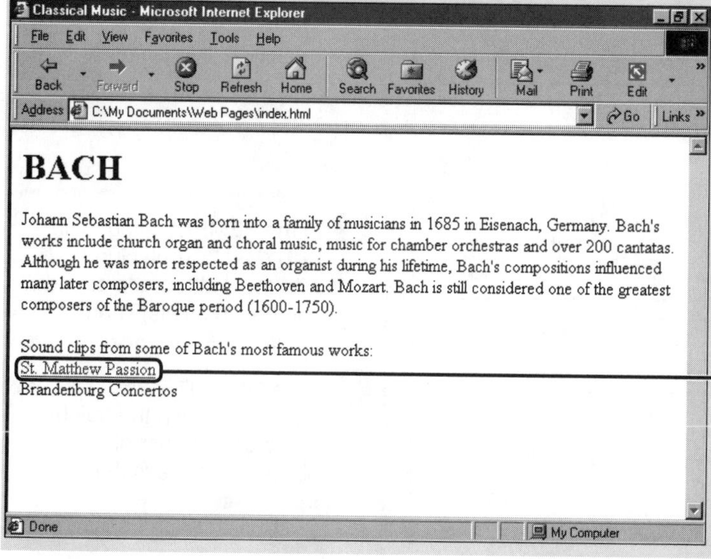

```
Classical Music - Microsoft Internet Explorer
File  Edit  View  Favorites  Tools  Help

Back  Forward  Stop  Refresh  Home  Search  Favorites  History  Mail  Print  Edit

Address  C:\My Documents\Web Pages\index.html                      Go   Links
```

# BACH

Johann Sebastian Bach was born into a family of musicians in 1685 in Eisenach, Germany. Bach's
works include church organ and choral music, music for chamber orchestras and over 200 cantatas.
Although he was more respected as an organist during his lifetime, Bach's compositions influenced
many later composers, including Beethoven and Mozart. Bach is still considered one of the greatest
composers of the Baroque period (1600-1750).

Sound clips from some of Bach's most famous works:
St. Matthew Passion
Brandenburg Concertos

```
Done                                              My Computer
```

**4** Display the Web page in a
Web browser.

■ The Web browser displays
the sound link on your Web
page.

■ When users select the
sound link, the sound will
transfer to their computers
and the sound will play. If a
user's Web browser cannot
play the sound, the browser
may allow the user to play
the sound in a different
program.

# ADD AN EMBEDDED SOUND

You can add an embedded sound that will play directly on your Web page. When you add an embedded sound, your Web page will display sound controls that allow users to start and stop the sound. You can specify the size for the sound controls. You can also specify whether you want the sound to play automatically when users visit the Web page and whether you want the sound to play continuously until a user stops the sound.

## ADD AN EMBEDDED SOUND

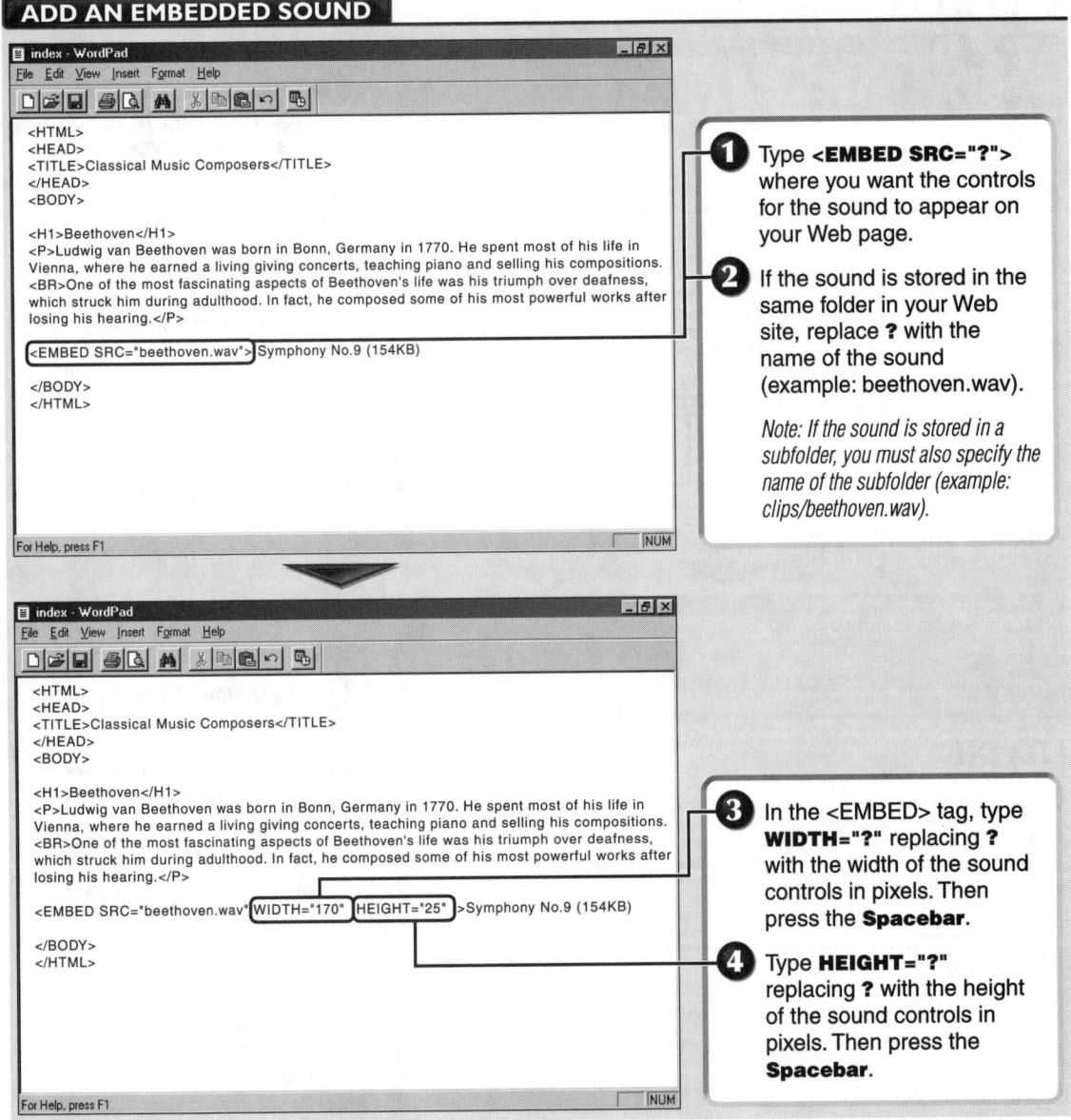

**1** Type **<EMBED SRC="?">** where you want the controls for the sound to appear on your Web page.

**2** If the sound is stored in the same folder in your Web site, replace **?** with the name of the sound (example: beethoven.wav).

*Note: If the sound is stored in a subfolder, you must also specify the name of the subfolder (example: clips/beethoven.wav).*

**3** In the <EMBED> tag, type **WIDTH="?"** replacing **?** with the width of the sound controls in pixels. Then press the **Spacebar**.

**4** Type **HEIGHT="?"** replacing **?** with the height of the sound controls in pixels. Then press the **Spacebar**.

# in an *instant*

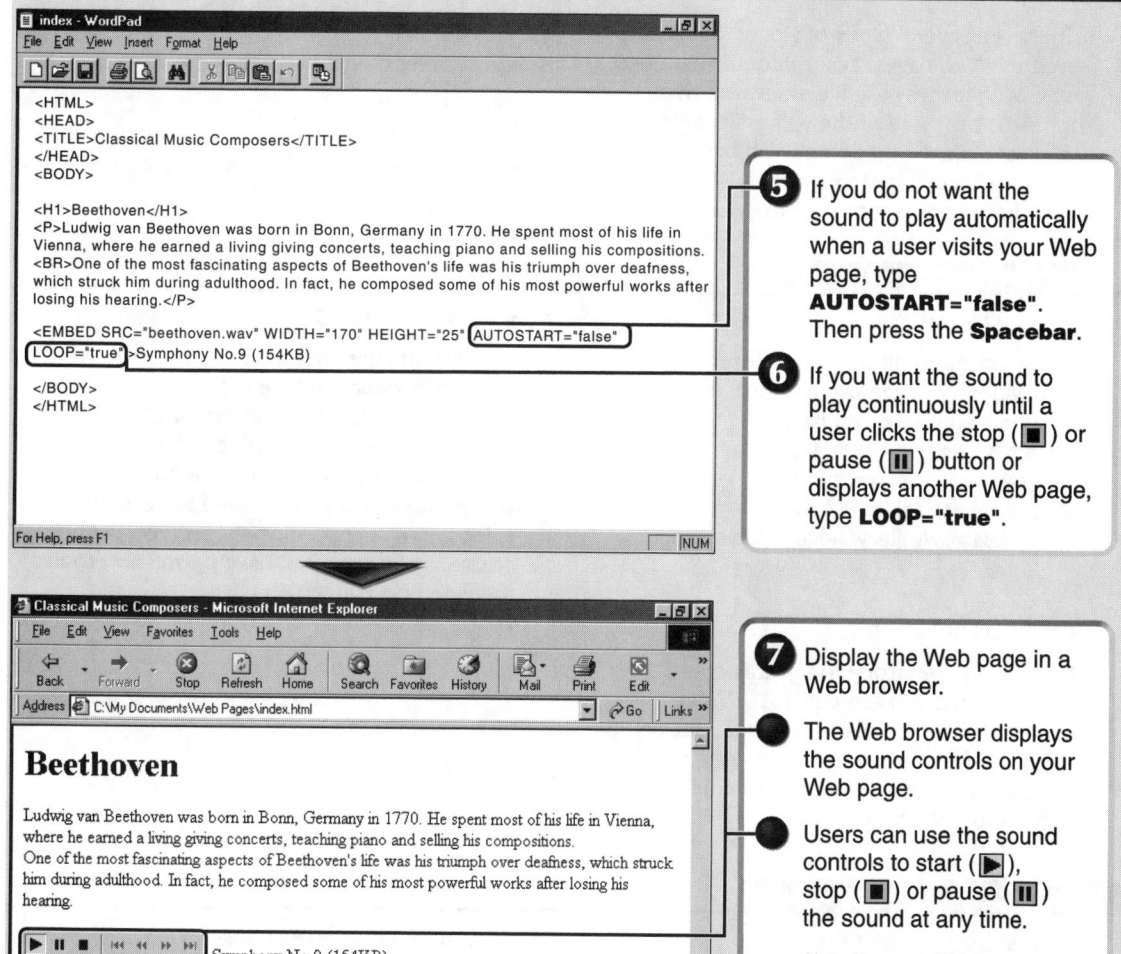

**5** If you do not want the sound to play automatically when a user visits your Web page, type **AUTOSTART="false"**. Then press the **Spacebar**.

**6** If you want the sound to play continuously until a user clicks the stop (■) or pause (❚❚) button or displays another Web page, type **LOOP="true"**.

**7** Display the Web page in a Web browser.

● The Web browser displays the sound controls on your Web page.

● Users can use the sound controls to start (▶), stop (■) or pause (❚❚) the sound at any time.

*Note: If a user's Web browser does not have the correct plug-in, or software, to play the sound, the browser may allow the user to download the plug-in from the Web.*

# INTRODUCTION TO VIDEOS

Entertainment is one of the most popular reasons for including videos on Web pages. You can include videos to present eye-catching visual effects, movie clips, animation or home videos. You can also include videos, such as TV broadcasts, interviews or product demonstrations, to provide information about a company, organization or topic of interest.

## TYPES OF VIDEOS

There are several types of videos commonly used on Web pages. You can determine the type of a video by the file extension that appears at the end of the video filename (example: plane.avi). Some Web browsers can play only certain types of videos, while other Web browsers cannot play any videos.

| TYPE OF VIDEO | EXTENSION |
|---------------|-----------------|
| AVI | .avi |
| MPEG | .mpg or .mpeg |
| QuickTime | .mov or .qt |

## WHERE TO GET VIDEOS

### THE INTERNET

There are many places on the Internet that offer videos you can use on your Web pages for free. Make sure you have permission to use any videos you obtain on the Internet. You can find videos at the www.jurassicpunk.com and www.nasa.gov/gallery/video Web sites.

### COMPUTER STORES

Many computer stores offer collections of videos that you can purchase. Video collections can include movie clips, special effects and nature clips. Make sure videos you purchase are in a format commonly used on the Web, such as AVI.

### RECORD VIDEOS

If your computer has a video capture card or built-in video capture capabilities, you can connect a VCR, video camera or DVD player to your computer to record videos. Video capture cards usually include all the necessary cables and software you need to record videos. When recording a video you did not create, make sure you have permission to use the video on your Web page.

## VIDEO CONSIDERATIONS

### USE SMALL VIDEO FILES

Video files tend to be the largest files on the Web. Videos with large file sizes can take a long time to transfer to a computer. Whenever possible, you should use videos with small file sizes.

### PROVIDE DESCRIPTIONS

Provide a short description of a video you add to your Web page, including the type, size and length of time the video will play. Visitors to your Web page can use this information to decide if they want to play the video.

You can create a link on your Web page that users can select to play a video. A video that users play by selecting a link is called an external video. When creating a link to a video, you should make sure the video is in a format commonly used on the Web, such as AVI or MPEG.

## CREATE A LINK TO A VIDEO

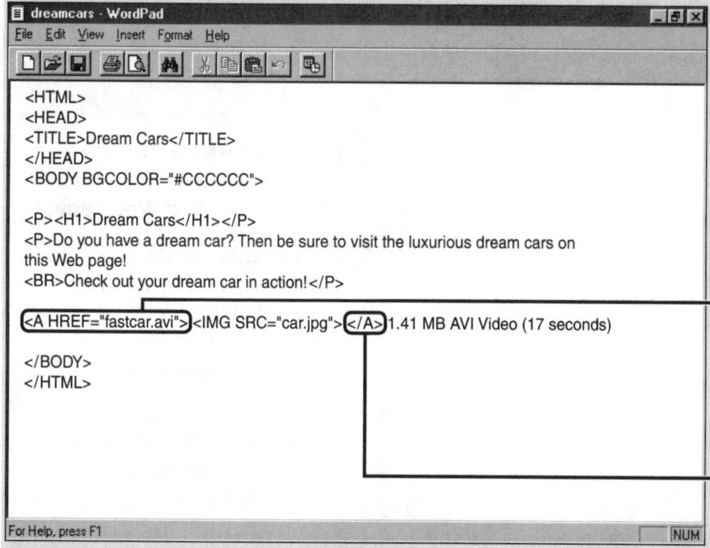

```
dreamcars - WordPad
File  Edit  View  Insert  Format  Help

<HTML>
<HEAD>
<TITLE>Dream Cars</TITLE>
</HEAD>
<BODY BGCOLOR="#CCCCCC">

<P><H1>Dream Cars</H1></P>
<P>Do you have a dream car? Then be sure to visit the luxurious dream cars on
this Web page!
<BR>Check out your dream car in action!</P>

<A HREF="fastcar.avi"><IMG SRC="car.jpg"></A>1.41 MB AVI Video (17 seconds)

</BODY>
</HTML>

For Help, press F1                                                    NUM
```

1 In front of the text or image you want users to select to play a video, type **<A HREF="?">**.

2 If the video is stored in the same folder in your Web site, replace **?** with the name of the video (example: fastcar.avi).

*Note: If the video is stored in a subfolder, you must also specify the name of the subfolder (example: videos/fastcar.avi).*

3 Type **</A>** after the text or image.

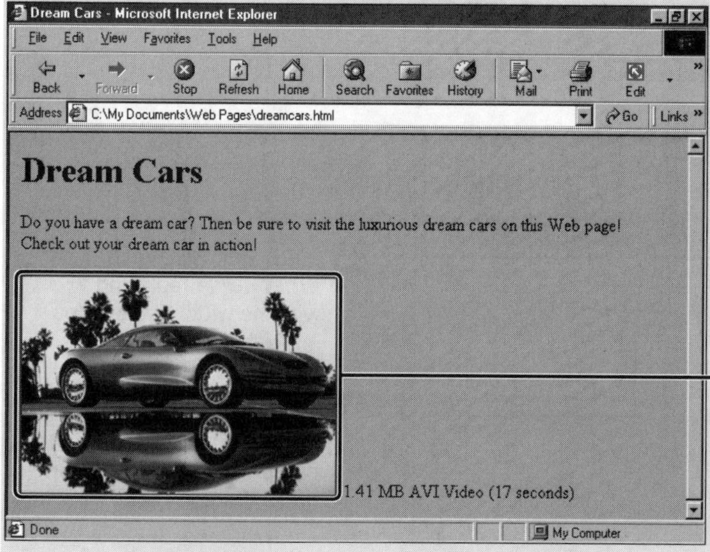

```
Dream Cars - Microsoft Internet Explorer
File  Edit  View  Favorites  Tools  Help

Back  Forward  Stop  Refresh  Home  Search  Favorites  History  Mail  Print  Edit

Address  C:\My Documents\Web Pages\dreamcars.html          Go  Links

Dream Cars

Do you have a dream car? Then be sure to visit the luxurious dream cars on this Web page!
Check out your dream car in action!

1.41 MB AVI Video (17 seconds)

Done                                              My Computer
```

4 Display the Web page in a Web browser.

● The Web browser displays the video link on your Web page.

● When users select the video link, the video will transfer to their computers and the video will play. If a user's Web browser cannot play the video, the browser may allow the user to open the video in a different program.

You can add an internal video that will play directly on your Web page. When adding an internal video, you should specify the correct dimensions for the video to make sure the video appears correctly in a Web browser. You can use a video player such as Windows Media Player or QuickTime Player to determine the correct width and height of a video.

## ADD AN INTERNAL VIDEO

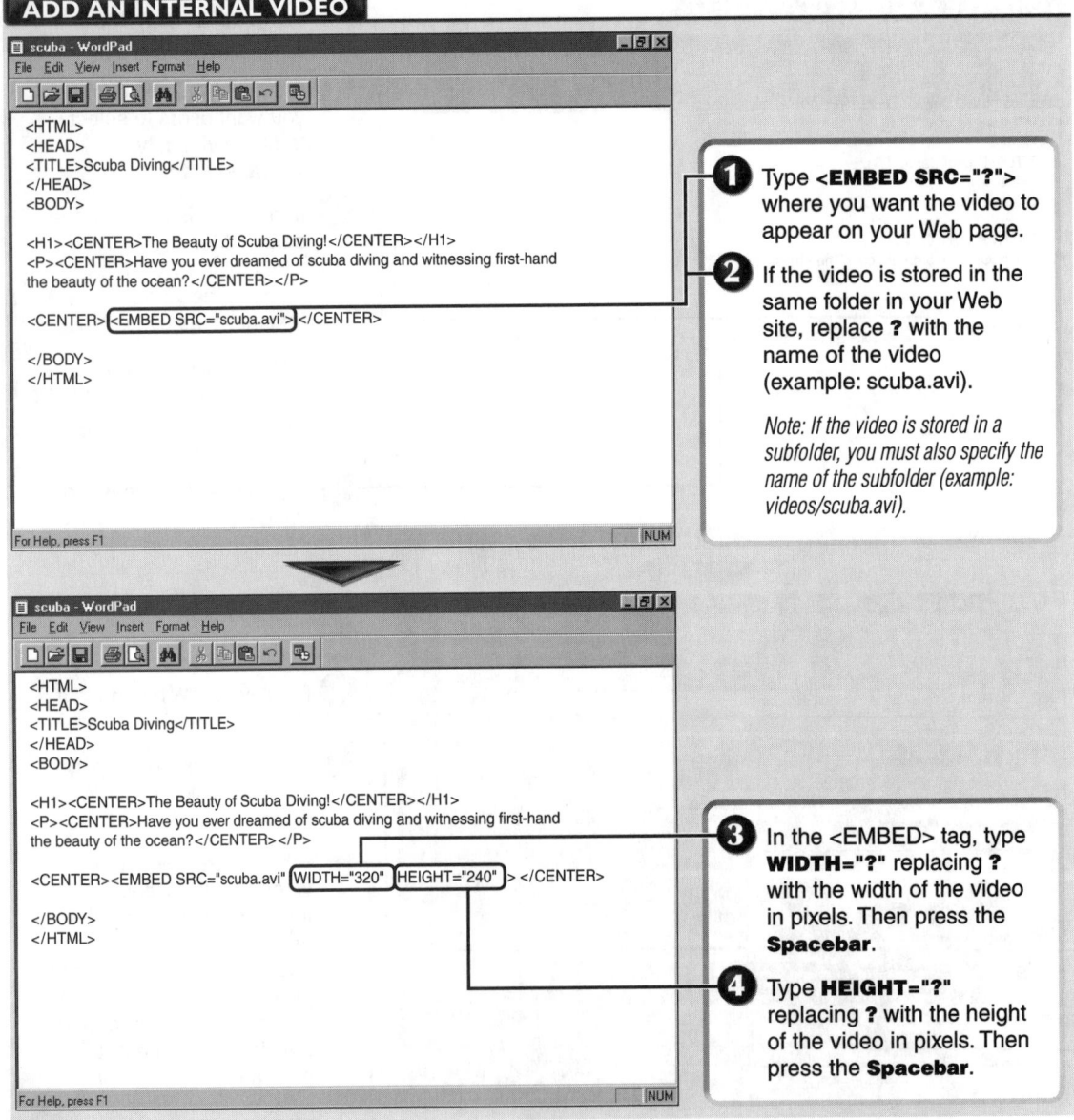

**1** Type **<EMBED SRC="?">** where you want the video to appear on your Web page.

**2** If the video is stored in the same folder in your Web site, replace **?** with the name of the video (example: scuba.avi).

*Note: If the video is stored in a subfolder, you must also specify the name of the subfolder (example: videos/scuba.avi).*

**3** In the <EMBED> tag, type **WIDTH="?"** replacing **?** with the width of the video in pixels. Then press the **Spacebar**.

**4** Type **HEIGHT="?"** replacing **?** with the height of the video in pixels. Then press the **Spacebar**.

# in an *Instant*

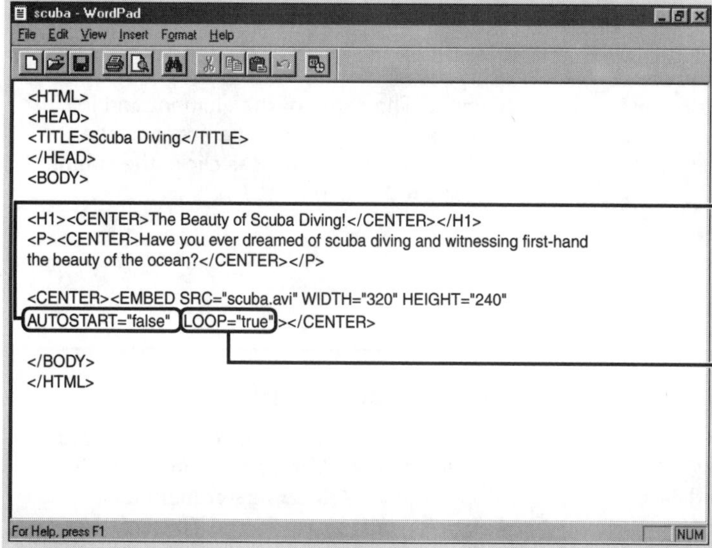

```
scuba - WordPad                                              _ □ ×
File  Edit  View  Insert  Format  Help

<HTML>
<HEAD>
<TITLE>Scuba Diving</TITLE>
</HEAD>
<BODY>

<H1><CENTER>The Beauty of Scuba Diving!</CENTER></H1>
<P><CENTER>Have you ever dreamed of scuba diving and witnessing first-hand
the beauty of the ocean?</CENTER></P>

<CENTER><EMBED SRC="scuba.avi" WIDTH="320" HEIGHT="240"
AUTOSTART="false" LOOP="true"></CENTER>

</BODY>
</HTML>

For Help, press F1                                            NUM
```

**5** If you do not want the video to play automatically when a user visits your Web page, type **AUTOSTART="false"**. Then press the **Spacebar**.

**6** If you want the video to play continuously until a user clicks the stop (■) or pause (❙❙) button or displays another Web page, type **LOOP="true"**.

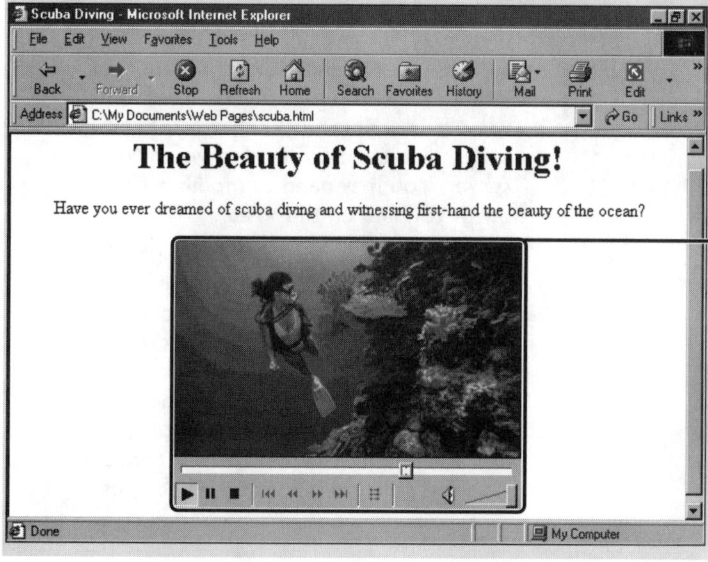

```
Scuba Diving - Microsoft Internet Explorer                   _ □ ×
File  Edit  View  Favorites  Tools  Help
← Back   → Forward   ✗ Stop   ↻ Refresh   ⌂ Home   🔍 Search   📁 Favorites   🕐 History   📧 Mail   🖨 Print   ✎ Edit   »
Address  C:\My Documents\Web Pages\scuba.html              ▼  → Go   Links »
```

# The Beauty of Scuba Diving!

Have you ever dreamed of scuba diving and witnessing first-hand the beauty of the ocean?

**7** Display the Web page in a Web browser.

● The Web browser displays the video on your Web page.

● A user can use the video controls to start (▶), stop (■) or pause (❙❙) the video at any time.

*Note: If a user's Web browser does not have the correct plug-in, or software, to play the video, the browser may allow the user to download the plug-in from the Web.*

# INTRODUCTION TO FORMS

Forms allow you to gather information from users who visit your Web pages. You can create a form that lets users send you questions or comments about your Web pages. You can also create a form that allows users to purchase products and services on the Web.

## HOW FORMS WORK

### GATHER INFORMATION

Form elements such as text areas and check boxes allow users to enter information and select options on a form.

When adding an element to a form, you must usually provide a name for the element. When a user enters information or selects an option

using the element, a value is assigned to the element. The name of the element and its corresponding value are then sent to the Web server when the user clicks the submit button on the form.

## CGI SCRIPTS

### PROCESS INFORMATION

When a Web server receives information from a form, the server runs a program called a Common Gateway Interface (CGI) script that processes the information. The CGI script the Web server uses determines how the information is processed. For example, a CGI script can send you the results of a form in an e-mail message, save the results in a document or add the results to a database stored on the Web server.

Once a CGI script has processed the form results, the script usually displays a message in the user's Web browser, indicating that the information was successfully sent.

### OBTAIN CGI SCRIPTS

Before including forms on your Web pages, make sure your Web server can run CGI scripts. Most Web servers contain CGI scripts for processing forms. These scripts are often stored in a directory named "cgi-bin."

If your Web server does not offer CGI scripts, you can find CGI scripts on the Web. The www.cgi-resources.com and www.free-scripts.net Web sites offer CGI scripts you can download to your Web server. You may need to modify a CGI script you find on the Web.

Some Internet Service Providers (ISPs) do not allow CGI scripts on their Web servers for security reasons. If your ISP does not allow you to use CGI scripts on your Web server, you may want to use a form hosting service to process your form results. Form hosting services are available at the www.creative-dr.com and www.response-o-matic.com Web sites.

Forms allow users to purchase products and services or send you questions or comments. You can set up a form that will allow you to gather information from users who visit your Web pages. Web servers use a program called a Common Gateway Interface (CGI) script to process the information users submit in a form.

## SET UP A FORM

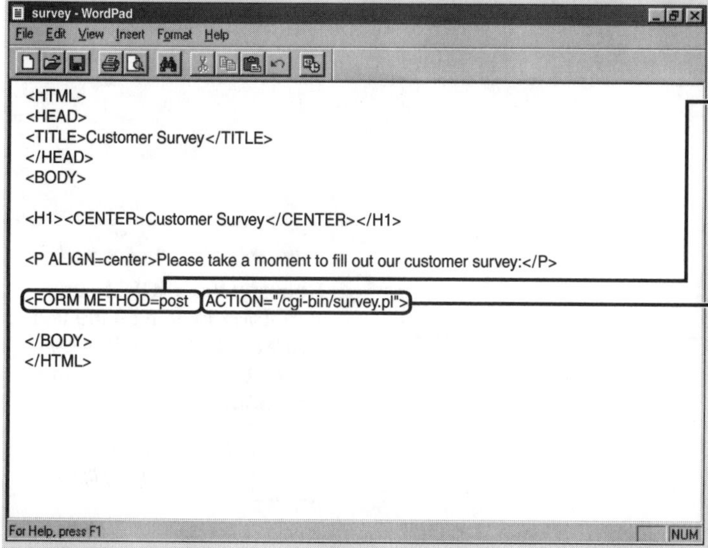

```
survey - WordPad                                          _ 8 X
File  Edit  View  Insert  Format  Help

<HTML>
<HEAD>
<TITLE>Customer Survey</TITLE>
</HEAD>
<BODY>

<H1><CENTER>Customer Survey</CENTER></H1>

<P ALIGN=center>Please take a moment to fill out our customer survey:</P>

<FORM METHOD=post   ACTION="/cgi-bin/survey.pl">

</BODY>
</HTML>



For Help, press F1                                        NUM
```

**1** Type **<FORM METHOD=post** where you want the form to appear on your Web page. Then press the **Spacebar**.

**2** Type **ACTION="?">** replacing **?** with the location of the CGI script on the Web server that will process the information submitted by the form.

*Note: To determine the location of the CGI script on your Web server, contact your Web server administrator.*

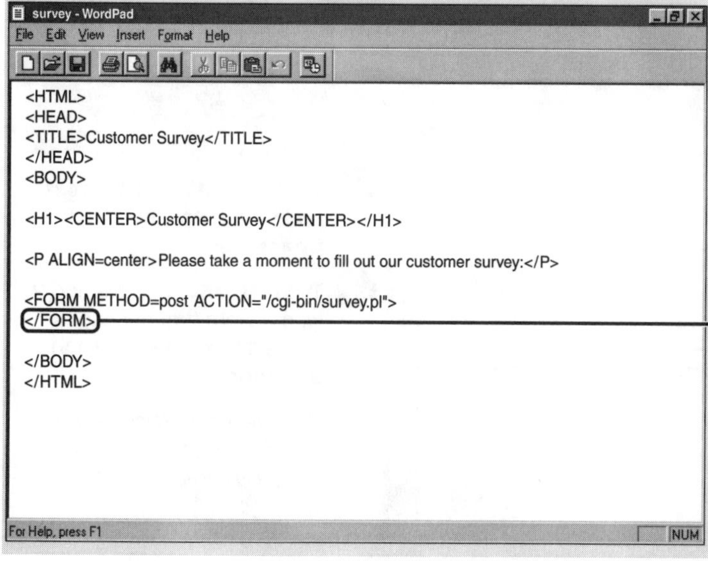

```
survey - WordPad                                          _ 8 X
File  Edit  View  Insert  Format  Help

<HTML>
<HEAD>
<TITLE>Customer Survey</TITLE>
</HEAD>
<BODY>

<H1><CENTER>Customer Survey</CENTER></H1>

<P ALIGN=center>Please take a moment to fill out our customer survey:</P>

<FORM METHOD=post ACTION="/cgi-bin/survey.pl">
</FORM>

</BODY>
</HTML>



For Help, press F1                                        NUM
```

**3** Type **</FORM>** to complete the form.

● You have now set up a form on your Web page. You can now add elements to the form that will allow users to select options and submit information to the Web server.

**133**

# CREATE A TEXT BOX

You can create a text box that allows users to enter a line of text such as a name, address or short response. By default, a text box is approximately 20 characters wide, but you can specify a width for the text box. If you want to limit the amount of text a user can enter in the text box, you must also specify the maximum number of characters the text box will accept.

## CREATE A TEXT BOX

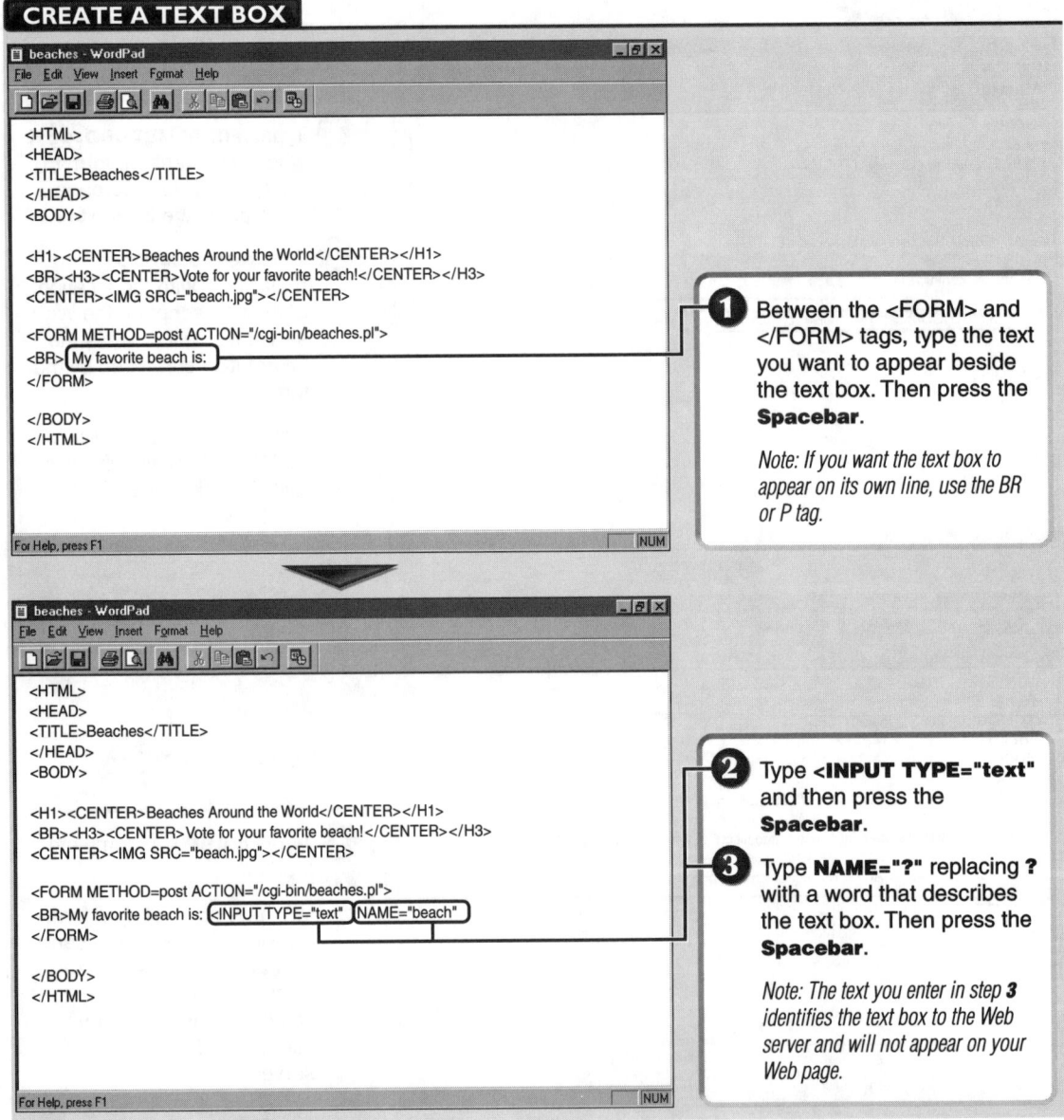

**1** Between the <FORM> and </FORM> tags, type the text you want to appear beside the text box. Then press the **Spacebar**.

*Note: If you want the text box to appear on its own line, use the BR or P tag.*

**2** Type **<INPUT TYPE="text"** and then press the **Spacebar**.

**3** Type **NAME="?"** replacing **?** with a word that describes the text box. Then press the **Spacebar**.

*Note: The text you enter in step 3 identifies the text box to the Web server and will not appear on your Web page.*

# in an *instant*

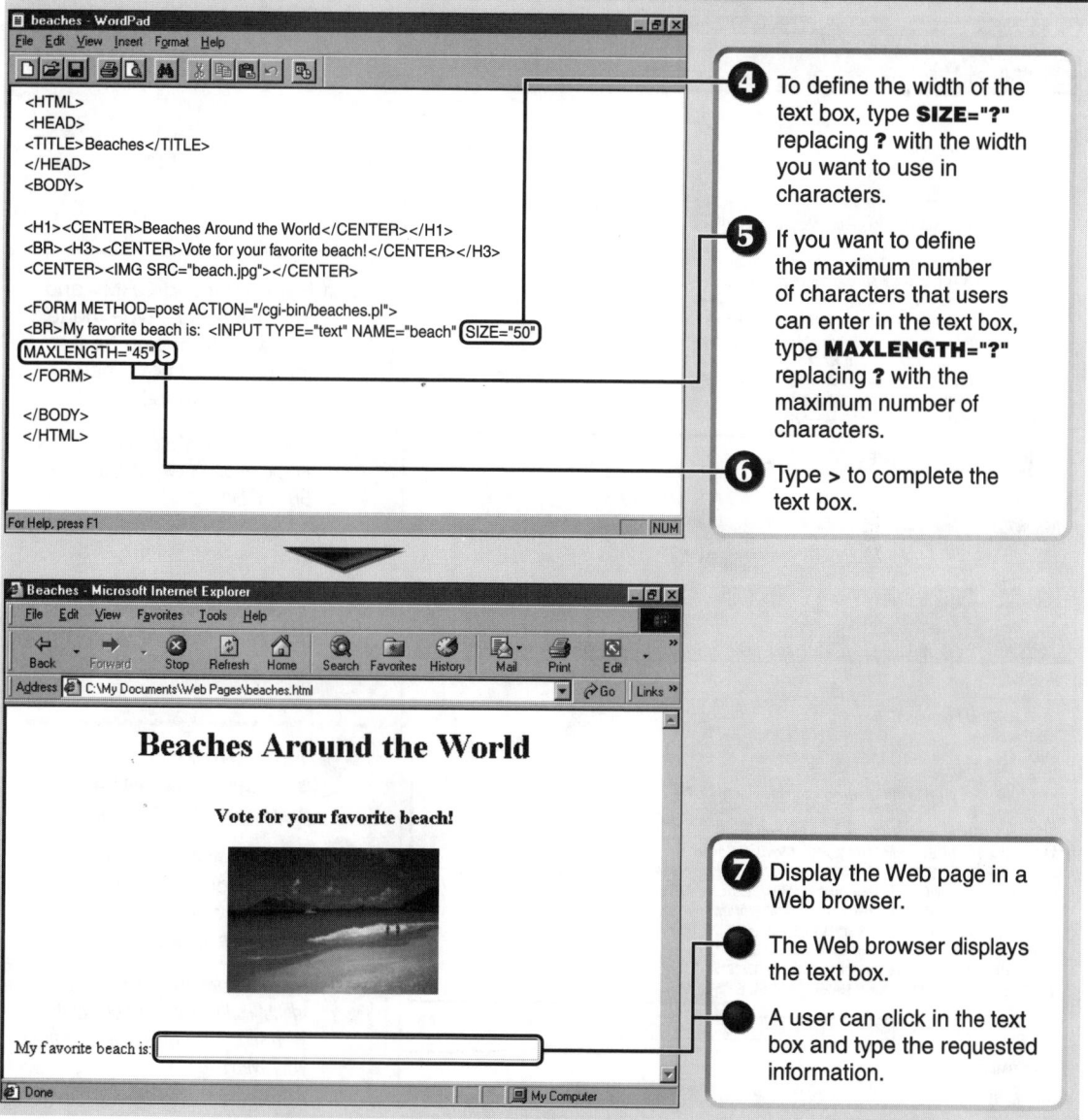

**4** To define the width of the text box, type **SIZE="?"** replacing **?** with the width you want to use in characters.

**5** If you want to define the maximum number of characters that users can enter in the text box, type **MAXLENGTH="?"** replacing **?** with the maximum number of characters.

**6** Type > to complete the text box.

**7** Display the Web page in a Web browser.

● The Web browser displays the text box.

● A user can click in the text box and type the requested information.

# CREATE A PASSWORD BOX

You can create a password box that allows users to enter a password or other confidential information. When a user types information in a password box, an asterisk (*) appears for each character so other people cannot view the information. A password box will not protect the information as it transfers over the Internet.

## CREATE A PASSWORD BOX

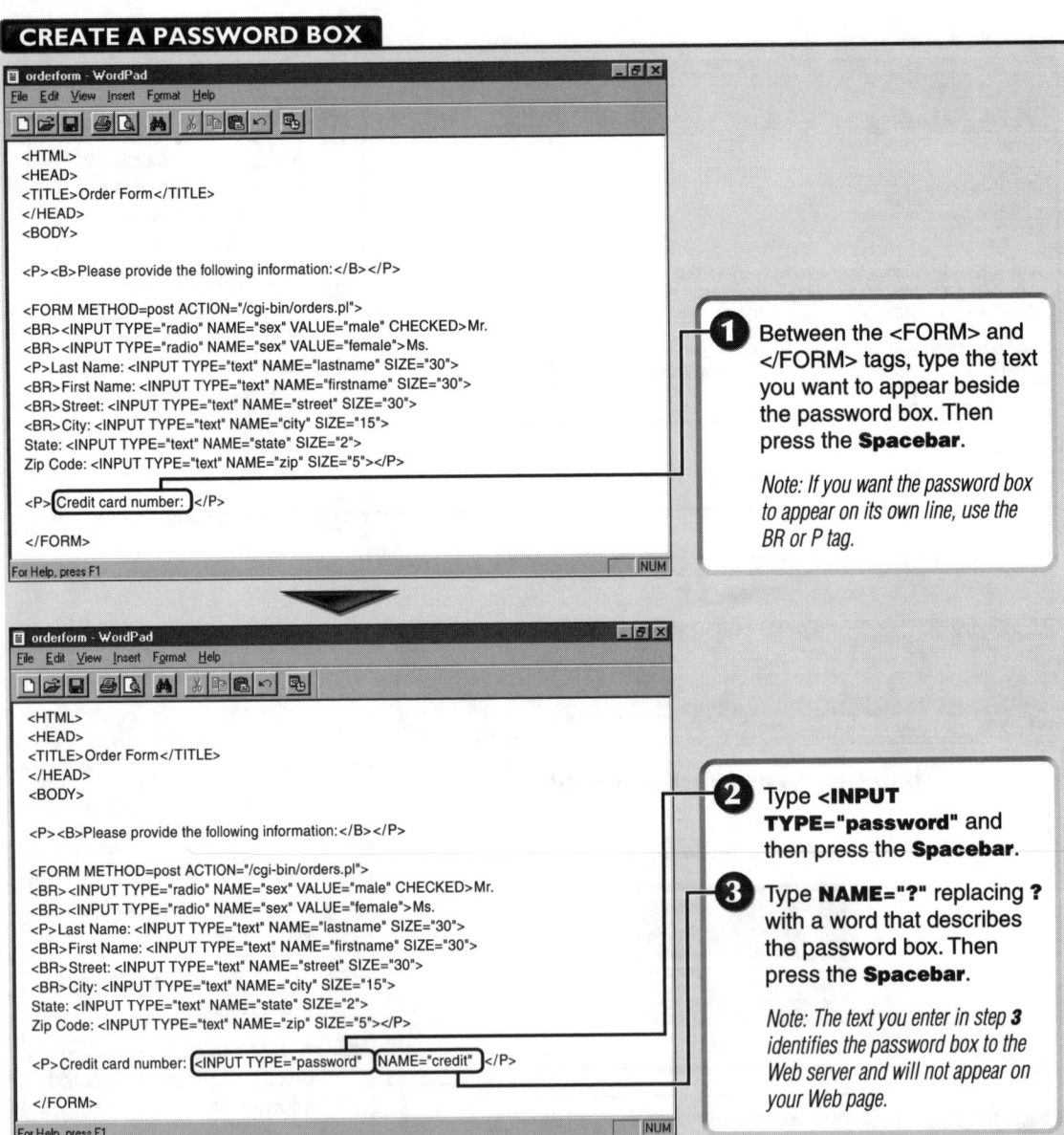

**①** Between the <FORM> and </FORM> tags, type the text you want to appear beside the password box. Then press the **Spacebar**.

*Note: If you want the password box to appear on its own line, use the BR or P tag.*

**②** Type **<INPUT TYPE="password"** and then press the **Spacebar**.

**③** Type **NAME="?"** replacing **?** with a word that describes the password box. Then press the **Spacebar**.

*Note: The text you enter in step 3 identifies the password box to the Web server and will not appear on your Web page.*

**136**

# in an instant

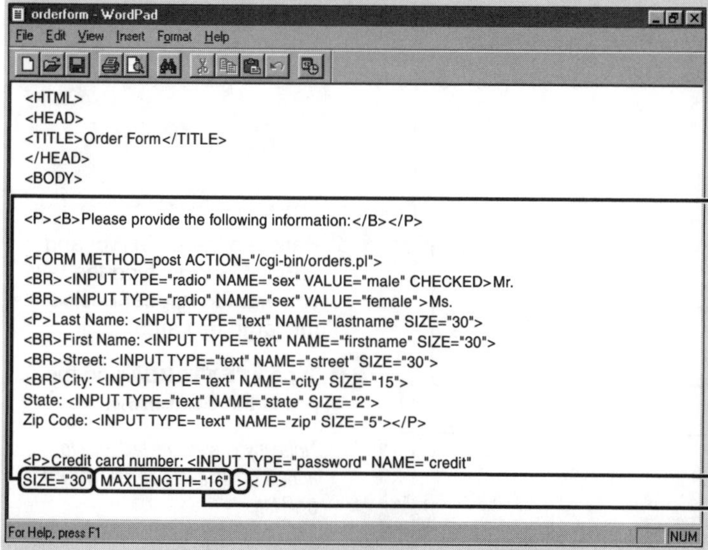

```
orderform - WordPad                                          _ 8 X
File  Edit  View  Insert  Format  Help

<HTML>
<HEAD>
<TITLE>Order Form</TITLE>
</HEAD>
<BODY>

<P><B>Please provide the following information:</B></P>

<FORM METHOD=post ACTION="/cgi-bin/orders.pl">
<BR><INPUT TYPE="radio" NAME="sex" VALUE="male" CHECKED>Mr.
<BR><INPUT TYPE="radio" NAME="sex" VALUE="female">Ms.
<P>Last Name: <INPUT TYPE="text" NAME="lastname" SIZE="30">
<BR>First Name: <INPUT TYPE="text" NAME="firstname" SIZE="30">
<BR>Street: <INPUT TYPE="text" NAME="street" SIZE="30">
<BR>City: <INPUT TYPE="text" NAME="city" SIZE="15">
State: <INPUT TYPE="text" NAME="state" SIZE="2">
Zip Code: <INPUT TYPE="text" NAME="zip" SIZE="5"></P>

<P>Credit card number: <INPUT TYPE="password" NAME="credit"
SIZE="30"  MAXLENGTH="16"  >  </P>

For Help, press F1                                            NUM
```

**4** To define the width of the password box, type **SIZE="?"** replacing **?** with a width in characters.

**5** If you want to define the maximum number of characters that users can enter in the password box, type **MAXLENGTH="?"** replacing **?** with the maximum number of characters.

**6** Type > to complete the password box.

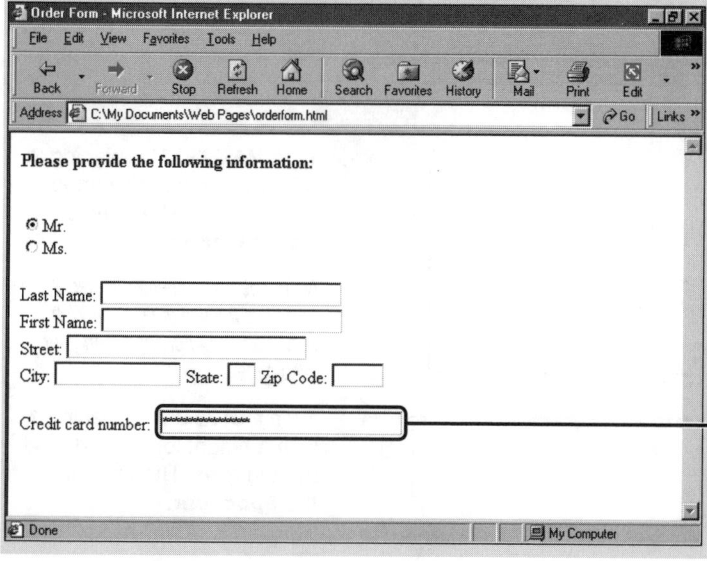

```
Order Form - Microsoft Internet Explorer                     _ 8 X
File  Edit  View  Favorites  Tools  Help

 Back   Forward   Stop  Refresh  Home  Search Favorites History  Mail  Print  Edit

Address  C:\My Documents\Web Pages\orderform.html          Go  Links »

Please provide the following information:

 (•) Mr.
 ( ) Ms.

Last Name: [                    ]
First Name: [                    ]
Street: [                    ]
City: [          ]  State: [  ]  Zip Code: [    ]

Credit card number: [ ************ ]

Done                                        My Computer
```

**7** Display the Web page in a Web browser.

● The Web browser displays the password box.

● A user can click in the password box and type the requested information. An asterisk (*) appears for each character a user types to prevent others from seeing the password.

# CREATE A LARGE TEXT AREA

You can create a large text area that allows users to enter several lines or paragraphs of text in a form. A large text area is ideal for gathering comments or questions from users. You should make sure the dimensions you specify for the text area will allow the text area to fit on a computer screen and clearly display the text that a user types.

## CREATE A LARGE TEXT AREA

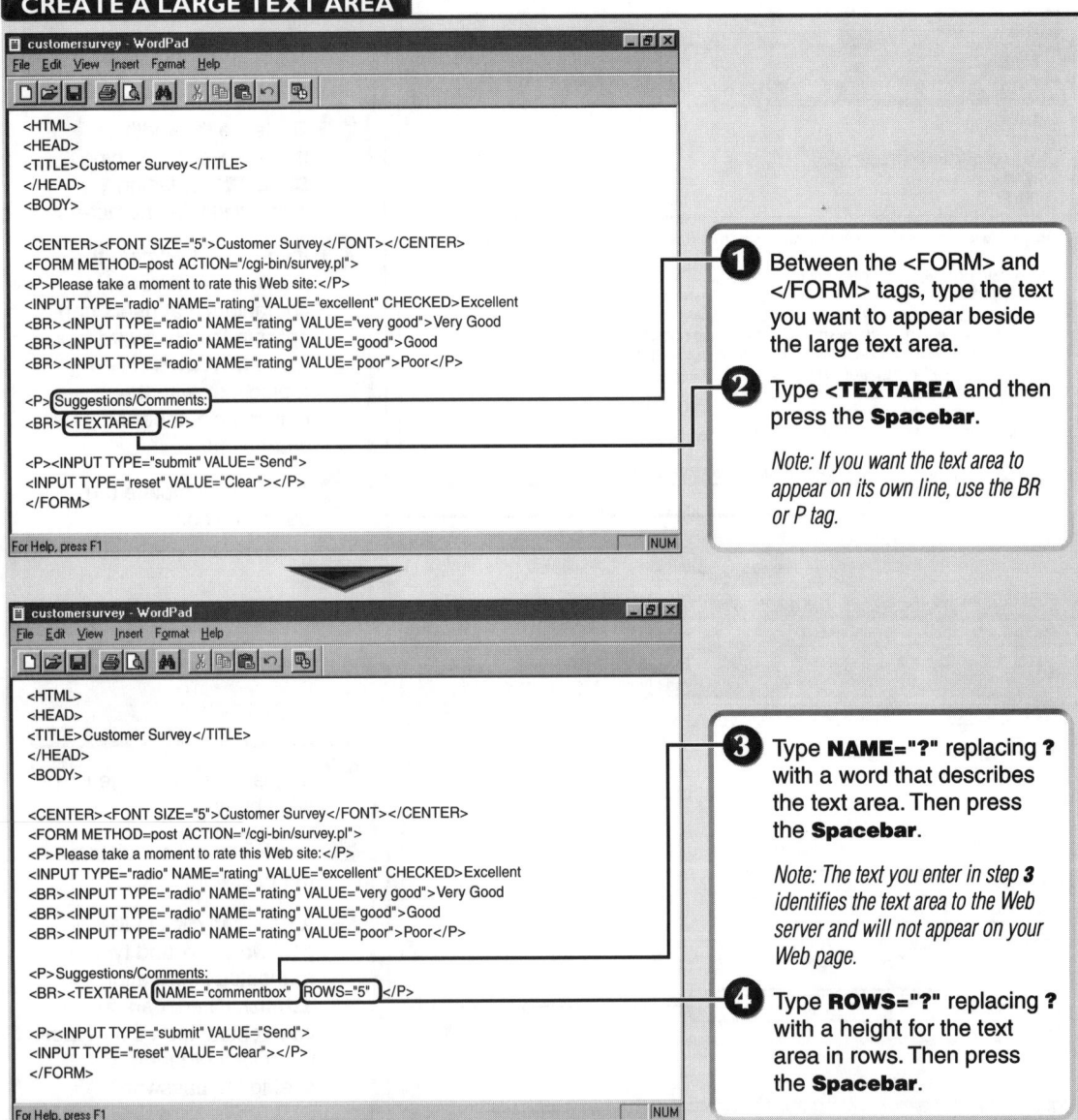

**①** Between the <FORM> and </FORM> tags, type the text you want to appear beside the large text area.

**②** Type **<TEXTAREA** and then press the **Spacebar**.

*Note: If you want the text area to appear on its own line, use the BR or P tag.*

**③** Type **NAME="?"** replacing **?** with a word that describes the text area. Then press the **Spacebar**.

*Note: The text you enter in step 3 identifies the text area to the Web server and will not appear on your Web page.*

**④** Type **ROWS="?"** replacing **?** with a height for the text area in rows. Then press the **Spacebar**.

in an *instant*

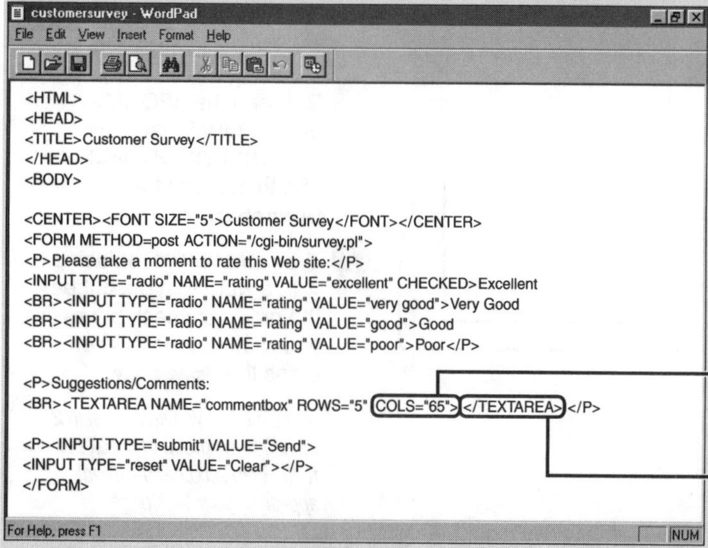

---

**customersurvey - WordPad**

File  Edit  View  Insert  Format  Help

```
<HTML>
<HEAD>
<TITLE>Customer Survey</TITLE>
</HEAD>
<BODY>

<CENTER><FONT SIZE="5">Customer Survey</FONT></CENTER>
<FORM METHOD=post ACTION="/cgi-bin/survey.pl">
<P>Please take a moment to rate this Web site:</P>
<INPUT TYPE="radio" NAME="rating" VALUE="excellent" CHECKED>Excellent
<BR><INPUT TYPE="radio" NAME="rating" VALUE="very good">Very Good
<BR><INPUT TYPE="radio" NAME="rating" VALUE="good">Good
<BR><INPUT TYPE="radio" NAME="rating" VALUE="poor">Poor</P>

<P>Suggestions/Comments:
<BR><TEXTAREA NAME="commentbox" ROWS="5" COLS="65"></TEXTAREA></P>

<P><INPUT TYPE="submit" VALUE="Send">
<INPUT TYPE="reset" VALUE="Clear"></P>
</FORM>
```

For Help, press F1                                                    NUM

**5** Type **COLS="?">** replacing **?** with a width for the text area in characters.

**6** Type **</TEXTAREA>** to complete the text area.

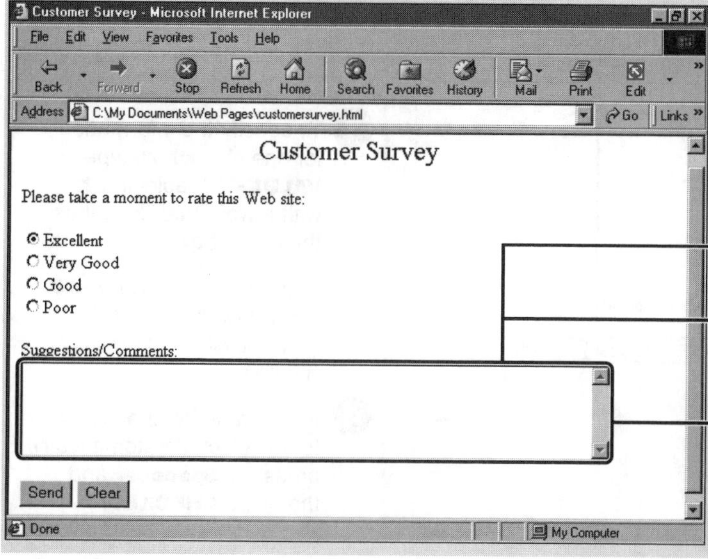

---

**Customer Survey - Microsoft Internet Explorer**

File  Edit  View  Favorites  Tools  Help

Back  Forward  Stop  Refresh  Home  Search  Favorites  History  Mail  Print  Edit

Address  C:\My Documents\Web Pages\customersurvey.html                 Go   Links

### Customer Survey

Please take a moment to rate this Web site:

- ⦿ Excellent
- ○ Very Good
- ○ Good
- ○ Poor

Suggestions/Comments:

Send   Clear

Done                                               My Computer

**7** Display the Web page in a Web browser.

● The Web browser displays the text area.

● A user can click in the text area and type the requested information.

● If the text a user types does not fit in the text area, the user can use the scroll bar to scroll through the text.

# CREATE CHECK BOXES

You can include check boxes on a form if you want users to be able to select one or more options. When creating check boxes, you need to specify a name that identifies each group of check boxes. To help you determine which options a user selected from a group of check boxes, you also need to specify a name for each check box.

## CREATE CHECK BOXES

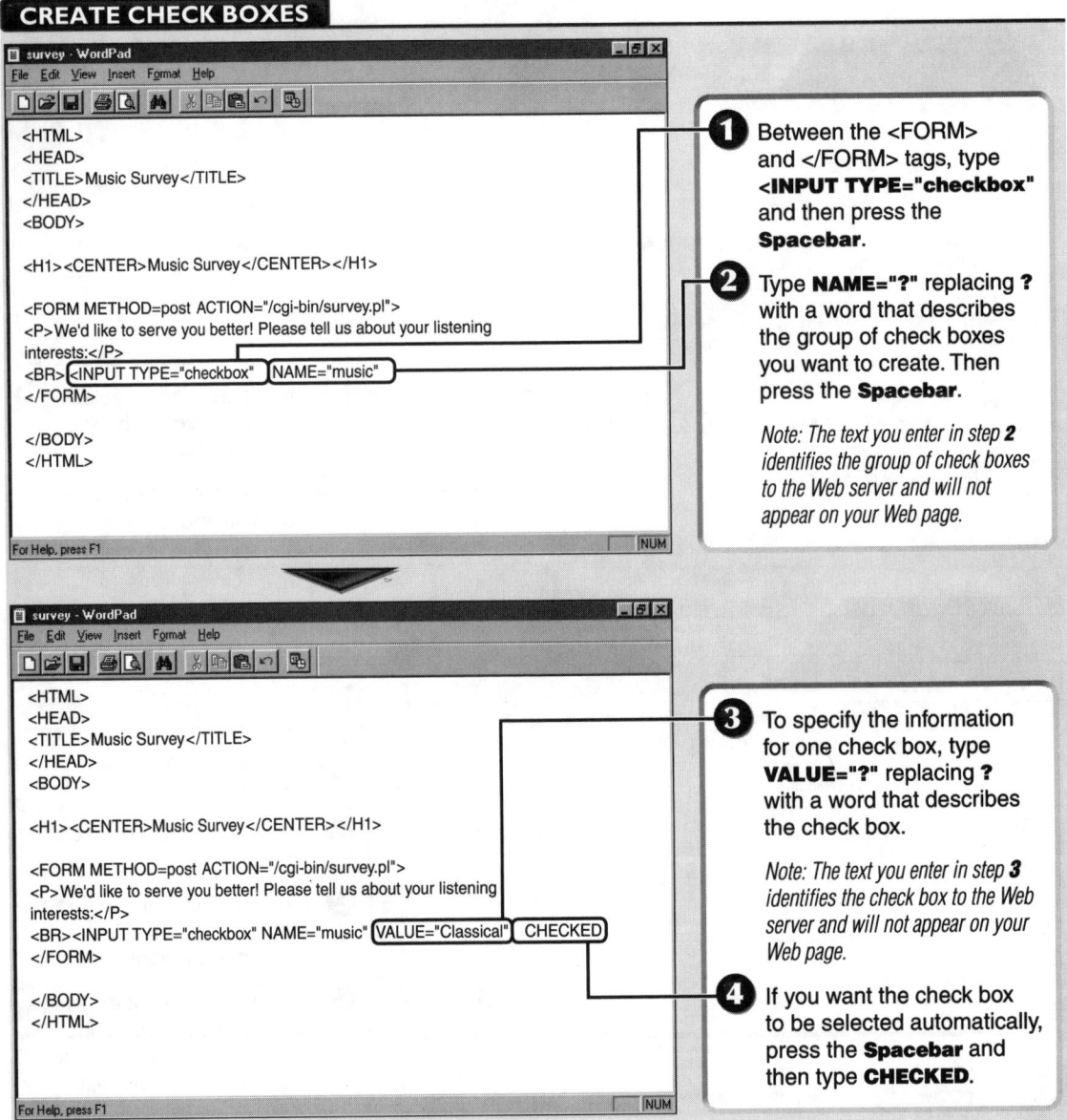

**1** Between the <FORM> and </FORM> tags, type **<INPUT TYPE="checkbox"** and then press the **Spacebar**.

**2** Type **NAME="?"** replacing **?** with a word that describes the group of check boxes you want to create. Then press the **Spacebar**.

*Note: The text you enter in step 2 identifies the group of check boxes to the Web server and will not appear on your Web page.*

**3** To specify the information for one check box, type **VALUE="?"** replacing **?** with a word that describes the check box.

*Note: The text you enter in step 3 identifies the check box to the Web server and will not appear on your Web page.*

**4** If you want the check box to be selected automatically, press the **Spacebar** and then type **CHECKED**.

**in an** *Instant*

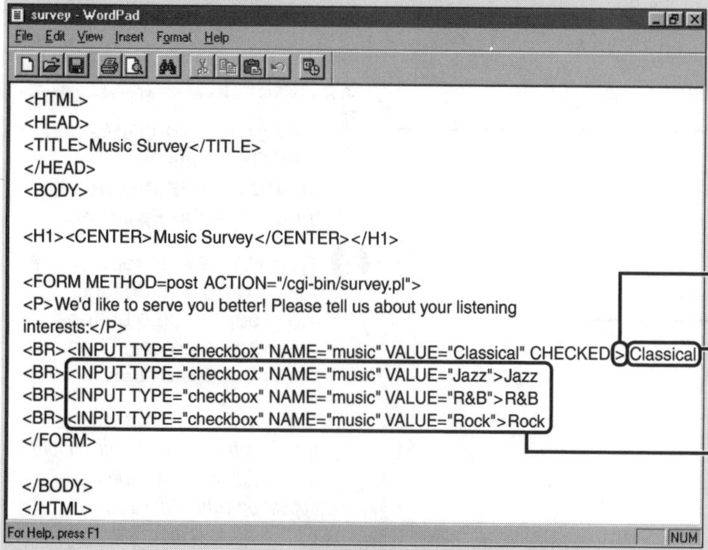

```
survey - WordPad                                      _ 8 X
File  Edit  View  Insert  Format  Help

D | ☞ 🖫 | 🖨 🔍 | 🏤 | 🖁 🖻 🖺 ▫ | 🖳 |

<HTML>
<HEAD>
<TITLE>Music Survey</TITLE>
</HEAD>
<BODY>

<H1><CENTER>Music Survey</CENTER></H1>

<FORM METHOD=post ACTION="/cgi-bin/survey.pl">
<P>We'd like to serve you better! Please tell us about your listening
interests:</P>
<BR><INPUT TYPE="checkbox" NAME="music" VALUE="Classical" CHECKED>Classical
<BR><INPUT TYPE="checkbox" NAME="music" VALUE="Jazz">Jazz
<BR><INPUT TYPE="checkbox" NAME="music" VALUE="R&B">R&B
<BR><INPUT TYPE="checkbox" NAME="music" VALUE="Rock">Rock
</FORM>

</BODY>
</HTML>
For Help, press F1                                          NUM
```

**5** Type > to complete the check box.

**6** Type the text you want to appear beside the check box on your Web page.

**7** Repeat steps **1** to **6** for each check box you want to create.

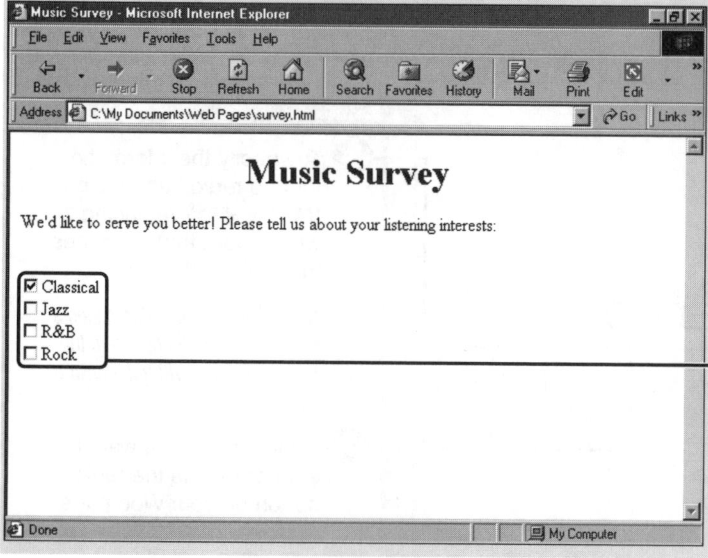

```
Music Survey - Microsoft Internet Explorer                 _ 8 X
File  Edit  View  Favorites  Tools  Help

 ⇦      ➡       ⊗       ↻       ⌂        🔍       🗀         🕒       🖳·     🖨      🖾      »
Back  Forward   Stop   Refresh   Home    Search  Favorites  History   Mail    Print    Edit

Address 🖉 C:\My Documents\Web Pages\survey.html              ▼  ⭆ Go  Links »
```

## **Music Survey**

We'd like to serve you better! Please tell us about your listening interests:

☑ Classical
☐ Jazz
☐ R&B
☐ Rock

```
🖉 Done                                        🖳 My Computer
```

**8** Display the Web page in a Web browser.

● The Web browser displays the check boxes.

● Users can click the check box for each option they want to select (☐ changes to ☑).

# CREATE RADIO BUTTONS

You can include radio buttons on a form if you want users to select only one of several options. When creating radio buttons, you need to specify a name for the group of radio buttons as well as a name that identifies each radio button. You can also have one radio button in the group appear automatically selected when a user displays the form.

## CREATE RADIO BUTTONS

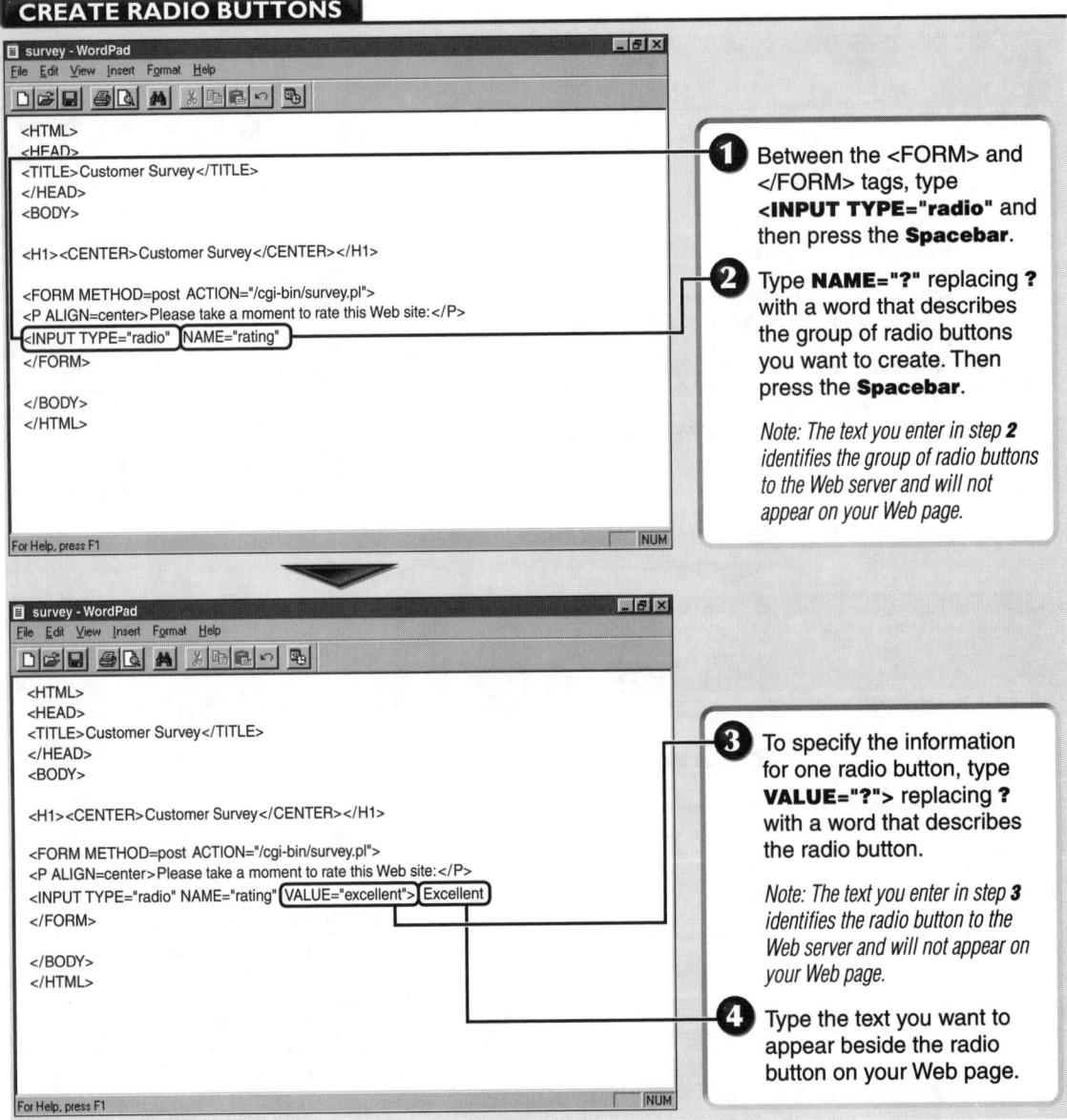

**1** Between the <FORM> and </FORM> tags, type **<INPUT TYPE="radio"** and then press the **Spacebar**.

**2** Type **NAME="?"** replacing **?** with a word that describes the group of radio buttons you want to create. Then press the **Spacebar**.

*Note: The text you enter in step 2 identifies the group of radio buttons to the Web server and will not appear on your Web page.*

**3** To specify the information for one radio button, type **VALUE="?">** replacing **?** with a word that describes the radio button.

*Note: The text you enter in step 3 identifies the radio button to the Web server and will not appear on your Web page.*

**4** Type the text you want to appear beside the radio button on your Web page.

# in an *instant*

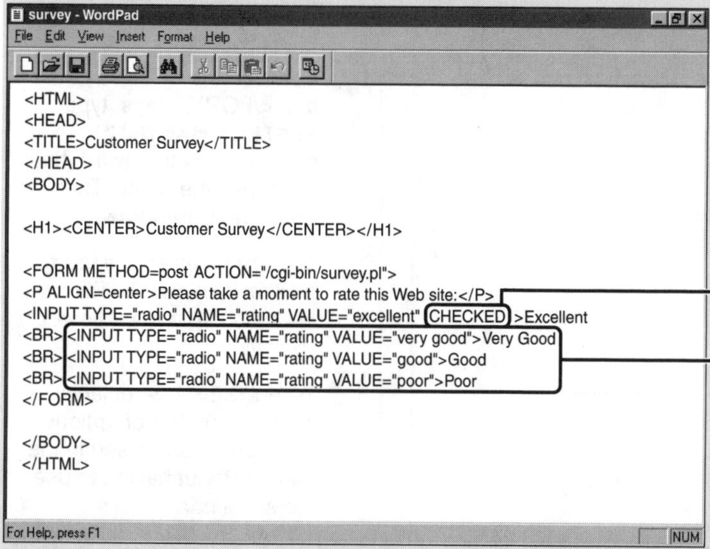

---

**survey - WordPad**

File Edit View Insert Format Help

```
<HTML>
<HEAD>
<TITLE>Customer Survey</TITLE>
</HEAD>
<BODY>

<H1><CENTER>Customer Survey</CENTER></H1>

<FORM METHOD=post ACTION="/cgi-bin/survey.pl">
<P ALIGN=center>Please take a moment to rate this Web site:</P>
<INPUT TYPE="radio" NAME="rating" VALUE="excellent" CHECKED >Excellent
<BR><INPUT TYPE="radio" NAME="rating" VALUE="very good">Very Good
<BR><INPUT TYPE="radio" NAME="rating" VALUE="good">Good
<BR><INPUT TYPE="radio" NAME="rating" VALUE="poor">Poor
</FORM>

</BODY>
</HTML>
```

For Help, press F1    NUM

**5** Repeat steps **1** to **4** for each radio button you want to create.

*Note: If you want each radio button to appear on its own line, use the P or BR tag.*

**6** If you want a radio button to be selected automatically, type **CHECKED** after the VALUE attribute for the radio button.

*Note: You can have only one radio button in a group selected automatically.*

---

**Customer Survey - Microsoft Internet Explorer**

File Edit View Favorites Tools Help

Back  Forward  Stop  Refresh  Home  Search  Favorites  History  Mail  Print  Edit

Address  C:\My Documents\Web Pages\survey.html    Go  Links

## Customer Survey

Please take a moment to rate this Web site:

○ Excellent
○ Very Good
○ Good
○ Poor

Done    My Computer

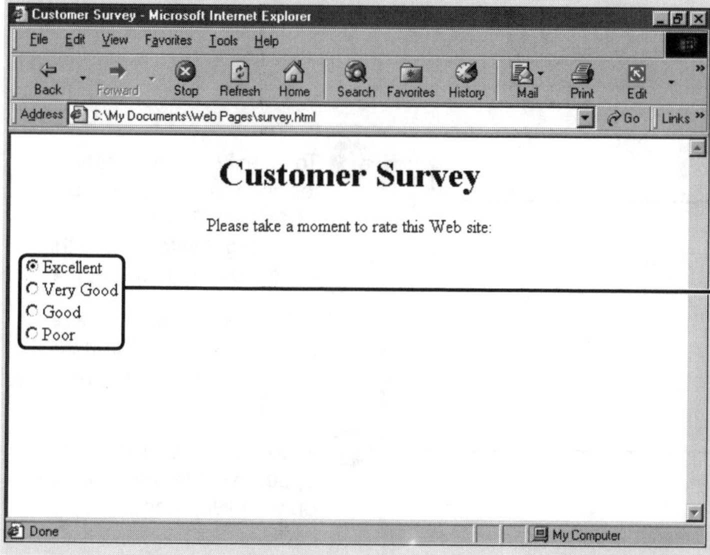

**7** Display the Web page in a Web browser.

■ The Web browser displays the radio buttons.

■ A user can click a radio button to select one of several options (○ changes to ⊙).

# CREATE A MENU

You can create a menu that offers users a list of options to choose from. Menus are commonly used for displaying lists of age groups, states and products. By default, a menu appears on a form as a drop-down menu with only the first option visible, but you can specify the number of options you want the menu to initially display.

## CREATE A MENU

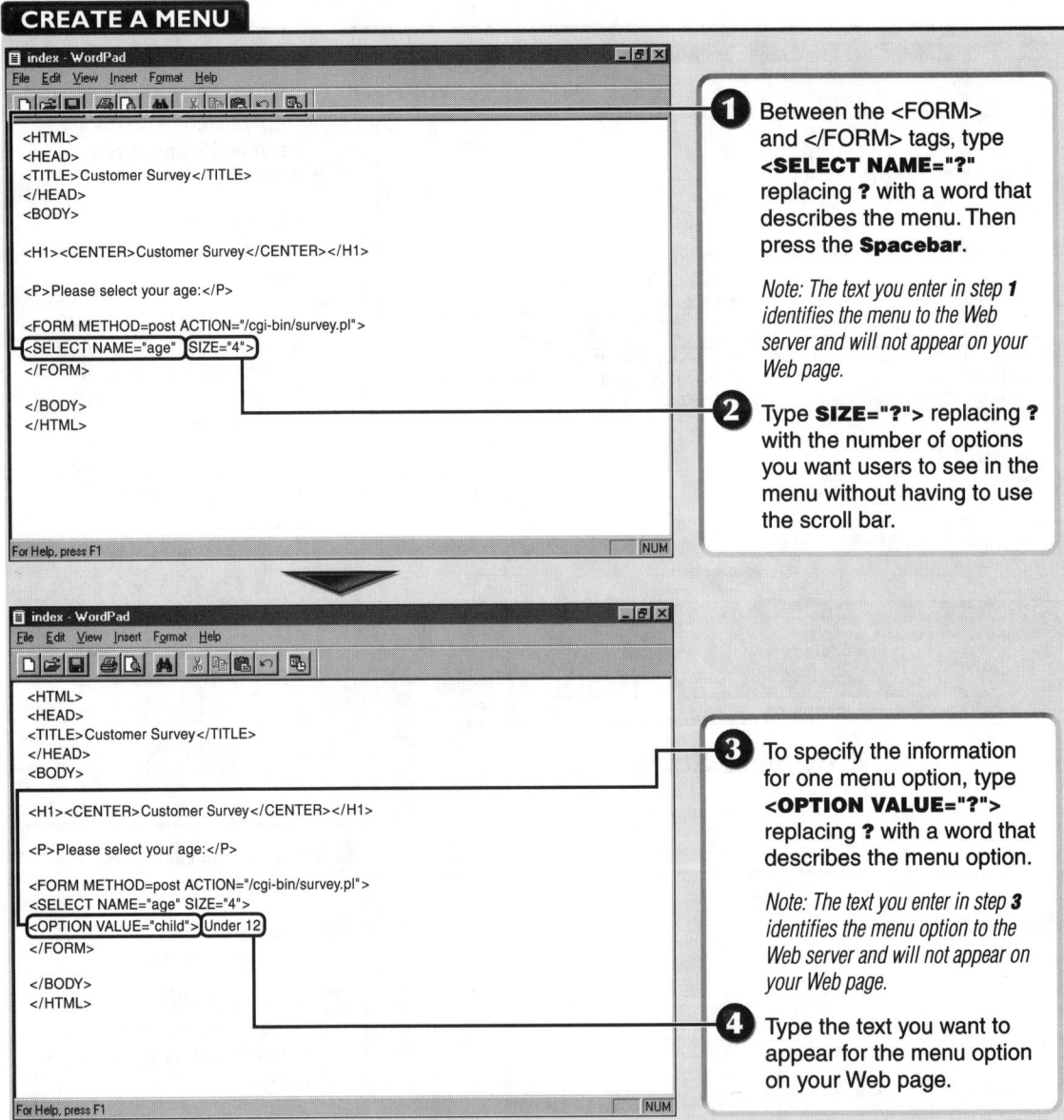

**1** Between the <FORM> and </FORM> tags, type **<SELECT NAME="?"** replacing **?** with a word that describes the menu. Then press the **Spacebar**.

*Note: The text you enter in step 1 identifies the menu to the Web server and will not appear on your Web page.*

**2** Type **SIZE="?">** replacing **?** with the number of options you want users to see in the menu without having to use the scroll bar.

**3** To specify the information for one menu option, type **<OPTION VALUE="?">** replacing **?** with a word that describes the menu option.

*Note: The text you enter in step 3 identifies the menu option to the Web server and will not appear on your Web page.*

**4** Type the text you want to appear for the menu option on your Web page.

**in an instant**

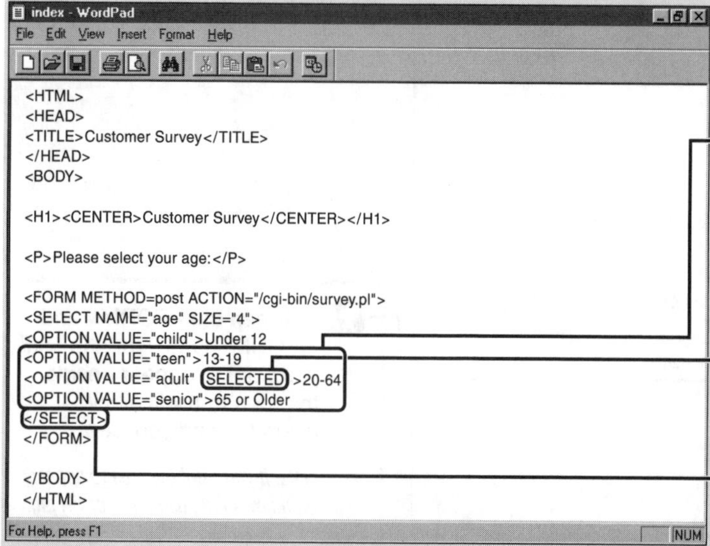

```
index - WordPad                                                    _ 8 X
File  Edit  View  Insert  Format  Help

[toolbar]

<HTML>
<HEAD>
<TITLE>Customer Survey</TITLE>
</HEAD>
<BODY>

<H1><CENTER>Customer Survey</CENTER></H1>

<P>Please select your age:</P>

<FORM METHOD=post ACTION="/cgi-bin/survey.pl">
<SELECT NAME="age" SIZE="4">
<OPTION VALUE="child">Under 12
<OPTION VALUE="teen">13-19
<OPTION VALUE="adult" SELECTED >20-64
<OPTION VALUE="senior">65 or Older
</SELECT>
</FORM>

</BODY>
</HTML>

For Help, press F1                                                 NUM
```

**5** Repeat steps **3** and **4** for each menu option you want to appear in the menu.

**6** If you want a menu option to be selected automatically, type **SELECTED** after the VALUE attribute for the menu option.

*Note: You can have only one menu option selected automatically.*

**7** Type **</SELECT>** to complete the menu.

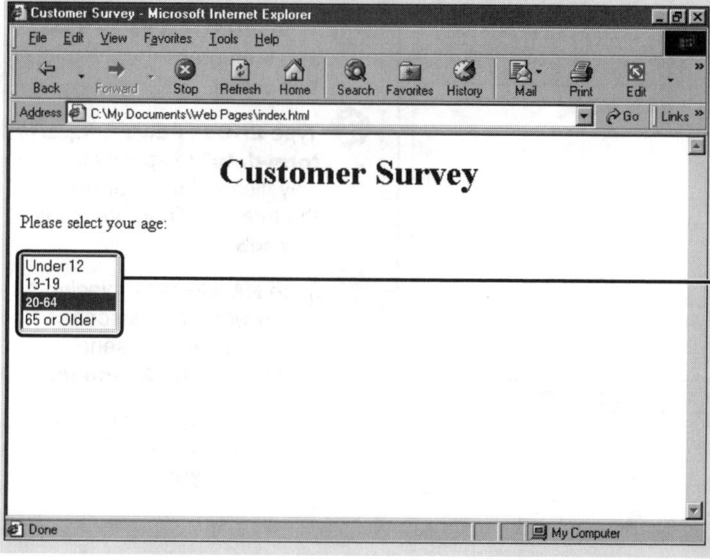

```
Customer Survey - Microsoft Internet Explorer                      _ 8 X
File  Edit  View  Favorites  Tools  Help

Back  Forward  Stop  Refresh  Home  Search  Favorites  History  Mail  Print  Edit

Address  C:\My Documents\Web Pages\index.html              Go    Links

                    Customer Survey

Please select your age:

Under 12
13-19
20-64
65 or Older

Done                                           My Computer
```

**8** Display the Web page in a Web browser.

The Web browser displays the menu.

A user can click a menu option to select the option. A selected menu option appears highlighted.

# ALLOW USERS TO SEND YOU FILES

You can create an area on your form that allows users to send you files. Allowing users to send you files is useful for collecting information that is best displayed in a separate file, such as a résumé or an order form. The files users send are stored on your Web server. Contact your Web server administrator for information about accessing these files.

## ALLOW USERS TO SEND YOU FILES

```
index - WordPad
File  Edit  View  Insert  Format  Help

<HTML>
<HEAD>
<TITLE>Employment Opportunities</TITLE>
</HEAD>
<BODY>

<P><B>Interested in working for our company? Please fill out the information
below:</B></P>

<FORM METHOD=post ACTION="/cgi-bin/employment.pl">
<BR><INPUT TYPE="radio" NAME="sex" VALUE="male" CHECKED>Mr.
<BR><INPUT TYPE="radio" NAME="sex" VALUE="female">Ms.
<P>First Name: <INPUT TYPE="text" NAME="name" SIZE="25">
<BR>Last Name: <INPUT TYPE="text" NAME="name" SIZE="25"></P>

<P>Files:</P>

<P><INPUT TYPE="submit" VALUE="Send"></P>
</FORM>

</BODY>

For Help, press F1                                    NUM
```

**1** Between the <FORM> and </FORM> tags, type the text you want to appear beside the area that will allow users to send you files.

*Note: If you want the area to appear on its own line, use the P or BR tag.*

```
index - WordPad
File  Edit  View  Insert  Format  Help

<HTML>
<HEAD>
<TITLE>Employment Opportunities</TITLE>
</HEAD>
<BODY>

<P><B>Interested in working for our company? Please fill out the information
below:</B></P>

<FORM METHOD=post ACTION="/cgi-bin/employment.pl">
<BR><INPUT TYPE="radio" NAME="sex" VALUE="male" CHECKED>Mr.
<BR><INPUT TYPE="radio" NAME="sex" VALUE="female">Ms.
<P>First Name: <INPUT TYPE="text" NAME="name" SIZE="25">
<BR>Last Name: <INPUT TYPE="text" NAME="name" SIZE="25"></P>

<P>Files:<INPUT TYPE="file" ENCTYPE="multipart/form-data" NAME="resume"></P>

<P><INPUT TYPE="submit" VALUE="Send"></P>
</FORM>

</BODY>

For Help, press F1                                    NUM
```

**2** Type **<INPUT TYPE="file"** and then press the **Spacebar**.

**3** Type **ENCTYPE="multipart/form-data"** to specify the way files will transfer over the Internet. Then press the **Spacebar**.

**4** Type **NAME="?"** replacing **?** with a word that describes the files users will send. Then press the **Spacebar**.

*Note: The text you enter in step **4** identifies the files to the Web server and will not appear on your Web page.*

in an Instant

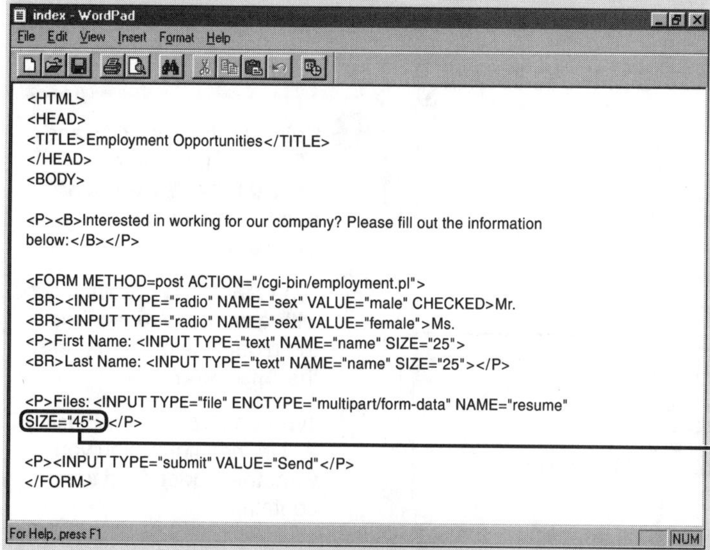

```
index - WordPad                                          _ 8 X
File  Edit  View  Insert  Format  Help

<HTML>
<HEAD>
<TITLE>Employment Opportunities</TITLE>
</HEAD>
<BODY>

<P><B>Interested in working for our company? Please fill out the information
below:</B></P>

<FORM METHOD=post ACTION="/cgi-bin/employment.pl">
<BR><INPUT TYPE="radio" NAME="sex" VALUE="male" CHECKED>Mr.
<BR><INPUT TYPE="radio" NAME="sex" VALUE="female">Ms.
<P>First Name: <INPUT TYPE="text" NAME="name" SIZE="25">
<BR>Last Name: <INPUT TYPE="text" NAME="name" SIZE="25"></P>

<P>Files: <INPUT TYPE="file" ENCTYPE="multipart/form-data" NAME="resume"
SIZE="45"></P>

<P><INPUT TYPE="submit" VALUE="Send"></P>
</FORM>

For Help, press F1                                          NUM
```

**5** To define the width of the box where users will enter the location and name of the file they want to send, type **SIZE="?">** replacing **?** with a width in characters.

*Note: You should use a width of at least 40 characters to make sure there is enough room for users to enter the location and name of a file.*

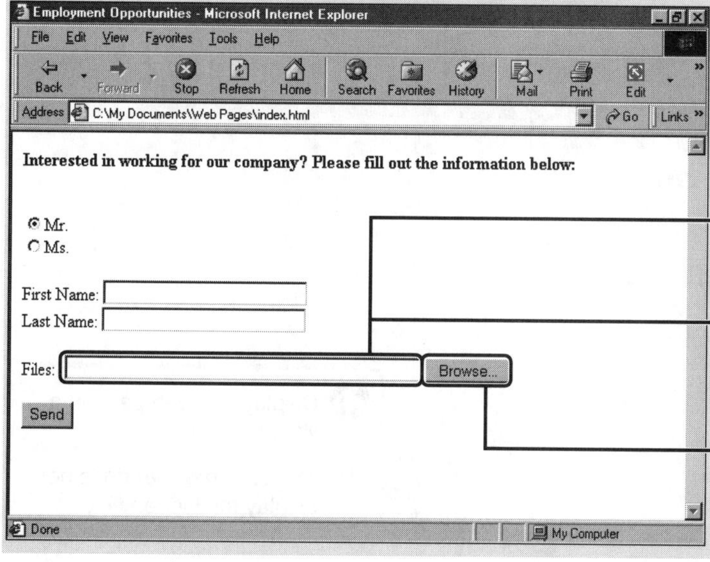

```
Employment Opportunities - Microsoft Internet Explorer        _ 8 X
File  Edit  View  Favorites  Tools  Help

Back  Forward  Stop  Refresh  Home   Search Favorites History   Mail  Print  Edit
Address  C:\My Documents\Web Pages\index.html          Go   Links

Interested in working for our company? Please fill out the information below:

○ Mr.
○ Ms.

First Name: [          ]
Last Name:  [          ]

Files: [                              ]  Browse...

Send

Done                                          My Computer
```

**6** Display the Web page in a Web browser.

● The Web browser displays an area that allows users to send you files.

● Users can click in the box and type the location and name of the file they want to send.

● Users can also click the **Browse** button to locate the file on their computers.

# CREATE A HIDDEN FIELD

You can create a hidden field in your form to include additional information that you want to appear only in the form results. The information from a hidden field will not appear on the Web page. If your Web pages contain multiple forms, you can use hidden fields to assign each form a different name. The name that appears in the form results can help you identify which form the user submitted.

## CREATE A HIDDEN FIELD

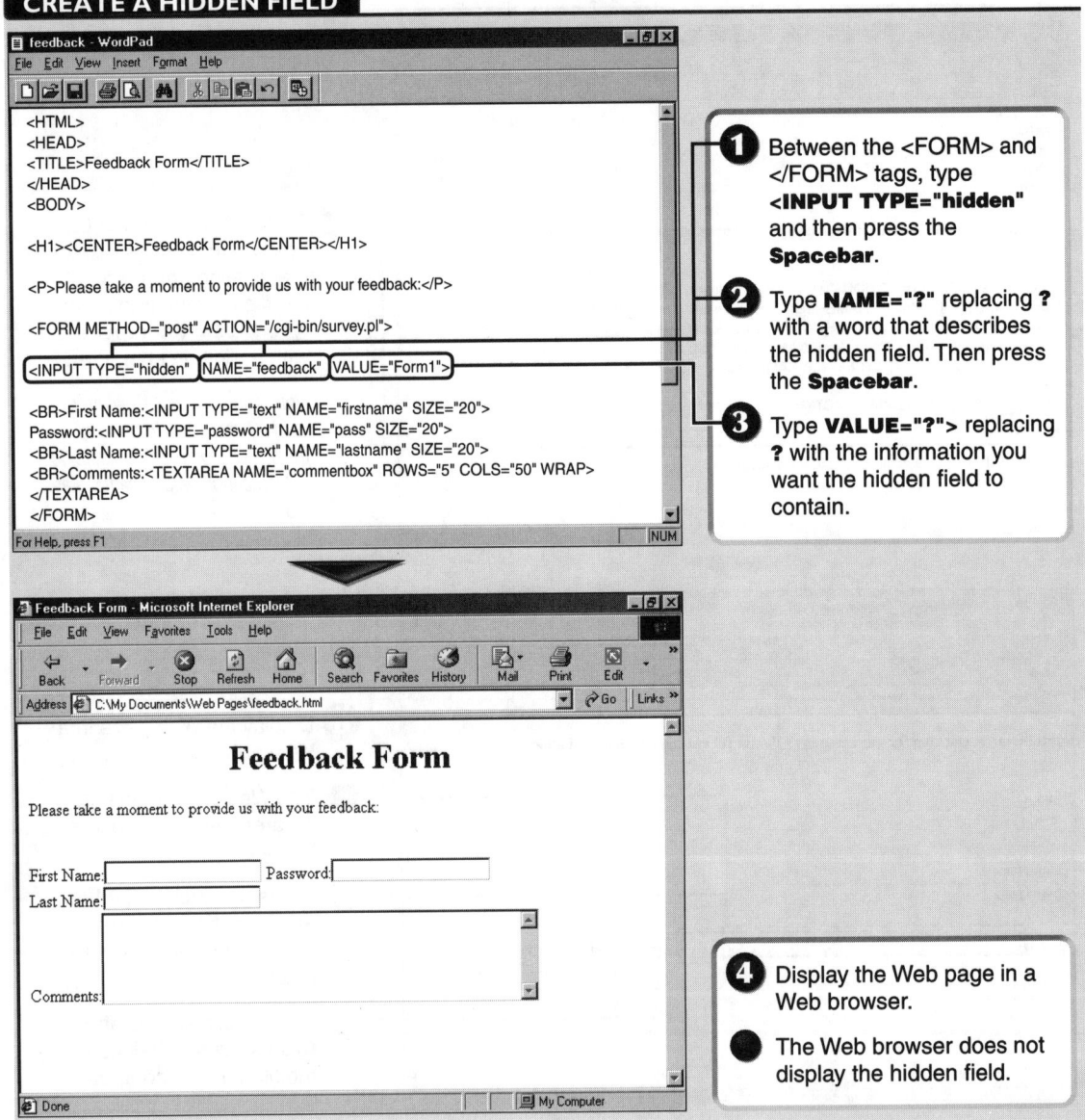

**1** Between the <FORM> and </FORM> tags, type **<INPUT TYPE="hidden"** and then press the **Spacebar**.

**2** Type **NAME="?"** replacing **?** with a word that describes the hidden field. Then press the **Spacebar**.

**3** Type **VALUE="?">** replacing **?** with the information you want the hidden field to contain.

**4** Display the Web page in a Web browser.

● The Web browser does not display the hidden field.

# CREATE A RESET BUTTON

You can create a reset button that users can click to clear the information they entered in your form. This allows users to start over if they make a mistake while filling out your form. When a user clicks the reset button, the Web browser will clear the information in all the form elements.

## CREATE A RESET BUTTON

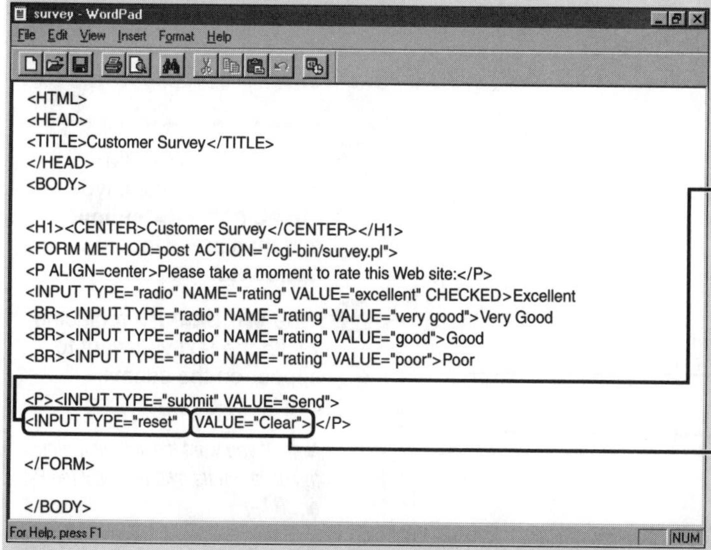

```
survey - WordPad
File  Edit  View  Insert  Format  Help

<HTML>
<HEAD>
<TITLE>Customer Survey</TITLE>
</HEAD>
<BODY>

<H1><CENTER>Customer Survey</CENTER></H1>
<FORM METHOD=post ACTION="/cgi-bin/survey.pl">
<P ALIGN=center>Please take a moment to rate this Web site:</P>
<INPUT TYPE="radio" NAME="rating" VALUE="excellent" CHECKED>Excellent
<BR><INPUT TYPE="radio" NAME="rating" VALUE="very good">Very Good
<BR><INPUT TYPE="radio" NAME="rating" VALUE="good">Good
<BR><INPUT TYPE="radio" NAME="rating" VALUE="poor">Poor

<P><INPUT TYPE="submit" VALUE="Send">
<INPUT TYPE="reset" VALUE="Clear"></P>

</FORM>

</BODY>
For Help, press F1                                          NUM
```

**1** Between the <FORM> and </FORM> tags, type **<INPUT TYPE="reset"** and then press the **Spacebar**.

**2** Type **VALUE="?">** replacing **?** with the text you want to appear on the reset button.

*Note: If you want the reset button to appear on its own line, use the P or BR tag.*

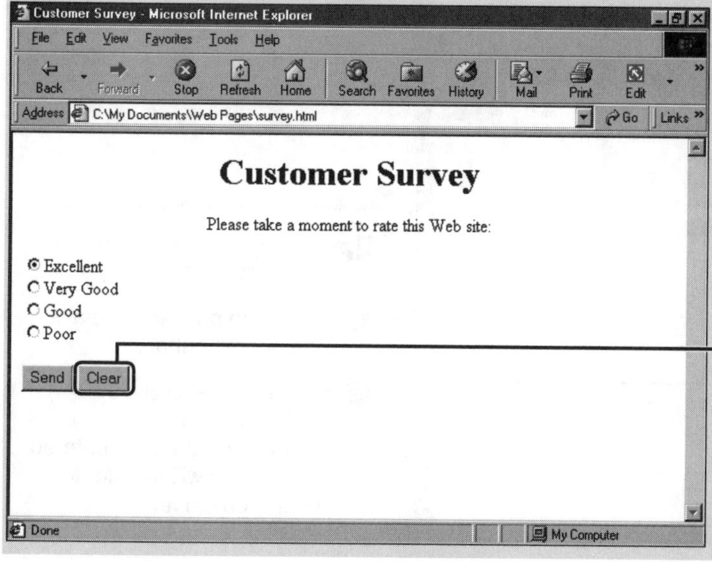

```
Customer Survey - Microsoft Internet Explorer
File  Edit  View  Favorites  Tools  Help

Back  Forward  Stop  Refresh  Home  Search  Favorites  History  Mail  Print  Edit

Address  C:\My Documents\Web Pages\survey.html          Go   Links
```

### Customer Survey

Please take a moment to rate this Web site:

⦿ Excellent
○ Very Good
○ Good
○ Poor

[ Send ]  [ Clear ]

Done                                        My Computer

**3** Display the Web page in a Web browser.

■ The Web browser displays the reset button.

■ When a user clicks the reset button, the form clears and once again displays its original settings.

# CREATE A SUBMIT BUTTON

You can create a submit button that users can click to send the information they entered in your form to your Web server. When creating a submit button, you can specify the text you want the button to display. Once a user clicks the submit button, the user will not be able to reverse submitting the form.

CREATE A SUBMIT BUTTON

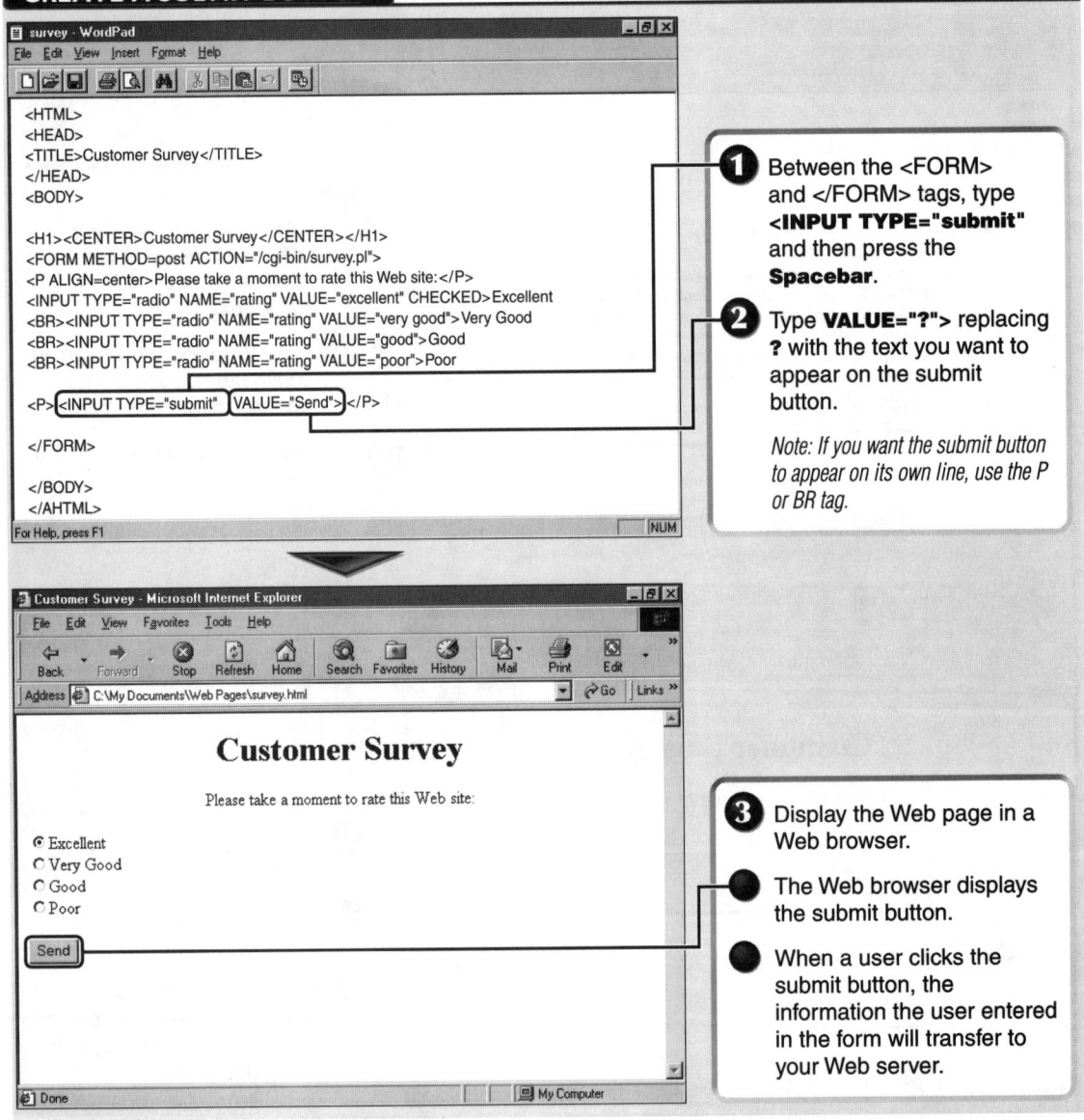

```
<HTML>
<HEAD>
<TITLE>Customer Survey</TITLE>
</HEAD>
<BODY>

<H1><CENTER>Customer Survey</CENTER></H1>
<FORM METHOD=post ACTION="/cgi-bin/survey.pl">
<P ALIGN=center>Please take a moment to rate this Web site:</P>
<INPUT TYPE="radio" NAME="rating" VALUE="excellent" CHECKED>Excellent
<BR><INPUT TYPE="radio" NAME="rating" VALUE="very good">Very Good
<BR><INPUT TYPE="radio" NAME="rating" VALUE="good">Good
<BR><INPUT TYPE="radio" NAME="rating" VALUE="poor">Poor

<P><INPUT TYPE="submit" VALUE="Send"></P>

</FORM>

</BODY>
</AHTML>
```

For Help, press F1                                                            NUM

**Customer Survey**

Please take a moment to rate this Web site:

⦿ Excellent
○ Very Good
○ Good
○ Poor

[ Send ]

Address: C:\My Documents\Web Pages\survey.html

① Between the <FORM> and </FORM> tags, type **<INPUT TYPE="submit"** and then press the **Spacebar**.

② Type **VALUE="?">** replacing **?** with the text you want to appear on the submit button.

*Note: If you want the submit button to appear on its own line, use the P or BR tag.*

③ Display the Web page in a Web browser.

● The Web browser displays the submit button.

● When a user clicks the submit button, the information the user entered in the form will transfer to your Web server.

**150**

# CREATE A GRAPHICAL SUBMIT BUTTON

You can use an image to allow users to enter information and submit the results of their form at the same time. When a user clicks a graphical submit button, the coordinates of the user's mouse pointer are submitted with the form information. This is useful when the areas of an image represent different options, such as the locations on a map.

## CREATE A GRAPHICAL SUBMIT BUTTON

**feedback - WordPad**

File Edit View Insert Format Help

```
<HTML>
<HEAD>
<TITLE>Feedback Form</TITLE>
</HEAD>
<BODY>

<H1><CENTER>Feedback Form</CENTER></H1>

<P>Please take a moment to provide us with your feedback:</P>

<FORM METHOD="post" ACTION="/cgi-bin/survey.pl">
Comments:<TEXTAREA NAME="commentbox" ROWS="5" COLS="50" WRAP></TEXTAREA>
<P>Click your region below to submit your comments:</P>

<BR><INPUT TYPE="image" SRC="map.gif" NAME="location">

</FORM>

</BODY>
</HTML>
```

For Help, press F1                                    NUM

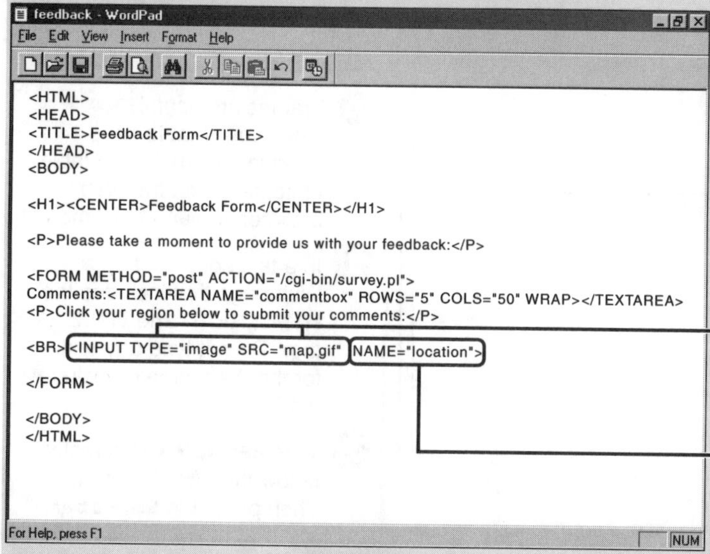

**1** Between the <FORM> and </FORM> tags, type **<INPUT TYPE="image" SRC="?"** and then press the **Spacebar**.

**2** If the image you want to use is stored in the same folder in your Web site, replace **?** with the name of the image.

● If the image is stored in a subfolder, also specify the name of the subfolder.

**3** Type **NAME="?">** replacing **?** with a word that describes the image.

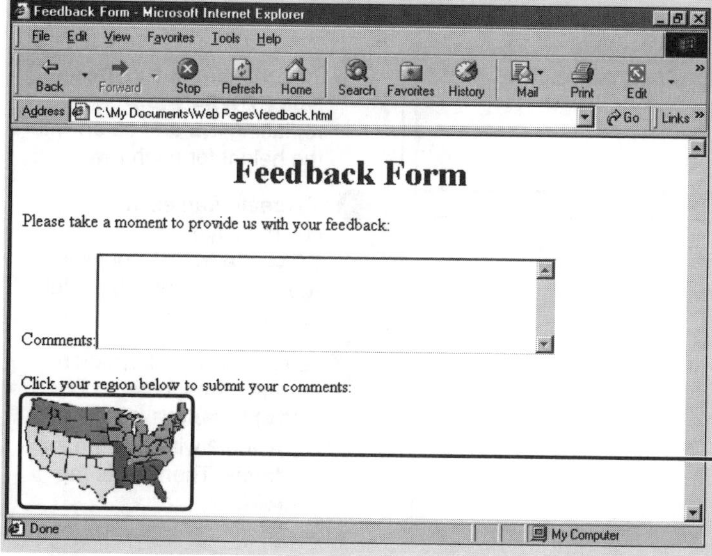

---

**Feedback Form - Microsoft Internet Explorer**

File Edit View Favorites Tools Help

Back  Forward  Stop  Refresh  Home  Search  Favorites  History  Mail  Print  Edit

Address  C:\My Documents\Web Pages\feedback.html            Go  Links

# Feedback Form

Please take a moment to provide us with your feedback:

Comments:

Click your region below to submit your comments:

Done                                My Computer

**4** Display the Web page in a Web browser.

● The Web browser displays the image.

● When a user clicks the image, the horizontal (x) and vertical (y) coordinates of the mouse pointer will be sent to the Web server along with the rest of the information in the form.

# CREATE FRAMES

You can create frames to divide a Web browser window into sections that will each display a different Web page. You can specify the height or width of each frame you create in pixels, as a percentage of the screen or as an asterisk (*). If you specify an asterisk, the size of the frame will depend on the size of the other frames.

## CREATE FRAMES

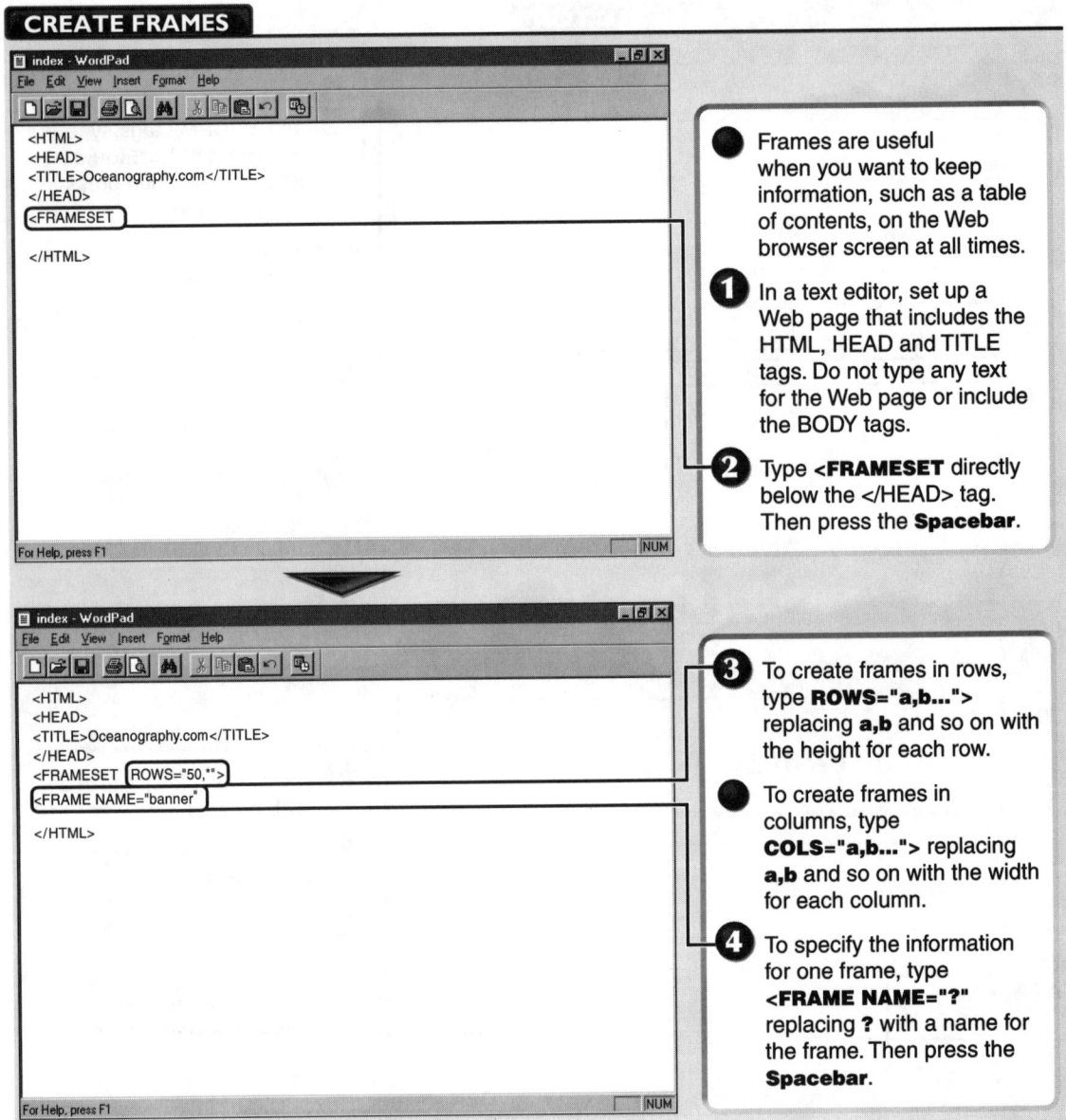

● Frames are useful when you want to keep information, such as a table of contents, on the Web browser screen at all times.

**1** In a text editor, set up a Web page that includes the HTML, HEAD and TITLE tags. Do not type any text for the Web page or include the BODY tags.

**2** Type **<FRAMESET** directly below the </HEAD> tag. Then press the **Spacebar**.

**3** To create frames in rows, type **ROWS="a,b..."**> replacing **a,b** and so on with the height for each row.

● To create frames in columns, type **COLS="a,b..."**> replacing **a,b** and so on with the width for each column.

**4** To specify the information for one frame, type **<FRAME NAME="?"** replacing **?** with a name for the frame. Then press the **Spacebar**.

# in an instant

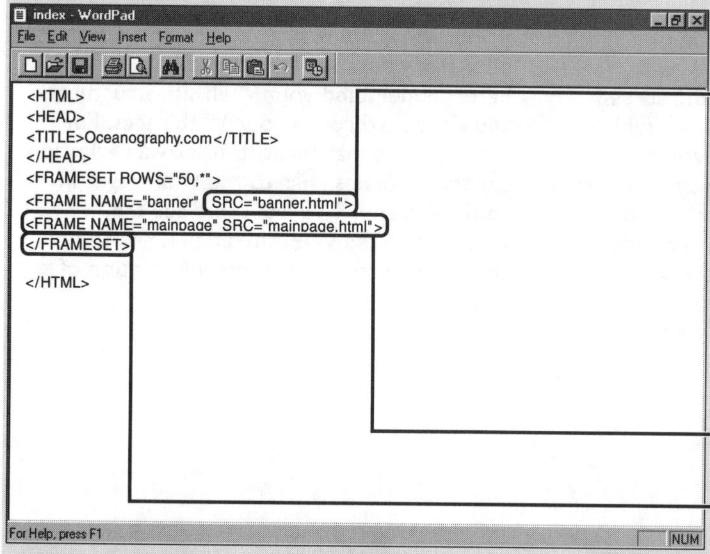

```
index - WordPad
File  Edit  View  Insert  Format  Help

<HTML>
<HEAD>
<TITLE>Oceanography.com</TITLE>
</HEAD>
<FRAMESET ROWS="50,*">
<FRAME NAME="banner" SRC="banner.html">
<FRAME NAME="mainpage" SRC="mainpage.html">
</FRAMESET>

</HTML>

For Help, press F1                                          NUM
```

**5** To specify the Web page in your Web site you want to appear in the frame, type **SRC="?">**.

**6** If the Web page is stored in the same folder, replace **?** with the name of the page.

*Note: If the Web page is stored in a subfolder, you must also specify the name of the subfolder.*

**7** Repeat steps **4** to **6** for each frame you created.

**8** Type **</FRAMESET>**.

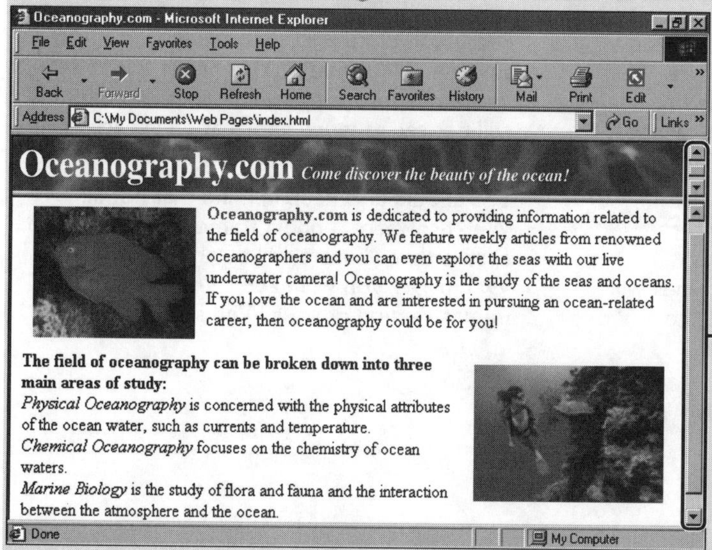

---

```
Oceanography.com - Microsoft Internet Explorer
File  Edit  View  Favorites  Tools  Help

Back  Forward  Stop  Refresh  Home  Search  Favorites  History  Mail  Print  Edit

Address  C:\My Documents\Web Pages\index.html                     Go   Links
```

## Oceanography.com  *Come discover the beauty of the ocean!*

Oceanography.com is dedicated to providing information related to the field of oceanography. We feature weekly articles from renowned oceanographers and you can even explore the seas with our live underwater camera! Oceanography is the study of the seas and oceans. If you love the ocean and are interested in pursuing an ocean-related career, then oceanography could be for you!

**The field of oceanography can be broken down into three main areas of study:**

*Physical Oceanography* is concerned with the physical attributes of the ocean water, such as currents and temperature.

*Chemical Oceanography* focuses on the chemistry of ocean waters.

*Marine Biology* is the study of flora and fauna and the interaction between the atmosphere and the ocean.

```
Done                                                      My Computer
```

**9** Display the Web page in a Web browser.

● The Web browser displays the frames.

● Scroll bars appear automatically when a frame is too small to display the contents of an entire Web page. Users can use the scroll bars to move through the Web page.

# FRAME CONSIDERATIONS

Designing a frames-based Web site requires careful organization and planning. While frames are useful for effectively presenting your Web site in an easy-to-navigate format, there are several factors you should take into consideration before using frames. Consider the following advantages and disadvantages of frames to determine if frames are appropriate for your Web site.

## ADVANTAGES OF USING FRAMES

Frames display multiple Web pages in one Web browser window. This allows you to display a variety of information on the screen at once. For example, you can display a table of contents for your Web site, copyright information and the current Web page on the screen at the same time. Using frames also allows you to keep information, such as your company logo or a disclaimer, on the screen at all times without having to add the information to every Web page in your Web site.

If your Web site is large and complex, frames offer many advantages that can help users better understand your Web site structure and navigate through your Web pages. For example, you may want to display a navigation bar that contains links to the Web pages in your Web site. This lets users see the structure of the Web site at all times and allows them to easily access information of interest.

## DISADVANTAGES OF USING FRAMES

Since frames divide a Web browser window into sections, the viewing area for each Web page is reduced. Web pages designed to be displayed in an entire Web browser window may not fit well in frames. Although users can scroll through the information in a frame, they may become annoyed if they have to continually scroll to view important information.

It is difficult to predict how your frames will appear on a user's computer, since the

resolution of a user's monitor determines the amount of information that appears in the frames. People using lower screen resolutions will not see as much information in each frame.

You should also keep in mind that not all Web browsers support frames. If you want to ensure that all users will be able to view your Web pages, you will need to design a non-frames version of your Web site.

You can provide text that you want to appear if a user's Web browser does not display frames. If you do not provide alternative text, users with Web browsers that do not display frames will see a blank screen. The text you provide can include information from your Web pages or a short explanation of why users cannot see the Web pages.

## PROVIDE ALTERNATIVE TEXT

```
index - WordPad
File  Edit  View  Insert  Format  Help

<HTML>
<HEAD>
<TITLE>Oceanography.com</TITLE>
</HEAD>

<FRAMESET ROWS="50,*">
<FRAME NAME="banner" SRC="banner.html">
<FRAME NAME="mainpage" SRC="oceanography.html">
</FRAMESET>
<NOFRAMES>
This Web page uses frames. Your current Web browser does not display
frames or frame viewing has been turned off.
</NOFRAMES>

</HTML>

For Help, press F1                                          NUM
```

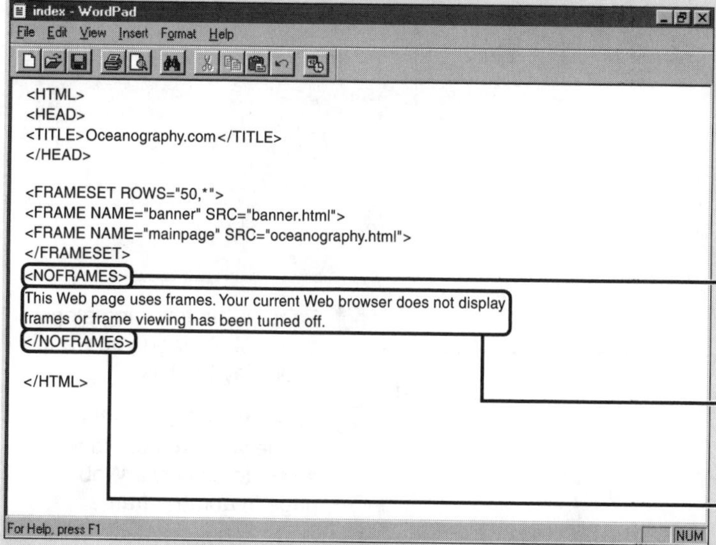

● Perform the following steps on the Web page that defines the structure of your frames.

**1** Type **<NOFRAMES>** directly below the **</FRAMESET>** tag.

**2** Type the text you want to appear if a Web browser does not display frames.

**3** Type **</NOFRAMES>**.

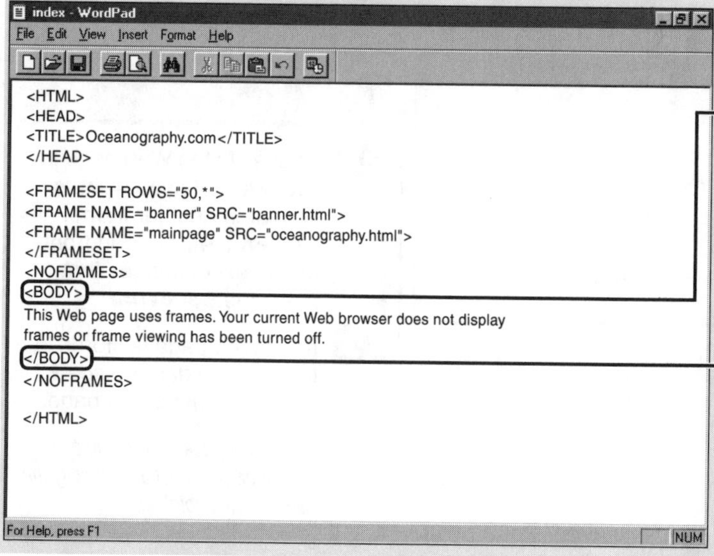

```
index - WordPad
File  Edit  View  Insert  Format  Help

<HTML>
<HEAD>
<TITLE>Oceanography.com</TITLE>
</HEAD>

<FRAMESET ROWS="50,*">
<FRAME NAME="banner" SRC="banner.html">
<FRAME NAME="mainpage" SRC="oceanography.html">
</FRAMESET>
<NOFRAMES>
<BODY>
This Web page uses frames. Your current Web browser does not display
frames or frame viewing has been turned off.
</BODY>
</NOFRAMES>

</HTML>

For Help, press F1                                          NUM
```

**4** Type **<BODY>** directly above the text you typed in step **2**.

**5** Type **</BODY>** directly below the text you typed in step **2**.

*Note: The <BODY> and </BODY> tags are optional.*

● If a user views your Web page in a Web browser that does not display frames, the information you specified will appear.

# CREATE A LINK TO A FRAME

You can create a link on a Web page that users can select to display a Web page in another frame. Creating links to frames can help users move through your Web site. For example, creating navigation links that will open in a different frame lets you keep the navigation links on the screen while users browse through your Web pages.

## CREATE A LINK TO A FRAME

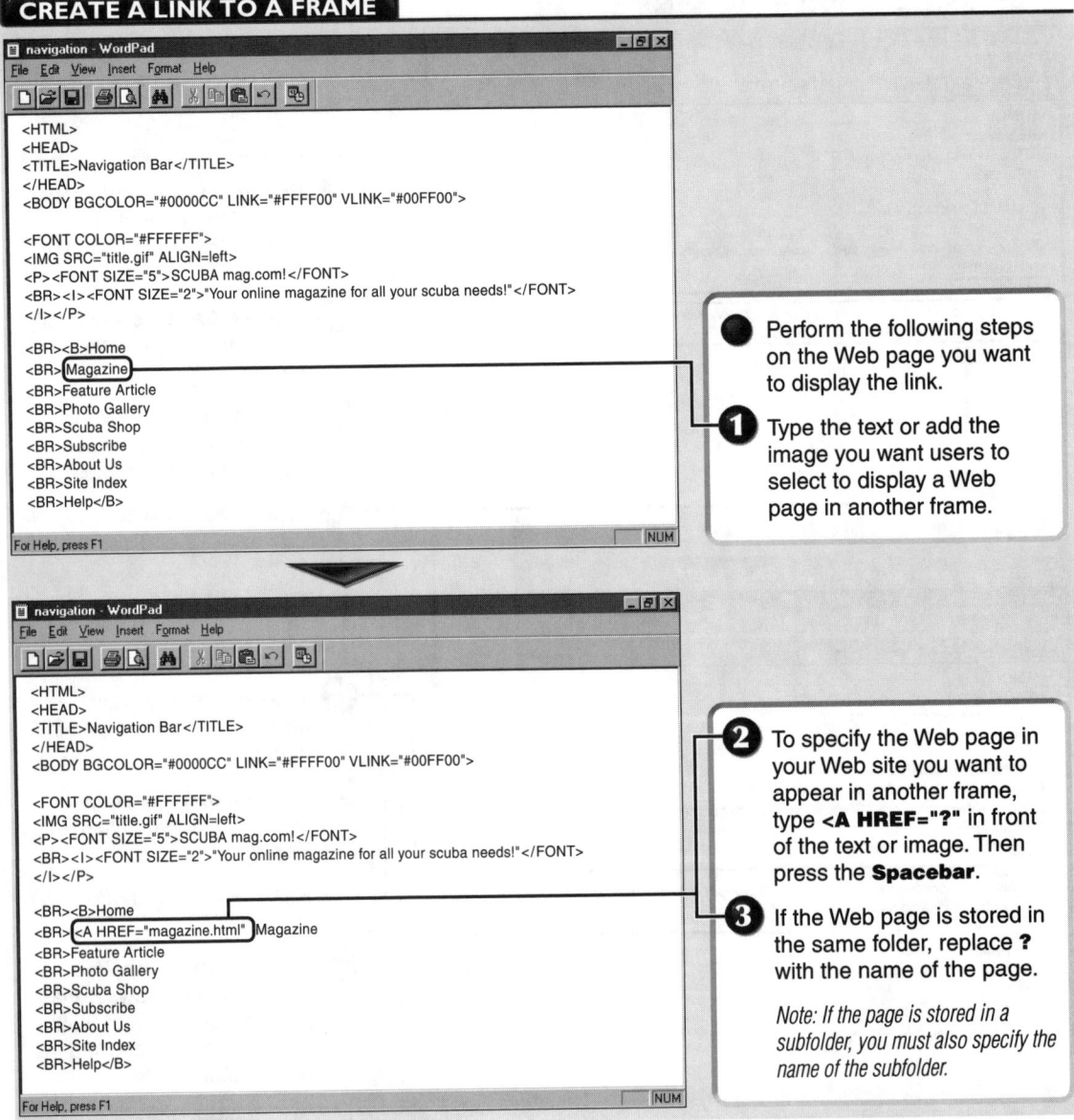

● Perform the following steps on the Web page you want to display the link.

**1** Type the text or add the image you want users to select to display a Web page in another frame.

**2** To specify the Web page in your Web site you want to appear in another frame, type **<A HREF="?"** in front of the text or image. Then press the **Spacebar**.

**3** If the Web page is stored in the same folder, replace **?** with the name of the page.

*Note: If the page is stored in a subfolder, you must also specify the name of the subfolder.*

# in an instant

---

**navigation - WordPad**

File  Edit  View  Insert  Format  Help

```
<HTML>
<HEAD>
<TITLE>Navigation Bar</TITLE>
</HEAD>
<BODY BGCOLOR="#0000CC" LINK="#FFFF00" VLINK="#00FF00">

<FONT COLOR="#FFFFFF">
<IMG SRC="title.gif" ALIGN=left>
<P><FONT SIZE="5">SCUBA mag.com!</FONT>
<BR><I><FONT SIZE="2">"Your online magazine for all your scuba needs!"</FONT>
</I></P>

<BR><B>Home
<BR><A HREF="magazine.html" TARGET="mainpage">Magazine</A>
<BR>Feature Article
<BR>Photo Gallery
<BR>Scuba Shop
<BR>Subscribe
<BR>About Us
<BR>Site Index
<BR>Help</B>
```

For Help, press F1                                     NUM

**4** To specify the frame where you want the Web page to appear, type **TARGET="?">** replacing **?** with the name of the frame.

*Note: You assigned names to your frames in step 4 on page 152.*

● To open the Web page in a new Web browser window instead of another frame, replace **?** with **_blank**.

**5** Type **</A>** after the text or image.

---

**SCUBA mag.com - Microsoft Internet Explorer**

File  Edit  View  Favorites  Tools  Help

Back  Forward  Stop  Refresh  Home  Search  Favorites  History  Mail  Print  Edit

Address  C:\My Documents\Web Pages\index.html                    Go  Links

**SCUBA mag.com!**

*"Your online magazine for all your scuba needs!"*

Home
Magazine
Feature Article
Photo Gallery
Scuba Shop
Subscribe
About Us
Site Index
Help

**Welcome to SCUBA mag.com!**

Thinking about learning to scuba dive, or are you an experienced diver? Scuba diving is an exciting sport that many can enjoy! SCUBA mag.com is the perfect place for divers of all ages! Each week we feature articles about learning to scuba dive, diving safety, planning your dive vacation and divers' experiences.

Two-thirds of the earth is under water! Scuba divers experience an exciting world of marine life, caves and untold treasures such as shipwrecks! If you've ever dreamed of seeing such wonders, or

Done                                         My Computer

**6** Display the Web page in a Web browser.

● The Web browser displays the link.

● A user can click the link to display the Web page in the frame you specified.

---

# SET THE DEFAULT TARGET

You can set a default target to specify the frame where you want all the links on a Web page to open. Setting a default target saves time since you do not need to specify a frame for each link you create. If you do not specify a frame for links, each link will open in the frame that contains the link.

## SET THE DEFAULT TARGET

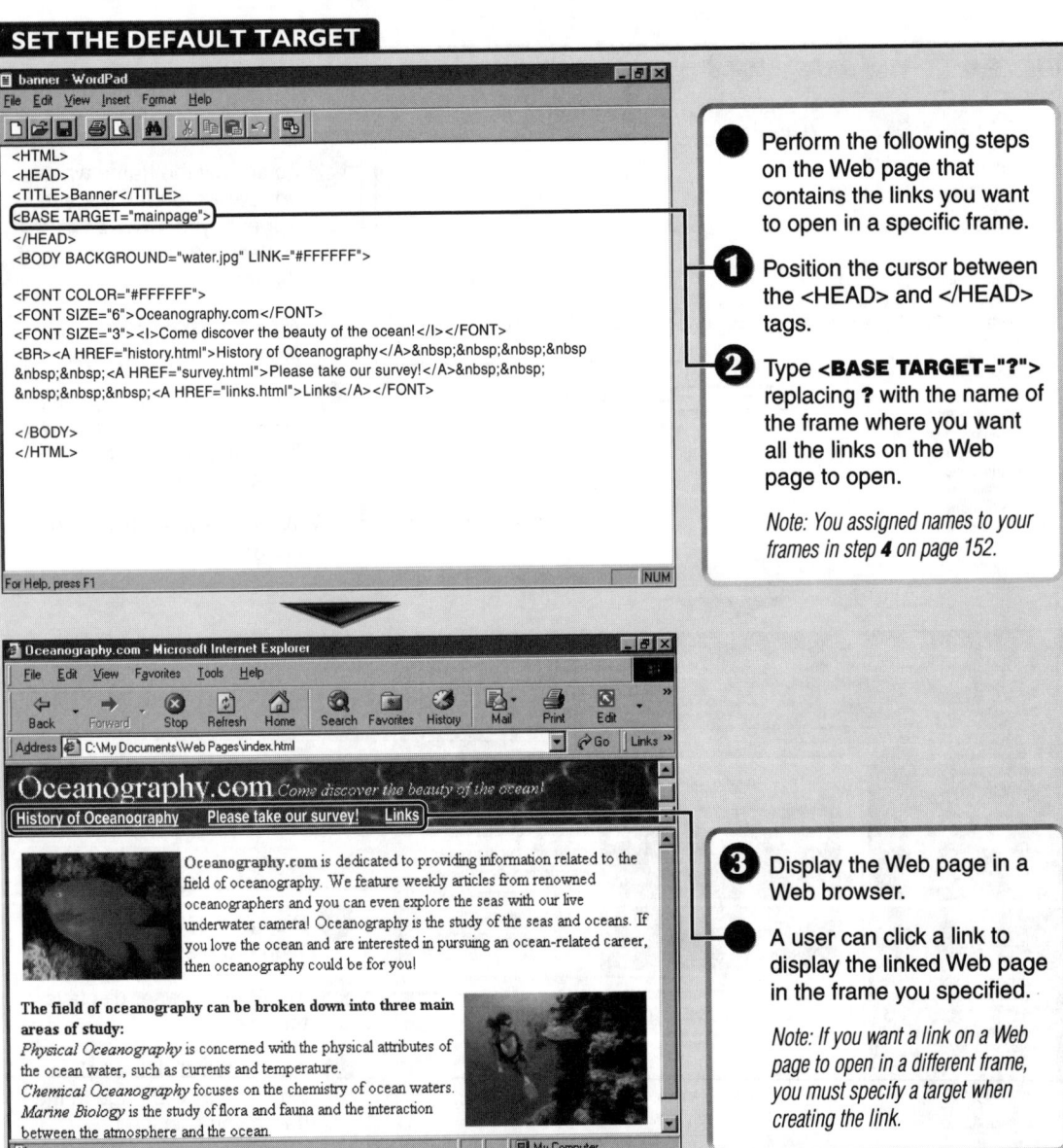

● Perform the following steps on the Web page that contains the links you want to open in a specific frame.

**1** Position the cursor between the <HEAD> and </HEAD> tags.

**2** Type **<BASE TARGET="?">** replacing **?** with the name of the frame where you want all the links on the Web page to open.

*Note: You assigned names to your frames in step **4** on page 152.*

**3** Display the Web page in a Web browser.

● A user can click a link to display the linked Web page in the frame you specified.

*Note: If you want a link on a Web page to open in a different frame, you must specify a target when creating the link.*

# PREVENT USERS FROM RESIZING FRAMES

You can prevent users from resizing frames on your Web page. This is useful when you do not want the layout of your frames to change. If you do not prevent users from resizing a frame, users can drag the frame border to a new location to resize the frame.

## PREVENT USERS FROM RESIZING FRAMES

```
<HTML>
<HEAD>
<TITLE>Oceanography.com</TITLE>
</HEAD>

<FRAMESET ROWS="50,*">
<FRAME NAME="banner" SRC="banner.html" NORESIZE >
<FRAME NAME="mainpage" SRC="oceanography.html">
</FRAMESET>

</HTML>
```

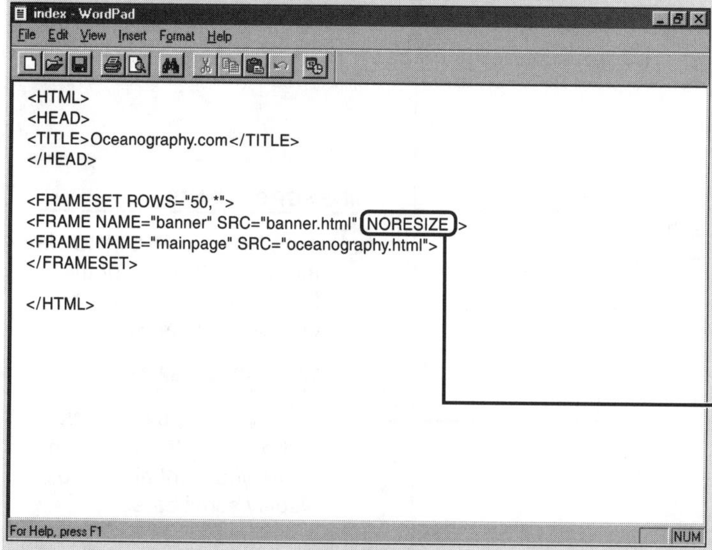

**1** Position the cursor in the <FRAME> tag for the frame you do not want users to resize.

**2** Type **NORESIZE**.

● You can repeat steps **1** and **2** for each frame you do not want users to resize.

---

**Oceanography.com**
*Come discover the beauty of the ocean!*

Oceanography.com is dedicated to providing information related to the field of oceanography. We feature weekly articles from renowned oceanographers and you can even explore the seas with our live underwater camera! Oceanography is the study of the seas and oceans. If you love the ocean and are interested in pursuing an ocean-related career, then oceanography could be for you!

**The field of oceanography can be broken down into three main areas of study:**

*Physical Oceanography* is concerned with the physical attributes of the ocean water, such as currents and temperature.
*Chemical Oceanography* focuses on the chemistry of ocean waters.
*Marine Biology* is the study of flora and fauna and the interaction between the atmosphere and the ocean.

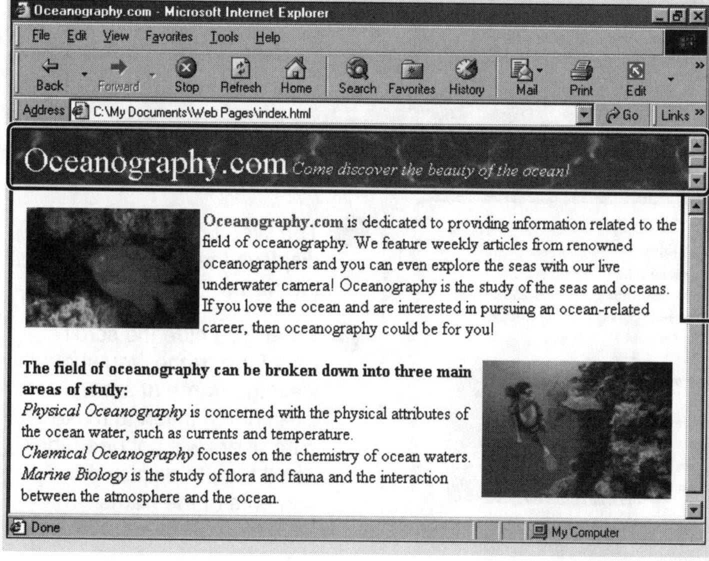

**3** Display the Web page in a Web browser.

● The Web browser will not allow users to resize the frame you specified.

*Note: When you prevent users from resizing a frame, they will not be able to use the borders of the frame to resize neighboring frames.*

# HIDE OR DISPLAY SCROLL BARS

You can hide or display scroll bars for a frame at all times. By default, a Web browser will display scroll bars only when a Web page contains too much information to fit in the frame. Hiding the scroll bars is useful for reducing clutter in a small frame, while displaying scroll bars may improve the layout of some frames.

## HIDE OR DISPLAY SCROLL BARS

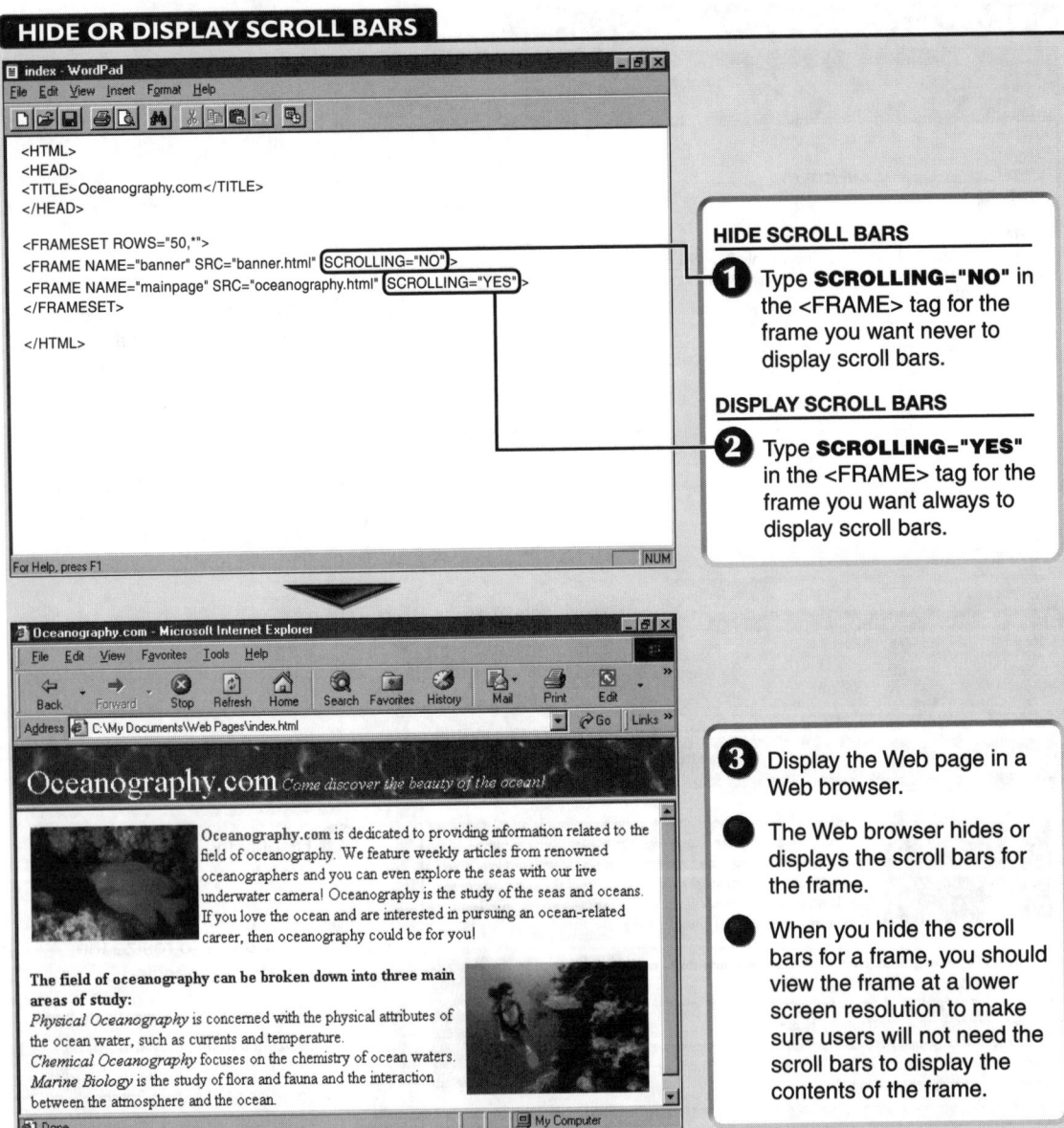

### HIDE SCROLL BARS

**1** Type **SCROLLING="NO"** in the <FRAME> tag for the frame you want never to display scroll bars.

### DISPLAY SCROLL BARS

**2** Type **SCROLLING="YES"** in the <FRAME> tag for the frame you want always to display scroll bars.

**3** Display the Web page in a Web browser.

■ The Web browser hides or displays the scroll bars for the frame.

■ When you hide the scroll bars for a frame, you should view the frame at a lower screen resolution to make sure users will not need the scroll bars to display the contents of the frame.

You can change the margins of a frame to adjust the amount of space between the contents of the frame and the edges of the frame. By default, most Web browsers display frame margins of approximately 10 pixels. You can set a frame margin to 0 to have the contents of the frame appear directly beside the edges of the frame.

## CHANGE FRAME MARGINS

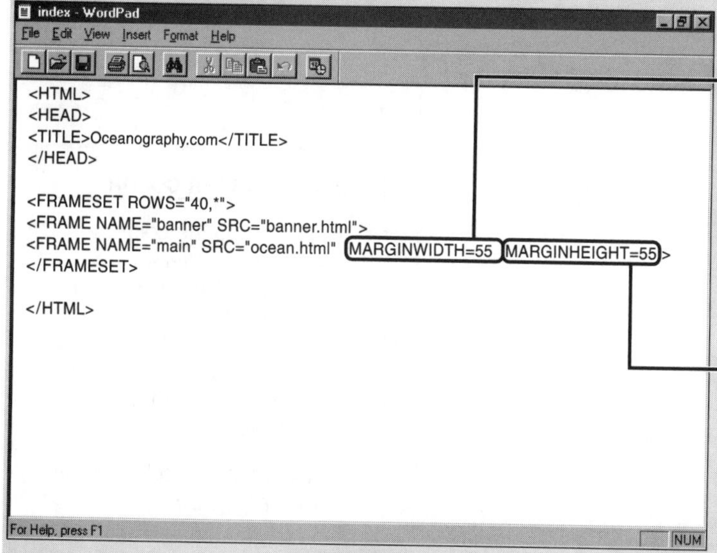

```
index - WordPad
File  Edit  View  Insert  Format  Help

<HTML>
<HEAD>
<TITLE>Oceanography.com</TITLE>
</HEAD>

<FRAMESET ROWS="40,*">
<FRAME NAME="banner" SRC="banner.html">
<FRAME NAME="main" SRC="ocean.html" MARGINWIDTH=55 MARGINHEIGHT=55>
</FRAMESET>

</HTML>

For Help, press F1                                                    NUM
```

**1** Position the cursor in the <FRAME> tag for the frame you want to change.

**2** To change the left and right margins, type **MARGINWIDTH=?** replacing **?** with the amount of space you want to use in pixels. Then press the **Spacebar**.

**3** To change the top and bottom margins, type **MARGINHEIGHT=?** replacing **?** with the amount of space you want to use in pixels.

```
Oceanography.com - Microsoft Internet Explorer
File  Edit  View  Favorites  Tools  Help

Back  Forward  Stop  Refresh  Home  Search  Favorites  History  Mail  Print  Edit
Address  C:\My Documents\Web Pages\index.html                    Go  Links

Oceanography.com  Come discover the beauty of the ocean!

    Oceanography is the study of the seas and oceans. If you love the ocean and are
    interested in pursuing an ocean-related career, then oceanography could be for you!

    The field of oceanography can be broken down into three main areas of
    study:
    Physical Oceanography is concerned with the physical attributes of the ocean
    water, such as currents and temperature.
    Chemical Oceanography focuses on the chemistry of ocean waters.
    Marine Biology is the study of flora and fauna and the interaction between the
    atmosphere and the ocean.

Done                                                    My Computer
```

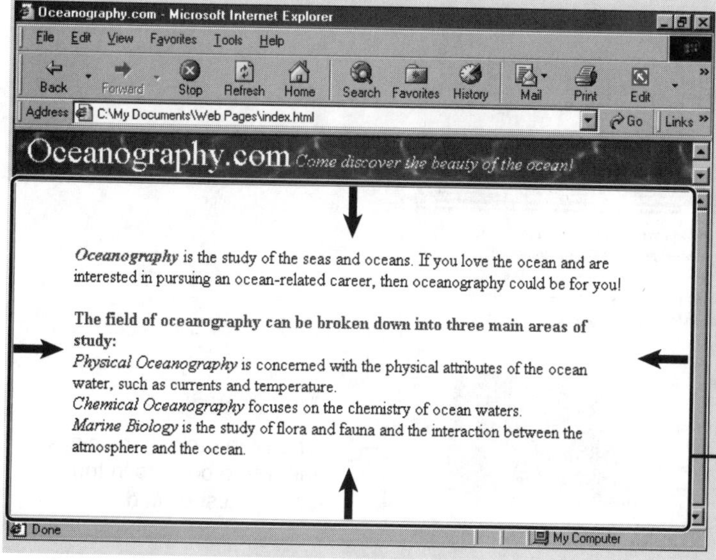

**4** Display the Web page in a Web browser.

● The Web browser displays the frame with the margins you specified.

# CHANGE FRAME BORDERS

You can customize the borders between your frames by changing the color or thickness of the borders. You can also hide the borders between your frames to make the contents of the frames appear as one Web page. For example, you may want to remove the frame borders between images in separate frames to have the images appear as a single image.

## CHANGE FRAME BORDERS

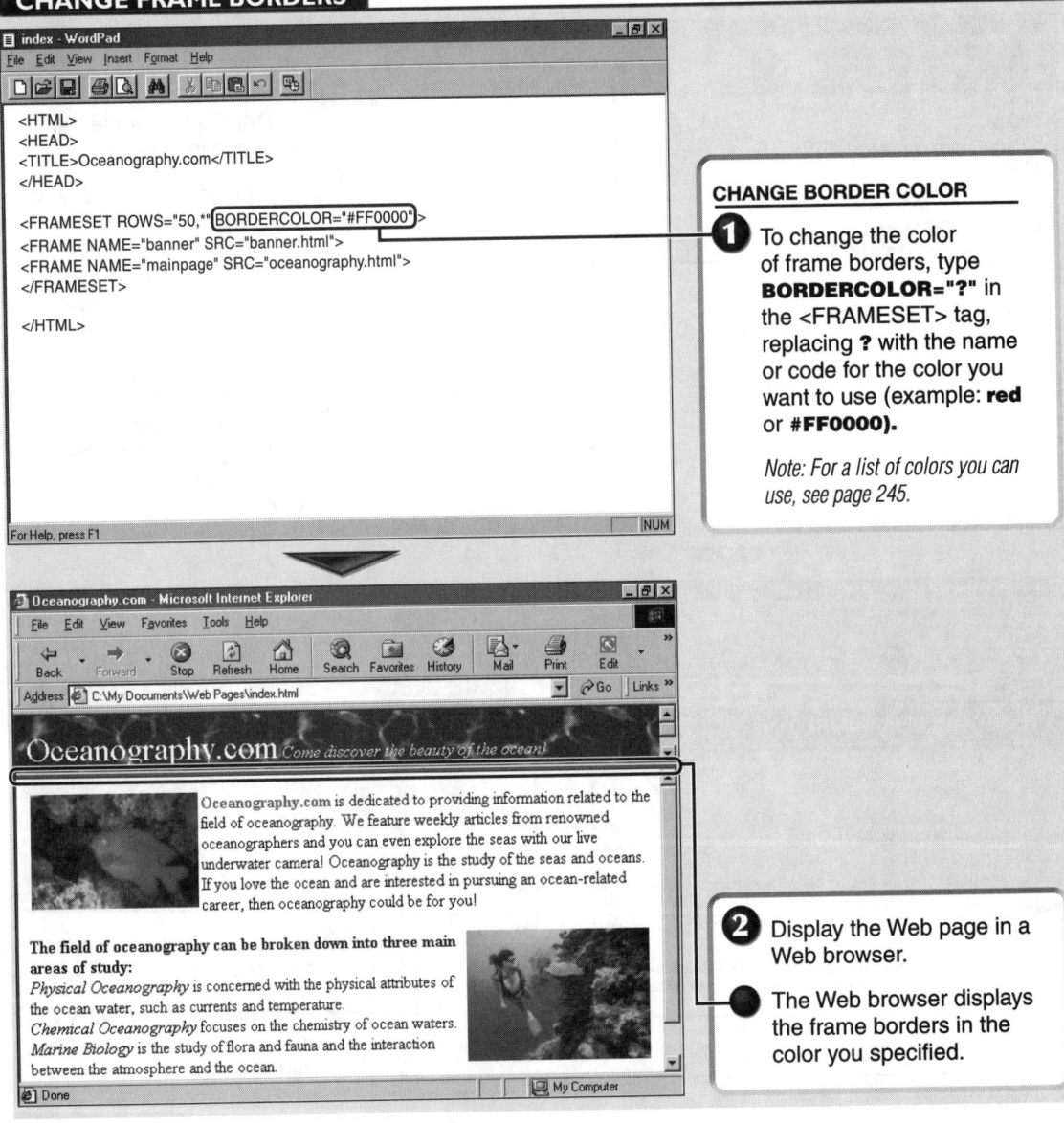

### CHANGE BORDER COLOR

**1** To change the color of frame borders, type **BORDERCOLOR="?"** in the <FRAMESET> tag, replacing **?** with the name or code for the color you want to use (example: **red** or **#FF0000).**

Note: For a list of colors you can use, see page 245.

**2** Display the Web page in a Web browser.

● The Web browser displays the frame borders in the color you specified.

# in an *instant*

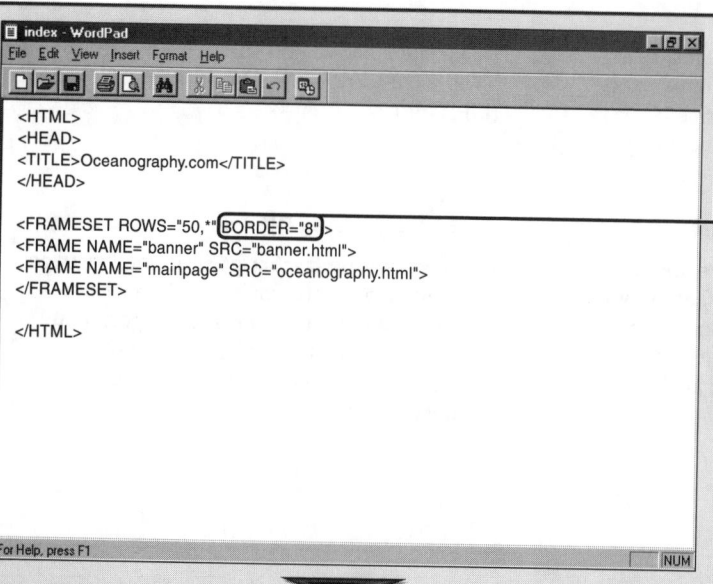

```
<HTML>
<HEAD>
<TITLE>Oceanography.com</TITLE>
</HEAD>

<FRAMESET ROWS="50,*" BORDER="8">
<FRAME NAME="banner" SRC="banner.html">
<FRAME NAME="mainpage" SRC="oceanography.html">
</FRAMESET>

</HTML>
```

## CHANGE BORDER THICKNESS

**1** To change the thickness of frame borders, type **BORDER="?"** in the **<FRAMESET>** tag, replacing **?** with the thickness you want to use in pixels.

● To hide the frame borders, replace **?** with **0** in step **1**.

*Note: To completely remove the space between the contents of the frames when hiding frame borders, you can set the width and height of the margins for each frame to 0.*

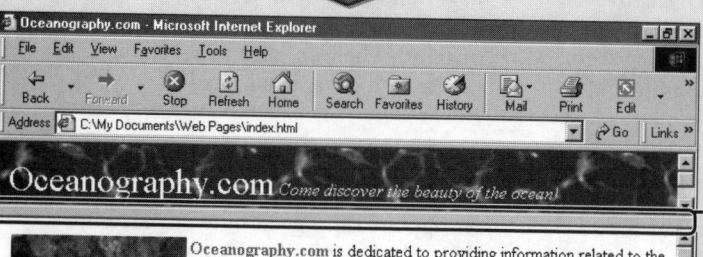

Oceanography.com *Come discover the beauty of the ocean!*

Oceanography.com is dedicated to providing information related to the field of oceanography. We feature weekly articles from renowned oceanographers and you can even explore the seas with our live underwater camera! Oceanography is the study of the seas and oceans. If you love the ocean and are interested in pursuing an ocean-related career, then oceanography could be for you!

**The field of oceanography can be broken down into three main areas of study:**
*Physical Oceanography* is concerned with the physical attributes of the ocean water, such as currents and temperature.
*Chemical Oceanography* focuses on the chemistry of ocean waters.
*Marine Biology* is the study of flora and fauna and the interaction between the atmosphere and the ocean.

**2** Display the Web page in a Web browser.

● The Web browser changes the thickness of the borders between your frames.

# JAVASCRIPTS AND JAVA APPLETS

JavaScripts and Java applets allow you to add animated and interactive elements to your Web pages. This can help make your Web pages more interesting and entertaining. Although the names are similar, JavaScripts and Java applets have very little in common.

## JAVASCRIPTS

JavaScripts can display alert messages, offer drop-down menus, open new windows and change images in response to mouse movements in your Web pages. Including

JavaScripts allows you to create dynamic Web pages, known as Dynamic HTML (DHTML).

### FIND JAVASCRIPTS ON THE INTERNET

There are many places on the Internet that offer JavaScripts you can use for free on your Web pages. Make sure you have permission to use any JavaScripts you obtain on the Internet. You can find JavaScripts at the javascript.internet.com and www.javascripts.com Web sites.

### CREATE JAVASCRIPTS

If you know the JavaScript scripting language, you can also create your own JavaScripts that you can add to your Web pages. You can learn about the JavaScript scripting language at the www.htmlgoodies.com/primers/jsp Web site.

## JAVA APPLETS

A Java applet is a program written using the Java programming language. Java applets can make your Web pages more entertaining by adding special effects such as rotating

images and fireworks. Java applets are also ideal for displaying information that constantly changes, such as stock market updates and news headlines.

### WHERE TO GET JAVA APPLETS

There are many places on the Internet that offer Java applets, such as the javaboutique.internet.com and www.javashareware.com Web sites. If you know the Java programming language, you can also create your own Java applets that you can add to your Web pages.

### CONSIDERATIONS

Java applets can significantly increase the time a Web page takes to transfer over the Internet and appear on a screen. If a Web page takes too long to appear, users may lose interest and move to another Web page.

You should also keep in mind that the Java applets on your Web pages may not appear for some users. Some users may have older Web browsers that cannot run Java applets.

# ADD A JAVASCRIPT

You can add a JavaScript to make your Web pages dynamic and
interactive. JavaScripts are often placed between the <HEAD> and
</HEAD> tags on a Web page, but can also be included between
the <BODY> and </BODY> tags. A JavaScript you obtain on the
Internet usually has instructions that indicate where you should
place the JavaScript on your Web page.

## ADD A JAVASCRIPT TO ONE PAGE

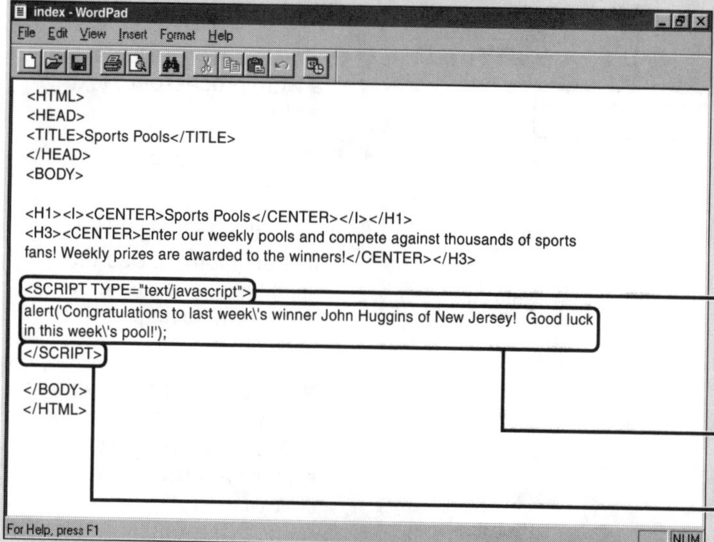

**index - WordPad**

File   Edit   View   Insert   Format   Help

```
<HTML>
<HEAD>
<TITLE>Sports Pools</TITLE>
</HEAD>
<BODY>

<H1><I><CENTER>Sports Pools</CENTER></I></H1>
<H3><CENTER>Enter our weekly pools and compete against thousands of sports
fans! Weekly prizes are awarded to the winners!</CENTER></H3>

<SCRIPT TYPE="text/javascript">
alert('Congratulations to last week\'s winner John Huggins of New Jersey!  Good luck
in this week\'s pool!');
</SCRIPT>

</BODY>
</HTML>
```

For Help, press F1                                                    NUM

**1** Type **<SCRIPT
TYPE="text/javascript">**
on your Web page.

*Note: To determine where to place
the JavaScript on your Web page,
check the instructions included with
the JavaScript.*

**2** Type the code for the
JavaScript.

**3** Type **</SCRIPT>**.

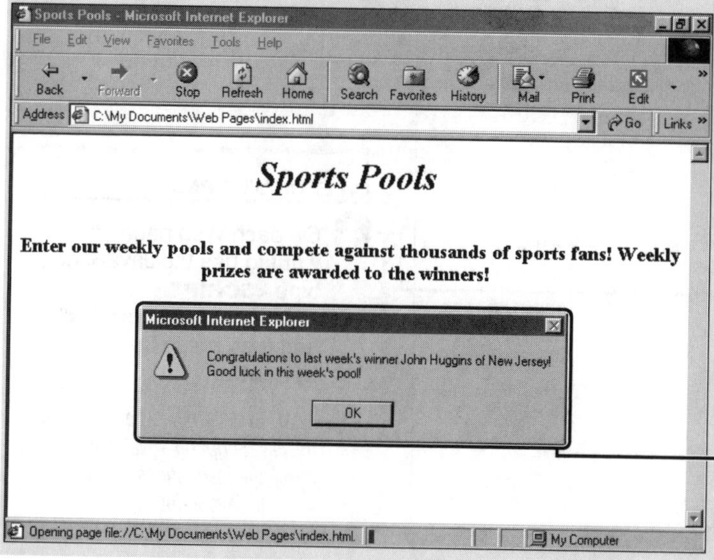

---

**Sports Pools - Microsoft Internet Explorer**

File   Edit   View   Favorites   Tools   Help

Back   Forward   Stop   Refresh   Home   Search   Favorites   History   Mail   Print   Edit

Address  C:\My Documents\Web Pages\index.html              Go   Links

### *Sports Pools*

**Enter our weekly pools and compete against thousands of sports fans! Weekly
prizes are awarded to the winners!**

**Microsoft Internet Explorer**

⚠ Congratulations to last week's winner John Huggins of New Jersey!
Good luck in this week's pool!

OK

Opening page file://C:\My Documents\Web Pages\index.html         My Computer

**4** Display the Web page in a
Web browser.

● The Web browser runs the
JavaScript on your Web
page.

CONTINUED

If you want to use a JavaScript on several Web pages, you can store the JavaScript code in a separate file. You can then include a reference to the file on each Web page. Storing the JavaScript code in a separate file prevents you from having to type the JavaScript code on each Web page you want to use the JavaScript.

## ADD A JAVASCRIPT TO SEVERAL WEB PAGES

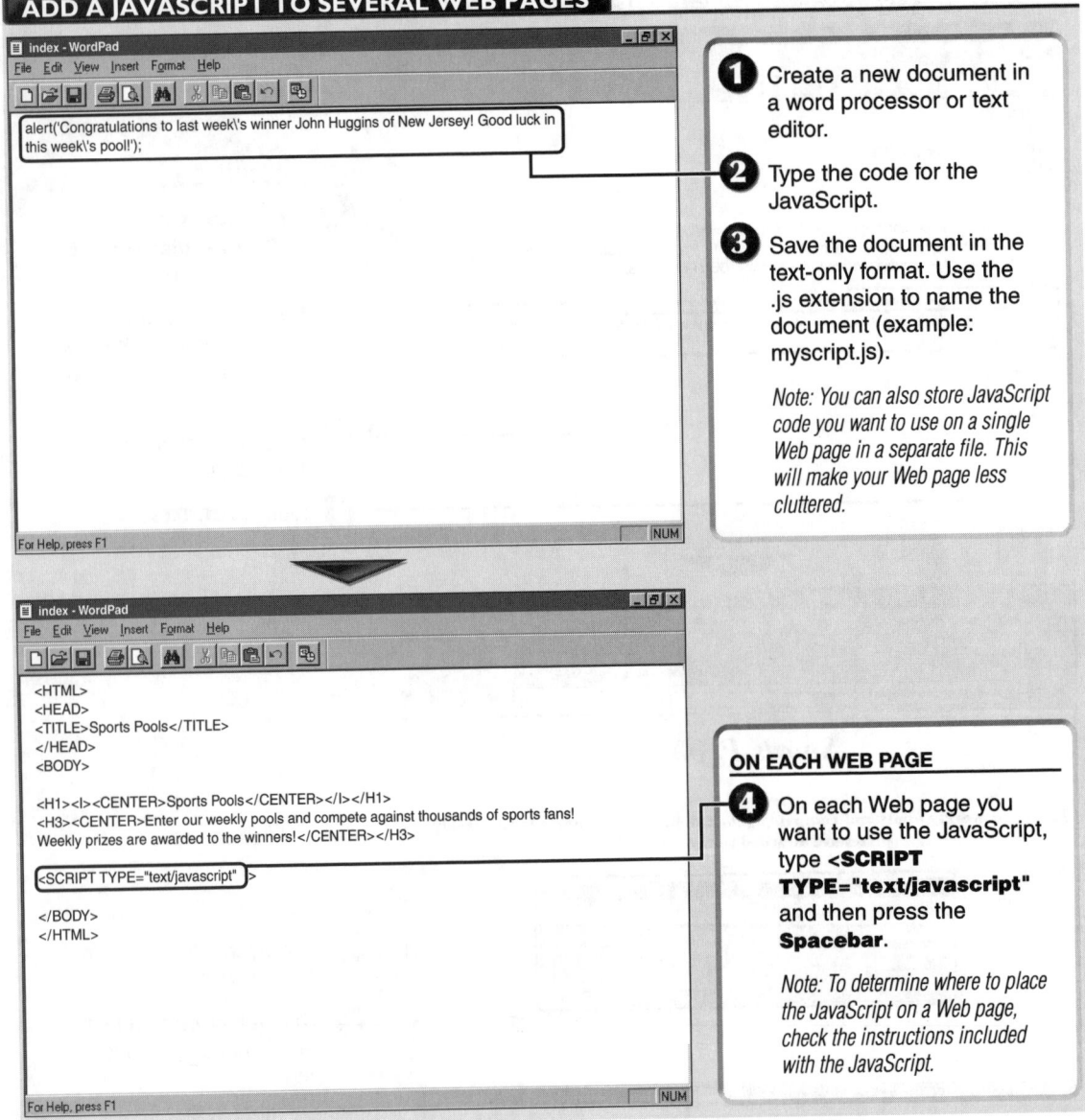

**1** Create a new document in a word processor or text editor.

**2** Type the code for the JavaScript.

**3** Save the document in the text-only format. Use the .js extension to name the document (example: myscript.js).

*Note: You can also store JavaScript code you want to use on a single Web page in a separate file. This will make your Web page less cluttered.*

**ON EACH WEB PAGE**

**4** On each Web page you want to use the JavaScript, type **<SCRIPT TYPE="text/javascript"** and then press the **Spacebar**.

*Note: To determine where to place the JavaScript on a Web page, check the instructions included with the JavaScript.*

in an **instant**

```
index - WordPad
File  Edit  View  Insert  Format  Help

<HTML>
<HEAD>
<TITLE>Sports Pools</TITLE>
</HEAD>
<BODY>

<H1><I><CENTER>Sports Pools</CENTER></I></H1>
<H3><CENTER>Enter our weekly pools and compete against thousands of sports fans!
Weekly prizes are awarded to the winners!</CENTER></H3>

<SCRIPT TYPE="text/javascript" SRC="myscript.js">
</SCRIPT>

</BODY>
</HTML>

For Help, press F1                                              NUM
```

**5** Type **SRC="?">**.

**6** If the JavaScript is stored in the same folder in your Web site, replace **?** with the name of the JavaScript (example: myscript.js).

*Note: If the JavaScript is stored in a subfolder, you must also specify the name of the subfolder (example: scripts/myscript.js).*

**7** Type **</SCRIPT>** to complete the JavaScript.

```
Sports Pools - Microsoft Internet Explorer
File  Edit  View  Favorites  Tools  Help

Back  Forward  Stop  Refresh  Home  Search  Favorites  History  Mail  Print  Edit

Address  C:\My Documents\Web Pages\index.html                    Go   Links


                     Sports Pools

Enter our weekly pools and compete against thousands of sports fans! Weekly
                prizes are awarded to the winners!

    Microsoft Internet Explorer

          Congratulations to last week's winner John Huggins of New Jersey!
          Good luck in this week's pool!

                        OK

Opening page file://C:\My Documents\Web Pages\index.html        My Computer
```

**8** Display the Web page in a Web browser.

● The Web browser runs the JavaScript on the Web page.

You can hide a JavaScript on your Web page from older Web browsers that cannot run JavaScript. If you do not hide the JavaScript, older Web browsers may display the code for the JavaScript on your Web page.

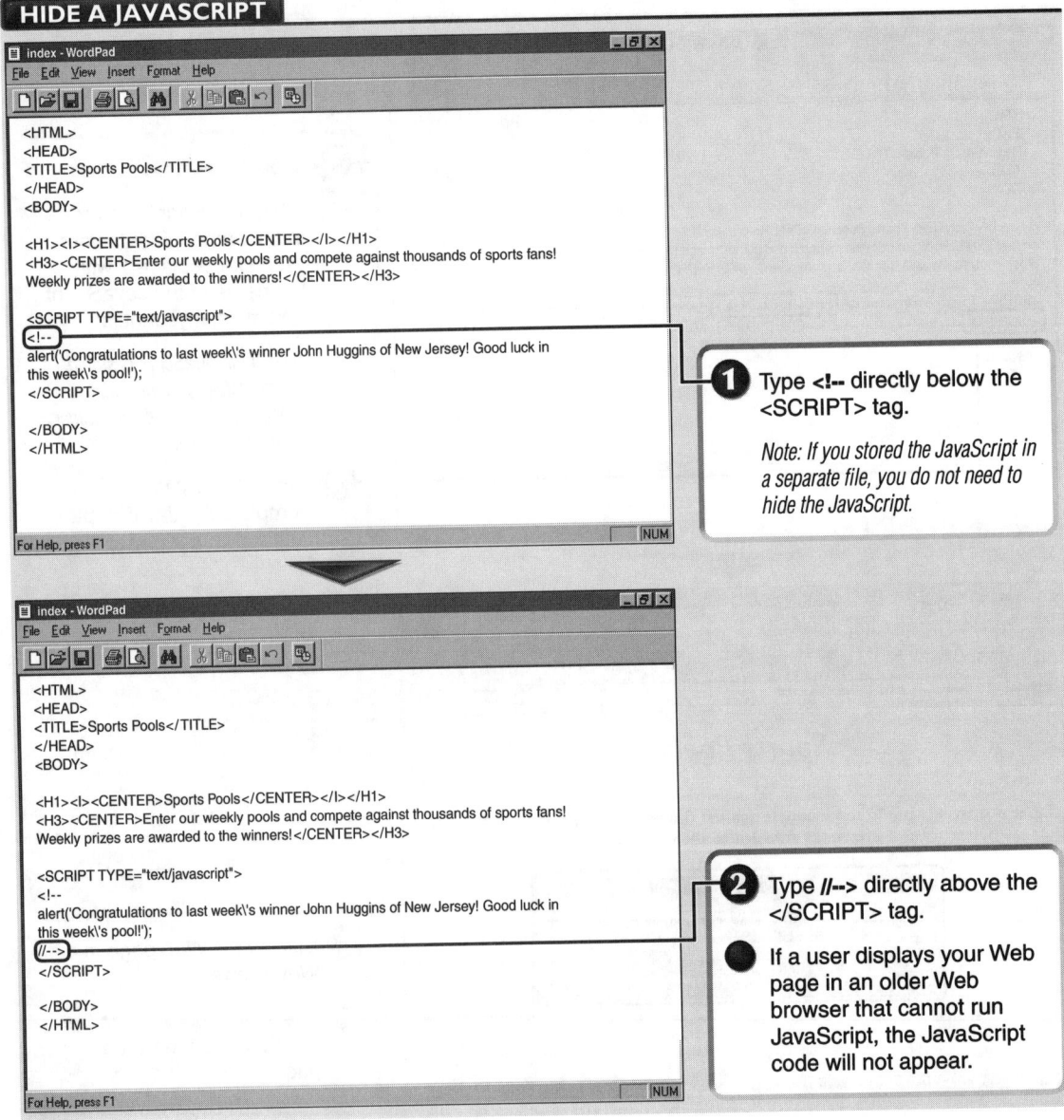

**1** Type **<!--** directly below the **<SCRIPT>** tag.

*Note: If you stored the JavaScript in a separate file, you do not need to hide the JavaScript.*

**2** Type **//-->** directly above the **</SCRIPT>** tag.

● If a user displays your Web page in an older Web browser that cannot run JavaScript, the JavaScript code will not appear.

# PROVIDE ALTERNATIVE TEXT

You can provide text that you want to display for users whose Web browsers cannot run JavaScript or who may have turned off JavaScript in their Web browsers. The text you provide can include information about the JavaScript or a short explanation of why users cannot see the JavaScript.

## PROVIDE ALTERNATIVE TEXT

```
<HTML>
<HEAD>
<TITLE>Sports Pools</TITLE>
</HEAD>
<BODY>

<H1><I><CENTER>Sports Pools</CENTER></I></H1>
<H3><CENTER>Enter our weekly pools and compete against thousands of sports fans!
Weekly prizes are awarded to the winners!</CENTER></H3>

<SCRIPT TYPE="text/javascript">
<!--
alert('Congratulations to last week\'s winner John Huggins of New Jersey! Good luck in
this week\'s pool!');
//-->
</SCRIPT>
<NOSCRIPT> Congratulations to last week's winner, John Huggins! </NOSCRIPT>

</BODY>
</HTML>
```

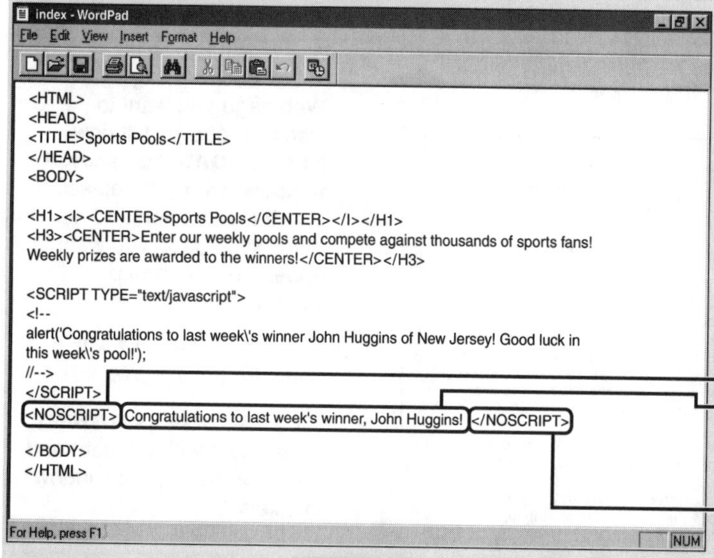

**1** Type **<NOSCRIPT>** directly below the </SCRIPT> tag.

**2** Type the text you want to display if a Web browser does not run JavaScript.

**3** Type **</NOSCRIPT>**.

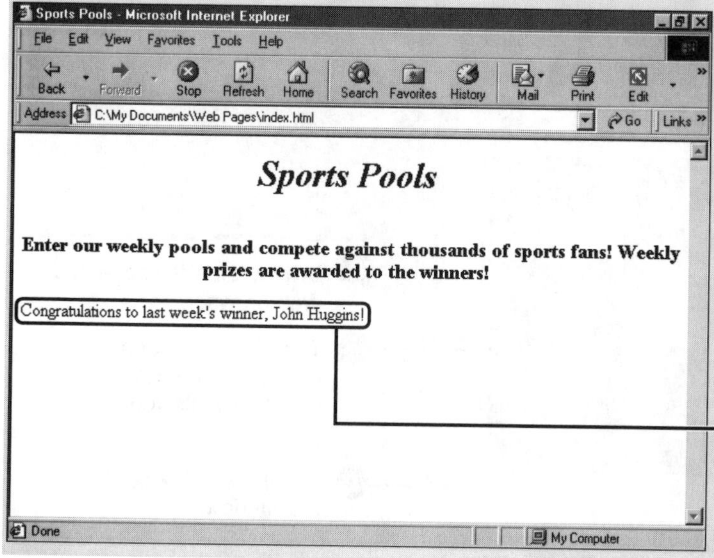

### Sports Pools

**Enter our weekly pools and compete against thousands of sports fans! Weekly prizes are awarded to the winners!**

Congratulations to last week's winner, John Huggins!

**4** Display the Web page in a Web browser.

● If the JavaScript does not run, the Web browser will display the text you specified.

**169**

# DISPLAY A POP-UP WINDOW

You can use JavaScript to create a pop-up window that will appear when a user visits your Web page. Pop-up windows can display other Web pages that provide additional information about the Web site or announce events, such as sales. When specifying a size for a pop-up window, you should make the window large enough to display the contents without blocking the main Web page.

## DISPLAY A POP-UP WINDOW

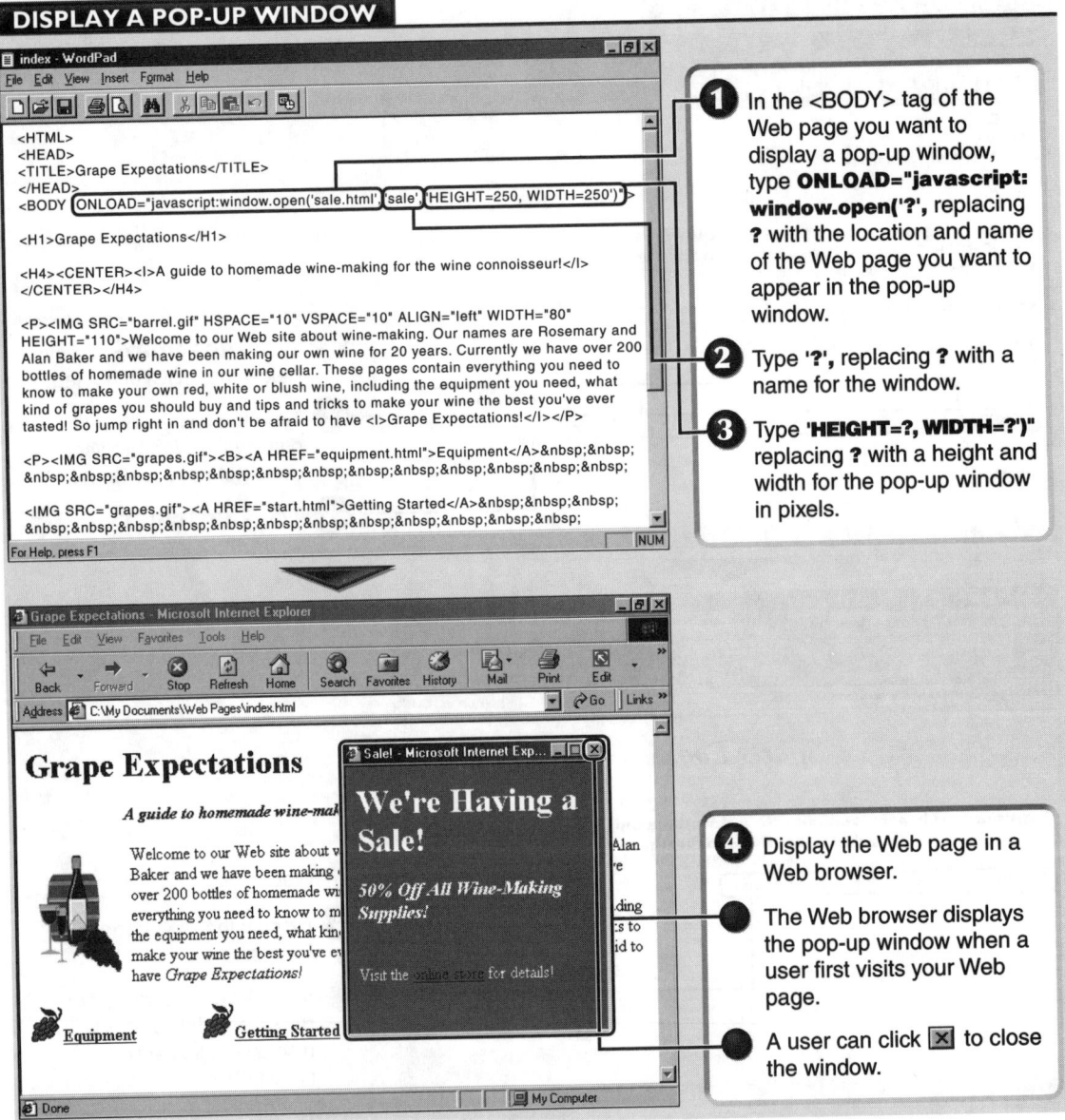

**1** In the <BODY> tag of the Web page you want to display a pop-up window, type **ONLOAD="javascript: window.open('?'**, replacing **?** with the location and name of the Web page you want to appear in the pop-up window.

**2** Type **'?'**, replacing **?** with a name for the window.

**3** Type **'HEIGHT=?, WIDTH=?')"** replacing **?** with a height and width for the pop-up window in pixels.

**4** Display the Web page in a Web browser.

● The Web browser displays the pop-up window when a user first visits your Web page.

● A user can click ☒ to close the window.

You can use JavaScript to customize the text that appears in the status bar of the Web browser window when a user positions the mouse over a link on the Web page. By default, the address of the linked Web page appears in the status bar. Specifying your own text allows you to give users extra information about a link. This is particularly useful for links that have complex URLs.

## CHANGE STATUS BAR FOR A LINK

```
index - WordPad
File  Edit  View  Insert  Format  Help

<HTML>
<HEAD>
<TITLE>Foster City Zoo</TITLE>
</HEAD>
<BODY>

<H1><CENTER>Foster City Zoo</CENTER></H1>
<CENTER><IMG SRC="tiger.jpg"></CENTER>
<P>The spacious grounds of Foster City Zoo were established in 1960 on 350 acres of forest
and farmland located five miles west of Foster City, NY. Our primary commitment is to educate
the public about the animal kingdom.</P>
<P>Foster City Zoo is proud to announce the completion of our newest exhibit, The World of
Cats. This week, in keeping with The World of Cats exhibit, the featured site of the week is all
about tigers!

<BR><A HREF="http://www.tigerkingdom.com" ONMOUSEOVER="window.status=' More About
Tigers '; return true">Click here</A> to find out more about tigers!</P>

</BODY>
</HTML>

For Help, press F1                                                    NUM
```

**1** In the <A> tag for the link you want to display descriptive text in the status bar, type **ONMOUSEOVER= "window.status='**.

**2** Type the text you want to appear in the status bar.

**3** Type **'; return true"** to complete the JavaScript.

```
Foster City Zoo - Microsoft Internet Explorer
File  Edit  View  Favorites  Tools  Help

Back  Forward  Stop  Refresh  Home  Search  Favorites  History  Mail  Print  Edit
Address  C:\My Documents\Web Pages\index.html              Go  Links

                        Foster City Zoo


The spacious grounds of Foster City Zoo were established in 1960 on 350 acres of forest and
farmland located five miles west of Foster City, NY. Our primary commitment is to educate the
public about the animal kingdom.

Foster City Zoo is proud to announce the completion of our newest exhibit, The World of Cats.
This week, in keeping with The World of Cats exhibit, the featured site of the week is all about
tigers!

Click here to find out more about tigers!

More About Tigers                                    My Computer
```

**4** Display the Web page in a Web browser.

● The Web browser displays the link.

● The text you specified appears in the status bar when a user positions the mouse over the link.

# VALIDATE FORM INFORMATION

Validating the information users enter in a form on your Web page is useful for detecting errors that users may make, such as accidentally entering a name in a text box that requests a telephone number. Using JavaScript, you can have an error message appear when a user enters the wrong type of characters or too few characters in a text box.

## VALIDATE CHARACTERS

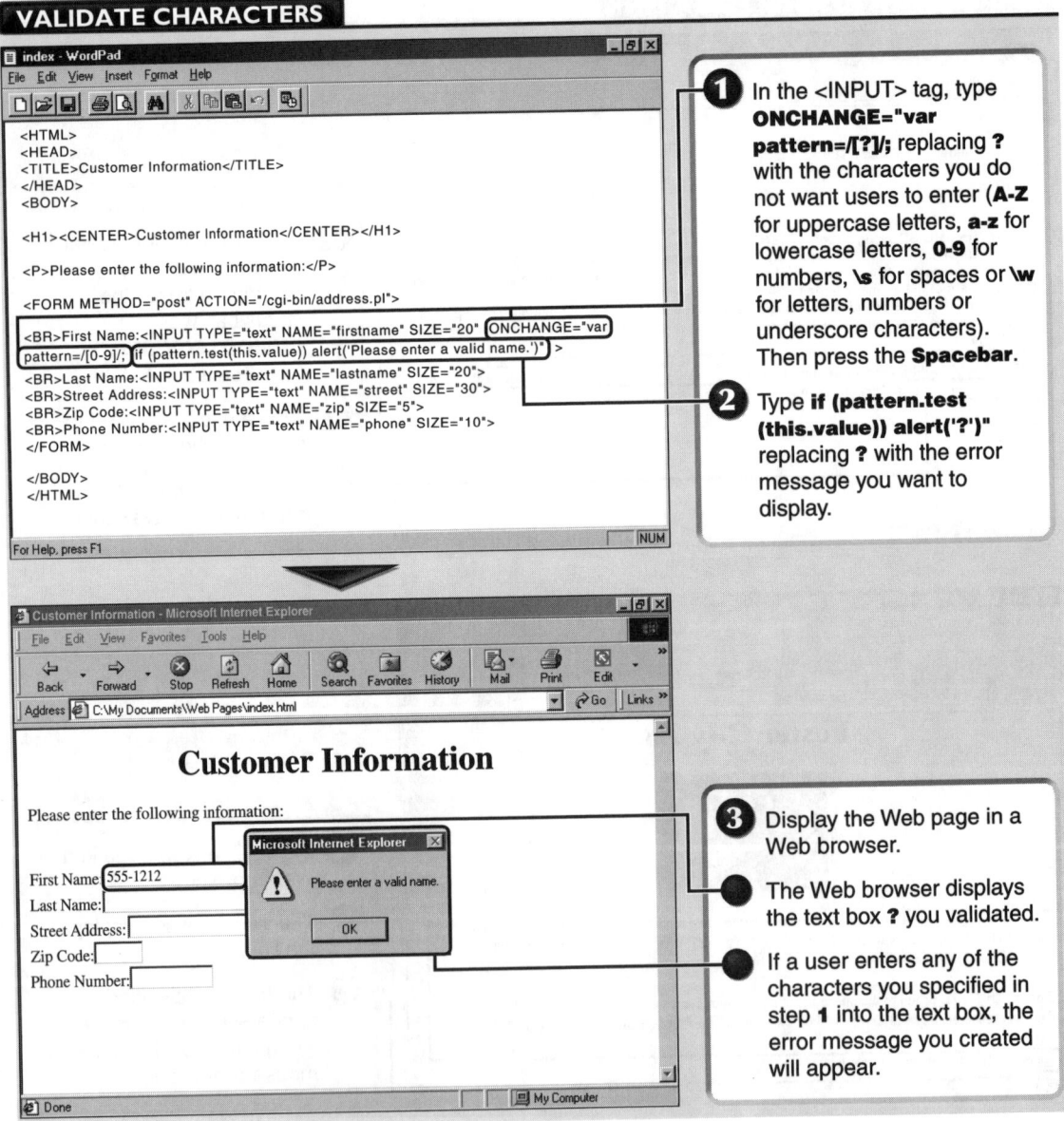

**1** In the <INPUT> tag, type **ONCHANGE="var pattern=/[?]/;** replacing **?** with the characters you do not want users to enter (**A-Z** for uppercase letters, **a-z** for lowercase letters, **0-9** for numbers, **\s** for spaces or **\w** for letters, numbers or underscore characters). Then press the **Spacebar**.

**2** Type **if (pattern.test (this.value)) alert('?')"** replacing **?** with the error message you want to display.

**3** Display the Web page in a Web browser.

● The Web browser displays the text box **?** you validated.

● If a user enters any of the characters you specified in step **1** into the text box, the error message you created will appear.

172

# in an *instant*

## VALIDATE MINIMUM LENGTH

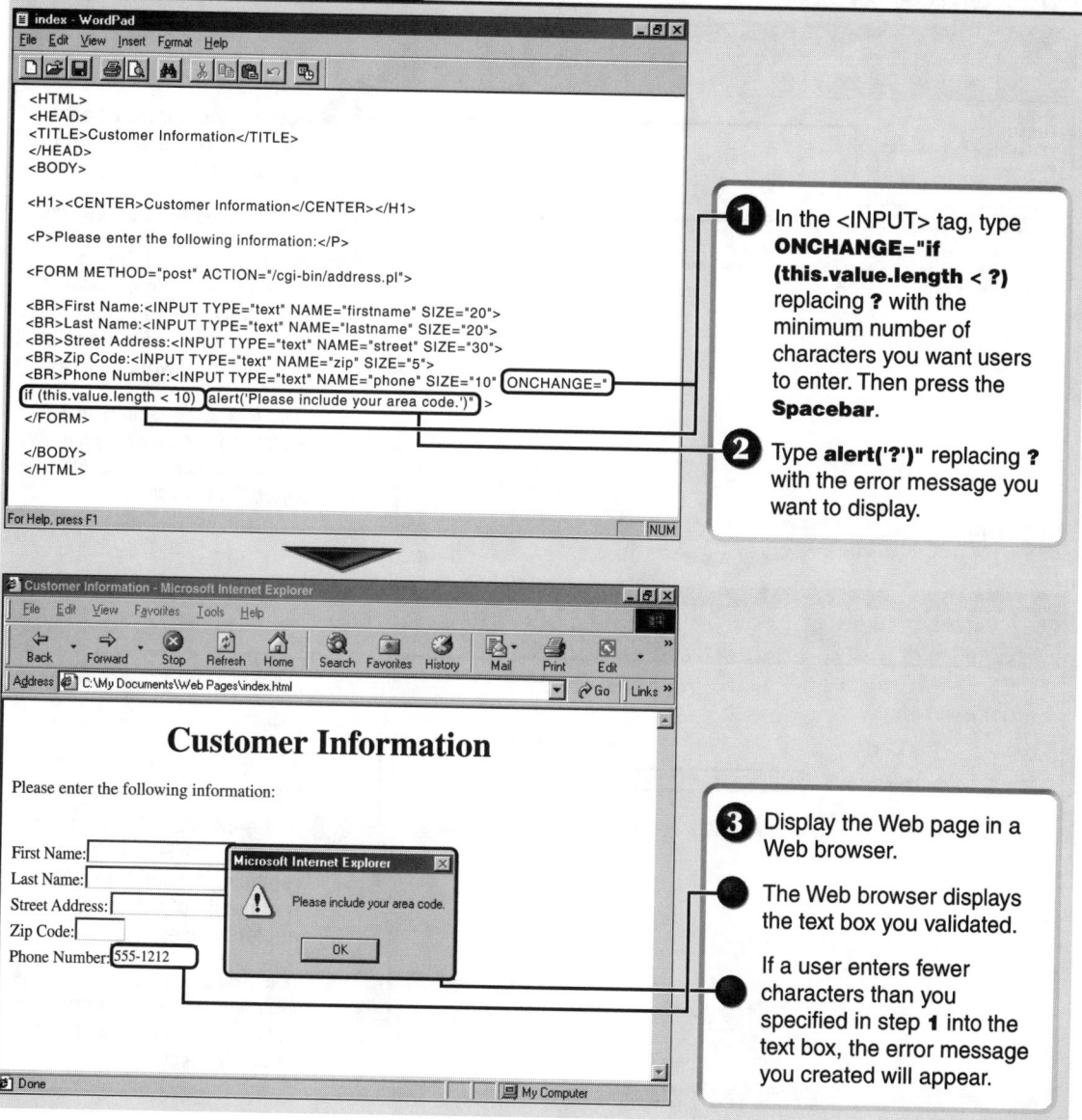

```
index - WordPad
File  Edit  View  Insert  Format  Help

<HTML>
<HEAD>
<TITLE>Customer Information</TITLE>
</HEAD>
<BODY>

<H1><CENTER>Customer Information</CENTER></H1>

<P>Please enter the following information:</P>

<FORM METHOD="post" ACTION="/cgi-bin/address.pl">

<BR>First Name:<INPUT TYPE="text" NAME="firstname" SIZE="20">
<BR>Last Name:<INPUT TYPE="text" NAME="lastname" SIZE="20">
<BR>Street Address:<INPUT TYPE="text" NAME="street" SIZE="30">
<BR>Zip Code:<INPUT TYPE="text" NAME="zip" SIZE="5">
<BR>Phone Number:<INPUT TYPE="text" NAME="phone" SIZE="10" ONCHANGE="
if (this.value.length < 10) alert('Please include your area code.')" >
</FORM>

</BODY>
</HTML>

For Help, press F1                                                    NUM
```

**1** In the <INPUT> tag, type
**ONCHANGE="if
(this.value.length < ?)**
replacing **?** with the
minimum number of
characters you want users
to enter. Then press the
**Spacebar**.

**2** Type **alert('?')"** replacing **?**
with the error message you
want to display.

```
Customer Information - Microsoft Internet Explorer
File  Edit  View  Favorites  Tools  Help

Back  Forward  Stop  Refresh  Home  Search  Favorites  History  Mail  Print  Edit

Address  C:\My Documents\Web Pages\index.html              Go   Links

                    Customer Information

Please enter the following information:

First Name:
Last Name:          Microsoft Internet Explorer
Street Address:        ⚠  Please include your area code.
Zip Code:
Phone Number: 555-1212        OK

Done                                                  My Computer
```

**3** Display the Web page in a
Web browser.

● The Web browser displays
the text box you validated.

● If a user enters fewer
characters than you
specified in step **1** into the
text box, the error message
you created will appear.

You can add a Java applet to your Web page to entertain or inform users. When you add a Java applet, you need to specify the correct width and height of the applet to ensure the applet will appear properly on your Web page. You can also specify text that you want to appear if a user's Web browser does not run the applet.

## ADD A JAVA APPLET

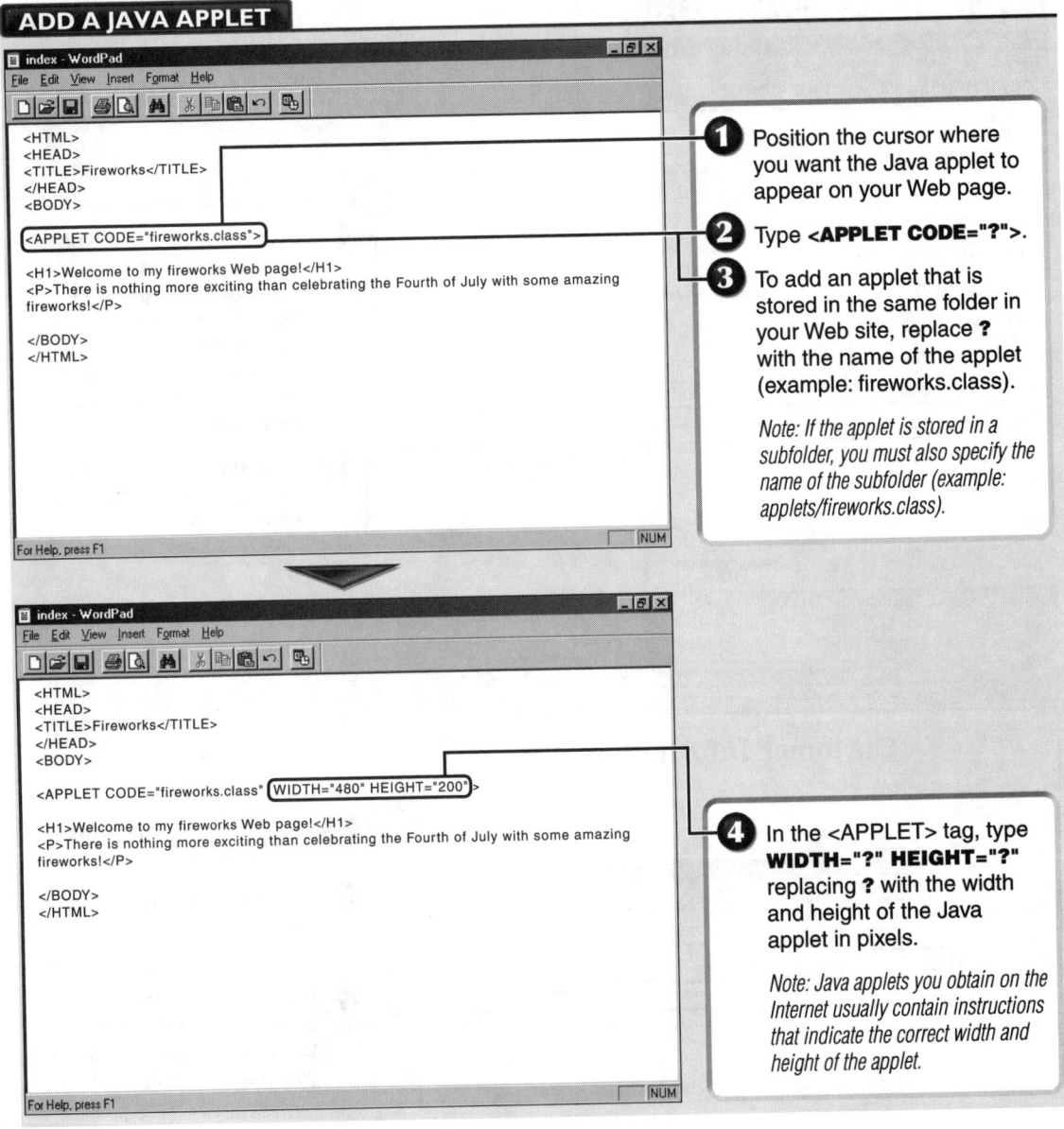

**1** Position the cursor where you want the Java applet to appear on your Web page.

**2** Type **<APPLET CODE="?">**.

**3** To add an applet that is stored in the same folder in your Web site, replace **?** with the name of the applet (example: fireworks.class).

*Note: If the applet is stored in a subfolder, you must also specify the name of the subfolder (example: applets/fireworks.class).*

**4** In the <APPLET> tag, type **WIDTH="?" HEIGHT="?"** replacing **?** with the width and height of the Java applet in pixels.

*Note: Java applets you obtain on the Internet usually contain instructions that indicate the correct width and height of the applet.*

in an *instant*

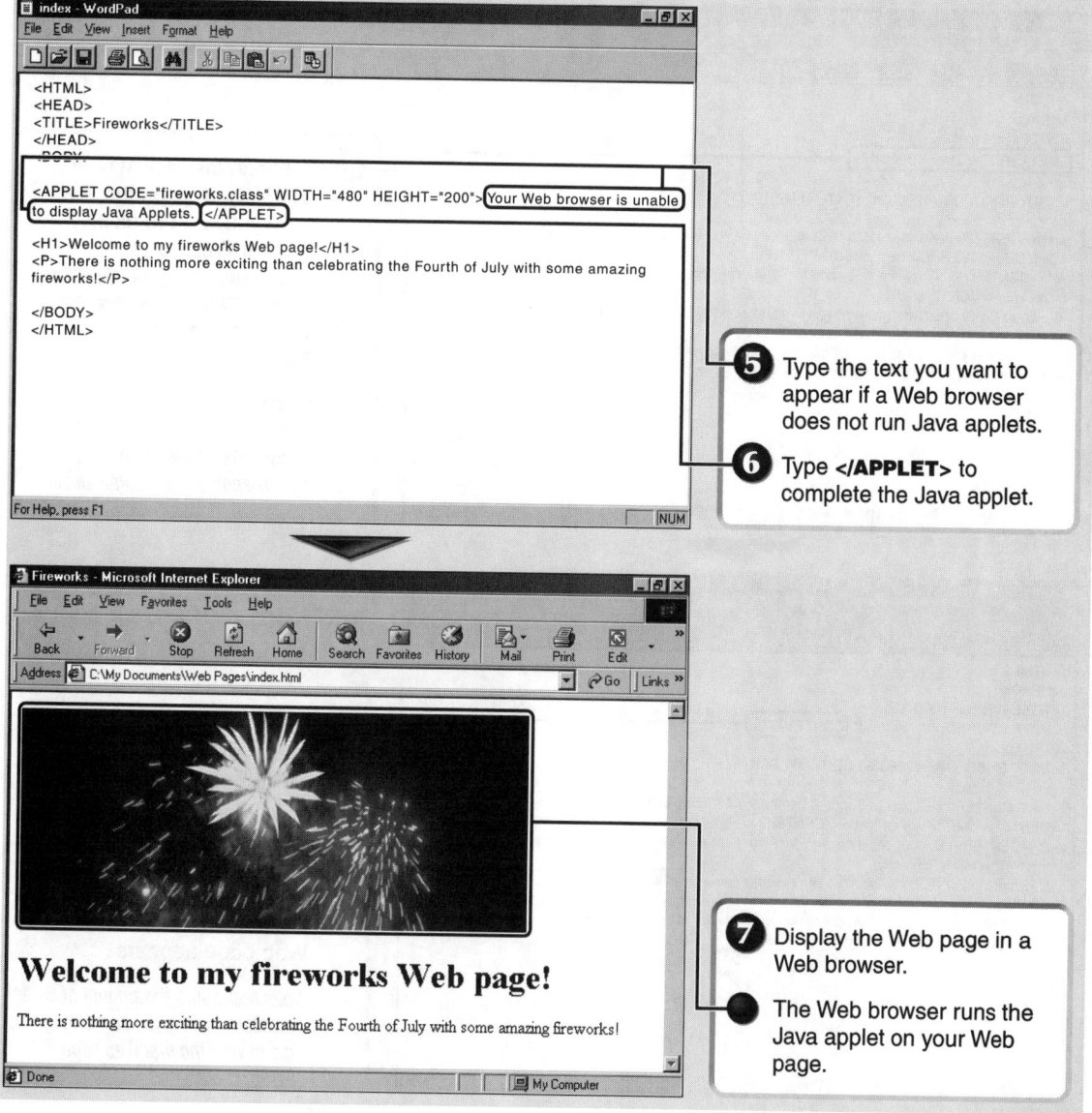

**5** Type the text you want to appear if a Web browser does not run Java applets.

**6** Type **</APPLET>** to complete the Java applet.

**7** Display the Web page in a Web browser.

■ The Web browser runs the Java applet on your Web page.

# DISPLAY ANOTHER WEB PAGE AUTOMATICALLY

You can have a Web page display another Web page automatically after a certain period of time. This is useful for creating title pages for your Web site and for redirecting Web browsers when a Web page has moved. You can also display a series of Web pages automatically to create a slide show effect.

## DISPLAY ANOTHER WEB PAGE AUTOMATICALLY

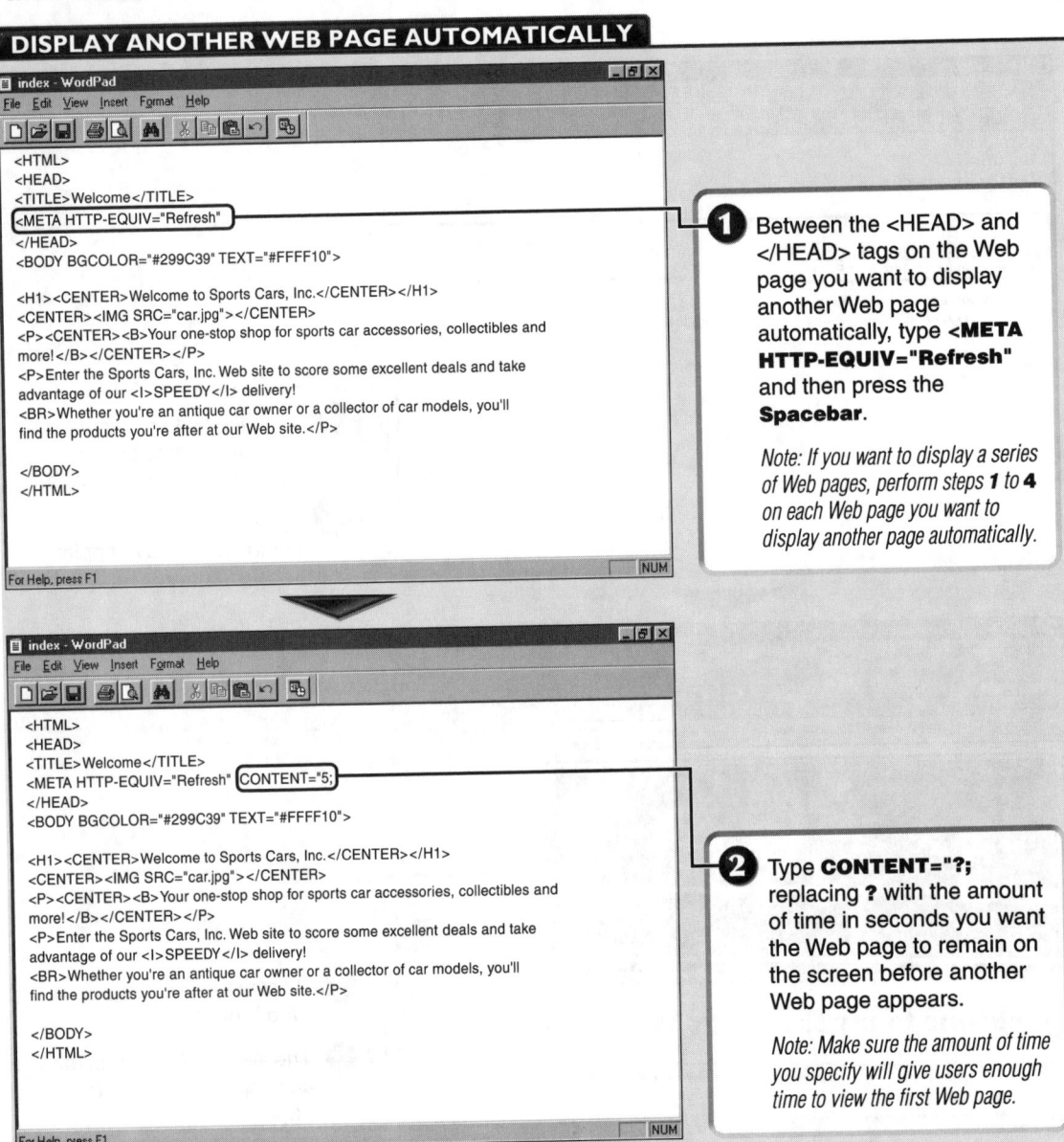

**1** Between the <HEAD> and </HEAD> tags on the Web page you want to display another Web page automatically, type **<META HTTP-EQUIV="Refresh"** and then press the **Spacebar**.

*Note: If you want to display a series of Web pages, perform steps 1 to 4 on each Web page you want to display another page automatically.*

**2** Type **CONTENT="?;** replacing **?** with the amount of time in seconds you want the Web page to remain on the screen before another Web page appears.

*Note: Make sure the amount of time you specify will give users enough time to view the first Web page.*

in an *instant*

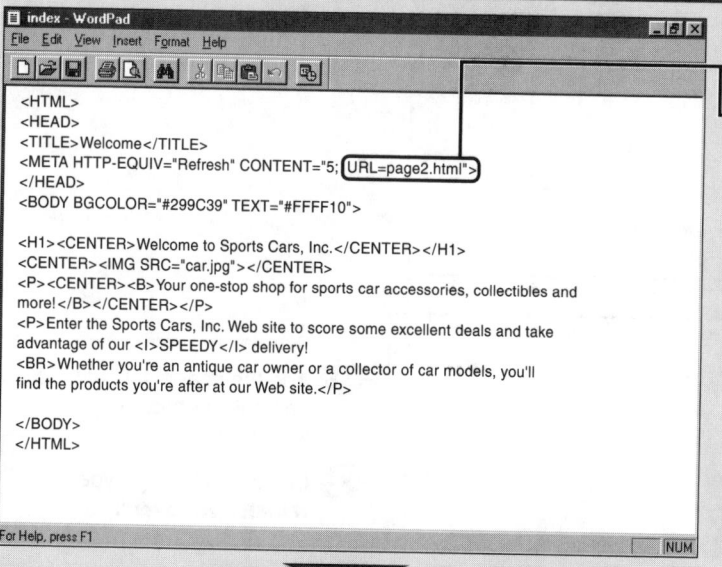

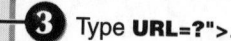

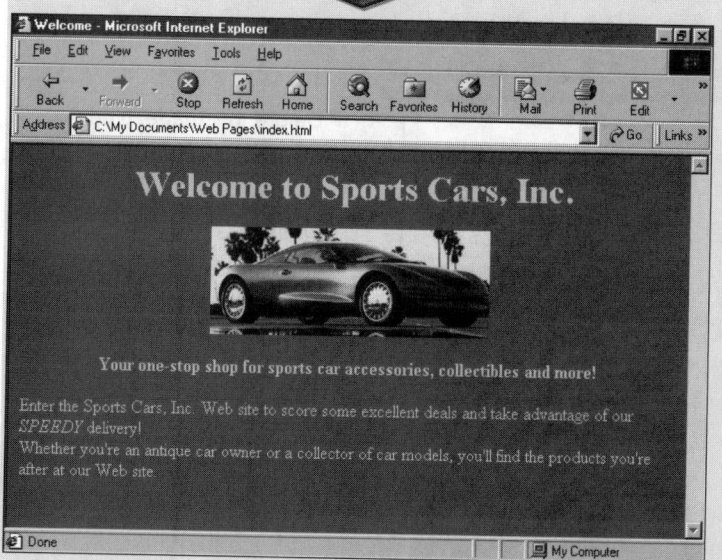

**3** Type **URL=?">**.

**4** To display a Web page that is stored in the same folder in the Web site, replace **?** with the name of the Web page.

● If the Web page is stored in a subfolder, you must also specify the name of the subfolder.

*Note: To have a series of Web pages loop continuously, make sure the last Web page specifies the location of the first Web page in the series.*

**5** Display the Web page in a Web browser.

● The Web browser displays the first Web page.

● After the time period you specified, the other Web page will automatically appear.

# CREATE AN IMAGE ROLLOVER

You can use JavaScript to create an image link that will change to another image when a user moves the mouse over the link. This is called an image rollover and is useful when you want to make your Web page more interactive. For example, creating an image rollover for each item in a menu can help users determine which item they are selecting.

## CREATE AN IMAGE ROLLOVER

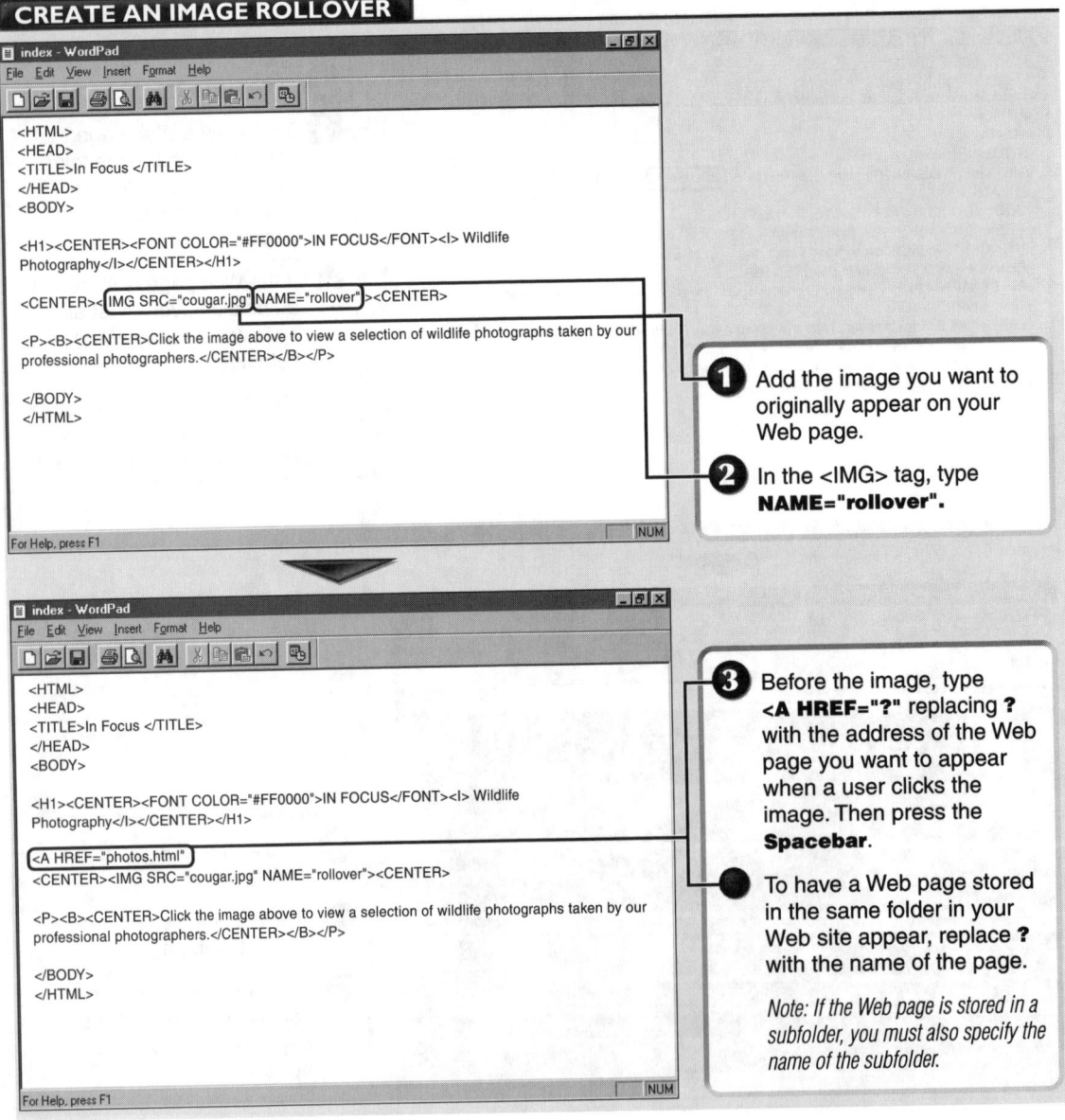

**1** Add the image you want to originally appear on your Web page.

**2** In the <IMG> tag, type **NAME="rollover"**.

**3** Before the image, type **<A HREF="?"** replacing **?** with the address of the Web page you want to appear when a user clicks the image. Then press the **Spacebar**.

● To have a Web page stored in the same folder in your Web site appear, replace **?** with the name of the page.

*Note: If the Web page is stored in a subfolder, you must also specify the name of the subfolder.*

# in an *instant*

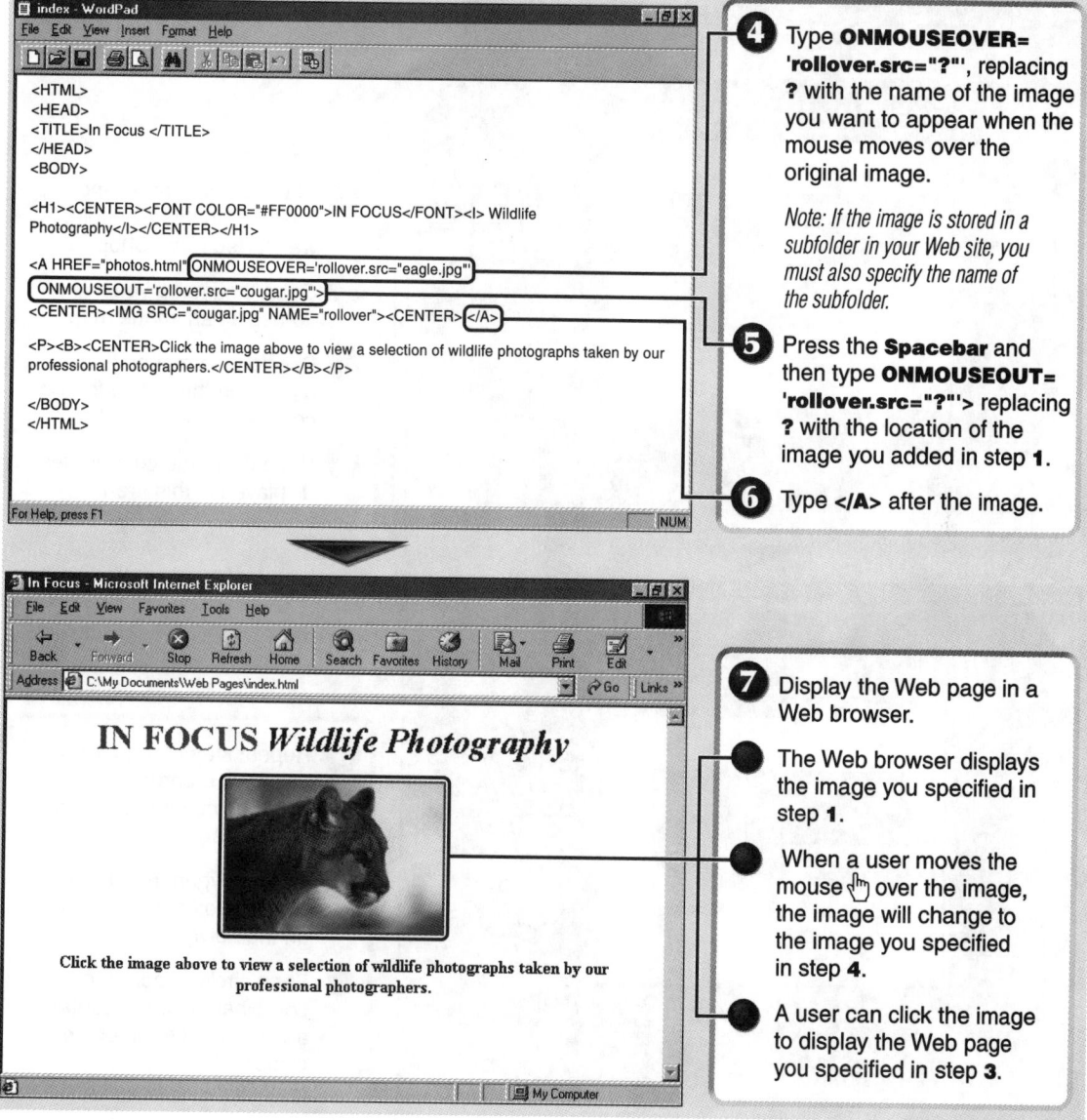

**4** Type **ONMOUSEOVER= 'rollover.src="?"'**, replacing **?** with the name of the image you want to appear when the mouse moves over the original image.

*Note: If the image is stored in a subfolder in your Web site, you must also specify the name of the subfolder.*

**5** Press the **Spacebar** and then type **ONMOUSEOUT= 'rollover.src="?"'>** replacing **?** with the location of the image you added in step **1**.

**6** Type **</A>** after the image.

**7** Display the Web page in a Web browser.

● The Web browser displays the image you specified in step **1**.

● When a user moves the mouse ⌐ᵐ⌐ over the image, the image will change to the image you specified in step **4**.

● A user can click the image to display the Web page you specified in step **3**.

# CREATE AN IMAGE MAP

You can create an image map by dividing an image into different areas that each link to a different Web page. Images that have several distinct areas that users can select, such as a floor plan or world map, are ideal for image maps. When creating an image map, you must first determine the coordinates of each image area using an image editing program.

## DETERMINE COORDINATES OF IMAGE AREAS

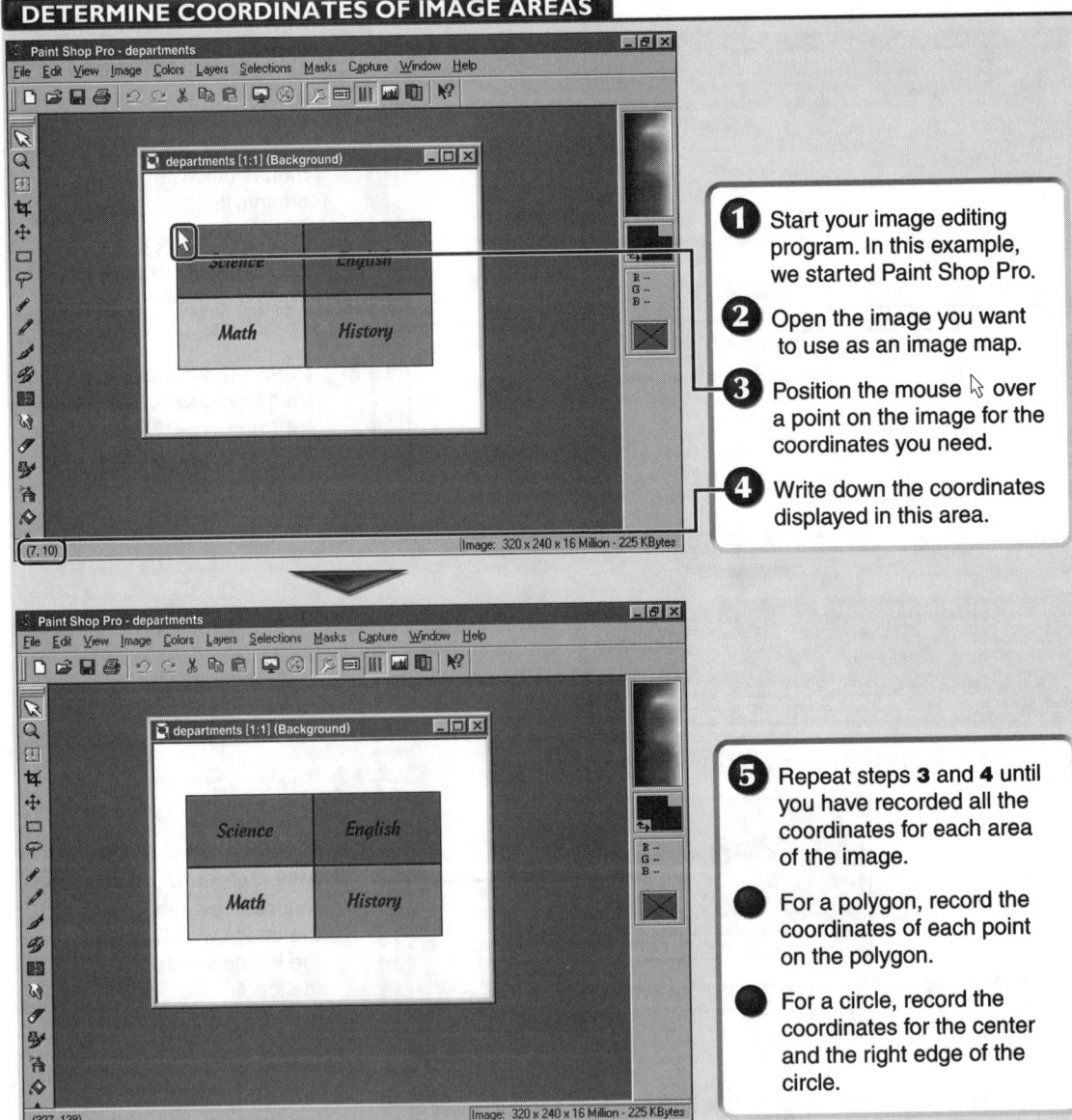

1 Start your image editing program. In this example, we started Paint Shop Pro.

2 Open the image you want to use as an image map.

3 Position the mouse ⬚ over a point on the image for the coordinates you need.

4 Write down the coordinates displayed in this area.

5 Repeat steps **3** and **4** until you have recorded all the coordinates for each area of the image.

● For a polygon, record the coordinates of each point on the polygon.

● For a circle, record the coordinates for the center and the right edge of the circle.

# in an *instant*

## CREATE AN IMAGE MAP

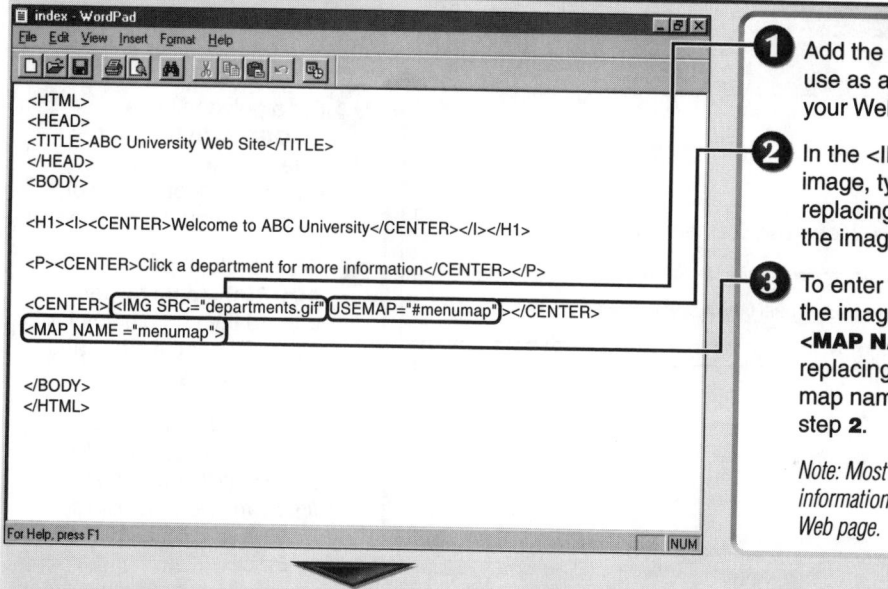

**1** Add the image you want to use as an image map on your Web page.

**2** In the <IMG> tag for the image, type **USEMAP="#?"** replacing **?** with a name for the image map.

**3** To enter the information for the image map, type **<MAP NAME="?">** replacing **?** with the image map name you typed in step **2**.

*Note: Most people enter this information at the bottom of the Web page.*

**4** Type **<AREA** to specify the information for one area of the image map. Then press the **Spacebar**.

**5** Type **SHAPE="?"** replacing **?** with the shape of the area (**poly** for polygon or **circle** for circle). Then press the **Spacebar**.

CONTINUED

# CREATE AN IMAGE MAP

When creating an image map, you must define each area of the image in your Web page. If you accidentally enter coordinates that cause two image areas to overlap, most Web browsers will interpret the overlapping area as part of the first image area you defined.

## CREATE AN IMAGE MAP (CONTINUED)

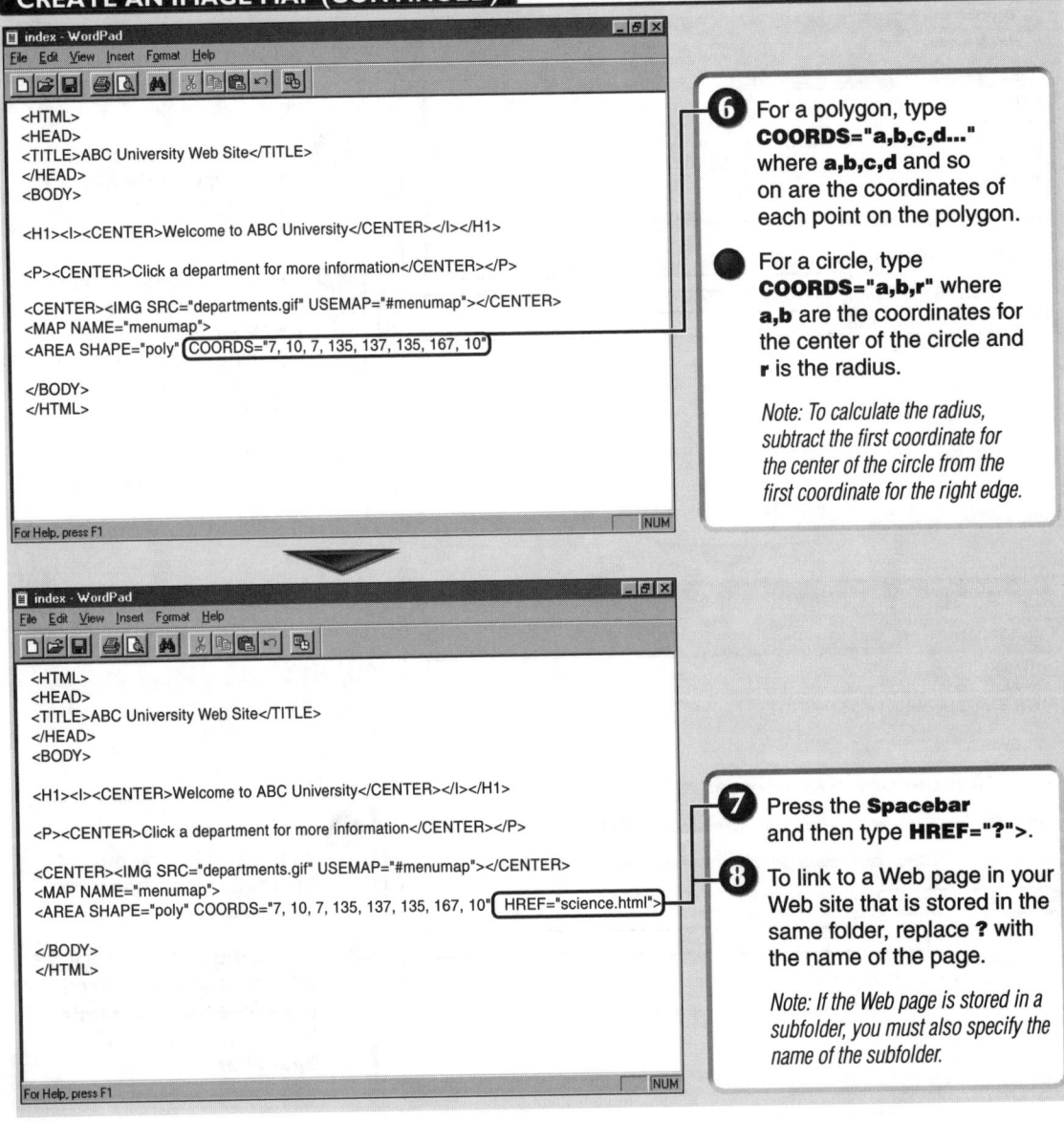

**6** For a polygon, type **COORDS="a,b,c,d..."** where **a,b,c,d** and so on are the coordinates of each point on the polygon.

For a circle, type **COORDS="a,b,r"** where **a,b** are the coordinates for the center of the circle and **r** is the radius.

*Note: To calculate the radius, subtract the first coordinate for the center of the circle from the first coordinate for the right edge.*

**7** Press the **Spacebar** and then type **HREF="?">**.

**8** To link to a Web page in your Web site that is stored in the same folder, replace **?** with the name of the page.

*Note: If the Web page is stored in a subfolder, you must also specify the name of the subfolder.*

in an *instant*

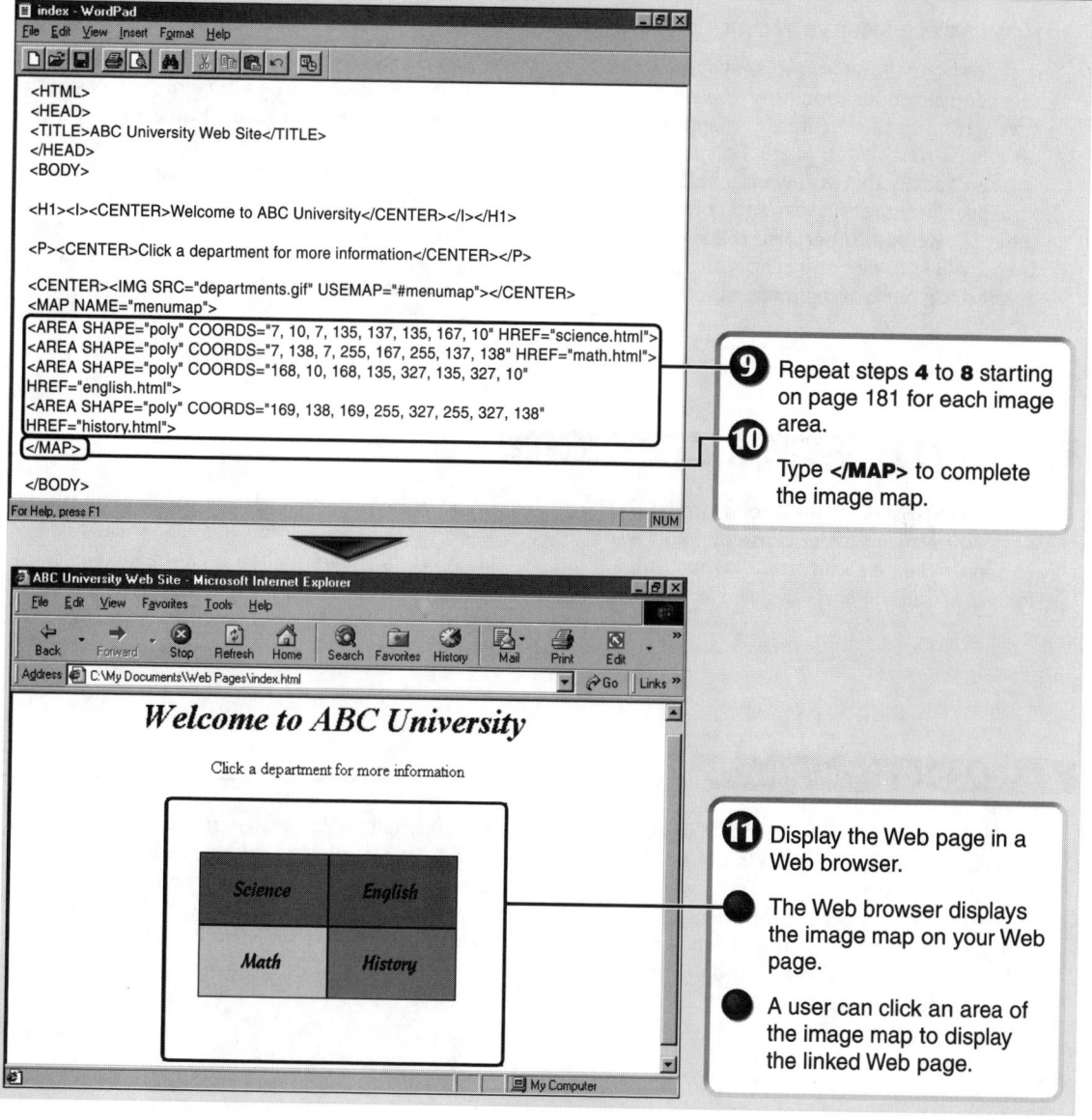

**index - WordPad**

File Edit View Insert Format Help

```
<HTML>
<HEAD>
<TITLE>ABC University Web Site</TITLE>
</HEAD>
<BODY>

<H1><I><CENTER>Welcome to ABC University</CENTER></I></H1>

<P><CENTER>Click a department for more information</CENTER></P>

<CENTER><IMG SRC="departments.gif" USEMAP="#menumap"></CENTER>
<MAP NAME="menumap">
<AREA SHAPE="poly" COORDS="7, 10, 7, 135, 137, 135, 167, 10" HREF="science.html">
<AREA SHAPE="poly" COORDS="7, 138, 7, 255, 167, 255, 137, 138" HREF="math.html">
<AREA SHAPE="poly" COORDS="168, 10, 168, 135, 327, 135, 327, 10"
HREF="english.html">
<AREA SHAPE="poly" COORDS="169, 138, 169, 255, 327, 255, 327, 138"
HREF="history.html">
</MAP>

</BODY>
```

For Help, press F1                                                          NUM

**9** Repeat steps **4** to **8** starting on page 181 for each image area.

**10** Type **</MAP>** to complete the image map.

**ABC University Web Site - Microsoft Internet Explorer**

File Edit View Favorites Tools Help

Back Forward Stop Refresh Home Search Favorites History Mail Print Edit

Address C:\My Documents\Web Pages\index.html                    Go   Links »

*Welcome to ABC University*

Click a department for more information

| Science | English |
| Math | History |

**11** Display the Web page in a Web browser.

● The Web browser displays the image map on your Web page.

● A user can click an area of the image map to display the linked Web page.

My Computer

# INTRODUCTION TO STYLE SHEETS

You can use style sheets to define the formatting and layout of information on your Web pages. Style sheets are also known as Cascading Style Sheets (CSS). You can find more information about style sheets at the www.w3.org Web site.

## INTRODUCTION TO STYLE SHEETS

### HOW STYLE SHEETS WORK

A style sheet allows you to specify in one centralized location how you want information for a specific tag to appear on one or more Web pages. For example, you can specify that you want all H1 headings to appear in a specific font and color. A style sheet allows you to perform the same tasks as many HTML tags and is now the preferred method for performing these tasks.

### STYLE SHEET STRUCTURE

When creating a style sheet, you enter a tag you want to define properties for, such as H1 (H1 headings), P (paragraphs) or B (bold text) and then list the properties you want the tag to use. The list of properties must be enclosed in braces { } and a semi-colon (;) must separate each property in the list. The properties you define for a tag will affect all the information that uses the tag on your Web page(s).

## EMBEDDED VERSUS LINKED STYLE SHEETS

Embedding a style sheet directly in the Web page you want to affect is useful if you want to simply create a consistent layout and format for all the parts of a single Web page.

If you want your style sheets to affect all the Web pages in your Web site, you should use linked style sheets. When creating linked style sheets, you specify the information for each tag in a file that is linked to each Web page you want to affect.

## CASCADING STYLE SHEETS

Style sheets can be very useful in large Web sites because the style sheets can be linked, or cascaded, to form a hierarchy of related style sheets. This allows you to re-use the properties specified in another style sheet without having to retype all the properties in a new style sheet.

For example, if you assign properties to the BODY tag in one style sheet, all the style sheets cascading from that style sheet will automatically be able to use and alter the properties specified for the BODY tag.

# in an *instant*

### ADDITIONAL FEATURES

Style sheets allow you to format and lay out text and images in ways you cannot accomplish with HTML tags. You can create sophisticated Web pages that look like pages from a magazine. For example, you can change the line spacing or margins for the page. You can also use style sheets to specify the position of text and images on a Web page.

### SAVE TIME

Style sheets allow you to define in one location how you want information that uses a tag to appear throughout your Web page(s). This saves time since you do not have to type the same information in each individual tag. For example, you can define how you want all the text that uses the P (paragraph) tag to appear throughout a Web page.

### EASY TO UPDATE

When you use style sheets, you can make changes to your Web page(s) in one centralized location. This prevents you from having to change each tag on your Web page(s) individually and helps maintain a consistent appearance for your Web page(s). For example, you can change the font, size and color of every heading that uses the H1 tag in your Web pages at once.

### DISPLAY WEB PAGES FASTER

Since style sheets allow you to save all your formatting and layout information in a separate file, the file sizes of your Web pages are smaller. This allows the Web pages to transfer faster to users' computers and appear more quickly on the screen.

### WEB BROWSER SUPPORT

When using style sheets in your Web site, you should keep in mind that not all Web browsers support style sheets. For best results, you should make sure that your Web pages will continue to work even when style sheets are disabled. This will ensure that all visitors to your Web site will be able to view your Web pages.

### PERFORM GENERAL SETS OF TASKS

When creating style sheets, you should design each style sheet to perform only a general set of formatting or layout tasks. Specialized style sheets can then be linked to the general style sheets. This prevents the style sheets from becoming overloaded and maximizes the efficiency of the style sheets. When a style sheet becomes too large, additional memory and resources are required to display the Web pages that use the style sheet.

# SET UP A STYLE SHEET

You can set up a style sheet that will define the formatting
and layout for a single Web page or multiple Web pages.
Setting up a style sheet for multiple Web pages allows you
to give your Web pages a consistent appearance. Changes
you make to the style sheet will affect all the Web pages
that use the style sheet.

## FOR A SINGLE WEB PAGE

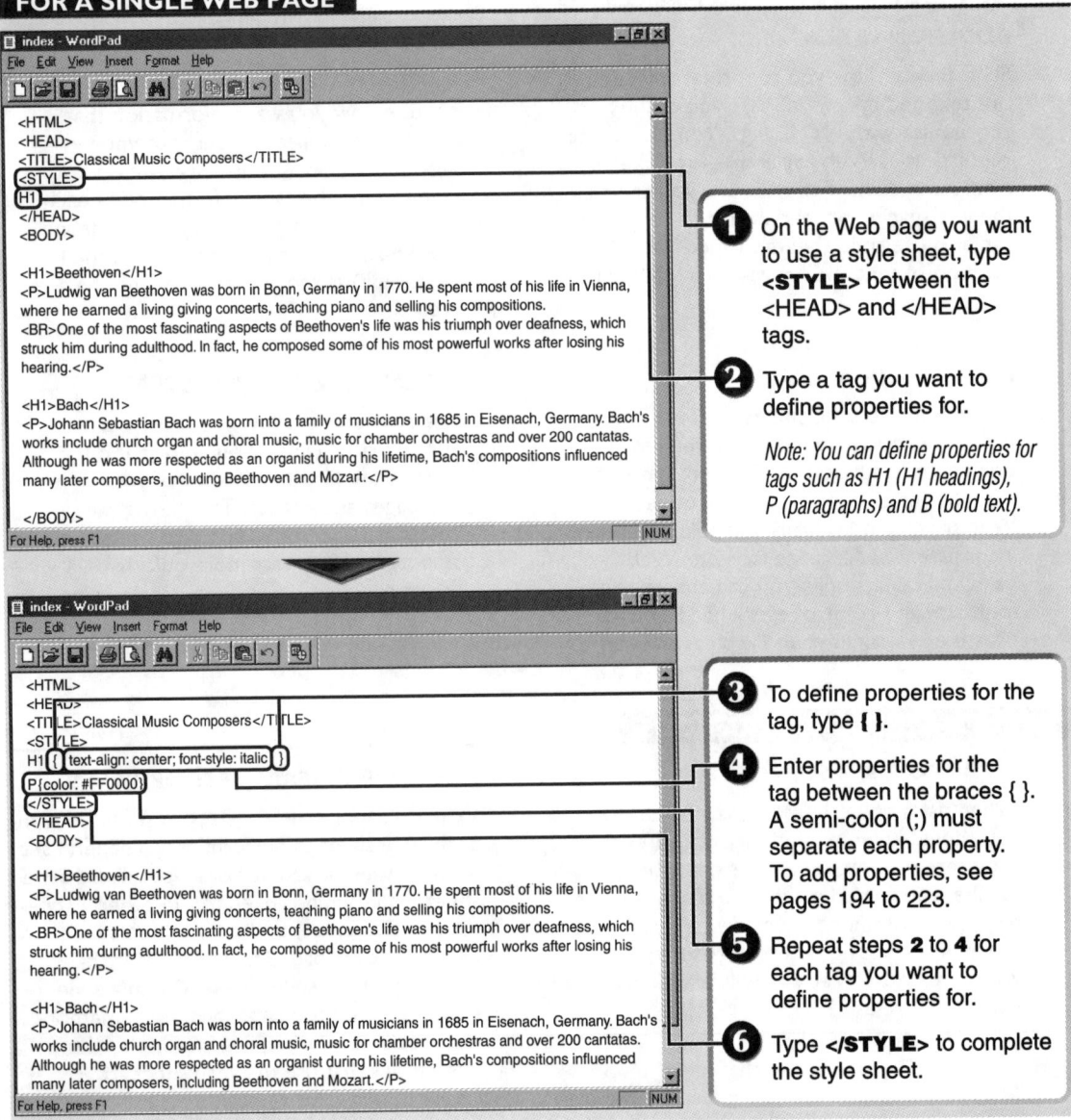

**1** On the Web page you want
to use a style sheet, type
**<STYLE>** between the
<HEAD> and </HEAD>
tags.

**2** Type a tag you want to
define properties for.

*Note: You can define properties for
tags such as H1 (H1 headings),
P (paragraphs) and B (bold text).*

**3** To define properties for the
tag, type **{ }**.

**4** Enter properties for the
tag between the braces { }.
A semi-colon (;) must
separate each property.
To add properties, see
pages 194 to 223.

**5** Repeat steps **2** to **4** for
each tag you want to
define properties for.

**6** Type **</STYLE>** to complete
the style sheet.

# in an *instant*

## FOR MULTIPLE WEB PAGES

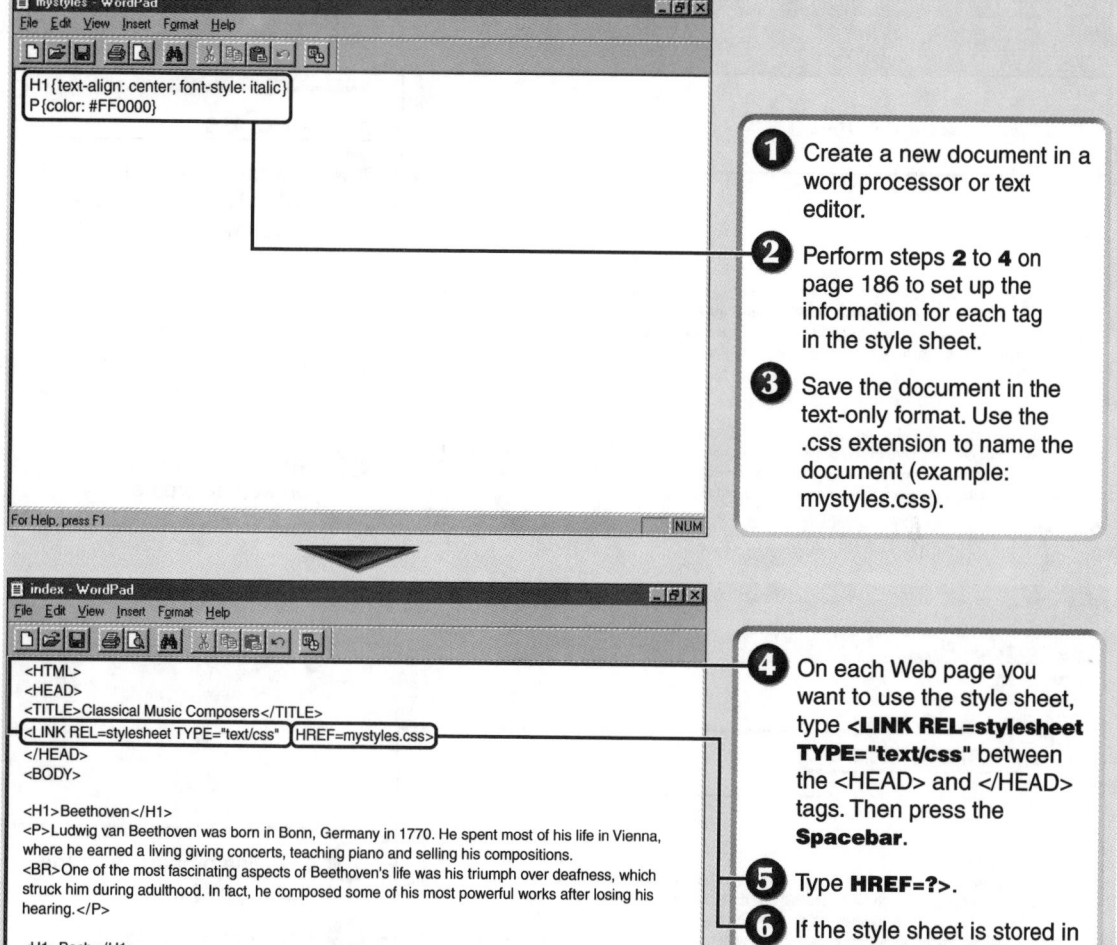

**mystyles - WordPad**

File Edit View Insert Format Help

```
H1 {text-align: center; font-style: italic}
P {color: #FF0000}
```

For Help, press F1    NUM

**index - WordPad**

File Edit View Insert Format Help

```
<HTML>
<HEAD>
<TITLE>Classical Music Composers</TITLE>
<LINK REL=stylesheet TYPE="text/css"  HREF=mystyles.css>
</HEAD>
<BODY>

<H1>Beethoven</H1>
<P>Ludwig van Beethoven was born in Bonn, Germany in 1770. He spent most of his life in Vienna,
where he earned a living giving concerts, teaching piano and selling his compositions.
<BR>One of the most fascinating aspects of Beethoven's life was his triumph over deafness, which
struck him during adulthood. In fact, he composed some of his most powerful works after losing his
hearing.</P>

<H1>Bach</H1>
<P>Johann Sebastian Bach was born into a family of musicians in 1685 in Eisenach, Germany. Bach's
works include church organ and choral music, music for chamber orchestras and over 200 cantatas.
Although he was more respected as an organist during his lifetime, Bach's compositions influenced
many later composers, including Beethoven and Mozart.</P>

</BODY>
</HTML>
```

For Help, press F1    NUM

**1** Create a new document in a word processor or text editor.

**2** Perform steps **2** to **4** on page 186 to set up the information for each tag in the style sheet.

**3** Save the document in the text-only format. Use the .css extension to name the document (example: mystyles.css).

**4** On each Web page you want to use the style sheet, type **<LINK REL=stylesheet TYPE="text/css"** between the <HEAD> and </HEAD> tags. Then press the **Spacebar**.

**5** Type **HREF=?>**.

**6** If the style sheet is stored in the same folder, replace **?** with the style sheet name.

*Note: If the style sheet is stored in a subfolder, you must also specify the name of the subfolder.*

# CREATE A CLASS

You can create a class to format only some of the elements on your Web page that use a specific tag. Creating a class gives you more control over the formatting and layout of information on your Web page. For example, you can create a class of important paragraphs (P.important) that will display slightly different formatting than regular paragraphs (P).

## CREATE A CLASS

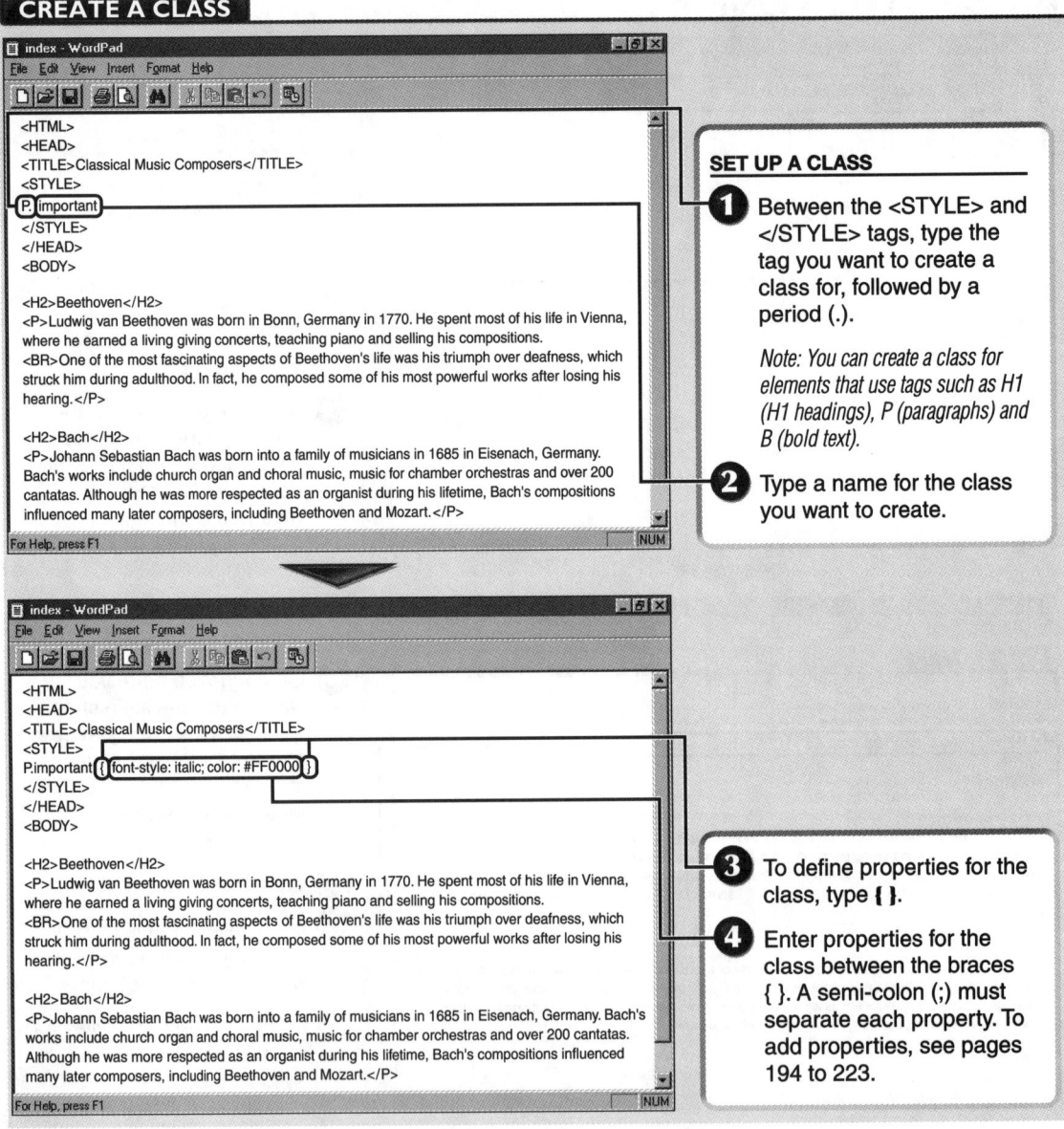

### SET UP A CLASS

**1** Between the <STYLE> and </STYLE> tags, type the tag you want to create a class for, followed by a period (.).

*Note: You can create a class for elements that use tags such as H1 (H1 headings), P (paragraphs) and B (bold text).*

**2** Type a name for the class you want to create.

**3** To define properties for the class, type { }.

**4** Enter properties for the class between the braces { }. A semi-colon (;) must separate each property. To add properties, see pages 194 to 223.

# in an *instant*

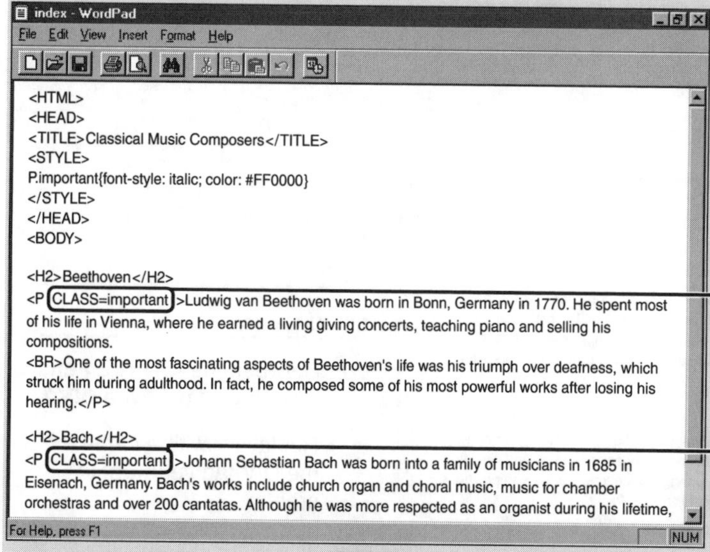

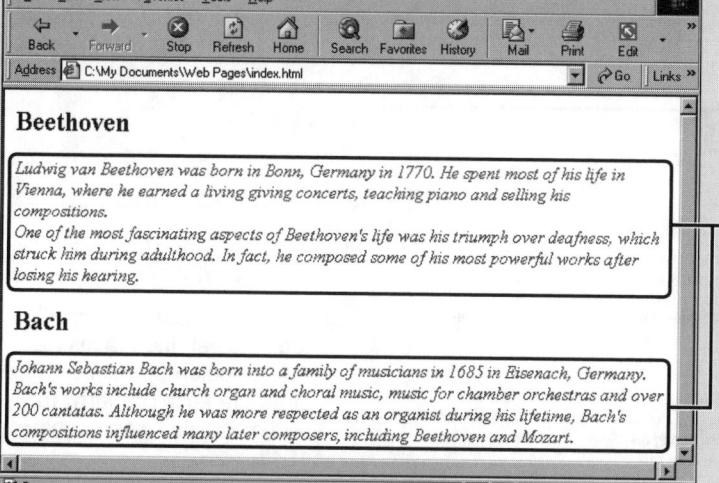

```
index - WordPad                                                    _ 5 X
File  Edit  View  Insert  Format  Help

[toolbar icons]

<HTML>
<HEAD>
<TITLE>Classical Music Composers</TITLE>
<STYLE>
P.important{font-style: italic; color: #FF0000}
</STYLE>
</HEAD>
<BODY>

<H2>Beethoven</H2>
<P CLASS=important >Ludwig van Beethoven was born in Bonn, Germany in 1770. He spent most
of his life in Vienna, where he earned a living giving concerts, teaching piano and selling his
compositions.
<BR>One of the most fascinating aspects of Beethoven's life was his triumph over deafness, which
struck him during adulthood. In fact, he composed some of his most powerful works after losing his
hearing.</P>

<H2>Bach</H2>
<P CLASS=important >Johann Sebastian Bach was born into a family of musicians in 1685 in
Eisenach, Germany. Bach's works include church organ and choral music, music for chamber
orchestras and over 200 cantatas. Although he was more respected as an organist during his lifetime,

For Help, press F1                                                    NUM
```

## DEFINE EACH CLASS AREA

**5** Position the cursor in the tag before an element you want to include in the class.

*Note: The element must use the tag you typed in step 1.*

**6** Type **CLASS=?** replacing **?** with the name of the class you typed in step **2**.

**7** Repeat steps **5** and **6** for each element you want to include in the class.

```
Classical Music Composers - Microsoft Internet Explorer           _ 5 X
File  Edit  View  Favorites  Tools  Help

Back   Forward   Stop   Refresh   Home   Search  Favorites  History   Mail   Print   Edit
Address   C:\My Documents\Web Pages\index.html          Go   Links

Beethoven

Ludwig van Beethoven was born in Bonn, Germany in 1770. He spent most of his life in
Vienna, where he earned a living giving concerts, teaching piano and selling his
compositions.
One of the most fascinating aspects of Beethoven's life was his triumph over deafness, which
struck him during adulthood. In fact, he composed some of his most powerful works after
losing his hearing.

Bach

Johann Sebastian Bach was born into a family of musicians in 1685 in Eisenach, Germany.
Bach's works include church organ and choral music, music for chamber orchestras and over
200 cantatas. Although he was more respected as an organist during his lifetime, Bach's
compositions influenced many later composers, including Beethoven and Mozart.

Done                                                        My Computer
```

**8** Display the Web page in a Web browser.

■ The Web browser displays each element you included in the class with the formatting you specified.

*Note: The elements you included in the class display the properties you defined for the class as well as the properties you defined for the original tag.*

# APPLY STYLES USING DIV

You can use the DIV tag to apply styles to specific areas of your Web page. Unlike creating a class, which allows you to define properties for only one type of element, using the DIV tag lets you define properties for several types of elements at once. For example, you can use the DIV tag to center headings and paragraphs at the same time.

## APPLY STYLES USING DIV

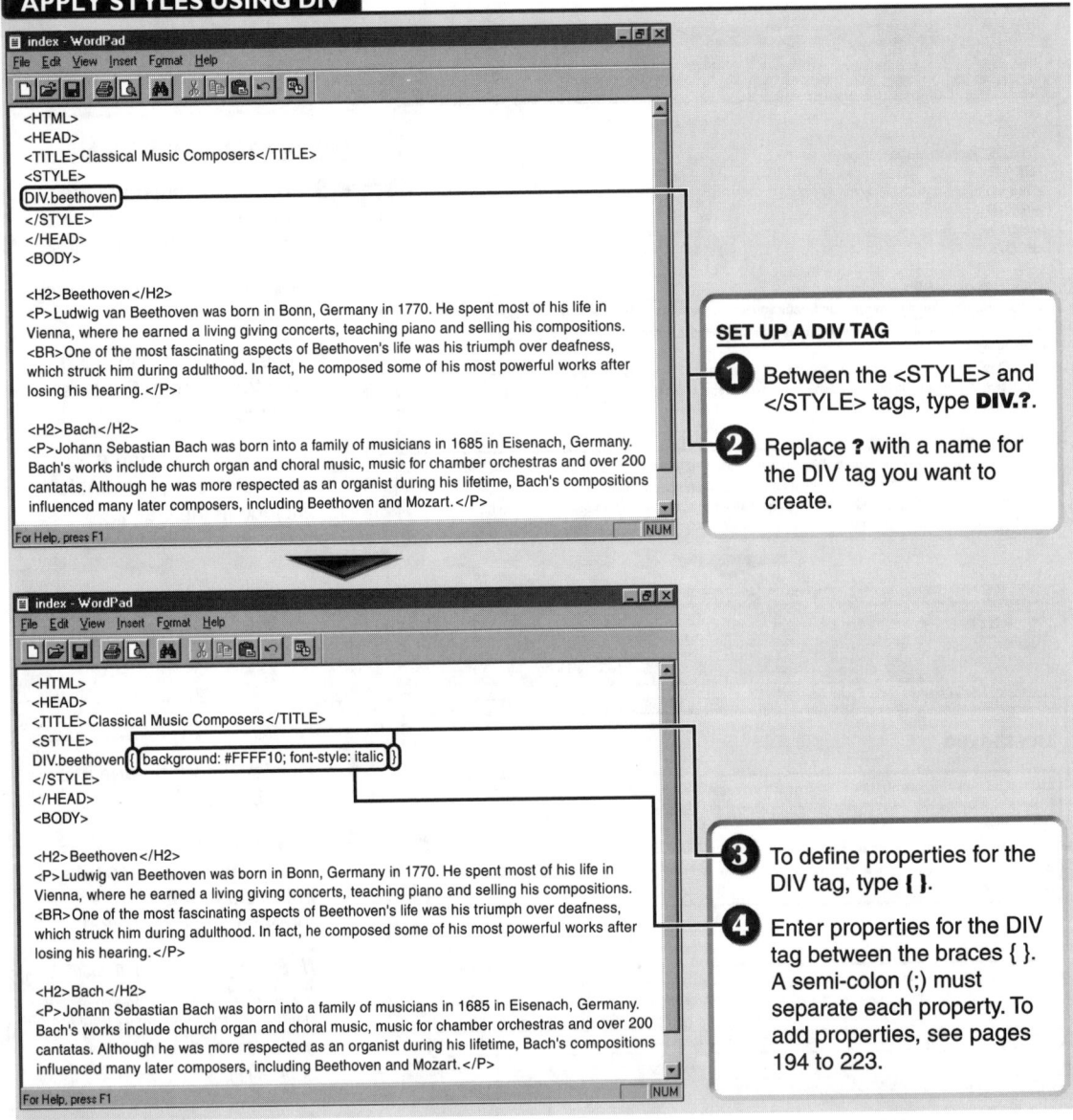

**SET UP A DIV TAG**

**1** Between the <STYLE> and </STYLE> tags, type **DIV.?**.

**2** Replace **?** with a name for the DIV tag you want to create.

**3** To define properties for the DIV tag, type **{ }**.

**4** Enter properties for the DIV tag between the braces { }. A semi-colon (;) must separate each property. To add properties, see pages 194 to 223.

in an **instant**

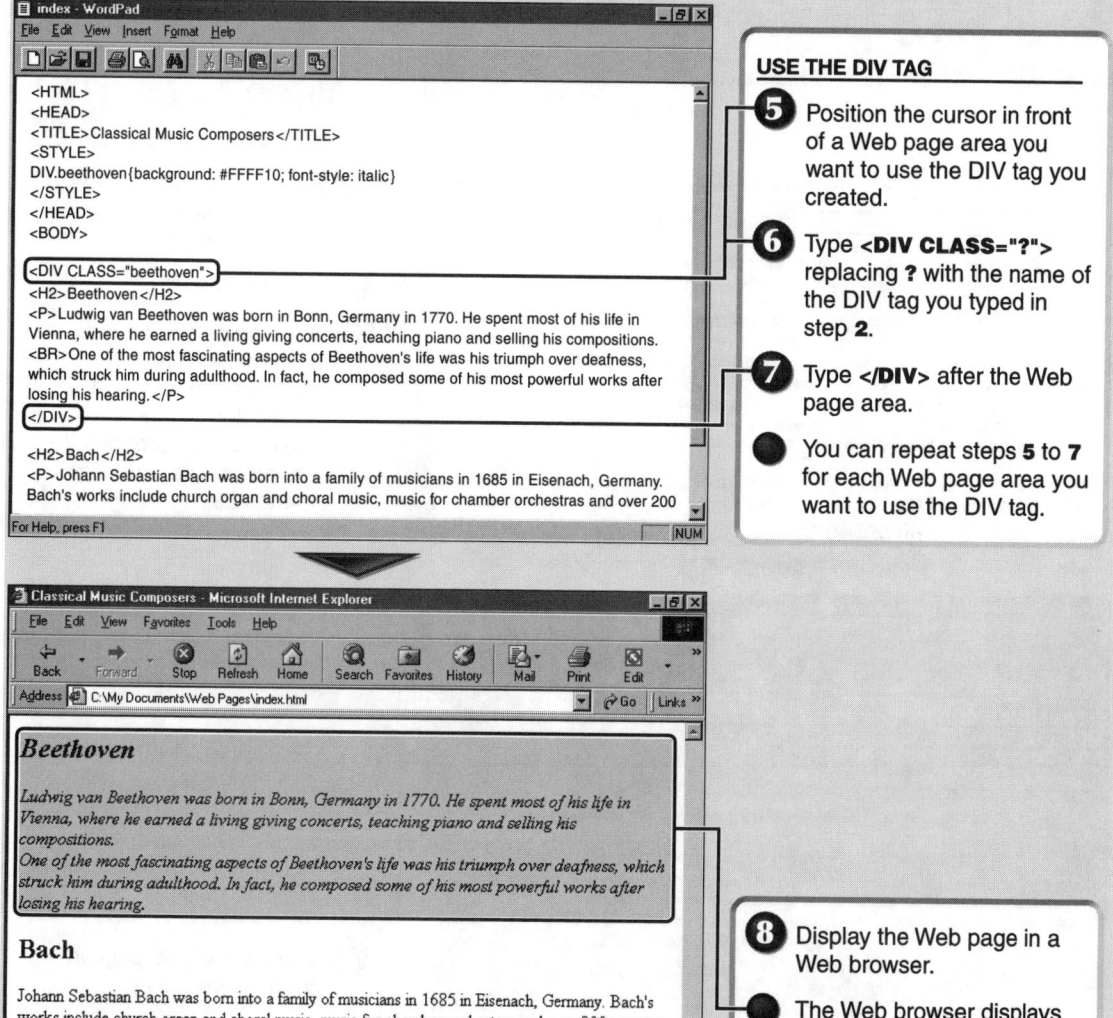

**USE THE DIV TAG**

**5** Position the cursor in front of a Web page area you want to use the DIV tag you created.

**6** Type **<DIV CLASS="?">** replacing **?** with the name of the DIV tag you typed in step **2**.

**7** Type **</DIV>** after the Web page area.

● You can repeat steps **5** to **7** for each Web page area you want to use the DIV tag.

**8** Display the Web page in a Web browser.

● The Web browser displays the Web page area(s) with the properties you specified.

# APPLY STYLES INDIVIDUALLY

You can apply styles to an individual element on your Web page. For example, you can change the appearance of an element such as a heading (H1 to H6), paragraph (P) or table (TABLE). Applying styles individually allows you to take advantage of the features offered by styles without having to create a style sheet.

APPLY STYLES INDIVIDUALLY

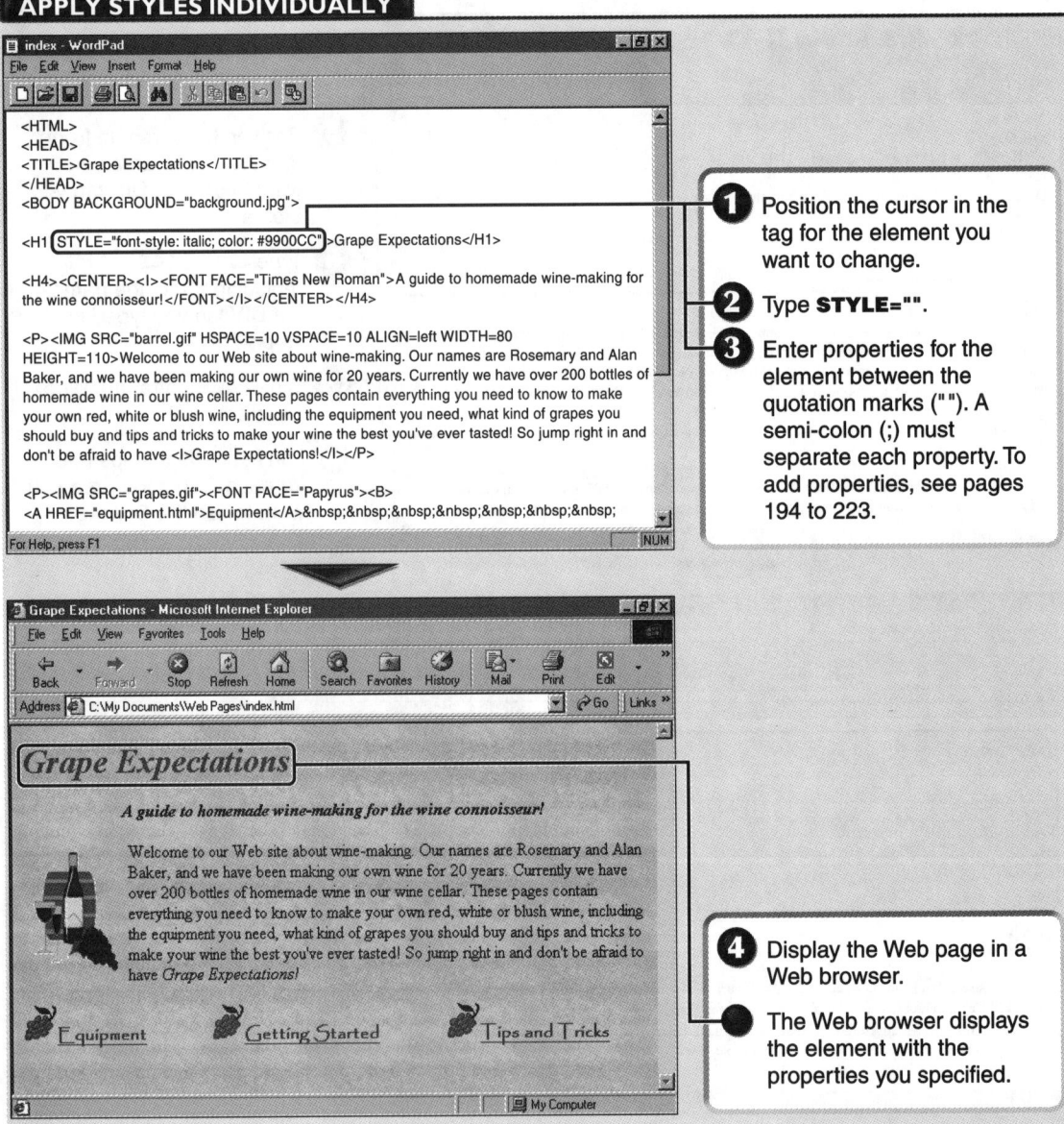

**1** Position the cursor in the tag for the element you want to change.

**2** Type **STYLE=""**.

**3** Enter properties for the element between the quotation marks (" "). A semi-colon (;) must separate each property. To add properties, see pages 194 to 223.

**4** Display the Web page in a Web browser.

The Web browser displays the element with the properties you specified.

You can hide a style sheet on a Web page so older Web browsers that cannot understand style sheets will ignore the information. If you do not hide the style sheet, an older Web browser may display the information for the style sheet on your Web page when a user displays the page.

## HIDE A STYLE SHEET

```
<HTML>
<HEAD>
<TITLE>Classical Music Composers</TITLE>
<STYLE>
<!--
H2{text-align: center; font-style: italic}
P{color: #FF0000}
</STYLE>
</HEAD>
<BODY>

<H2>Beethoven</H2>
<P>Ludwig van Beethoven was born in Bonn, Germany in 1770. He spent most of his life in Vienna,
where he earned a living giving concerts, teaching piano and selling his compositions.
<BR>One of the most fascinating aspects of Beethoven's life was his triumph over deafness, which
struck him during adulthood. In fact, he composed some of his most powerful works after losing his
hearing.</P>

<H2>Bach</H2>
<P>Johann Sebastian Bach was born into a family of musicians in 1685 in Eisenach, Germany.
Bach's works include church organ and choral music, music for chamber orchestras and over 200
```

**1** Type **<!--** directly below the **<STYLE>** tag.

*Note: You do not need to hide a style sheet you created as a separate document.*

```
<HTML>
<HEAD>
<TITLE>Classical Music Composers</TITLE>
<STYLE>
<!--
H2{text-align: center; font-style: italic}
P{color: #FF0000}
-->
</STYLE>
</HEAD>
<BODY>

<H2>Beethoven</H2>
<P>Ludwig van Beethoven was born in Bonn, Germany in 1770. He spent most of his life in Vienna,
where he earned a living giving concerts, teaching piano and selling his compositions.
<BR>One of the most fascinating aspects of Beethoven's life was his triumph over deafness, which
struck him during adulthood. In fact, he composed some of his most powerful works after losing his
hearing.</P>

<H2>Bach</H2>
<P>Johann Sebastian Bach was born into a family of musicians in 1685 in Eisenach, Germany.
```

**2** Type **-->** directly above the **</STYLE>** tag.

● If a user displays your Web page in an older Web browser that cannot understand style sheets, the Web browser will ignore the style sheet information.

**193**

# BOLD OR ITALICIZE TEXT

You can bold or italicize all the text on your Web page that uses a specific tag. Bolding or italicizing text is useful for emphasizing information on your Web page. You can also remove bold or italic formatting from text that uses a specific tag, such as H1 (H1 headings).

## BOLD OR ITALICIZE TEXT

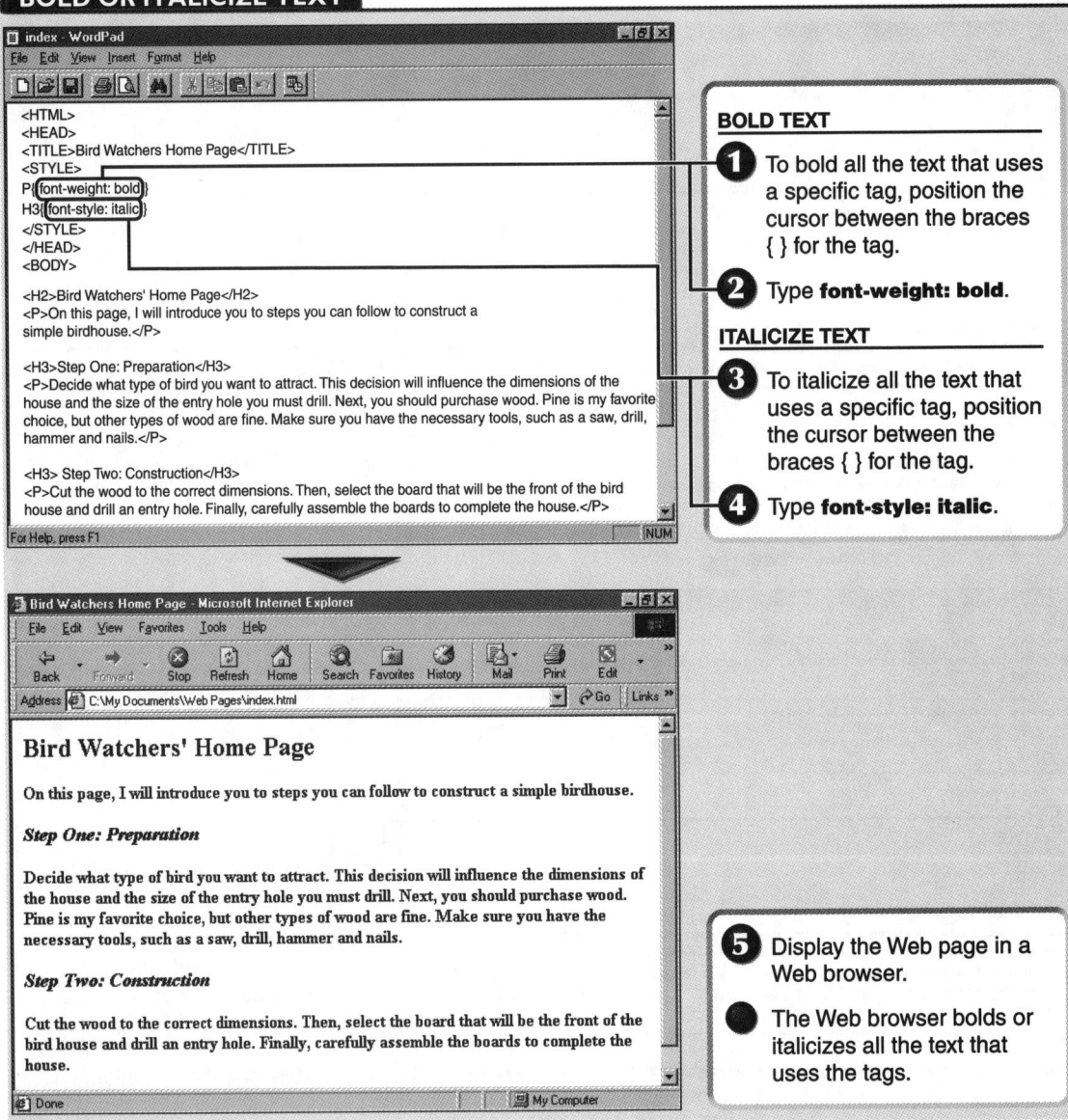

**BOLD TEXT**

**1** To bold all the text that uses a specific tag, position the cursor between the braces { } for the tag.

**2** Type **font-weight: bold**.

**ITALICIZE TEXT**

**3** To italicize all the text that uses a specific tag, position the cursor between the braces { } for the tag.

**4** Type **font-style: italic**.

**5** Display the Web page in a Web browser.

● The Web browser bolds or italicizes all the text that uses the tags.

**194**

# in an *instant*

## REMOVE BOLD OR ITALIC FORMATTING

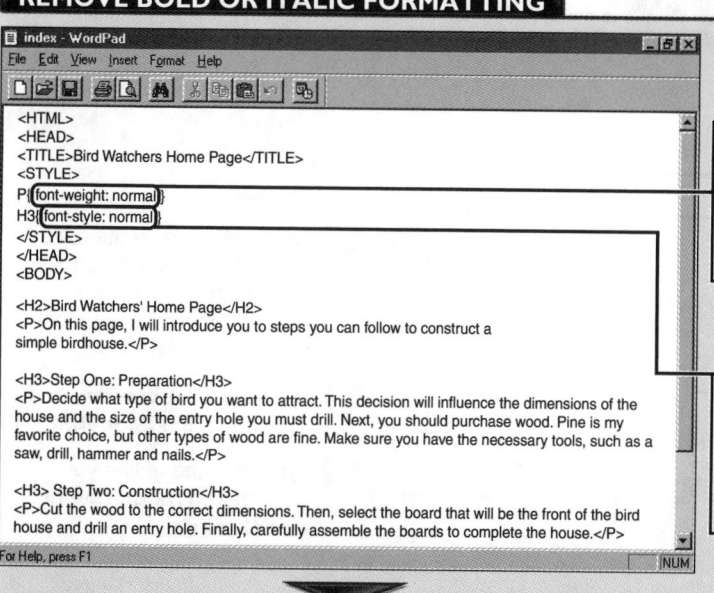

```
<HTML>
<HEAD>
<TITLE>Bird Watchers Home Page</TITLE>
<STYLE>
P{font-weight: normal}
H3{font-style: normal}
</STYLE>
</HEAD>
<BODY>

<H2>Bird Watchers' Home Page</H2>
<P>On this page, I will introduce you to steps you can follow to construct a
simple birdhouse.</P>

<H3>Step One: Preparation</H3>
<P>Decide what type of bird you want to attract. This decision will influence the dimensions of the
house and the size of the entry hole you must drill. Next, you should purchase wood. Pine is my
favorite choice, but other types of wood are fine. Make sure you have the necessary tools, such as a
saw, drill, hammer and nails.</P>

<H3> Step Two: Construction</H3>
<P>Cut the wood to the correct dimensions. Then, select the board that will be the front of the bird
house and drill an entry hole. Finally, carefully assemble the boards to complete the house.</P>
```

**REMOVE BOLDING**

**1** To remove bold formatting from text that uses a specific tag, position the cursor between the braces { } for the tag.

**2** Type **font-weight: normal**.

**REMOVE ITALICS**

**3** To remove italic formatting from text that uses a specific tag, position the cursor between the braces { } for the tag.

**4** Type **font-style: normal**.

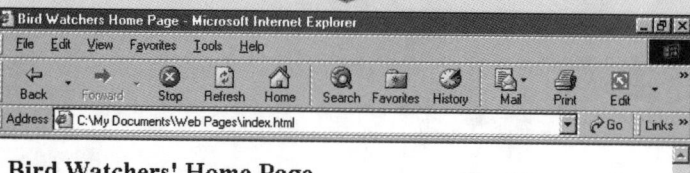

### Bird Watchers' Home Page

On this page, I will introduce you to steps you can follow to construct a simple birdhouse.

**Step One: Preparation**

Decide what type of bird you want to attract. This decision will influence the dimensions of the house and the size of the entry hole you must drill. Next, you should purchase wood. Pine is my favorite choice, but other types of wood are fine. Make sure you have the necessary tools, such as a saw, drill, hammer and nails.

**Step Two: Construction**

Cut the wood to the correct dimensions. Then, select the board that will be the front of the bird house and drill an entry hole. Finally, carefully assemble the boards to complete the house.

**5** Display the Web page in a Web browser.

● The Web browser removes the bold or italic formatting from all the text that uses the tags.

# UNDERLINE OR STRIKE OUT TEXT

You can underline or strike out all the text on your Web page that uses a specific tag. You should be careful when underlining text, since users may mistake the text for a link. Striking out text is useful for indicating that the information is being revised.

UNDERLINE OR STRIKE OUT TEXT

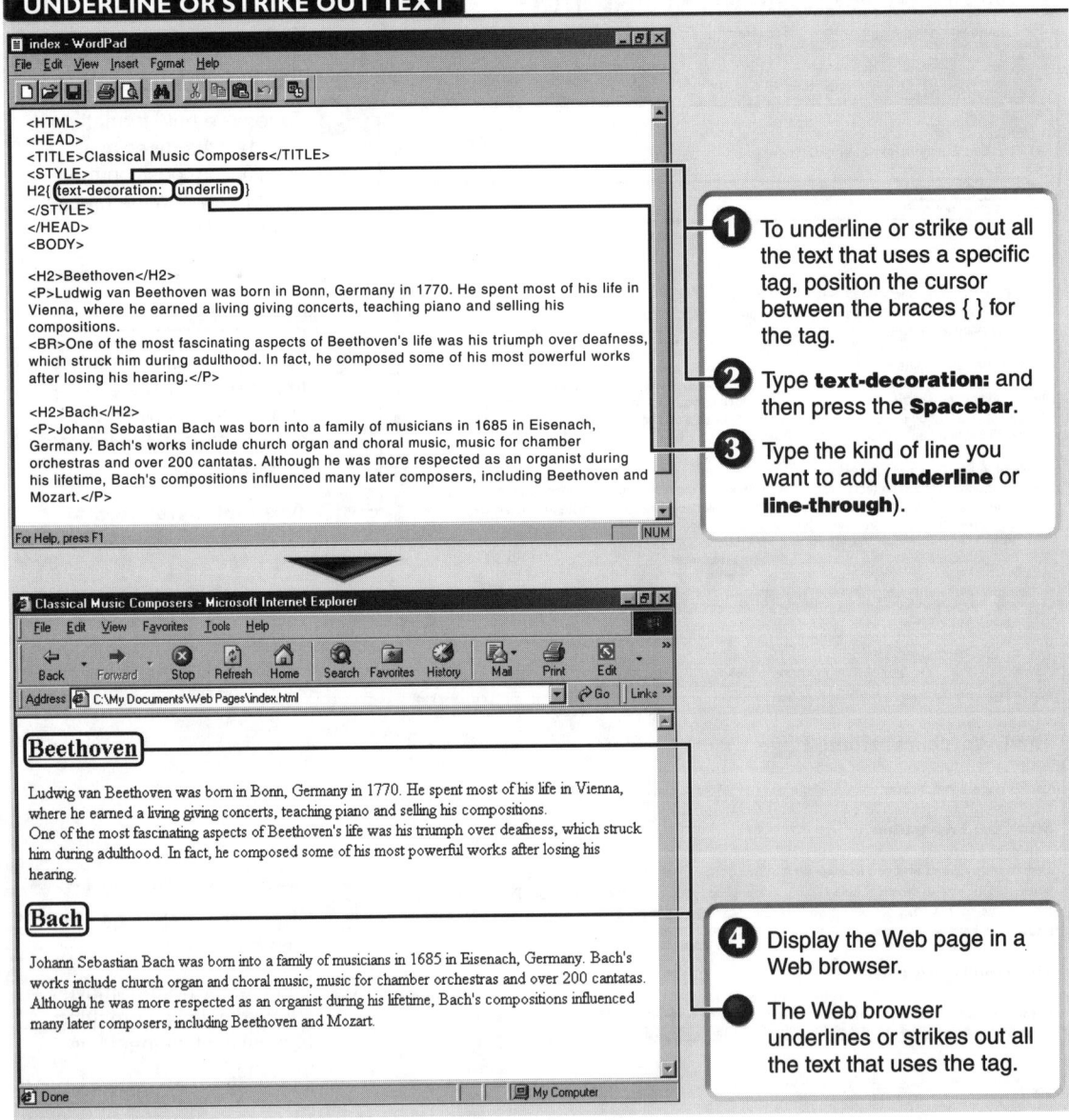

**1** To underline or strike out all the text that uses a specific tag, position the cursor between the braces { } for the tag.

**2** Type **text-decoration:** and then press the **Spacebar**.

**3** Type the kind of line you want to add (**underline** or **line-through**).

**4** Display the Web page in a Web browser.

● The Web browser underlines or strikes out all the text that uses the tag.

# CHANGE TEXT CASE

You can change the case of all the text on your Web page that uses a specific tag. When changing the case of text, you can change the first letter of each word to uppercase, change all the letters in each word to uppercase or change all the letters in each word to lowercase.

## CHANGE TEXT CASE

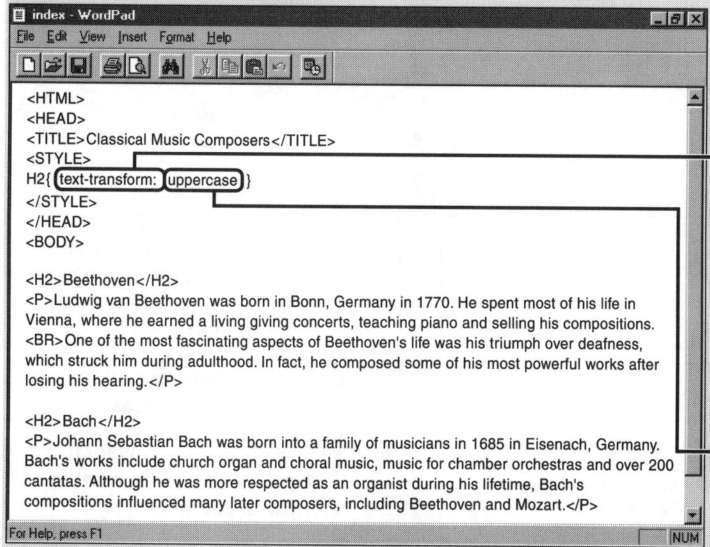

```
index - WordPad
File  Edit  View  Insert  Format  Help

<HTML>
<HEAD>
<TITLE>Classical Music Composers</TITLE>
<STYLE>
H2{ text-transform: uppercase }
</STYLE>
</HEAD>
<BODY>

<H2>Beethoven</H2>
<P>Ludwig van Beethoven was born in Bonn, Germany in 1770. He spent most of his life in
Vienna, where he earned a living giving concerts, teaching piano and selling his compositions.
<BR>One of the most fascinating aspects of Beethoven's life was his triumph over deafness,
which struck him during adulthood. In fact, he composed some of his most powerful works after
losing his hearing.</P>

<H2>Bach</H2>
<P>Johann Sebastian Bach was born into a family of musicians in 1685 in Eisenach, Germany.
Bach's works include church organ and choral music, music for chamber orchestras and over 200
cantatas. Although he was more respected as an organist during his lifetime, Bach's
compositions influenced many later composers, including Beethoven and Mozart.</P>

For Help, press F1                                                          NUM
```

**1** To change the case of all the text that uses a specific tag, position the cursor between the braces { } for the tag.

**2** Type **text-transform:** and then press the **Spacebar**.

**3** Type the case you want to use (**capitalize, uppercase** or **lowercase**).

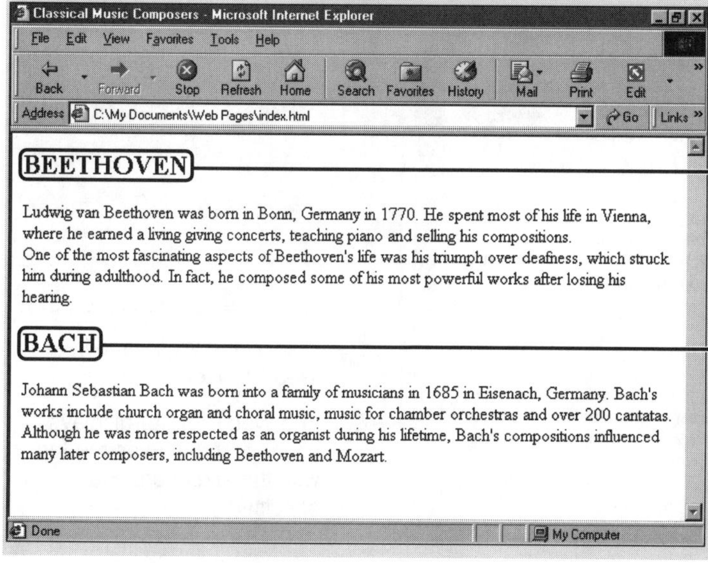

```
Classical Music Composers - Microsoft Internet Explorer
File  Edit  View  Favorites  Tools  Help

Back  Forward  Stop  Refresh  Home  Search  Favorites  History  Mail  Print  Edit

Address  C:\My Documents\Web Pages\index.html                    Go  Links

BEETHOVEN

Ludwig van Beethoven was born in Bonn, Germany in 1770. He spent most of his life in Vienna,
where he earned a living giving concerts, teaching piano and selling his compositions.
One of the most fascinating aspects of Beethoven's life was his triumph over deafness, which struck
him during adulthood. In fact, he composed some of his most powerful works after losing his
hearing.

BACH

Johann Sebastian Bach was born into a family of musicians in 1685 in Eisenach, Germany. Bach's
works include church organ and choral music, music for chamber orchestras and over 200 cantatas.
Although he was more respected as an organist during his lifetime, Bach's compositions influenced
many later composers, including Beethoven and Mozart.

Done                                                          My Computer
```

**4** Display the Web page in a Web browser.

■ The Web browser displays all the text that uses the tag in the case you specified.

# CHANGE TEXT ALIGNMENT

You can change the alignment of all the text on your Web page that uses a specific tag. The text you want to align must use a block-level tag. A block-level tag, such as a heading (H1 to H6) or P, displays a blank line before and after elements that use the tag.

## CHANGE TEXT ALIGNMENT

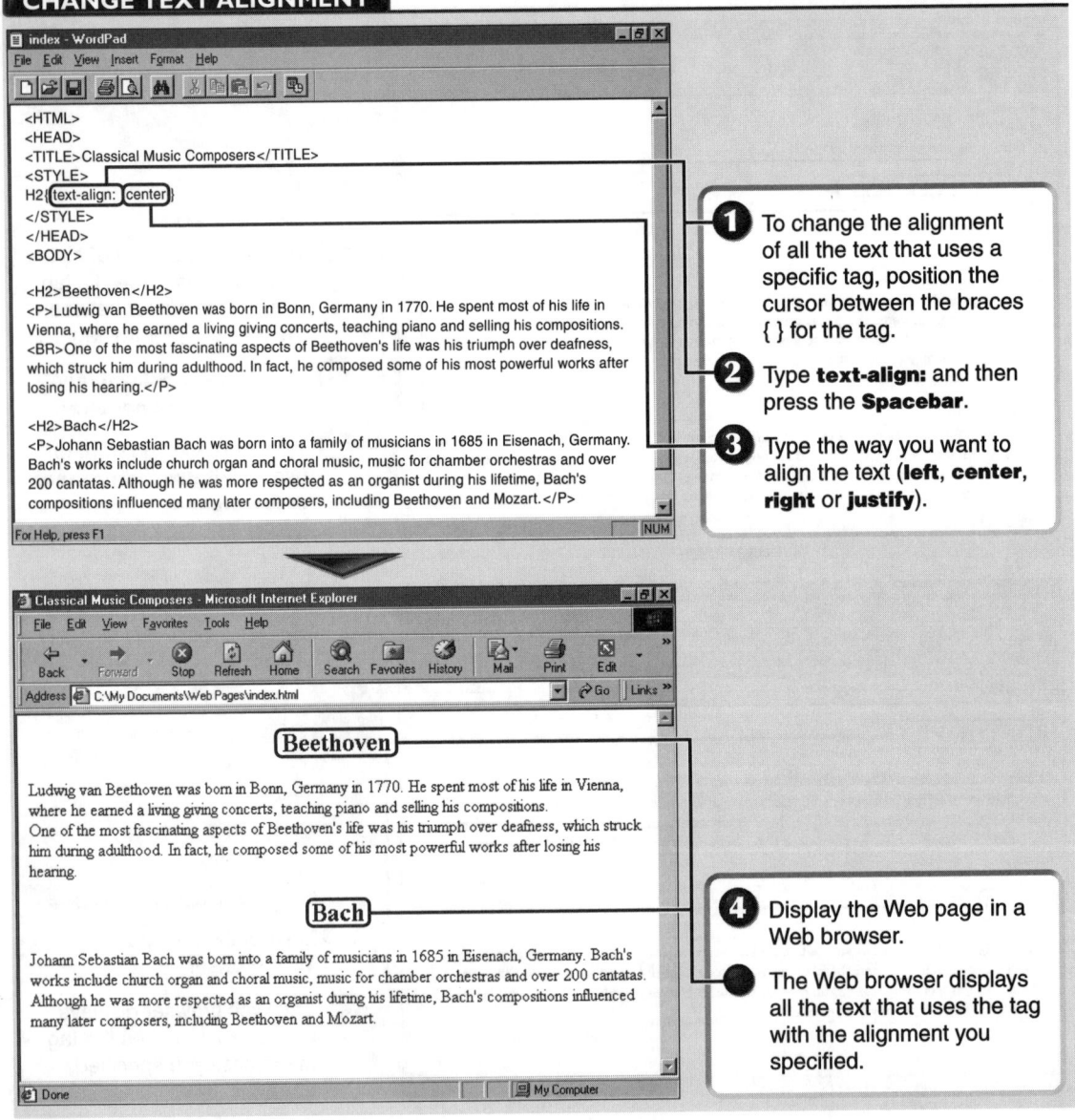

**1** To change the alignment of all the text that uses a specific tag, position the cursor between the braces { } for the tag.

**2** Type **text-align:** and then press the **Spacebar**.

**3** Type the way you want to align the text (**left**, **center**, **right** or **justify**).

**4** Display the Web page in a Web browser.

● The Web browser displays all the text that uses the tag with the alignment you specified.

You can change the color of all the text on your Web page that uses a specific tag. The color you choose for the text may not appear the way you expect on some computers since some users can set their Web browsers to display the colors they prefer.

## CHANGE TEXT COLOR

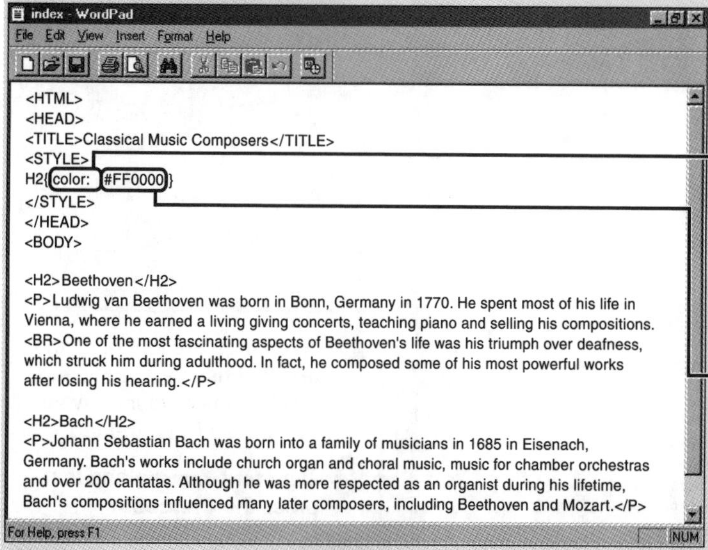

```
index - WordPad
File  Edit  View  Insert  Format  Help

<HTML>
<HEAD>
<TITLE>Classical Music Composers</TITLE>
<STYLE>
H2{color:  #FF0000}
</STYLE>
</HEAD>
<BODY>

<H2>Beethoven</H2>
<P>Ludwig van Beethoven was born in Bonn, Germany in 1770. He spent most of his life in
Vienna, where he earned a living giving concerts, teaching piano and selling his compositions.
<BR>One of the most fascinating aspects of Beethoven's life was his triumph over deafness,
which struck him during adulthood. In fact, he composed some of his most powerful works
after losing his hearing.</P>

<H2>Bach</H2>
<P>Johann Sebastian Bach was born into a family of musicians in 1685 in Eisenach,
Germany. Bach's works include church organ and choral music, music for chamber orchestras
and over 200 cantatas. Although he was more respected as an organist during his lifetime,
Bach's compositions influenced many later composers, including Beethoven and Mozart.</P>

For Help, press F1                                                                    NUM
```

**1** To change the color of all the text that uses a specific tag, position the cursor between the braces { } for the tag.

**2** Type **color:** and then press the **Spacebar**.

**3** Type the name or code for the color you want to use (example: **red** or **#FF0000**).

*Note: For a list of colors you can use, see page 245.*

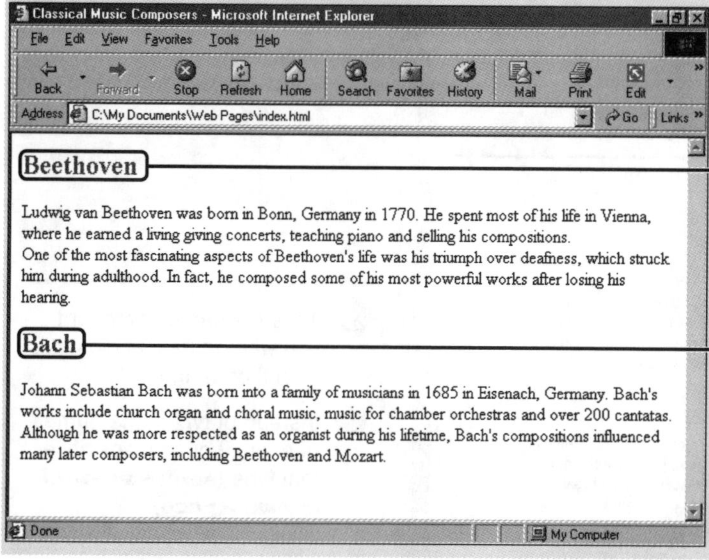

```
Classical Music Composers - Microsoft Internet Explorer
File  Edit  View  Favorites  Tools  Help

 Back    Forward   Stop   Refresh  Home    Search  Favorites  History    Mail    Print     Edit

Address  C:\My Documents\Web Pages\index.html                          Go   Links

Beethoven

Ludwig van Beethoven was born in Bonn, Germany in 1770. He spent most of his life in Vienna,
where he earned a living giving concerts, teaching piano and selling his compositions.
One of the most fascinating aspects of Beethoven's life was his triumph over deafness, which struck
him during adulthood. In fact, he composed some of his most powerful works after losing his
hearing.

Bach

Johann Sebastian Bach was born into a family of musicians in 1685 in Eisenach, Germany. Bach's
works include church organ and choral music, music for chamber orchestras and over 200 cantatas.
Although he was more respected as an organist during his lifetime, Bach's compositions influenced
many later composers, including Beethoven and Mozart.

Done                                                          My Computer
```

**4** Display the Web page in a Web browser.

● The Web browser displays all the text that uses the tag in the color you specified.

*Note: You can also specify a color by providing the amount of red, green and blue (r,g,b) in the color as values or as percentages. For example, type **rgb (255,0,0)** or **rgb (100%,0%,0%)** in step 3 to display the text in red.*

# CHANGE THE FONT

You can change the font of all the text on your Web page that uses a specific tag. You can specify a font by name, such as Courier, or by type, such as monospace. If you specify a font by name, you should specify more than one font in case your first choice is not available on a user's computer.

## CHANGE THE FONT

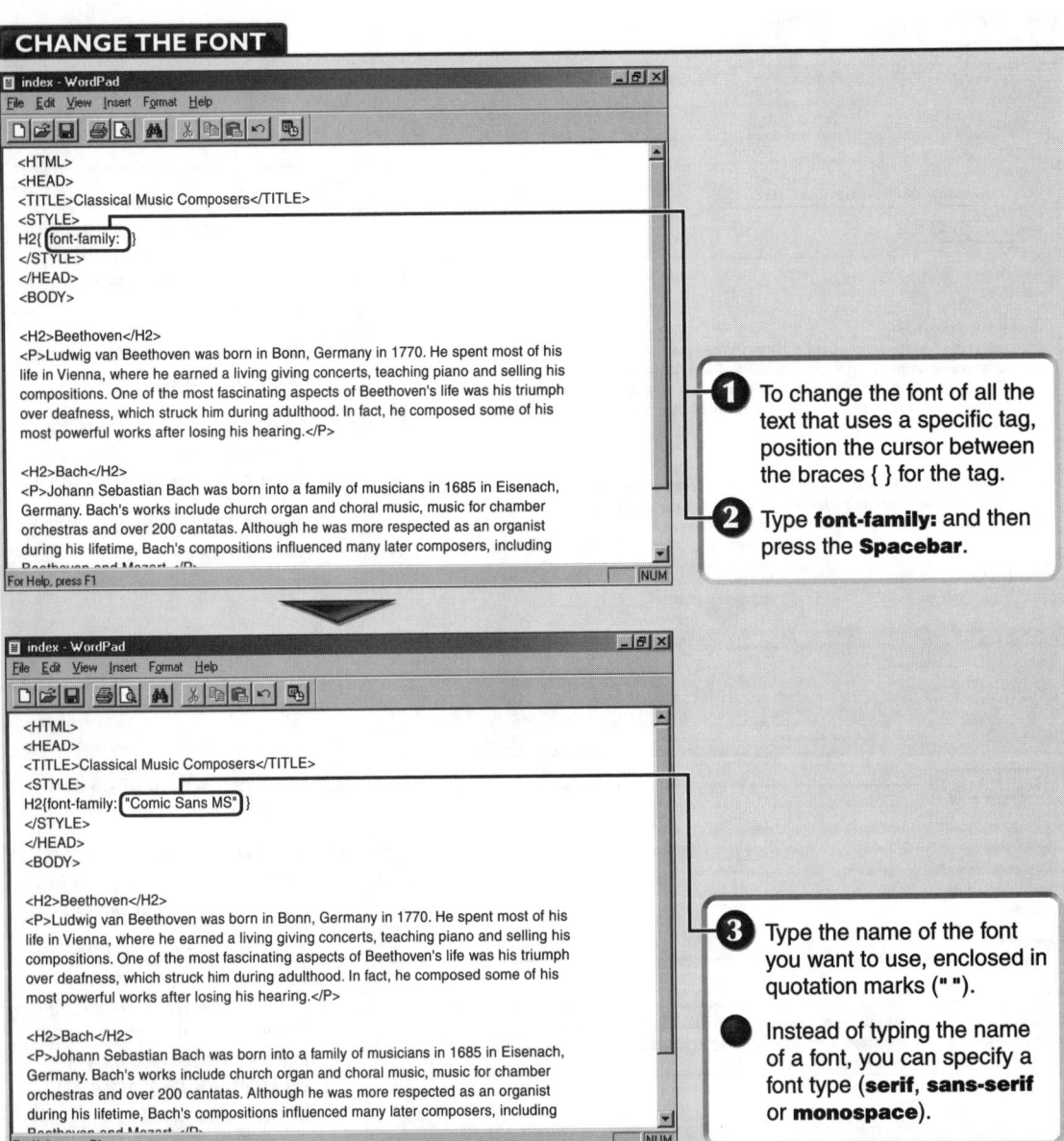

**1** To change the font of all the text that uses a specific tag, position the cursor between the braces { } for the tag.

**2** Type **font-family:** and then press the **Spacebar**.

**3** Type the name of the font you want to use, enclosed in quotation marks (" ").

● Instead of typing the name of a font, you can specify a font type (**serif**, **sans-serif** or **monospace**).

# in an *instant*

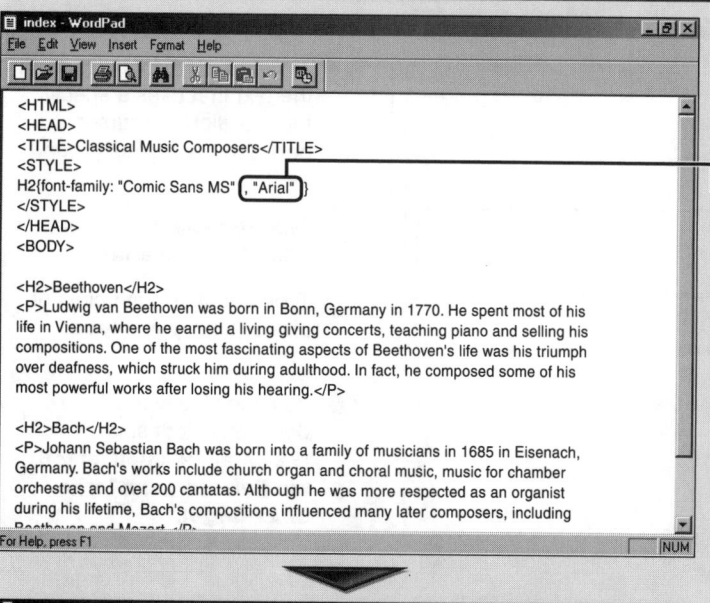

**4** To specify a second font choice, type a comma (**,**) and then press the **Spacebar**. Then type your second font choice, enclosed in quotation marks (**" "**).

*Note: One of the fonts you specify should be a common font, such as Arial, to increase the probability that the Web page will display one of your font choices.*

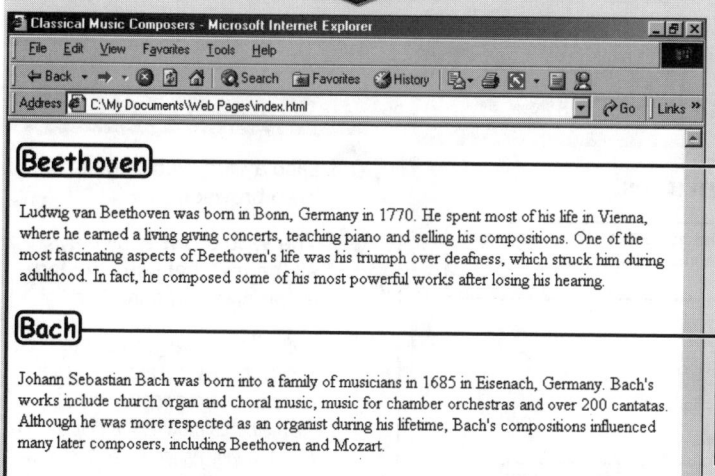

**5** Display the Web page in a Web browser.

● The Web browser displays all the text that uses the tag in the font you specified.

# CHANGE FONT SIZE

You can change the font size of all the text on your Web page that uses a specific tag. Larger text is easier to read, but smaller text allows you to fit more information on a screen. You can specify a new font size in points, in pixels or as a descriptive size, such as small, medium or large.

## CHANGE FONT SIZE

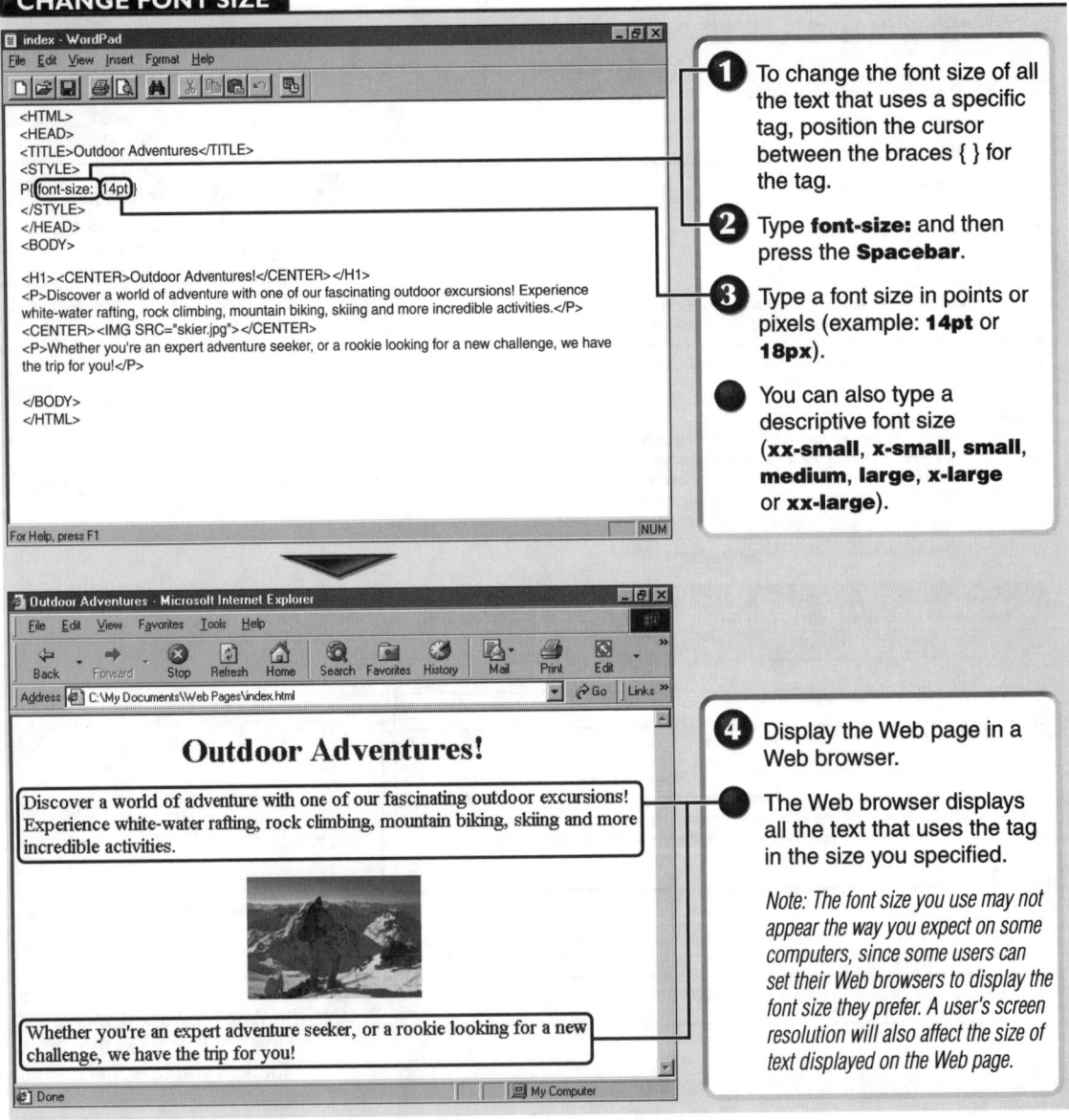

1. To change the font size of all the text that uses a specific tag, position the cursor between the braces { } for the tag.

2. Type **font-size:** and then press the **Spacebar**.

3. Type a font size in points or pixels (example: **14pt** or **18px**).

● You can also type a descriptive font size (**xx-small, x-small, small, medium, large, x-large** or **xx-large**).

4. Display the Web page in a Web browser.

● The Web browser displays all the text that uses the tag in the size you specified.

*Note: The font size you use may not appear the way you expect on some computers, since some users can set their Web browsers to display the font size they prefer. A user's screen resolution will also affect the size of text displayed on the Web page.*

You can change the line spacing of all the text on your Web page that uses a specific tag. Increasing the line spacing can make text easier to read. You can determine the new line spacing by specifying a number that will be multiplied by the current font size. If you later change the font size, the line spacing will also change.

## CHANGE LINE SPACING

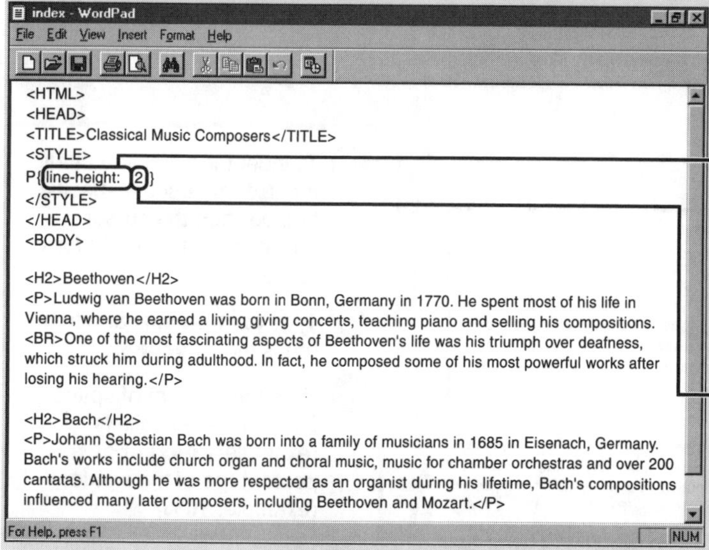

```
index - WordPad
File  Edit  View  Insert  Format  Help

<HTML>
<HEAD>
<TITLE>Classical Music Composers</TITLE>
<STYLE>
P{line-height: 2}
</STYLE>
</HEAD>
<BODY>

<H2>Beethoven</H2>
<P>Ludwig van Beethoven was born in Bonn, Germany in 1770. He spent most of his life in
Vienna, where he earned a living giving concerts, teaching piano and selling his compositions.
<BR>One of the most fascinating aspects of Beethoven's life was his triumph over deafness,
which struck him during adulthood. In fact, he composed some of his most powerful works after
losing his hearing.</P>

<H2>Bach</H2>
<P>Johann Sebastian Bach was born into a family of musicians in 1685 in Eisenach, Germany.
Bach's works include church organ and choral music, music for chamber orchestras and over 200
cantatas. Although he was more respected as an organist during his lifetime, Bach's compositions
influenced many later composers, including Beethoven and Mozart.</P>

For Help, press F1                                                      NUM
```

**1** To change the line spacing of all the text that uses a specific tag, position the cursor between the braces { } for the tag.

**2** Type **line-height:** and then press the **Spacebar**.

**3** Type the number that you want to multiply by the current font size to determine the line spacing (example: **2**).

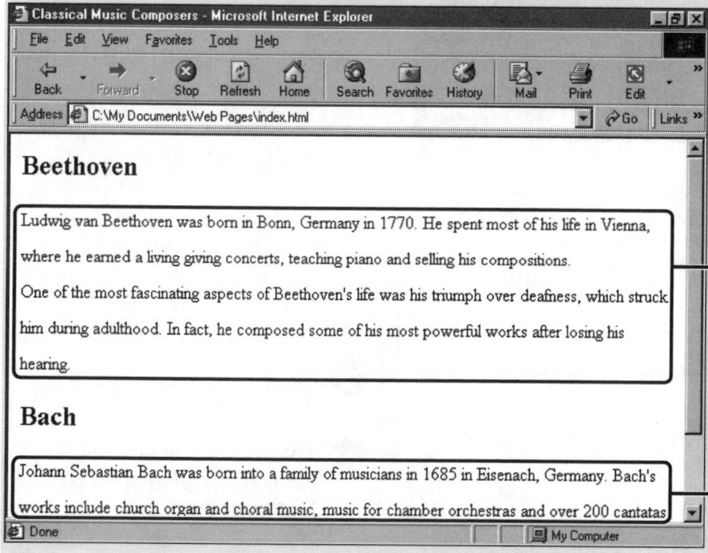

```
Classical Music Composers - Microsoft Internet Explorer
File  Edit  View  Favorites  Tools  Help

Back  Forward  Stop  Refresh  Home   Search  Favorites  History   Mail  Print  Edit
Address  C:\My Documents\Web Pages\index.html                          Go  Links

Beethoven

Ludwig van Beethoven was born in Bonn, Germany in 1770. He spent most of his life in Vienna,

where he earned a living giving concerts, teaching piano and selling his compositions.

One of the most fascinating aspects of Beethoven's life was his triumph over deafness, which struck

him during adulthood. In fact, he composed some of his most powerful works after losing his

hearing.

Bach

Johann Sebastian Bach was born into a family of musicians in 1685 in Eisenach, Germany. Bach's

works include church organ and choral music, music for chamber orchestras and over 200 cantatas

Done                                                       My Computer
```

**4** Display the Web page in a Web browser.

■ The Web browser displays all the text that uses the tag with the line spacing you specified.

*Note: You can also specify the line spacing in pixels (example: 30px), points (example: 20pt) or as a percentage of the current text size (example: 150%).*

# INDENT TEXT

You can indent the first line of all the text on your Web page that uses a specific tag. For example, you may want to indent the first line of each paragraph on your Web page to emphasize the paragraphs. You can specify the amount of space for the indent in pixels or as a percentage of the Web browser window.

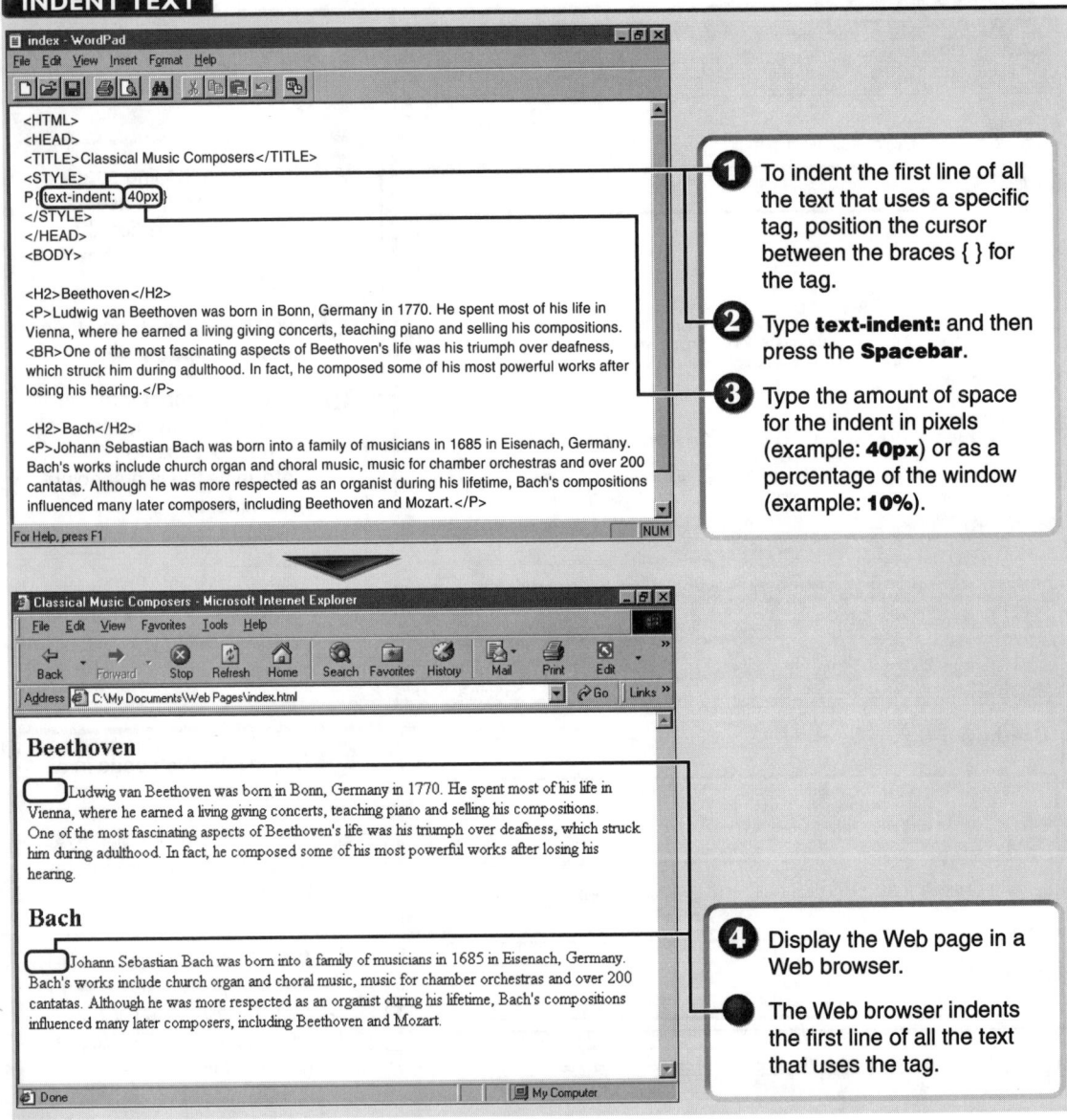

**1** To indent the first line of all the text that uses a specific tag, position the cursor between the braces { } for the tag.

**2** Type **text-indent:** and then press the **Spacebar**.

**3** Type the amount of space for the indent in pixels (example: **40px**) or as a percentage of the window (example: **10%**).

**4** Display the Web page in a Web browser.

● The Web browser indents the first line of all the text that uses the tag.

You can change the margins for every element on your Web page that uses a specific tag. The margins define the amount of space that appears around an element. You can change the margins for elements such as headings (H1 to H6), paragraphs (P) and images (IMG).

## CHANGE MARGINS

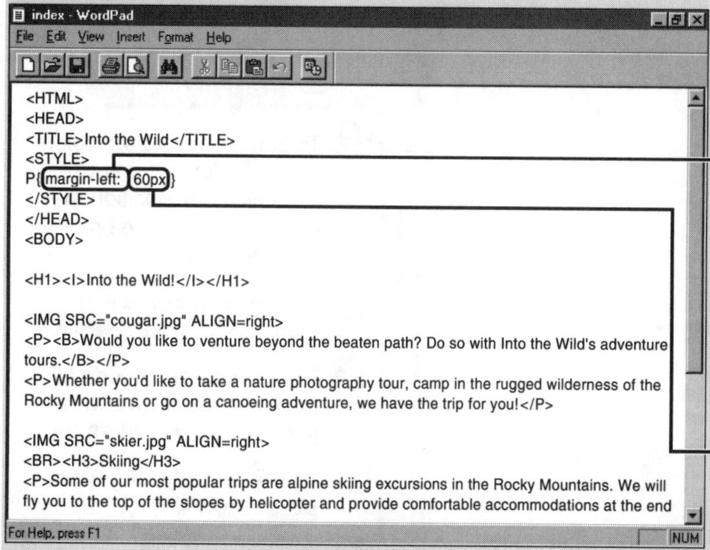

```
<HTML>
<HEAD>
<TITLE>Into the Wild</TITLE>
<STYLE>
P{margin-left: 60px}
</STYLE>
</HEAD>
<BODY>

<H1><I>Into the Wild!</I></H1>

<IMG SRC="cougar.jpg" ALIGN=right>
<P><B>Would you like to venture beyond the beaten path? Do so with Into the Wild's adventure tours.</B></P>
<P>Whether you'd like to take a nature photography tour, camp in the rugged wilderness of the Rocky Mountains or go on a canoeing adventure, we have the trip for you!</P>

<IMG SRC="skier.jpg" ALIGN=right>
<BR><H3>Skiing</H3>
<P>Some of our most popular trips are alpine skiing excursions in the Rocky Mountains. We will fly you to the top of the slopes by helicopter and provide comfortable accommodations at the end
```

For Help, press F1                                    NUM

**1** To change a margin for every element that uses a specific tag, position the cursor between the braces { } for the tag.

**2** Type **margin-?:** replacing **?** with the margin you want to change (**top**, **bottom**, **left** or **right**). Then press the **Spacebar**.

**3** Type the amount of space for the margin in pixels (example: **60px**).

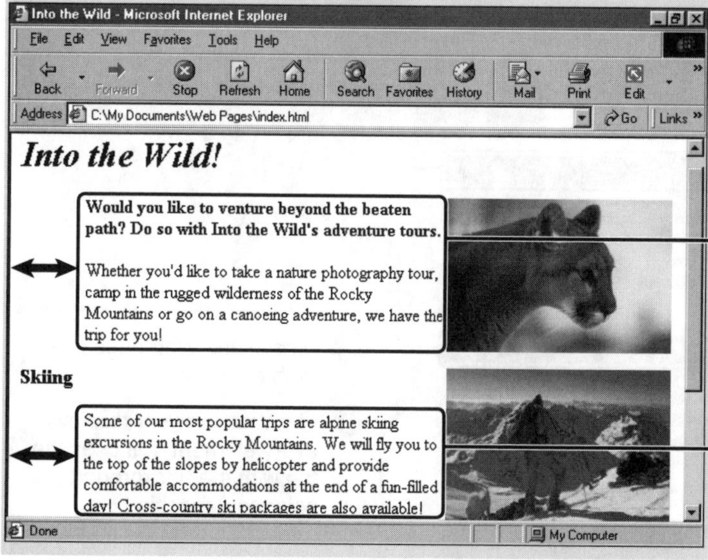

---

### Into the Wild - Microsoft Internet Explorer

File   Edit   View   Favorites   Tools   Help

Back   Forward   Stop   Refresh   Home   Search   Favorites   History   Mail   Print   Edit

Address  C:\My Documents\Web Pages\index.html        Go   Links »

## *Into the Wild!*

**Would you like to venture beyond the beaten path? Do so with Into the Wild's adventure tours.**

Whether you'd like to take a nature photography tour, camp in the rugged wilderness of the Rocky Mountains or go on a canoeing adventure, we have the trip for you!

**Skiing**

Some of our most popular trips are alpine skiing excursions in the Rocky Mountains. We will fly you to the top of the slopes by helicopter and provide comfortable accommodations at the end of a fun-filled day! Cross-country ski packages are also available!

Done                                    My Computer

**4** Display the Web page in a Web browser.

■ The Web browser displays every element that uses the tag with the margin you specified.

*Note: To change more than one margin for every element that uses a specific tag, repeat steps 1 to 3 for each margin. Make sure you separate each margin setting with a semi-colon (;).*

# ADD A BACKGROUND COLOR

You can add a background color to every element on your Web page that uses a specific tag. When adding a background color, you should make sure the color you select works well with the elements on your Web page. You can add a background color to elements such as headings (H1 to H6) and paragraphs (P).

## ADD A BACKGROUND COLOR

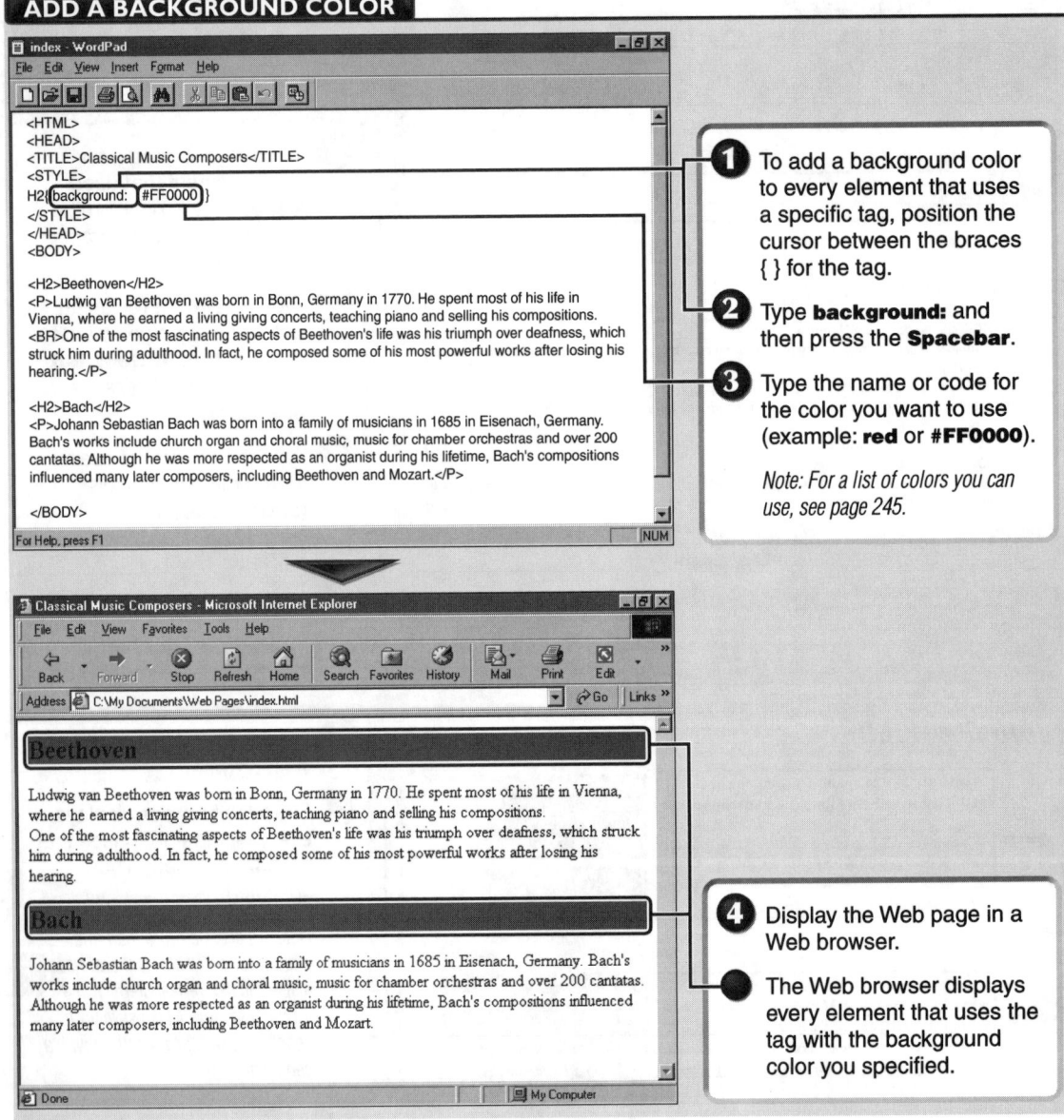

1 To add a background color to every element that uses a specific tag, position the cursor between the braces { } for the tag.

2 Type **background:** and then press the **Spacebar**.

3 Type the name or code for the color you want to use (example: **red** or **#FF0000**).

*Note: For a list of colors you can use, see page 245.*

4 Display the Web page in a Web browser.

■ The Web browser displays every element that uses the tag with the background color you specified.

You can add a background image to every element on your Web page that uses a specific tag. Interesting background images are available at the imagine.metanet.com and www.nepthys.com/textures Web sites. Make sure the background image you select does not make the text on your Web page difficult to read.

## ADD A BACKGROUND IMAGE

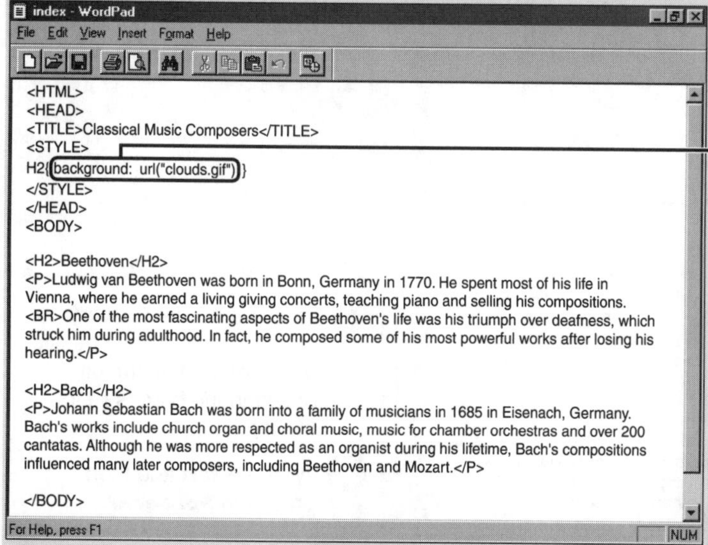

```
index - WordPad
File  Edit  View  Insert  Format  Help

<HTML>
<HEAD>
<TITLE>Classical Music Composers</TITLE>
<STYLE>
H2{background:  url("clouds.gif")}
</STYLE>
</HEAD>
<BODY>

<H2>Beethoven</H2>
<P>Ludwig van Beethoven was born in Bonn, Germany in 1770. He spent most of his life in
Vienna, where he earned a living giving concerts, teaching piano and selling his compositions.
<BR>One of the most fascinating aspects of Beethoven's life was his triumph over deafness, which
struck him during adulthood. In fact, he composed some of his most powerful works after losing his
hearing.</P>

<H2>Bach</H2>
<P>Johann Sebastian Bach was born into a family of musicians in 1685 in Eisenach, Germany.
Bach's works include church organ and choral music, music for chamber orchestras and over 200
cantatas. Although he was more respected as an organist during his lifetime, Bach's compositions
influenced many later composers, including Beethoven and Mozart.</P>

</BODY>
For Help, press F1                                                    NUM
```

**1** To add a background image to every element that uses a specific tag, position the cursor between the braces { } for the tag.

**2** Type **background: url("?")**.

**3** If the background image is stored in the same folder as the Web page, replace **?** with the name of the image.

*Note: If the image is stored in a subfolder, you must also specify the name of the subfolder.*

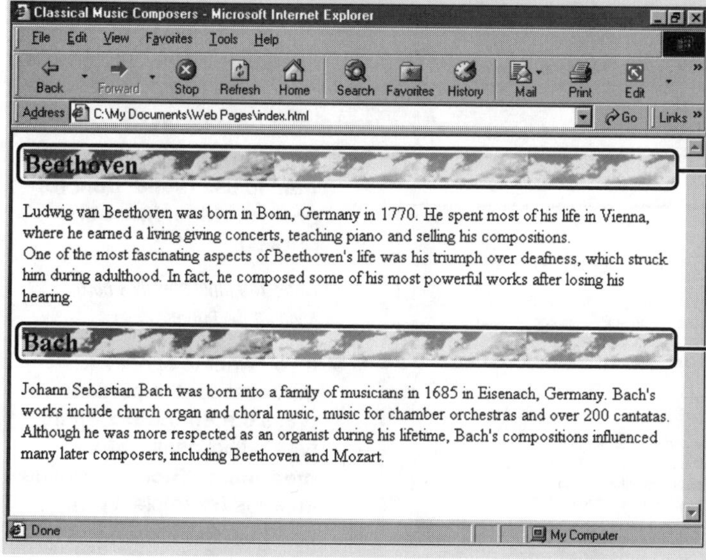

```
Classical Music Composers - Microsoft Internet Explorer
File  Edit  View  Favorites  Tools  Help

Back  Forward  Stop  Refresh  Home  Search  Favorites  History  Mail  Print  Edit
Address  C:\My Documents\Web Pages\index.html                        Go  Links
```

### Beethoven

Ludwig van Beethoven was born in Bonn, Germany in 1770. He spent most of his life in Vienna, where he earned a living giving concerts, teaching piano and selling his compositions.
One of the most fascinating aspects of Beethoven's life was his triumph over deafness, which struck him during adulthood. In fact, he composed some of his most powerful works after losing his hearing.

### Bach

Johann Sebastian Bach was born into a family of musicians in 1685 in Eisenach, Germany. Bach's works include church organ and choral music, music for chamber orchestras and over 200 cantatas. Although he was more respected as an organist during his lifetime, Bach's compositions influenced many later composers, including Beethoven and Mozart.

```
Done                                                    My Computer
```

**4** Display the Web page in a Web browser.

■ The Web browser displays every element that uses the tag with the background image you specified.

■ The background image repeats until it fills the background area of each element.

# ADD A BORDER

You can add a border to every element on your Web page that uses a specific tag. Adding borders is useful for making elements stand out. You can add a border to elements such as headings (H1 to H6), paragraphs (P) and images (IMG). Web browsers may display borders you add to your Web pages in slightly different ways.

## ADD A BORDER

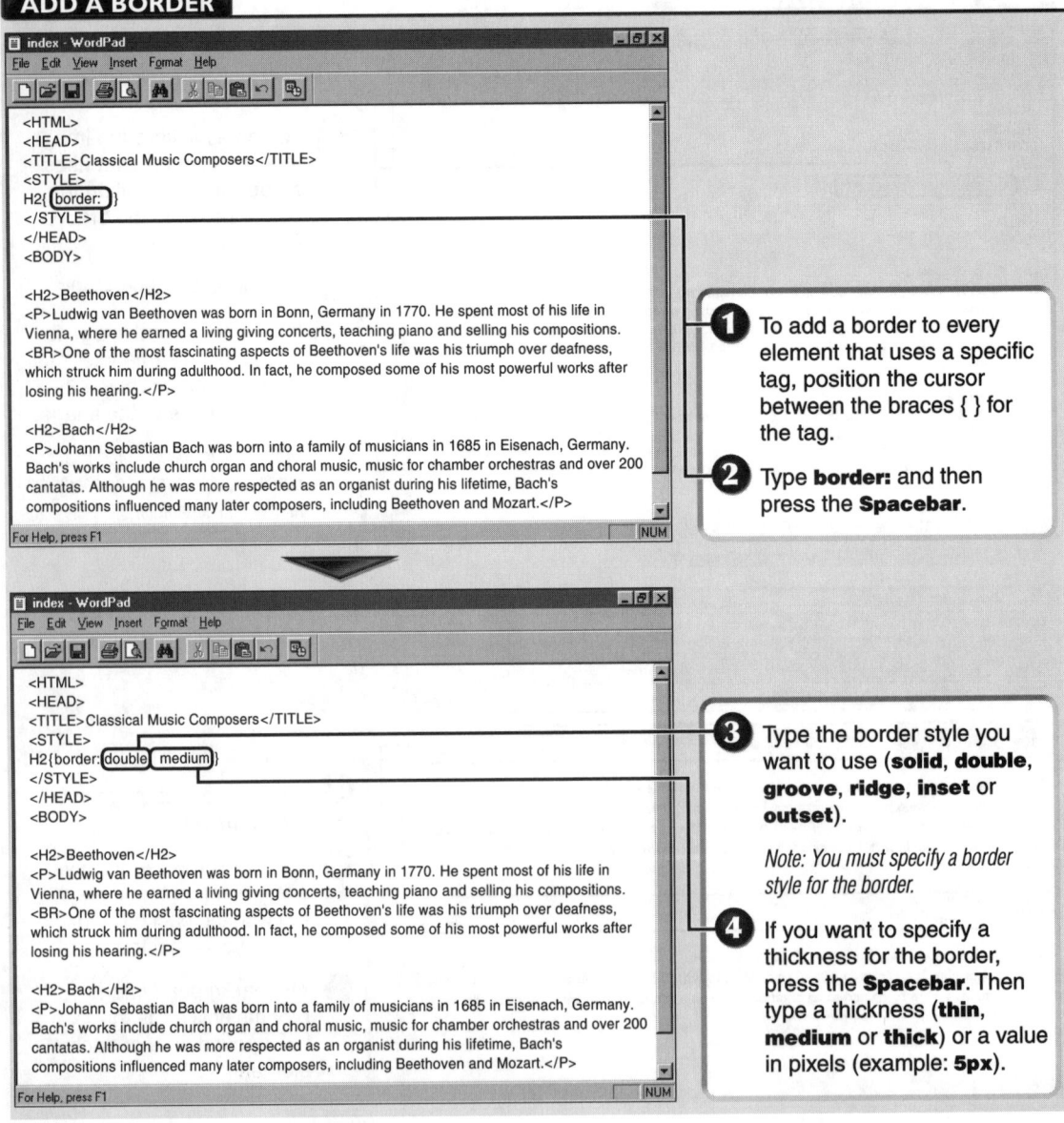

**1** To add a border to every element that uses a specific tag, position the cursor between the braces { } for the tag.

**2** Type **border:** and then press the **Spacebar**.

**3** Type the border style you want to use (**solid**, **double**, **groove**, **ridge**, **inset** or **outset**).

*Note: You must specify a border style for the border.*

**4** If you want to specify a thickness for the border, press the **Spacebar**. Then type a thickness (**thin**, **medium** or **thick**) or a value in pixels (example: **5px**).

in an *instant*

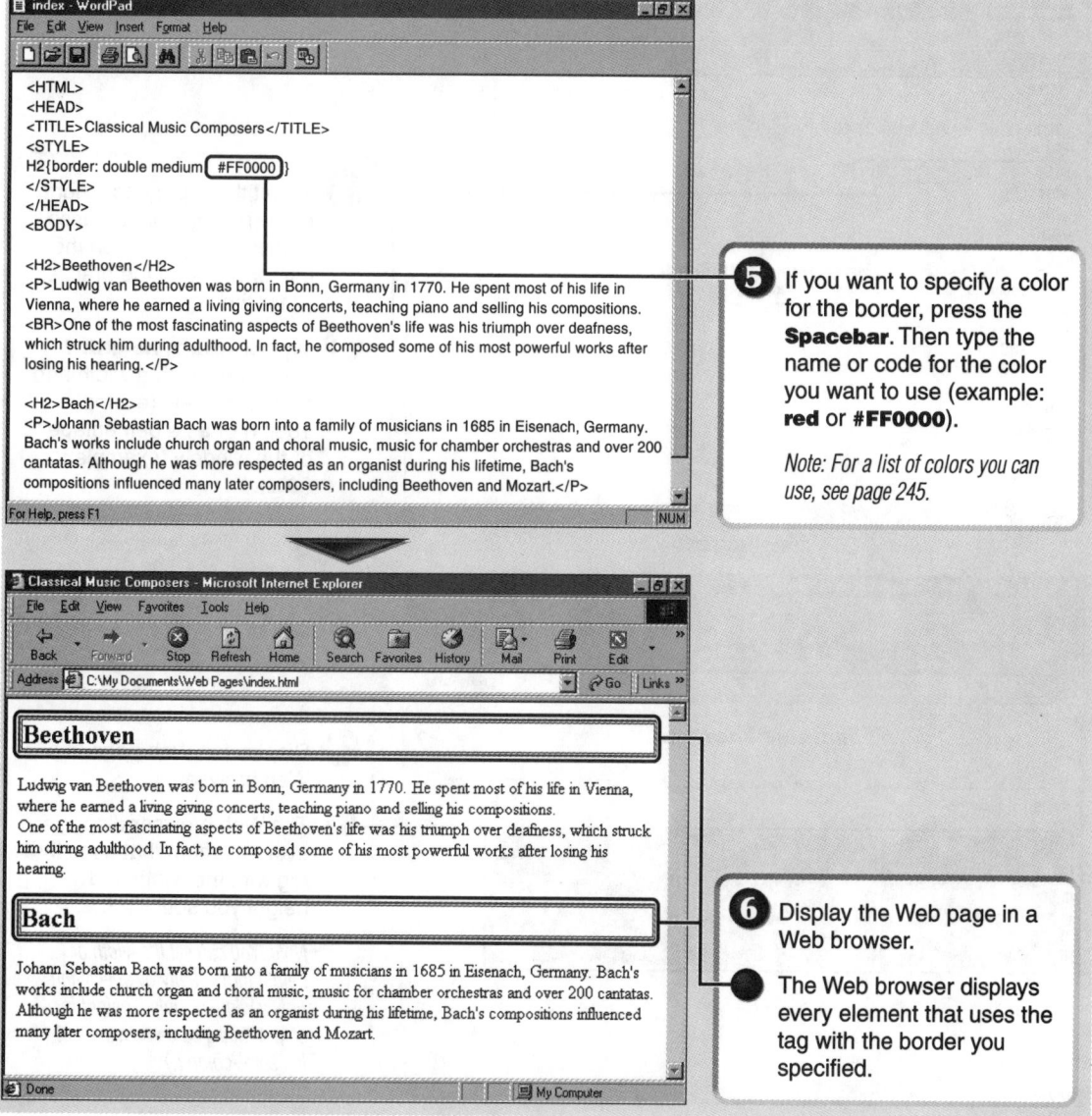

```
index - WordPad

File  Edit  View  Insert  Format  Help

<HTML>
<HEAD>
<TITLE>Classical Music Composers</TITLE>
<STYLE>
H2{border: double medium  #FF0000  }
</STYLE>
</HEAD>
<BODY>

<H2>Beethoven</H2>
<P>Ludwig van Beethoven was born in Bonn, Germany in 1770. He spent most of his life in
Vienna, where he earned a living giving concerts, teaching piano and selling his compositions.
<BR>One of the most fascinating aspects of Beethoven's life was his triumph over deafness,
which struck him during adulthood. In fact, he composed some of his most powerful works after
losing his hearing.</P>

<H2>Bach</H2>
<P>Johann Sebastian Bach was born into a family of musicians in 1685 in Eisenach, Germany.
Bach's works include church organ and choral music, music for chamber orchestras and over 200
cantatas. Although he was more respected as an organist during his lifetime, Bach's
compositions influenced many later composers, including Beethoven and Mozart.</P>

For Help, press F1                                                                      NUM
```

**5** If you want to specify a color
for the border, press the
**Spacebar**. Then type the
name or code for the color
you want to use (example:
**red** or **#FF0000**).

*Note: For a list of colors you can
use, see page 245.*

```
Classical Music Composers - Microsoft Internet Explorer

File  Edit  View  Favorites  Tools  Help

Back   Forward   Stop   Refresh   Home   Search  Favorites  History   Mail   Print   Edit

Address  C:\My Documents\Web Pages\index.html                              Go   Links
```

## Beethoven

Ludwig van Beethoven was born in Bonn, Germany in 1770. He spent most of his life in Vienna,
where he earned a living giving concerts, teaching piano and selling his compositions.
One of the most fascinating aspects of Beethoven's life was his triumph over deafness, which struck
him during adulthood. In fact, he composed some of his most powerful works after losing his
hearing.

## Bach

Johann Sebastian Bach was born into a family of musicians in 1685 in Eisenach, Germany. Bach's
works include church organ and choral music, music for chamber orchestras and over 200 cantatas.
Although he was more respected as an organist during his lifetime, Bach's compositions influenced
many later composers, including Beethoven and Mozart.

```
Done                                                                       My Computer
```

**6** Display the Web page in a
Web browser.

The Web browser displays
every element that uses the
tag with the border you
specified.

# SET THE WIDTH AND HEIGHT

You can set the width and height of every element on your Web page that uses a specific tag. This is useful when you want all the elements to display the same size. For example, you can set the width and height of all your images (IMG) or the width of all your paragraphs (P).

## SET THE WIDTH AND HEIGHT

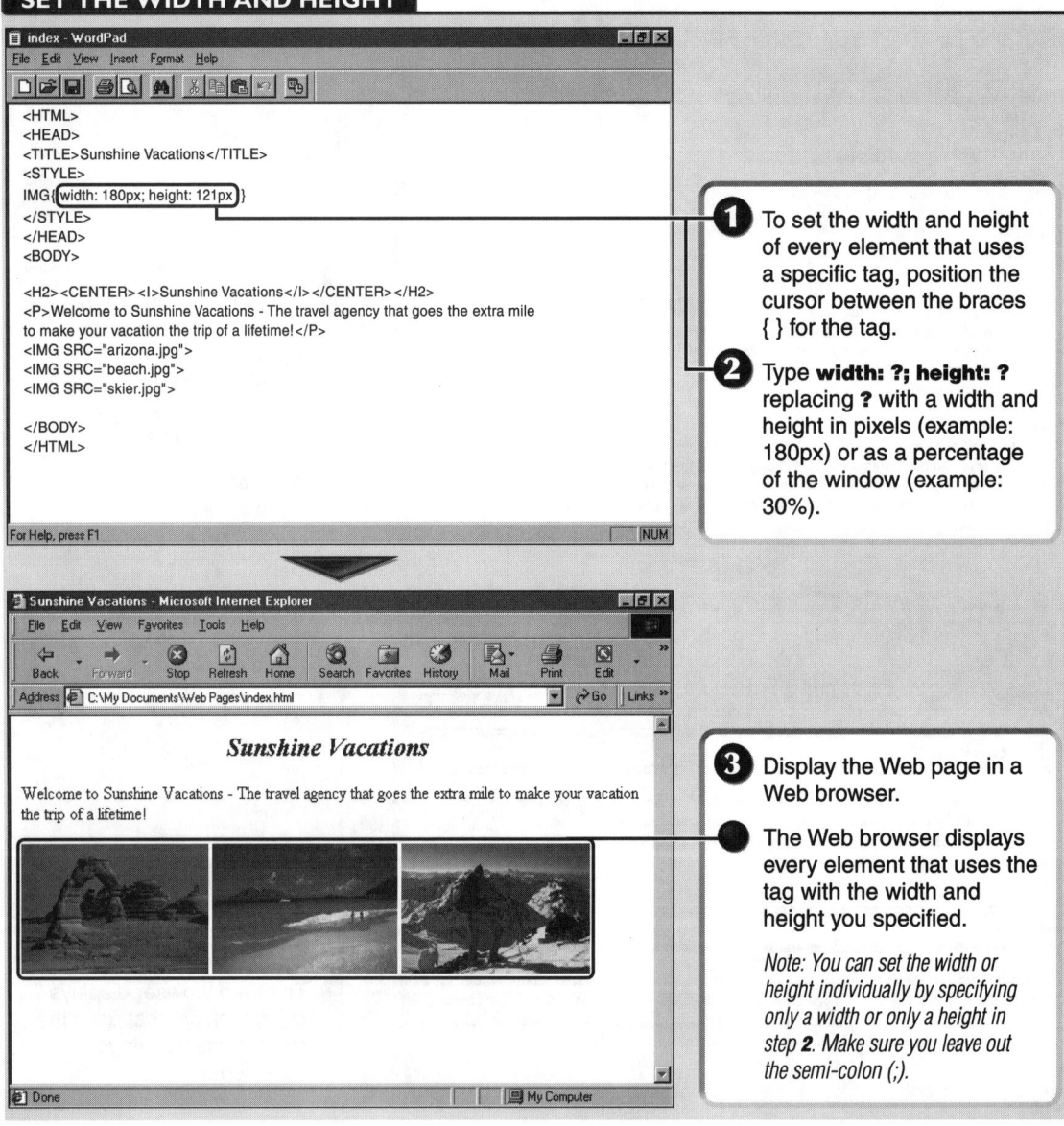

**1** To set the width and height of every element that uses a specific tag, position the cursor between the braces { } for the tag.

**2** Type **width: ?; height: ?** replacing **?** with a width and height in pixels (example: 180px) or as a percentage of the window (example: 30%).

**3** Display the Web page in a Web browser.

The Web browser displays every element that uses the tag with the width and height you specified.

*Note: You can set the width or height individually by specifying only a width or only a height in step 2. Make sure you leave out the semi-colon (;).*

# WRAP TEXT AROUND ELEMENTS

You can wrap text around every element on your Web page that uses a specific tag. For example, you may want to wrap text around images (IMG) or tables (TABLE). To ensure text wraps correctly, each element should appear directly before the text you want to wrap around the element.

## WRAP TEXT AROUND ELEMENTS

```
<HTML>
<HEAD>
<TITLE>Into the Wild</TITLE>
<STYLE>
IMG{float: left}
</STYLE>
</HEAD>
<BODY>

<H1><I>Into the Wild!</I></H1>

<IMG SRC="cougar.jpg">
<P><B>Would you like to venture beyond the beaten path? Do so with Into the
Wild's adventure tours.</B>
<BR>Whether you'd like a nature photography tour, camp in the
rugged wilderness of the Rocky Mountains or go on a canoeing adventure, we
have the trip for you!
<BR>We provide once-in-a-lifetime adventures for groups or individuals. Call
today for information on our packages and sign up for an unforgettable
experience!</P>
```

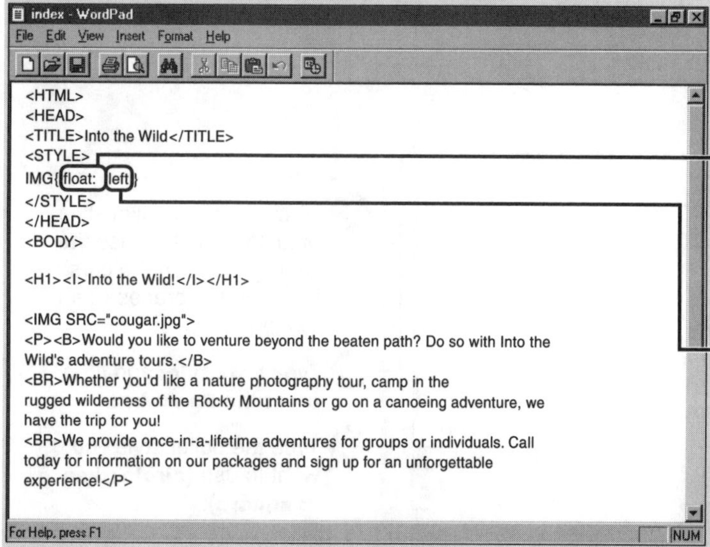

**1** To wrap text around every element on your Web page that uses a specific tag, position the cursor between the braces { } for the tag.

**2** Type **float:** and then press the **Spacebar**.

**3** To wrap text around the right side of each element, type **left**.

To wrap text around the left side of each element, type **right**.

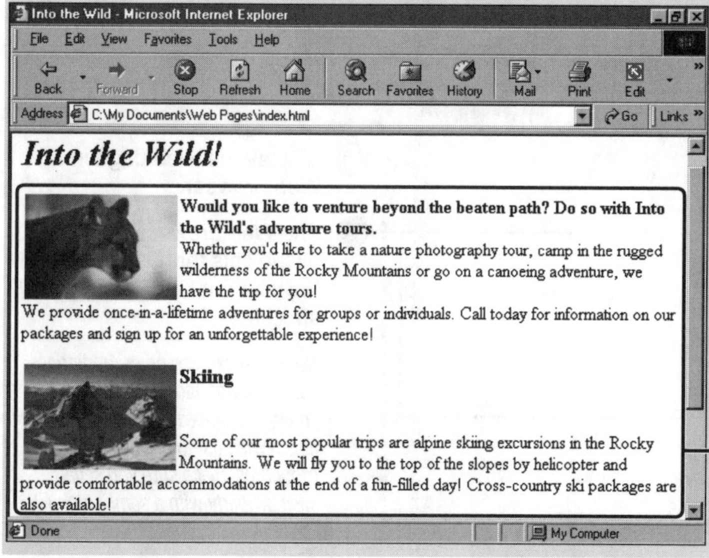

---

*Into the Wild!*

**Would you like to venture beyond the beaten path? Do so with Into the Wild's adventure tours.**
Whether you'd like to take a nature photography tour, camp in the rugged wilderness of the Rocky Mountains or go on a canoeing adventure, we have the trip for you!
We provide once-in-a-lifetime adventures for groups or individuals. Call today for information on our packages and sign up for an unforgettable experience!

**Skiing**

Some of our most popular trips are alpine skiing excursions in the Rocky Mountains. We will fly you to the top of the slopes by helicopter and provide comfortable accommodations at the end of a fun-filled day! Cross-country ski packages are also available!

**4** Display the Web page in a Web browser.

The Web browser wraps text around each element that uses the tag.

You can change the bullet style of all the unordered lists (UL) or change the number style of all the ordered lists (OL) on your Web page. By default, Web browsers display unordered lists with the disc bullet style and ordered lists with the decimal number style.

## CHANGE BULLET STYLE

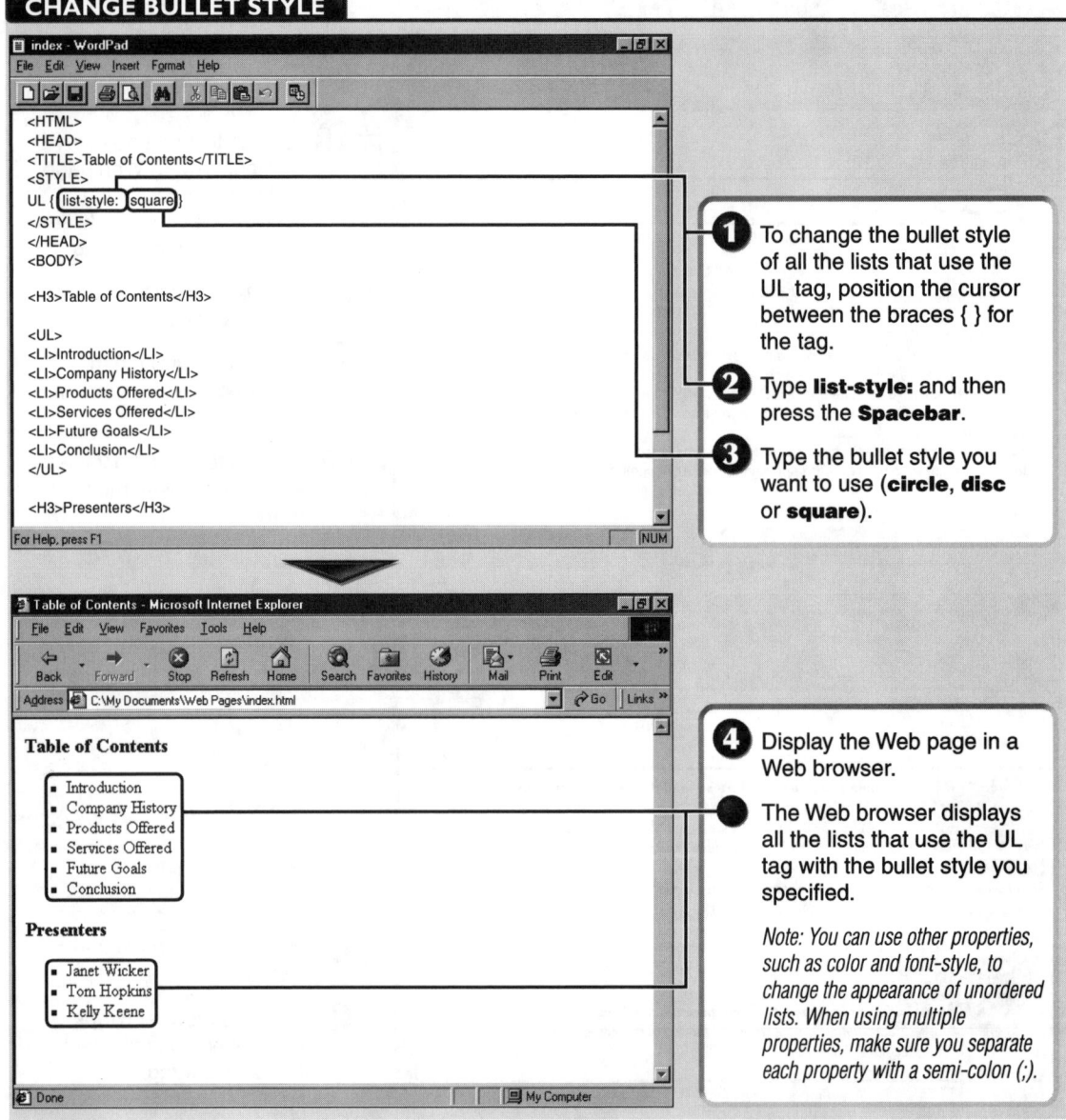

**1** To change the bullet style of all the lists that use the UL tag, position the cursor between the braces { } for the tag.

**2** Type **list-style:** and then press the **Spacebar**.

**3** Type the bullet style you want to use (**circle**, **disc** or **square**).

**4** Display the Web page in a Web browser.

■ The Web browser displays all the lists that use the UL tag with the bullet style you specified.

*Note: You can use other properties, such as color and font-style, to change the appearance of unordered lists. When using multiple properties, make sure you separate each property with a semi-colon (;).*

# in an *instant*

## CHANGE NUMBER STYLE

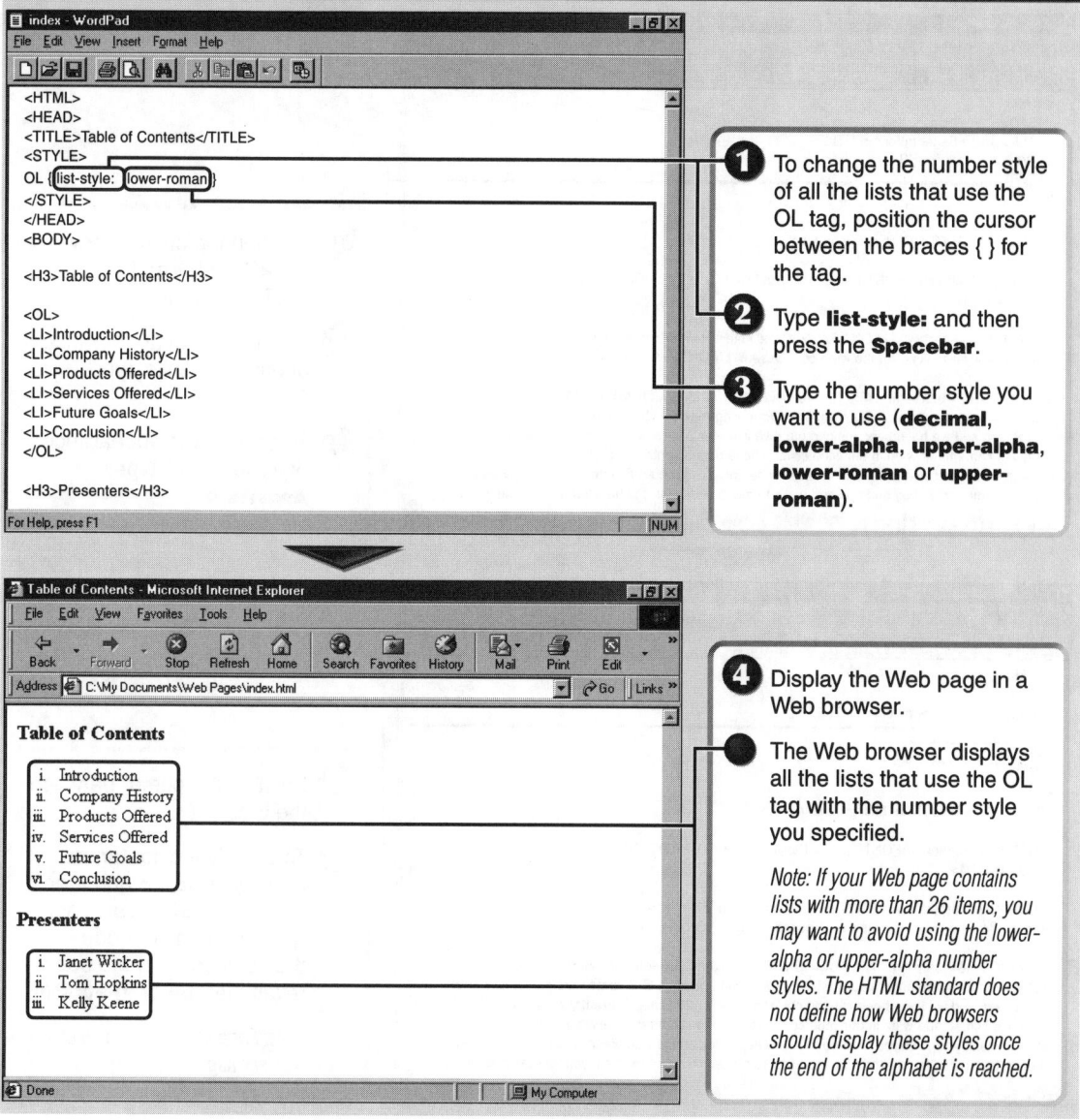

**1** To change the number style of all the lists that use the OL tag, position the cursor between the braces { } for the tag.

**2** Type **list-style:** and then press the **Spacebar**.

**3** Type the number style you want to use (**decimal**, **lower-alpha**, **upper-alpha**, **lower-roman** or **upper-roman**).

**4** Display the Web page in a Web browser.

■ The Web browser displays all the lists that use the OL tag with the number style you specified.

*Note: If your Web page contains lists with more than 26 items, you may want to avoid using the lower-alpha or upper-alpha number styles. The HTML standard does not define how Web browsers should display these styles once the end of the alphabet is reached.*

# CHANGE APPEARANCE OF LINKS

You can change the appearance of unvisited and visited text links on your Web page. An unvisited link is a link a user has not previously selected. A visited link is a link a user has previously selected. You can change the color of the links or remove the underline that automatically appears under each link.

## CHANGE APPEARANCE OF LINKS

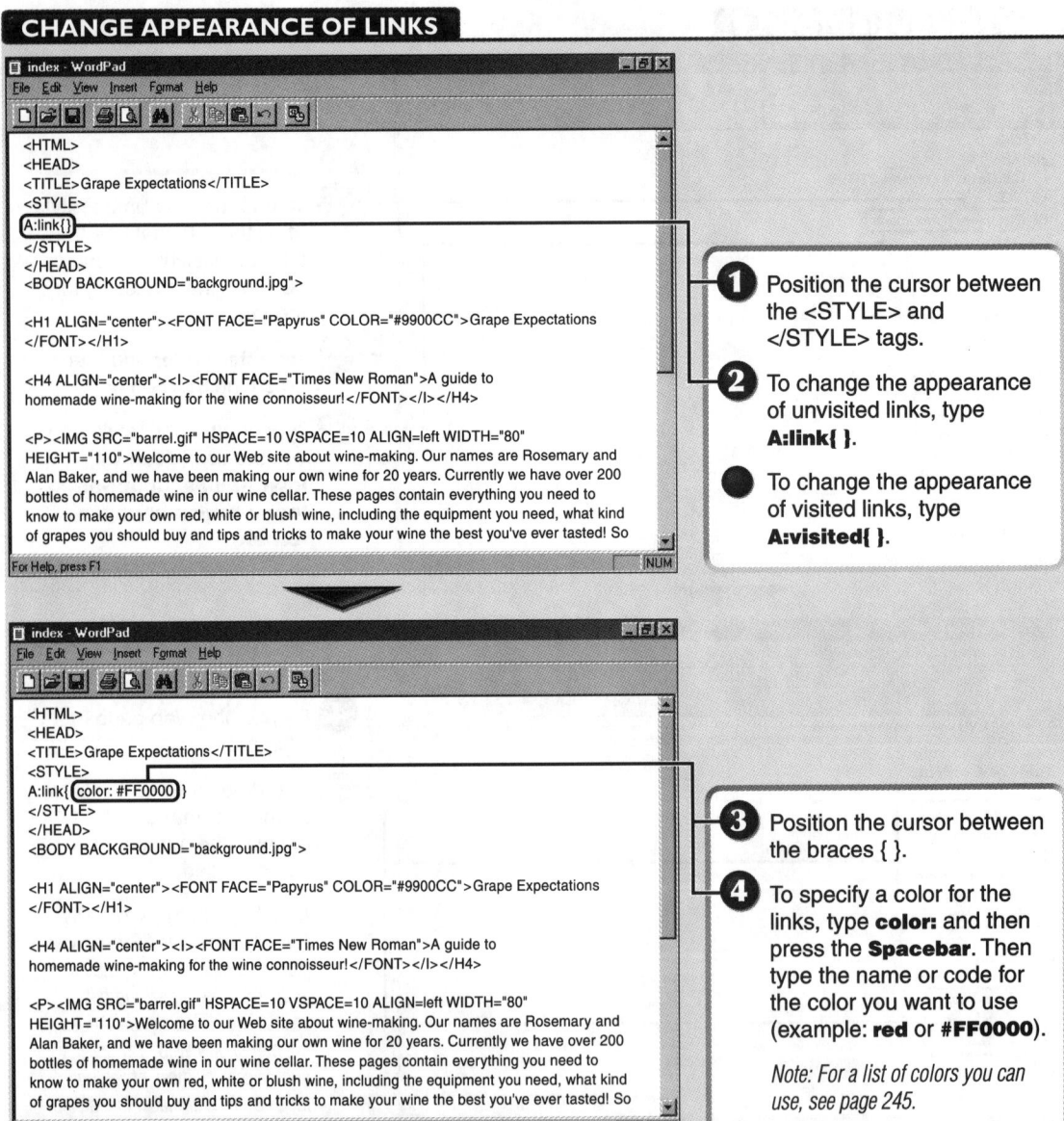

**1** Position the cursor between the <STYLE> and </STYLE> tags.

**2** To change the appearance of unvisited links, type **A:link{ }**.

● To change the appearance of visited links, type **A:visited{ }**.

**3** Position the cursor between the braces { }.

**4** To specify a color for the links, type **color:** and then press the **Spacebar**. Then type the name or code for the color you want to use (example: **red** or **#FF0000**).

Note: For a list of colors you can use, see page 245.

in an *instant*

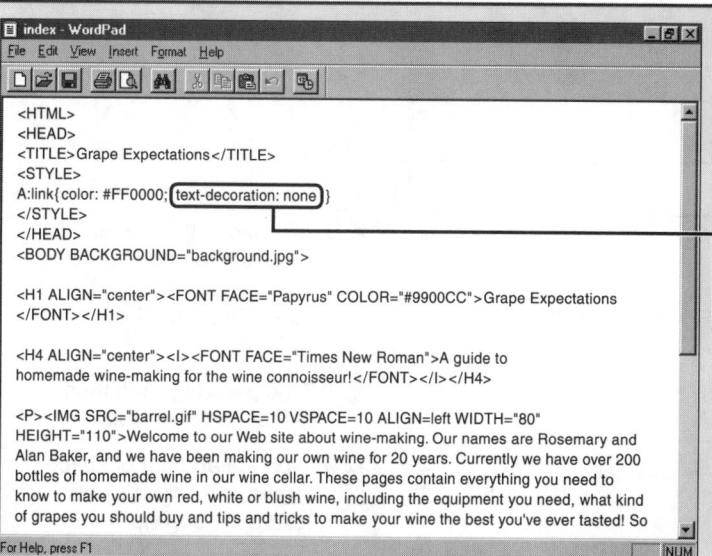

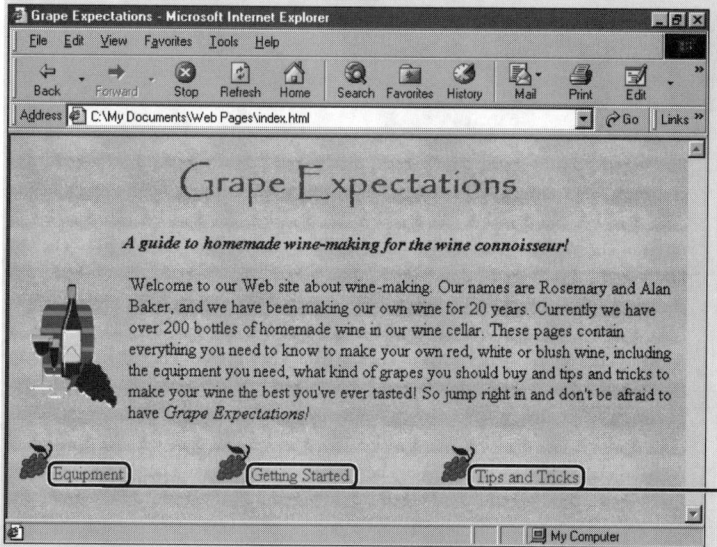

**6** Display the Web page in a
Web browser.

■ The Web browser displays
the unvisited or visited links
in the color you specified,
without underlines.

*Note: You can also use other
style sheet properties, such as
background or font-weight, to
change the appearance of links.
When using multiple properties,
make sure you separate each
property with a semi-colon (;).*

# ADD PADDING

You can add space, or padding, around every element on your Web page that uses a specific tag. Think of the elements on your Web page as appearing centered in invisible boxes. The padding you specify for elements will appear between each element and the edges of the invisible box.

## ADD PADDING

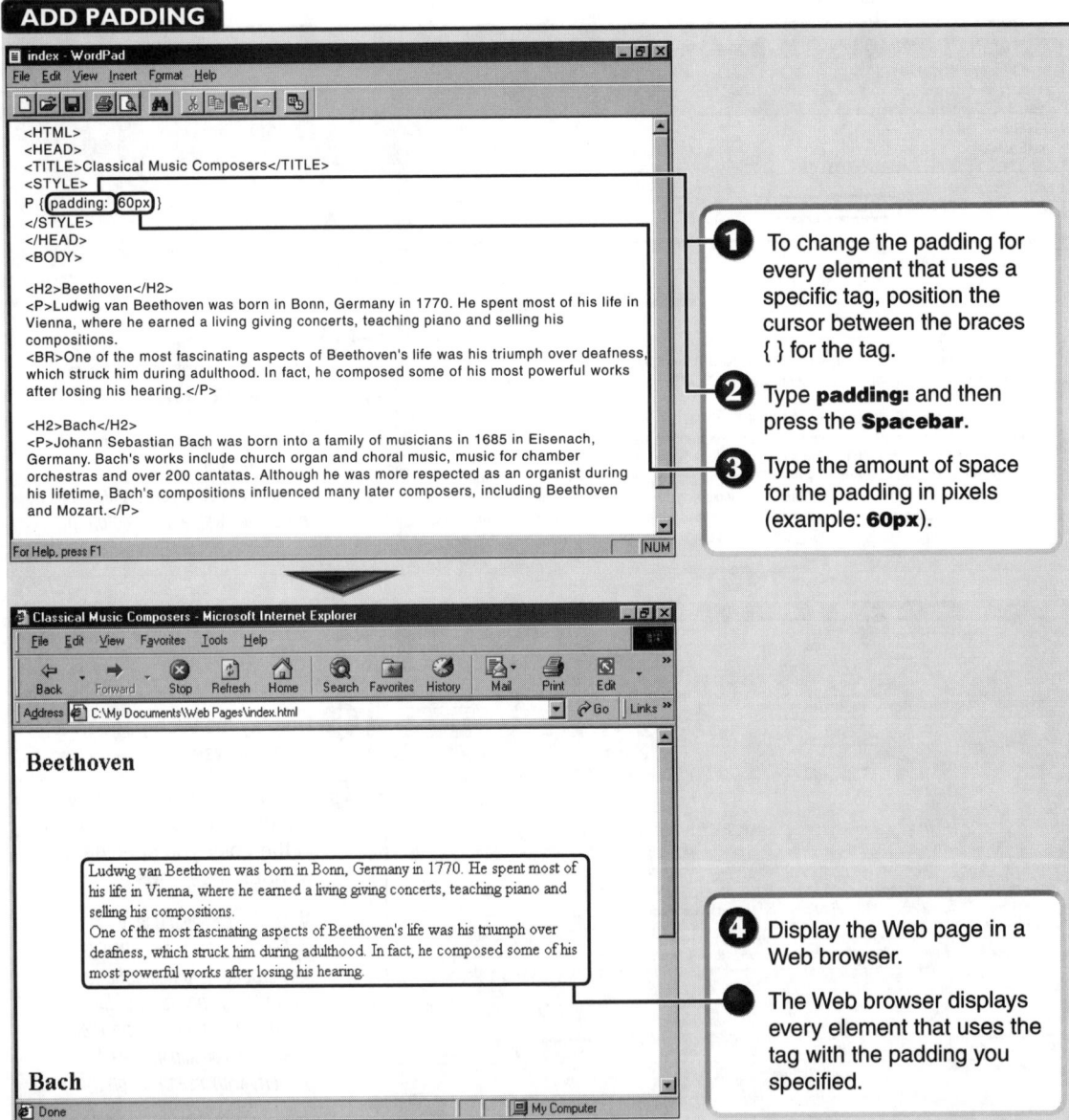

1 To change the padding for every element that uses a specific tag, position the cursor between the braces { } for the tag.

2 Type **padding:** and then press the **Spacebar**.

3 Type the amount of space for the padding in pixels (example: **60px**).

4 Display the Web page in a Web browser.

■ The Web browser displays every element that uses the tag with the padding you specified.

216

# CHANGE DISPLAY OF ELEMENTS

You can change the display of all the elements on your Web page that use a specific tag. You can use the block value to display elements with a blank line above and below each element or use the inline value to display elements on the same line as surrounding elements. You can also use the none value to temporarily hide elements on your Web page.

## CHANGE DISPLAY OF ELEMENTS

```
index - WordPad
File  Edit  View  Insert  Format  Help

<HTML>
<HEAD>
<TITLE>Classical Music Composers</TITLE>
<STYLE>
H2 { display: inline }
</STYLE>
</HEAD>
<BODY>

<P><H2>Beethoven: </H2>
Ludwig van Beethoven was born in Bonn, Germany in 1770. He spent most of his life in
Vienna, where he earned a living giving concerts, teaching piano and selling his
compositions.
<BR>One of the most fascinating aspects of Beethoven's life was his triumph over deafness,
which struck him during adulthood. In fact, he composed some of his most powerful works
after losing his hearing.</P>

<P><H2>Bach: </H2>
Johann Sebastian Bach was born into a family of musicians in 1685 in Eisenach, Germany.
Bach's works include church organ and choral music, music for chamber orchestras and over
200 cantatas. Although he was more respected as an organist during his lifetime, Bach's
compositions influenced many later composers, including Beethoven and Mozart.</P>

</BODY>
For Help, press F1                                                          NUM
```

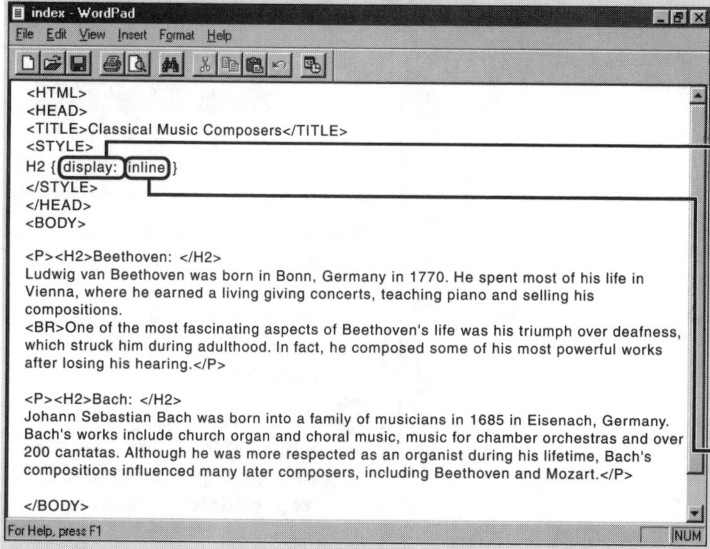

**1** To change the display of all the elements that use a specific tag, position the cursor between the braces { } for the tag.

**2** Type **display:** and then press the **Spacebar**.

**3** Type the way you want to display the elements (**block**, **inline** or **none**).

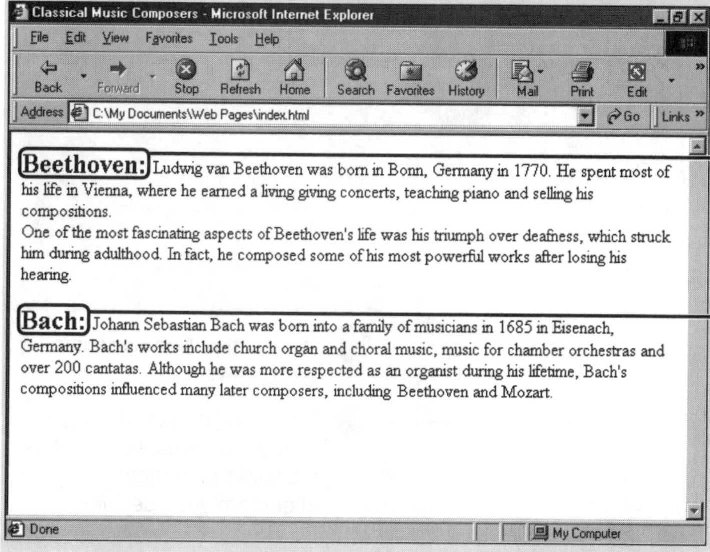

```
Classical Music Composers - Microsoft Internet Explorer
File  Edit  View  Favorites  Tools  Help
Back  Forward  Stop  Refresh  Home  Search  Favorites  History  Mail  Print  Edit
Address  C:\My Documents\Web Pages\index.html                    Go   Links
```

**Beethoven:** Ludwig van Beethoven was born in Bonn, Germany in 1770. He spent most of his life in Vienna, where he earned a living giving concerts, teaching piano and selling his compositions.
One of the most fascinating aspects of Beethoven's life was his triumph over deafness, which struck him during adulthood. In fact, he composed some of his most powerful works after losing his hearing.

**Bach:** Johann Sebastian Bach was born into a family of musicians in 1685 in Eisenach, Germany. Bach's works include church organ and choral music, music for chamber orchestras and over 200 cantatas. Although he was more respected as an organist during his lifetime, Bach's compositions influenced many later composers, including Beethoven and Mozart.

```
Done                                                    My Computer
```

**4** Display the Web page in a Web browser.

■ The Web browser displays all the elements that use the tag with the display style you specified.

*Note: If you specified the none value, the elements will not appear on your Web page.*

# ALIGN ELEMENTS VERTICALLY

You can specify a vertical alignment for all the inline elements on your Web page that use a specific tag. Inline elements, such as images, are elements that do not automatically appear on a new line. You can align elements with the top of the highest element on the current line, with the middle of the surrounding elements or with the bottom of the lowest element.

## ALIGN ELEMENTS VERTICALLY

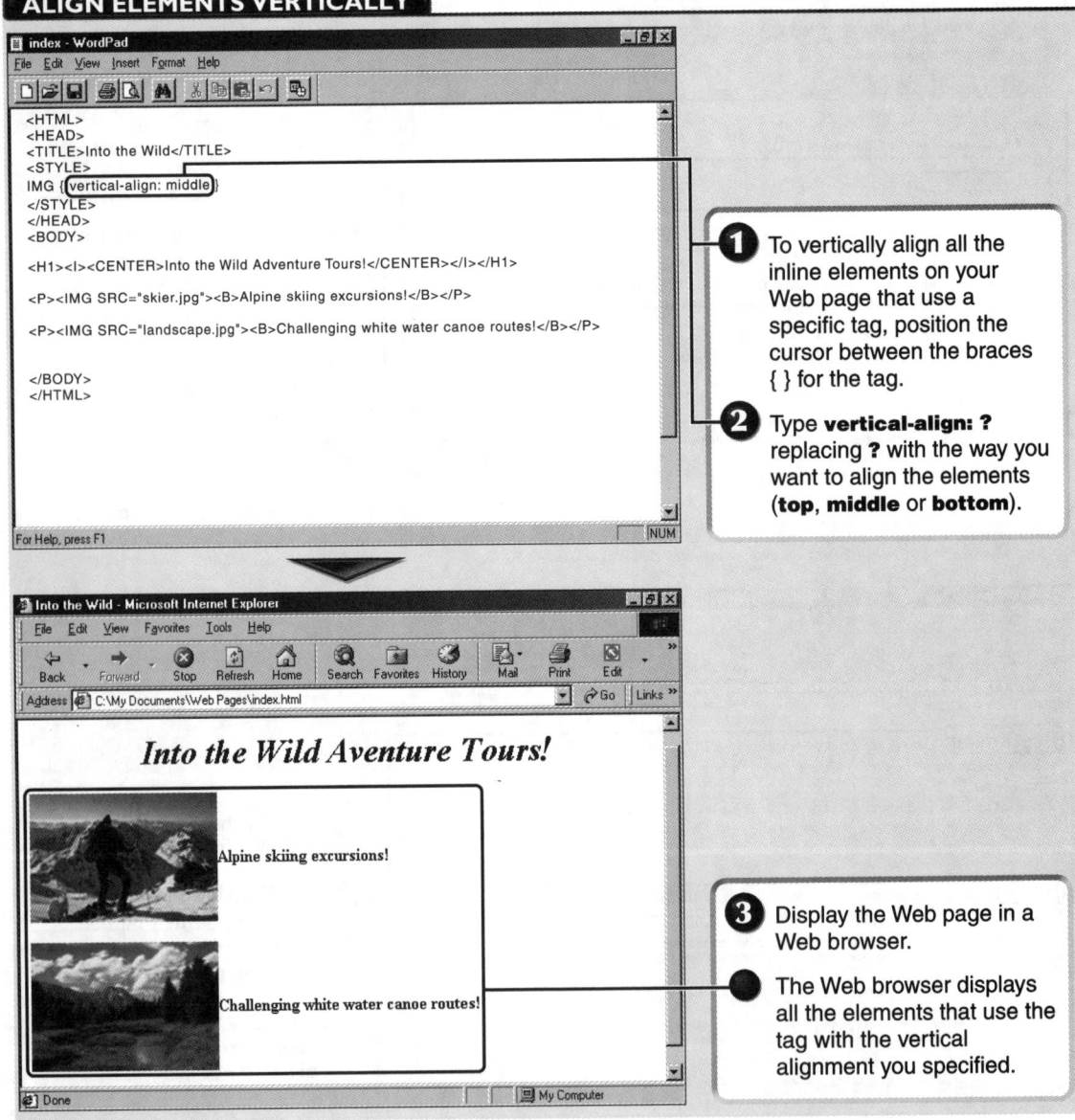

**1** To vertically align all the inline elements on your Web page that use a specific tag, position the cursor between the braces { } for the tag.

**2** Type **vertical-align: ?** replacing **?** with the way you want to align the elements (**top**, **middle** or **bottom**).

**3** Display the Web page in a Web browser.

■ The Web browser displays all the elements that use the tag with the vertical alignment you specified.

You can add a page break before or after every element on your Web page that uses a specific tag. Adding page breaks allows you to control where page breaks will occur when a user prints your Web page. Some Web browsers may not allow you to specify where page breaks will occur on your Web page.

## ADD PAGE BREAKS

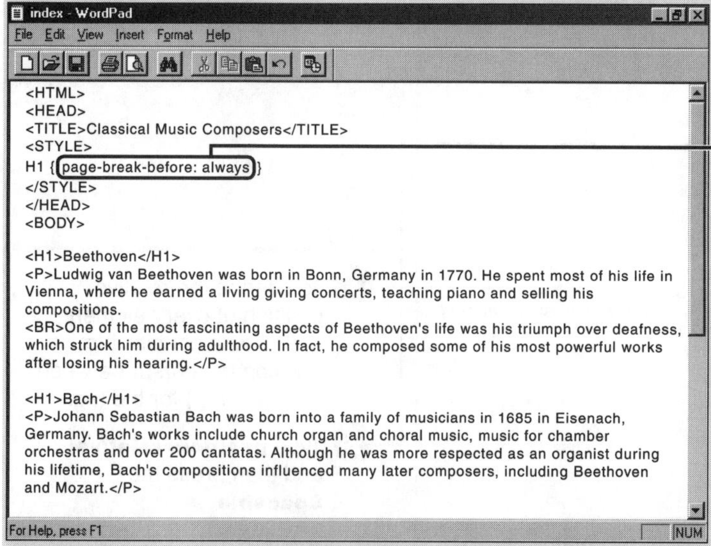

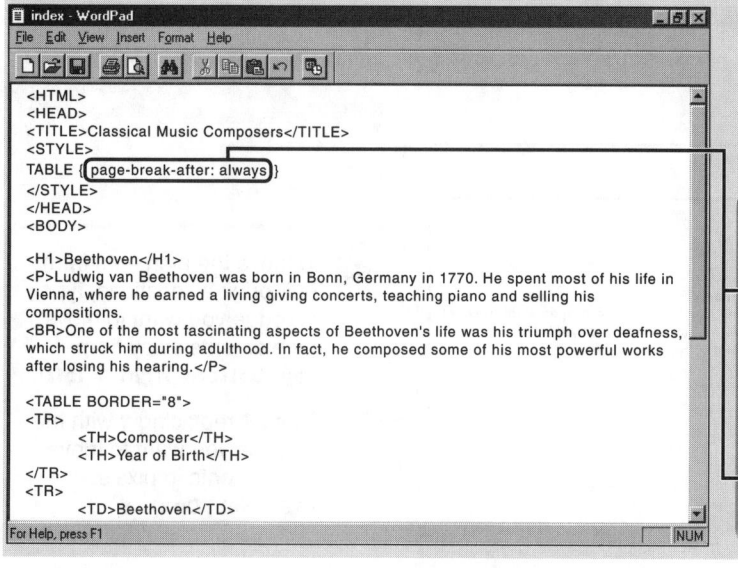

```
<HTML>
<HEAD>
<TITLE>Classical Music Composers</TITLE>
<STYLE>
H1 { page-break-before: always }
</STYLE>
</HEAD>
<BODY>

<H1>Beethoven</H1>
<P>Ludwig van Beethoven was born in Bonn, Germany in 1770. He spent most of his life in
Vienna, where he earned a living giving concerts, teaching piano and selling his
compositions.
<BR>One of the most fascinating aspects of Beethoven's life was his triumph over deafness,
which struck him during adulthood. In fact, he composed some of his most powerful works
after losing his hearing.</P>

<H1>Bach</H1>
<P>Johann Sebastian Bach was born into a family of musicians in 1685 in Eisenach,
Germany. Bach's works include church organ and choral music, music for chamber
orchestras and over 200 cantatas. Although he was more respected as an organist during
his lifetime, Bach's compositions influenced many later composers, including Beethoven
and Mozart.</P>
```

### ADD PAGE BREAKS BEFORE ELEMENTS

**1** To add a page break before every element on your Web page that uses a specific tag, position the cursor between the braces { } for the tag.

**2** Type **page-break-before: always**.

```
<HTML>
<HEAD>
<TITLE>Classical Music Composers</TITLE>
<STYLE>
TABLE { page-break-after: always }
</STYLE>
</HEAD>
<BODY>

<H1>Beethoven</H1>
<P>Ludwig van Beethoven was born in Bonn, Germany in 1770. He spent most of his life in
Vienna, where he earned a living giving concerts, teaching piano and selling his
compositions.
<BR>One of the most fascinating aspects of Beethoven's life was his triumph over deafness,
which struck him during adulthood. In fact, he composed some of his most powerful works
after losing his hearing.</P>

<TABLE BORDER="8">
<TR>
        <TH>Composer</TH>
        <TH>Year of Birth</TH>
</TR>
<TR>
        <TD>Beethoven</TD>
```

### ADD PAGE BREAKS AFTER ELEMENTS

**1** To add a page break after every element on your Web page that uses a specific tag, position the cursor between the braces { } for the tag.

**2** Type **page-break-after: always**.

# POSITION ELEMENTS RELATIVELY

You can move every element that uses a specific tag to a new position relative to its original location on your Web page. For example, you can move elements away from the top, bottom, right or left edge of their original locations. Changing the relative position of elements is useful for moving elements, such as images, without changing the position of the surrounding elements.

## POSITION ELEMENTS RELATIVELY

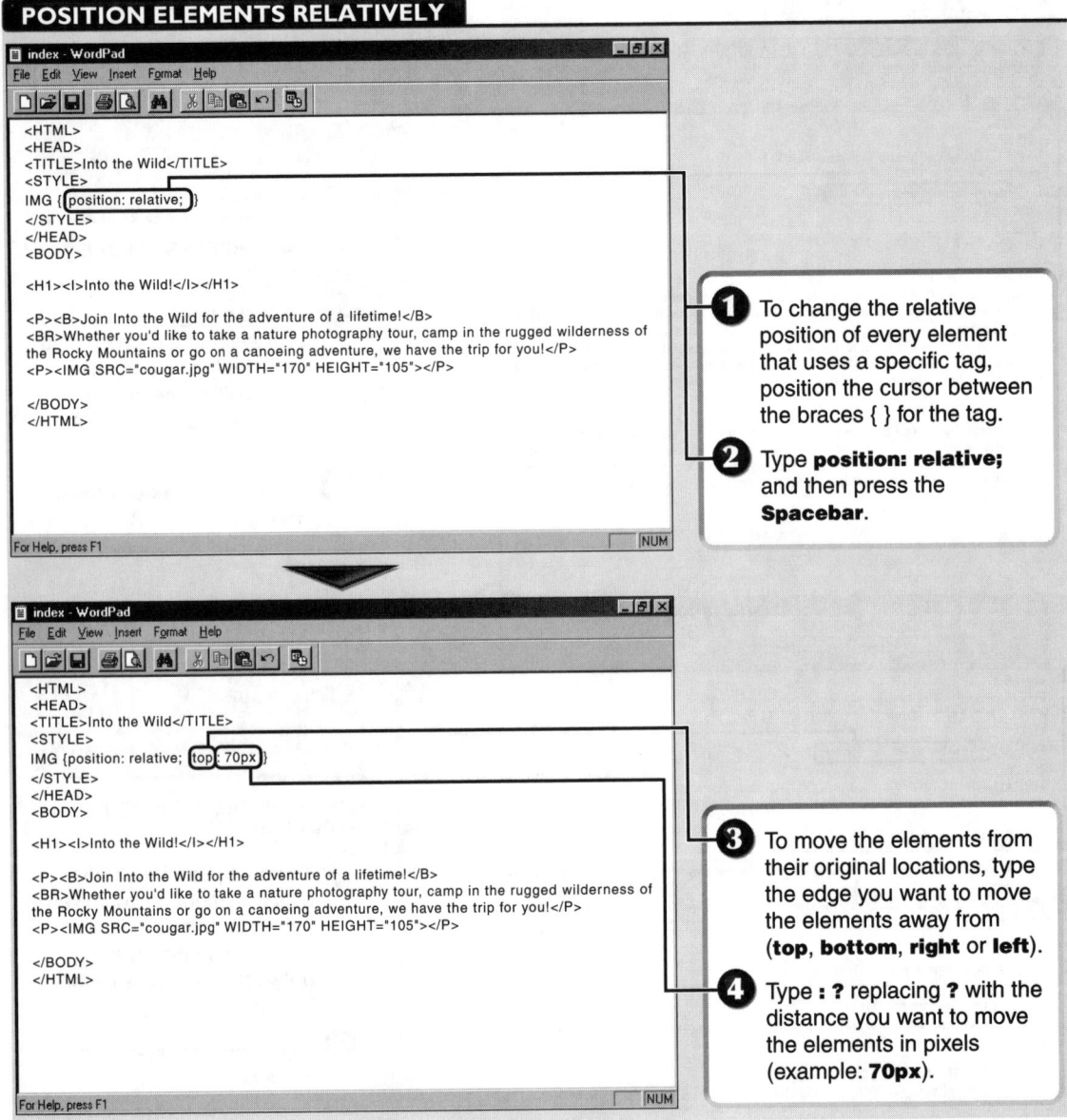

**1** To change the relative position of every element that uses a specific tag, position the cursor between the braces { } for the tag.

**2** Type **position: relative;** and then press the **Spacebar**.

**3** To move the elements from their original locations, type the edge you want to move the elements away from (**top, bottom, right** or **left**).

**4** Type **: ?** replacing **?** with the distance you want to move the elements in pixels (example: **70px**).

in an *instant*

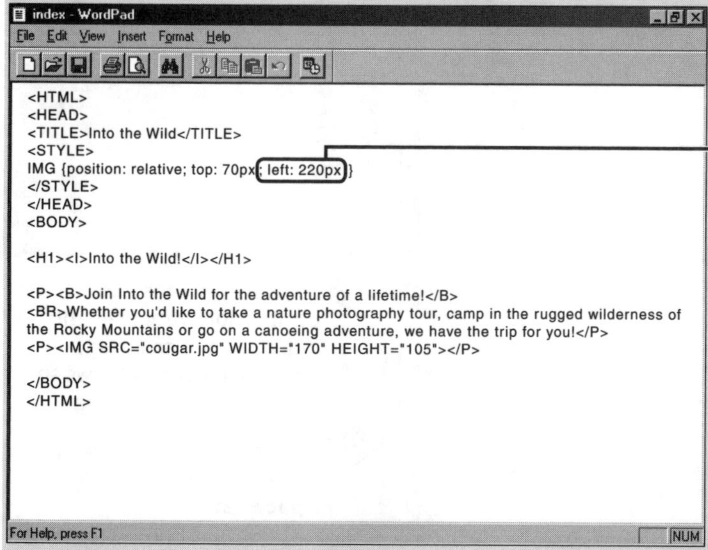

```
index - WordPad                                          _ 5 X
File  Edit  View  Insert  Format  Help

<HTML>
<HEAD>
<TITLE>Into the Wild</TITLE>
<STYLE>
IMG {position: relative; top: 70px; left: 220px }
</STYLE>
</HEAD>
<BODY>

<H1><I>Into the Wild!</I></H1>

<P><B>Join Into the Wild for the adventure of a lifetime!</B>
<BR>Whether you'd like to take a nature photography tour, camp in the rugged wilderness of
the Rocky Mountains or go on a canoeing adventure, we have the trip for you!</P>
<P><IMG SRC="cougar.jpg" WIDTH="170" HEIGHT="105"></P>

</BODY>
</HTML>

For Help, press F1                                              NUM
```

**⑤** To move the elements in more than one direction at a time, type a semicolon (**;**) followed by a space and then repeat steps **3** and **4**.

*Note: Moving elements in more than one direction allows you to move the elements diagonally.*

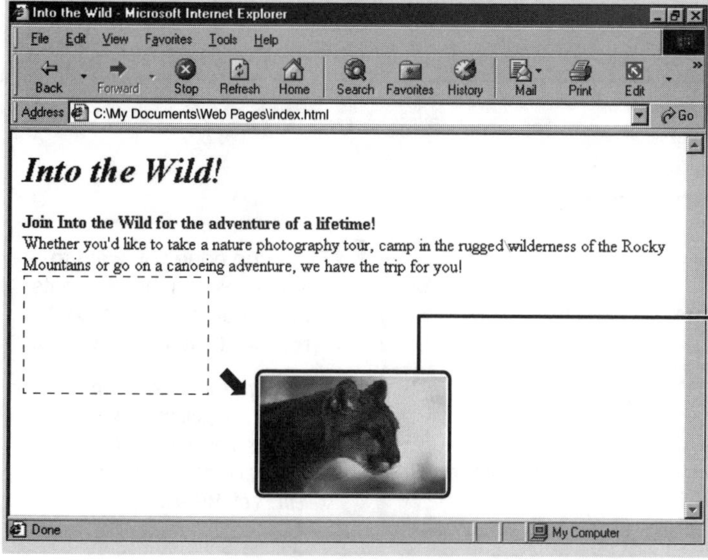

```
Into the Wild - Microsoft Internet Explorer                 _ 5 X
File  Edit  View  Favorites  Tools  Help

 ⇦      ⇨       ⊗      ⟳      ⌂      ⊚       ⌧       ⊛       ⊠ -     ⊜      ⊡
Back   Forward   Stop   Refresh  Home   Search  Favorites  History   Mail    Print    Edit
Address  C:\My Documents\Web Pages\index.html                         ▼  ⟶Go
```

## Into the Wild!

**Join Into the Wild for the adventure of a lifetime!**
Whether you'd like to take a nature photography tour, camp in the rugged wilderness of the Rocky
Mountains or go on a canoeing adventure, we have the trip for you!

**⑥** Display the Web page in a Web browser.

● The Web browser displays all the elements that use the tag with the positioning you specified.

*Note: Positioning elements relatively may cause elements on your Web page to overlap.*

# POSITION ELEMENTS ABSOLUTELY

You can specify an absolute position for every element on your Web page that uses a specific tag. Positioning elements absolutely removes the elements from the natural flow of the Web page and allows other elements on the page to shift to fill the space previously occupied by the elements you positioned.

## POSITION ELEMENTS ABSOLUTELY

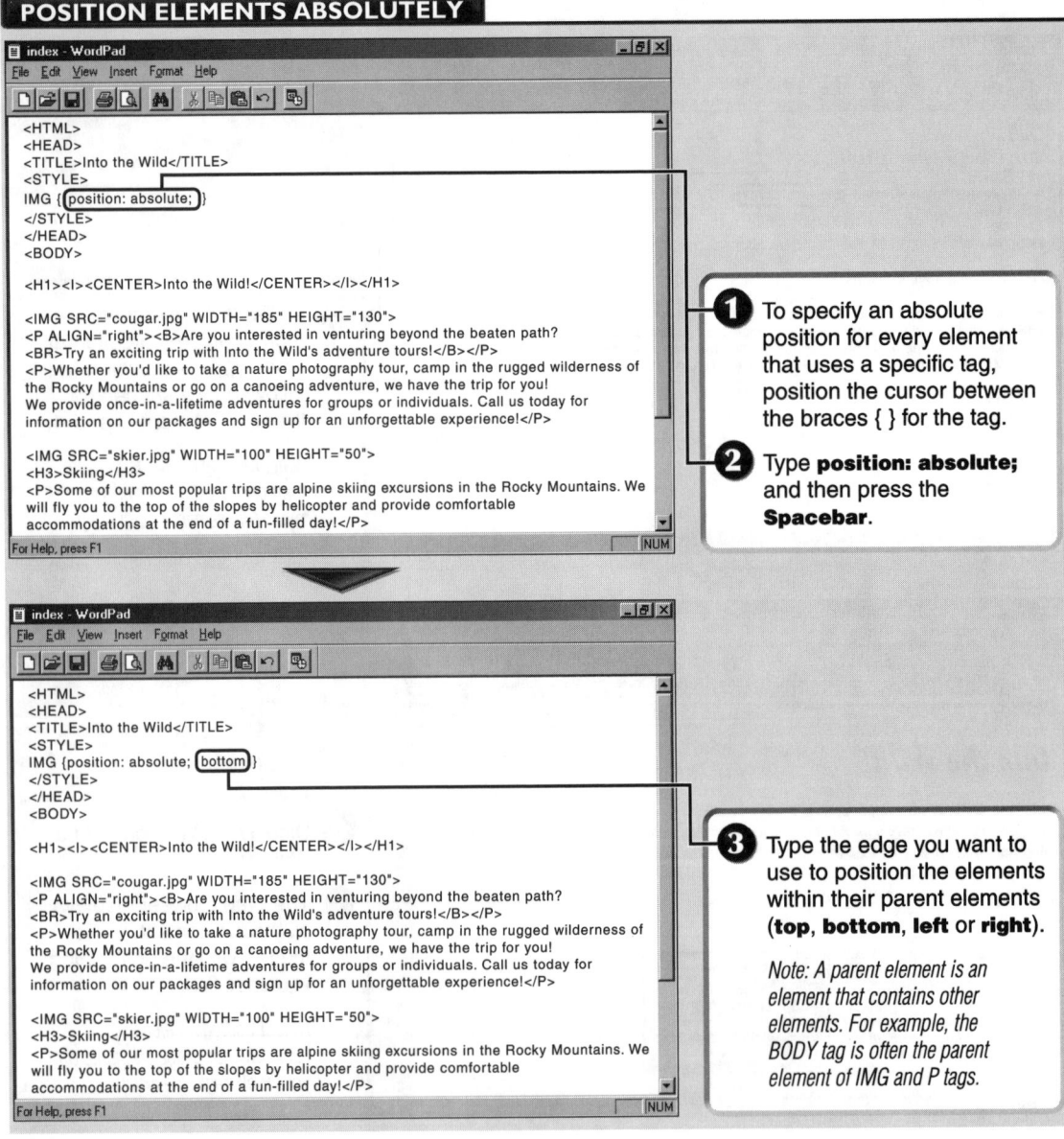

① To specify an absolute position for every element that uses a specific tag, position the cursor between the braces { } for the tag.

② Type **position: absolute;** and then press the **Spacebar**.

③ Type the edge you want to use to position the elements within their parent elements (**top, bottom, left** or **right**).

*Note: A parent element is an element that contains other elements. For example, the BODY tag is often the parent element of IMG and P tags.*

in an *instant*

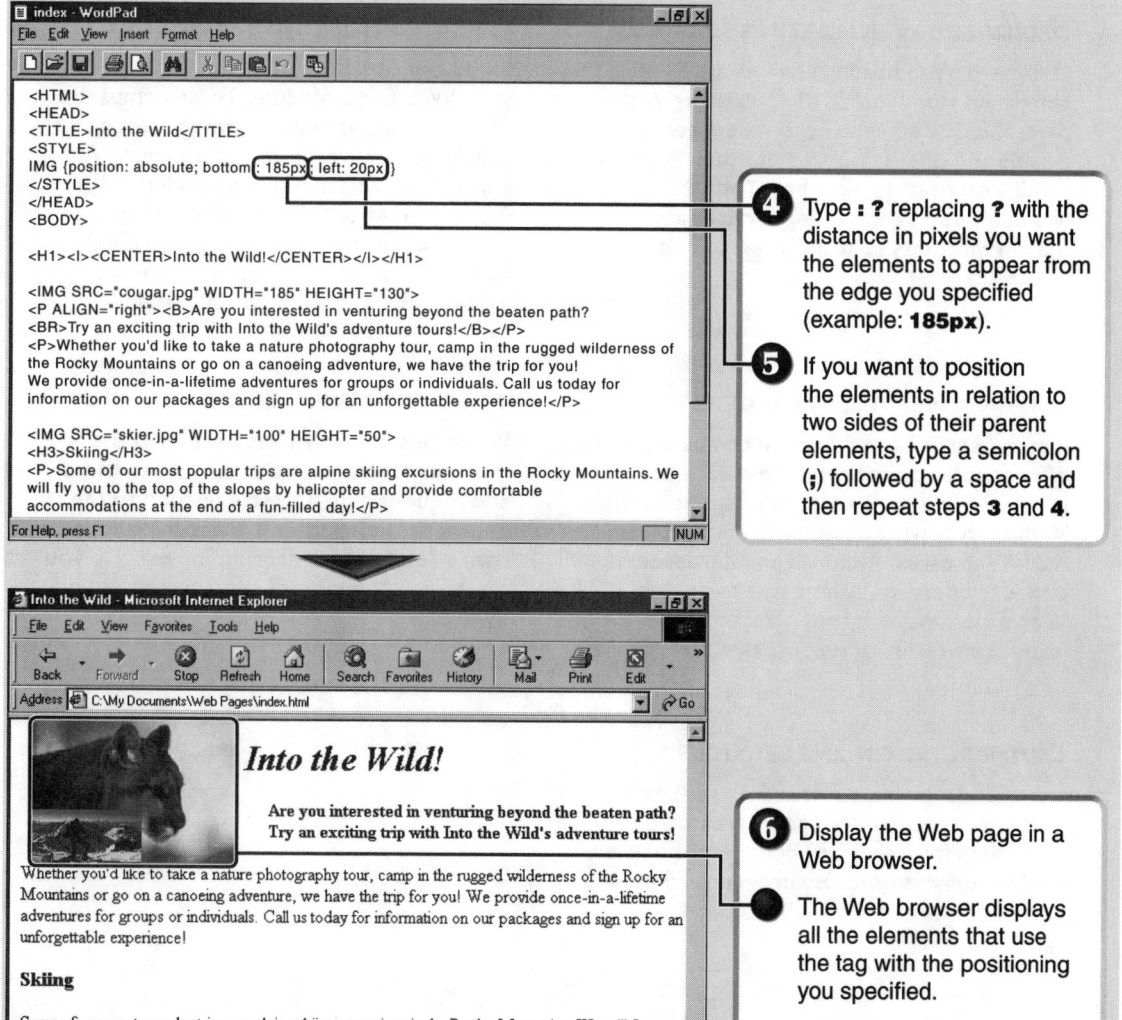

**4** Type **: ?** replacing **?** with the distance in pixels you want the elements to appear from the edge you specified (example: **185px**).

**5** If you want to position the elements in relation to two sides of their parent elements, type a semicolon (**;**) followed by a space and then repeat steps **3** and **4**.

**6** Display the Web page in a Web browser.

■ The Web browser displays all the elements that use the tag with the positioning you specified.

*Note: Positioning elements absolutely may cause elements on your Web page to overlap.*

# CHOOSE A WEB HOSTING SERVICE

Web hosting services are companies that store Web pages and make them available on the Web for people to view. Web hosting services store Web pages on computers called Web servers. Web servers monitor and control access to Web pages.

## TYPES OF WEB HOSTING SERVICES

### DEDICATED WEB HOSTING SERVICES

Dedicated Web hosting services are companies that specialize in publishing Web pages. Dedicated Web hosting services are flexible and offer features that other Web hosting services do not offer. You can find dedicated Web hosting services at the www.hostess.com and www.pair.com Web sites.

### INTERNET SERVICE PROVIDERS

Internet service providers are companies that offer people access to the Internet. Most Internet service providers offer space on their Web servers where customers can publish their Web pages. Although an Internet service provider offers the easiest way to publish Web pages, they may not provide all the features or technical support that you require.

### COMMERCIAL ONLINE SERVICES

Commercial online services such as America Online will publish Web pages created by customers for free. Many commercial online services offer easy-to-use programs to help people create and publish Web pages.

### FREE WEB HOSTING SERVICES

Some companies on the Web will publish your Web pages for free. These companies offer a limited amount of storage space and usually place advertisements on your Web pages. They also may not offer all the features you need. Companies such as Yahoo! GeoCities (geocities.yahoo.com) and Tripod (www.tripod.lycos.com) are examples of free Web hosting services.

### YOUR OWN WEB SERVER

Purchasing your own Web server is the most expensive way to publish Web pages and requires a full-time connection to the Internet. Setting up and maintaining your own Web server is difficult but will give you the greatest amount of control over your Web pages.

# in an instant

## WEB HOSTING SERVICE CONSIDERATIONS

### TRAFFIC LIMIT

When users view your Web pages, information transfers from the Web server to their computers. The amount of information that transfers from the Web server depends on the number of people that view your Web pages and the file size of your pages.

Most Web hosting services limit the amount of information that can transfer in one month. If more information transfers, you usually have to pay extra.

### DOMAIN NAME REGISTRATION

A domain name is the address that people type to access your Web pages, such as www.maran.com. If you want your own personalized domain name, most Web hosting services can register a domain name for you. A personalized domain name is easy for people to remember and will not change if you switch to another Web hosting service. For information on registering your own domain name, visit the internic.net Web site.

### TECHNICAL SUPPORT

A Web hosting service should have a technical support department to answer your questions. You should be able to contact a Web hosting service by telephone or e-mail and get a response to your questions within a day.

### RELIABILITY

A Web hosting service should be able to tell you how often their Web servers shut down. You should take into consideration that Web hosting services occasionally shut down their Web servers for maintenance and upgrades. You may want to ask a Web hosting service for customer references.

### STORAGE SPACE

Most Web hosting services limit the amount of space you can use to store your Web site. If your Web site is larger than the space provided, you will have to pay extra. Choose a Web hosting service that provides enough space to store all the information for your Web site.

### ACCESS LOGS

A good Web hosting service will supply you with statistics about your Web pages, such as which Web pages are the most popular and where your users are from. You should also be able to view any error messages users may see when viewing your Web pages, such as "Page Not Found." Access logs can help you determine if you need to make changes to your Web pages.

CONTINUED

## WEB HOSTING SERVICE CONSIDERATIONS (CONTINUED)

### AVAILABLE BANDWIDTH

Bandwidth is the amount of data that can transfer over the Internet in a set amount of time. The speed and number of connections to the Internet determine a Web hosting service's bandwidth. A high bandwidth can decrease the amount of time users spend waiting to view your Web pages. Keep in mind that the available bandwidth is more important than the maximum bandwidth. You should ensure that a Web hosting service has enough available bandwidth to suit the needs of your Web site.

### SHOPPING SOFTWARE

If you plan to use your Web pages to sell products on the Web, you should consider a Web hosting service that offers shopping software. Shopping software simplifies the task of creating Web pages that allow users to purchase products. You can easily create Web pages that accept orders, verify credit card numbers, generate invoices and organize product shipments.

### DATABASE ACCESS

If you want to give users access to a large amount of information, you should choose a Web hosting service that lets you use a database program on the Web server. A database program can store a large amount of information, such as a product list. When a user requests information, the Web server will search the database for the information and then display the requested information on a Web page.

### CGI SCRIPT ACCESS

Web pages can include forms that allow users to send you questions and comments, order products or fill out questionnaires. If you plan to use forms on your Web pages, make sure your Web hosting service allows you to use CGI scripts. CGI scripts are programs that process information sent by a form.

### SECURE WEB SERVER

If you require users of your Web site to enter confidential information, such as credit card numbers, you should use a Web hosting service with a secure Web server. Secure Web servers encode the information that transfers over the Internet so that only the sending and receiving computers can read the information.

# PREPARE TO PUBLISH WEB PAGES

Before publishing your Web pages on the Web, you must prepare to transfer the pages to a Web server. By properly preparing your Web pages for publishing, you can avoid problems such as broken links and error messages when users view the Web pages.

## PREPARE TO PUBLISH WEB PAGES

### CHECK WEB PAGE FILE NAMES

Your Web page file names should all have the .htm or .html extension (example: garden.html) and should not include spaces or unusual characters, such as * or &. You should check with your Web hosting service to ensure that you use the correct name for your home page. Home pages are usually named index.html.

### CHECK FILE REFERENCES

After you organize your Web page files, you should check all references to the files on your Web pages. For example, if an image on a Web page is stored in the same folder as the Web page, make sure you specified just the name of the image (example: porsche.jpg).

If an image on a Web page is stored in a subfolder, make sure you specified both the name of the subfolder and the name of the image (example: images/porsche.jpg).

### OBTAIN AN FTP PROGRAM

You need a File Transfer Protocol (FTP) program to transfer your Web pages to a Web server. You can obtain popular FTP programs at the following Web sites:

**WS_FTP Pro (Windows)**

www.ipswitch.com

**Fetch (Macintosh)**

www.fetchsoftworks.com

### ORGANIZE WEB PAGE FILES

You should store all your Web pages in one folder on your computer. Make sure the folder also contains all the images, sounds, videos and other files you included on your Web pages. If the folder contains many files, you may want to store some of the files in subfolders. For example, you can store all the images for your Web pages in a subfolder of the folder that stores your Web pages.

### CHECK TOTAL FILE SIZE OF WEB PAGES

Make sure the total file size of all your Web pages does not exceed the amount of space that your Web hosting service allows. If the total file size is too large, an error message will appear when you try to transfer the Web pages.

You can specify keywords to help search tools catalog your Web page. When users enter words in a search tool that match your keywords, your Web page will be more likely to appear in the search results. The keywords you use should be common words that accurately describe your Web page.

## SPECIFY KEYWORDS

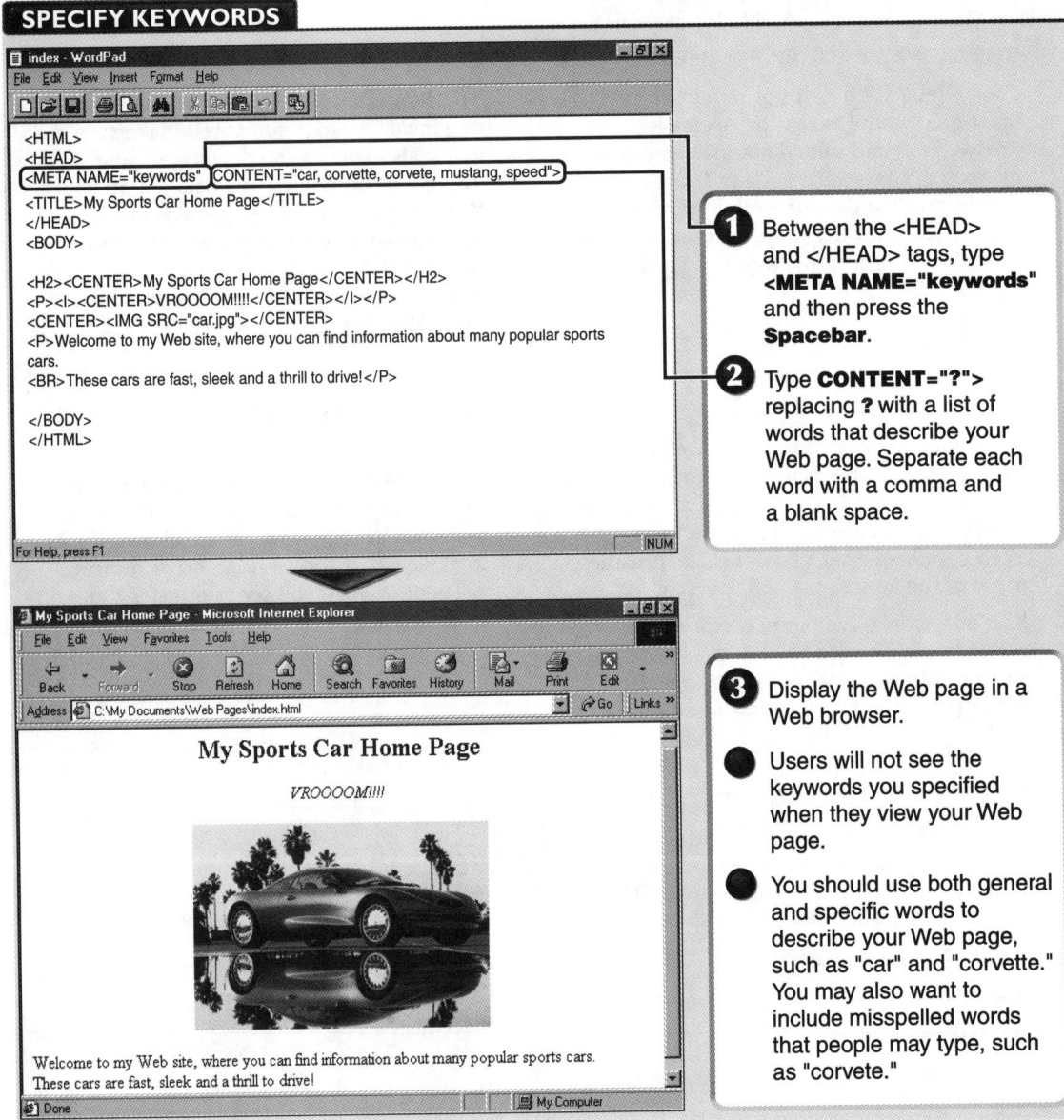

**1** Between the <HEAD> and </HEAD> tags, type **<META NAME="keywords"** and then press the **Spacebar**.

**2** Type **CONTENT="?">** replacing **?** with a list of words that describe your Web page. Separate each word with a comma and a blank space.

**3** Display the Web page in a Web browser.

● Users will not see the keywords you specified when they view your Web page.

● You should use both general and specific words to describe your Web page, such as "car" and "corvette." You may also want to include misspelled words that people may type, such as "corvete."

You can specify a summary that you want search tools to display when they find your Web page. You should ensure the summary is concise and descriptive, since most search tools will not display more than three lines for a summary. If you do not specify a summary, search tools will use text from the top of your Web page for the summary.

## SPECIFY WEB PAGE SUMMARY

**index - WordPad**

File  Edit  View  Insert  Format  Help

```
<HTML>
<HEAD>
<META NAME="description"  CONTENT="Information and pictures of sports cars.">
<TITLE>My Sports Car Home Page</TITLE>
</HEAD>
<BODY>

<H2><CENTER>My Sports Car Home Page</CENTER></H2>
<P><I><CENTER>VROOOOM!!!!</CENTER></I></P>
<CENTER><IMG SRC="car.jpg"></CENTER>
<P>Welcome to my Web site, where you can find information about many popular
sports cars.
<BR>These cars are fast, sleek and a thrill to drive!</P>

</BODY>
</HTML>
```

For Help, press F1                                                      NUM

**1** Between the <HEAD> and </HEAD> tags, type **<META NAME="description"** and then press the **Spacebar**.

**2** Type **CONTENT="?">** replacing **?** with a summary of your Web page.

*Note: Try to limit the summary to one or two sentences.*

**My Sports Car Home Page - Microsoft Internet Explorer**

File  Edit  View  Favorites  Tools  Help

Back  Forward  Stop  Refresh  Home  Search  Favorites  History  Mail  Print  Edit

Address  C:\My Documents\Web Pages\index.html          Go    Links

### My Sports Car Home Page

*VROOOOM!!!!*

Welcome to my Web site, where you can find information about many popular sports cars. These cars are fast, sleek and a thrill to drive!

Done                                                My Computer

**3** Display the Web page in a Web browser.

● Users will not see the summary you specified when they view your Web page.

# SPECIFY AUTHOR AND COPYRIGHT INFORMATION

You can specify information about your Web page, including the name of the author and a copyright statement. Specifying copyright information lets you indicate that you do not want the information on your Web page copied without your permission. Only users who view the HTML code for your Web page will see the author and copyright information you specify.

## SPECIFY AUTHOR AND COPYRIGHT INFORMATION

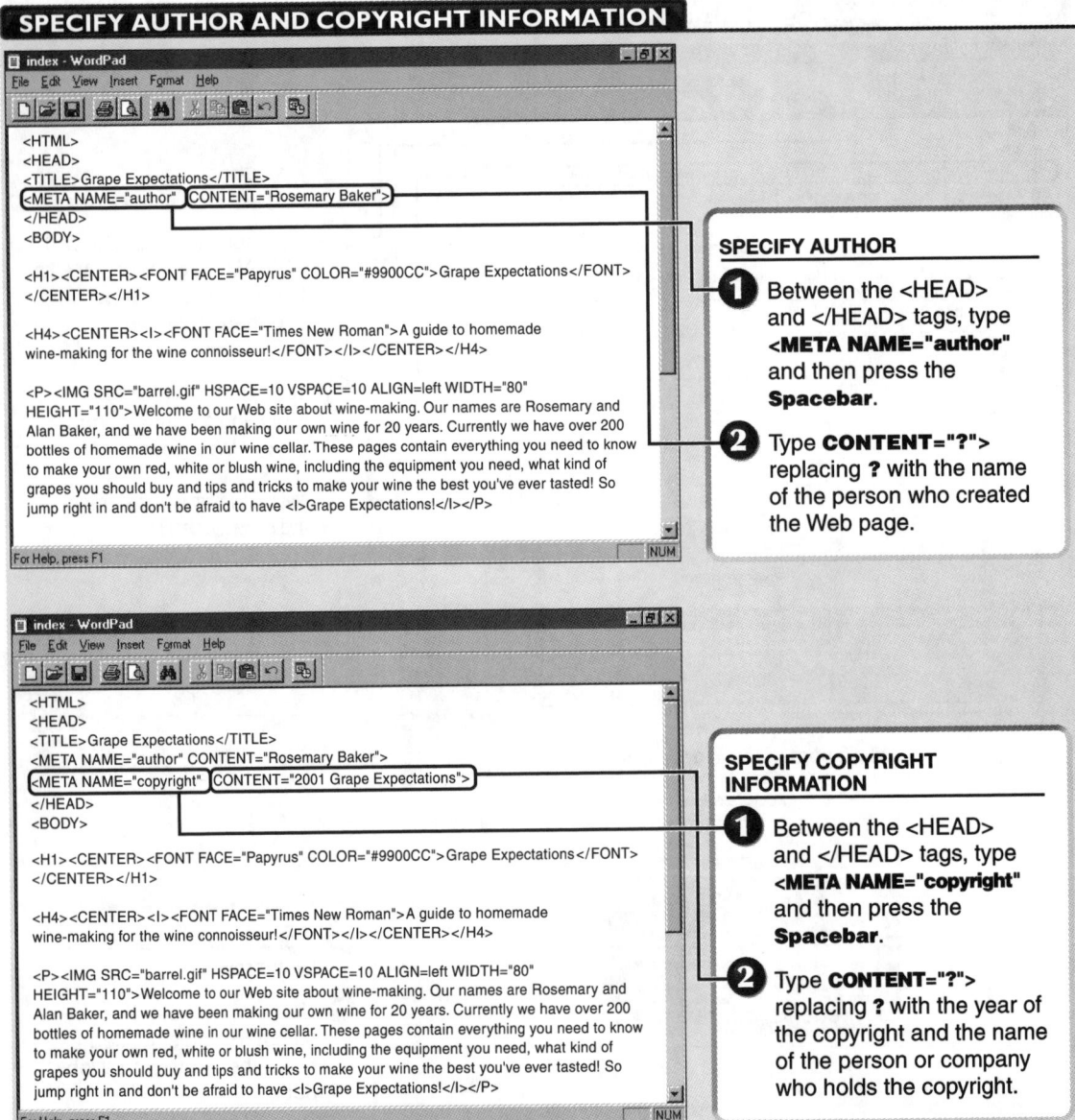

**SPECIFY AUTHOR**

1. Between the <HEAD> and </HEAD> tags, type **<META NAME="author"** and then press the **Spacebar**.

2. Type **CONTENT="?">** replacing **?** with the name of the person who created the Web page.

**SPECIFY COPYRIGHT INFORMATION**

1. Between the <HEAD> and </HEAD> tags, type **<META NAME="copyright"** and then press the **Spacebar**.

2. Type **CONTENT="?">** replacing **?** with the year of the copyright and the name of the person or company who holds the copyright.

# PREVENT ROBOTS FROM INDEXING

Many search tools use programs, called robots or spiders, to find new and updated pages on the Web. You can prevent most robots from indexing your Web page. This is useful when you have created a Web page for a specific audience, such as your family or company, and do not want other people to access the Web page.

## PREVENT ROBOTS FROM INDEXING

```
index - WordPad                                                    _ ß x
File  Edit  View  Insert  Format  Help

<HTML>
<HEAD>
<TITLE>Smith Family Home Page</TITLE>
<META NAME="robots" CONTENT="NOINDEX, NOFOLLOW">
</HEAD>
<BODY>

<H1><CENTER>Welcome Smith Family Members and Friends!</CENTER></H1>
<P>The Smith Family has grown over the years, and now we have created a Web site to keep
in touch and update each other about family events.
<BR>It will be updated regularly, and anyone who would like to post some family-related news
should contact the
<A HREF="mailto:webmaster@smithfamily.com">Webmaster</A>.</P>

<H3>New Addition!</H3>
<P>There is a new addition to the Smith family! Mike and Janet Smith have given birth to a
baby boy named Justin. He is doing very well. Congratulations!</P>

</BODY>
</HTML>

For Help, press F1                                                    NUM
```

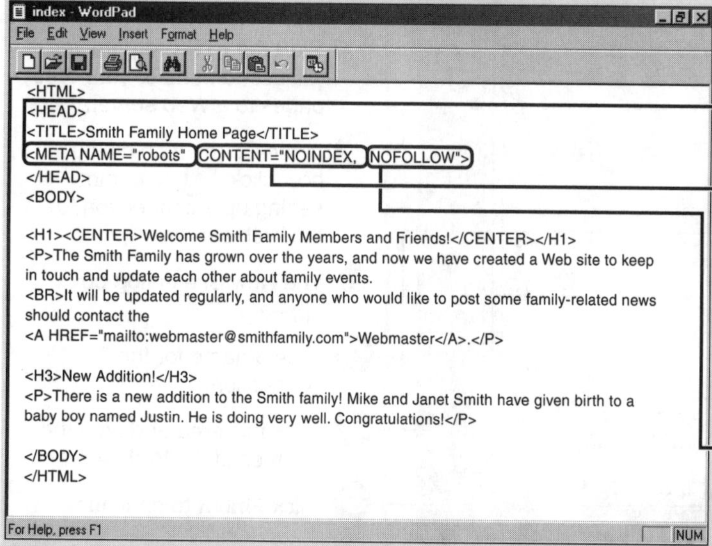

**1** Between the <HEAD> and </HEAD> tags, type **<META NAME="robots"** and then press the **Spacebar**.

**2** Type **CONTENT="NOINDEX,** to prevent robots from indexing your Web page. Then press the **Spacebar**.

**3** Type **NOFOLLOW">** to prevent robots from indexing any Web pages

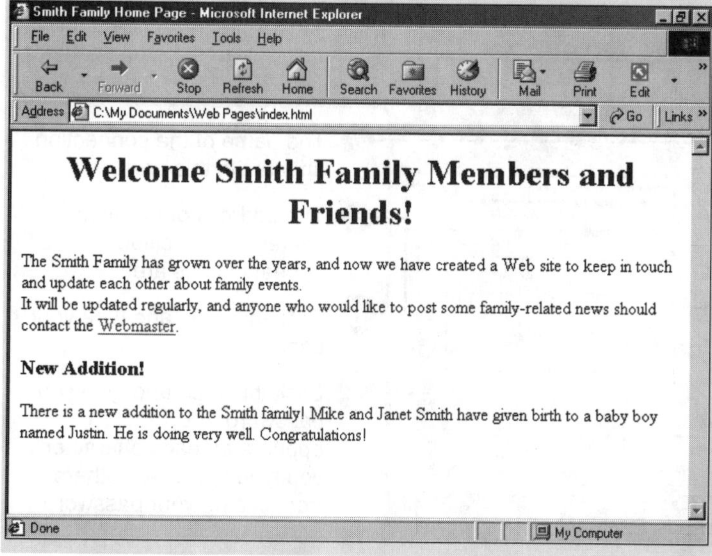

```
Smith Family Home Page - Microsoft Internet Explorer                 _ ß x
File  Edit  View  Favorites  Tools  Help

 ⇐      ⇒       ⊗      ⊡      ⌂       ⊛       ⊡      ⊛      ⊡·     ⊜      ⊠       »
Back   Forward   Stop   Refresh   Home   Search   Favorites  History   Mail    Print    Edit

Address  C:\My Documents\Web Pages\index.html                      ▼  ∂Go  Links »
```

# **Welcome Smith Family Members and Friends!**

The Smith Family has grown over the years, and now we have created a Web site to keep in touch and update each other about family events.
It will be updated regularly, and anyone who would like to post some family-related news should contact the Webmaster.

**New Addition!**

There is a new addition to the Smith family! Mike and Janet Smith have given birth to a baby boy named Justin. He is doing very well. Congratulations!

```
Done                                                    My Computer
```

**4** Display the Web page in a Web browser.

When users view your Web page, the information you specified to prevent robots from indexing the page will not appear.

# TRANSFER WEB PAGES TO WEB SERVER

To make your Web pages available on the Web, you must transfer the pages to a Web server using a File Transfer Protocol (FTP) program such as WS_FTP Pro. You can obtain WS_FTP Pro at the www.ipswitch.com Web site. To set up a connection to the Web server, you must know the address of the server and your user ID and password. If you do not know this information, contact your Web hosting service.

## SET UP A CONNECTION

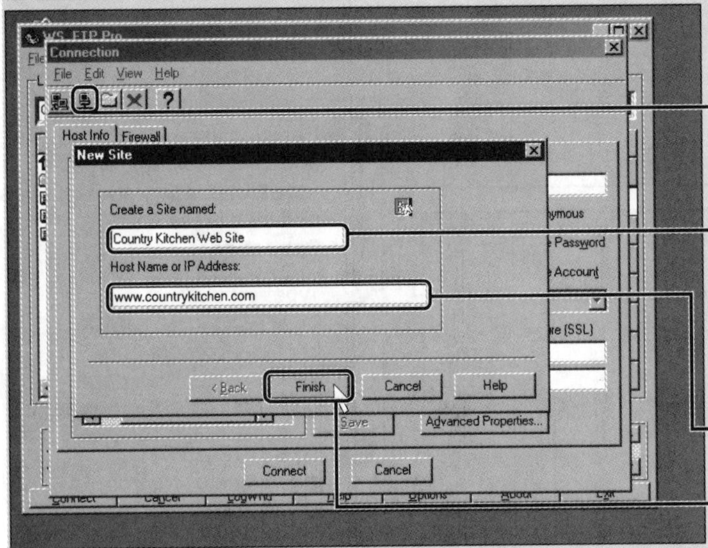

**1** Start the FTP program you will use to transfer your Web pages to a Web server.

**2** In the Connection dialog box, click 🖳 to begin setting up a connection to the Web server.

● The New Site dialog box appears.

**3** Type a name for the connection.

**4** Click this area and type the address of the Web server.

**5** Click **Finish** to continue.

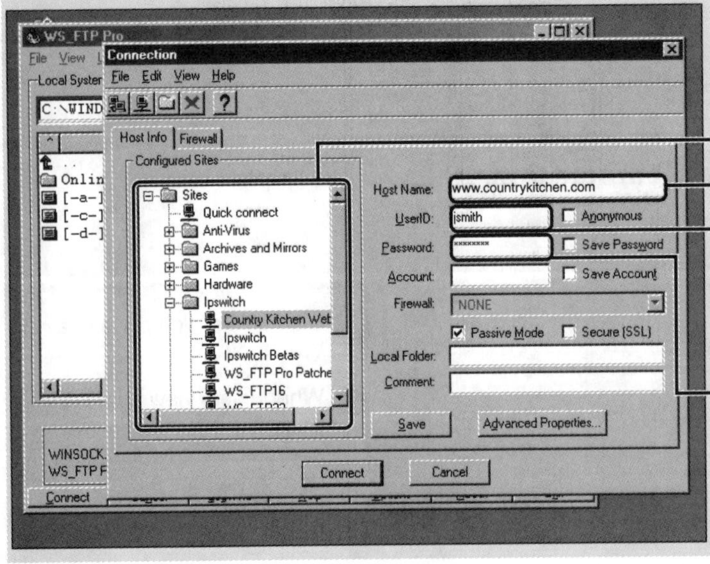

● The name of the connection appears in this area.

● The address of the Web server you specified appears in this area.

**6** Click this area and type your user ID.

**7** Click this area and type your password. A symbol (x) appears for each character you type to prevent others from seeing your password.

# in an *instant*

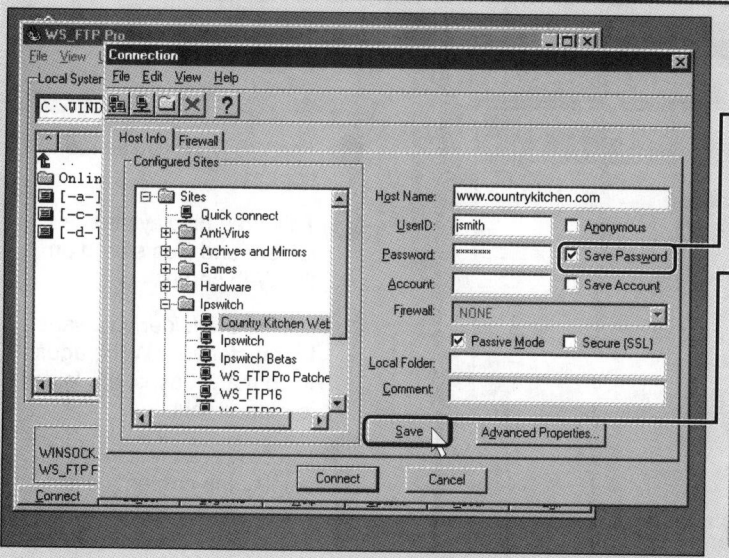

**8** To save your password so you will not need to retype the password again later, click this option ( ☐ changes to ☑).

**9** Click **Save** to have the program store the information you entered for the connection.

*Note: You need to set up a connection to a Web server only once. After you set up a connection, you can connect to the Web server at any time.*

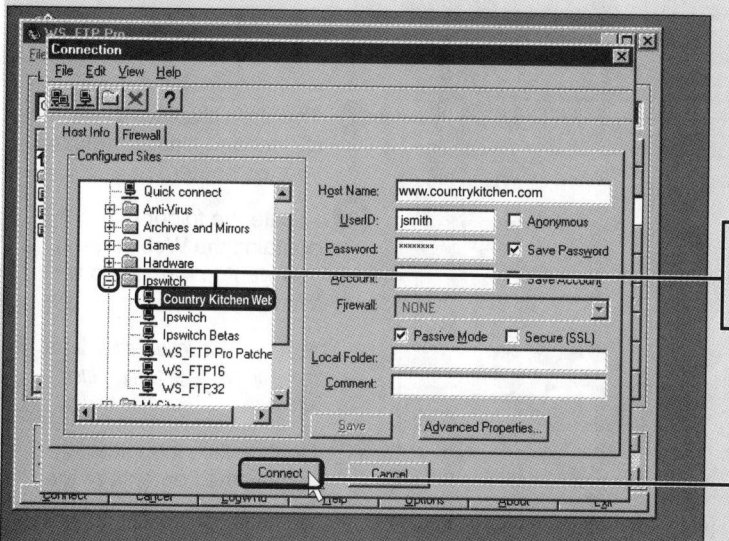

### TRANSFER WEB PAGES TO WEB SERVER

**1** Click the connection for the Web server you want to transfer your Web pages to.

■ If the connection you set up is not displayed, click the plus sign (⊞) beside the Ipswitch directory (⊞ changes to ⊟).

**2** Click **Connect** to connect to the Web server.

CONTINUED

Once you have connected to a Web server, you can transfer information to the server. You can transfer a single file, multiple files or an entire folder to the Web server at once. To ensure that the Web server's resources are available for other people, the Web server may automatically disconnect you if your connection is idle for an extended period of time.

## TRANSFER WEB PAGES TO WEB SERVER (CONTINUED)

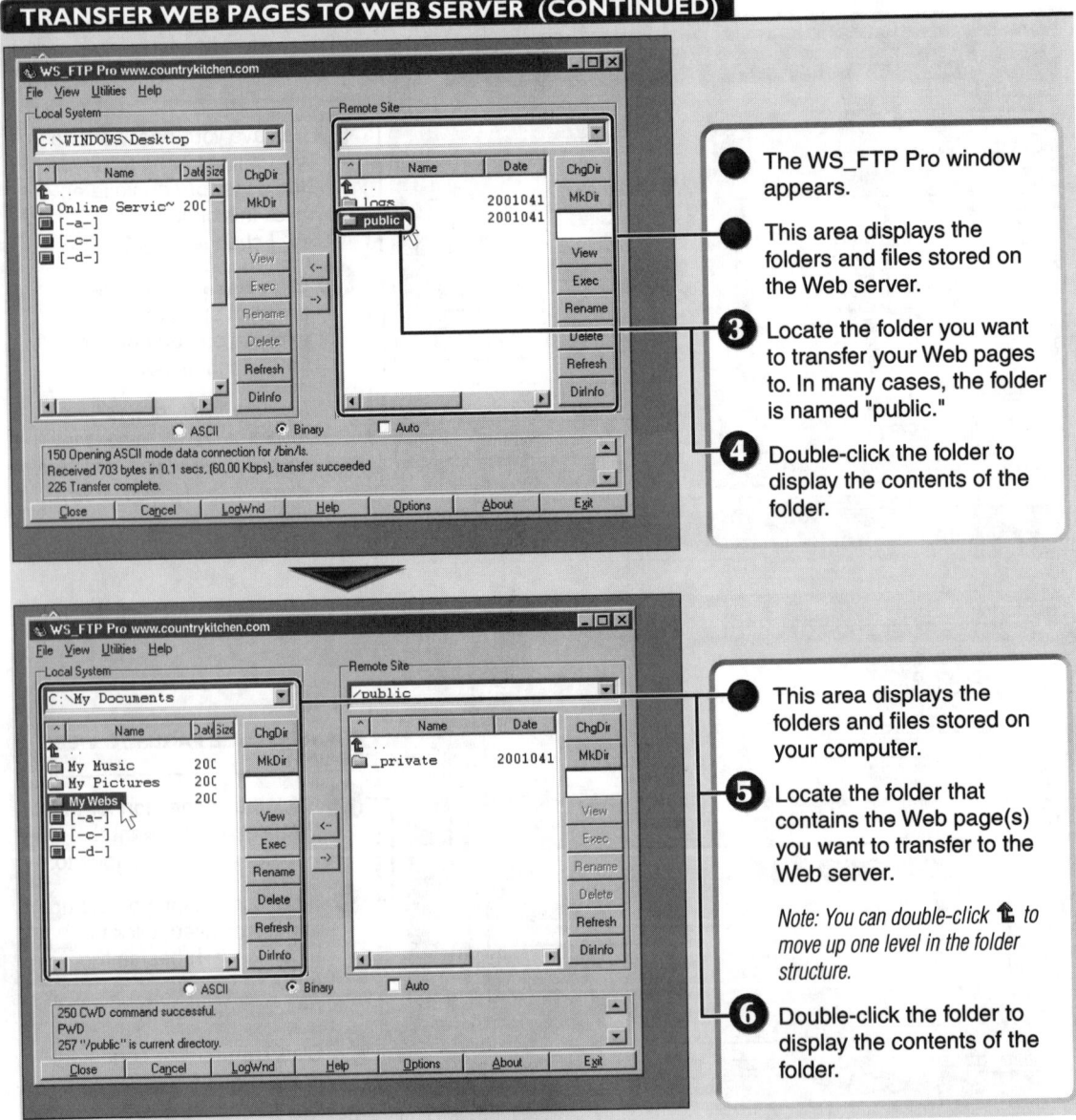

● The WS_FTP Pro window appears.

● This area displays the folders and files stored on the Web server.

③ Locate the folder you want to transfer your Web pages to. In many cases, the folder is named "public."

④ Double-click the folder to display the contents of the folder.

● This area displays the folders and files stored on your computer.

⑤ Locate the folder that contains the Web page(s) you want to transfer to the Web server.

Note: You can double-click 🔼 to move up one level in the folder structure.

⑥ Double-click the folder to display the contents of the folder.

# in an instant

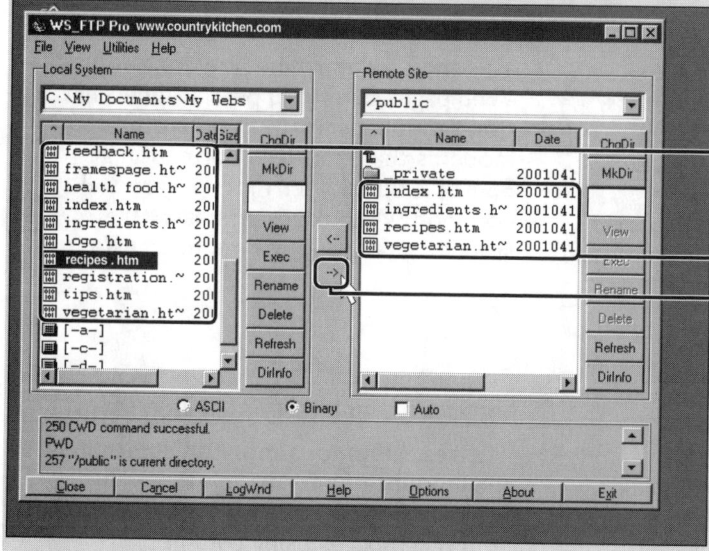

**WS_FTP Pro** www.countrykitchen.com

File  View  Utilities  Help

**Local System**

C:\My Documents\My Webs

| ^ | Name | Date | Size | ChgDir |
|---|---|---|---|---|
| | feedback.htm | 20| | MkDir |
| | framespage.ht~ | 20| | |
| | health food.h~ | 20| | |
| | index.htm | 20| | View |
| | ingredients.h~ | 20| | |
| | logo.htm | 20| | Exec |
| | recipes.htm | 20| | |
| | registration.~ | 20| | Rename |
| | tips.htm | 20| | Delete |
| | vegetarian.ht~ | 20| | |
| | [-a-] | | | Refresh |
| | [-c-] | | | |
| | [-d-] | | | DirInfo |

**Remote Site**

/public

| ^ | Name | Date | ChgDir |
|---|---|---|---|
| | .. | | MkDir |
| | _private | 2001041 | |
| | index.htm | 2001041 | |
| | ingredients.h~ | 2001041 | View |
| | recipes.htm | 2001041 | |
| | vegetarian.ht~ | 2001041 | Exec |
| | | | Rename |
| | | | Delete |
| | | | Refresh |
| | | | DirInfo |

○ ASCII  ● Binary  ☐ Auto

250 CWD command successful.
PWD
257 "/public" is current directory.

Close | Cancel | LogWnd | Help | Options | About | Exit

**7** Click the file or folder you want to transfer to the Web server.

**8** Click ▣ to transfer the file or folder to the Web server.

● The file or folder appears on the Web server.

**9** Repeat steps **5** to **8** for each file and folder you want to transfer.

---

**WS_FTP Pro** www.countrykitchen.com

File  View  Utilities  Help

**Local System**

C:\My Documents\My Webs

| ^ | Name | Date | Size | ChgDir |
|---|---|---|---|---|
| | framespage.ht~ | 200| | MkDir |
| | health food.h~ | 200| | |
| | index.htm | 200| | |
| | ingredients.h~ | 200| | View |
| | logo.htm | 200| | |
| | recipes.htm | 200| | Exec |
| | registration.~ | 200| | Rename |
| | tips.htm | 200| | |
| | vegetarian.ht~ | 200| | Delete |
| | WS_FTP.LOG | 200| | Refresh |
| | [-a-] | | | |
| | [-c-] | | | DirInfo |
| | [-d-] | | | |

**Remote Site**

/public

| ^ | Name | Date | ChgDir |
|---|---|---|---|
| | .. | | MkDir |
| | _private | 2001041 | |
| | index.htm | 2001041 | |
| | ingredients.h~ | 2001041 | View |
| | recipes.htm | 2001041 | |
| | vegetarian.ht~ | 2001041 | Exec |
| | | | Rename |
| | | | Delete |
| | | | Refresh |
| | | | DirInfo |

○ ASCII  ● Binary  ☐ Auto

150 Opening ASCII mode data connection for /bin/ls.
Received 357 bytes in 0.1 secs, (30.00 Kbps), transfer succeeded
226 Transfer complete.

Close | Cancel | LogWnd | Help | Options | About | Exit

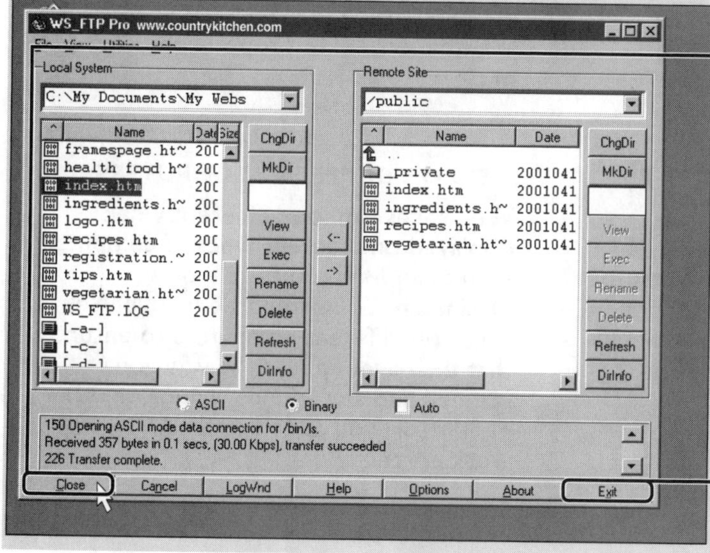

**10** Click **Close** to end the connection to the Web server.

**11** Click **Exit** to exit the program.

### UPDATE WEB PAGES

● If you make changes to the Web pages on your computer, you must replace the old Web pages on the Web server with the updated pages. To transfer updated Web pages to the Web server, perform steps **1** to **11** starting on page 233.

# TEST WEB PAGES

Testing your Web pages helps make sure they look and work the way you planned. For example, you should test your Web pages to determine how easily users will be able to browse through the information. You should also make sure your Web pages have a consistent design and writing style and do not contain formatting or layout errors.

## WAYS TO TEST YOUR WEB PAGES

### CHECK HTML CODE AND LINKS

You can use a validation service to check your Web pages for HTML errors. You can find a validation service at the validator.w3.org Web site. You should also regularly check the links on your Web pages to make sure they take users to the intended destinations. Make sure the linked Web pages still exist and contain useful information.

### TRY DIFFERENT TRANSFER SPEEDS

You should determine how long your Web pages take to appear at different transfer speeds. Many people use modems that transfer information at 56 Kbps, but slower modems are still common. Web pages with large file sizes may take a long time to transfer.

### TURN OFF IMAGES

Some people turn off the display of images to browse the Web more quickly, while others use Web browsers that cannot display images. You should view your Web pages without images to ensure that users who do not see images will still find your pages useful.

### VIEW AT DIFFERENT RESOLUTIONS

The resolution of a monitor determines the amount of information that will appear on a screen. You should view your Web pages using common resolutions, such as 640x480 and 800x600, to determine if your information will fit properly on most screens.

### VIEW IN DIFFERENT WEB BROWSERS

You should view your Web pages in different Web browsers, such as Microsoft Internet Explorer and Netscape Navigator, to make sure the pages look the way you planned. Each Web browser will display your Web pages in a slightly different way.

### VIEW ON DIFFERENT COMPUTERS

Web pages can look different when displayed on different types of computers, such as an IBM-compatible or a Macintosh. You should view your Web pages on different computers to ensure that the pages appear the way you planned and any sounds, videos or other multimedia you added to the Web pages work correctly.

After you publish your Web pages, there are several ways you can let people know about the pages. Publicizing your Web pages is important if you want many people to view your pages. You can publicize your Web pages using traditional methods or by using the Internet.

## WAYS TO PUBLICIZE YOUR WEB PAGES

### TRADITIONAL METHODS

You can mail an announcement about your Web pages to family, friends, colleagues and customers. You can also send information about your Web pages to local newspapers and magazines that may be interested in your Web pages. If you created Web pages for your company, make sure you include your Web page address on business cards, letterhead and any print advertisements you produce.

### SEARCH TOOLS

Search tools help people quickly find information on the Web. Adding your Web pages to various search tools can help people easily find your Web pages. Some popular search tools include Google (www.google.com) and Yahoo! (www.yahoo.com). The www.submit-it.com Web site allows you to add your Web pages to many search tools at once.

### EXCHANGE LINKS

If another Web site offers information, products or services related to your Web site, you can ask the individual or company to include a link to your Web pages if you will do the same. This allows people reading the other Web pages to easily visit your Web site.

### WEB PAGE ADVERTISEMENTS

Many companies set aside areas on their Web pages where you can advertise your Web site for a fee. You can also use the bCentral Banner Network, which is a service that brings organizations together to exchange Web page advertisements. The bCentral Banner Network is located at the www.bcentral.com/services/bn Web site.

### NEWSGROUPS

You can send an announcement about your Web pages to discussion groups on the Internet, called newsgroups. Make sure you choose newsgroups that discuss topics related to your Web pages.

### E-MAIL MESSAGES

Most e-mail programs include a feature, called a signature, that allows you to add the same information to the end of every e-mail message you send. You can use a signature to include information about your Web pages in all your e-mail messages.

# TROUBLESHOOT WEB PAGES

If your Web pages do not appear the way you expect when you display the pages in a Web browser, there are several common HTML errors you can check for to troubleshoot the problem. Locating errors in a Web page can be difficult, since Web browsers display pages containing incorrect HTML code as best they can rather than generating error messages.

## COMMON ERRORS

### TYPING ERRORS

Typing errors are the most common errors in HTML code. Web browsers usually ignore HTML tags and attributes they do not recognize, so mistyped HTML code is usually ignored. For example, if you type <A HERF="webpage.html"> for a link, the link will not appear on your Web page.

### INCORRECT PATH OR EXTENSION

If you specify the incorrect path or extension when adding an element such as an image or sound to your Web page, the element will not appear on the page. For example, if you use the .gif extension for an image that is saved using the .jpg extension, a Web browser will not be able to locate and display the image.

### MISSING QUOTATION MARKS OR ANGLE BRACKETS

If you forget to type a closing quotation mark (") for a value or a closing angle bracket (>) for a tag, Web browsers will not know where the information for the value or tag ends. This may cause Web browsers to omit a section of your Web page or display the HTML code on your Web page.

### UNSUPPORTED HTML CODE

Even if your HTML code does not contain errors, your Web page may not appear correctly in a Web browser if the browser does not yet support the code you are using. For example, some features of style sheets are not yet fully supported by Web browsers.

### MISSING END TAGS

While some end tags are optional in HTML, such as the </P> tag, others are necessary to properly display elements. For example, if you leave off the </FONT> tag, Web browsers will not know when to stop formatting text on your Web page using the font settings you specified.

# in an instant

## COMMON PROBLEMS

### MISSING IMAGES

If an image does not appear on your Web page, check the filename of the image. Make sure you spelled the name correctly, using the correct uppercase and lowercase letters. You should also verify that the image is saved in a format that Web browsers support, such as JPEG or GIF.

### SOUNDS OR VIDEOS DO NOT PLAY

A Web browser's ability to play sounds and videos depends on the plug-ins that are installed for the browser. A plug-in is software that adds features to a Web browser. If you are having difficulty playing a sound or video, make sure that your Web browser has the correct plug-ins. You should also verify that you successfully transferred the sound or video file to your Web server.

### WEB BROWSER CANNOT FIND WEB PAGE

If an error message appears stating that your Web page cannot be found, you may have placed the Web page in the wrong directory on the Web server. Contact your Web hosting service to confirm where you should store your Web pages. You should also make sure that you have given your home page the correct name. Home pages are usually named index.html.

### WEB BROWSER DISPLAYS BLANK SCREEN

If your Web browser displays a blank screen, you may have a missing or incorrectly typed end tag for a large element such as a table (</TABLE>) or frameset (</FRAMESET>). You should also check HTML tags that appear between the <HEAD> and </HEAD> tags on your Web page. For example, if the <STYLE> tag is incomplete or misspelled, your Web page may appear blank in a Web browser window.

### WEB BROWSER DISPLAYS HTML CODE

If you did not save your Web page with the .html or .htm extension, some Web browsers will display your HTML code. Check that you did not accidentally give your Web page the .txt extension. Some word processors may automatically add the .txt extension to your Web page file. You should also make sure that you used the <HTML> tag on your Web page. Without this tag, a Web browser may not recognize your document as a Web page.

# SUMMARY OF HTML TAGS

| TAG/ATTRIBUTE | DESCRIPTION | REFERENCES |
|---|---|---|
| **BASIC HTML TAGS** | | |
| **!--** | Adds a comment | 29, 193 |
| **BODY** | Identifies the main content of a Web page | 17 |
| **BR** | Starts a new line | 22 |
| **H1 to H6** | Creates headings | 24 |
| ALIGN | Aligns headings | 25 |
| **HEAD** | Contains information about a Web page | 16 |
| **HTML** | Identifies a document as an HTML document | 16 |
| **NOBR** | Keeps text on one line | 27 |
| **P** | Starts a new paragraph | 20 |
| ALIGN | Aligns a paragraph | 21 |
| **TITLE** | Creates a title for a Web page | 17 |
| **FORMAT TEXT** | | |
| **B** | Bolds text | 32 |
| **BASEFONT** | Changes the appearance of all text | 38 |
| SIZE | Changes the size of all text | 38 |
| **BIG** | Makes text larger than the surrounding text | 35 |
| **BLOCKQUOTE** | Separates a section of text from the main text | 51 |
| **BODY** | | |
| BGCOLOR | Changes the background color of a Web page | 42 |
| TEXT | Changes the color of all text | 40 |
| **CENTER** | Centers text | 26 |
| **FONT** | Changes the appearance of text | 36, 39, 41 |
| COLOR | Changes the color of text | 41 |
| FACE | Changes the font of text | 36 |
| SIZE | Changes the size of text | 39 |
| **I** | Italicizes text | 32 |
| **PRE** | Retains the spacing of text you type | 28 |
| **SMALL** | Makes text smaller than the surrounding text | 35 |
| **STRIKE** | Places a line through text | 33 |
| **SUB/SUP** | Places text slightly below or above the main text | 34 |
| **TT** | Creates typewriter text | 43 |
| **U** | Underlines text | 33 |

| TAG/ATTRIBUTE | DESCRIPTION | REFERENCES |
|---|---|---|

## FORMS

| TAG/ATTRIBUTE | DESCRIPTION | REFERENCES |
|---|---|---|
| **FORM** | Creates a form | 133 |
| ACTION | Identifies the location of a CGI script for a form | 133 |
| METHOD | Specifies how information from a form transfers to a Web server | 133 |
| **INPUT** | Creates an item on a form | 134, 136, 140, 142, 146, 148-151 |
| CHECKED | Selects a radio button or check box automatically | 140, 143 |
| ENCTYPE | Specifies how files will transfer over the Internet | 146 |
| MAXLENGTH | Specifies the maximum number of characters an item will accept | 135, 137 |
| NAME | Identifies an item on a form to a Web server | 134, 136, 140, 142, 146, 148, 151 |
| SIZE | Specifies the size of an item on a form | 135, 137, 147 |
| SRC | Specifies the location of the image for a graphical submit button | 151 |
| TYPE | Specifies the type of an item on a form | 134, 136, 140, 142, 146, 148-151 |
| VALUE | Identifies an item on a form | 140, 142, 144, 148-150 |
| **OPTION** | Creates a menu option | 144 |
| SELECTED | Selects a menu option automatically | 145 |
| VALUE | Identifies a menu option to a Web server | 144 |
| **SELECT** | Creates a menu on a form | 144 |
| NAME | Identifies a menu to a Web server | 144 |
| SIZE | Specifies the number of options visible in a menu | 144 |
| **TEXTAREA** | Creates a large text area on a form | 138 |
| COLS/ROWS | Specifies a width or height for a large text area | 138, 139 |
| NAME | Identifies a large text area to a Web server | 138 |

## FRAMES

| TAG/ATTRIBUTE | DESCRIPTION | REFERENCES |
|---|---|---|
| **A** | | |
| HREF | Specifies the location of a linked Web page to appear in a frame | 156 |
| TARGET | Specifies the frame where a linked Web page will appear | 157 |
| **BASE** | Specifies information about the links on a Web page | 158 |
| TARGET | Specifies the frame where all linked Web pages will appear | 158 |
| **FRAME** | Specifies information for one frame | 152 |
| MARGINHEIGHT | Changes the top and bottom margins for a frame | 161 |
| MARGINWIDTH | Changes the left and right margins for a frame | 161 |
| NAME | Names a frame | 152 |
| NORESIZE | Prevents users from resizing a frame | 159 |
| SCROLLING | Hides or displays scroll bars for a frame | 160 |
| SRC | Specifies the location of a Web page that will appear in a frame | 153 |
| **FRAMESET** | Specifies the structure for frames | 153 |
| BORDER | Specifies a thickness for frame borders | 163 |
| BORDERCOLOR | Specifies the color of the borders for a frame | 162 |
| COLS/ROWS | Creates frames in columns or rows | 152 |
| **NOFRAMES** | Displays alternative text when frames do not appear | 155 |

CONTINUED

# SUMMARY OF HTML TAGS

| TAG/ATTRIBUTE | DESCRIPTION | REFERENCES |
|---|---|---|
| **IMAGE MAPS** | | |
| **AREA** | Specifies the information for one image area | 181 |
| COORDS | Specifies all the coordinates for one image area | 182 |
| HREF | Specifies the location of a Web page linked to an image area | 182 |
| SHAPE | Specifies the shape of one image area | 181 |
| **IMG** | Adds an image | 181 |
| USEMAP | Identifies the image map for an image | 181 |
| **MAP** | Creates an image map | 181 |
| NAME | Names an image map | 181 |
| | | |
| **IMAGES** | | |
| **BODY** | | |
| BACKGROUND | Adds a background image to a Web page | 65 |
| **BR** | | |
| CLEAR | Stops text from wrapping around an image | 59 |
| **CENTER** | Centers an image | 55 |
| **HR** | Adds a horizontal rule | 66 |
| ALIGN | Aligns a horizontal rule | 69 |
| SIZE | Changes the thickness of a horizontal rule | 67 |
| WIDTH | Changes the width of a horizontal rule | 68 |
| **IMG** | Adds an image | 54, 64, 110 |
| ALIGN | Aligns an image with text or wraps text around an image | 58, 60, 61, 71 |
| ALT | Displays alternative text when an image does not appear | 57 |
| BORDER | Adds a border to an image | 56 |
| HEIGHT/WIDTH | Specifies the height or width of an image | 74, 75 |
| HSPACE | Adds space to the left and right sides of an image | 62, 71 |
| SRC | Specifies the location of an image | 54, 64, 70, 110 |
| VSPACE | Adds space above and below an image | 63 |
| | | |
| **JAVA APPLETS** | | |
| **APPLET** | Adds a Java applet | 174 |
| CODE | Specifies the location of a Java applet | 174 |
| HEIGHT/WIDTH | Specifies the height or width of a Java applet | 174 |

| TAG/ATTRIBUTE | DESCRIPTION | REFERENCES |
|---|---|---|
| **JAVASCRIPT** | | |
| **NOSCRIPT** | Displays alternative text when JavaScript does not run | 169 |
| **SCRIPT** | Adds JavaScript to a Web page | 165, 166 |
| SRC | Specifies the location of a JavaScript | 167 |
| TYPE | Identifies a script as JavaScript | 165, 166 |
| **LINKS** | | |
| **A** | Creates a link | 90, 92, 94, 96, 98, 100, 102 |
| HREF | Specifies the location of a linked item | 90, 95, 96, 98, 100, 102 |
| NAME | Names a Web page area displayed by selecting a link | 92, 94 |
| TARGET | Specifies where linked information will appear | 103 |
| **BODY** | | |
| LINK | Changes the color of an unvisited link | 104 |
| VLINK | Changes the color of a visited link | 105 |
| **LISTS** | | |
| **DD** | Identifies a definition in a list | 49 |
| **DL** | Creates a list of terms with definitions | 49 |
| **DT** | Identifies a term in a list | 49 |
| **LI** | Identifies an item in an ordered or unordered list | 44, 46 |
| **OL** | Creates an ordered list | 44 |
| START | Specifies a starting number | 45 |
| TYPE | Specifies a number style | 45 |
| **UL** | Creates an unordered list | 46, 50 |
| TYPE | Specifies a bullet style | 47 |
| **PUBLISH WEB PAGES** | | |
| **META** | Provides information about a Web page | 220-223 |
| CONTENT | Specifies custom information about a Web page | 220-223 |
| NAME | Adds information to a Web page, such as a description or copyright information | 220-223 |
| **SOUNDS AND VIDEOS** | | |
| **A** | | |
| HREF | Specifies the location of a linked sound or video | 125, 129 |
| **EMBED** | Adds a sound or video to a Web page | 126, 130 |
| AUTOSTART | Plays a sound or video automatically | 127, 131 |
| HEIGHT/WIDTH | Specifies the height or width of sound controls or a video | 126, 130 |
| LOOP | Plays a sound or video continuously | 127, 131 |
| SRC | Specifies the location of a sound or video | 126, 130 |

CONTINUED

**243**

# SUMMARY OF HTML TAGS

| TAG/ATTRIBUTE | DESCRIPTION | REFERENCES |
|---|---|---|
| **STYLE SHEETS** | | |
| CLASS | Divides elements that use the same tag into groups | 189 |
| STYLE | Applies a style to one element | 192 |
| **DIV** | Applies a style to specific areas of a Web page | 191 |
| CLASS | Identifies the style for elements | 191 |
| **LINK** | Links a Web page to a style sheet stored in a separate document | 187 |
| HREF | Specifies the location of a style sheet stored in a separate document | 187 |
| REL | Specifies a link to a style sheet | 187 |
| TYPE | Specifies the format of a style sheet | 187 |
| **STYLE** | Creates a style sheet | 186 |

| TAG/ATTRIBUTE | DESCRIPTION | REFERENCES |
|---|---|---|
| **STYLE SHEET CHARACTERISTICS** | | |
| **background** | Specifies a background color or image for elements | 206, 207 |
| **border** | Specifies a border for elements | 208 |
| **bottom** | Positions elements with respect to the bottom edge of elements | 220 |
| **color** | Specifies a color for text | 214, 222 |
| **display** | Changes the display of elements | 217 |
| **float** | Wraps text around images | 211 |
| **font-family** | Specifies a font for text | 200 |
| **font-size** | Specifies a font size for text | 202 |
| **font-style** | Italicizes text | 194 |
| **font-weight** | Bolds text | 194 |
| **height** | Specifies a height for elements | 210 |
| **left** | Positions elements with respect to the left edge of elements | 220, 222 |
| **line-height** | Specifies a line spacing for text | 203 |
| **list-style** | Specifies a bullet or number style for lists | 212, 213 |
| **margin** | Specifies a margin for elements | 205 |
| **padding** | Adds space around all four sides of elements | 216 |
| **page-break-after** | Adds a page break after elements | 219 |
| **page-break-before** | Adds a page break before elements | 219 |
| **position** | Specifies an absolute or relative position for elements | 220, 222 |
| **right** | Positions elements with respect to the right edge of elements | 220, 222 |
| **text-align** | Aligns text | 198 |
| **text-decoration** | Specifies an underline for text | 196, 215 |
| **text-indent** | Indents the first line of text | 204 |
| **text-transform** | Specifies a case for text | 197 |
| **top** | Positions elements with respect to the top edge of elements | 220, 222 |
| **vertical-align** | Specifies a vertical alignment for inline elements | 218 |
| **width** | Specifies a width for elements | 210 |

| TAG/ATTRIBUTE | DESCRIPTION | REFERENCES |
|---|---|---|

## TABLES

| TAG/ATTRIBUTE | DESCRIPTION | REFERENCES |
|---|---|---|
| **CAPTION** | Adds a caption to a table | 111 |
| **CENTER** | Centers a table | 108 |
| **TABLE** | Creates a table | 106 |
| BACKGROUND | Adds a background image to a table | 117 |
| BGCOLOR | Adds a background color to a table | 116 |
| BORDER | Adds a border to a table | 109 |
| CELLPADDING | Changes the amount of space around the contents of cells | 121 |
| CELLSPACING | Changes the amount of space between cells | 120 |
| HEIGHT/WIDTH | Changes the height or width of a table | 118 |
| **TD** | Creates a data cell in a table | 107 |
| BGCOLOR | Adds a background color to a data cell | 116 |
| COLSPAN | Combines two or more data cells across columns | 112 |
| HEIGHT/WIDTH | Changes the height or width of a data cell | 119 |
| NOWRAP | Keeps text in a data cell on one line | 122 |
| ROWSPAN | Combines two or more data cells down rows | 113 |
| **TH** | Creates a header cell in a table | 107 |
| BGCOLOR | Adds a background color to a header cell | 116 |
| COLSPAN | Combines two or more header cells across columns | 112 |
| HEIGHT/WIDTH | Changes the height or width of a header cell | 119 |
| NOWRAP | Keeps text in a header cell on one line | 122 |
| ROWSPAN | Combines two or more header cells down rows | 113 |
| **TR** | Creates a row in a table | 106 |
| ALIGN | Horizontally aligns data in a table | 114 |
| BGCOLOR | Adds a background color to a row | 116 |
| VALIGN | Vertically aligns data in a table | 115 |

## HTML COLOR CODES

Here are the names and color codes for some colors commonly used on Web pages. A color code is also known as a hexadecimal value. There are only 16 colors you can specify by name. You can find a more complete list of colors at the www.maran.com/colorchart Web site.

| COLOR NAME | COLOR CODE | COLOR NAME | COLOR CODE |
|---|---|---|---|
| Aqua | #00FFFF | Navy | #000080 |
| Black | #000000 | Olive | #808000 |
| Blue | #0000FF | Purple | #800080 |
| Fuchsia | #FF00FF | Red | #FF0000 |
| Gray | #808080 | Silver | #C0C0C0 |
| Green | #008000 | Teal | #008080 |
| Lime | #00FF00 | White | #FFFFFF |
| Maroon | #800000 | Yellow | #FFFF00 |

# INDEX

# INDEX

## G

**GIF (Graphics Interchange Format).** *See also* **images**
    convert images to, 72-73
    interlace, 86-87
    make background transparent
        multicolored, 84-85
        solid, 82-83
**graphical submit button, create, 151**

## H

**HEAD tags, Web pages, set up, 16**
**header cells, in tables, 106**
**headings**
    add, 24
    align, 25
**height**
    of cells, change, 119
    of frames, specify, 152
    of images
        define, 74
        increase, 75
    of tables, change, 118
    of Web page elements, set, using style sheets, 210
**hidden fields, create, 148**
**hide**
    JavaScript, 168
    scroll bars for frames, 160
    style sheets, 193
**home page, plan, 10**
**horizontal rules**
    add, 66-69
    alignment, change, 69
    thickness, change, 67
    width, change, 68
**horizontally, align data in tables, 114**
**HTML (HyperText Markup Language)**
    codes, view for Web pages, 13
    editors, 12
    overview, 11
    steps to creating Web pages, 7
    tags, Web pages, set up, 16
**http (HyperText Transfer Protocol), 3**

## I

**image maps, create, 180-183**
**image rollovers, create, 178-179**
**images**
    add, 54
        spaces around, 62-63
        to tables, 110
    align
        in lists, 71
        with text, 61
    background, add, 65
        to tables, 117
        using style sheets, 207
    banners, add, 64
    borders, add, 56
    center, 55

colors, reduce, 80-81
considerations, 53
convert
    to GIF or JPEG, 72-73
    to Web browser, safe colors, 88-89
create links to, 96-97
crop, 78-79
GIF
    background, make transparent
        multicolored, 84-85
        remove, 83
        solid, 82-83
    interlace, 86-87
links, create, to other Web pages, 96-97
in lists, 70-71
overview, 52-53
provide alternative text for, 57
resolution, 53
sizes
    define, 74
    increase, 75
    reduce, 76-77
stop text wrap, 59
thumbnail, 53
turn off display, 236
view Web pages without, 53
where to obtain, 52
wrap text
    around, 58
        using style sheets, 211
        between two, 60
**increase image size, 75**
**indent text**
    using lists, 50
    using style sheets, 204
**indexing, prevent robots from, 231**
**insert**
    blank spaces, 23
    special characters, 30-31
**interlace GIF images, 86-87**
**internal videos, add, 130-131**
**Internet**
    connect to, 5
    overview, 2-3
**Internet Service Providers (ISPs), 5, 132, 224**
**ISDN (Integrated Services Digital Network), 5**
**italicize text, 32**
    using style sheets, 194-195

## J

**Java applets, 164**
    add, 174-175
**JavaScript, 164**
    add, 165-167
        to several Web pages, 166-167
    hide, 168
    provide alternative text for, 169
**JPEG (Joint Photographic Experts Group).** *See also* **images**
    add to Web pages, 54
    convert images to, 72-73

# INDEX

# INDEX

# New *from the Award-Winning Visual*™ *Series*

**Windows XP In an Instant**
(0-7645-3625-7)

## in an *instant*

- *Fast*
- *Focused*
- *Visual*

### —and a great value!

- Zeroes in on the core tools and tasks of each application
- Features hundreds of large, super-crisp screenshots
- Straight-to-the-point explanations get you up and running—instantly

## *Titles* In Series

**Dreamweaver 4 In an Instant**
(0-7645-3628-1)

**Flash 5 In an Instant**
(0-7645-3624-9)

**FrontPage 2002 In an Instant**
(0-7645-3626-5)

**HTML In an Instant**
(0-7645-3627-3)

**JavaScript In an Instant**
(0-7645-3659-1)

**Office XP In an Instant**
(0-7645-3637-0)

**Outlook 2002 In an Instant**
(0-7645-3669-9)

**Photoshop 6 In an Instant**
(0-7645-3629-X)

*in an Instant*

*fast, focused, visual*

# Other Visual Series That Help You Read Less - Learn More™

Simplified®

Teach Yourself VISUALLY™

Master VISUALLY™

Visual Blueprint

## Available wherever books are sold

To view a complete listing of our publications, please visit **www.maran.com**

Wiley Publishing, Inc.